Social Psychology

SOCIAL PSYCHOLOGY

MARILYNN B. BREWER
Ohio State University

William D. Crano
University of Arizona

WARNER MEMORIAL LIBRARY
EASTERN COLLEGE
ST. DAVIDS, PA. 19087

WEST PUBLISHING COMPANY
Minneapolis/St. Paul   New York   Los Angeles   San Francisco

Copy Editor: Elaine Levin
Composition: Parkwood Composition Service
Index: Terry Casey
Cover Art: Color Box, FPG

Photo credits and acknowledgements appear following the subject index.

West's Commitment to the Environment

In 1906, West Publishing Company began recycling materials left over from the production of books. This began a tradition of efficient and responsible use of resources. Today, up to 95 percent of our legal books and 70 percent of our college and school texts are printed on recycled, acid-free stock. West also recycles nearly 22 million pounds of scrap paper annually—the equivalent of 181,717 trees. Since the 1960s, West has devised ways to capture and recycle waste inks, solvents, oils, and vapors created in the printing process. We also recycle plastics of all kinds, wood, glass, corrugated cardboard, and batteries, and have eliminated the use of Styrofoam book packaging. We at West are proud of the longevity and the scope of our commitment to the environment.

Production, Prepress, Printing and Binding by West Publishing Company.

COPYRIGHT ©1994   By WEST PUBLISHING COMPANY
                    610 Opperman Drive
                    P.O. Box 64526
                    St. Paul, MN 55164-0526

Library of Congress Cataloging-in-Publication Data

Brewer, Marilynn B., 1942-
    Social psychology / Marilynn B. Brewer, William D. Crano.
        p.   cm.
    Includes index.
    ISBN 0-314-02840-4
    1. Social psychology.   I. Crano, William D., 1942-
II. Title.
HM251.B643   1994
302--dc20

93-41156

 ∞ CIP

CONTENTS IN BRIEF

CHAPTER ONE
Introduction: The Way of Social Psychology   1

■ PART I SOCIAL ATTITUDES:
   WAYS OF VIEWING THE WORLD   21
CHAPTER TWO
Attitudes: Measurement, Structure, and Behavior   23
CHAPTER THREE
Attitude Change: The Study of Communication
   and Persuasion   41
CHAPTER FOUR
Models of Attitude Change: How and Why
   Persuasion Works   63
CHAPTER FIVE
Cognitive Dissonance: Persuading Ourselves   81

■ PART II SOCIAL PERCEPTIONS:
   UNDERSTANDING OURSELVES AND OTHERS   105
CHAPTER SIX
Nonverbal Communication of Moods and Emotions:
   Perceiving What Others Are Feeling   107
CHAPTER SEVEN
Forming Impressions: What Do We See In Other People?   125
CHAPTER EIGHT
Social Cognition: Impression Formation Revisited   145
CHAPTER NINE
Attribution: The Social Consequences of Causual
   Perception   167
CHAPTER TEN
Social Inference: From Behavior to Personality   185
CHAPTER ELEVEN
The Social Self: Self-Concept in Its Social Context   207

■ PART III SOCIAL INTERACTION: RELATING TO OTHERS   229

CHAPTER TWELVE
Social Exchange: the Economics of Interpersonal
    Relationships   231
CHAPTER THIRTEEN
Attraction and Affiliation: Choosing Our Friends
    and Lovers   253
CHAPTER FOURTEEN
Bystander Intervention: People Helping People   279
CHAPTER FIFTEEN
Aggression: People Hurting People   303
CHAPTER SIXTEEN
Interpersonal Expectancies: and the Self-fulfilling
    Prophecy   327

■ PART IV SOCIAL INFLUENCE:
    THE PSYCHOLOGY OF GROUPS   347

CHAPTER SEVENTEEN
Obedience: Doing What You're Told   349
CHAPTER EIGHTEEN
Conformity and Independence: Going Along with
    the Crowd   367
CHAPTER NINETEEN
Minority Influence: When Dissidents Prevail   387
CHAPTER TWENTY
Group Performance: The Effects of Working Together   403
CHAPTER TWENTY ONE
Group Decision Making: Making Choices Collectively   423
CHAPTER TWENTY TWO
Social Identity: The Group in the Individual   439

■ PART V INTERGROUP RELATIONS:
    THE PSYCHOLOGY OF CONFLICT   459

CHAPTER TWENTY THREE
Intergroup Attitudes: Prejudice and Stereotypes   461
CHAPTER TWENTY FOUR
Discrimination: The Behavioral Consequences of Prejudice 481
CHAPTER TWENTY FIVE
Intergroup Relations: Conflict or Cooperation?   499

TABLE OF CONTENTS

■■■ **CHAPTER ONE**
INTRODUCTION: THE WAY OF SOCIAL PSYCHOLOGY   **1**

WHAT IS SOCIAL PSYCHOLOGY?   2

A FEW ILLUSTRATIONS   3
    The Invasion from Mars: A Study of Panic   3
    Facing Shock: Affiliation and Uncertainty   4
    Getting Acquainted: A Study of College Friendships   5
    The Law of Attraction   6
    Learning Political Values: The Bennington Study   7
    A Light in the Dark: The Formation of Group Norms   8

LESSONS ABOUT SOCIAL PSYCHOLOGY   8
    Levels of Explanation: From Individuals to Social Groups   9
    Hypothesis-testing Research   10
    The Context of Research: Laboratory and Field   11

METHODOLOGY: THE TOOLS OF SOCIAL PSYCHOLOGICAL RESEARCH   11
    Correlational and Experimental Research   12
    Research Validity   14

VALUES AND ETHICS IN SOCIAL PSYCHOLOGICAL RESEARCH   15

APPLYING SOCIAL PSYCHOLOGY   17

SUMMARY   19

■ **PART I**
SOCIAL ATTITUDES: WAYS OF VIEWING THE WORLD   **21**

■ ■ ■ CHAPTER TWO
ATTITUDES: MEASUREMENT, STRUCTURE, AND BEHAVIOR   23

SOCIAL ATTITUDES: CONCEPTION AND MEASUREMENT   25
    Beginnings: Thurstone's Approach   25
    The Three-part Distinction   26
APPLYING SOCIAL PSYCHOLOGY TO   The Attitudes = Evaluations Approach   27
            HEALTH   Psychophysiological Approaches   28
              ■
   UNOBTRUSIVE METHODS   ATTITUDES AS EVALUATIONS: CONCEPTIONS AND STANDARD DEFINITIONS   30
            29
                                THE ATTITUDE-BEHAVIOR CONSISTENCY DEBATE   30

                                FACTORS THAT AFFECT THE ATTITUDE-BEHAVIOR LINK 31
                                    Generality/Specificity of Attitude and Behavior 31
                                    Intention   32
                                    Direct Experience   33
                                    Extremity and Mere Thought   34
                                    Accessibility and Knowledge   35

                                APPLYING SOCIAL PSYCHOLOGY TO THE ENVIRONMENT:
APPLYING SOCIAL PSYCHOLOGY TO   ATTITUDES AND RECYCLING   35
        THE ENVIRONMENT   Ego Involvement and Vested Interest   36
              ■   Individual Differences: Self-Monitoring 38
   ATTITUDES AND RECYCLING
            35   SOME CONCLUDING THOUGHTS   39

                                SUMMARY   39

■ ■ ■ CHAPTER THREE
ATTITUDE CHANGE: THE STUDY OF COMMUNICATION AND PERSUASION   41

                                HOVLAND'S MESSAGE-LEARNING APPROACH   42

                                THE SOURCE OF A COMMUNICATION   43
APPLYING SOCIAL PSYCHOLOGY TO   Expertise   44
        ADVERTISING   Trustworthiness   44
              ■   Credibility Research: The Sleeper Effect 44
   ATTRACTIVENESS AND SALES
            47   THE MESSAGE   49
                                    Drawing A Conclusion   49
                                    Delivery: Force, Speed, Number and Intensity 50

One or Two Sides?   51
Fear Arousal   52

APPLYING SOCIAL PSYCHOLOGY TO   Inoculation Effects   54
HEALTH
■   THE SETTING   55
INOCULATING AGAINST STRESS   Situational Distractions   55
55   "Overheard" or Confusing Communications   57

CHARACTERISTICS OF THE AUDIENCE   58
Individual Differences in Intelligence and Self-Esteem   58
Mood   59

SOME CONCLUDING THOUGHTS   60

SUMMARY   60

■ ■ ■ CHAPTER FOUR
MODELS OF ATTITUDE CHANGE: HOW AND WHY PERSUASION WORKS   **63**

SOCIAL JUDGMENT THEORY   65
Components of the Theory   65
Evidence for the Theory   66

APPLYING SOCIAL PSYCHOLOGY TO   THE ELABORATION-LIKELIHOOD MODEL   68
THE ELECTORATE   Central versus Peripheral Processing   68
■   Factors that Determine Elaboration   69
WHO GETS YOUR VOTE?
73   THE HEURISTIC-SYSTEMATIC MODEL   74
Systematic Processing   74
Heuristic Processing   74
Efficiency + Sufficiency = Confidence   75
APPLYING SOCIAL PSYCHOLOGY TO   Elm and the Heuristic-Systematic Model: Some Comparisons   77
MARKETING
■   SOME CONCLUDING THOUGHTS   78
THE XT-100
76   SUMMARY   78

■ ■ ■ CHAPTER FIVE
COGNITIVE DISSONANCE: PERSUADING OURSELVES   **81**

DISSONANCE   82
The Theory   83
Preconditions to Dissonance   85

Applying Social Psychology to Health
■
Dissonance and Weight Loss
91

Applying Social Psychology to Health
■
Dissonance and AIDS
94

The Three Faces of Dissonance   86
    Insufficient Justification   86
    Free Choice   87
    Effort Justification   89

Cognitive Dissonance Reconsidered: Alternative Explanations   92
    Alterations to the Basic Theory   92

Replacements to the Basic Theory   95
    Impression Management   95
    Self-Perception   96
    Motivating Properties of Dissonance   99
    A Reconciliation   101

Some Concluding Thoughts   102

Summary   103

■ Part II
Social Perceptions: Understanding Ourselves and Others   105

■■■ Chapter Six
Nonverbal Communication of Moods and Emotions:
Perceiving What Others Are Feeling   107

Applying Social Psychology to the Law
■
The "Lie Detector" Controversy
113

Applying Social Psychology to the Law
■
Baby Faces in the Courtroom
118

Communicating Without Words: An Evolutionary Perspective   109

Expressing Emotions: Sending Nonverbal Messages   109
    Is There a Universal Code?   109
    Expression or Communication?   110
    Is Nonverbal Expression Controllable?   112

Decoding Emotions: Interpreting Nonverbal Messages   114
    Nonverbal Message as "Affordances"   116
    Reading More Than There Is to Know   118
    Accuracy of Interpreting Expressions: Are Some Individuals
      Better Decoders than Others?   119
    Can We Detect Deception?   120
    Understanding Others' Emotions: Recognition or Empathy?   121

SOME CONCLUDING THOUGHTS   123

SUMMARY   123

■ ■ ■ **CHAPTER SEVEN**
       FORMING IMPRESSIONS: WHAT DO WE SEE IN OTHER PEOPLE?   **125**

                    PERSON PERCEPTION: SOME BASIC PRINCIPLES   128
APPLYING SOCIAL PSYCHOLOGY TO   Order Effects: The Primacy of First Impressions   128
        EDUCATION   Centrality: Some Traits Are More Important Than Others   131
            ■
FIRST IMPRESSIONS IN THE   IMPLICIT PERSONALITY THEORY: WHAT GOES WITH WHAT?   133
        CLASSROOM   Evaluate Bias: The Halo Effect   134
            131
                                   EVALUATION ISN'T EVERYTHING   137

                                   SIZING OTHERS UP: HOW DO WE PUT IT ALL TOGETHER?   139
APPLYING SOCIAL PSYCHOLOGY TO   Model I: Cognitive Algebra   139
        THE LAW   Model II: Holistic Impressions   141
            ■
ATTRACTIVE DEFENDANTS   SOME CONCLUDING THOUGHTS   142
            136
                                   SUMMARY   144

■ ■ ■ **CHAPTER EIGHT**
       SOCIAL COGNITION: IMPRESSION FORMATION REVISITED   **145**

                                   SOCIAL COGNITION AND THE "NEW LOOK"   146

                                   SCHEMAS: THE STRUCTURES OF SOCIAL KNOWLEDGE   147
                                       Scripts and Roles   148
                                       Person Schemas   149

                                   SCHEMA ACCESSIBILITY   152
                                       External Factors   152
                                       Internal Factors   153
APPLYING SOCIAL PSYCHOLOGY TO
        THE LAW   SCHEMATIC PROCESSING   157
            ■   Selective Attention and Recall   157
EYEWITNESS TESTIMONY   Confirmatory Biases: Cognitive Conservatism   160
            164   Reconstructing Memory   163

SOME CONCLUDING THOUGHTS   165

SUMMARY   165

■■■ CHAPTER NINE
ATTRIBUTION: THE SOCIAL CONSEQUENCES OF CAUSAL PERCEPTION   167

APPLYING SOCIAL PSYCHOLOGY TO   THE STRUCTURE OF PERCEIVED CAUSES   169
SOCIAL POLICY   Locus of Cause: The Internal-External Distinction   170
■   Stability of Cause: Expectations for the Future   172
CAUSAL ATTRIBUTIONS AND   Controllability of Cause: Could It Be Helped?   174
NEGATIVE LIFE CIRCUMSTANCES
172   ATTRIBUTIONS, EMOTIONS, AND SOCIAL BEHAVIOR   177
                                         Anger: You Did It On Purpose   177
APPLYING SOCIAL PSYCHOLOGY TO   Pity: You Need Help   178
EDUCATION   Manipulating Attributions: Strategies for Social Interaction   179
■
ATTRIBUTIONS AND SUCCESS IN   SELF-ATTRIBUTIONS: IMPLICATIONS FOR ACHIEVEMENT AND HEALTH   180
COLLEGE   Explanations for Success and Failure: Heads I Win;
174   Tails I Don't Lose   180

APPLYING SOCIAL PSYCHOLOGY TO   SOME CONCLUDING THOUGHTS   182
HEALTH
■   SUMMARY   182
DEPRESSION VERSUS EFFICACY
181

■■■ CHAPTER TEN
SOCIAL INFERENCE: FROM BEHAVIOR TO PERSONALITY   185

APPLYING SOCIAL PSYCHOLOGY TO   ATTRIBUTION AS SOCIAL INFERENCE   186
EDUCATION   The Covariation Principle   187
■   Deviations from the Principle of Covariation   190
UNDERMINING INTRINSIC   Causal Inference from Single Observations   192
MOTIVATION   Correspondent Inference Theory   193
195   Attributions of Motivation   194

                                      THE PERSON ATTRIBUTION BIAS   196
APPLYING SOCIAL PSYCHOLOGY TO   Person or Role?   198
THE LAW   Why Do We make Person Attributions?   198
■   The Actor or the Observer: A Matter of Perspective 201
CONFESSION OR COERCION?
200   PERSON-SITUATION ATTRIBUTION: SIMULTANEOUS OR SEQUENTIAL?   201

SOME CONCLUDING THOUGHTS 203

SUMMARY 204

■■■ CHAPTER ELEVEN
THE SOCIAL SELF: SELF-CONCEPT IN ITS SOCIAL CONTEXT 207

APPLYING SOCIAL PSYCHOLOGY TO
HEALTH
■
SELF-COMPLEXITY AND THE
BUFFERING EFFECT
212

APPLYING SOCIAL PSYCHOLOGY TO
THE LAW
■
DELINQUENCY AND SELF-CONCEPT
215

APPLYING SOCIAL PSYCHOLOGY TO
THE WORKPLACE
■
SELF-ESTEEM IN THE WAITING
ROOM
220

WHO AM I? THE NATURE OF THE SELF-CONCEPT 209
Self-schema: The Cognitive Component 209
Self-esteem: The Evaluative Component 215
Self-perception: The Behavioral Component 217

YOU AND ME: THE COMPARATIVE BASIS OF SELF-CONCEPT 219
Social Comparison and Self-evaluation 219
Distinctiveness and Social Comparison 221
Some Comparisons Matter More Than Others 221
The Ups and Downs of Social Comparison 222

THE MAINTAINING AND PROTECTING A SELF-IMAGE 222
Do We Want Others to See Us as We See Ourselves? 223
Cross-cultural perspectives on the Self 225

SOME CONCLUDING THOUGHTS 227

SUMMARY 227

■ PART III
SOCIAL INTERACTION: RELATING TO OTHERS 229

■■■ CHAPTER TWELVE
SOCIAL EXCHANGE: THE ECONOMICS OF INTERPERSONAL
RELATIONSHIPS 231

THE ELEMENTS OF SOCIAL EXCHANGE 232
The Pivotal Concept: Interdependence 234
The Nature of Outcome Values 236

REGULATING SOCIAL EXCHANGE: LIMITS ON PURE HEDONISM 237
Types of Relationships: Communal and Exhange 238

	Transformations	239
	Social Norms	240
APPLYING SOCIAL PSYCHOLOGY TO THE ENVIRONMENT ■ **REAL-WORLD RESOURCE CONSERVATION** **246**	BARGAINING AND NEGOTIATION: CONTROLLING NET OUTCOMES	241
	Fate Control	241
	Behavior Control	242
	SOCIAL DILEMMAS: INDIVIDUAL VERSUS COLLECTIVE OUTCOMES	243
	Tragedy of the Commons	243
	The Prisoners' Dilemma	247
	SOME CONCLUDING THOUGHTS	251
	SUMMARY	251

■ ■ ■ **CHAPTER THIRTEEN**
ATTRACTION AND AFFILIATION: CHOOSING OUR FRIENDS AND LOVERS 253

	COMMUNAL VERSUS EXCHANGE RELATIONSHIPS	255
	FACTORS THAT INFLUENCE INITIAL ATTRACTION: HOW IT BEGINS	255
	Physical Attractiveness	256
	Does Beauty Equal Goodness?	257
APPLYING SOCIAL PSYCHOLOGY TO THE ENVIRONMENT ■ **THE ARCHITECTURE OF FRIENDSHIP** **263**	The Market Value of Physical Attractiveness	258
	Is it a Good Match? The Role of Physical Similarity	260
	FROM ATTRACTION TO LIKING	262
	Physical Proximity	262
	Attitude Similarity and Reciprocity of Positive Feelings	264
	Self-Disclosure	265
	FROM LIKING TO LOVING: DIFFERENT FORMS OF CLOSENESS	266
	Measurement of Liking and Love	266
	Forms of Love	269
	Attachment Theory	270
	PERSISTENCE AND DISSOLUTION OF RELATIONSHIPS	271
	Equity Theory	272
APPLYING SOCIAL PSYCHOLOGY TO HEALTH ■ **PEOPLE AS GOOD MEDICINE** **276**	The Investment Model	272
	Jealousy	274
	Loneliness	275
	SOME CONCLUDING THOUGHTS	276
	SUMMARY	277

■■■ **CHAPTER FOURTEEN**
BYSTANDER INTERVENTION: PEOPLE HELPING PEOPLE   **279**

THE MURDER OF KITTY GENOVESE   280

BYSTANDER INTERVENTION RESEARCH   282
    The Epileptic Seizure Study   283
    The Smoke-Filled Room   285
    A General Model   286

THE AROUSAL-COST-REWARD MODEL   286
    Arousal   287
    Costs and Rewards: Normative Factors   289
    Costs and Rewards: Nonnormative Factors   292

MOTIVES FOR HELPING   294
    Image Repair and Negative-State Relief   294
    The Urban Environment and Helping   295
    Helping Because It Feels Good: The Emphatic Joy Hypothesis   297
    The Empathy-Altruism Model   298

SOME CONCLUDING THOUGHTS   300

SUMMARY   300

■■■ **CHAPTER FIFTEEN**
AGGRESSION: PEOPLE HURTING PEOPLE   **303**

WHAT IS IT? DEFINING AGGRESSION   304
    Types of Aggression: Instrumental and Hostile   305
    Sources of Aggression: Where Does It Come From?   306

EXPLANATIONS BASED ON INSTINCT OR INHERITANCE   307
    Instinct Theories   307

**APPLYING SOCIAL PSYCHOLOGY TO
THE ENVIRONMENT**
■
**HEAT AND AGGRESSION
315**

    Inheritance Theories   307

EXPLANATIONS BASED ON MOTIVATION AND LEARNING   309
    Frustration—Aggression Theory   309
    Frustration—Aggression Theory: Revised Edition   310
    Excitation Transfer   312
    Social Learning of Aggression   317
    Cues to Aggression   318

APPLYING SOCIAL PSYCHOLOGY TO THE LAW

■

ALCOHOL AND AGGRESSION
323

IMPORTANT SOCIAL ISSUES IN THE STUDY OF AGGRESSION   319
    Race and Ethnicity   319
    Media Aggression   320

SOME CONCLUDING THOUGHTS   323

SUMMARY   324

■ ■ ■ **CHAPTER SIXTEEN**
INTERPERSONAL EXPECTANCIES: AND THE SELF-FULFILLING PROPHECY   **327**

APPLYING SOCIAL PSYCHOLOGY TO EDUCATION

■

EXPECTANCY EFFECTS IN THE CLASSROOM
331

APPLYING SOCIAL PSYCHOLOGY TO WORK

■

EXPECTATIONS ON THE JOB
338

APPLYING SOCIAL PSYCHOLOGY TO THE LAW

■

EFFECTS OF INNUENDO AND LEADING QUESTIONS
341

THE PLACEBO STUDIES   329
    Ancient History   329
    Contemporary Pharmacology   330

EXPERIMENTER EXPECTANCIES   330
    Laboratory Biases   330
    Accuracy versus Expectancy   332
    The Transmission of Expectations in the Classroom   334

THE SELF-FULFILLING PROPHECY   334
    Effects of Appearance on Expectations   335
    Effects of Race on Expectations   337
    Effects of Sex on Expectations   338

BIASED INFORMATION SEARCH   339
    "Proving" (versus Testing) One's Hypotheses   339

ARE SELF-FULFILLING PROPHECIES INEVITABLY FULFILLED?   342
    Self-Affirmation versus the Self-Fulfilling Prophecy   342
    The Self-Fulfilling Prophecy and High Stakes   343

SOME CONCLUDING THOUGHTS   345

SUMMARY   346

■ **PART IV**
SOCIAL INFLUENCE: THE PSYCHOLOGY OF GROUPS   **347**

■ ■ ■ **CHAPTER SEVENTEEN**
OBEDIENCE: DOING WHAT YOU'RE TOLD **349**

APPLYING SOCIAL PSYCHOLOGY TO
HEALTH
■
THE OBEDIENT NURSE
358

APPLYING SOCIAL PSYCHOLOGY TO
THE WORK FORCE
■
USING REAL MANAGERS
361

MILGRAM'S RESEARCH PROGRAM   351
    The Basic Paradigm   351
    Variations on the Theme   355

OBJECTIONS TO THE PROGRAM OF RESEARCH   356
    Ethics   356
    Generalizability   358

ADMINISTRATIVE OBEDIENCE   359
    Distinguishing Features   359
    Extending the Series   361
    How Does It Happen? the Postexperimental Questionnaire   362

FORCES FOR COMPLIANCE OR RESISTANCE   363

SOME CONCLUDING COMMENTS   364

SUMMARY   364

■ ■ ■ **CHAPTER EIGHTEEN**
CONFORMITY AND INDEPENDENCE: GOING ALONG WITH THE CROWD **367**

SHERIF'S AUTOKINETIC ILLUSIONS   369
    Study 1: Isolated Respondents   369
    Study 2: Paired Respondents   369
    Study 3: Conflicting Response Norms   371

A DIFFERENT PERSPECTIVE: ASCH'S LINES   372
    The Standard Paradigm   372
    Extensions   373
    Sherif and Asch: Are the Implications of Their Research
      Contradictory?   374
    Some Theoretical Distinctions   376

CONTEXTUAL AND PERSONAL VARIABLES THAT AFFECT SOCIAL INFLUENCE   377
    Ambiguity and Task Difficulty   377
    Gender   377
    Other's Expertise   378
    Individual Differences   379

COMPLIANCE-GAINING STRATEGIES   380
    The Foot-in-the-Door   380
    The Door-in-the-Face   381
    The Law-Ball Technique   381

**APPLYING SOCIAL PSYCHOLOGY TO
THE ENVIRONMENT**
■

**THE LOW BALL AND
CONSERVATION
382**

RESISTANCE TO SOCIAL INFLUENCE   383
    Anticonformity   383
    Independence   383

SOME CONCLUDING THOUGHTS   384

SUMMARY   385

■■■ CHAPTER NINETEEN
MINORITY INFLUENCE: WHEN DISSIDENTS PREVAIL   387

AN ALTERNATIVE VIEW   389
    Symmetry versus Asymmetry   389
    Models of Influence   390
    Rigidity, Consistency and Originality   392
    Direct versus Indirect Influence   395

**APPLYING SOCIAL PSYCHOLOGY TO
THE ENVIRONMENT**
■

**FIGHTING POLLUTION
394**

EXTENSIONS OF THE MINORITY INFLUENCE EFFECT   397
    Convergent and Divergent Thought   397
    Diffusion of Influence Effects   398

SOME UNRESOLVED ISSUES   399
    Who or What is a Minority?   399
    One Process or Two?   400

SOME CONCLUDING THOUGHTS   401

SUMMARY   401

■■■ CHAPTER TWENTY
GROUP PERFORMANCE: THE EFFECTS OF WORKING TOGETHER   403

WHY PEOPLE WORK IN GROUP SETTINGS   404

APPLYING SOCIAL PSYCHOLOGY TO WORK
■
WORK-GROUP NORMS
415

SOCIAL FACILITATION: THE PRESENCE OF OTHERS — 407
  General Arousal — 408
  Evaluation Apprehension — 409
  Distraction — 410

INTERACTIVE GROUPS: WORKING TOGETHER — 411
  Participant Characteristics — 411
  Commitment and Cohesion — 415
  Participant Behavior — 416
  Task Demands — 418

APPLYING SOCIAL PSYCHOLOGY TO WORK
■
DOES PAY DISTRIBUTION MATTER?
419

SOME CONCLUDING THOUGHTS — 420

SUMMARY — 420

■■■ **CHAPTER TWENTY ONE**
GROUP DECISION MAKING: MAKING CHOICES COLLECTIVELY — **423**

APPLYING SOCIAL PSYCHOLOGY TO ORGANIZATIONS
■
THE USE OF DECISION SCHEMES
427

EXPERIMENTAL STUDIES OF GROUP DECISION MAKING — 424
  The Group Decision-Making Process — 425

INDIVIDUAL PREFERENCES AND COLLECTIVE DECISION — 428
  Decision Making in Juries — 429
  Task Solution Certainty: Can We Tell If We're Right? — 429
  Group Polarization — 430

APPLYING SOCIAL PSYCHOLOGY TO POLITICS
■
THE PSYCHOLOGY OF GROUPTHINK
434

THREATS TO THE QUALITY OF GROUP DECISIONS — 343

SOME CONCLUDING THOUGHTS — 437

SUMMARY — 438

■■■ **CHAPTER TWENTY TWO**
SOCIAL IDENTITY: THE GROUP IN THE INDIVIDUAL — **439**

APPLYING SOCIAL PSYCHOLOGY TO HEALTH
■
CHANGING SEXUAL BEHAVIOR
442

IN-GROUP LOYALTY AND ETHNOCENTRISM — 441
  Changing Groups or Individuals — 441
  Membership Groups and Reference Groups — 442

WHY DO IN-GROUPS MATTER?   444
    Social Comparison: The Search for Consensus   444
    Social Identity: Groups and the Sense of Self   447
    The Importance of Distinctiveness   449
    The Importance of Positive Identity   451
    Minority Self-esteem   452

APPLYING SOCIAL PSYCHOLOGY TO
POLITICS
■
RESPONSE TO INJUSTICE—
ACCEPTANCE VERSUS COLLECTIVE
ACTION
456

FROM SOCIAL IDENTITY TO SOCIAL CHANGE   455
    Relative Deprivation: When Is Inequality Unfair?   455

SOME CONCLUDING THOUGHTS   457

SUMMARY   457

■ PART V
INTERGROUP RELATIONS: THE PSYCHOLOGY
OF CONFLICT   459

■ ■ ■ CHAPTER TWENTY THREE
INTERGROUP ATTITUDES: PREJUDICE AND STEREOTYPES   461

APPLYING PSYCHOLOGY TO THE
LAW
■
CROSS-RACIAL RECOGNITION AND
THE EYEWITNESS
471

ATTITUDES TOWARD SOCIAL GROUPS: COGNITION AND EMOTION   462
    Stereotypes: The Content of Category Schemas   462
    Prejudice: The Emotional Side of Intergroup Perceptions   464
    The Relationship Between Stereotypes and Prejudice   464

CATEGORIZATION: THE COGNITIVE BASIS OF STEREOTYPES AND PREJUDICE   465
    Accentuation: Enhancing Category Distinctions   465
    Learning Stereotypes: Illusory Correlation's   467
    In-group-Out-group Categorization   468

APPLYING PSYCHOLOGY TO SOCIAL
ISSUES
■
OVERCOMING THE HABIT OF
PREJUDICE
478

OTHER CONTRIBUTING FACTORS: PERSONALITY AND SOCIETY   471
    Personality Factors   472
    Social Learning Factors   474
    Unconscious Prejudice   476

SOME CONCLUDING THOUGHTS   479

SUMMARY   479

■■■ **CHAPTER TWENTY FOUR**
DISCRIMINATION: THE BEHAVIORAL CONSEQUENCES OF PREJUDICE　　**481**

DISCRIMINATION IN THE MINIMAL INTERGROUP SITUATION　483
　Discrimination and the Rules of Fairness　484
　Social Identity and Self-Esteem　486

INTERPERSONAL DISCRIMINATION　486
　Social Distance　487
　Nonverbal Behavior, Anxiety, and Ambivalence　488

APPLYING SOCIAL PSYCHOLOGY TO POLITICS
■
INSTITUTIONALIZED DISCRIMINATION: RACISM AND SEXISM　492
　The Role of Political Ideologies: Symbolic Racism　495

REACTIONS TO POLITICAL CHANGE 496
SOME CONCLUDING THOUGHTS　496

SUMMARY　497

■■■ **CHAPTER TWENTY FIVE**
INTERGROUP RELATIONS: CONFLICT OR COOPERATION?　　**499**

APPLYING SOCIAL PSYCHOLOGY TO POLITICS
■
MISSILES VERSUS FACTORIES 503
ROBBERS CAVE: A CLASSIC EXPERIMENT IN INTERGROUP RELATIONS　501
　The Lessons of Robbers Cave　502

INTERGROUP COMPETITIVENESS: CAUSE OR CONSEQUENCE?　504

IGNORANCE AND MISPERCEPTION IN INTERGROUP RELATIONS　505

APPLYING SOCIAL PSYCHOLOGY TO POLITICS
■
THE IMAGE OF THE ENEMY 505
INTERGROUP CONTACT: THE SOCIAL PSYCHOLOGY OF DESEGREGATION　508
　The Role of Social Science in Desegregation　509
　Contact Experiments; Defining the Limits　511

SOME CONCLUDING THOUGHTS　515

SUMMARY　516

APPLYING SOCIAL PSYCHOLOGY TO EDUCATION
■
COOPERATION IN THE CLASSROOM 512
Glossary　519
References　525
Name Index　I-1
Subject Index　I-13

The experience of more than fifty (combined) years of teaching social psychology and the thoughtful suggestions and comments of our students have encouraged us to develop this text. We believe that the result of our efforts presents the complex information of the field of social psychology in a way that both meets students' requirements and maximizes their understanding. We do this through brief focused chapters that emphasize social phenomena that all of us encounter in our daily lives, in their historical and cultural context. By knowing why a phenomenon is investigated, not just what has been found, students can appreciate its importance, understand how it relates to them, and place the work in the more involving framework of their own lives.

Our text consists of twenty-five chapters—nearly twice the usual number. Each chapter begins with one or more scenarios to help personalize the chapter's topic and then describes the events, ideas, and research findings that illuminate the central focus of the chapter. We trace the development of ideas in social psychology by highlighting critical research and theory that changed the way people thought about an issue, provoked a controversy, or settled one. We emphasize why an issue is important and why a particular line of research has been followed, not just what has been done. In our experience, this approach not only helps to generate enthusiasm for social psychology but also leads to a more exciting classroom environment.

Although we think it is crucial for understanding today's social psychology to know the origins of the phenomena that occupy our research and theorizing, this is not a "history of ideas in social psychology" book. Our coverage is as up to date as any book available—but we also discuss why certain studies or approaches have been adopted and, by implication, why others have been avoided. If we have accomplished what we have set out to do, the common question, "Why is this study relevant?" will not be asked by readers of this book.

Presentation Strategy

In addition to making social psychology more approachable, we believe the presentation strategy we have adopted is pedagogically sound. Because the chapters are relatively brief, and tightly focused, their information is more easily learned. Our approach enables us to introduce material in a manner that maximizes understanding and recall. Brief chapters also facilitate the review of material. Also, each chapter can stand alone, and can be linked with other chapters in any number of combinations. For the instructor, this organizational flexibility has clear advantages. Chapters can be arranged and presented in a manner that coincides with the instructor's, rather than the text writer's, understanding of the structure of the field.

We do not present separate chapters on some of the theoretical branches that link social psychological knowledge with specific applications or problems. For example, we have no chapters specifically devoted to environmental psychology, legal psychology, health psychology, gender, or racism. Rather, we integrate information about these important issues within chapters to show its relevance to the general field of social psychology.

Organization

This text is divided into five sections. After the introduction, which offers a general framework for integrating the content and methods of social psychology, we first consider the most individualistic aspect of our field, social attitudes: the measurement of attitudes, attitude change, and models of persuasion.

Section 2 moves beyond attitudes to the larger arena of social perception—how we conceptualize ourselves and others and how these conceptualizations affect our social interactions. Here we examine the ways we form impressions and attributions, social cognition, and the self-concept.

Section 3 is even more socially or other-oriented, and deals with the ways in which we interact with other people. Topics are social exchange and interpersonal attraction, bystander intervention and aggression, and interpersonal expectations and their impact on our own and others' actions.

Section 4 considers the effects of social groups on behavior, with a special emphasis on social influence. This section is devoted to obedience and conformity to both majority and minority influence, group performance, and the impact of groups on self-identity.

Section 5 is concerned with intergroup conflict and the ever-timely issues of prejudice, stereotyping, and discrimination. It concludes with a discussion of intergroup contact and the effects of contact on cooperation and conflict.

Pedagogy

At the beginning of each chapter, we present a list of key concepts and a chapter outline. The key concepts are the fundamental building blocks of the material in the chapter. The outline guides the reader to the chapter organization. In addition, marginal notes help to link important concepts with related ideas in other areas of the text. We have been liberal in our use of marginal cross-references both to help the interested reader form a network of related links among phenomena and to show the extent to which themes recur in social psychological research. The glossary at the end of the book will be helpful for review purposes. The terms included in the glossary are printed in bold in the text.

Each chapter ends with a summary of material and a "concluding thoughts" section, a more personalized statement of our perspective on the topic at hand.

Complementing an extensive reference section is a list of suggested readings at the end of each chapter. These readings typically are review articles or books that discuss in depth the topics covered in the chapters. Students who might have to prepare a term paper on a given issue, or who simply are particularly interested in a topic, should consult these suggested readings.

Supplementary Materials

Along with the text, our text package includes an instructor's manual, a computerized test bank, a student study guide, and 35 transparencies for instructors' use. These materials should enhance the clarity of the information and facilitate its learning and integration.

Acknowledgments

Writing this book has occupied three years of our lives and considerable time and effort of others as well. We are indebted to the many people who gave unstintingly of their time, ideas, and effort to help us realize our vision. We are most grateful to Lawrence Messé, whose work on Chapters 20 and 21, Group Performance and Group Decisions, laid the basic foundations for these chapters. Without his help and advice (and initial chapter drafts), these chapters could not have been written. We are also grateful to host of reviewers whose comments are reflected throughout the text:

Judith Allen, Drake University
Scott T. Allison, University of Richmond
Craig A. Anderson, University of Missouri-Columbia
Steve R. Baumgardner, University of Wisconsin-Eau Claire
Galen V. Bodenhausen, Michigan State University
Craig Bowman, California State University, Fullerton
Kelly A. Brennan, University of Texas at Austin
Bernardo J. Carducci, Indiana University, Southeast
James E. Collins II, Carson-Newman College
Mark K. Covey, Concordia College
Christian S. Crandall, The University of Kansas
Brian M. Earn, University of Guelph
Steve L. Ellyson, Youngstown State University
Ralph Erber, University of Virginia
Robert W. Fuhrman, The University of Texas at San Antonio
Bert H. Hodges, Gordon College
Keith James, Colorado State University
Robert D. Johnson, Arkansas State University
George S. Larimar, West Liberty State College
Leonard L. Martin, The University of Georgia
Carol T. Miller, The University of Vermont
Richard Reardon, The University of Oklahoma
Ronald Riggio, California State University, Fullerton
Carol Sansone, The University of Utah
Mark Schaller, The University of Montana
Jerry Shaw, California State University, Northridge
Jeffry Simpson, Texas A&M University
Laurie A. Skokan, Portland State University
Charles Stangor, University of Maryland
Mark A. Stewart, American River College
Michael J. Strube, Washington University
Ellen Sullins, Northern Arizona University
David Wiesenthal, York University
Wendy Wood, Texas A&M University
Elissa Wurf, Lehigh University
Michael A. Zarate, The University of Texas at El Paso

We also would like to thank Dr. Karl N. Kelley, (North Central College) who prepared the instructor's manual to accompany the text, and Drs. Shelagh Towson (University of Windsor) and Brian Earn, who prepared the test bank and Steve Baumgardner, who wrote the study guide.

Our editors at West Educational Publishing, especially Steve Schonebaum and Beth A. Kennedy, deserve special thanks for all their help. They have been supportive and prodding at the same time, and have helped us produce a book of which we are proud.

Finally, on a personal note, our work on this book has occupied many of our nights and most of our weekends and spare time for a long time. For us, this sacrifice was worthwhile. We were able to learn lots of new information about a field that we both find captivating. But for those close to us, it may have proved much less advantageous. It was not our intention to be "away" so long, but the book seemed to require it. We are very grateful to our families for understanding, for enduring our self-imposed exile during this time, and promise not to do it again. At least, not for a while.

Marilynn B. Brewer and William D. Crano

Marilynn Brewer is Ohio State Regents Professor of Social Psychology at Ohio State University. In 1993 she was elected President of the American Psychological Society and has also served as President of the Society for Personality and Social Psychology and of the Society for the Psychological Study of Social Issues (SPSSI). She is author of numerous books and articles on the social psychology of intergroup relations, stereotyping, and person perception.

William Crano is Professor of Psychology and Communication and Head of the Department of Communication at the University of Arizona. Previously, he taught at Michigan State University and Texas A&M University. He has been a Fulbright Fellow and a NATO Senior Scientist. He also served as the director of the Program in Social Psychology at the National Science Foundation, and as Liaison Scientist in the behavioral sciences for the Office of Naval Research, London. In 1993, he was the elected Chairman of the Society for Experimental Social Psychology. He has written books and articles on social influence, persuasion, research methods, and cross-cultural psychology.

Crano and Brewer are also co-authors of *Principles and Methods of Social Research,* a well-known research methods text in social psychology.

CHAPTER 1

INTRODUCTION
The Way of Social Psychology

■ **Key Concepts**

Levels of explanation
Hypotheses
Field research
Laboratory experiment
Correlation
Independent variable
Dependent variable
Random assignment
Internal validity
External validity
Informed consent
Deception
Debriefing
Invasion of privacy

■ **Chapter Outline**

WHAT IS SOCIAL PSYCHOLOGY?

A FEW ILLUSTRATIONS
    The Invasion from Mars: A Study of Panic
    Facing Shock: Affiliation and Uncertainty
    Getting Acquainted: A Study of College Friendships
    The Law of Attraction
    Learning Political Values: The Bennington Study
    A Light in the Dark: The Formation of Group Norms

LESSONS ABOUT SOCIAL PSYCHOLOGY
    Levels of Explanation: From Individual to Group
    Hypothesis-testing Research
    The Context of Research: Laboratory and Field

METHODOLOGY: THE TOOLS OF SOCIAL PSYCHOLOGICAL RESEARCH
    Correlational and Experimental Research
    Research Validity

VALUES AND ETHICS IN SOCIAL PSYCHOLOGICAL RESEARCH

APPLYING SOCIAL PSYCHOLOGY

SUMMARY

Sue sits in front of her mirror, trying to imagine what kind of an impression she will make during her job interview later that morning. She decides that the Gucci scarf will be just the right touch to give her that competent career-woman look she is striving for.

■ ■ ■

Ten minutes into the interview, Sue is feeling a lot more confident than she did at the start. Although the personnel director has not yet said anything directly, Sue knows that the job is hers.

■ ■ ■

Later that evening, the euphoria wears off and Sue starts to feel anxious about whether she is really ready for the new responsibilities ahead. Three close friends stop by and suggest they all go out for a celebration. Their enthusiasm and excitement restore Sue's positive outlook.

■

Meeting new people, judging others' actions, sharing experiences with friends—these are the everyday events that illustrate how much life is played out in a social context. Almost everything we think, feel, say, or do is affected in some way by what other people are thinking, feeling, saying, or doing. It is no wonder, then, that a science of human behavior must include a field of study devoted to explaining social processes. This is the mission of social psychology.

■ ■ ■ WHAT IS SOCIAL PSYCHOLOGY?

According to Gordon Allport (1985), "Social psychologists regard their discipline as an attempt to understand how the thought, feeling, and behavior of individuals are influenced by the actual, imagined, or implied presence of others" (p. 3).

Any attempt to define a whole field of scientific study in just a few words is bound to be oversimplified, but Allport's definition comes as close as any to capturing the scope of the field of social psychology as it is represented in this book. By emphasizing the thoughts, feelings, and behaviors of *individuals,* Allport's definition places social psychology within the broader discipline of psychology as a whole. By emphasizing the role of other persons, Allport's definition tells us what is unique about social psychology.

Social psychology is concerned with the links between individuals and their social world. That world consists of other individuals, groups, organizations, and social institutions. But note that social psychology is not limited to situations in which more than one person is physically present. An individual can be influenced by the social world even when he or she is quite alone. Sue's behavior in front of her mirror, although solitary, was definitely social, influenced by the evaluations of imagined others.

Allport's description is a very abstract view of social psychology. A more concrete approach to defining this field is to say that "social psychology *is* what social psychologists *do*." By learning what goes on under the label of social psychology, we come to understand what that label means.

Reaching such a concrete understanding of social psychology is what this book is all about. By providing a broad sampling of what social psychologists do by way of research and theory, we hope to convey the meaning of social psychology. We will consider the kinds of questions social psychologists are interested in, how they go about answering those questions, and how they interpret the results of their inquiry. This text is a banquet of social psychological fare. Some of the dishes will be quite familiar, others more exotic, but until you have tasted all of the courses, you will not really know the cuisine.

■ ■ ■ A FEW ILLUSTRATIONS

In this chapter we briefly describe six studies that are classic examples of social psychological research. Taken together, they represent the *what* and the *how* of social psychology—the sorts of issues that social psychologists are interested in and the ways they go about investigating those interests.

The Invasion from Mars: A Study of Panic

On Halloween Eve, 1938, H. G. Wells's "War of the Worlds" was broadcast nationwide on CBS radio. Although the production was preceded by an announcement that this was a fictitious drama (and the announcement was repeated during the course of the one-hour production), the script resembled a realistic news bulletin reporting the events that transpired after the landing of "a huge flaming object" in the small town of Grovers Mill, New Jersey. As the script unfolded, the "news announcer" told of creatures emerging from the object, which were later identified as a "vanguard of an invading army from the planet Mars." According to the dramatic newscast, more Martian landings were reported in cities across the country, violence and destruction were rampant, and martial law was declared. Ultimately, the news reporter declared, "This is the end now," and an interview with the U.S. secretary of interior advised that there was nothing to do but "place our faith in God."

Many of the listeners who tuned in to the broadcast that night did not realize it was only a play. Later news stories estimated that of the six million Americans who heard the production, almost one million believed it was a legitimate news program. As a consequence, throughout the country people reacted with panic, terror, and hysteria in the belief that we had been invaded from Mars.

Shortly after the "War of the Worlds" broadcast (when panic had subsided and things returned to normal), social psychologist Hadley Cantril of Princeton University interviewed 135 New Jersey listeners about their reactions to the

When Orson Welles produced a radio drama based on the novel "War of the Worlds" by H. G. Wells in 1938, many who tuned into the broadcast thought it was an actual news bulletin reporting an invasion from Mars. Later, social psychologists studied this event to understand how people respond to uncertainty and impending disaster. (Reprinted with permission from The New York Times.) ■

broadcast (Cantril, 1940). Many of those interviewed had not known that the news reports were a dramatic production and thus had been very uncertain about how to interpret the situation. How did they respond to this uncertainty? The most frequently reported reactions included *seeking out other people for information*—calling friends or relatives on the telephone, running to a next-door neighbor's apartment, and so on. Sometimes other people provided information that served to correct misperceptions. In many cases, however, those who had been sought out were equally misinformed. Groups of people developed a shared perception that the world was coming to an end and there was nothing they could do about it. Cantril's interviews offer vivid documentation of social psychological responses to impending disaster.

Facing Shock: Affiliation and Uncertainty

Twenty years after the infamous "War of the Worlds" production, another social psychologist, Stanley Schachter (1959), conducted a very different kind of investigation of the idea that when people are faced with danger or uncertainty, they turn to other people to relieve their uncertainty. In this case, the sense of uncertainty or "impending disaster" was created in the laboratory. The research

College roommates spend time getting acquainted. In 1954, social psychologist Theodore Newcomb studied friendship formation among college students at the University of Michigan. ■

was conducted with female college students who had come to Schachter's laboratory to participate in a psychology experiment. When they arrived at the research session, the participants were told that the experiment would require receiving a series of electric shocks.

In some cases, this information was immediately followed by much reassurance that the shocks would be "like a tickle" and that the experiment would probably be enjoyable. In other cases, however, the participants in the experiment were left with the impression that the shocks could be quite painful, perhaps even dangerous. These participants were placed in a state of uncertainty much like that of the listeners of news of an invasion from Mars.

Before any shocks were administered, participants were given a choice about how to spend a waiting period. They could either be alone or wait in a room with other students facing the same series of shocks. Those who had not been reassured by the experimenter (participants in the high-fear condition) were much more likely to choose to spend their time with other people. As Cantril had found earlier in his study of responses to the "War of the Worlds" broadcast, Schachter demonstrated that facing an uncertain future increased people's desire to seek the company of others. Why does this happen? The answer to this question lies in social psychology's theory of social comparison.

The theory of social comparison explains people's desire to seek others' company under conditions of uncertainty: See Chapter 22.

Getting Acquainted: A Study of College Friendships

In September 1954, seventeen male transfer students arrived at the University of Michigan in Ann Arbor and moved into a rent-free residence provided by social psychologist Theodore Newcomb (1961). In exchange for a semester of free residence, these college men participated in a research study designed to document their experiences in the Project House. On a regular basis, participants completed questionnaires reporting on their current attitudes towards college and their relationships with their housemates. All of the men who participated in the research project were initially strangers to each other. Thus, Newcomb created an unusual opportunity to study the process of acquaintance and friendship formation as it unfolded over time.

What Newcomb found was that patterns of mutual interpersonal attraction did change across the six months. In initial stages, everyone in the house generally liked everyone else, and the intensity of interaction between individuals was determined by physical proximity. Roommates or floormates reported more friendly relations than those who were spatially separated from each other. Gradually, however, friendships became more differentiated. In later stages, the housemates subdivided into small groups of two or three individuals who developed close relationships to one another and interacted less with other members of the household. Ultimately, the strongest determinant of these friendship groupings proved to be *similarity of attitudes and values*. Across time, physical proximity became less important, and individuals gravitated toward others who shared the same views of the world.

The Law of Attraction

While Newcomb was studying friendship formation over time, Donn Byrne and his colleague Don Nelson (Byrne & Nelson, 1965) were investigating the determinants of interpersonal attraction in a very different context. Byrne and Nelson were also interested in the initial attraction between strangers, but in this case the stranger was a fictitious person, created by the researcher. At the beginning of Byrne and Nelson's study, each participant completed an extensive questionnaire indicating his or her own positions on a number of social issues. Later the participants were told they would learn about one other student who had also responded to the same questionnaire. In order to "get acquainted" with this other student, the participant was shown a copy of the attitude survey as it had been filled out by the unknown person.

In reality, this attitude survey the research participants received was bogus. It had been doctored to create the impression that the "other person" was very similar to them, very dissimilar, or some point in between. For some participants, the responses they saw were virtually identical to their own. For others, the stranger's responses were more dissimilar—with two-thirds or one-half or one-third of the responses the same as those of the participant.

After reading the stranger's questionnaire responses, participants were asked, "How much do you think you would like this person?" and "How much do you think you would enjoy working with this person?" Responses to this two-item measure of attraction produced results consistent with those from Newcomb's study of friendship formation. The greater the proportion of similar attitudes, the more participants liked the stranger (Figure 1.1). Just knowing that another person is highly dissimilar is apparently sufficient to assume that you will dislike each other, while knowing that you share a large proportion of attitudes is sufficient to assume you will enjoy each other's company. This relationship between attitude similarity and interpersonal liking proved to be so pervasive that Byrne (1971) dubbed it the "law of attraction."

Why do people show strong preference for similar others? See Chapter 13.

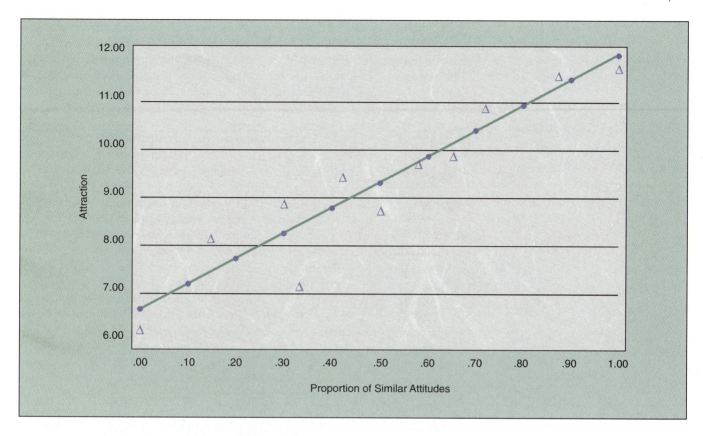

FIGURE 1.1

■

The correlation between attraction toward a stranger and proportion of similar attitudes. (From Byrne & Nelson, 1965, p. 661.)

Learning Political Values: The Bennington Study

Almost twenty years before his study of friendship formation at the University of Michigan, Newcomb (1943) had conducted another study of a different group of college students. In this case, the students were all females, and the study was conducted at an exclusive women's college in Vermont.

Bennington College was founded in 1932 as an experimental liberal arts college. The philosophy of education at the college was quite radical for the times, and the faculty tended to hold highly liberal social and political values. The student body, on the other hand, was drawn from wealthy, upper-class, East Coast families that held quite conservative political views. Thus, the women who entered Bennington College in the 1930s came with conservative political values into a social milieu in which the liberal politics of President Franklin D. Roosevelt's New Deal were the norm.

Newcomb arrived at Bennington College in 1935 to conduct a four-year study of its students. Through questionnaires and interviews, he assessed the social and political attitudes of Bennington students from the time they entered as freshmen until their graduation. What he found was a general pattern of attitude change among students, from conservative attitudes to the more liberal views current at the college at the time. But not all students exhibited a dramatic change in values.

Some, who were not as engaged in the activities of the college, steadfastly maintained their original positions. For these students, home and family remained the most important source of values, insulating them from the norms of the college. The results of Newcomb's study led to important insights about the circumstances under which individual attitudes are shaped by prevailing group norms.

A Light in the Dark: The Formation of Group Norms

Before Newcomb demonstrated that individuals' views of what is correct or valued can be influenced by group norms, Muzafer Sherif (1936) conducted an experimental study of mutual influence in groups in the laboratory. His experiment made use of an optical illusion called the *autokinetic effect*. This effect occurs when an individual stares at a small pinpoint of light presented in an otherwise totally darkened room. After a minute or two, the light appears to move around in various directions, even though it actually is stationary. The illusion of movement is impossible to control—all individuals perceive it even when they know it is illusory. However, when an individual is asked how *much* movement is occurring (less than an inch? two inches? six inches?), it is very difficult to make a judgment because there is no good frame of reference to establish the extent of movement.

In his experiment, Sherif placed pairs of participants together in a darkened room to make judgments of autokinetic movement. Each time the light was shown, respondents were asked to estimate aloud how much movement was occurring. After making several such judgments, members of the pair tended to converge on a common estimate. Further, when these students were separated from each other and made new judgments individually, they remained consistent with their previous group judgments and were more committed to the correctness of their estimates than judges who had not been in a group previously. Shared judgments apparently have more validity than isolated judgments—even when they are based on an illusion.

Groups can dramatically influence individual beliefs and values: See Chapters 18 and 22.

■■■ LESSONS ABOUT SOCIAL PSYCHOLOGY

These six research studies provide only a small sampling of the range and diversity of issues that interest social psychologists. But together they illustrate quite a bit about what social psychologists do.

First, these examples demonstrate that social psychology is a relatively new area of scientific research. We have identified these studies as "classics" in the field, but the oldest dates back to 1935 and some are as recent as 1965. This thirty-year period is, indeed, the time when the field of social psychology took shape. Historically, one of the first experiments now identified as social psychological in nature was conducted in 1897. Two books with the title of *Social Psychology* appeared in 1908 (McDougall, 1908; Ross, 1908). However, it was not until the 1930s that the content and methods of social psychology, as we

One of the first social psychological experiments was conducted to study social facilitation: See Chapter 20.

know it today, began to develop. In the sixty years since then, social psychology has expanded in scope and research sophistication. The chapters that follow furnish many illustrations of recent research that build on the ideas and concepts represented in the six studies described here, but using new research techniques and theoretical perspectives.

Levels of Explanation: From Individuals to Social Groups

The six studies just described also illustrate the different **levels of explanation**★ that are covered in social psychology. As a branch of the discipline of psychology, social psychology focuses on the thoughts and behaviors of individuals. But when individuals interact with other individuals, they create social structures in the form of interpersonal relationships and groups that have interesting properties of their own, above and beyond the characteristics of the individuals who participate in them. Thus, social psychology encompasses individual, interpersonal, and group processes.

Individual processes. Some of the questions that social psychologists pursue are about processes that take place inside a particular person—*individual* perceptions and behaviors. The first two studies described earlier are examples of this level of phenomena. Uncertainty and fear are states experienced by individuals, and seeking out company is an individual's response to those feelings. True, the result of such responses is social (affiliation, creation of a social group), but the feelings and motives exist at the individual level. Attitudes toward social issues, perceptions of other people, self-esteem and identity are other examples of individual processes of interest to social psychologists.

Interpersonal processes. The studies of similarity and attraction are examples of research at the *interpersonal* level. Similarity and friendship are "dyadic" concepts. They describe *relationships between individuals,* not features of the individuals taken alone. The study of interpersonal processes such as mutual attraction, helping, reciprocity, competition, and social exchange is unique to social psychology as a field of research.

Group processes. The studies of conformity to norms represent research at the level of the social *group.* Although individuals can hold beliefs and values, those beliefs are not social norms unless they are shared by other individuals who think of themselves as a social group. Conformity, consensus formation, and intergroup conflict are examples of group-level processes of interest to social psychology.

The topics and areas of research covered in this textbook include the full range of individual, interpersonal, and group processes. The organization of chapters follows a traditional sequence of coverage from those topics that are primarily individual (attitudes and social perception), to those that are interpersonal in

---

★*Boldfaced terms are defined in the glossary.*

nature (social exchange, affiliation, altruism and aggression), to those that involve group processes and intergroup relations. However, within each of these topics, the relationships between individuals and their social groups is of primary concern. Because the phenomena of concern to social psychologists cross levels of explanation from individual to interpersonal to group, the challenge of social psychology is to understand how processes at these different levels are linked to one another (Doise, 1986).

Hypothesis-testing Research

In addition to illustrating the scope of social psychological research, our six studies portray the nature of social psychology as a scientific enterprise. Social psychological research is designed to answer questions about human behavior using established empirical methods of inquiry.

More specifically, social psychological research is guided by **hypotheses** about how and why aspects of the social environment influence individual thoughts, feelings, and behavior. Hypotheses are guesses or predictions about how people will react to different circumstances or experiences. Hypotheses may be derived from previous observations of social behavior or from formal theories about underlying psychological processes. Empirical research is designed and conducted to test such hypotheses, and the results of research generate new questions and hypotheses about how it all works.

The research of Newcomb and of Byrne and Nelson on friendship formation and attraction, for instance, was initially motivated by the question of whether people are more attracted to similar or dissimilar others. Do "birds of a feather flock together"? or do "opposites attract"? Once it was established that similarity and attraction are positively related (in general, we like similar others more than dissimilar others), the question shifts to *why* similarity has such positive effects. Is it because similarity itself is rewarding? because we expect similar people to like us? because it is easier to interact with people we agree with? The course

Some social psychological research is conducted in a laboratory setting where participants come to the research site. Other research takes place outside the laboratory, where the researcher finds participants in their own setting. ■

TABLE 1.1
■
Classifying the Classics

Level of Explanation	Type of Research	
	FIELD RESEARCH	LABORATORY EXPERIMENT
INDIVIDUAL	Cantril (1940): A Study of Panic	Schachter (1959): Affiliation and Uncertainty
INTERPERSONAL	Newcomb (1961): Getting Acquainted	Byrne & Nelson (1965): The Law of Attraction
GROUP	Newcomb (1943): The Bennington Study	Sherif (1936): Norm Formation

The positive effect of similarity on attraction has been explored from several aspects: See Chapter 13.

of research in social psychology is often a branching pathway, with many interesting hypotheses generated from an initial core idea or study. In the chapters that follow, we trace some of these pathways from their early research origins to current theories of social behavior.

The Context of Research: Laboratory and Field

The same hypothesis can be investigated in many different ways. As the alert reader may well have recognized by now, the illustrative studies were selected to include pairs of studies that investigated a similar question in very different research contexts. One of each pair was an example of **field research,** where events and individual responses were systematically recorded as they occurred in their natural setting. The other study in each pair was a **laboratory experiment,** where the same phenomenon was investigated in a setting controlled by the researcher.

As illustrations of different levels of explanation and types of research, our six studies can be classified as in Table 1.1. This table distinguishes among major types of research in social psychology and gives us a framework for discussing methodological issues associated with these categories of research.

■ ■ ■ METHODOLOGY: THE TOOLS OF SOCIAL PSYCHOLOGICAL RESEARCH

The standing of social psychology as a scientific discipline rests on a commitment to systematic, empirical research. Our ideas and theories about how things work are tested against systematic observations and recording of actual human behavior.

Like the content of social psychology, its research methodology is best understood through exposure to many concrete examples of social psychological studies. Our six selected studies represent a variety of research methods characteristic of social psychology and help to illustrate some of the basic distinctions among different kinds of research.

Correlational and Experimental Research

Research in which events and behaviors are studied as they occur naturally provides the basis for assessing **correlations** between variables, or characteristics. A correlation is simply evidence that two variables are associated—if one changes, the other can also be expected to change. Cantril (1940), for instance, reported a relationship between uncertainty and affiliation—when individuals' feelings of uncertainty and fear went up, their desire to be with other people also increased. Newcomb's (1961) field study of friendship formation also obtained a correlation between measures of attitude similarity and degree of liking in pairs of individuals. High similarity was associated with liking and friendship formation; low similarity was associated with less attraction and little likelihood of becoming good friends over time.

These two findings illustrate *positive correlations*—higher values on one variable (uncertainty, similarity) correspond to higher values on the other (affiliation, attraction). A *negative correlation* exists when high values on one characteristic are associated with low values on the other. In his study of Bennington College students, for instance, Newcomb (1943) found that students who remained closely attached to their families showed less attitude change than other students. In other words, he found a negative relationship between family attachment and degree of conformity to college norms.

Correlations are often very interesting in their own right, but one must be cautious in interpreting the meaning of any correlational finding. The existence of an association between two variables (A and B) could indicate any of three different things. Figure 1.2 illustrates these alternatives with three possible explanations for the positive correlation between attitude similarity and interpersonal attraction. The correlation could mean that *A causes B*—people with similar attitudes are attracted to each other because of their similarity. Alternatively, the correlation may mean that *B causes A*—when people like each other, they develop similar attitudes. Or, it could be that there is no direct causal relationship between A and B at all, but instead both are caused by some other factor, C. For instance, people with common socioeconomic background may have similar attitudes (C causes A) and they may be highly likely to get to know each other and develop friendships (C causes B).

To take another example, Cantril (1940) reported a positive association between uncertainty and affiliation as responses to the "invasion from Mars" broadcast. We could interpret this to mean that feelings of fear and uncertainty *caused* individuals to feel greater need for the company of others (A causes B). However, it could be the other way around. Maybe people who have a high need for affiliation with others experienced more fear and uncertainty when they were alone; thus, affiliation need *caused* increases in uncertainty (B causes A). Or maybe the association had something to do with what people will report in an interview.

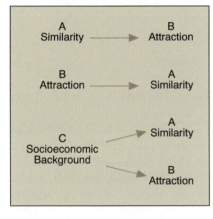

FIGURE 1.2

■

Alternative interpretations of a correlation between attitude similarity and attraction.

Perhaps gregarious individuals are more likely to affiliate with others under any circumstances *and* more likely to be willing to admit that they experienced fear and uncertainty. Shy people, on the other hand, may avoid seeking out other people and be unwilling to report to a strange interviewer that they felt fearful. The obtained relationship between reported uncertainty and affiliation may both be effects of individual differences in gregariousness (C causes both A and B).

It is just this kind of ambiguity in interpreting correlational associations that leads researchers to the use of experiments to test causal hypotheses. The logic of an experiment is this: If it is true that *A causes B,* then if we create a change in A, a change in B should follow. The factor that is varied by the experimenter is called the **independent variable.** Different levels (conditions) of the independent variable are created by alterations in the environment or in the instructions given to participants. The participants' responses to these alterations (the effects) are the **dependent variables** of the experiment. In most social psychological studies, measures of the dependent variables are obtained either by observing behaviors in the setting or by asking research participants to report on their responses to the situation.

To resolve the causal ambiguity about the relationship between similarity and attraction, Byrne and Nelson (1965) designed an experiment in which similarity was an independent variable. In their study, the degree of similarity between the participant and the fictitious other person was determined by the researcher. Since the participants had never interacted with this other person, they could not have influenced one another's attitudes, and other factors such as socioeconomic background were eliminated from the situation as well. When participants in the high-similarity condition liked the fictitious other person more than those in the low-similarity condition, there was little reason to doubt that differences in similarity *caused* the obtained differences in degree of attraction.

To test causal hypotheses adequately, an experiment must have two essential ingredients—*control* over the independent variable and **random assignment** of participants to the different experimental conditions. Randomization requires that all individuals available for a study be potentially able to participate in any conditions of the study. Only chance determines the condition to which any individual is assigned. These two criteria are closely related. The researcher must define and control the conditions of the experiment in order to determine what experiences specific participants are exposed to. And random assignment assures that any research participant has an equal chance of exposure to any of the conditions of the independent variable.

Random assignment of participants is necessary to assure that differences in the independent variable (experimental conditions) are unrelated to personal differences among individuals who participate in the experiment. To illustrate the importance of random assignment, consider Schachter's experimental study of uncertainty and affiliation. In order to test the causal hypothesis that uncertainty causes need for affiliation, Schachter (1959) exposed participants to different levels of fear and uncertainty (independent variable), and then assessed their desire to affiliate with other people (dependent variable) (Figure 1.3).

In this experiment, it was very important that the women exposed to the high-fear condition and those exposed to the low-fear manipulation did not differ initially in their overall level of affiliation need. If participants had been allowed to choose whether to face the anticipated shock, under high-fear conditions very

FIGURE 1.3

■

Experimental manipulations in Schachter (1959).

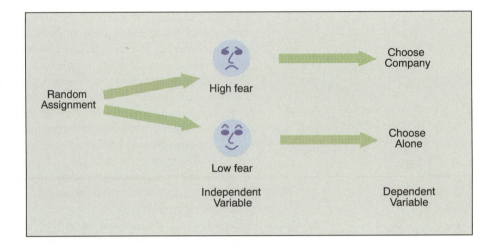

affiliative women may have been more likely to volunteer (to help the experimenter) than less affiliative women. This difference in personality could then have accounted for any later differences in desire to wait with other people. But students in the experiment were not given the choice of participating in the high- or low-fear condition. They were assigned at random to one of the two manipulations. Any differences among participants in affiliative need were evenly (randomly) distributed between the high- and low-fear conditions. Thus, when those in the high-fear condition showed more interest in being with others than those in the low-fear condition, we knew this was not due to existing personality differences between the two groups of participants.

Research Validity

Experiments that effectively control the independent variable and randomly assign participants to experimental conditions are said to have **internal validity** (Campbell & Stanley, 1966). When a study has high internal validity we can conclude with some confidence that any effects on the dependent variables were caused by variations in the independent variable (or variables) in the experiment.

Internal validity is essential for testing causal hypotheses, but it is achieved at some cost. Because manipulation and random assignment require a high level of control over the situation, the setting in which experiments take place is often very constrained or artificial. Research participants are usually aware that they are taking part in an experimental study, so they may respond in ways that are peculiar to that particular setting. Features in an experiment that may influence how participants respond are known as *demand characteristics*.

Research participants may be influenced by the nature of the experimental setting: See Chapter 16.

To reduce the effects of demand characteristics in experiments, researchers often have to develop elaborate cover stories, explanations about the nature of the experiment that get participants involved and encourage them to respond as naturally and honestly as possible. Efforts to get participants fully engaged in the setting enhance what Aronson, Brewer, and Carlsmith (1985) call *experimental realism*. The idea is that if participants are caught up in the situation, they will not artificially control their responses to the experimental conditions. Sometimes experiments are conducted in natural settings, outside the laboratory, to further enhance realism. It often is more difficult to control the independent variable in such field experiments, but participants may respond more naturally (less self-consciously) in nonlaboratory settings.

Despite efforts to increase experimental realism, many researchers question whether social psychological experiments have **external validity.** Can the results be generalized to nonexperimental settings where the causal variable has not been artificially created? Can we assume that this same causal relationship holds in natural situations? This is why it is so important that research on social psychological problems be conducted in both laboratory experiments and field settings. When experimental variations in A are found to cause changes in B *and* these two variables are found to be correlated in natural situations, we have much more confidence in the finding than we could achieve from either result taken alone.

■■■ VALUES AND ETHICS IN SOCIAL PSYCHOLOGICAL RESEARCH

Because the subject matter of social psychology is human behavior, social psychological research is itself a social enterprise, subject to the norms of interpersonal behavior and social conduct. In many cases, there is a conflict or tension between the values that govern normal interpersonal interaction and the requirements of objective, scientific research. Such conflicts raise important ethical issues that influence the conduct of social psychological studies. In designing research procedures, the social psychologist must be continually concerned with this question: To what extent could human subjects be harmed or exploited by their participation in this enterprise?

Since social psychological research rarely places research participants at risk of *physical* harm (even those experiments that lead participants to anticipate receiving electric shock almost never actually deliver those shocks), our concern is directed to potential psychological harm such as embarrassment, loss of self-esteem, anxiety, or even extreme boredom. The primary ethical issues faced by social psychologists differ somewhat depending on whether the research they are conducting is a laboratory experiment or a field study.

For experimental studies, the primary ethical conflict is between the principle of **informed consent** and the need for **deception** to create controlled experimental conditions. Ideally, individuals should not participate in research unless they fully understand and consent to what will happen to them during the course of the study. However, for many experimental manipulations, if participants fully understood the nature of the manipulations in advance, their responses would be meaningless. The use of deceptive cover stories to create experimental realism is often essential to the validity of research results. Yet any such deception is essentially a violation of interpersonal trust, even when done in the service of scientific goals.

Under the code of ethics developed by the American Psychological Association to guide the conduct of human research (1982), the necessity for deception in some social psychological experiments is acknowledged, but it is redressed in two ways. First, researchers are required to inform participants as fully as possible in advance about what procedures and activities the experiment will involve. Only the most critical elements required by the experimental design are not revealed. (Participants may even be informed in advance that some of what they are told during the experiment may be untrue.) Second, once the experimental session is over, each participant should be fully **debriefed.** At this point, any deceptions are explained and the purposes of the experiment are discussed. Good experimenters will take advantage of the debriefing session to determine whether their experimental procedures are causing participants any grief or embarrassment.

Although laboratory experiments may involve ethically sensitive deception, in most laboratory studies participants are at least fully aware that they are being observed and have consciously consented to take part in a research study. In many field research settings, this is not the case. When behaviors are observed in public places outside the laboratory, respondents may not be aware that they are subjects of a research study. In such situations, the researchers must be concerned that their observation methods do not constitute an **invasion of privacy.** In this domain, there are also two principal ethical guidelines. First, the events being recorded should be generally agreed to be "public behaviors." Even though individuals may not know their responses are being recorded, it should be within a context in which they know their behavior could be observed by others. Secret recordings in places where individuals believe they are not observable would be ethically questionable, at best.

Second, recordings should be made in a way that protects the anonymity of the person observed. Once the response has been coded, it should not be possible for someone later to track down the individual who made that response. If recording techniques (such as the use of videotape) make the respondent identifiable, then it is mandatory that the subject be made aware of the recording and give permission for its use for research purposes.

Even when respondents are aware that they are participating in a field research study—as in the case of survey questionnaires or interviews—issues of invasion of privacy must be considered. The primary ethical directive governing survey research is maintenance of confidentiality of information provided by respondents. In addition, it is important that respondents feel free to refuse to answer questions that might be excessively embarrassing or sensitive.

How do we know whether social psychological research is being conducted in an ethically acceptable way? There is no simple answer to that question, but over the years we have developed rules and procedures that guide the conduct of research with human subjects. Research that is conducted in universities or research institutes supported by government funds is monitored by Institutional Review Boards (IRBs). Before conducting any research, investigators are required to submit a description of their research purposes and procedures for review by members of their IRB. The board is charged with evaluating the proposed research for consistency with ethical guidelines and concern for the welfare of human subjects. Only proposals that have been approved by the IRB can be conducted under the auspices of the institution or receive federal research funding.

Even with the development of IRBs, the evaluation of the ethics of research is ultimately a matter of judgment of costs and benefits. The potential costs to individual research participants (temporary embarrassment, deception, anxiety) are

One earlier social psychological research program might be considered unethical today: See Chapter 17.

weighed against the potential benefits to be gained through greater understanding of human behavior. Not all research survives this cost–benefit analysis. And standards of judgment sometimes change across time. Research that was considered acceptable in the 1950s and 1960s is not always judged to be ethical today. For instance, later in the text we describe a dramatic program of research in which participants were faced with a very stressful situation, believing they were administering severe electric shocks to another person. The controversy that ensued after the publication of these studies (Baumrind, 1964; Milgram, 1964) had considerable influence on ethical standards for subsequent social psychological research.

■ ■ ■ APPLYING SOCIAL PSYCHOLOGY

As a scientific discipline, the goal of social psychological research is basic understanding of human behavior in its social context. Ultimately, however, the pursuit of knowledge is justified by the social consequences of understanding ourselves. Knowledge should be useful.

By its very nature, social psychology has implications for many aspects of social life—from interpersonal relationships to social policy. Because the subject matter touches on major social issues, social psychologists must be continually aware of the potential applications of their research conclusions.

The results of social psychological research have been put to practical use in many arenas—advertising, marriage counseling, jury selection, courtroom testimony, prevention of violence, behavioral medicine, conservation, and school desegregation, to name a few. Health psychology, consumer behavior, environmental psychology, psychology and law, and organizational behavior are among the applied specializations that draw heavily from social psychological research and theory as their scientific base.

Social psychology as a discipline is concerned with the scientific exploration of basic processes of human interaction. To fulfill this mission, we study those processes both in laboratory settings specially designed for experimental research and in real-world contexts where the processes of interest take place naturally. Once research moves into the real-world settings, its potential applications become evident. The next step is to develop actual programs, procedures, and systems that make use of research findings. Entire industries have been built around principles discovered through social psychological research efforts. Personnel selection, political polling, advertising and marketing, management training, and self-help groups are all enterprises that represent social psychology in action.

The primary purpose of this book is to introduce readers to social psychology as a basic research field. However, we want students to be aware of the relevance of theory and research discoveries to specific areas of application. As we have already pointed out, the processes that interest social psychologists can be studied at the individual, interpersonal, and group levels of explanation (see Table 1.1). At each of these levels, research is focused on specific topic areas that are the component parts of social psychology. For instance, at the individual level, we

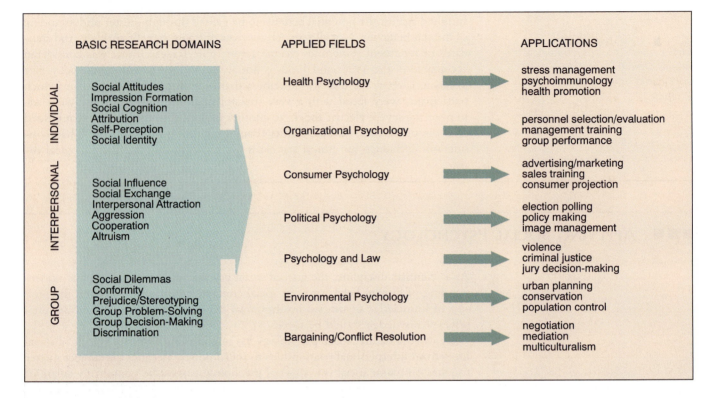

FIGURE 1.4

■

Linkages between subject matter of social psychology and its use in applied settings.

study attitudes, expectations and judgments of other people, and self-perceptions. At the interpersonal level we investigate communication of emotions, social exchange, friendship, and social interactions that hurt or help others. Topics at the group level include group problem solving, conformity to social norms, crowd behavior, and intergroup relations.

For each of these research domains, there are many areas of application that are informed by social psychological research and theory. Research on social influence and persuasion is used regularly in the development of advertising campaigns for commercial products, political candidates, and public health. Research on self-esteem, social support, and group affiliation has proved to have important implications for health and coping with stress. Principles of social exchange are used to counsel couples through marital difficulties and to develop effective methods of negotiation and conflict resolution. Figure 1.4 illustrates these and other linkages between the subject matter of social psychology and its use in applied settings.

Even though the arrows in Figure 1.4 are drawn in only one direction, the link between basic research on social psychological processes and its application to social problems is actually a two-way street. Social psychological theory suggests directions for solving practical problems, and applied research provides a testing ground for assessing the validity of those theories. In the chapters that follow, the relationships between basic research and applied problems are featured in the discussion of specific areas of research. Our purpose is to show the close connections between the development of social psychology as a scientific discipline and its application to real-life concerns.

■■■ SUMMARY

Social psychology is defined as the study of how individuals are influenced by other people—their social environment. Social psychological research takes place at three different levels of explanation: the individual level, which includes the study of attitudes and social perception; the interpersonal level, which includes the study of affiliation and attraction; and the group level, which includes the study of conformity, consensus, and intergroup relations.

Social psychological research is designed to test hypotheses about relationships between individuals and their social environment. Research takes place in both field settings and in laboratory experiments. Most field research assesses the correlations between variables as they occur naturally. Experiments are designed to test causal relationships between variables by manipulating independent variables and determining their effect on dependent variables. A critical feature of experimental design is random assignment of participants to different conditions of the independent variable.

Social psychological experiments are evaluated in terms of their internal and external validity. To achieve validity, experimenters often mislead research participants about the true purposes of the experimental study. The use of deception in psychological research must be balanced against the principles of informed consent that underlie the ethics of research. When research requires some degree of deception, a thorough debriefing is essential to the conduct of good experiments.

In addition to conducting research that meets high ethical standards, social psychologists are concerned about the implications and applications of their research findings in real-world settings. Basic topics of research in social psychology have given rise to major fields of applied research, including health psychology, organizational psychology, consumer research, environmental psychology, and political psychology. These applied fields have, in turn, provided the links for applications of social psychology to problems as diverse as stress reduction, resource conservation, and multicultural training.

■■■ SUGGESTED READINGS

1. Allport, G. W. (1985). The historical background of social psychology. In G. Lindzey & E. Aronson (Eds.), *Handbook of social psychology* (Vol. 1, 3rd ed., pp. 1–46). New York: Random House.

2. Aronson, E., Brewer, M. B., & Carlsmith, J. M. (1985). Experimentation in social psychology. In G. Lindzey & E. Aronson (Eds.), *Handbook of social psychology* (Vol. 1, 3rd ed., pp. 441–486). New York: Random House.

3. Crano, W. D., & Brewer, M. B. (1986). *Principles and methods of social research.* Boston: Allyn and Bacon.

4. Doise, W. (1986). *Levels of explanation in social psychology.* Cambridge, England: Cambridge University Press.

PART I

SOCIAL ATTITUDES

Ways of Viewing the World

CHAPTER 2
Attitudes: Measurement, Structure, and Behavior

CHAPTER 3
Attitude Change: The Study of Communication and Persuasion

CHAPTER 4
Models of Attitude Change: How and Why Persuasion Works

CHAPTER 5
Cognitive Dissonance: Persuading Ourselves

ATTITUDES
Measurement, Structure, and Behavior

■ Key Concepts

Thurstone scale
Likert scale
Semantic differential scale
Attitudes = evaluations
Galvanic skin response (GSR)
Facial electromyogram (EMG)
Unobtrusive methods
Attitude–behavior consistency
Generality/Specificity of Attitude
  and Behavior
Intention
Direct experience
Extremity
Mere thought
Accessibility
Knowledge
Involvement
Vested interest

■ Chapter Outline

SOCIAL ATTITUDES: CONCEPTION AND MEASUREMENT
  Beginnings: Thurstone's Approach
  The Three-part Distinction
  The Attitudes = Evaluations Approach
  Psychophysiological Approaches
  ■ Unobtrusive Methods

ATTITUDES AS EVALUATIONS: CONCEPTION AND STANDARD DEFINITIONS

THE ATTITUDE–BEHAVIOR CONSISTENCY DEBATE

FACTORS THAT AFFECT THE ATTITUDE–BEHAVIOR LINK
  Generality/Specificity of Attitude and Behavior
  Intention
  Direct Experience
  Extremity and Mere Thought
  Accessibility and Knowledge
  ■ Attitudes and Recycling
  Ego Involvement and Vested Interest
  Individual Differences: Self-Monitoring

SOME CONCLUDING THOUGHTS

SUMMARY

Charlie is anticipating another boring Friday evening at the local pub, but as he approaches his usual barstool, his heart nearly stops. Less than twenty feet away is the most beautiful woman he has ever encountered. Who is this person? He plunges through the crowd and, forgetting all his standard opening lines, blurts out, "Hi, I'm Charlie. What's your name?" The stranger answers, "I'm Joy." Charlie responds, "You certainly are." His mind is blank. He can think of nothing but getting to know her.

■ ■ ■

In a recent commercial, Lee Iacocca, the persuasive former president of Chrysler Motors, talks about the airbags that are standard in all Chrysler minivans. The gist of his pitch: If you want airbags in your van, buy Chrysler—"Nobody else has 'em."

■ ■ ■

After her busy work day, Alicia takes a taxi home and sinks into the soft pillows of her sofa. It is election day. As usual at this time of year, the wind is howling, it is cold, and a downpour seems inevitable. Alicia has followed the campaign with interest. She was won over to the Democratic challenger, whom she believes will be an effective leader. But the weather is abominable. And she has a cold. And she has dinner to prepare. Still, the election is important. Reluctantly, she puts on her raincoat and trudges to the polls.

Should the death penalty be abolished? Are American cars better than Japanese cars? Should we feed starving people in other lands? Who was more responsible for the Cold War, the U.S. or Russia?

Your answers to these questions reflect your attitudes—toward the death penalty, American and Japanese cars, foreign aid, and the like. Attitudes are everywhere—they are expressed by everyone about almost everything. If you reflect on your last three conversations, it is a safe bet that in at least two of them you stated an attitude—a belief or evaluation that would be difficult, if not impossible, to prove objectively. In addition to being pervasive, attitudes are big business. Think of the constant bombardment you experience every day, from advertisers, politicians, people supporting one cause or another. Why do some appeals cause you to change your mind, or attitude, about an issue, while others have no effect at all? Why are some companies successfully selling their products, while others, with an equally good commodity, fail? Why do we vote for some politicians and not others? The answers to all of these questions lie at the heart of attitude research. In this chapter, we describe the ways attitudes are measured, and then consider their effects on action. Do attitudes influence behavior? The answer seems apparent, but as we shall see, considerable controversy surrounds this issue.

■ ■ ■ SOCIAL ATTITUDES: CONCEPTION AND MEASUREMENT

More than a half-century ago, Allport (1935) observed that attitude was "the most distinctive and indispensable concept in contemporary social psychology" (p. 798). Had he written the same words today, he would be equally correct. In the decade of the 1970s, more than 20,000 books and articles were devoted to attitudes and attitude change. Today, the pace has quickened (Dawes & Smith, 1985). Why? Because the stakes in the "attitude game" are enormous. Ask any advertiser or politician. This is one reason why social psychologists have lavished such attention on them. But what are attitudes? And how are they measured?

Beginnings: Thurstone's Approach

The origin of the idea of attitude can be traced to Aristotle. His treatise on *Rhetoric* described the principles that governed persuasion—the ways people change others' attitudes. For our purposes, we need not journey to the Aegean hills of the fourth century B.C. It is sufficient instead to travel to Hyde Park, Illinois, where in the 1920s Louis Thurstone developed a scientific measure of attitudes (Thurstone, 1928; Thurstone & Chave, 1929). Before Thurstone, the study of attitudes was confined to the realm of poets and philosophers. With the development of a method to measure them (the **Thurstone scale**), attitudes became the fundamental building block of social psychology (McGuire, 1985).

Let's consider the method Thurstone used when he conceived the first attitude scale. To build his measure, meant to assess attitudes toward the church, Thurstone presented statements that covered a broad spectrum of possible evaluations. People judged the implicit favorability of each item toward the church. Table 2.1 lists a sample of the items Thurstone used. Many readers will be familiar with scales of this type. They are common in marketing, psychology, politics, and business.

Thurstone calculated an item's value on the basis of the average score it received from all judges. Then, items whose values were evenly distributed across the range of possible evaluations were presented to a new sample of respondents. These people checked the two or three items that best represented their feelings. The parenthesized numbers that follow the items of Table 2.1 are the average values each item received from Thurstone's judges in 1929. Because values can range from 1 to 11, we can see that item 5 was rated as the most negative statement possible. If a person endorsed this item (and item 3) we would infer that he or she held a very negative attitude toward the church. If the person endorsed only the more positive statements (items 2 and 4), we would infer a positive attitude. The endorsed items define, or quantify, the rater's attitude.

TABLE 2.1

■

**Sample items drawn from Thurstone and Chave's (1929)
"Attitude Toward Church" Scale**

1. I do not receive any benefit from attending church services but I think it helps some people. (5.7)
2. I believe church membership is almost essential to living life at its best. (1.5)
3. I think the country would be better off if the churches were closed and the ministers set to some useful work. (10.4)
4. I find the services of the church both restful and inspiring. (2.3)
5. I think the church is a parasite on society. (11.0)
6. When I go to church I enjoy a fine ritual service with good music. (4.0)
7. I think the teaching of the church is altogether too superficial to have much social significance. (8.3)

Note: Parenthesized values refer to judges' average ratings of the favorability of items. Typically, they are not presented when subjects are completing the scale. An individual's attitude score is the median scale value of all items checked.

The Three-part Distinction

Thurstone defined attitudes in terms of feelings or evaluations. Such feelings and evaluations are implicit in the items of his scales. Thus, information about people's feelings is inferred, or extracted, from the attitude statements. Evaluation is inferred on the basis of people's agreement with one item over the others that are available.

Some researchers conceive of attitudes as more than evaluative feelings; they believe that attitudes contain elements of knowledge and action as well, and these components should not be merged, as Thurstone suggested (e.g., Breckler & Wiggins, 1989, 1991). The vignettes presented at the beginning of this chapter were written to emphasize these different features of attitudes. Charlie's emotional rush when he encounters Joy is almost purely affective—he knows nothing about her, not even her name, but his feelings are evident. The appeal of the car commercial is primarily cognitive, or knowledge based. Iacocca is saying, "It is not important if you like the looks of our product. We have an innovation no one else has. You should consider this information and act reasonably—buy our van." In the voting vignette, we find Alicia deciding to *act* on her strong feelings for one candidate over another despite the inconvenience of voting.

All three attitudes contain elements of evaluation, cognition, and behavior, but we stressed a different component in each. The three-part division of attitude is appealing because it promises greater precision. However, precise measurement can be costly, and the added precision often is more apparent than real. One difficulty involves the relationships among components. Do we need to use all

Attraction is one emotional expression of attitudes: See Chapter 13.

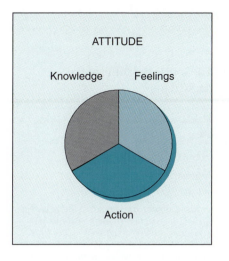

ATTITUDE

Knowledge   Feelings

Action

FIGURE 2.1

◼

The Three Part Approach to the Definition of Attitude. Some attitude theorists reject the "attitudes = evaluations" approach, and prefer instead to think that attitudes consist of knowledge, feeling, and action components.

three components if they are highly related? If evaluation conveys most of the information, why go to the trouble of trying to measure the other two? On the other hand, if the components are not related, do we have a unitary measure of attitude? Which feature should concern us? Which is the best representative of the attitude?

The Attitudes = Evaluations Approach

Because of such ambiguities, most researchers today restrict their definition of attitude to a person's *evaluative* (good–bad) response. Thus, when social psychologists measure attitudes, they are interested in evaluations. What are the ingredients of evaluations? Zanna and Rempel (1986) state that evaluations consist of emotion and knowledge components. An attitude is the combination of *feelings* and *knowledge* about an object. We know that a particular politician is dishonest and stupid, and we do not like these traits. Our negative evaluation is the summary of these feelings, based on our knowledge.

Likert Scales.   Developments in attitude measurement following Thurstone are consistent with his emphasis on evaluation. Likert (1932), for example, devised a method that bypassed some of the difficulties involved in developing Thurstone-style scales, but still generated a solid attitude measure. His method is used widely today. Many will be familiar with the format of the items in Table 2.2, which is an example of a **Likert**-style **scale**. Like Thurstone, Likert emphasized the evaluative feature of attitudes, but the evaluations are inferred from people's ratings, based on knowledge and feelings about that knowledge.

Osgood's semantic differential.   Osgood, Suci, and Tannenbaum's (1957/ 1978) method also is based on evaluation. Their **semantic differential** technique requires respondents to describe an attitude object through scales bounded

---

TABLE 2.2

◼

An Example of a Likert-type Attitude Scale, with the Response Options Typically Employed

Circle the response (strongly agree, agree, don't know, disagree, strongly disagree) that best expresses your feeling on each question.

SA A ? D SD   It is natural to fear the future.

SA A ? D SD   Man on his own is helpless and miserable.

SA A ? D SD   I hate some people because of what they stand for.

SA A ? D SD   To know what's going on, rely on leaders.

SA A ? D SD   Most people don't know what's good for them.

(From Rokeach, 1960).

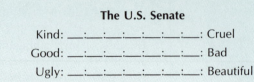

TABLE 2.3

■

An Example of the Format Used in a Semantic Differential Approach to Attitude Scaling

---

The U.S. Senate

Kind: __:__:__:__:__:__:__: Cruel

Good: __:__:__:__:__:__:__: Bad

Ugly: __:__:__:__:__:__:__: Beautiful

Note: Respondents are asked to characterize the attitude object by checking the scales provided. To score responses, a scale value of +3 to −3 is assigned to each scale value. Thus, a person checking the category nearest "Kind" would receive a score of +3 on this scale, while a person checking the middle category would receive a score of 0 on the item. Scores on all evaluative items are summed to arrive at an estimate of the person's attitude toward the attitude object. Notice the versatility of this approach: To form a new scale, we need merely to change the attitude object (which in this case is the U.S. Senate).

by pairs of antonyms (Table 2.3). Osgood found that people used *evaluative* words as their chief method of signifying their reaction to an attitude object. Our primary reaction to another person, event, or object is a judgment of its goodness or badness—an evaluation. This finding has been replicated in many cultures around the world, across a host of different languages. Based on these findings, many attitude researchers have adopted Osgood's semantic differential as the measurement technique of choice. The semantic differential is the most purely evaluative measure we have. It does not extract evaluation from people's expressed beliefs about an attitude object, as do Thurstone and Likert (see Tables 2.1 and 2.2). Rather, it attempts to tap into those evaluations directly.

Psychophysiological Approaches

GSR. The assessment methods discussed so far rely on information that people want to provide about themselves. Over the years, researchers have tried to construct measures that do not depend so much on people's consciously monitored responses. The reason is obvious—sometimes, people cannot or will not tell the truth. Psychophysical approaches were developed to compensate for this weakness. These techniques are based on the assumption that people's feelings are reflected in their physiological state. The **galvanic skin response (GSR)** is a method used to tap such states. This technique assesses skin conductivity through electrodes attached to a person's palm. If the skin is sweaty, it conducts electricity better. Since arousal causes sweating, the GSR is used to indicate positive or negative emotional states. The GSR can provide useful information. The stronger or more arousing their attitude, the greater are people's GSRs (Dawson, Schell, & Filion, 1990). Unfortunately, the GSR does not tell us the *direction* of the attitude—a person will display a high GSR in response to an object that is loved **or** detested. The GSR merely reflects intensity. Another drawback is that the GSR is affected by other factors as well—for example, novelty, surprise, or anxiety—making it less than the perfect physiological indicator (Raskin, 1973).

Facial EMG.   A promising method of inferring attitude from physiological states is the **facial electromyogram (EMG).** The EMG is based on the assumption that the face reflects feelings. This assumption dates back at least to Charles Darwin (1872). The EMG detects differences in electrical activity among the various facial muscles via electrodes attached to the participant's face (Cacioppo & Tassinary, 1990; Tassinary & Cacioppo, 1992). Some facial muscles are good indicators of positive reactions, others of negative reactions. For example, Schwartz, Fair, Salt, Mandel, and Klerman (1976) asked people to "think happy thoughts," and EMG activity was greater in their depressor and zygomatic muscles than when they were asked to "think unhappy thoughts." Tiny contractions of the facial muscles are promising indicators of attitude strength and direction.

Facial expression is a guide to feelings: See Chapter 6.

APPLYING SOCIAL PSYCHOLOGY TO HEALTH
■ ■ ■

Unobtrusive Methods

Concealed, or indirect, attitude measures also are popular in today's social psychology. These *unobtrusive methods* require the researcher to infer attitudes from people's actions. Leventhal provides an interesting example of an unobtrusive measure. He wanted to know if high- or low-fear-arousing messages would convince people to quit smoking and take a precautionary chest X-ray. To answer this question, Leventhal and Watts (1966) set up an exhibit at the New York State Exposition (see also Leventhal, 1970). In their exhibit, they projected three health-relevant films, and the people who wandered into the exhibit saw one of them. All films focused on the dangers of smoking, but they varied in their graphic depiction of these dangers. The most arousing film showed a vivid and horrifying operation on a lung cancer patient. The point of the study was to see if one film was more effective than the others. Rather than ask participants if they planned to follow the film's advice, Leventhal placed a mobile X-ray unit at the exit. The measure of each film's effect was the proportion of people who obtained a chest X-ray. (In this study, high-fear arousal had the greatest impact.)

The effect of fear arousal on attitude change has been the focus of considerable research on persuasion: See Chapter 3.

The point of this example is that participants did not know they were the subject of investigation—they simply had viewed a free movie. The experimenters inferred the effectiveness of the three films from participants' behavior. In this instance, the inference seems relatively safe. In some contexts, the translation is not so easy, and data must be interpreted very carefully. In an engaging and entertaining book, Webb and his colleagues suggest some solutions to these problems, and discuss a host of interesting unobtrusive measures that have been employed over the years (Webb, Campbell, Schwartz, Sechrest, & Grove, 1981). For example, to determine the popularity of museum exhibits, researchers in Chicago's Field Museum noted the frequency with which the floor tiles were replaced. Of course, to be confident of this measure's validity, we would need to be sure that the exhibit was not on a highly traveled path (such as the only way to the cafeteria or to other popular exhibits).

■ ■ ■ **ATTITUDES AS EVALUATIONS: CONCEPTIONS AND STANDARD DEFINITIONS**

How do the approaches we have surveyed correspond to the commonly accepted definitions of attitude? As we will see, the focus on evaluation in measurement is matched by a theoretical emphasis on evaluation as well. Consider some popular definitions of attitudes:

■ Attitudes are likes and dislikes (Bem, 1970, p. 14).

■ [An attitude is] a feeling that an attitude object is good or bad, fair or unfair (Collins, 1970, p. 71).

■ [Attitudes are] evaluative beliefs about objects, classes of people, ideas, and events (Crano & Messé, 1982, p. 110).

■ [Attitudes are] predispositions to respond, but are distinguished from other such states of readiness in that they predispose toward an *evaluative* response (Osgood et al., 1957/1978, p. 189).

■ [Attitudes are] general evaluations based on affect and cognition (Millar & Tesser, 1989).

Clearly, there is consensus about the meaning of attitude—what it is and how it is measured. But does this agreement matter? Do attitudes really have anything to do with behavior? For years, this question was the stimulus for heated debate. Let's review some of the research on this issue to see how the fight has turned out.

■ ■ ■ **THE ATTITUDE–BEHAVIOR CONSISTENCY DEBATE**

Is it not obvious that attitudes affect behavior? If a person's favorite flavor of ice cream is chocolate, isn't it reasonable that he or she would order this flavor more often than not? If Charlie loves Joy, should he marry her rather than Judy? The answers to these questions seem trivially simple. But the obvious answer is not the one that is always given. Sometimes, attitudes do not predict actions, and the volume of research devoted to the study of *attitude–behavior consistency* reflects this fact.

Why attitudes do not predict behavior has been an issue of debate since one of the earliest studies on attitude–behavior consistency. To gather data for this study, Richard LaPiere (1934) traveled throughout the southwestern United States accompanied by a Chinese couple. During this period in America's past, many held unfavorable attitudes toward Asian people. LaPiere wanted to know if people's actions—their treatment of his traveling companions—would reflect their attitudes. In their travels, the trio visited more than 250 restaurants and hotels, and were given courteous service in all but one.

Prejudice and discrimination are major topics of research in social psychology: See Chapters 23 and 24.

After returning home, LaPiere wrote to each of the establishments he had visited, and asked if they would serve an Asian person. Of those who responded (approximately 50% of the total group), 90% said they would not! There was a great gulf between the attitudes expressed by personnel of the establishments they visited and their actions. Over the years, many flaws in LaPiere's study have been identified. The people who extended service to the couple were probably not the same people who answered the attitude questionnaire. That one person's attitude does not predict another person's actions should not cause surprise. Nevertheless, many researchers used LaPiere's study to argue that attitudes had few, if any, implications for actual behavior. Later research that avoided some of the more glaring errors of LaPiere's study did not alter his conclusions. When Wicker (1969) reviewed more than forty studies of the attitude–action link, he found only a weak relationship between attitude and behavior. As a result, he suggested it might be reasonable to dismiss the attitude concept and focus instead on behavior. Many researchers strongly disagreed. Let's see why, and how they pressed their case.

An early defense of attitude–behavior consistency was advanced by Calder and Ross (1973), who proposed a number of reasons why research had failed to show a strong link between attitudes and actions. An obvious reason is that it is much easier to induce people to *express* an attitude than to get them to *act* on it. For example, it is easy for many of us to express the attitude that we weigh too much, but it is very difficult to reduce caloric intake. The lack of a consistent relation between attitude and behavior in this case does not necessarily mean that the attitude is irrelevant, but rather that other forces (habit, genetics, appetite) operate against its behavioral expression.

Another problem has to do with the relative importance of the attitudes that we study. In many studies, investigators focused on attitudes that were unimportant to their participants. They avoided strongly held beliefs because they are difficult to change. Unimportant attitudes can affect behavior, but their impact will not be great. What other factors affect attitude–behavior consistency? On the pages that follow, we consider some of the more important variables.

■■■ FACTORS THAT AFFECT THE ATTITUDE–BEHAVIOR LINK

Generality/Specificity of Attitude and Behavior

Fishbein and Ajzen (1975) took a leading role in promoting the idea that attitudes can predict behavior (see also Doll & Ajzen, 1992). They observed that much early work measured attitudes and behavior at different levels of *specificity*. They argued that it was not reasonable to assume that an attitude measured at a very *general* level would predict a very *specific* action. For example, suppose we measure people's general political orientation, and arrange these people along a dimension from extremely liberal to extremely conservative. If we question respondents after the election, we will find that their general attitudes are not good indicators of choice of one candidate over another. Does this result suggest that attitudes are irrelevant? Not necessarily, because the components of the attitude–action relationship were measured at different levels of specificity. The political attitude (liberal or conservative) is measured at a very general, nonspecific level, whereas the action (a vote for a given candidate) is quite specific. In this circumstance, inconsistent attitude–behavior relationships are common.

Suppose we controlled the generality/specificity of the attitude and the behavior measures. Would this affect attitude–behavior consistency? Weigel and his colleagues suggest that it would (Weigel, Vernon, & Tognacci, 1974). These researchers measured participants' attitudes about environmental problems at three different levels of specificity. At the least specific level, participants expressed their attitudes about general environmental problems. At the middle level, they stated their evaluations of specific ecological concerns of environmental organizations like Greenpeace or the Sierra Club. At the most specific level, they evaluated the Sierra Club, an established and important environmental organization.

Five months later, participants received a fund-solicitation and membership form from the Sierra Club. Weigel and his colleagues wanted to determine (unobtrusively) the extent of relationship between environmental attitudes measured at various levels of specificity and a specific proenvironmental action—joining the Sierra Club. As specificity between attitude and action increased, so too did the relationship between attitude and behavior. No relation was found between participants' general ecological attitudes and their specific behavior. Participants with strong, positive, but *general,* attitudes toward conservation did not necessarily choose to join the Sierra Club. However, a strong positive relationship was discovered between attitudes and behavior at the highest level of specificity. Those who expressed positive attitudes toward the Sierra Club were much more likely to join when asked to do so. When specificity of attitude *and* behavior measures match, behavior is more likely to be consistent with attitude.

Intention

Another important mediator of the attitude–behavior link is the extent to which people *intend* to act on their attitude. Fishbein and Ajzen's (1981) theory linking attitudes to behavior specifically includes an *intention* component. Their research suggests that people's intention to behave in a certain way is the most immediate determinant of behavior (cf. Sheppard, Hartwick, & Warshaw, 1988). In a test of this idea, Madden, Ellen, and Azjen (1992) assessed people's attitudes toward, and intentions to perform, a series of commonplace acts—washing the car, exercising, talking to a friend, taking vitamins, avoiding caffeine, and the like. The results disclosed that people's attitudes affected their intentions, which in turn influenced behavior. Intention substantially increased the researchers' ability to predict action. If an attitude stimulated an intention, the attitude-consistent action was performed. If the attitude did not produce an intention, its link with behavior was weak.

Intention is a major component of an interesting model of attitude change, the theory of reasoned action, developed by Ajzen and Fishbein (1980). This model predicts that behavior is the result of people's behavioral intentions which, in turn, are caused by people's attitudes and their estimates that a specific action will result in a given outcome. In a theoretical extension, Ajzen (1985) added a predictive component to the model, which he termed perceived behavior control. This component reflects the extent to which the individual feels *capable* of performing a behavior. Madden and colleagues (1992) suggest that adding this

FIGURE 2.2

■

Theory of Planned Behavior (adapted from Madden et al., 1992). The arrows indicate the effect of one variable on another.

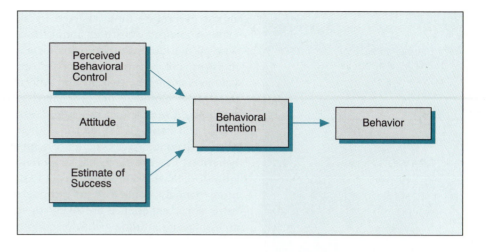

component results in a better model, which has been dubbed the theory of planned behavior. Figure 2.1 summarizes the components of this theory, and the ways they influence each other.

How does it work? Let's return to Alicia from our chapter opening. We know that Alicia is strongly in favor of the Democratic challenger in the election. In the model's terms, her positive attitude will affect her behavioral intention—to vote. However, suppose she feels that her vote will not really matter much, or that she is feeling so tired that she simply cannot make it to the polling place. In either case, because of subjective norms (low probability of success) or perceived behavioral control ("I'm too tired to vote"), the model suggests that the desired action (voting) will not occur. Although it requires considerable information—we must know participants' attitudes, intentions, perceived capabilities, and so forth—the theory is a powerful predictive device when sufficient information is available.

Direct Experience

Direct experience with attitude-relevant people, objects, or events enhances attitude–behavior consistency. Such experiences increase our certainty in the attitude, and our knowledge about the attitude object. Fazio and Zanna (1981) found that attitudes formed through direct experience are almost always more predictive of later actions than attitudes formed without such experience. For example, a young boy may express a positive attitude toward dogs, but if the attitude is not grounded in experience, he may run away from even the smallest Yorkie when he encounters one. If the attitude had been based on experience, the behavior would be more likely to match the expressed attitude.

Regan and Fazio (1977) demonstrated the importance of experience on attitude–behavior consistency in a study that took place at Cornell University. At the time of the experiment, Cornell was experiencing such serious overcrowding that some unfortunate freshmen found themselves occupying a cot in their dormitory's lobby during their first semester. This probably was not the college experience they had anticipated. Students' attitudes were measured, and

Will direct experience affect these inmates' actions toward prison reform? ▪

almost everyone—those affected by the problem and those who were not—expressed negative attitudes about this arrangement. How could they feel otherwise? When these same students were asked to work to solve the overcrowding problem, the researchers found a substantial difference in the proportions of volunteers from the two groups. Affected students were three times more likely to work to eliminate the problem than those who had not been consigned to the lobby, even though the attitudes of the two groups were indistinguishable. Regan and Fazio (1977) explained their results in terms of experience. Attitudes of those having direct experience with the problem were linked more firmly to behaviors. Later research has supported the link between direct experience and attitude–behavior consistency (e.g., Fazio & Williams, 1986). In addition to being more strongly connected to attitude-relevant behaviors, evaluations resulting from direct experience are likely to involve firsthand knowledge, which also contributes to attitude–behavior consistency (Wood, Rhodes & Biek, in press).

Extremity and Mere Thought

Most attitude theorists believe that extreme attitudes are more likely than moderate ones to be expressed behaviorally, and there is strong evidence for this supposition (Chaiken & Yates, 1985; Liberman & Chaiken, in press). Many factors promote attitude *extremity*. For example, an attitude is likely to be extreme if it has important personal consequences (see "Ego Involvement and Vested Interest" later in this chapter). If an attitude is expressed frequently, it will be more extreme (Downing & Judd, in press). One of the least obvious factors known to affect extremity (and hence attitude–behavior consistency) is *mere thought*. In a series of studies, Tesser and his colleagues have shown that merely thinking about one's attitude toward an object tends to make the evaluation more extreme (Tesser, Martin, & Mendolia, in press).

In an early study of the "mere thought" effect, for example, Sadler and Tesser (1973) had pairs of participants interact via an intercom and describe themselves to each other. Actually, people were studied in isolation—their "partner" was a tape recording. In some interactions, the partner appeared to be a very likeable guy who complimented his partners on their self-descriptions. In turn, he described himself positively but realistically. Other participants were paired with a very unpleasant fellow, who criticized their self-descriptions and was boastful and conceited. Afterward, participants rated their partner. For some, the ratings were taken after they had been given time to sit quietly and think about him. The other participants were occupied with a distracting task until the rating task, and hence could not think much about their partner before rating him. There were large differences in evaluations as a result of this difference. Those given a chance to think about their partner evaluated him more *extremely* than did participants not given this opportunity. "Thoughtful" participants rated the likeable partner more positively, and the unpleasant partner more negatively, than distracted participants. Later research extended this finding by demonstrating that the effect was stronger if the issue was ambiguous (Tesser & Cowan, 1975), if the attitude object was not physically present (Leone, Taylor, & Adams, 1991; Tesser, 1978), and if the measure was delayed rather than immediate (Sanbonmatsu, Kardes, & Sansone, in press).

How does mere thought influence attitude–behavior consistency? As attitudes become more extreme, they become more accessible—that is, they more readily come to mind. Accessible attitudes, in turn, are more likely to cause belief-consistent behavior. Mere thought produces more extreme (and therefore more accessible) attitudes, which are more likely to be expressed.

Accessibility and Knowledge

Accessibility.   We learned earlier that direct experience heightens attitude–behavior consistency. Fazio (1990) has explained this relationship by showing that direct experience magnifies attitude *accessibility*. Accessible attitudes are easier to recall, and more likely to come to mind spontaneously. Attitudes that more readily come to mind are more likely to influence behavior (Fazio, Powell, & Williams, 1989). During the 1984 presidential election campaign, for example, Fazio and Williams (1986) measured the accessibility of people's attitudes toward the candidates. Three months later, after the election had taken place, the participants were asked to reveal their vote. Attitude was an almost perfect predictor of the vote of those classified as having attitudes of high accessibility. For those of low accessibility, attitude was much less strongly related to candidate choice.

Attitude accessibility is magnified by direct experience: See Chapter 8.

Knowledge.   Another factor that affects accessibility of attitudes is *knowledge*. Theoretically, the more one knows about an object, the more accessible its evaluation, and the more likely it is to guide behavior. In an important series of investigations, Wendy Wood (1982; Wood, Rhodes, & Biek in press) confirmed these hypotheses. She demonstrated that attitudes characterized by high knowledge are more accessible and more strongly related to attitude-consistent action. Wood's research supports Zanna and Rempel's (1986) view that evaluations consist of knowledge and feeling components. Strengthening one or the other of these components appears to strengthen accessibility and thereby enhances attitude–behavior consistency.

APPLYING SOCIAL PSYCHOLOGY TO THE ENVIRONMENT

■ ■ ■

Attitudes and Recycling

Kalgren and Wood (1986) tested the effects of accessibility on behavior in an interesting and persuasive study. They estimated the accessibility of participants' proenvironmental beliefs by asking them to list in two minutes all the ecologically responsible actions they had ever performed. Their idea was that if people were really concerned about the environment, they would have a number of actions readily available to list. Then they measured participants' attitudes toward conservation, recycling, and so on. Two weeks later, they called the same individuals and asked them to join a recycling project. Those who agreed were visited and directed to place recyclable materials in a specific location each week. Kalgren and Wood's weekly collection of recycled cans and bottles constituted the study's behavioral measure.

The results leave little doubt that the accessibility of participants' ecological attitudes affected their behavior. Participants' attitudes of low accessibility did not predict behavior. However, for participants of high accessibility, ecological attitudes strongly predicted their diligence in recycling. These results affirm that knowledge affects attitude accessibility, which in turn influences the likelihood that the attitude will direct and guide behavior. Bassili and Fletcher (in press) reconfirmed this result in a study of voting behavior. They found that survey respondents who responded rapidly to the question of their favored candidate demonstrated greater attitude–behavior consistency (that is, were more likely to vote for the candidate they favored) than those whose choice was less rapid, and thus, presumably, less accessible. How do these findings translate into practical actions? Quite simply, they show that the more you know, the more likely you are to act in accord with your knowledge. From the other perspective, the data suggest that attitudes backed up by little knowledge are not likely to be accompanied by actions that logically follow from the attitude. Thus, two people might have attitudes that appear identical (in terms of extremity and direction), but they will act differently as a result of differences in the amount of knowledge on which the attitudes are based.

Ego Involvement and Vested Interest

It stands to reason that if an attitude object has nothing to do with a person's life, there will be little correspondence between the attitude and the person's actions. However, if the attitude has implications for the person's well-being, if it is "hedonically relevant," it will guide and direct action.

Involvement.   Two lines of research bear on this observation. Muzafer Sherif and his associates theorized that the extent to which a person was personally *involved* with an attitude object would determine whether the attitude would be expressed behaviorally. To test this possibility, Sherif, Sherif, and Nebergall (1965) studied the degree of people's involvement in a presidential election. They found that people who were highly involved were much more likely to be engaged in organized political actions. Later research by Sherif, Kelly, Rodgers, Sarup, and Tittler, (1973) reconfirmed this finding—the more involvement, the greater the correspondence between attitude and action.

Involvement also plays a role in communication and persuasion: See Chapter 3.

Vested interest.   *Vested interest* refers to the extent to which a person perceives an issue to be associated with his or her well-being (Crano, in press). The greater a person's stake in the outcome of an attitude-relevant action, the stronger the attitude–action link. A useful example of vested interest in action is seen in a study by Sivacek and Crano (1982). At the time of the study, a referendum was being held in the state of Michigan to raise the legal drinking age from nineteen to twenty-one years. Prevailing opinion on the college campuses of the state was hostile to the referendum. An opinion survey conducted at Michigan State University, for example, found that more than 70% of the students opposed the law's change. Note, however, that whatever their opinion, only some of the students would be affected by the new law. Those who would be twenty-one by the time the law was implemented would not be affected by the referendum's outcome, no matter what that outcome was.

The Michigan referendum afforded Sivacek and Crano a naturalistic opportunity to assess the effect of vested interest on attitude–behavior consistency on

Suppose your lawmakers wanted to raise the drinking age in your state to 25 years. Are you opposed to such a change? If so, would you work against it? Much depends upon the extent to which the change would affect you personally. ■

a real and (to some students) important issue. To capitalize on this opportunity, they measured attitudes of a large number of students toward the referendum. Two weeks later, all participants who said they were opposed to the referendum were called by a representative of a fictitious (antireferendum) organization and asked to volunteer to work against its passage. Respondents were classified according to their degree of vested interest, which in this case was defined by age. Those who would not be able to drink in bars for at least two years as a result of the law change were defined as being of high vested interest; those who would be at least twenty-one years old by the time the change took effect were classed as having low vested interest; between these extremes, people were defined as moderately vested.

The three groups were indistinguishable in their (negative) attitude toward the referendum. Also, there were no differences among them in reported alcohol consumption or in their patronage of drinking establishments. However, there was a significant difference in the proportion of participants from the three subgroups who were willing to work to defeat the referendum. More than 47% of the youngest respondents (those defined as being of high vested interest) volunteered to work against the referendum. In contrast, only 26% of the moderately invested participants volunteered, and only 12% of the oldest (low-vested interest) subgroup would work to defeat the referendum. These findings demonstrate that vested interest can be an important moderator of the extent to which attitudes are expressed in overt behavior. It is important to understand that the contribution of vested interest to attitude–behavior consistency was independent of the extremity of the participants' attitudes. Participants shared identical attitudes, but only some were willing to translate their attitudes into action.

TABLE 2.4

■

Some Selected Items from a Self-monitoring Scale

Indicate whether each of the following statements is true or false about yourself.

1. I am not always the person I appear to be.

2. I can only argue for ideals which I already believe.

3. In order to get along and be liked, I tend to be what people expect me to be, rather than anything else.

4. I rarely need the advice of my friends to choose movies, books, or music.

5. In different situations and with different people, I often act like very different persons.

6. My behavior is usually an expression of my true inner feelings, attitudes, and beliefs.

Note: The scale consists of 25 true-false self-descriptive statements. (From Snyder, 1974.)

Individual Differences: Self-Monitoring

A final moderator of attitude–behavior consistency is an individual difference variable first proposed by Mark Snyder and his colleagues (Snyder, 1974, 1979; Snyder & Tanke, 1976). Snyder observed that some people act consistently, no matter what the social context of their actions, while others are more attuned to the situation. He labeled this difference "self-monitoring." This term refers to the extent to which people use their surroundings to guide their actions. High self-monitors act in accordance with their reading of the situation and in response to the reactions their behaviors elicit from others. Low self-monitors are guided more by internal beliefs than external situational cues. Do you salt your food before tasting it? If so, you are probably a low self-monitor. High self-monitors taste their food before seasoning it (McGee & Snyder, 1975). For low self-monitors, internal cues (I love salty food) are given great weight, and contextual cues (the food already is very salty) are largely ignored. High self-monitors use contextual cues before acting, and often downplay internal cues (attitudes) when deciding on a course of action.

Snyder (1974) developed a brief questionnaire to measure the extent to which people differ in their tendency to monitor themselves. A sample of these items is presented in Table 2.4. Research making use of this scale has produced some interesting evidence of the effects of individual differences on attitude–behavior consistency. Snyder and Swann (1976), for example, categorized participants on self-monitoring, and then measured their attitudes toward affirmative action. Two weeks later, they had participants play the role of jurors in a mock trial. They were to evaluate a case involving a female job applicant's sex discrimination suit against an employer who had rejected her in favor of a male applicant.

Participants were given information about the qualifications of the applicants, as well as the arguments advanced by both attorneys. They were asked to render their verdict and to discuss the reasons for their decision. The central issue of the study was the extent to which participants' pretrial attitudes about sex discrimination and affirmative action influenced their decision. A strong relationship between pretrial attitudes and decisions was found in the low-self-monitor group, as predicted. Their attitudes toward affirmative action were an accurate guide to their verdict. Those who had a positive attitude toward affirmative action were much more likely to find in favor of the plaintiff; low self-monitors opposed to affirmative action were more likely to find for the defense. The information presented in the mock court case did not appear to make much difference to low self-monitors.

In contrast, no appreciable relationship existed between the pretrial attitudes and the decisions of the high self-monitors. These people were influenced by the evidence given in the trial. Their actions were unrelated to their pretrial attitudes. These are provocative findings. They suggest that personal characteristics can have important effects on the consistency with which people express their attitudes. Other researchers have studied the impact of a variety of personal characteristics on attitude–behavior consistency (e.g., Bem & Allen, 1974).

The relationship between personality and attitude has been explored by a number of researchers: See Chapters 3 and 4.

■ ■ ■ SOME CONCLUDING THOUGHTS

The study of attitudes is a continuing preoccupation and a distinguishing feature of social psychology. It has been this way since Thurstone's ground-breaking research in the 1920s. Why? The answer is simple. We care about attitudes because they reflect people's feelings. And this is important because the way we feel about something affects our actions toward it. Future work in social psychology will witness even greater attention to attitudes. As shown in other chapters, we are now beginning to focus our attention not only on the effects of attitudes on the attitude holder's actions but also on the actions of the target of the attitude. In the past, debate raged over the usefulness of attitudes for predicting behavior. Today, that debate is largely resolved. We no longer ask if attitudes predict actions, but rather the circumstances under which they do so.

Recent attitude research also focuses on the target of the attitude: See Chapters 12, 15, and 16.

■ ■ ■ SUMMARY

Attitudes represent an important concern of social psychology. Over the years, a number of measurement approaches have been developed to assess these mental constructions. The first was invented by Thurstone, who conceived of attitudes as evaluative responses toward some person or object. This emphasis on evaluation is evident in later approaches—Likert scales and the semantic differential approach. Other attempts at assessing attitudes, including the psychophysiological and unobtrusive measurement approaches, offer less reactive methods of inferring attitudes.

The relevance of attitudes for predicting behavior has been studied at length, in research concerned with attitude–behavior consistency. Many factors affect the likelihood of attitudinally consistent action, including the generality or specificity of the attitude and behavior measures, the intention of the individual to act on a belief, the amount of prior direct experience the person has had with the attitude object, the accessibility of the attitude, and the extent to which the attitude is of deep personal relevance (vested interest). Individual differences, (for example, self-monitoring) also affect the likelihood that an action will follow from a specific attitude.

▪ ▪ ▪ Suggested Readings

1. Cacioppo, J. T., & Tassinary, L. G. (Eds.) (1990). *Principles of psychophysiology: Physical, social, and inferential elements.* Cambridge, England: Cambridge University Press.

2. McGuire, W. J. (1985). Attitudes and attitude change. In G. Lindzey & E. Aronson (Eds.), *The handbook of social psychology* (Vol. 2, 3rd ed.), pp. 233–336. New York: Random House.

3. Pratkanis, A. R., Breckler, S. J., & Greenwald, A. G. (Eds.) (1989). *Attitude structure and function.* Hillsdale, NJ: Erlbaum.

4. Webb, E. J., Campbell, D. T., Schwartz, R. D., & Sechrest, L., & Grove, J. B. (1981). *Nonreactive measures in the social sciences* (2nd ed.). Boston: Houghton Mifflin.

5. Zanna, M. P., & Rempel, J. K. (1986). Attitudes: A new look at an old concept. In D. Bar-Tal & A. Kruglanski (Eds.), *The social psychology of knowledge.* New York: Cambridge University Press.

CHAPTER 3

ATTITUDE CHANGE
The Study of Communication and Persuasion

■ Key Concepts

Counter-argumentation
Source credibility
Expertise
Trustworthiness
Sleeper effect
Role playing
Conclusion drawing
One-sided versus two-sided
 message
Inoculation hypothesis
Distraction
Intelligence, self-esteem, and
 persuadability
Mood and persuasion

■ Chapter Outline

HOVLAND'S MESSAGE-LEARNING APPROACH

THE SOURCE OF A COMMUNICATION
 Expertise
 Trustworthiness
 Credibility Research: The Sleeper Effect
 ■ Attractiveness and Sales

THE MESSAGE
 Drawing a Conclusion
 Delivery: Force, Speed, Number, and Intensity
 One or Two Sides?
 Fear Arousal
 Inoculation Effects
 ■ Inoculating against Stress

THE SETTING
 Situational Distractions
 "Overheard" or Confusing Communications

CHARACTERISTICS OF THE AUDIENCE
 Individual Differences in Intelligence and Self-Esteem
 Mood

SOME CONCLUDING THOUGHTS

SUMMARY

Which message will have the greater effect on smokers? On non-smokers? For answers see page 52.

■■■

■■■ HOVLAND'S MESSAGE-LEARNING APPROACH

Carl Hovland worked for the U.S. Army during World War II. His job was to create and analyze propaganda. At the time many believed there was no more important job in the army, and this may be true. Hovland and his colleagues had to know how to keep the morale of both civilians and fighting troops high. They had to keep people engaged in the war effort, working hard for democracy,

Thurstone pioneered the field of attitude measurement: See Chapter 2.

fighting the enemy on two fronts. After the war, Hovland established and directed the Communication and Attitude Change Program at Yale University. For psychology, the timing of his enterprise could not have been more auspicious. Thanks to the work of Thurstone and his successors, social psychology had a firm grasp on attitude measurement. And, by the war's end, Hovland possessed a wealth of practical knowledge about the ways attitudes could be changed. Combined with his organizational ability, these factors helped Hovland build a science of persuasion. Wartime demands had forced attention on how to apply persuasion. From his experiences Hovland knew what worked, but often did not know why. At Yale he was determined to focus on developing a *basic theory* of persuasion. He used controlled laboratory methods to allow him to explain *how,* and not merely predict *when,* persuasion would succeed.

Hovland assumed that we change attitudes by exposing people to information that is inconsistent with what they believe. If the new information is convincing, people will change their attitudes. But what makes information convincing? Obviously, not all communications produce change, even those that contain lots of information. Hovland hypothesized that before a message could persuade, it had to be noticed, understood, and remembered. To pass these tests, the message had to stimulate two responses: First, it had to raise a question about an attitude's validity. Second, it had to offer an alternative position, and give the receiver a reason to accept it. These two-pronged communications induce people to carry on an internal debate, in which they defend their positions against the one advocated. This process is called **counter-argumentation** (Hovland, Lumsdaine, & Sheffield, 1949). The outcome of the internal debate determines whether the original attitude is maintained or modified. Factors that affect people's ability to counter-argue affect persuasion. For example, if a setting is so distracting that counter-argumentation is next to impossible, attitude change is more likely to occur. Advertisers sometimes take advantage of this fact by presenting their persuasive message in a context that is so rich with distractions that counter-argumentation is difficult, if not impossible. Levi's jeans commercials often use this strategy. They feature lots of movement, loud music, and a subtle sales pitch that seems little more than an afterthought. If the message is comprehensible, this strategy can sell lots of jeans.

Hovland thought the ability to counter-argue was the critical determinant of attitude change, and so he directed his group to learn about factors that affected this ability. The factors they settled on reduced to the following: characteristics of the message source, features of the message itself, the setting in which the message is delivered, and the characteristics of the audience. In Lasswell's (1948) terms, the study of attitude change boils down to the question, "Who says what to whom, under what circumstances?" In the pages that follow, we consider each of these factors.

◼◼◼ THE SOURCE OF A COMMUNICATION

There is little question that *who* communicates a message (the source) can be as important as *what* is said. Think about your response to a Bayer aspirin commercial, which states, "Taking one aspirin every night will significantly reduce your risk of heart attack." Now suppose you hear this same sentence, but it is delivered by your doctor. Will your reaction to the two presentations be different? For most people, it would. Although the message is the same, the source differs, and this difference matters. Hovland devoted considerable attention to this issue in his study of *source credibility*. He wanted to discover if there were characteristics of a source that, by themselves, lead to greater acceptance of a persuasive message. To research this question, Hovland and his colleagues exposed respondents to a persuasive message that had been attributed to one of two different sources (Hovland, Janis, & Kelley, 1953). In one study, for instance, the communication considered the future of the movie industry (competition from TV was just beginning). The message was attributed to one of two sources, a well-known gossip columnist or *Fortune* magazine. Hovland and his team theorized that the nature of the source could have a considerable impact on the persuasiveness of the message. Why? Because affiliating with a positively evaluated source is reinforcing. Hovland distinguished between two source characteristics he thought would affect people's susceptibility to a message—expertise and trustworthiness.

Expertise

Expertise refers to the credentials of the source that bear on the validity of its assertions. Mario Andretti discussing the latest trends in automotive design is an example of a source of high expertise. Expertise is issue dependent. If Mario were to offer his ideas on the probable winner of the Super Bowl, he would probably be less influential than the local bookie, though the respect accorded him might be much greater.

Trustworthiness

Trustworthiness is a second major component of source credibility. It refers to the manipulative intent of the source. The answer to the question, "What does the source stand to gain by my accepting his or her position?" helps define trustworthiness. If the source has no stake in the issue, the message will be more persuasive than if the source stands to gain by the target's acquiescence. Research carried out over the past forty years is generally consistent with these theoretical expectations (Hass, 1981). Think back to the advice you received about using aspirins. If you are like most people, it would have more effect when presented by your doctor. Why? Trustworthiness. Your doctor has nothing to gain by your taking aspirins. Bayer's bottom line depends on it.

Credibility Research: The Sleeper Effect

In an early study of source credibility, Hovland and Weiss (1951) measured participants' attitudes toward the feasibility of nuclear submarines. At that time, the cold war era of the 1950s, the issue was still in doubt—nuclear subs were a matter of attitude, not fact. Then, they presented participants with a written communication that argued in favor of their feasibility, a position that was contrary to the beliefs of most participants. For one group, the message was attributed to J. Robert Oppenheimer, a famous and respected American nuclear scientist. For the other participants, the same communication was attributed to Pravda, the leading newspaper of the Soviet Union. The same communication was significantly more persuasive when attributed to Oppenheimer (the highly credible source), than when it was attributed to the Soviet journal.

That's all there is to it—connect a message with a credible source, and you can sell anything, right? Not exactly. When Hovland and Weiss remeasured their participants three weeks after the original session, they found that source-related differences in attitude had disappeared. The researchers could not distinguish between those exposed to the different sources. This reversal, in which attitudes return after a short period to their original position, is called a *sleeper effect,* because the attitude seemed to have reverted to its original position overnight. To explain this result, they hypothesized that as time passed, the source had somehow become dissociated from its message. In other words, three weeks after the original attitude change session, everyone remembered something about the feasibility of nuclear submarines, but they had forgotten where they obtained their information. Depending on the credibility of the original information source, this dissociation of source and message would have very different effects. The positive attitudes of those provided information by a high-credibility source would become less positive. Why? Because their original attitudes were the result of *both* the credible source and the information it presented. When the source was forgotten, the positive attitude change attributed to the source diminished.

For those exposed to a source of low credibility *(Pravda),* the opposite effect occurred. These respondents' feasibility estimates also were a combined function of the source's message and their evaluation of the source's credibility. In this instance, credibility was low, and detracted from the positive change recommended in the communication. When the source was forgotten, the impact of the message was unfettered by its association with a negative source. Thus, attitudes became more positive.

This explanation suggests that reminding people about the source of a message would reinstate the original source credibility effects. Figure 3.1 depicts the hypothesized relationships. These hypotheses are based on the source dissociation explanation. Research by Kelman and Hovland (1953) produced results that confirmed these predictions. Figure 3.1 tells the story of this experiment: Participants who shared the same general opinion at Time 1 were exposed to sources of high or low credibility. Immediately after exposure to the communication their attitudes were remeasured (Time 2). Source credibility effects are evident at this measurement session. Three weeks later (Time 3), respondents' attitudes are measured again. Change persists among those for whom the source is reinstated. Attitudes of those for whom the source is not reinstated undergo a sleeper effect. Their attitudes revert to their original position.

Years of research on the sleeper effect have helped social psychologists understand more about source effects and their persistence (Allen & Stiff, 1989; Gillig & Greenwald, 1974; Petty & Cacioppo, 1981; Pratkanis, Greenwald, Leippe, & Baumgardner, 1988). What do we know? First, we have learned that

FIGURE 3.1

■

Effects of Source Credibility and Source Reinstatement on Attitude Change Over Time. (Adapted from Kelman and Hovland, 1953.) Notice that the effects of source credibility dissipate over time. However, when the source is reinstated—when people are reminded of the source of the information on which their attitude is based—source credibility effects reappear.

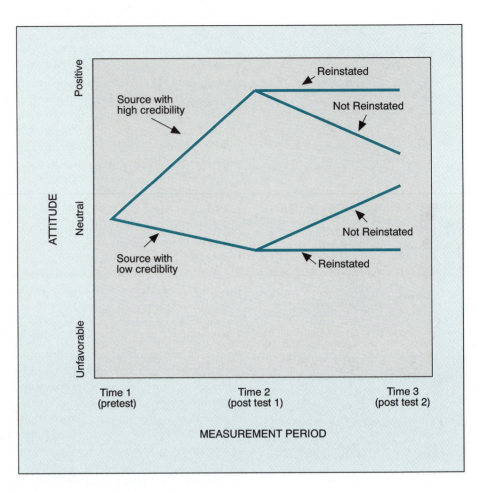

source credibility does affect persuasion. We discount information presented by sources of low credibility and appreciate (identical) information presented by highly credible sources. These effects *persist* if we are aware of the credibility of the source *before* receiving its message or if we are reminded of the source when attitudes are remeasured at some later time. A sleeper effect is likely to occur if we do not know the status of the source until *after* the message is received (as was done in Hovland and Weiss's study). Gruder and his associates showed that source information presented after message reception has an immediate effect on our expressed attitudes, but the source effect dissipates over time, and only the message exerts a long-term influence on attitudes (Gruder, Cook, Hennigan, Flay, Alessi, & Halamaj, 1978). Thus, if we read a persuasive message *and then* learn that it originated from a source of low credibility, our attitude apparently will not be influenced by the message at first. However, change consistent with the communication is likely when the attitude is measured later. Over time, we will have dissociated the (incredible) source from the message, and the message itself will exert its influence. If we knew the source was not credible *before* the communication, its message would have neither immediate nor delayed effects. This pattern suggests that information about the source affects the manner in which we process its message.

Ever wonder why advertisers use physically attractive models to sell their goods? ■

Attractiveness and Sales

Did you ever wonder why advertisers use attractive models to sell their products? Common sense suggests that physical attractiveness might heighten, or reinforce, a source's persuasive power. Why? Because it is more rewarding to look at an attractive spokesperson. Greater attention may facilitate persuasion. A review of relevant research is consistent with this interpretation (Chaiken, 1986). In general, we like people more if they are good looking, and this response affects our attitudes toward influence sources as well (DeBono & Harnish, 1988). But there may be more to it than reinforcement.

Is it possible that we do not process the messages of attractive and unattractive sources in the same way? Do we counter-argue less strongly against a beautiful source? In their study, DeBono and Telesca (1990) searched for the processes responsible for the effects of attractiveness. They showed some participants a slide of a woman who was both beautiful and darkly tanned. Other subjects saw the same woman, but her dress and hairstyle were altered so that she was quite unattractive. Each picture was accompanied by one of two audio tracks prepared for this study. The audio presented persuasive arguments for Savage Tan, a new tanning oil.

Some subjects heard the model give a strong pitch for the new product ("proven protection from ultraviolet rays, special ingredients to prevent premature aging and wrinkling," and the like). Others heard much weaker arguments ("it's silky smooth and easy to apply"). Figure 3.2 shows the effects of these variations on people's attitudes. The results indicate that attractive sources are more effective than unattractive ones in general. And, they are particularly effective when their message is strong. With weak messages, attractiveness does not make much difference. The message to advertisers who make use of attractive sources is to ensure that their messages are strong.

In addition to attitude data, DeBono and Telesca (1990) assessed the amount of information their participants could recall and the favorableness of their thoughts during recall. When the argument was strong, the attractive source stimulated greater recall and more positive thoughts than the unattractive one. Attractive sources stimulate us to process their messages more intently and to do so in a more positive and accepting mental state.

Multiple Sources

If one source can make a difference, can many sources make an even greater difference? Recent investigations have considered this question by expanding the research design to include more than one source. This expansion makes sense, because persuasive messages often originate not from one, but from many, sources. During a presidential campaign, for example, we are confronted with the images of scores of (hired) spokespersons, all of whom extol the virtues of their candidate over the others. Should the wise presidential hopeful concentrate all her advertising money on one spokesperson or on many? The results of research on this issue are clear. If the information presented is strong, logical, and compelling, multiple sources are more effective than solitary ones. This is especially true if the sources promote different ideas or different features of the candidate that appeal to different audiences. However, if the message arguments are weak, or if the multiple sources all say the same thing rather than presenting a diverse set of arguments, the multiple source effect is diminished. In such cases, a solitary source is more effective (Harkins & Petty, 1983, 1987).

FIGURE 3.2

Source Attractiveness and Message-Strength Effects on Attitude. (From DeBono and Telesca, 1990.) Attractive sources are even more influential when their message is strong.

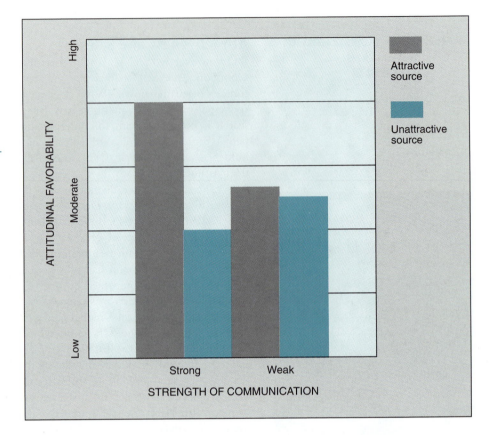

Role-playing also has been used extensively in the study of the theory of cognitive dissonance: See Chapter 5.

Role Playing: Another Kind of Source Effect

We know that a source's characteristics can have a major effect on persuasion. Will this result hold if the receiver of a message is also the person who is creating it? If we combine the roles of source and target, we might be able to create very strong pressure for attitude change. But how can we make the source of a message the simultaneous target of the message? By having the subject play the role of the source. *Role playing* is a technique in which people act out a position with which they might disagree. It is a relatively popular method of studying attitude change. In role-playing research, a person is asked to enact a role—usually, to argue a position to which he or she does not really subscribe. Will such an act influence attitudes? At first glance, it would not appear so. The role player would know all through the performance that it was just that—a performance—and thus would not be influenced. Hovland and his colleagues (1953) saw it differently. They reasoned that in playing a role, communicators encounter a very credible source—themselves. In addition, for all but the most experienced actors, the task is inherently distracting. Being exposed to information, by a credible source (one's self), under distracting conditions, should enhance susceptibility to the message because it would impair counter-argumentation. Hovland's team predicted that role playing will produce attitude change even if the role being enacted is contrary to the role player's established attitude. Were they right?

Let's consider the striking study of Janis and Mann (1965), who asked women who were smokers to play the role of a person who had just been informed by her doctor that she had developed lung cancer. The women were given a set of recommendations by the physician, and encouraged to express the emotions such a patient would experience. Other female smokers, a control group, did not actively play a role, but heard a tape recording of a doctor–patient interaction. The results showed that women who had actively played the role of cancer victim felt more vulnerable to the disease and were more determined to quit smoking than women in the control group. Did these good intentions amount to anything? They certainly did. Follow-up research by Mann and Janis (1968) found that the role-playing women were smoking significantly less than the control group participants eighteen months after the original experiment.

Hovland would explain these results as follows: The women in the role-playing condition were not likely to counter-argue the antismoking message because (1) they were too busy role playing to mount a defense of their smoking behavior, (2) the task itself was not obviously meant to affect their attitudes—thus, they were less defensive, less likely to counter-argue, and (3) the source of the persuasive message was a person each woman trusted implicitly—herself. Other theoretical approaches would handle these findings differently. One possibility is that the smoking became an issue of great vested interest for the role players. The theory of cognitive dissonance would explain the results in terms of effort justification. The role players worked hard in their presentation and needed to justify their effort to themselves. Although many possible explanations exist, we should not lose sight of the central result—role playing had a powerful impact on attitudes *and* subsequent actions. When people play a role, they become susceptible to the information they themselves create.

The concept of vested interest is one explanation of the results of Janis and Mann's (1965) study: See Chapter 2.

The theory of cognitive dissonance is another explanation of the results of Janis and Mann's (1965) study: See Chapter 5.

■ ■ ■ THE MESSAGE

Clearly, the source of a message can have a powerful effect on the message's persuasiveness. If this is not so, advertisers have been wasting millions of dollars annually by hiring famous sports and entertainment personalities to endorse their products. There's more to persuasion, however, than a pretty (or famous) face. What is said and how it is said are important considerations. We discuss these and related aspects of the communication on the pages that follow.

Drawing A Conclusion

Recall that one of the central assumptions of Hovland's theory is that a persuasive message is most effective when it stimulates a question in the mind of the recipient and then *suggests an answer*. Should a persuasive message draw an explicit conclusion, or should receivers be free to form their own? Hovland's answer is clear, but is it right? Research on the issue of *conclusion drawing* generally supports

Hovland's thinking. In an early study, Hovland and Mandell (1952) asked participants to listen to one of two tape-recorded communications which discussed the advisability of devaluating the U.S. dollar. For one group, the message ended with an explicit conclusion that the dollar should be devalued. The other participants heard the same message, but its explicit conclusion was omitted. Did this minor variation matter? It did. More than half of those for whom the conclusion was drawn changed in the direction advocated, whereas less than one-third of the participants denied the conclusion changed in the advocated direction. Conclusions work, and lots of research agrees with this observation (Feingold & Knapp, 1977; Ferris and Wicklund, 1974; Geller, 1975).

Conclusions seem to make the most difference when the persuasive material is complex or presented under distracting conditions. The advantage of a conclusion diminishes with simple communications. If people can be motivated to draw their own conclusions, they are more persuaded than if the conclusion is drawn for them (Linder & Worchel, 1970). This result probably owes a debt to source credibility—when the receiver of a message draws a conclusion, the receiver is one of his or her own most credible sources. (In our discussion of role playing, we saw how combining the functions of source and receiver in the same person enhances attitude change.) When the source does not draw a conclusion, it might seem less organized, less confident, and so on, and this would diminish its impact. Perhaps the best summary of the effects of conclusion drawing was provided by McGuire (1969) who observed:

> It may well be that if the person draws the conclusion himself he is more persuaded than if the source draws it for him; the problem is that in the usual communication situation the subject is either insufficiently intelligent or insufficiently motivated to draw the conclusion for himself, and therefore misses the point of the message . . . In communication, it appears, it is not sufficient to lead the horse to water; one must also push his head underneath to get him to drink. (p. 209)

Delivery: Force, Speed, Number and Intensity

When persuasive messages are presented, their impact is at least partly dependent on features of their delivery. Considerable research has shown that more forceful presentations have greater impact. Forcefulness is affected by a number of variables. For example, if a speaker uses greater volume when presenting a persuasive message, more variations in pitch, more concrete (versus abstract) arguments, and more extreme adjectives or adverbs, the message will be more persuasive (cf. Burgoon & Miller, 1971; Ginosar & Trope, 1980; Robinson & McArthur, 1982). More rapid delivery sometimes has been shown to enhance the persuasiveness of communications (Apple, Streeter, & Krauss, 1979). Electronic compression of advertisements, which accelerates the speed with which information is presented, also enhances the persuasive power of a message. It is possible that these delivery-speed effects occur because they make the message more difficult to counterargue. Although the data are suggestive, the case for delivery speed is far from decided; many studies have failed to show such effects. However, of these failures, many used presentation speeds within the boundaries of normal speech.

How do you suppose these Marines responded to the message that the war would last another two years? ■

Possibly, participants do not find processing too difficult in these circumstances (cf., Woodall & Burgoon, 1983), and hence distraction, which facilitates persuasion, does not operate.

One or Two Sides?

Suppose you want to convince someone to take your side on an important and controversial issue. Should you present arguments favoring both sides of the issue and then show why your position should be accepted, or should you present only arguments that favor your stance? The answer to this question depends on the initial attitude of the person you are trying to persuade. In an early study performed shortly after the Allies had defeated Nazi Germany, but before Japan had surrendered, Hovland and his associates (1949) exposed groups of GIs to messages that argued that the war with Japan would continue for another two years. As you can imagine, this message was extremely contrary to what the soldiers wanted to hear. Some heard only arguments in favor of the two-year position. Others heard these arguments along with a few messages that held that the war would be over much sooner.

Compared with a control group that received no communication, the soldiers who heard either message were more convinced that the war would drag on. There appeared to be no persuasive difference in the effectiveness of the *one-sided versus two-sided message.* But then the researchers inspected the attitudes the soldiers held *before* they were exposed to messages. When they factored in this information, the experimenters found that a soldier's prior attitude had a lot to do with the effectiveness of one- or two-sided messages. Soldiers who indicated on the pretest that they thought the war was going to last a long time were much more persuaded by the one-sided message, which was in agreement with their established position. Soldiers who thought the war would be over soon were more persuaded by the two-sided message.

Jones and Brehm (1970) conducted a study with results consistent with Hovland's. Their research shows that one-sided messages are most persuasive when recipients are not aware that another position even exists. When recipients know the issue is controversial or if the issue is prominent, then two-sided messages are more persuasive (Baumgardner, Leippe, Ronis, & Greenwald, 1983).

Fear Arousal

You've seen it a hundred times. Parents want to ensure that their young children act appropriately. So what do they do? They try to scare them. Most of us were told at one time or another, "Be a good child or Santa will bring you coal!" Such messages are meant to arouse fear. But are messages that arouse emotion more effective than those that do not? Sometimes. The link between arousal and attitude change has been studied extensively. We discuss some of these studies in the paragraphs that follow, and propose a model that accounts for the pattern of findings in this area.

Most of the research on arousing communications is patterned after an early study of Janis and Feshbach (1953). In this study, junior high school students received one of three presentations dealing with dental hygiene. The persuasive messages took the form of a fifteen-minute lecture, accompanied by illustrative slides. The information presented in the three messages was essentially identical, but the presentations differed markedly in their use of gory details and personalized threats. In the highly arousing presentation condition, the painful consequences of neglected teeth were explained to the participants. Some of the threats used in this condition were extraordinary: "If you ever develop an infection of this kind from improper care of your teeth, it will be an extremely serious matter because these infections are really dangerous. They can spread to your eyes, or your heart, or your joints and cause secondary infections which may lead to diseases such as arthritis, paralysis, kidney damage, or total blindness." Pass the Crest! These words were accompanied by slides dramatically and graphically depicting some of the problems being discussed. They included disgusting pictures of decayed teeth, gum infections, and the like. At the other extreme (in the low-arousal condition) students learned about how teeth develop, were shown pictures of healthy teeth, X-rays of teeth with cavities, and so on.

The results of this study are still controversial after forty years. First, it is clear that the arousal manipulation worked. Students in the high-arousal group were scared, and very determined to take care of their teeth. However, when the researchers returned to the scene of the experiment one week later, they found that the frightened students had retained *less* information than those who had not had the wits scared out of them. The researchers reasoned that fear had caused participants to respond defensively to the communication. The communication contained advice about how dental health could be maintained, but their defensiveness precluded their taking advantage of the information.

This explanation is consistent with results of a later study (Janis & Terwilliger, 1962), in which smokers received either a high- or low-fear-arousing message about the dangers of tobacco. While reading these messages, the smokers talked about their reactions to the information. The study revealed that smokers in the high-fear-arousing condition were more frightened than their counterparts, more likely to react defensively, and more likely to *reject* the information presented. As a consequence of their defensive reactions, smokers who received the fear-arousing message were less likely to change their attitudes.

Janis's "high fear causes less change" hypothesis held sway for a time, but the results of later studies contradicted this position. In some research, high-fear-arousing messages were *more effective* attitude change agents. For example, Insko, Arkoff, and Insko (1965) replicated Janis and Terwilliger's study and found the high-fear-arousing message more effective. The difference between their study and Janis and Terwilliger's lies in the sample. Insko's participants were seventh-grade school children, none of whom smoked, whereas the subjects of Janis and Terwilliger were all confirmed smokers who were trying hard to quit. These two groups probably had very different attitudes toward smoking and its effects, and these initial differences predisposed them to different reactions when fear-arousing messages were presented.

Later research by Leventhal and his colleagues, which also found high-fear-arousing messages more effective than low-arousing messages, supports this explanation. Leventhal (1970, 1974) usually chose issues that could be made frightening (for example, the dangers of tetanus), but that were not ordinarily part of people's daily concerns. In addition, his fear-arousing messages typically offered solutions to the problems that were discussed. So, to avoid tetanus, go to the doctor and get a tetanus shot. Leventhal found that when a solution to the fear-arousing problem is contained in the communication, high-fear-arousing messages are more effective than low. When the issue is one on which the individual is already worried, and the fear-arousing communication offers no solution, it will be avoided or dismissed. In such circumstances, nonarousing communications are more persuasive.

Leventhal's work suggests an interplay of message arousal and chronic arousal. If a person is already worried about an issue, then adding fuel to the fire probably will not help matters. The already anxious receiver will find a highly arousing message unduly uncomfortable and refuse to process it. If a person is not already scared about an issue, then a highly arousing message might motivate him or her to attend to its arguments. These possibilities suggest that the persuasive power of a communication will increase as its fear-inducing quality increases—but only up to a point. Receptivity to the message and consequent attitude change diminish sharply when arousal passes beyond some threshold of discomfort.

Figure 3.3 presents a predictive model that is consistent with earlier findings in the fear-arousal literature. The model assumes that a message must evoke some arousal to be effective. If the recipient of the message is not already anxious about the issue at hand, then the greater the arousal, the greater the impact of the message. Higher levels of arousal also will prove increasingly effective if solutions are included in the message. With individuals who are already aroused about the topic under consideration, increasing levels of arousal causes defensive reactions. Message recipients will be more and more likely to disengage from the communication as the fear-arousal level of the message increases. Such individuals will respond better to a low-fear-arousal message (Witte, 1992).

FIGURE 3.3

◼

Chronic Anxiety and Receptivity to High- and Low-Fear-Arousing Messages. High fear appeals will work best on targets who are not already scared about the issue under attack. For those of very low fear, a more frightening message may provide the motivation necessary to cause belief or behavior change.

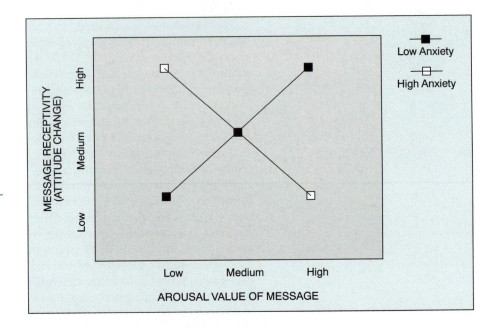

Inoculation Effects

So far we have discussed the factors that enhance the persuasive power of communication. This is consistent with the general thrust of Hovland's theory. But the other side of the coin is also worthy of study, namely, the factors that induce *resistance* to persuasion. William McGuire (1964) proposed an interesting extension of Hovland's theory, which he calls the **inoculation hypothesis.** McGuire begins with the assumption that an idea or attitude that had never been questioned will be particularly susceptible to persuasion, because the attitude has never had to be defended. When is the last time you had to argue with someone about the desirability of brushing one's teeth after meals? How can unchallenged beliefs be defended? In a clever analogy, McGuire reminded us of the medical practice of inoculation. By injecting a weakened dose of a virus into the body, we stimulate the body's defenses to resist a more full-blown attack. McGuire suggested a similar process might operate in persuasion. By overcoming a weak attack mounted against our beliefs, we learn to build defenses against more powerful future attacks.

To test the inoculation hypothesis, McGuire and Papageorgis (1961) assembled a set of "cultural truisms"—ideas that almost everyone believes unreservedly, without question, and which almost never come under attack. Such statements as "Brush your teeth after every meal" or "Get eight hours of sleep every night" are the kinds of positions that are widely accepted, rarely questioned, and hence, according to McGuire, very susceptible to change pressures. How would one render these truisms resistant to change? By giving an "inoculation"—exposing people to *weak* messages that question their validity. McGuire and Papageorgis did just this. Some participants were presented a very weak counter-argument (for example, "Brushing too often might weaken the teeth's enamel"). Others were not given the inoculation. Then, all were exposed to *strong* persuasive messages that argued against the truism ("Research has shown without question that brushing after every meal is definitely harmful to teeth. It can cause gum damage, greater susceptibility to decay, and more cavities."). McGuire and Papageorgis then assessed vulnerability to the strong argument. The results support the inoculation hypothesis. Those who had been inoculated with a weak counter-attitudinal message were substantially more resistant to the strong message than were those who had not dealt with the weak argument directed against the truism. It is not necessary that the inoculation use arguments identical to those of the major attack (Miller & Burgoon, 1979), nor that the topic be a cultural truism. Even controversial attitudes are strengthened by inoculation (Bither, Dolich, & Nell, 1971; Szybillo & Heslin, 1973). Apparently, a weak persuasive communication helps people learn defenses that they can use against a stronger message. Those whose defenses are not stimulated by the prior (weak message) inoculation are more easily persuaded later.

APPLYING SOCIAL PSYCHOLOGY TO HEALTH
■ ■ ■

Inoculating against Stress

An interesting application of the inoculation metaphor was developed by Donald Meichenbaum, a clinical psychotherapist interested in helping people cope with extreme stress reactions. Meichenbaum (1985) developed an approach in which patients are inoculated against the debilitating stress that brought them into therapy in the first place. How is this done? A three-step approach is employed (Meichenbaum & Deffenbacher, 1988). First, with the help of a therapist, patients learn to recognize the factors that cause stress ("Whenever my boss calls me into her office, I get stressed out."). Then, patient and therapist design ways to cope with it ("Suppose you try this relaxation technique whenever the phone rings."). Finally, the patients test these coping strategies within the protected confines of the clinic ("Let's practice this. We'll pretend the boss has just called. What do you do?"). This final (inoculation) component of the therapy allows patients to experience the factors that cause problems for them, but to do so in a way that controls and curtails the magnitude of stress they will have to endure. (After all, the boss really is not at the other end of the line.) By experiencing *controlled* stress and learning strategies that allow them to cope with it, patients who have undergone stress inoculation training are more capable of dealing with the effects of more extreme stress in their daily lives.

■ ■ ■ THE SETTING

Situational Distractions

We have stressed the importance of counter-argumentation in Hovland's theory of persuasion, and have shown how different aspects of sources and messages (such as attractiveness, credibility, speed of delivery) can add or detract from a person's ability to defend against a persuasive message. In addition to these source

Distraction weakens resistance to persuasion. How persuadable is this man in the context pictured here? ▪

and message factors, the *setting* in which a communication is presented also can have a significant impact on persuasion. If the setting itself hinders counter-argumentation, then message targets will be more susceptible to attitude change. In an interesting role-playing study conducted by Zimbardo (1965), participants, who had been fitted with earphones, read a message that was contrary to their beliefs into a complicated recording device. For some people, the device altered the aural feedback so that they heard the words they spoke approximately a half second after saying them. This form of delayed auditory feedback is horribly disruptive, and the respondents had to work hard just to keep on track. The *distraction* inherent in this context increased their susceptibility to the message they had struggled to read. Those who read the belief-inconsistent message under normal conditions were much less persuaded by it.

Petty, Wells, and Brock (1976) followed Zimbardo's experiment with an attitude change study in which a persuasive communication was presented under varying conditions of distraction. While listening to a recorded message, students had to count the number of Xs that appeared at random intervals on a screen in front of them. For some, lots of Xs appeared, and they were kept busy counting them. They were distracted from their primary job—to listen to and analyze the communication. For others, the Xs were infrequent, and hence not disruptive. The researchers manipulated one other variable in their study, message quality. Some heard a well-crafted, logical, and well-argued message; others heard a message that called for the same outcome as the first, but it was not strong, nor logical, nor well-reasoned.

Consistent with Hovland's expectations, the more distracting the context, the more effective the persuasive message. However, this result held only for those who heard the poorly argued case. For those exposed to the strong and logical message, *less* distraction resulted in *greater* attitude change. Why? Petty argued that distraction operated as Hovland had hypothesized—that is, it interfered with participants' ability to process and critically analyze incoming information. In the case of a poorly constructed persuasive message, this inability to analyze and counter-argue enhanced the message's effectiveness, because its weak points were not readily identified. However, distraction weakened the impact of the well-constructed, well-documented communication. Its high-quality arguments could not be recognized by the distracted receivers. As a result, the message did not have the impact it would have, had the receivers not been distracted.

These results suggest that Hovland's ideas were correct, but that he had not pushed them far enough. Distraction does affect persuasion, but its effect depends on the quality of the persuasive message. With low-quality messages, distraction intensifies attitude change; with high-quality messages, a nondistracting setting results in greater change. Distraction is a two-edged sword; it prevents people from fully appreciating the logic of high-quality messages, and thus detracts from the persuasiveness of well-crafted arguments. On the other hand, distraction interferes with the ability to see the weakness of a poorly conceived argument. In these instances, distraction enhances attitude change. Advertisers appear well aware of this. They usually present strong arguments in a nondistracting context. When they have little to say other than "Please buy our stuff, even though there's not much difference between it and our competitors'," they do so in as distracting a manner as possible.

"Overheard" or Confusing Communications

As Petty and his colleagues (1976) show, distraction interferes with receivers' ability to process persuasive messages. Other factors within the context in which the message is presented can have a similar effect. For example, if something in the context induces message receivers to let their guard down, they may prove more susceptible to persuasion. In an interesting test of this possibility, Walster and Festinger (1962) took the students in their introductory psychology class on a tour of the psychology labs. As part of the tour, they were shown a laboratory control room fitted with a one-way mirror. On the other side of the mirror, they listened to two people talking about smoking. The speakers came to the conclusion that there was no good research linking lung cancer to smoking. Some groups of participants were told that the speakers knew they were being observed, while others thought they were eavesdropping (that is, the speakers were not aware that their conservation was monitored). Walster and Festinger thought that the "eavesdropping" students might let their guard down, and thus be more susceptible to persuasion. (Of course, in both instances the speakers gave the same message—it was all an act.)

A week later, in class, participants' attitudes toward smoking were assessed, as well as their beliefs about the link between smoking and cancer. No mention was made of the laboratory tour. Analysis showed that those who had "overheard" the prosmoking message were much more persuaded by it than those who knew the communication had been staged. Apparently, those who were eavesdropping on the communication felt no need to defend against it—the source certainly was not trying to persuade them, and hence was judged trust-worthy. In this circumstance, the receivers were easy prey.

■ ■ ■ CHARACTERISTICS OF THE AUDIENCE

Individual Differences in Intelligence and Self-Esteem

There can be little doubt that people differ in the extent to which they can be persuaded. All of us know people with no sales resistance whatever, who can be persuaded to buy almost anything a salesperson wants to unload on them. Other people won't agree to anything. Considerable research has been conducted to discover the factors that account for these individual differences. Over the years, *intelligence* and *self-esteem* have received most of the attention (Rhodes & Wood, 1992). Early studies (Janis & Hovland, 1959) suggested that self-esteem mattered—people of low self-esteem were easier to influence than those of high esteem. However, the findings regarding the effects of intelligence on persuasion were more complex. Sometimes intelligence is associated with stronger resistance to persuasion. Sometimes the opposite is found. In the case of either variable, it is fair to say that the early research was largely unsuccessful in isolating personal differences that *strongly* affected susceptibility. Much appeared to depend on respondents' experience with the issue.

Investigation of personal factors that affect susceptibility has continued, how-ever, and recent research that integrates this body of work suggests that self-esteem and intelligence have consistent and systematic effects on persuadability—but they operate in different ways (Rhodes & Wood, 1992). Let's consider in-telligence. How should it affect persuasion? Obviously, intelligence facilitates people's ability to understand communications. If a message is well constructed and logical, then intelligence should be *positively* related to susceptibility. With weak messages, the opposite should occur. Smart people should be able to see through the fog of a weak argument and reject it. In their analysis, Rhodes and Wood found this interpretation consistent with the results of the many studies in this area of research.

Self-esteem is not related to people's ability to process information, but rather to their tendency to protect their beliefs against attack. People with high self-esteem are better *able* to defend themselves, and thus should be resistant to in-fluence. On the other hand, people with a fragile self-esteem are *more highly motivated* to protect themselves. It is reasonable to predict that people who are either very high or very low in self-esteem may be highly resistant to persuasion. Those between these extremes should be more susceptible. This predicted pattern is described by an inverted U-shaped relationship between self-esteem and sus-ceptibility, as shown in Figure 3.4. Those very high and those very low in self-esteem are most resistant to persuasion—for very different reasons—while the bulk of people in the middle of the self-esteem distribution are the most suscep-tible. Rhodes and Wood's analysis supports this conclusion.

FIGURE 3.4

■

Relationship between Self-Esteem and Persuadability. People of very high and very low levels of self-esteem should prove strongly resistant to persuasion—but for very different reasons. At moderate levels, we find the greatest susceptibility to persuasive messages.

Would these two be more likely to purchase raffle tickets because of their mood? ■

Mood

Intelligence and self-esteem are relatively enduring characteristics. Mood is a more transient state, but it too affects susceptibility to persuasion. Most of the mood research undertaken over the years is based on the premise that happy people are easier to persuade. Workers seeking a raise, for example, often wait until the boss is in a good mood. Public speakers, politicians, advertisers, and others attempting to win people to their side often try to soften up their audience by inducing positive feelings (Belch, Belch, & Villareal, 1987; Holman, 1986). Does the research support this strategy? Almost without exception. More than fifty years ago, Razran (1940) presented political propaganda to people who were either enjoying a free lunch or sitting in a lab suffused with a very disagreeable odor. Those in the positive state were substantially more susceptible to the persuasive slogans. Janis, Kaye, and Kirchner (1965) found that people snacking on nuts and sodas were more susceptible to persuasive communications than those without such accompaniments. How does it work? Isen (1987) discovered that positive mood affects the way we process information. People in a good mood process information more quickly, with less effort and less thought. They base decisions on less information, and generally hold them with greater confidence. Positive mood does not improve the quality of decisions, but it does improve the speed of decision making. Consistent with Isen's results, Mackie and Worth (1989, 1990) found that people in a good mood tended to respond more to the qualifications of a source than to the quality of the source's message. They were

People use various information-processing strategies when responding to messages: See Chapter 4.

prone to accept the recommendations of a high-credibility source without bothering to examine closely what the source had to say. People in a neutral mood were not likely to use this superficial form of information processing. Along with Isen's, Mackie and Worth's results are especially informative because they demonstrate that mood affects the way messages are processed (see also Bless, Bohner, & Schwarz, 1990).

What causes these processing differences? Mood effects on persuasion appear *not* to be a result of motivational differences; that is, happy people are not more easily persuaded simply because they do not bother to process information. As Worth and her colleagues show, positive mood does not stop people from processing information when they are given the opportunity to do so or when they are asked to do so (Worth, Mackie, & Asunsion, 1989; also see Bohner, Crow, Erb, & Schwarz, 1992). It seems their processing is simply less efficient. Why should this be so? Some theorists (Frijda, 1988; Isen, 1987) hypothesize that a positive mood increases our cognitive flexibility—it enables us to consider more alternatives. Under such conditions, "happy" receivers may have too much on their minds to process efficiently. Though rose-colored glasses make things seem prettier, they interfere with efficient information processing.

■ ■ ■ SOME CONCLUDING THOUGHTS

The message-learning approach laid the foundation for powerful models of attitude development and change: See Chapter 4.

Hovland's work laid the foundation for much that characterizes today's social psychology. Although this program did not provide many definitive answers, the questions he posed are still major preoccupations of the field. We know a lot about the effects of different types of message sources and of features of messages that enhance or retard persuasion. We understand how fear-arousing appeals work, and have a much more clear understanding of the role of mood on persuasion. We understand the ways that different factors in a message, or a message context, influence our capacity to process persuasive communications. We owe much of this understanding to Hovland's pioneering work, which succeeded in laying the foundation for some of today's most important research on attitude development and change.

■ ■ ■ SUMMARY

Hovland's message-learning explanation of attitude change assumes that people are persuaded because they accept and learn information that is contrary to their established beliefs. Factors that influence this process are the source of the persuasive message, the structure of the message, the setting in which it is delivered, and the characteristics of the people exposed to it. The power to influence is affected by a source's expertise, trustworthiness, and number.

Communications that draw a conclusion are generally more persuasive, as are messages delivered with intensity and speed. Whether a message should contain both sides of an issue depends on the attitude of the receiver. Fear arousal can facilitate or hinder message effectiveness depending on the receiver's existing level of anxiety about the issue. Attitude change can be forestalled by inoculation, a process by which a weak attack is mounted against a belief, and defeated, thereby strengthening the receiver's ability to withstand a later, stronger attack.

Aspects of the situation in which a message is presented also influence its power to persuade. Situational distractions hinder the effects of strong messages and enhance the impact of weak ones. Similarly, if the intent to persuade is not obvious, the communication is generally more persuasive. Receiver differences also affect the likelihood of persuasion. Intelligent recipients are more susceptible than less intelligent receivers to logical, well-constructed communications and more resistant to weak or illogical ones. Self-esteem is related in a curvilinear fashion to susceptibility. People with either very high or very low levels of self-esteem are most resistant to persuasion. Mood too affects persuasion: More positive mood is associated with greater susceptibility to persuasive communications. Mechanisms for this effect are uncertain, but it appears that happy people generally consider many alternatives when responding to a persuasive communication, and this may interfere with their ability to counter-argue.

■■■ SUGGESTED READINGS

1. O'Keefe, D. J. (1990). *Persuasion: Theory and research.* Newbury Park, CA: Sage.

2. Pratkanis, A. R., & Aronson, E. (1992). *Age of propaganda: The everyday use and abuse of persuasion.* New York: W. H. Freeman.

3. Zanna, M. P., Olson, J. M. & Herman, C. P. (Eds.) (1987). *Social influence: The Ontario Symposium* (Vol. 5). Hillsdale, NJ: Erlbaum.

CHAPTER 4

MODELS OF ATTITUDE CHANGE

How and Why Persuasion Works

■ **Key Concepts**

Social judgment theory
Latitude of acceptance
Latitude of rejection
Assimilation effect
Contrast (or boomerang) effect
Elaboration likelihood model
  (ELM)
Central (processing) route
Peripheral (processing) route
Need for cognition
Heuristic-systematic model
Systematic processing
Heuristic processing
Efficiency and sufficiency
  principles

■ **Chapter Outline**

SOCIAL JUDGMENT THEORY
  Components of the Theory
  Evidence for the Theory

THE ELABORATION-LIKELIHOOD MODEL
  Central versus Peripheral Processing
  Factors that Determine Elaboration
  ■ Who Gets Your Vote?

THE HEURISTIC–SYSTEMATIC MODEL
  Systematic Processing
  Heuristic Processing
  Efficiency + Sufficiency = Confidence
  ■ The XT-100

ELM AND THE HEURISTIC–SYSTEMATIC MODEL: SOME COMPARISONS

SOME CONCLUDING THOUGHTS

SUMMARY

On a walk across campus, you stumble across your good friend Jim, who is involved in an animated conversation with Jules, a student that both you and Jim have scorned in the past. Jules dresses strangely, does not appear to be bright, and is very awkward in social situations. When you kid Jim about his new friend, he responds, "You should get to know Jules—he's an interesting guy." Do you change your attitude about Jules? About Jim? About Jules and Jim?

■■■

Skip and John are best friends. Neither has given much thought to the future, but here it is, senior year in high school, and they have no idea of what they will do after the last dance at the senior prom. Earlier, they had attended the navy recruiter's talk at the high school—mostly to get out of third-period English class. They found the recruiter, Lieutenant McCloskey, extremely personable. He had driven up to the school in a new Corvette, dressed well, and spoke the language of the boys' own group. Before long, Skip and John decide they will join up. Skip made his decision without really thinking much about it—the uniform, the $3,000 signing bonus, and the certainty of knowing that he would be on his own in September was enough for him. John, however, listened to McCloskey very carefully; he knew what was being offered and what the personal costs would be. After careful deliberation, he decided it was worth it, and he too signed up. Two days later, when he thought about the six-year commitment he had made and all it entailed, Skip wondered how he had ever been talked into something like this. John had no second thoughts. Why?

Your attitudes are important, not only to you, but to businesses, politicians, and many other groups who spend vast sums of money trying to influence them. You should know how tactics of attitude change work, if only to be able to resist them. This chapter offers some useful information on this topic. Along the way, we will learn about the factors that might affect your attitudes toward Jules and Jim, and about the personal features that differentiate Skip and John.

Over the past forty years, social psychologists have discovered a multitude of ways to influence attitudes. The message source's expertise, the setting in which the message is presented, the speed of message presentation, the receiver's mood—all of these factors have an important bearing on the success or failure of the persuader. The theory that guided much of the early research on attitudes was developed by Carl Hovland, his students, and colleagues. Although his theory accounts for some of the factors uncovered by attitude researchers, it does not account for all of them. In this chapter, we discuss models of attitude change that have developed since Hovland's pioneering work. These models all owe a debt to Hovland's seminal work, but as you will see, they have developed in

■ Many factors affect the success or failure of a persuasive message: See Chapter 3.

ways that allow more precise prediction of attitude change. Given the stakes, even a small advantage in the capability to affect the magnitude and direction of attitude change can be worth a lot. More than Hovland's, the new models are concerned with the *processes* that underlie change. They help to tell us why attitudes change, not merely how to change them. Although the new models represent major advances over Hovland's approach, there is an obvious continuity from his program to today's work.

■■■ SOCIAL JUDGMENT THEORY

One of the early attitude change models is an extension of Hovland's original theory. It is termed **social judgment theory** (Sherif & Hovland, 1961). It holds that the effects of a persuasive message are a consequence of variations in people's *ego involvement* with a critical issue. Ego involvement has to do with the degree to which a person finds an issue personally relevant. In Hovland's original (message-learning) theory, communication recipients were considered passive receivers of information (messages). Their ability to process and store persuasive information determined the extent to which they changed their attitudes. This capability, in turn, was determined by external forces (source expertise, distraction, conclusion drawing, and so on). In social judgment theory, people are more active participants in the change process. Factors *within the receiver* determine the receiver's susceptibility to change.

Components of the Theory

Social judgment theory conceives of attitude not as a discrete point on a mental continuum but as the range of positions about an object of belief that an individual finds acceptable. This range of positions, which differs from person to person, is defined as the individual's *latitude of acceptance*. Conversely, there is a range of positions the person rejects as unacceptable, or untrue. These positions constitute the *latitude of rejection*. The relative size of people's latitudes of acceptance and rejection vary as a consequence of their ego involvement in the attitude (Petty, Cacioppo, & Haugtvedt, 1992). With greater involvement, the latitude of rejection widens, and the latitude of acceptance shrinks, as shown in Figure 4.1a. With little involvement, the latitude of involvement is very wide and the latitude of rejection inconsequential—people will accept almost any statement about an issue with which they are generally unconcerned (Figure 4.1b).

How does this relate to our everyday experience? Consider the continuing debate on abortion in the United States. In this debate, we often encounter people who are highly involved with this issue. Typically, they are extremely resistant to positions that differ even slightly from their own, no matter what side of the issue they have chosen. On the other hand, on issues with which they are not concerned, these same people might be willing to entertain a wide variety of positions. Sherif and Hovland believed that these differences in willingness to consider contrary positions are the result of people's ego involvement.

FIGURE 4.1

∎

Latitudes of acceptance and rejection vary in size as a consequence of involvement with the issue. Compared to uninvolving attitudes, highly involving attitudes have wider latitudes of rejection, and more narrow latitudes of acceptance.

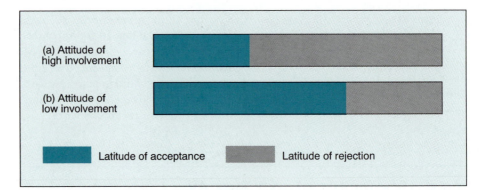

The implications of this theory for attitude change are straightforward. Social judgment theory assumes that if a communication is to be effective, it must fall within the recipient's latitude of acceptance. If this occurs, the theory predicts an *assimilation effect;* that is, the receiver will perceive the message as being more similar to his or her attitude than it really is, and as such will not raise strong defenses against it. The message will be accepted, and little counter-argumentation will ensue. If the message falls into the person's latitude of rejection, a *contrast (or boomerang) effect* is expected; the message will be perceived as being even more antagonistic to the recipient's established position than it actually is, and the receiver will counter-argue strongly against its acceptance.

Evidence for the Theory

During the war in Vietnam, Peterson and Koulack (1969) measured the attitudes and ego involvement of college-age subjects toward the war. Three weeks later, they brought the participants back to the laboratory to write an essay that advocated a position at odds with their expressed beliefs. For some, the position they were asked to support was only slightly different from their stated attitude (that is, the message fell into their latitude of acceptance). Others were asked to advocate a position that was very discrepant from their attitudes (the message was in their latitude of rejection).

Asking people to role play (in this case through writing) can be an effective means of altering attitudes, but Peterson and Koulack found that the effectiveness of the technique depended on the distance between participants' original attitudes and the position they were asked to advocate. As social judgment theory predicts, attitude change toward the advocated position increased as discrepancy between the original attitude and the communication increased—but only up to a point. When the position they advocated fell into their latitudes of rejection, the participants did not change.

A study whose results reinforce Peterson and Koulack's was performed by Rhine and Severance (1970), who assessed the attitudes of California college students on two issues of markedly different levels of ego involvement. The involving issue concerned their views on the advisability of a tuition increase in the California college system, a controversial possibility under consideration at the time by state officials. The noninvolving topic concerned the amount of new

Role playing can be an effective means of altering attitudes: See Chapters 3 and 5.

How wide is this woman's latitude of acceptance on the issue of abortion? Does your assessment have any implications for the likelihood that her attitude will be easy or difficult to change? ■

park acreage that should be developed in Allentown, Pennsylvania—probably not high on most California students' list of worries.

Consistent with the theory, how wide the participants' latitudes of acceptance and rejection were differed as a consequence of the issue. On the park acreage topic, respondents displayed narrow latitudes of rejection and wide latitudes of acceptance—they were willing to go along with almost any proposed increase in park acreage in Allentown. On the tuition issue, respondents' latitudes of rejection were very wide and their corresponding latitudes of acceptance very narrow. The amount of tuition increase they found tolerable was very small.

After establishing that the latitude widths were consistent with theoretical expectations, the experimenters presented one of two persuasive messages on each issue. The two messages differed in terms of the discrepancy between the respondents' attitudes and the position advocated. Thus, for some, the message advocated a position that fell into the latitude of acceptance; for others, it fell into the latitude of rejection.

In the low-involvement condition (park acreage), the more extreme the discrepancy between participants' attitudes and the position advocated in the communication, the greater the attitude change. On the involving topic (tuition), small discrepancies produced change, but larger discrepancies did not—the tuition-raise message landed in receivers' latitudes of rejection, and its impact on attitudes diminished substantially. These results indicate that the impact of a persuasive message on attitudes varies as a consequence of the latitude into which the advocated position falls, which in turn is determined by the receiver's degree of involvement with the issue.

■■■ THE ELABORATION-LIKELIHOOD MODEL

Although recent research (e.g., Leippe & Elkin, 1987) has produced results consistent with Sherif and Hovland's model, social judgment theory has stimulated little research. This is partly attributable to the complexities in its application. Measuring involvement, tailoring communications to each receiver's latitude of acceptance, and avoiding the latitude of rejection makes implementing Sherif and Hovland's ideas difficult.

A model that shares some of the assumptions of social judgment theory—in that it considers participants' involvement with the issue under study—has proved much more effective in stimulating research. This "new generation" theory is the **elaboration-likelihood model (ELM)** of Richard Petty and John Cacioppo. The ELM is concerned with the ways people process the information presented in a persuasive communication. The term *elaboration likelihood* refers to the probability that an individual will either elaborate (that is, think about, analyze, draw out the implications of) the information contained in a communication or attend instead to peripheral cues surrounding the message's delivery (the attractiveness of the message source, the speed or intensity of the presentation, the setting and circumstances in which messages are presented, and so on). Elaboration differences determine both the extent to which a message affects attitude change and the persistence of change.

Central versus Peripheral Processing

Petty and Cacioppo (1981, 1986a,b) believe that people process, or respond to, persuasive messages in two very different ways. We take the *central route* to persuasion when we are stimulated to think about (or elaborate, in ELM terms) the information presented in a persuasive communication, to concentrate on the logic of the arguments it contains, to analyze the quality of the message, and to consider its implications. The *peripheral route* is characterized by a more shallow message analysis. In this processing mode, we are concerned with features that are irrelevant to the content, quality, or logical merit of the message itself. Self-presentation (how do I look in the eyes of the experimenter), the expertise or attractiveness of the source of the message, and so on, dominate the message-processing concerns in the peripheral mode.

How does this theory connect with social judgment theory? Recall Sherif and Hovland's stress on ego involvement. As with social judgment theory, the ELM assumes that a person's self-interest in an issue determines the particular route to persuasion that is taken. If an issue has lots to do with people's well-being, people will elaborate any message concerned with the issue. Communications about issues of low self-interest will not be elaborated, and the quality of the information such messages contain will not matter so much. Instead, persuasion will depend on factors extraneous to message quality—source expertise, message speed, and so forth.

Although both routes to persuasion can result in change, the persistence of change differs as a consequence of elaboration. Attitudes changed via the peripheral route are expected to revert to their original (prepersuasion) position when the peripheral cue (for example, source attractiveness) is no longer salient. This is because the attitude change that occurs as a result of peripheral processing is not based on information contained in the message itself, but on message-irrelevant factors. When these irrelevancies are removed, the foundation of the changed attitude is destroyed, and the attitude reverts to its original position.

When the attitude is changed via the central route, the change is based on the recipient's elaboration of the *information* contained in the message. The material is considered carefully, its implications drawn out. It is this elaborated information that is remembered. The irrelevant features that accompany the communication do not affect recipients' internalized understandings. These understandings are based on message content, not on the manner in which the message was presented, the character of the source, or the setting in which it was delivered. Such information-based knowledge will persist and bolster the new attitude. In a comprehensive review of the factors that moderate the persistence of attitude change, Cook and Flay (1978) found that factors that promoted recipients' *active involvement* in processing the persuasive message resulted in long-lasting change. This observation is in complete accord with Petty and Cacioppo's ELM.

Factors that Determine Elaboration

Motivation.   What determines the intensity of message elaboration? Petty and Cacioppo (1981) have proposed a number of factors that may determine whether the central or peripheral route is taken (and therefore how intense elaboration will be). One of the most important is *motivation*. If a person is motivated to think about a communication carefully, there is a much greater chance of message elaboration than if the appropriate motivation is lacking. Many techniques have been employed to induce such motivation. If the message has high personal relevance or is ego involving, it is likely to be elaborated (Petty & Cacioppo, 1990). In a typical manipulation, students are faced with a communication that argues for a 30% tuition hike at their school. Most students consider tuition a very relevant issue. As such, they are expected to process the communication very carefully (that is, to elaborate it). In these circumstances, Petty and Cacioppo have found well-constructed, logical messages stimulate more attitude change than messages that are poorly argued or illogical. When students are asked to consider the advisability of a 30% tuition hike at *another* school, they do not process it as carefully because the message is of relatively low self-interest. In this circumstance, variations in the quality of the message's arguments do not matter much—message-irrelevant factors, such as source credibility or attractiveness determine whether (nonaffected) students accept the recommendations of the communication. In this case, that is, the peripheral route is taken. Factors that suggest a topic is of low self-relevance result in peripheral processing (Petty, Harkins, & Williams, 1980).

Ability.   Circumstances may arise in which careful processing does not occur, even though a recipient might be motivated. For example, if a communication is too difficult to understand, if it is presented under conditions of extreme confusion or distraction, or if it is focused on an obscure topic, then the receiver may not be able to elaborate the information despite being motivated to do so. In circumstances such as these, one of two accommodations occur: (1) People reflect on their preexisting attitudes. The attitude will be reviewed and rehearsed and probably become more polarized. The expectation of increased polarization is based on Tesser's (1978; Tesser et al., in press) findings that merely thinking about an attitude results in its becoming more extreme. Thus, initially positive attitudes will become even more positive after the attempt at elaboration has failed. If the attitude is initially negative, it will become even more negative. (2) Because of the obscurity of an issue, a person may be unable to understand the arguments presented in a communication. If, in addition, the individual has no established attitude on the issue, he or she will adopt the peripheral processing mode.

When a person thinks about an attitude, it can become more extreme: See Chapter 2.

Message Factors.   The ELM emphasizes the importance of message quality in determining the outcome of persuasion. When processing in the central mode, receivers are motivated to think about, understand, and elaborate on the arguments contained in the communication. If the message is found wanting—if its arguments are weak or illogical, these weaknesses will be glaringly obvious to the person engaged in its critical analysis, and the persuasion attempt will fail. On the other hand, if the message is well constructed, logical, and forceful, these strengths will be evident to the individual who is concentrating on the content of the message, and it will prove persuasive.

Receivers who lack motivation or ability to embark on the central route will show a different response to messages of differing quality. Well-constructed messages will be less persuasive for peripheral processors because they will not analyze the message carefully, and hence will not appreciate its strength and logic. Also, these same receivers are much less likely to discover the weaknesses of a poorly constructed communication. They are prone to concentrate on peripheral features (source, message intensity, and so on).

Processes of Resistance and Change.   We can now trace the manner in which attitudes are changed, according to the ELM. Figure 4.2 depicts the expectations of the model. This figure will serve as our road map as we trace the routes to persuasion hypothesized by Petty and Cacioppo.

To know how people will respond to a persuasive communication, we first must know whether they are motivated to process it. If they are, we then ask whether they have the ability to do so. If both questions are answered affirmatively, the central processing mode is engaged. In this mode, receivers carefully consider argument quality. If the message is strong and well crafted, thoughts consistent with its arguments are elaborated or created. Consequently, the receiver's attitude changes in the direction of the message. This new attitude will persist, given the manner in which the change was generated. On the other hand, if the message is weak and not compelling, the central route receiver

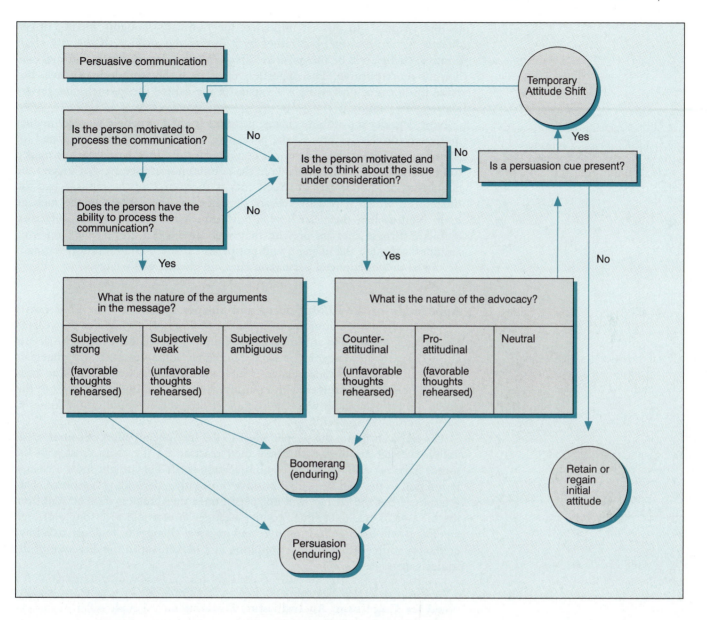

FIGURE 4.2

The elaboration-likelihood model of attitude change. (From Petty & Cacioppo, 1982, p. 264.) This complex model specifies the conditions under which attitude change is most likely, and the circumstances that increase the likelihood that the change will persist.

develops thoughts that are contrary to the recommendations contained in the communication. These contrary thoughts cause resistance to change. The original attitude is maintained or polarized.

When the communication is ambiguous in central mode processing—when it is not clear which position it is advocating—the receiver will fall back on pre-existing attitudes that are relevant to the communication. In this circumstance, the ELM predicts that preexisting attitudes will become more polarized.

What of the person who is either unmotivated to think about a communication or unable to process it? The individual still might be able to think about the issue under discussion. Such a situation might occur when a person is confronted with a communication on an extremely important topic, but is unable to understand it. In this circumstance, the receiver's thoughts are not driven directly by the message, but rather by a preexisting attitude. If the attitude is positive, change will be in a positive direction—the already positive attitude will become more positive. The opposite will occur if the attitude is negative. Because this form of processing is a variant of the central mode, such changes are expected to endure.

Now consider the attitude change pattern expected of people who are neither motivated (or able) to process the persuasive communication nor motivated (or able) to think about the issue under consideration. In these conditions, we need to know if there are cues available in the communication setting that suggest the desirability of attitude change. Such cues as the source of the message and the situation in which it is delivered are peripheral to the content of the message itself. Nonetheless, they can have a powerful, if relatively transient, effect on attitudes. If these cues are present, they will cause a shift in receivers' reported attitudes, although the changes will not persist. If the communication setting is devoid of these peripheral persuasion cues, no change will occur.

Application of the ELM: Source and Sleeper Effects.   The ELM casts a very different interpretation on many of the findings produced over the years in the study of attitude and attitude change. Consider the sleeper effect. The sleeper effect refers to the tendency of a highly credible source to exert an immediate positive impact on attitude change, which then dissipates over time. The messages of noncredible sources have a negative impact on attitudes initially, but this effect also dissipates, and with the passage of time the communication comes to have a persuasive impact.

The ELM attributes the sleeper effect to the (peripheral) effect of source credibility. Message recipients who base their reaction on the characteristics of the source have not elaborated the communication itself. They might show a change in reaction to the source—either positive or negative, depending on source characteristics—but the change will not persist once the source is disassociated from the message. Thus, over time, positive changes in response to a source of high credibility will become less positive, and negative changes in response to a low-credibility source will moderate, resulting in a movement in the direction of the source's message.

Need for Cognition: An Individual Difference.   People differ in the extent to which they characteristically analyze (elaborate) or fail to analyze persuasive messages. The second vignette of the chapter, the story of Skip, John, and the U.S. Navy, portrays an obvious difference. Skip is predisposed to quick judgments, even judgments that involve six years of his life. He seems unwilling or unable to invest much of his energy in thinking about issues. John is a different kind of person, one who likes, perhaps needs, to think about things that affect him. Cacioppo and Petty (1982) devised a scale that measures variations in people's *need for cognition,* the motivation to engage in effortful thought. To give a flavor of their work, some of the items that constitute their scale are presented in Table 4.1. Theoretically, people who are high in the need for cognition are more likely to think about a persuasive communication than those who are low in the need. They are more likely to traverse the central route to persuasion.

Hovland has suggested another explanation of the sleeper effect: See Chapter 3.

TABLE 4.1

◼

Selected Items from the Need for Cognition Scale (From Cacioppo and Petty, 1982.)

1. I really enjoy a task that involves coming up with new solutions to problems.

2. I would prefer a task that is intellectual, difficult, and important to one that is somewhat important but does not require much thought.

3. I would prefer complex to simple problems.

4. The notion of thinking abstractly is appealing to me.

5. Learning new ways to think doesn't excite me very much.

6. I think only as hard as I have to.

7. Thinking is not my idea of fun.

8. It's enough for me that something gets the job done; I don't care how or why it works.

Note: Responses are indicated through the use of a +4 (strongly agree) to −4 (strongly disagree) Likert-type scale. The last 4 items are worded in a direction opposite to the first, and are scored accordingly.

APPLYING SOCIAL PSYCHOLOGY TO THE ELECTORATE
◼ ◼ ◼

Who Gets Your Vote?

In a test of these ideas, Cacioppo, Petty, Kao, & Rodriguez (1986) assessed the need for cognition of a group of voters. At this test, which took place two months before the 1984 presidential election, voters also were asked to indicate their preferred candidate. After the election, participants were contacted again and asked their actual vote. Results indicated that high-need-for-cognition voters engaged in more issue-relevant thinking than participants who were low in need for cognition, and were much more likely to exhibit attitude–behavior consistency. These results are consistent with the general predictions of the ELM. They suggest that when individual traits or dispositions prompt people to engage in intensive message processing, they will exhibit a pattern of change that is different from that shown by people who focus on the peripheral information accompanying a message. The central route not only results in longer-lasting change, should change take place, but also produces attitudes that are more predictive of later attitude-relevant behavior.

Considerable research supports the assumptions that underlie the ELM. People clearly differ in the ways in which they process persuasive messages, and these differences have implications for the longevity of the resultant attitudes. Circumstances surrounding the presentation of a persuasive message can affect the manner in which the message is processed. People's motivation or ability to process messages affects their use of central or peripheral processing modes. These modes, in turn, determine the persistence of changed attitudes and the likelihood that subsequent actions will be consistent with the newly formed beliefs.

■ ■ ■ THE HEURISTIC–SYSTEMATIC MODEL

Although it is a powerful and successful predictive model, the ELM is not the only contemporary theory of attitude change. An interesting alternative that has stimulated much research and also has proved successful in predicting attitude change is the **heuristic–systematic model** of Shelly Chaiken and her associates (Chaiken, 1980, 1987; Chaiken, Liberman, & Eagly, 1989; Eagly & Chaiken, 1984). In many cases, the ELM and the heuristic–systematic model make similar predictions. However, their predictions are based on very different assumptions about the way people deal with information. Both models have much to offer, and both may be right—at least partially. Understanding both gives us a more complete picture of the ways our attitudes are modified in response to persuasive communications.

Systematic Processing

The central premise of the model is that people are motivated to hold accurate, or valid, attitudes—attitudes that are in accord with reality. To maximize the validity of their attitudes, people may process attitude-relevant information in one of two ways, systematically or heuristically. When engaged in *systematic processing,* message recipients actively engage in judging the truth of the message. They study the message's arguments and use knowledge they already possess to evaluate its validity. Systematic processing is intentional—it is under the individual's conscious control—and requires motivation, effort, and ability. It makes heavy demands on the information-processing capacity of the receiver. Certain contextual variables (such as distraction) and some individual difference variables (like low need for cognition) make systematic processing difficult or unlikely. Under conditions of stress, time restriction, and so forth, systematic processing may be impossible. Similarly, lack of expertise or information about the issue may put systematic processing beyond the reach of the individual.

Systematic processing is not necessarily open-minded and unbiased (Chaiken et al., 1989). A prochoice abortion advocate, for example, might process an antiabortion message systematically, but his or her existing attitude might bias the ultimate result of such processing. Such an individual would be thinking diligently about information that might be used to counteract the message's arguments, and failing to find it, might misinterpret or distort the counter-attitudinal message so that it could be more easily discounted or denied.

Heuristic Processing

In contrast to systematic processing, *heuristic processing* makes many fewer demands on the thought processes of the receiver. When processing heuristically, people use simple decision rules (heuristics) to rapidly estimate the validity of a position. In this form of processing, message recipients are less intent on understanding the content of a persuasive message than on focusing on non–content-related aspects of the communication that can be used to judge its validity.

What are heuristics? They are general rules of thumb that one uses to determine how to act. One common heuristic is "Experts are usually right." People will be persuaded by a message attributed to an expert if (1) they are processing heuristically, (2) they possess this particular heuristic, and (3) the heuristic is accessed from memory. Heuristics can be accessed either by a conscious action on the part of the receiver or by the circumstances within which the persuasive message is delivered. They substitute for a more informed and detailed understanding of the communication. Consider the "experts are right" heuristic in terms of your own actions. Think about the last time your doctor gave you some advice on a health issue. You may or may not have taken the advice, but you probably spent little time thinking, "Is this person qualified to give me this advice?" If you were processing heuristically, you probably intended to comply with the suggestions. If you were processing systematically, however, your judgment of the quality of the advice would have a greater effect on your ultimate action.

Heuristic processing is qualitatively different from systematic processing. It makes use of minimal information search and analysis, and relies instead on information (attitudes, personal theories, stereotypes, and so on) the receiver already possesses. Heuristic processing is a spontaneous, automatic response to a persuasive message. Because heuristic processing is so much easier than systematic processing, it is the preferred processing mode among those who are not highly motivated to ensure the validity of a particular position. With issues of high self-interest, systematic processing is preferred, and if the individual has the ability to process systematically, this mode will be employed. However, even when systematic processing is preferred, circumstances may mitigate against its adoption. Under conditions of extreme time pressure, for example, the careful, deliberate weighing of the pros and cons of an argument is not possible, and systematic processing cannot be employed. Similarly, if receivers have little or no knowledge about the information contained in a persuasive message, they will not be able to process it systematically, because such processing demands the ability to determine the validity of arguments. Lacking knowledge, such a determination cannot be made, and again systematic processing will prove impossible.

Efficiency + Sufficiency = Confidence

The principles of efficiency and sufficiency govern people's use of systematic or heuristic processing modes. The guiding principle in this determination is simple: Whatever the process employed, it must produce attitudes in whose validity the individual is confident. The *efficiency principle* asserts that people will attempt to achieve their goal as easily as possible. Thus, if heuristic processing is adequate, people will not engage in more effortful systematic processing. The *sufficiency principle* asks whether the mode of information processing being used is capable of generating sufficient confidence in the validity of the resultant attitude. Efficiency and sufficiency interact in such a way that the least-effortful processing model will be employed *if* it allows the receiver to be confident that the extracted information leads to a valid conclusion.

Personal estimates of efficiency and sufficiency vary from person to person, from issue to issue, and from situation to situation. With issues of extreme self-

When will other people's opinions have more impact than the technical quality of the equipment? When will technical quality matter most? ■

interest, a high degree of effort may be necessary before a person achieves sufficient confidence. With issues of less importance, less effort will be necessary. Individual differences also influence perceptions of efficiency and sufficiency. As Cacioppo and Petty (1982) have shown, people differ in their need for cognition. Making use of this variable, Chaiken, Axom, Yates, Wilson, Hicks, and Liberman (1988) showed that participants low in need for cognition were more frequent users of heuristics—and were more influenced by heuristic cues—than people high in the need for cognition.

APPLYING SOCIAL PSYCHOLOGY TO MARKETING
■ ■ ■

The XT-100

An interesting test of the efficiency–sufficiency hypothesis was conducted by Maheswaran & Chaiken (in press). They gave participants two types of information about a product, the "XT-100 answering machine." Participants learned that either a minority or majority of customers liked the machine, and then read a report in which the XT-100 was described either very positively or very negatively. Participants' motivation for processing the message was manipulated by instructions indicating that their responses had very important, or very unimportant, personal implications.

The researchers predicted that participants who had been led to believe that their responses were very important would engage in systematic processing. This hypothesis was confirmed through the use of a thought-listing procedure. In this test, participants wrote all the thoughts that occurred to them as they read the persuasive material. The participants in the high-importance condition generated a large number of issue-relevant thoughts. In addition, information regarding the quality of the machine had a strong effect on these cognitions and on the attitudes the participants subsequently expressed. The heuristic cue—the consensus information, which advised the participant that a majority (or minority) of consumers liked the machine—had very little effect on their thoughts or attitudes.

A different processing pattern emerged among participants for whom the task was characterized as unimportant. As would be expected of people who processed heuristically, participants in this condition did not produce many product-relevant cognitions when asked to do so in the thought-listing task. However, they were swayed by the consensus information. "If everyone else thinks the XT-100 is swell it must be." The consensus heuristic can have a powerful effect when the decision is unimportant.

ELM and the Heuristic–Systematic Model: Some Comparisons

Festinger's (1954) theory of social comparison presumes that people are motivated to hold "correct" attitudes: See Chapter 11.

The ELM and the heuristic–systematic approaches generate predictions of attitude change effects that are broadly consistent, but the reasons that underlie the predictions are quite distinct. Both models begin with the presumption that people are motivated to hold "correct" attitudes, a postulate that dates back at least to Festinger's (1954) theory of social comparison. How people arrive at correct attitudes, however, differs from model to model. The ELM looks at the particular elaboration route that is taken. Do people focus on the arguments presented in the communication or on peripheral aspects of the communicator or the communication setting? If receivers are attuned to the message itself, the resultant attitude is expected to persist. What determines the particular route to persuasion a receiver will traverse? Motivation and ability. If the attitude is important, receivers will be motivated to elaborate the persuasive message. What ultimately determines attitude change? The strength of the persuasive communication.

The heuristic–systematic model begins at the same point as the ELM, with the assumption that people are motivated to hold correct attitudes. How do people arrive at their attitudes? By processing information presented to them either systematically or heuristically. And what determines the particular mode of processing people will adopt? Motivation and ability, just as in the ELM. At this juncture, the models diverge. Heuristics are learned knowledge structures that the receiver brings into the persuasion situation. Examples of heuristics are "Experts give good advice," or "Consensus means correctness," or "Beautiful people are more sociable." They are part of the baggage that accompanies a person, not a consequence of information that accompanies the message. If a preexisting heuristic is activated in the communication context, it will be used as a cue to the appropriate attitude to extract from the message. Heuristic processing is rapid, efficient, and in some situations leads to the appropriate conclusion. Experts usually *do* give good advice, consensus often *is* associated with a correct view, and beautiful people *are* more sociable. Sometimes, however, speed and efficiency come at a cost. Heuristic-based attitudes often result in a position that is far off the mark, and in such circumstances the costs of heuristic processing can be great.

There is evidence that beautiful people *are* more sociable than others: See Chapter 13.

Unlike the ELM, Chaiken's model admits the possibility that both heuristic and systematic processing can be undertaken more or less simultaneously. While it is very unlikely that people could traverse both the central and peripheral routes concurrently, it is conceivable that systematic processing can activate the use of heuristics and vice versa.

■■■ SOME CONCLUDING THOUGHTS

The search for better methods of assessing and predicting attitudes and attitude change, which began with Thurstone's (1928) original measurement work, has led to current theoretical models that predict when people will change and when they will resist changing their attitudes. These models, in addition to predicting the direction of attitude change, also stipulate some of the major factors responsible for it. The near future of the social psychology of attitude and attitude change will be dominated by Petty and Cacioppo's ELM and the heuristic–systematic model of Chaiken and her colleagues. Clearly, both models have much to tell us about the manner in which people respond to persuasive communications. While compatible, neither model completely subsumes the other—and neither accounts for everything. This suggests that there is yet another attitude model on social psychology's horizon, one that integrates the insights of both the ELM and the systematic–heuristic model into a broader representation of attitude change.

■■■ SUMMARY

Social judgment theory is an extension of Hovland's message-learning model of persuasion. The extended theory holds that people may be susceptible to a range of statements about an attitude object. This range is the person's latitude of acceptance. The theory also postulates a latitude of rejection, a range of positions that a person finds objectionable and rejects. Latitude widths are affected by a person's ego involvement with the attitude object. Greater involvement is associated with smaller latitudes of acceptance and wider latitudes of rejection. The theory presupposes that the placement of a persuasive message is critical: If a message falls into the latitude of acceptance, it will be assimilated. If it falls into the latitude of rejection, it will have an effect opposite from that intended, a contrast or boomerang effect.

The elaboration-likelihood model (ELM) focuses on the manner in which people process persuasive communications to arrive at valid attitudes. If people elaborate the information presented, because of the social context or variations in their need for cognition, they will be influenced by message quality, not by peripheral cues. This central-processing strategy stands in contrast to peripheral processing, in which features extraneous to the quality of arguments (for example, source attractiveness) are most critical.

The heuristic–systematic model also assumes that people are motivated to develop valid attitudes. To do so, people can engage in thoughtful (systematic) or rule-based (heuristic) information processing. When stakes are high, people attend to message quality (that is, they process systematically). In low-stakes conditions or in contexts in which people are unable to comprehend a communication, they process heuristically on the basis of cues to message quality, which are derived from non-content-related aspects (source credibility, attractiveness, and so on) of the communication.

■ ■ ■ **SUGGESTED READINGS**

1. Ajzen, I. (1985). From intentions to actions: A theory of planned behavior. In J. Kuhl & J. Beckman (Eds.), *Action control: From cognitions to behavior* (pp. 11–39). Heidelberg: Springer.

2. Chaiken, S., Liberman, A., & Eagly, A. H. (1989). Heuristic and systematic processing within and beyond the persuasion context. In J. S. Uleman & J. A. Bargh (Eds.), *Unintended thought.* New York: Guilford Press.

3. Granberg, D., & Sarup, G. (Eds.) (1992). *Social judgment and intergroup relations: Essays in honor of Muzafer Sherif.* New York: Springer/Verlag.

4. Petty, R. E., & Cacioppo, J. T. (1986). The elaboration likelihood model of persuasion. In L. Berkowitz (Ed.), *Advances in experimental social psychology* (Vol. 19, pp. 123–205). New York: Academic Press.

CHAPTER 5

COGNITIVE DISSONANCE
Persuading Ourselves

■ **Key Concepts**

Cognitive dissonance
Reverse incentive effect
Commitment
Insufficient justification
Postdecision regret
Free choice
Effort justification
Aversive consequences
Hypocrisy
Self-affirmation
Impression management
Self-perception
Misattribution

■ **Chapter Outline**

DISSONANCE
  The Theory
  Preconditions to Dissonance

THE THREE FACES OF DISSONANCE
  Insufficient Justification
  Free Choice
  Effort Justification
  ■ Dissonance and Weight Loss

COGNITIVE DISSONANCE RECONSIDERED: ALTERNATIVE EXPLANATIONS
  Alterations to the Basic Theory
  The Aversive Consequences Revision
  ■ Dissonance and AIDS

REPLACEMENTS TO THE BASIC THEORY
  Impression Management
  Self-Perception
  Motivating Properties of Dissonance
  A Reconciliation

SOME CONCLUDING THOUGHTS

SUMMARY

Joe has followed the presidential election campaign with great interest. Although the candidates are very different in their personal style and advocate different programs and approaches, both have much to offer. Joe is hard put to decide between them. Just before Joe enters the voting booth, a friend asks him what he thinks of the candidates. Joe replies that he likes them both, almost equally. In the booth, Joe finally decides. Soon after he has voted, Bob asks him his opinion of the candidates. Forcefully as he can, Joe tries to convince Bob to vote for his candidate.

■ ■ ■

The next evening, Joe goes out on a blind date with Kathy. He doesn't really enjoy himself much, but at the end of the evening, perhaps to be polite, he tells Kathy he had a wonderful time. A few days later, he finds himself thinking warmly about the date. Almost to his surprise, he calls Kathy and asks if she would like to go out again.

■ ■ ■

Two weeks later, Joe buys the car he has been dreaming about for years, a beautiful lemon-yellow Corvette Stingray. He spends two solid weeks working under the car, with grease up to his elbows. Finally, it's ready to go. On the way to Kathy's, the gas tank falls off. On top of this, Joe learns at the garage that he will need a new transmission. The repair bill is equal to two months' pay. After all this, can you estimate Joe's attitude toward his car? Does he now hate it? Surprisingly, Joe now may have a more *positive* attitude about the car than on the day he bought it.

Two questions should spring to mind when reading these scenarios. First, is there a way to make sense of Joe's actions and attitudes? And second, can a single theory be made to explain all three of them? The answer to both questions is yes. The name of the theory is **cognitive dissonance,** the focus of this chapter.

■ ■ ■ Dissonance

During the 1960s, social psychology theory developed around the general principle that people are motivated to maintain consistency in their beliefs and attitudes. A number of variations on this consistency theme were proposed (Abelson, Aronson, McGuire, Newcomb, Rosenberg, & Tannenbaum, 1968). It was in this context that the theory of **cognitive dissonance** was proposed by Leon Festinger. Dissonance proved to be the most influential of all the consistency

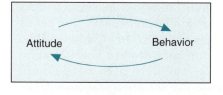

FIGURE 5.1

■

Classic and dissonance-inspired interpretation of the relationship between attitudes and behavior.

The theory of cognitive dissonance has influenced research on attribution: See Chapters 9 and 10; prejudice and discrimination: See Chapters 23 and 24; and social cognition: See Chapter 8.

"Attitudes cause behavior" was a central idea of early attitude studies: See Chapter 2.

theories that arose during that period. Even today, more than three decades since it first appeared, dissonance theory has a powerful effect on the ways social psychologists frame their research and explain their results. Dissonance has spurred more research and debate in social psychology than any theory before or since. In this chapter, we attempt to give a sense of the intensity of concern, scientific and otherwise, that greeted the study of cognitive dissonance. The debates the theory stimulated were exhilarating and fun. And, although some ultimately proved pointless, some of the theoretical confrontations laid the groundwork for much of what constitutes social psychology in the 1990s (cf. Aronson, in press; Bagby, Parker & Bury, 1990; Berkowitz & Devine, 1989; Cooper & Fazio, 1984; 1989; Freedman, Cunningham, & Krismer, 1992; Lord, 1989; Stone, Aronson, Crain, Winslow, & Fried, in press). Research on attribution, prejudice and discrimination, and social cognition has been influenced by this theory. The theory and the research that flowed from it are a fine example of the ways science advances and how we accumulate reliable knowledge.

The Theory

You might assume that a theory that stimulated such wide debate would be long and complicated. Not true. In fact, Festinger (1957) summarized his theory in one sentence, by stating that "two elements [beliefs and/or behaviors] are in a dissonant relation if, considering these two alone, the obverse of one element would follow from the other" (p. 13). An extended and somewhat more informative version of the theory, all of three sentences long, takes the following form:

■ Inconsistencies can exist among a person's cognitions (beliefs, attitudes, values) or between a cognition and an action.
■ *Cognitive inconsistency* (which Festinger called *cognitive dissonance*) is unpleasant, and gives rise to pressures to reduce it.
■ Cognitive dissonance can be reduced (cognitive consistency restored) through a change of attitudes or beliefs or through a change of behavior.

That's it—the theory that launched a thousand experiments! Why?

In part, the answer is found in the ingenuity of the experiments designed to test the theory. Festinger and his students had a knack for developing studies that produced findings contrary to everyday expectations, yet in perfect accord with dissonance theory's predictions. They did this by subtly inducing a conflict between people's beliefs and actions. The conflict was stage managed in such a way that the action could be undone. Thus, all the change pressure arising from attitude–action inconsistency fell on the actor's beliefs.

Before Festinger's research, social psychological studies of attitude and attitude change centered on the idea that attitudes cause behavior. This relationship is depicted in the top portion of Figure 5.1. Festinger reversed the usual assumption. From the perspective of dissonance theory, behavior (especially behavior contrary to one's beliefs) causes attitudes, as shown in the bottom portion of the figure. Dissonance theory transposed the fundamental cause–effect relationship between attitudes and behavior. Today, it is widely recognized that both processes occur—behavior often follows from attitudes, but new behavior can lead to new attitudes as well.

A Research Example.   One of the classic studies in dissonance research offers a good example of the way inconsistency can be induced between people's beliefs and actions. Conducted by Festinger and Carlsmith (1959), the study took the guise of a motor coordination test. Research participants worked alone for thirty minutes on two boring tasks. On the first task, they were given a large board with forty-eight knobs, and asked to turn each one 90 degrees; then they repeated the operation over and over for fifteen minutes. On the second task, they were given a peg board and asked to place spools on each peg. When all the pegs were spooled, the time was noted, and they began again.

After all of this excitement, participants were given research credit and released. Before they reached the door, however, the experimenter asked if they would be willing to "introduce" the study to a waiting subject, and in the process, earn some money. The amount promised is the major manipulation of the study—some were given $20 to describe the tasks to the waiting subject as enjoyable, fun, intriguing, etc.; other participants are given only $1 to make this false description. The participants were perfectly free to refuse—but none did.

The "waiting subject" was actually an experimental accomplice who voiced strong doubts about the study she was about to undertake. After describing the tasks to this incoming "subject" and insisting that they were fun and enjoyable, the actual participant was given a questionnaire and asked to indicate his true feelings about the study. This questionnaire was purportedly part of a general evaluation of students' reactions to psychological research, conducted under the auspices of the Psychology Department.

What would most people predict in this situation? Wouldn't the participants who had been paid $20 to describe the tasks as enjoyable express more positive attitudes toward tasks than those who had been paid only $1? This is what the prevailing learning theories in psychology would have predicted. The more one is rewarded for an act, the more positive the act becomes. This is the basic principle of reinforcement.

The results of the Festinger and Carlsmith experiment were completely contrary to this expectation. Those paid $20 to say nice things about the study evaluated it much *less* favorably than those paid only $1 (Figure 5.2). Although this *reverse incentive effect,* as it is called, is contrary to reinforcement-based expectations, it makes perfect sense in the context of dissonance theory. Why?

Thinking Through the Results.   Let's break the study down in dissonance-theory terms to see how and why it worked the way it did. First, a conflict had been induced between the beliefs and actions of the participant. No one in his right mind could possibly think the tasks were fun and enjoyable. Yet the participant had described them in this way to an innocent and trusting fellow student. This created an inconsistency between a belief (the tasks were boring) and an action (describing the tasks in positive terms).

Consider the people who had been paid $20. When they were faced with the inconsistency between their beliefs about the tasks and their action, they had a ready justification for their behavior available to them—a $20 reward. Because of this reward, the theory predicts they would experience very little dissonance, and hence little need to change their attitude. Thus, when asked what they thought of the boring tasks, these participants responded that they thought they were boring.

FIGURE 5.2

Effects of payment differences on task evaluation. (From Festinger & Carlsmith, 1959.) This is the classic reverse-incentive effect. The more one is paid to *express* a favorable attitude, the less favorable is the actual attitude.

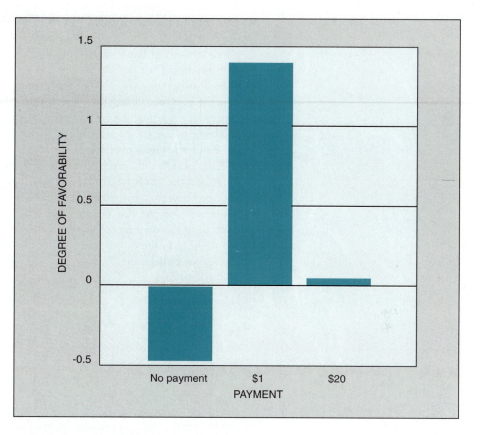

What about those who were paid only $1 for their performance? They *could not* justify their behavior on external grounds. Surely no one would tell so egregious a lie for a measly dollar. Nor could they undo their behavior—the waiting subject was not waiting any longer, she was in the middle of the dial-turning task. According to the theory, these people would experience high levels of dissonance, and the only means available to them to reduce dissonance was to modify their attitude about the tasks. If the tasks were not really so bad—if, in fact, they were even somewhat interesting—then the positive description they provided could be rationalized as not being really contradictory to their beliefs. Clearly, there was strong internal pressure on the low-paid participants to change one of the two dissonant elements in the attitude–behavior equation. The only element they *could* change was their attitude about the task, and this is what they did.

Preconditions to Dissonance

From this study and many others like it, we have learned some important lessons about the conditions under which dissonance will occur. First, dissonance will arise only if the belief-inconsistent action is induced with minimal pressure and with minimal justification. If the experimenter had pulled a gun on the hapless participant and demanded that he rave about the tasks to the waiting subject, do you think dissonance would have been aroused? The theory says not, because the participant easily would have rationalized his behavior—if he had not complied, he would have been shot. Under strong compliance pressure, dissonance will not occur.

Paying $20 for the lie not only increases the pressure on the participant to comply but also rationalizes the action. The behavior is perhaps not so unreasonable if accompanied by a large reward. It is when the conflict between attitude and action cannot be attributed to other, reasonable, factors ($20 or an armed experimenter) that dissonance is most likely (Baumeister & Tice, 1984).

A second factor that appears to matter is *commitment*. When the participant described the study as fun, interesting, and enjoyable, he was challenged by the waiting subject, who responded that her roommate had told her it was a boring waste of time. At this point, the participant was forced to elaborate the lie, to contradict the waiting subject's roommate, and to insist that the tasks really were wonderful. Forcing this kind of commitment enhanced the effects of belief-discrepant behavior.

■■■ THE THREE FACES OF DISSONANCE

Although other dissonance studies had preceded the work of Festinger and Carlsmith (1959), this experiment seemed to open the floodgates. Study after study was undertaken to investigate the novel theory. Some of these studies supported the theory, others did not. In the sections that follow, we describe this empirical debate. We have divided the dissonance literature into three subsections, which correspond roughly to the three major approaches taken to examine the theory. In each section, we give an example of each type of study, along with some of the critical reaction it generated.

Insufficient Justification

The Festinger and Carlsmith (1959) experiment falls into the general classification of **insufficient justification** research. In this variety of study, people are induced with as little pressure (or justification) as possible to perform an action contrary to their beliefs. The situation is set up so that the action cannot subsequently be undone. Then the effects of the conflict between belief and behavior are examined. The theory holds that if people cannot find (or invent) a plausible reason for a dissonant action and cannot undo the action, they will change their beliefs so as to bring them into line with their behavior. Insufficient justification has been used to induce attitude change on a wide variety of issues, including attitudes toward the police (Cohen, 1962), toward drafting students during the Vietnam War (Crano & Messé, 1970), purchasing condoms (Stone et al., in press), even eating grasshoppers (Smith, 1961).

This woman just chose a Saab over a Volvo. Obviously she is committed to her choice. Did her attitudes toward Saabs and Volvos change after buying the Saab? How? ■

Free Choice

One of the unique features of dissonance theory is that it was developed to predict the cognitive and behavioral adjustments that occur *after* a person makes a decision to act. Dissonance has been termed the theory of *postdecision regret,* because it assumes that we constantly second-guess ourselves after deciding on a course of action. This emphasis on postdecisional processes distinguishes dissonance from other social psychological theories that are concerned with the consistency between attitudes and behaviors. Most of these models focus on the processes that occur *before* a person decides on an action. Festinger reversed the usual approach.

This focus on postdecisional events is most evident in dissonance-inspired research on the cognitive consequences of **free choice.** In the usual free-choice experiment, participants are asked to consider and evaluate a group of objects, rating them from most desirable to least. Then they are made to choose between two of the rated objects. For some participants, the choice involves items they rated as very similar in desirability; for others, the choice is between items they rated very differently. After the choice, everyone is asked to reevaluate the objects. Dissonance predicts that people who have been made to choose between equally desirable items will need to justify their choice, because by choosing one, they have lost the positive features of the one they rejected. If the desirability of the rejected alternative is close to the chosen one, this will cause cognitive dissonance. How is the dissonance resolved? We may downgrade the rejected alternative or upgrade the chosen one. Either way, the rejected item is reevaluated subjectively as being less desirable than the chosen one.

One of the earliest dissonance experiments tested these predictions. In this study, Brehm (1956) asked college women to evaluate eight items of approximately equal value—a toaster, blender, radio, silk-screen print, and the like. As payment, they were promised a choice between two of the items. Half the women were asked to choose between two items they had rated very similarly; the others to choose between items they had evaluated very differently. After choosing, all participants were asked to rerate the items. Interestingly, the difference between the chosen and unchosen items was significantly greater after the choice was made—but only for those women who had to choose between items they had originally evaluated nearly identically. The greatest dissonance was aroused in this condition because by choosing one alternative, they had rejected another that was almost equally desirable. To justify the choice between the two nearly identical possibilities, the women enlarged the distance between them. Those who had been asked to choose between two options they had evaluated very differently did not experience much if any dissonance, as predicted, and hence did not adjust their original ratings.

Thirty years after Brehm's experiment, Zanna and Sande (1987) expanded on his investigation by demonstrating the importance of *commitment* in modifying the dynamics of the dissonance process. In their study, Zanna and Sande asked students to read some information about two people who were applicants for housing in a new project. Half the participants simply rated the two people; the remaining participants did the same, but they were told their ratings would determine which person would be admitted to the housing project. Since housing was in short supply, their decision was important. Then, all were asked to evaluate a group of seven housing applicants. The group included the two people they had already judged. The participants whose decision was crucial seemed to justify their initial choice by judging the two as very different when given the second judgment opportunity. Of course, the person they chose initially was evaluated in the subsequent judgment as being highly deserving. Participants whose first evaluation had no implications for assignment to the housing project did not alter their later judgments. Zanna and Sande's study reinforces Brehm's much earlier results and emphasizes the importance of commitment in the dissonance process. Making a decision does indeed alter our perception of the choices we had entertained before making the decision; and it alters our perceptions even more strongly when the decision means something to us.

Many of you might have experienced something similar if you had the good fortune to have had to choose between two (or more) desirable colleges. Initially, you might have had a difficult time. But after your decision was made, the chosen alternative somehow became more and more obvious and desirable and the unchosen alternative(s) progressively less so. Eventually, you might have even wondered why college X was ever even in the running. This is a common psychological process by which an unchosen alternative is successively displaced in a negative direction, and the chosen one viewed with growing positivity. There are many other examples of everyday postdecision justification processes. Frenkel and Doob (1976) obtained ratings of political candidates from voters either immediately before or immediately after they had voted. Like Joe, who voted at the beginning of this chapter, those polled after they had voted were significantly more positive about their candidate, and were more confident of victory, than were people who rated the candidates before voting. Apparently, to justify their vote, participants widened the gap between the chosen and the unchosen office

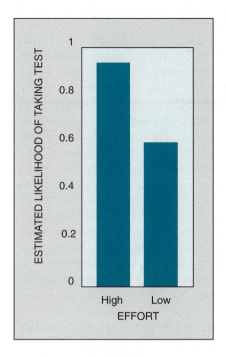

FIGURE 5.3

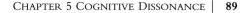

Effects of effort justification on test expectations. (From Yaryan & Festinger, 1961.) Higher levels of effort are "justified" by the actor's expectation that it will prove necessary.

seekers. The same process occurs at the racetrack, another fine arena in which to study free-choice behavior. Knox and Inkster (1968) asked bettors to estimate the chances of their horse's winning. Those who had just placed their bets were much more confident than those still waiting to put their money down! Making a choice arouses dissonance, and dissonance stimulates the consequent need to justify the choice (and thereby reduce dissonance).

Effort Justification

The third general division of dissonance research is concerned with **effort justification.** Dissonance holds that a person who works hard to attain a particular outcome will evaluate that outcome more highly than if it were attained with little effort expenditure. According to the theory, we love the things that cost us the most and devalue easy conquests. To study this hypothesis, Yaryan and Festinger (1961) performed an ingenious experiment in which people were made to expend different amounts of effort to prepare for a test that they might or might not have to take. In the experiment, participants reported in groups to a classroom. An index card was taped on each desk. They were instructed *not* to turn the card over. The experimenter explained that he was developing a new test of intelligence based on symbol manipulation; accordingly, participants were to review a set of symbols in preparation for the examination. Half were told they would need to memorize the symbols to take the test; the other participants were told they simply needed to familiarize themselves with them. For the memorization group, the task would take more than an hour of concerted effort. The familiarization group had only to look over the materials.

Before participants began this part of the test, the experimenter explained that he had underestimated the number of people who would sign up for his study, and had only enough test booklets for half the participants in the room. These people had already been randomly chosen via the index card that had been taped to each desk before their arrival. For half the participants, the index card indicated that they were to take the test; the other half of the cards dismissed the participant from further work. Before turning the cards over, the experimenter asked each participant to estimate the likelihood that he or she would have to take the test.

The scale on which participants recorded their answers is presented in Figure 5.3, along with their average responses. As shown, the high-effort participants were more certain that they would have to take the test. The low-effort participants' mean rating is near the middle of the scale, consistent with the odds. Analyzing the data in another way, Yaryan and Festinger found that 92% of the high-effort participants placed themselves on the positive side of the scale, while only 60% of the low-effort participants did so.

The results are surprising, but consistent with dissonance predictions. Those who had committed themselves to the hard work of memorization thought they would be tapped to take the test despite the fact that (1) they knew only 50% of the sample would receive it and (2) the identity of these participants had been determined completely by chance (the index cards), in advance of their having entered the laboratory. Because participants seated themselves, there was no way the experimenter could have picked on a specific person or group of persons to take the test. Obviously, the best bet was 50%, and this was approximately the guess of those who expected to expend little energy on the task. Dissonance apparently prompted the memorizers to justify their expected effort by assuming that the odds were in favor of their having to take the test, despite the fact that objectively they knew the odds were exactly 50–50. Apparently, those who had committed themselves to hard work assumed a higher likelihood that they would end up in the test group. In this way, their memorization efforts were justified.

The effort involved in effort justification need not be cognitive or even physical. Consider a classic study of Aronson and Mills (1959), who advertised in the student newspaper of a woman's university for volunteers to join a sex discussion group. The women who expressed an interest in joining the group were told that because of the press of volunteers and the material to be considered, each member would take a screening test. This test would ensure that the subject could contribute to the discussion in a frank and uninhibited manner. The test took one of two forms: In the *mild* form, women were asked to read aloud a series of mildly suggestive words (fondle, french kiss, and the like); in the *severe* form, the women were asked to read aloud a series of sexually explicit words and a passage from erotic fiction. After this test (which all passed), each participant was allowed, via intercom, to listen in to a meeting of the sex discussion club. It was explained to the participant that because her test had run late, she could not be admitted to the group immediately, because this would interrupt the flow of the discussion. In fact, the "group discussion" was a tape recording of a purposely dry and boring exchange on the secondary sex characteristics of lower animals.

The central issue of this study was the effect of the different screening tests on participants' ratings of the discussion they had monitored. Dissonance theory's effort justification orientation predicts that the more severe the screening experience—that is, the more psychological effort the women had to expend to join the group—the more dissonance they would experience when listening to the dull discussion. Those who had read the more explicit material had expended more effort, and hence would be more motivated to resolve dissonance. How would they do this? The effort already had been spent. If they quit the group, it would be totally wasted. However, if the discussion were judged really interesting, the dissonance would be resolved. Getting into the group *was* worth the effort. According to the theory, then, there was considerable pressure on the severe-initiation participants to evaluate the discussion more positively than their less severely initiated peers—and this is exactly what they did. Later research using different forms of "initiations" replicated Aronson and Mills's results (e.g., Gerard & Mathewson, 1966; Wicklund, Cooper, & Linder, 1967).

The Real World.   Real-world analogues of this work are readily available. Many institutions that have severe initiations—fraternities, college football teams, the marines—also have very committed followers. It is conceivable that the effort members have to expend to gain entry to the group is related to later allegiance. More systematic research on effort justification in nonlaboratory settings suggests this is so. For example, consider the research of Kahle and Beatty (1987). Many states now have laws that require a deposit on all soft-drink cans and bottles, presumably to foster conservation and reduce litter. Kahle and Beatty found that people's attitudes toward conservation were much less favorable before such bills were enacted than after the laws had been in effect for a while. Can effort justification account for this pattern of attitude change? We believe it can.

Realistically, the work of storing used cans and bottles, lugging them to the grocery, and waiting for a refund is not really worth the paltry deposit involved.

Somehow, the effort needs to be justified. How do we do this? According to Kahle and Beatty, by becoming more favorable to the law and its implications for a cleaner environment, to conservation of energy, and so on. These attitudes are all valid, of course. Bottle return does make ecological sense—but the point is, it made just as much sense before such bills were enacted, and attitudes then were much less favorable. Evidently, some cognitive response was required to justify the effort that such laws require.

APPLYING SOCIAL PSYCHOLOGY TO HEALTH
■ ■ ■

Another fascinating application of the effort justification principle is found in Axsom and Cooper's (1985) study on weight loss. In this experiment, participants signed up to see if they could shed a few pounds. All were 10%–20% above their ideal body weight. After everyone had completed a questionnaire on their exercise patterns and everyday eating habits, they were given information on diet, exercise, and so on, and then were exposed to tasks requiring different degrees of effort. The high-effort participants completed a series of very difficult *perceptual and cognitive* tasks. The tasks had nothing to do with losing weight. The low-effort participants did not participate in these tasks. This procedure was repeated over four weekly meetings.

Participants were weighed at the fifth meeting. The data, summarized in Figure 5.4, reveal a small but significant difference between the high- and low-effort groups, which had begun the study at identical average weights. The high-effort

FIGURE 5.4
■

Weight loss as a function of (cognitive) effort justification. (From Axsom & Cooper, 1985.) Cognitive effort is justified by weight loss. And, the loss persists.

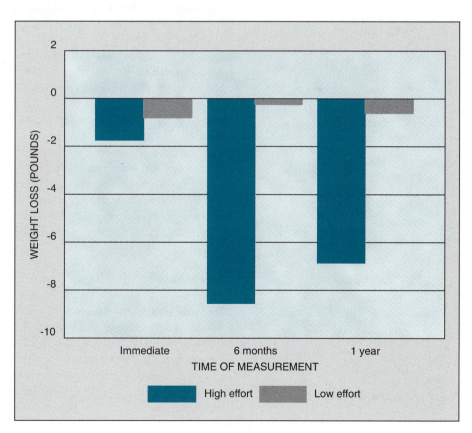

participants lost 1.75 pounds over the course of the "treatment," while the low-effort participants lost .80 pounds. Not dissuaded by the these minor differences, Axsom and Cooper reweighed their participants at six months and one year post-treatment. Here the differences were more dramatic: At six months, the high-effort participants had extended their weight loss to 8.5 pounds, while the low-effort group had slipped back to their original weight. After one year, the high-effort participants had maintained their weight loss (6.75 pounds), while the low-effort participants were approximately .5 pounds heavier than when they began the experiment. The effort justification manipulation not only made for differences but also the differences grew over time. The implications of these results for a host of real-world problems are wonderfully intriguing and are being investigated in other therapeutic settings—desensitization clinics, smoking treatment centers, and similar organizations (e.g., Axsom, 1989).

■ ■ ■ COGNITIVE DISSONANCE RECONSIDERED: ALTERNATIVE EXPLANATIONS

Any theory that stimulates more than a thousand studies is likely to encounter predictive failures as well as successes and to undergo a certain degree of revision to account for both. This is certainly true of the theory of cognitive dissonance (cf. Aronson, in press; Cooper & Fazio, 1984; 1989). The major revisions of dissonance theory are presented on the pages that follow. Some of these were suggested by researchers seeking to specify in finer detail the conditions under which dissonance would affect beliefs and actions. These revisions were developed to overcome some of the theory's limitations, and as such are best viewed as *alterations* to the original model. Other, more profound, alternatives to dissonance also have been suggested. These are designed to supplant or replace dissonance theory by postulating mechanisms other than dissonance that can account for the standard dissonance findings and by anticipating cause–effect relationships that are beyond the predictive domain of the theory. We term these types of revisions *replacements*. All the revisions, alterations and replacements alike, were developed to deal with issues that posed problems for the original theory. If nothing else, the revisions acknowledge dissonance as a powerful predictive model, but like all theories of social behavior, it is not perfect.

Alterations to the Basic Theory

The Aversive Consequences Revision. A revision that refines the theory of cognitive dissonance was proposed by Joel Cooper and Russell Fazio (1984). In their suggested alteration, Cooper and Fazio specified precisely the conditions under which dissonance effects would or would not occur. According to Cooper and Fazio, **aversive consequences** are necessary to trigger cognitive dissonance. If we perform an action that is inconsistent with our beliefs, it will not generate dissonance unless the action has negative consequences for ourselves or for people we like (Scher & Cooper, 1989). So, in Festinger and Carlsmith's (1959) study, the revised theory predicts that no reverse incentive effect would occur if the participant could not convince the waiting subject that the study in which she was about to participate was fun and interesting. Cooper and Worchel (1970) performed a study whose findings are consistent with this expectation. In their investigation, Cooper and Worchel found that the attitudes and actions of participants who gave a speech contrary to their beliefs were affected *only* if they thought their audience would be persuaded by their arguments. If participants were led to believe that their speech would have no effect on the audience, dissonance was not experienced, and attitude or behavior change did not occur.

Cooper, Zanna, and Goethals (1974) followed this research with a study that showed that if the participant disliked the waiting subject, then deceiving her did not result in dissonance-induced attitude change. If the participant liked the waiting subject, dissonance effects did occur. Thus, if aversive consequences result from our actions, we feel dissonance if we care about, or feel responsible for, the person who experiences them. If we don't care about the others, dissonance—and consequent attitude or behavior change—does not occur.

Aversive consequences alone are not sufficient, however. The individual must feel a sense of *personal responsibility* for the consequences. So, if one inadvertently tells another a story that turns out to be untrue and that causes harm, the teller may regret the action but it will not cause guilt or dissonance. Similarly, if a person advises another and the advice results in unforeseen problems, dissonance will not ensue. Aversive consequences must be intentional and foreseeable if they are to trigger dissonance. The aversive consequences revision of dissonance theory is reasonably explicit in its prediction that attitude or behavior changes will be directed to minimizing the negative consequences produced by the actor's behavior. Thus, the participant in Festinger and Carlsmith's study would rationalize his lie by forming the new impression that the boring tasks really were not so bad after all—the waiting subject probably was going to enjoy doing them. Behavior change is more likely to be directed toward *undoing* aversive consequences, if this is possible. Most dissonance experiments have been designed in such a way that this is not an option.

Hypocrisy Theory. Another friendly alteration to the basic theory, which fits well with the aversive consequences approach, was proposed by Aronson and his colleagues (Aronson, in press; Aronson, Fried, & Stone, 1991; Stone et al., in press). It is called **hypocrisy theory.** Aronson hypothesized that many past dissonance findings occurred because people had been induced to act hypocritically. Since this characterization is quite dissonant with our usual self-image, we are under some pressure to change either belief or action to reestablish a positive (nonhypocritical) self-evaluation. Consider the usual dissonance experiment—people are induced to act in ways at odds with their beliefs. These acts usually have aversive consequences for another person. Acting at odds with our beliefs is hypocritical, and calls for a cognitive or behavioral adjustment if we are to maintain a positive self-image. In most dissonance studies, behavioral adjustments are not possible. Thus, people induced to act hypocritically adjust their attitudes to lessen the perception of hypocrisy. They bring their beliefs into congruence with their actions, thereby reducing hypocrisy.

Dissonnance and AIDS

Aronson's revision of the standard dissonance explanation was studied in an important health context. In this investigation, Aronson and his colleagues tried to increase condom usage among sexually active young adults to lower the risk of HIV infection (Aronson et al., 1991). To do this, the researchers had college students read a communication that presented the rationale for using condoms. Some were asked to discuss instances in their recent past in which they had failed to use condoms; others were not asked to discuss their personal lives. After this, all presented a speech that argued strongly for greater condom usage.

Aronson reasoned that the students who had been made aware of their own past failings in condom usage *and* who had given a speech arguing for their consistent use would experience cognitive dissonance. Why? Because they were being hypocritical. They were urging condom use while failing to use them consistently themselves. How could they resolve the ensuing dissonance? Either by modifying their attitudes regarding AIDS (not likely—nobody is going to be in favor of becoming HIV positive) or by resolving to change their future behavior. Those for whom the inconsistency between speech and action was not emphasized were not expected to experience much dissonance, and thus were not be expected to modify either beliefs or behaviors. The data confirmed these expectations. The "hypocritical" students who gave the procondom speech were much more likely three months later to be using condoms consistently. Those students who were not made mindful of their past failures were not nearly as diligent in their practice of safer sex. Dissonance reduction apparently influenced the students' behavior for at least three months after it was aroused.

Self-Affirmation.   A variant of the hypocrisy interpretation that is somewhat less consonant with Festinger's model than Aronson's was proposed by Steele (1988; Steele & Liu, 1983). Steele's approach, termed **self-affirmation** theory, holds that the kinds of activities usually thought to produce cognitive dissonance also generate a need in people to reaffirm their integrity. This need, Steele argues, lies at the heart of most findings in dissonance research.

Self-affirmation differs from dissonance in that it focuses more broadly on the self-concept and the effects of threats to the self-concept on behavior. According to Steele, dissonance is only one such threat. In most dissonance research, people are induced to act in ways contrary to their beliefs. Such inconsistency threatens the self-concept. Dissonance resolution (via attitude or behavior change) is one way in which the self-affirmation process can proceed, but it is only one of many ways.

Considerable research has been focused on the effects of threat to the self-concept: See Chapter 11.

Like Aronson, Steele is not critical of the fundamental idea of dissonance; rather, he is concerned with a more fine-grained identification of the factors that cause the changes observed in dissonance studies. He suggests that the manipulations used in the three major areas of dissonance research—insufficient justification, postdecision regret, and effort justification—all compromise people's ability to maintain a positive self-image. In attempting to bolster or preserve the self, people make use of many different forms of defense. Some of these behaviors include, *but are not restricted to,* dissonance reduction mechanisms of behavior or attitude change.

To test his ideas, Steele (1988; Steele, Hopp, & Gonzales, 1986) asked participants in a free-choice experiment to rate ten record albums. Then, all chose between the albums they had rated fifth and sixth. After having chosen one album or the other, participants rated the entire group again. On the second rating task, the chosen album was rated more positively than it had been in the first session and the unchosen album less positively—the standard free-choice dissonance effect. However, this effect was not obtained for everyone. Before the experiment began, Steele had determined who among the participants was oriented strongly toward a career in science. Some of these participants, along with a portion of those who were not science oriented, were asked to don white lab coats in the interval between their choice of album and the second rating. They did this presumably to prepare for another study. In Steele's view, the science-oriented participants who donned lab coats had reaffirmed their identity. This reaffirmation allowed them to resolve the postdecision regret generated in the free-choice task. Because of the identity-reaffirmation process, they were not expected to show a displacement effect on their second ratings, which is predicted by dissonance theory. And they did not. By reestablishing or reaffirming an important part of their self-concept, Steele argued, these participants had reduced any self-uncertainty that might have resulted from the postdecision regret generated by their choice. The science-oriented participants who were not provided the lab coats showed the dissonance-displacement effect, as did the lab-coated participants who were not oriented toward science. For this latter group, the lab coat did not reaffirm their social identities, and hence dissonance still operated.

■■■ REPLACEMENTS TO THE BASIC THEORY

Do these possibilities end the story? Is the validity of dissonance theory, at least as revised by Cooper and Fazio, Aronson, or Steele, established beyond a doubt? No. As we shall see, many explanations counsel replacement rather than alteration of the theory.

Impression Management

Impression management is an alternative theory that suggests a radical reinterpretation of dissonance-related findings. The theory, developed by James Tedeschi and his colleagues, argues that dissonance phenomena are the result of people's attempts to "maintain face," to present themselves in the best possible light to others (Schlenker, 1982; Tedeschi & Rosenfeld, 1981; Tedeschi, Schlenker, & Bonoma, 1971). In Tedeschi's view, the attitude change that apparently occurs in the typical insufficient justification experiment is not the outcome of people's attempts to resolve an uncomfortable inconsistency between their behaviors and attitudes. Rather, it is the consequence of a conscious attempt to look good to the experimenter. According to impression management theory, people are motivated not to *be* consistent but to *appear* consistent.

The logic of impression management is as follows. Suppose at the request of an experimenter you have just written a strong essay, contrary your true position, and you have done so for the promise of a measly 50 cents (a typical insufficient justification manipulation). Then, the experimenter solicits your attitude on the issue you have just written about. What should you do? If you indicate your real attitude, the experimenter will think you are stupid. Otherwise, why would you have written an essay, for practically nothing, that argued a position exactly opposite to your beliefs? So as not to look ridiculous, therefore, you report an attitude that is in keeping with the essay you have just written. This *looks* like a dissonance effect. Dissonance proponents would interpret your attitude as the result of a motivated change brought about by cognitive dissonance aroused by the clash between your beliefs and your action. In the view of Tedeschi and his colleagues (1971), there really is no arousal or tension involved in any of this—the attitude you report is merely an attempt to fool the experimenter, a public demonstration undertaken so that you will not appear stupid.

What does the evidence say about this alternative? It is mixed. Let's consider research on insufficient justification. In these studies, people act in a counter-attitudinal fashion for large or very small inducements. Then, the effects of their action on subsequent attitudes are assessed. If impression management is to be a viable interpretation of these studies, participants must assume that the same experimenter will have access to both the counter-attitudinal essay and the subsequent attitude measure. If this is not so, then participants would be under no pressure to justify the position advocated by their action. If a witness to the action (such as the reader of a counter-attitudinal essay) does not have access to the attitude measure, he or she cannot know the participant's real belief. There would be no one to whom the participant would need to justify him- or herself.

Such a split between dissonance induction and attitude measurement was precisely the arrangement of Festinger and Carlsmith's (1959) classic study. The attitude scale was administered by a person other than the experimenter in a department-wide evaluation of students' reactions to psychological experimentation, and the scale was anonymous. Thus, the participant was under no obligation to justify himself to the experimenter by misreporting his attitude. Nonetheless, dissonance effects were found in this experiment. Much the same can be said of many other dissonance investigations, and this fact casts some doubt on the validity of Tedeschi's alternative explanation.

Self-Perception

Of all the replacement alternatives to dissonance theory proposed over the years, none has had the impact of Daryl Bem's **self-perception** theory (cf. Bem, 1965, 1972). Self-perception is based on B. F. Skinner's behavioristic philosophy, which holds that it is counter-productive to speculate about internal, unmeasured, psychological processes to understand behavior; rather, we should examine measurable, overt behavior. The theory is important, not only as an alternative to dissonance, but also because it has served as one of the foundations of attribution theory.

How does self-perception theory explain this happy couple's feelings for one another? Does the explanation seem plausible to you? ■

Self-perception is one of the foundations of attribution theory: See Chapters 9 and 10.

Many theorists view attitudes as motivating forces on action: See Chapter 2.

In Bem's scheme, attitudes are nothing more than after-the-fact explanations people create on the spot when asked about earlier actions or events. So, in answer to the question, "Do you like brown bread?" you might reply, "Yes, very much." According to Bem, you generate this answer by reviewing your past eating behavior and realizing that you eat brown bread all the time. On the basis of this realization, you conclude, "I must like it, I eat it a lot." This review of your past history is the basis of your "attitude" and consequent response, "Yes, very much." This is a radical revision of the meaning of attitude. Far from being an internal, motivating state of approach or avoidance toward a person or thing attitudes are historical behavior summaries, self-perceptions created after reviewing past actions and the circumstances in which they occurred. Attitudes do not guide behavior in Bem's scheme, they summarize them.

In short, we infer attitudes from past behavior and the context in which the behavior occurred. This inference process, which we call *attribution,* holds no matter who the actor is—we use behavior (and its context) not only to infer others' attitudes but our own as well. Implausible? Unconvincing? Then suppose you were to witness the following event: An old woman is walking down a busy city street. As she passes a beggar on the corner, she quietly slips a few coins into his cup. Would you infer that she was kind and generous or stingy and mean? The answer is obvious. Now suppose we alter the scenario a bit. We have the same actors on the same street, but this time the beggar accosts the woman and demands money. Clearly frightened, she gives him some change. What do you infer about the woman in these circumstances? Is she generous or stingy? It is impossible to tell, because her behavior was forced, whereas in the first instance she appeared to help the beggar of her own volition. Notice that we are forming inferences, or attributions, on the basis of minimal information— in this instance, by observing the woman's behavior and the circumstances under

FIGURE 5.5

Comparison of the results of Bem with those of Festinger and Carlsmith. (From Bem, 1967) Notice the overlap in findings in these two very different studies.

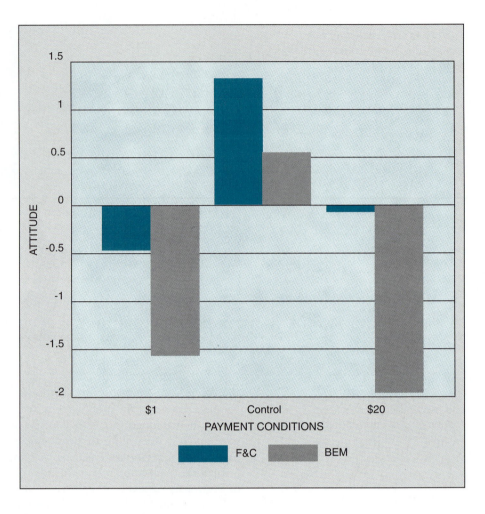

which it occurs. According to Bem, we do this all the time to infer attitudes—other people's *and our own.*

How does this orientation intersect with dissonance theory? Suppose you *observed* Festinger and Carlsmith's (1959) classic dissonance study. You see a young man perform a series of what seem to you to be mindless, boring, repetitive tasks. Then, for $.50 (and no other inducement) he describes the tasks to a fellow student as fun and interesting. On the basis of this action, and the circumstances under which it occurred, what would you infer his true attitude to be?

Bem (1967) studied this issue in a design in which participants were given a description of Festinger and Carlsmith's study, and then were asked to guess how they thought the actor would respond. Bem's results, along with those of Festinger and Carlsmith (1959), are summarized in Figure 5.5. Participants who observed the actor who had been paid only $1 praise the (boring) tasks thought that he was more favorably disposed to them than did participants who read the description in which the actor had been paid $20 to do so. This pattern of results duplicated that found in the original Festinger and Carlsmith experiment despite the fact that the observers probably were not experiencing any dissonance at all. A "dissonance" effect had been obtained without dissonance. Rather, Bem argued, people had observed a series of actions, the circumstances surrounding the actions, and had generated an inference about the probable attitude that motivated the actions. This self-perception based interpretation makes fewer assumptions about underlying motivational states that we cannot observe, and as such, Bem argued, was preferable to dissonance.

Motivating Properties of Dissonance

Despite these results, not all social psychologists find Bem's evidence completely compelling. To many, the theory seems too "cold" to be right, too devoid of the stuff that makes us human, such as feelings, emotions, and biases. By deemphasizing important internal states like love, passion, hate, wonder and depression, and replacing them with a purely objective information-processing orientation, Bem's theory describes an approach that is not the way most of us experience life. We *do* have motives, attitudes, hopes, fears, and other feelings that seem beyond the boundaries of self-perception. If self-perception is right, then the negative feeling Festinger hypothesized as a consequence of conflict between beliefs and actions simply would not occur.

Dissonance and Arousal. Do people experience negative feelings when they experience such conflicts? This critical question must be answered to judge the plausibility of these competing theories. Does dissonance produce arousal, or are dissonance-like responses attributable simply to information-based self-perception processes, as Bem assumed? From his opening statement on the theory, Festinger (1957) insisted that dissonance was arousing. It is unpleasant, and people are motivated to reduce it. Yet most dissonance research only assumes such motivation. When participants changed their attitudes in circumstances of attitude–behavior inconsistency, researchers attributed change to unpleasant arousal—dissonance—but a direct measure of a negative arousal state was never obtained. This lack of direct evidence of arousal undoubtedly benefited self-peception theory, which denied the necessity of arousal when explaining dissonance-like phenomena.

The question that social psychologists ultimately had to address, therefore, was, "Can the arousing nature of dissonance be demonstrated empirically?" The most straightforward investigation of the arousing properties of dissonance was conducted by Croyle and Cooper (1983), whose participants wrote essays contrary to their true attitudes under conditions of high or low choice. In research of this type, participants who have a great deal of free choice to refuse to write the essay (but do not do so) demonstrate attitude change consistent with their action. Those who have no choice in the matter, and who thus, theoretically, should not experience dissonance, give no evidence of attitude change. This is precisely what Croyle and Cooper found. Then the experimenters reran a variation of the study. In it, they took physiological measures of arousal as the participants executed their task. Results showed that all participants experienced heightened (presumably negative) arousal when writing the belief-discrepant essay. However, the arousal persisted only for those who, according to the theory, were experiencing dissonance—those who had undertaken the task under conditions of high choice. For the low-choice participants, arousal quickly faded. These results suggest that belief-discrepant (dissonant) actions are arousing and that the arousal persists when dissonance is great.

The Misattribution Paradigm.   An experiment of Zanna and Cooper (1974) further supports the dissonance perspective. In this study, participants were induced to write essays contrary to their beliefs. For some participants, the induction was very subtle—they felt very little pressure to comply with the experimenter's request, but they did so nonetheless. The remaining participants were given no choice.

Before they began the essay, all participants were given a pill. It was composed of milk powder, and could not possibly have had any pharmacological consequences. However, in some experimental conditions, participants were led to believe they would experience a reaction to the "drug": Some were told the tablet would prove mildly arousing; others were told it would relax them; and a final group was told the tablet would produce no side effects. This use of an inactive pill is known as a *misattribution* manipulation. Of most interest is the condition in which participants were told the tablet would have arousing effects. If they experienced any real emotional arousal during the course of the experiment, they were likely to think it was caused by the pill and thus ignore it as an indication of internal distress. In other words, they would misattribute the arousal to the pill.

After taking the pill, participants wrote an essay contrary to their beliefs, and their attitudes toward the topic of the essay were assessed. The pattern of results (summarized in Figure 5.6) conformed precisely to the expectations of dissonance theory. As shown, attitude change differed markedly as a combined consequence of (1) participants' expectations of side effects and (2) decision freedom—their perception of free choice to write, or to refuse to write, the essay. Those who believed the pill would have no impact on them exhibited the standard dissonance effect. Those in the high-choice condition were considerably more in favor of the originally contrary position than their peers, who had been given little choice in writing the essay.

The high-choice participants who expected the pills to be mildly arousing did not display a dissonance effect. Why not? Because, although they experienced dissonance when they wrote the counter-attitudinal essay, they misattributed the resulting arousal to the drug they had ingested. Given this attribution, they would not attempt to reduce their arousal through attitude change, because they attributed it to the pill, not their essay. Consequently, they did not change their attitudes, and their responses were indistinguishable from those of other, low-choice, participants in the same drug-arousal condition who did not have the freedom to refuse to write the essay and who consequently were not expected to experience dissonance.

The attitude change pattern of the participants who expected the pill to relax them shows a dissonance effect that is even stronger than that observed in the no-expectancy condition. These "relaxation" participants expected no unpleasant arousal. When dissonance was experienced by the high-choice participants, the arousal took them by surprise. It must have seemed to them that dissonance overwhelmed the relaxing side effects of the drug they had ingested. As a result, strong attitude change ensued.

FIGURE 5.6

■

Attitude as a function of decision freedom and expected drug reaction. (From Zanna and Cooper, 1974.) Notice how the standard dissonance effect (in the middle bars of the illustration) is enhanced among participants who expected the drug to relax them.

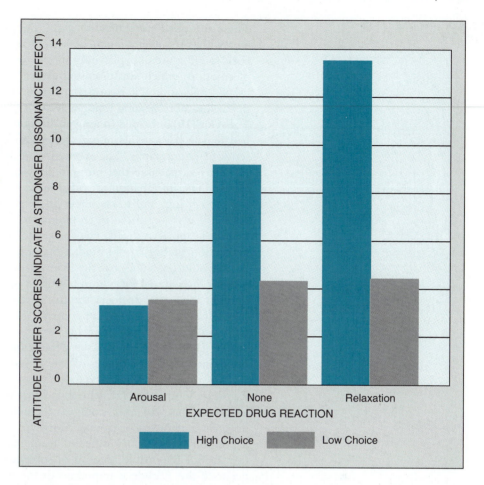

Results that complement these were produced in later misattribution research by Cooper, Zanna, and Taves (1978). In this experiment, participants were given either a mild tranquilizer, which would inhibit arousal, or a placebo. All were told to expect no side effects. Participants then engaged in the typical insufficient justification essay-writing task, and their attitudes were measured. The reverse incentive effect was found in the placebo group, consistent with dissonance theory predictions. Dissonance effects were not evident in the tranquilized group. As Cooper and Fazio (1984) observed, "Drug-induced inhibition of dissonance arousal inhibits the typical attitude-change process. Arousal . . . appears to be a necessary component of the attitude-change process" (p. 248) following counter-attitudinal advocacy for an insufficient reward.

A Reconciliation

Overjustification effects can be explained by self-perception theory: See Chapter 10.

The studies that employed physiological measures or misattribution all point to the arousing nature of dissonance, as Festinger speculated. But such findings do not necessarily rule out self-perception as a potential explanation of some behaviors. Dissonance theory cannot explain the changes that sometimes occur when people are bribed to perform an act consistent with their original attitudes.

These are called *overjustification effects*. They can be explained by, and are consistent with, the general tenets of self-perception theory. Similarly, the theory has been found a useful explanatory model for findings regarding the self-perception of emotion, which was discussed earlier in the chapter. Given these and other useful applications, it is important to understand where self-perception theory fits in the more general topography of social psychology.

Taylor (1975) helped to answer this question in an interesting experiment that had female participants rating the attractiveness of a set of men depicted in a series of photographs. The women were hooked up to a variant of the bogus pipeline—a machine that purportedly broadcast their heartbeat, an indicator of arousal. The information provided by the machine was a hoax. The "heartbeat" the participants heard was under the control of the experimenter. This information was manipulated in an interesting way. On a particular picture, the participant's apparent heart rate increased noticeably, suggesting arousal. Self-perception theory would predict that a person noticing her (apparently) racing heart would conclude that the man in the picture was arousing. It worked this way for the women for whom nothing was at stake. However, when participants thought they were to meet the man responsible for this enhanced arousal after the session, as part of the experiment, the bogus physiological feedback had no influence on their ratings of his attractiveness. On the basis of these findings, Taylor (1975) argued that self-perception effects are most likely to occur in situations involving attitudes of low importance or vested interest.

This conclusion is consistent with the results of Fazio and his colleagues (Fazio, Zanna, & Cooper, 1977), who found that when people were induced to perform an action that was very contrary to their established beliefs, dissonance—and dissonance reduction—ensued. However, when they were induced to advance a position only slightly different from their established beliefs, self-perception furnished a reasonable account of subsequent attitudes. Apparently, dissonance occurs if the attitude is important or the discrepancy between attitudes and actions great. When the issue is not critical or the attitude–behavior discrepancy small, then self-perception works.

■■■   SOME CONCLUDING THOUGHTS

The theory of cognitive dissonance has attracted its share of critics and reformers, many of whom are in agreement with the fundamental features of Festinger's original statement, but all of whom feel that the theory could stand at least a bit of fine tuning. Dissonance theory has evolved over the years, and has given rise to alternatives that have played a very positive role in the further development of social psychology. Cooper and Fazio's (1984) newer rendition of the theory promises to stimulate much research, as does Steele's (1988) theory of self-affirmation, and Aronson's (in press, 1991) hypocrisy theory. Self-perception has already had an important impact—the strong attributional flavor of much of today's social psychology owes an obvious debt to Bem's audacious theory.

■ ■ ■ SUMMARY

The theory of cognitive dissonance is one of social psychology's most intensively studied ideas. The theory holds that people strive to maintain consistency between their beliefs and actions. When this is not possible, an unpleasant cognitive state (dissonance) ensues. To reduce this state, people change one of the dissonant elements (either the belief or the action).

Research on dissonance has been conducted within three broad paradigms. In studies involving insufficient justification, participants perform an act that is contrary to their beliefs, for either a large or a trivial inducement. Typically, a belief-discrepant action that is performed for little inducement puts pressure on actors to change their attitudes, so the action becomes consonant with the action. Free-choice research requires participants to choose among a set of alternatives. The closer the alternatives in terms of desirability, the greater the dissonance. This dissonance causes subsequent reevaluation of the choices, such that later evaluations of the chosen alternative are displaced positively, while the unchosen alternative is displaced in a negative direction. Effort justification refers to the tendency to overvalue the things for which we have labored. To work for a worthless outcome arouses dissonance, and hence people rationalize their hard work by overvaluing the outcomes they have attained.

The revisions suggested to the theory of cognitive dissonance can be grouped in terms of alterations and replacements. Among the alterations, Cooper and Fazio's aversive consequences model holds that a person must be aware of the negative consequences of his or her actions and feel responsible for them before dissonance can occur. In a similar vein, Aronson's hypocrisy theory revision suggests that dissonance will be aroused most strongly if people are made aware of the discrepancy between their actions and their stated beliefs (hypocrisy). Steele's self-affirmation approach is in many ways similar to Aronson's, with the exception that for Steele, any action that allows the individual to reaffirm his or her self-worth can offset the arousal that a dissonant action has produced.

Impression management, a dissonance-replacement theory, argues that the insufficient justification results reflect participants' attempts to maintain face in the eyes of the experimenter. Tedeschi and his associates produced some intriguing evidence that pointed in this direction, but in much of the dissonance literature, participants knew that their face-saving gestures would not be witnessed by the experimenter, and they still made them.

Self-perception theory is at once the most persuasive and the least persuasive alternative to dissonance. It is persuasive because it appears to cover all the ground that dissonance does, while making very few appeals to unseen, and unmeasured, cognitive processes. It is unpersuasive because it is in direct conflict with the intensely real internal processes that all of us experience. Also, dissonance has been shown convincingly to be arousing—and this does not fit well with self-perception theory. Nonetheless, self-perception theory has played an important role in the growth of social psychology.

■ ■ ■   **SUGGESTED READINGS**

1. Aronson, E. (in press). The return of the repressed: Dissonance theory makes a comeback. *Psychological Inquiry*.

2. Bem, D. J. (1972). Self-perception theory. In L. Berkowitz (Ed.), *Advances in Experimental Social Psychology* (Vol. 6). New York: Academic.

3. Cooper, J., & Fazio, R. H. (1984). A new look at dissonance theory. In L. Berkowitz (Ed.), *Advances in Experimental Social Psychology* (Vol. 17), (pp. 229–266). Orlando, FL: Academic Press.

4. Festinger, L. (Ed.). (1980). *Retrospections on social psychology*. Oxford: Oxford University Press.

5. Schlenker, B. R. (1980). *Impression management: The self-concept, social identity, and interpersonal relations*. Monterey, CA: Brooks/Cole.

6. Steele, C. M. (1988). The psychology of self-affirmation: Sustaining the integrity of the self. In L. Berkowitz (Ed.), *Advances in Experimental Social Psychology* (Vol. 21) (pp. 261–302). San Diego: Academic Press.

7. Symposium on Theory in Social Psychology (1989). *Personality and Social Psychology Bulletin, 15,* 493–532.

PART II

SOCIAL PERCEPTION
Understanding Ourselves and Others

CHAPTER 6
Nonverbal Communication of Moods and Emotions: Perceiving What Others are Feeling

CHAPTER 7
Forming Impressions: What Do We See in Other People?

CHAPTER 8
Social Cognition: Impression Formation Revisited

CHAPTER 9
Attribution: The Social Consequences of Causal Perceptions

CHAPTER 10
Social Inference: From Behavior to Personality

CHAPTER 11
The Social Self: Self-Concept in its Social Context

CHAPTER 6

NONVERBAL COMMUNICATION OF MOODS AND EMOTIONS

Perceiving What Others Are Feeling

■ **Key Concepts**

Nonverbal communication
Kinesics
Paralinguistics
Proxemics
Transmission cues
Decoding
Polygraph
Affordances
Profile of Nonverbal Sensitivity
  (PONS)
Empathy

■ **Chapter Outline**

COMMUNICATING WITHOUT WORDS: AN EVOLUTIONARY PERSPECTIVE

EXPRESSING EMOTIONS: SENDING NONVERBAL MESSAGES
  Is There a Universal Code?
  Expression or Communication?
  Is Nonverbal Expression Controllable?
  ■ The "Lie Detector" Controversy

DECODING EMOTIONS: INTERPRETING NONVERBAL MESSAGES
  Nonverbal Messages as "Affordances"
  Reading More Than There Is to Know
  ■ Baby Faces in the Court Room
  Accuracy of Interpreting Expressions: Are Some Individuals Better
    Decoders Than Others?
  Can We Detect Deception?
  Understanding Others' Emotions: Recognition or Empathy?

SOME CONCLUDING THOUGHTS

SUMMARY

As soon as he walked into his boss's office, Brandon knew this was not the time to bring up the problem with the Baxter account. "Have a bad meeting with the CEO?" he asked. "Rotten," she answered. Brandon decided to keep out of her way until this bad mood blew over.

■ ■ ■

After sitting alone in the noisy bar for more than an hour, Harry was ready to call it a night. Somewhat dejected, he stood up to leave when he caught sight of an attractive woman in the booth nearest the door. Catching Harry's glance, the woman tilted her head slightly to one side and gave a slow smile. Maybe it's too soon to leave now, Harry thought to himself. After all, the night is young . . .

Many of our social interactions depend on our ability to interpret how another person is feeling—what kind of mood or emotional state that individual may be in at a particular time. Knowing what other people are experiencing is important to our decisions about how to behave toward them or how to react to the situation in which we find ourselves. Much of our knowledge about others' feelings and emotions comes not from what they tell us about themselves but from observation of how they look or sound. One of the fascinating achievements of social life is our ability to convey and interpret emotional states through *nonverbal communication.*

The channels of communication that convey feelings and moods include the visual displays in facial expression (Alley, 1988; Ekman, 1982) and the many aspects of body language, such as posture, movement, and direction of body orientation (Mehrabian, 1972). This is the category of nonverbal behavior known as **kinesics.** Nonverbal information is also contained in the way people talk— not what they say, but how they say it, including their tone of voice, pitch, volume, and speed of talking. These aspects of speech are known as **paralinguistic** features (Davitz, 1964). Yet another category of nonverbal language is **proxemics,** which includes the distance people maintain between themselves and others (Hall, 1966) and the direction of eye gaze (Exline, 1972), both important indicators of intimacy and attention during social interactions.

Each of these communication channels has been studied intensively in its own right, and a great deal has been learned about the information that is conveyed by specific features of body language, speech, and distance—even the contraction of individual facial muscles (Ekman & Friesen, 1978). Nonverbal behavior serves a number of different functions in social interaction, including expressing intimacy, regulating the course of interactions, and exercising social control or dominance (Patterson, 1983). In this chapter, however, we consider only general questions about the nature of nonverbal communication and its role in providing information about moods and emotions.

■ ■ ■ COMMUNICATING WITHOUT WORDS: AN EVOLUTIONARY PERSPECTIVE

Charles Darwin, a social psychologist before his time. ■

Although the expression and interpretation of moods and emotions is inherently social psychological, the classic work in this area was not produced by a social psychologist but by the naturalist Charles Darwin. In developing the theory of evolution, Darwin was interested in the continuity across species of emotional expressiveness and other forms of nonverbal communication. In *The Expression of the Emotions in Man and Animals,* Darwin (1872) raised some fascinating questions about the functions of facial expressions and other nonverbal cues, which have guided research in this area for more than a century. In effect, Darwin proposed that expressions of emotions are innate and that the meaning of certain patterns of nonverbal emotional expression is understood by all members of the species. Such expressive displays have adaptive value for social animals because they serve to control the behavior of other group members. If an individual can convey threat by way of facial expression and body posture, for instance, such a display may ward off attack by another individual without the expense of actual physical combat.

Darwin's speculations about the adaptive significance of emotional expression call attention to the two sides of nonverbal communication. On the one side is the **transmission** of emotional responses—their expression in the form of alterations of facial muscles, body posture, and vocalization **(cues).** On the other side is the **decoding** of such expressive displays by receivers—the ability to interpret the messages conveyed by others' emotional reactions. Both sides of the nonverbal communication system have generated interesting issues for research and theoretical analysis.

■ ■ ■ EXPRESSING EMOTIONS: SENDING NONVERBAL MESSAGES

Is There a Universal Code?

Darwin speculated that certain primary emotions are transmitted by the same cues in all humans, as well as other primates. If that were so, we would expect the same links between emotional experience and facial expressions to be evidenced across all cultures.

A number of lines of research support this contention that the expression of emotional states through specific physical cues (particularly facial configurations) is universal. Craig and Patrick (1985), for instance, induced pain by immersing volunteers' hands into icy water. Although there were individual differences in facial expression over time, at the outset of the immersion all respondents exhibited highly consistent facial reactions. Universally, these reactions included raised cheeks with tightened eyelids, raised upper eyelids, parting of the lips, and closed or blinking eyes. Keating, Mazur, and Segall, (1981) also report consistencies between humans and other primates in facial cues associated with dominance, including lowered eyebrows and nonsmiling mouth. Ekman (1972) observed, by means of a hidden camera, both Japanese and Americans watching

FIGURE 6.1

■

Video frames of attempts to pose emotion by subjects from the Fore of New Guinea. The instructions for the top left photograph was "your friend has come and you are happy"; for the top right "your child has died"; for the bottom left "you are angry and about to fight"; and for the bottom right "you see a dead pig that has been lying there for a long time." (From Ekman, 1973.)

either stress-inducing films (displaying bodily mutilation) or neutral films (nature scenes). When participants were unaware that they were being observed, virtually the same facial responses were emitted by members of both cultures in response to the stressful stimulus.

Perhaps the most impressive demonstration of cross-cultural similarities in facial expression of emotions is a study by Ekman and Friesen (1971) conducted among the South Fore, an isolated New Guinea culture whose members had never lived in a Western settlement or been exposed to Western media. Members of this culture were photographed with instructions to show how their face would look in response to six different emotional situations (for example, "You feel sad because your child died") (Figure 6.1). These facial photos were then shown to Americans who were asked to select the emotion being expressed in each. Consistently, the Americans were able to identify the portrayals of anger, disgust, happiness, and sadness with much higher-than-chance accuracy. (The portrayals of fear and surprise, however, were often confused with each other, though both were distinguished from the other emotions.)

Although the form of expression of several basic emotions has proven to be remarkably consistent across cultures, there are cultural differences in the degree or *intensity* of emotional expressiveness (Ekman, 1972) and in the frequency or circumstances in which the emotion is expressed (Scherer, Wallbott, & Summerfield, 1986). There is also considerable evidence for gender differences in encoding (that is, expressing) emotions. Across a wide range of studies using both posed and spontaneous emotional portrayals, female communicators are generally interpreted more accurately than male communicators by both male and female judges (Hall, 1984), and this is particularly true for judgments based on facial expression. Women apparently are more willing or more able than men to reveal their emotional state through nonverbal channels.

Expression or Communication?

The influence of culture and gender on the intensity and precision of emotional expressiveness suggests that the nonverbal display of moods and emotions is not simply an automatic response to emotion-arousing experiences. Darwin's hypothesis was that emotional displays serve as signals to influence the behavior of other members of the species. This implies that the degree of expression of emotion will be determined by its communication value rather than the intensity

Smiling is a form of social communication. ◼

of the felt emotion per se. In this view, the expression of emotion is more a form of social interaction than a private personal experience.

Strong evidence in favor of the social interaction interpretation of emotional expressiveness was obtained in a series of studies in naturalistic settings by Kraut and Johnston (1979). These researchers observed a particular form of nonverbal expression—smiling—in a number of different social settings, including bowling alleys, hockey games, and city streets. The question they were addressing in their studies was whether the incidence of smiling is associated with the occurrence of events that would be expected to induce happiness (emotional expression) or whether smiling occurs primarily in the context of social interaction. What they found in all three settings was that smiling was highly associated with social interaction, but occurred only rarely in the presence of positive events without social involvement.

Lone bowlers, for example, almost never smiled when they bowled a strike or spare, whereas those bowling with a group of friends smiled about 30% of the time following a successful shot. Even more interesting findings were obtained when Kraut and Johnston positioned observers behind the pins at the end of the alley to observe bowlers' facial expressions through binoculars. As reported in Table 6.1, when bowlers were facing the pins, the occurrence of smiling in response to a strike or spare was very low. When bowlers turned to face their companions, however, the incidence of smiling increased substantially.

TABLE 6.1

■

What Makes Us Smile?
The Incidence of Smiling in Different Social Settings*

	PERCENT OF TIME SMILING OCCURRED	
Bowling	STRIKE/SPARE	OTHER OUTCOMES
Facing pins	4%	3%
Facing companions	42%	28%
Hockey Game	GOOD OUTCOME	BAD OUTCOMES
Fans alone	12%	2%
Fans interacting	27%	22%
Pedestrians	GOOD WEATHER	BAD WEATHER
Alone	12%	5%
Socially interacting	61%	57%

*Data taken from Kraut and Johnston (1979)

Kraut and Johnston also found that whether fans at a hockey game smiled in response to a favorable outcome for their own team was determined by social context. Those who were not engaged in social interaction smiled only rarely on these occasions, but those who were socially involved with other individuals smiled much more often. Apparently, the happiness induced by favorable events is not sufficient to elicit smiling unless such expression also serves to communicate one's feelings to others as well.

Is Nonverbal Expression Controllable?

The existence of cultural, gender, and situational differences in the occurrence and intensity of nonverbal emotional displays all suggest that the expression of mood and emotion is to some extent controllable. Control over the intensity of emotional expressivity was demonstrated directly in Ekman's (1972) observational study of American and Japanese participants as they viewed stress-inducing film sequences. When they were not aware of being observed, respondents from both cultures exhibited the same facial reactions. However, when a researcher was visibly present, Japanese participants (more than Americans) masked negative facial expressions with smiles during the viewing of the stressful movie. These observations indicate that we can learn to manage facial displays in response to emotionally arousing situations, and that such management may obscure otherwise universal emotional expressions.

Despite our ability to mask or inhibit certain displays of emotion, there is widespread belief that nonverbal expression of feelings cannot be fully controlled. The idea that emotions that are being consciously inhibited in some channels of communication will be displayed in other nonverbal cues is known as "nonverbal leakage" (Ekman & Friesen, 1974). Ekman proposed that some channels are more difficult to control than others and hence more susceptible to leakage of true

When people interact, they communicate nonverbally as well as by words. Note how much information is conveyed by hand gestures, body orientation, and facial expression. ■

emotions. To test this, Ekman and Friesen showed a series of brief films to female nurses. Some of the films were pleasant, whereas others were selected to arouse disgust. As they were watching the films, participants were instructed either to display their honest impressions of the movie sequence or to try to conceal their true feelings.

The nurses were videotaped during the viewing and portions of the tapes were shown to other judges, who were asked to guess whether the respondent was exhibiting her true feelings or not. Observers who saw videotapes that focused on body language were better able to detect deception in emotional expression than observers who saw videotapes only of respondents' facial expressions. The nurses were better able to intentionally control their facial displays in response to the films than to control other nonverbal cues such as nervous movements of their hands or feet.

Concealed emotions may also be leaked in paralinguistic expression. Several studies, for instance, indicate that voice pitch is higher when individuals are trying to deceive than when they are giving truthful expressions (e.g., Ekman, Friesen, & Scherer, 1976). Such pitch changes are very difficult to hear, but can be consistently demonstrated with electronic vocal analysis. Thus, paralinguistic cues of deception may be difficult to control intentionally, although leakage on this channel may be more difficult to detect by human observers than nonverbal body cues.

APPLYING SOCIAL PSYCHOLOGY TO THE LAW ■ ■ ■

The "Lie Detector" Controversy

The use of the polygraph in police interrogation and security clearance processes is based on the idea that some subtle, nonverbal cues of deception are not subject to intentional control. The **polygraph** (or "lie detector") is an instrument that records physiological arousal during questioning, including measures of the person's breathing, pulse rate, and fingertip perspiration (skin conductance). Changes in these physiological measures are assessed during the course of a carefully structured set of questions, and the pattern of arousal while answering different questions is used as the basis for inferring the respondent's truthfulness or deception.

Contrary to popular misconceptions, the lie detector apparatus does not record whether the individual being interrogated is lying. There is no single, unique pattern of physiological response associated with deception. Rather, the determination is based on the *interpretation* of the physiological record by a polygraph expert. Not surprisingly, since human judgment is involved, there is considerable variability in outcomes of the test depending on who is conducting the interview and interpreting the results. Some experts report very high accuracy rates in detection of deception (e.g., Raskin, 1986), but others claim that use of the polygraph is subject to a great deal of error and abuse (Lykken, 1981).

A review of the scientific evidence related to polygraph testing by Saxe, Dougherty, and Cross (1985) concluded that the test results are heavily dependent on the nature of the question technique used, the situation established by the examiner, and the naiveté of the respondent. Results of a number of field experiments indicated that, under different conditions, the "false positive" rate of polygraph results (concluding that an innocent person was lying) ranged from 0% to as high as 75%! When outcomes are so dependent on the conditions of testing, it is wise that the results of polygraph tests not be admissible as evidence in court or as a basis of selection for most jobs.

■ ■ ■ DECODING EMOTIONS: INTERPRETING NONVERBAL MESSAGES

Clearly, if the function of emotional expression is primarily social communication, then we must be able to interpret one another's emotional displays just as consistently as we are able to produce them. It would be of no use to have a common code of expression if we did not also have a common understanding of the meaning of nonverbal cues. Much of the research on universality of facial and other nonverbal expression of emotions has also addressed the issue of universal interpretation of facial displays.

Some of the earliest psychological research on recognition of emotion was concerned with identifying the *dimensions* of emotional response that can be distinguished accurately (Woodworth, 1938). Observers (adults and children) are good at distinguishing positive emotions (happiness, excitement) from negative ones (fear, anger, disgust) and also at discriminating emotions associated with high arousal (excitement, anger) from those associated with low arousal (contentment, sadness) (Russell & Bullock, 1985). There is less consistency, however, in people's ability to distinguish accurately between emotional expressions that are similar in evaluation and arousal, such as surprise and excitement.

Ekman and Friesen's (1971) work among the South Fore in New Guinea also demonstrated the cross-cultural consistency of decoding emotional expressions. After participants had been photographed posing different emotional displays, they were shown photographs of Western faces depicting specific emotions. The photo displaying the target emotion was shown along with two other photos depicting different emotions. The New Guinea respondents were correct in selecting the face displaying the designated emotion more than 80% of the time.

TABLE 6.2

■

Single-Emotion Judgment Task: Percentage of Subjects Within Each Culture Who Chose the Predicted Emotion

Nation	Happiness	Surprise	Sadness	Fear	Disgust	Anger
Estonia	90	94	86	91	71	67
Germany	93	87	83	86	61	71
Greece	93	91	80	74	77	77
Hong Kong	92	91	91	84	65	73
Italy	97	92	81	82	89	72
Japan	90	94	87	65	60	67
Scotland	98	88	86	86	79	84
Sumatra	69	78	91	70	70	70
Turkey	87	90	76	76	74	79
United States	95	92	92	84	86	81

From Ekman et al. (1987).

Ekman and his colleagues later conducted a more extensive cross-cultural study of emotion recognition based on facial expression with participants from ten different Western and non–Western countries (Ekman et al., 1987). In this research, judges were shown photographs of Caucasian men and women displaying facial expressions of six different emotions, either posed or spontaneously elicited. For each photo, judges were asked to select from a list of seven emotions the one being portrayed in the picture. There was remarkably high agreement across cultures in the selection of depicted emotions. For photos exhibiting happiness, for instance, almost 90% of judges in nine of the countries identified the predicted emotion (Table 6.2). Only judges in Sumatra showed somewhat lower agreement, with only 69% identifying the photo as displaying happiness. Correct recognition of facial displays of surprise, fear, sadness, disgust, and anger was equally high across all ten cultures. Thus, the evidence for universal recognition of certain basic positive and negative emotions from static facial expression is quite strong.

Some emotions can be detected from even minimal cues of facial expression. Bassili (1979) used an interesting technique to demonstrate the effects of static versus dynamic (moving) visual displays. He blackened the faces of actors and then painted fifty white spots at various points all over each face. He then videotaped the actors portraying six basic emotions against a dark background. In the resulting videotapes, only the white spots of light were visible for display. Then, either still photographs of the faces or moving videos were shown to judges, who were asked to select which emotion was being portrayed in each segment. Even with static displays of dots, the emotions of happiness, sadness, surprise, and disgust were correctly recognized with more than chance accuracy. With dynamic displays, recognition of all six emotions was significantly improved (with as high as 90% correct identification for happiness).

Yet another type of evidence of the meaningfulness of facial displays of emotion comes from experimental research by Orr and Lanzetta (1980), who used a classical conditioning situation to demonstrate the interpretation of facial expres-

Bassili's facial expressions in light displays. ■

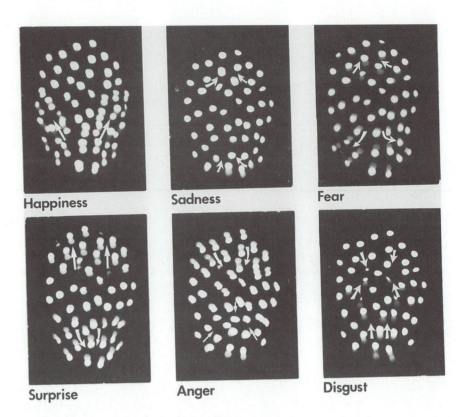

Happiness Sadness Fear

Surprise Anger Disgust

sion. Participants were shown a sequence of slides of faces and received a mild electric shock immediately following some of the slides. For some participants, faces displaying a fearful expression were accompanied by the electric shock, while happy faces were not followed by shock. For the remaining participants, the association was reversed—happy faces were followed by shock, and fearful faces were not. This is the usual experimental setup to test classical conditioning. If participants learn to associate facial expression with upcoming shock, they eventually develop an autonomic (involuntary) response to the facial cue itself.

Measures of skin conductance were used to assess physiological response to the faces that had been paired with shock. The results of Orr and Lanzetta's experiment revealed that participants learned the association between fearful faces and shock much more quickly than the association between shock and happy faces, indicating that fearful facial expressions served as a meaningful cue. Since participants already interpreted these expressions to convey something negative, they were more ready to associate the face with impending shock. Happy faces, on the other hand, carried positive associations that interfered with learning to expect a negative experience such as electric shock.

Nonverbal Messages as "Affordances"

Research on the accuracy of detection of nonverbal emotional displays is consistent with an *ecological perspective* on the nature of social perception (McArthur & Baron, 1983). The ecological approach to perception (Gibson, 1979) focuses on the perceiver's ability to detect useful information inherent in events. Gibson refers to this as perception of the **affordances** of the environment, affordances being those aspects of objects and events that are relevant to the organism's survival (such as their potential edibility or threat). According to this perspective, it is adaptive to be particularly sensitive or attuned to perceiving those aspects of the environment that help us function to meet goals of survival and reproduction.

For social species such as human beings, the information contained in nonverbal expression of moods and emotions can be seen as affordances. Recognizing that others are frightened, angry, or socially receptive clearly has survival value, making it possible for us to avoid situations or confrontations that may be costly and to encourage interactions that are likely to benefit us. (Recall from the chapter-opening vignettes Brandon's avoidance of unpleasant interaction with his boss and Harry's anticipation of a potentially positive exchange with an attractive stranger.) According to the ecological perspective, the universal recognition of basic positive and negative emotions has adaptive value for a social species such as ours.

Ecological theory also predicts that some emotional states will be more important—and hence more readily detectable—than others. For example, McArthur and Baron (1983) speculate that the negative emotions of anger and fear will be perceived more easily than more benign emotions because of their greater functional importance. This speculation is supported by results of research by Hansen and Hansen (1988), who tested perceivers' ability to detect particular emotional expressions in groups of faces. In one experiment, participants were shown a series of 108 slides, each containing nine faces. In some slides, the expression on all nine faces portrayed the same emotion (either anger or happiness) or were all neutral in expression. In other slides, a single discrepant face was embedded among the other eight, who all portrayed the same emotional state (for example, one angry face among a set of happy faces or one happy face in a group of otherwise neutral faces). As each slide was flashed on the screen, it was the participant's task to indicate whether all of the faces were the same in emotion or whether there was a discrepant face present and to record this judgment by pressing a button as fast as possible. As predicted, respondents were significantly faster in detecting an angry face present in a set of happy or neutral faces than they were at recognizing a happy face in an angry context.

The results of Hansen and Hansen's experiment support the contention that sensitivity of social perception is related to the perceiver's goals and needs. This hypothesis applies to the detection of states and characteristics other than emotions. Many nonverbal features and gestures convey status or power, and low-status individuals are particularly sensitive to such cues (Henley, 1977). Interviews with convicts in prison for assault crimes indicate that they use cues from an individual's gait or pattern of walking in order to select victims for a mugging (Grayson & Stein, 1981) (Exhibit 6.1). For these professionals, then, a person's "muggability" is an affordance to which they are particularly attuned.

For important social information, people appear to be quite sensitive to even minimal information from the environment. We have already mentioned Bassili's (1979) research indicating that facial expressions can be identified accurately from patterns of moving dots. Similar information is conveyed by patterns of body movement when all the perceiver can see is moving points of light attached to an actor's joints filmed in darkness. Kozlowski and Cutting (1977) demonstrated that a walker's sex can be recognized accurately from such moving points of light alone, and the rhythm, speed, and length of step of walking are used as cues to judgments of mood and power (Montepare & McArthur, 1988).

EXHIBIT 6.1

■

Who Is Ripe for a Mugging? It's in the Rhythm

Based on interviews with prison inmates convicted of assault crimes, Grayson and Stein (1981) used the following scale for rating an individual's potential for being a victim of assault:

1 = "very easy ripoff"
2 = "easy dude to corner"
3 = "you could take that one out"
4 = "looks like a fairly easy hit"
5 = "you could stand the problem"
6 = "could give you a little static"
7 = "would be a problem; could give you a hard time"
8 = "hard dude to knock off; wouldn't mess with him"
9 = "would be heavy; would give you a hard time"
10 = "would avoid it, too big a situation; too heavy"

Using this scale, 53 convicts rated videotapes of New York pedestrians. Not surprisingly, women and older people were rated as more likely victims than healthy young men, but nonverbal style also influenced the assessments. Regardless of sex or age, walkers who were rated 1, 2, or 3 on this scale differed significantly on a number of measures of gait and movement from those rated above 4. Those rated as potential victims walked less smoothly, shifting from side to side, and lifting rather than swinging their feet, compared to nonvictims whose gait was assessed as more synchronous and bilateral. In effect, those who are slightly "out of step" are more likely to be targeted as potential victims for a mugging. How you move can make a difference.

From Grayson and Stein (1981).

Reading More Than There Is to Know

Sometimes structural cues that are useful for identifying affordances in particular environments are overgeneralized to other contexts. There is considerable evidence in the person-perception research literature that both vocal characteristics and facial features have a strong influence on our impressions of a person's abilities and personality traits, regardless of the validity of those associations. Keating et al. (1981), for instance, found that features such as a broad face and receding hairline are associated with judgments of dominance by people from a variety of cultures. These particular cues are related to physical size and seniority, which in many cases are good predictors of dominant status, but they are overgeneralized as indicators of dominance when they are used in situations where they may be irrelevant to the person's actual status or position.

According to an ecological perspective, such impression biases represent "overgeneralizations of highly adaptive perceptual attunements" (McArthur & Baron, 1983, p. 231). Probably the most extensively researched instance of overgeneralized perceptions is associated with "baby-faced" features in adults (Berry & McArthur, 1986). Adult male (and female) faces are judged to be babyish when they have large, round eyes, high eyebrows, and a small chin. These are all characteristics of infant faces across a wide range of species, and as such are accurately associated with dependence, helplessness, and the need for nurturance. Again, however, cues that are appropriately interpreted in their natural ecological setting are overgeneralized when they appear in the context of an adult face. Ratings of the babyishness of adult male facial photographs are strongly correlated with impressions of warmth, honesty, kindness, and naiveté, and these findings have been replicated cross-culturally (McArthur & Berry, 1987).

APPLYING SOCIAL PSYCHOLOGY TO THE LAW
■ ■ ■

Baby Faces in the Courtroom

Based on evidence that baby-faced adults are perceived to be more naive and honest than those with mature faces, Berry and Zebrowitz-McArthur (1988) hypothesized that facial appearance would influence judgments of legal responsibility. Specifically, they predicted that baby-faced defendants would be less likely to be convicted of a charge involving *intentional* criminal behavior, but they would be more likely to be found guilty of crimes of negligence. These predictions were supported in a judgment experiment in which participants read a case study of a charge involving either intentional or negligent criminal actions (for example, either deliberately falsifying records or maintaining poor records). A photograph of the defendant attached to the case record was varied as either baby-faced or mature in appearance. Baby-faced defendants were significantly more likely than others to be judged guilty of negligence, but somewhat less likely to be convicted of intentional crimes. This finding fits with other research indicating that facial stereotypes are associated with particular types of crime and that facial appearance influences judgments of likelihood of guilt (Shoemaker, South, & Lowe, 1973).

Accuracy of Interpreting Expressions: Are Some Individuals Better Decoders than Others?

Consistent with the idea that accurate detection of social information depends on its relation to individual needs and goals, there is considerable evidence that people vary in their ability to recognize the moods and emotions of others. Robert Rosenthal and his colleagues (Rosenthal, Hall, DiMatteo, Rogers, & Archer, 1979) have conducted an extensive series of studies on individual differences in sensitivity to signals in nonverbal communication. Their research makes use of a test called the **Profile of Nonverbal Sensitivity (PONS),** a forty-five-minute film and soundtrack composed of 220 randomly ordered auditory and visual segments. Each segment provides information in one of eleven channels of nonverbal communication (facial, body, or auditory paralinguistic cues) from twenty short, emotionally expressive scenes enacted by a professional. (One such scene, for example, is an enactment of the script: "I love you. I think I'll always love you. I just want to do things with you and be with you." Other scenes include such acts as talking to a lost child, discussing one's divorce, returning a faulty item to a store, and criticizing someone for being late.) For each segment, the viewer is asked to circle one of two labels that identifies the scene being portrayed in that segment. The total number of correct identifications constitutes a measure of individual sensitivity to nonverbal information.

Based on the PONS test results, Rosenthal and his colleagues were able to identify a number of bases for individual differences in recognition accuracy. Scores on the PONS test, for instance, are related to performance on other tests of basic social skills (Riggio, 1986). Of particular interest is research on the relationship between occupation and nonverbal sensitivity. In Rosenthal's studies, actors and students of communication and visual arts scored significantly higher on the PONS test than other groups. On the other hand, clinicians, teachers, foreign service officers, and business executives did not generally score higher than the average college student. Within these occupations, however, those who were rated as more effective in their jobs also scored higher on the PONS, suggesting that success in people-oriented occupations is related to nonverbal decoding skills.

The most well-established difference in the ability to interpret nonverbal behavior is that between males and females (Hall, 1984; Riggio & Friedman, 1986; Rosenthal et al., 1979). We have already discussed research evidence that women encode emotions more expressively than do males, and this difference is even more pronounced on the decoding side. Across a wide range of studies, women have been found to be more sensitive to nonverbal visual cues, more accurate in identifying the emotion portrayed by both male and female actors, and more sensitive to paralinguistic cues in speech. Females score significantly higher than males on the PONS test among samples of elementary, high school, and college students and with samples outside the United States. In a review of 125 studies using different measures of nonverbal decoding skill, Hall (1984) found that more than 80% obtained differences favoring females, with the female advantage being most pronounced for interpretation of facial expression, somewhat less for body cues, and least for paralinguistic communication. In general, the sex differences are small but consistent.

We do not know for sure why women are better than men at decoding nonverbal communication, but the most popular social psychological explanation is as follows: Women have a lower power position than men in almost all societies. Being at a power disadvantage, it is argued, women are more dependent on others and thus more affected by how others are feeling. This motivates greater attention and practice of nonverbal decoding skills and more willingness to accommodate to others' emotional states or feelings.

There is much to support this social learning–motivational interpretation of sex differences in nonverbal skills, but the evidence is not definitive. For one thing, other power-disadvantaged groups, such as African Americans in the United States, do not show such consistent superiority in nonverbal sensitivity as women do. In addition, there is some evidence that sex differences appear in infancy, with female newborns being more likely than male newborns to cry in response to the sound of another infant's crying (Eisenberg & Lennon, 1983). Perhaps a predisposition to be responsive to nonverbal cues is inborn, but this is merely an interesting speculation at this point. As with all sex differences in social behavior, we have much yet to learn about why they occur.

Can We Detect Deception?

We have already seen that some nonverbal channels are susceptible to "leakage" when an actor is attempting to suppress or misrepresent emotional reactions. Some cues to deception are detectable only by sophisticated recording equipment, but others are evident to ordinary observers. The evidence is mixed, however, as to whether observers can judge accurately whether an individual is lying on the basis of nonverbal cues alone. Women seem to be slightly better than men at detecting deception but, in general, accuracy of detection is not high.

In a typical laboratory experiment on detection of deception, a target person is instructed to answer a series of questions either truthfully or by lying with the intention to deceive. Video and auditory recordings are made of both types of responses. These recordings are then shown to naive judges, either in whole or in part (for example, just the visual or auditory information alone or both together). The judge's task is to evaluate the responses and guess whether the sender was being truthful or not.

Based on a review of more than sixty such experiments, Zuckerman, DePaulo, and Rosenthal (1981) concluded that the ability to detect deception depends on the perceiver's ability to attend to multiple channels of communication at the same time. It is the *inconsistency* between what a person is saying and nonverbal behaviors that furnishes the best potential information about deception. Gestures such as wringing hands and tense posture are not necessarily indicators of deception by themselves. They may be undisguised expressions of anxiety or distress. However, when they occur simultaneously with a calm facial expression and verbal denial of distress, this is evidence that someone is being less than truthful.

When individuals intend to lie, they are most able to control their verbal content and their facial expression and less able to control other channels of nonverbal expression. Thus, the most sensitive cues to deception lie in the relationship between verbal and facial expression on the one hand and body and paralinguistic signals on the other. But many perceivers attend more to verbal content and facial expression than to other sources of nonverbal communication, missing the most important clues to the presence of deception.

Understanding Others' Emotions: Recognition or Empathy?

Some social psychologists believe there is more to understanding what others are feeling than merely recognizing what emotion or mood they are experiencing. Communication of affect also involves **empathy.** Empathy is sometimes defined simply as the accuracy with which a perceiver decodes another's emotional communication. But many psychologists argue that empathy is more than accurate perception—it is actually *feeling with* the other person, experiencing that person's emotional state for oneself. Empathy at its most direct is illustrated by young preschool children who begin crying when another child cries, without even knowing what caused the other child's distress. Among adults, empathic understanding takes somewhat more subtle forms.

One of the most intriguing questions in the study of nonverbal sensitivity is the role that the perceiver's own nonverbal expressions play in his or her ability to understand (empathize with) the emotional displays of others. The "facial feedback" hypothesis of emotional expression (Izard, 1977; Tomkins, 1962) states that facial displays are not simply the result of emotional experience but actually contribute to the emotion being felt. That is, when we display the facial activity associated with a particular emotion, we feel the emotion we are displaying (for example, if we lift the corners of our mouths in a smile, we feel happier). This idea, which goes back to the nineteenth century, is known as the *James–Lange*

In a moment, all three babies will be crying. "Contagious crying" is common in groups of infants and toddlers. ◼

theory of emotion. According to this theory, our subjective emotional experiences follow from automatic physiological reactions to events.

The effect of facial muscle movement on experienced emotion has been demonstrated in a variety of experimental studies (Laird, 1984). The studies show that manipulating facial muscles directly (for example, contracting eyebrows and lowering the corners of the mouth in an expression like anger or drawing up the corners of the mouth like smiling) has effects on subjective mood. Further, when individuals are exposed to emotionally arousing stimuli (such as films or pictures) and are instructed to suppress facial reactions to those stimuli, they report less emotional feeling in response to those stimuli than when they are free to display facial expression. One such study demonstrated that suppressing facial displays in response to electric shock not only lowered subjective ratings of pain but also decreased physiological reaction to the shock. By contrast, when facial reactions were freely expressed, pain reactions to the shock were greater (Lanzetta, Cartwright-Smith, & Kleck, 1976). Facial expression has also been found to enhance experience of happiness, anger, sadness, fear, and humor (e.g., Martin, Harlow, & Strack,1992).

The action of facial muscles alone has been found to influence subjective feelings, even when the muscle activity has nothing to do with emotional events or experiences. In one experiment, participants viewed cartoons while either holding a pen in their teeth (a task that facilitates use of muscles associated with smiling) or holding a pen with their lips (a mouth configuration incompatible with smiling—try it). The cartoons were rated as less humorous in the latter condition (Strack, Martin, & Stepper, 1988). In yet another series of experiments, participants merely repeated a series of vowel sounds (Zajonc, Murphy, & Inglehart, 1989). The facial action associated with certain vowels (such as the Germanic *u*) was found to increase forehead temperature and lower ratings of pleasantness, while the facial muscles associated with other vowel sounds (such as *ee* and *ah*) proved to lower forehead temperature and increase feelings of liking and pleasantness.

Of most relevance to theories of empathy is recent research indicating that even minute muscle actions in the face can influence emotional experience. In an experiment by McCane and Anderson (1987), individuals were taught to enhance or suppress muscle tension in very specific muscles of the face. This muscle action was imperceptible to the naked eye but could be detected with electronic (EMG) monitoring equipment. When participants were instructed to imagine positive emotional scenes, activation of zygomatic muscles (those associated with stretching the mouth, as in a smile) was associated with feelings of enjoyment, but suppression of zygomatic tension decreased ratings of enjoyment and increased feelings of distress.

So, the evidence is in that facial action influences our own emotional experiences. But what does this have to do with our understanding of other people's emotional states? Robert Zajonc has suggested that viewing emotional facial displays in others leads to imitative muscle movements in the perceiver's face (Zajonc, Adelman, Murphy, & Niedenthal, 1987). This muscle action may be imperceptibly small, but the research just described suggests that even tiny facial movements may alter our own feelings. There is evidence that observers do imitate facial expressions even when looking at photos, and these imitated facial expressions can later be used to identify the emotion that was being viewed at the time (Wallbott, 1991). It could be, then, that our ability to recognize another's moods and emotions and our empathic experience of those feelings are more closely linked than we previously imagined.

■■■ SOME CONCLUDING THOUGHTS

The study of nonverbal communication of emotions is not only a fascinating subject in its own right but it is also the area of research that brings social psychology in close contact with theories of human evolution. Communication of emotion is among the most primitive of social behaviors, and emotional displays have been documented in many species other than human beings. It is not surprising, then, that our ability to produce emotional expressions that can be "read" by others may be built in as part of our natural sociability, and that understanding how we encode and decode such displays may bring us in touch with our evolutionary past.

■■■ SUMMARY

Understanding what another person is experiencing or feeling often depends on the expression and interpretation of nonverbal communication. Channels of nonverbal communication include facial and other visual displays, body posture, paralinguistic features of speech, like voice pitch and speed, and proxemics, the distances that are maintained between persons by physical position and eye contact.

The study of nonverbal communication includes the study of transmission, or the expression of emotional cues, and decoding, the interpretation of others' emotional expressions. The most extensively studied form of emotional expression is facial displays that accompany emotion-arousing situations. Of particular interest is cross-cultural research on the presence of universal facial cues associated with specific emotional experience.

Some forms of nonverbal display (smiling, frowning) appear to be subject to intentional control, while others (such as body movements, voice pitch, and physiological arousal) are not easily controlled. The use of polygraph instruments to detect deception through the recording of uncontrollable cues is still the subject of much scientific and legal controversy.

The ability to recognize or interpret nonverbal cues to emotion also seems to have some universal aspects. Ecological theorists speculate that the information contained in nonverbal expressions of moods and emotions act as affordances, environmental cues that are functional for individual survival and reproduction. According to this view, individuals are particularly sensitive to signs of significant emotional states in others, such as anger and fear. Structural characteristics, such as baby-faced features, and dynamic features, like speed and rhythm of body movements, also serve as important nonverbal cues to other persons' moods, status, and power.

Although some recognition of nonverbal displays appears to be universal, individuals differ in their overall ability to detect the moods and emotions of others accurately. The PONS test (a measure of ability to interpret cues from eleven channels of visual and auditory communication) provides one measure of individual differences in decoding accuracy. In general, females tend to be better than males in sensitivity to nonverbal cues. Ability to recognize others' emotional states is also related to empathy, the vicarious experience and imitation of others' emotional reactions.

■ ■ ■ SUGGESTED READINGS

1. Alley, T. R. (1988). *Social and applied aspects of perceiving faces*. Hillsdale, NJ: Erlbaum.

2. Berry, D. S., & McArthur, L. (1986). Perceiving character in faces: The impact of age-related craniofacial changes on social perception. *Psychological Bulletin, 100,* 3–18.

3. Ekman, F. (1982). *Emotion in the human face*. Cambridge, England: Cambridge University Press.

4. Hall, J. A. (1984). *Nonverbal sex differences*. Baltimore: Johns Hopkins University Press.

5. Henley, N. M. (1977). *Body politics*. Englewood Cliffs, NJ: Prentice-Hall.

6. Saxe, L., Dougherty, D., & Cross, T. (1985). The validity of polygraph testing: Scientific analysis and public controversy. *American Psychologist, 40,* 355–366.

7. Zuckerman, M., DePaulo, B., & Rosenthal, R. (1981). Verbal and nonverbal communication of deception. In L. Berkowitz (Ed.), *Advances in experimental social psychology* (Vol. 14). New York: Academic Press.

CHAPTER 7

FORMING IMPRESSIONS
What Do We See In Other People?

■ **Key Concepts**

Gestalt perspective
Primacy effect
Trait centrality
Implicit personality theory
Halo effect
Negativity effect
Extremity effect
Cognitive algebra
Wholistic impressions

■ **Chapter Outline**

PERSON PERCEPTION: SOME BASIC PRINCIPLES
    Order Effects: The Primacy of First Impressions
    Centrality: Some Traits Are More Important Than Others
    ■ First Impressions in the Classroom

IMPLICIT PERSONALITY THEORY: WHAT GOES WITH WHAT?
    Evaluation Bias: The Halo Effect
    ■ Attractive Defendants
    Evaluation Isn't Everything

SIZING OTHERS UP: HOW DO WE PUT IT ALL TOGETHER?
    Model I: Cognitive Algebra
    Model II: Wholistic Impressions

SOME CONCLUDING THOUGHTS

SUMMARY

Andrea is preparing for a blind date with a new man in town named Jim. Her friend, Sue, has already met Jim and told Andrea that he is not only good-looking but warm and nice as well—a real sweetheart. Andrea checks her outfit one more time and decides that this blind date might turn out better than most.

■ ■ ■

Anthony approached the first class session of his Intro Psych course with a mixture of curiosity and suspense. Within ten minutes of the beginning of class, however, he felt very disappointed. The instructor was dressed formally, appeared nervous and stiff, and droned on and on about the history of psychology. This guy is pretty dull, Anthony concluded, I don't think I'm going to enjoy this class very much.

Observation of appearance and nonverbal communication help to form impressions of others: See Chapter 6.

Most of our social interactions are guided by the impressions we form about other people. Often these impressions are formed on the basis of little or no direct experience with the other person. The things we learn about a particular individual sometimes come from observation of his or her appearance and non-verbal communication. Anthony's evaluation of his psychology teacher shows how initial experiences can result in generalized impressions about what another person is like.

In other instances, as in the case of blind dates, the information we have about another person sometimes comes from the impressions provided by others. Informal conversations as well as official letters of recommendation are frequent sources of information about persons we have never actually met. We have many occasions during our lives to describe people we know or to form impressions about a person based on someone else's description.

Possibly because knowing and understanding other people is so important to us as a social species, we have available a rich vocabulary of terms and phrases to express our perceptions of what a particular individual is like. One lexicon of psychological terms lists more than 4,000 words in the English language that can be used to describe a person's character or personality (Allport & Odbert, 1936). The concepts that appear most often in our descriptions of other people are *personality traits*—terms that summarize the individual's characteristic behaviors, abilities, motives, or interpersonal style. Traits themselves are psychological constructs (Shweder, 1977); we do not "see" the dispositions or intentions that underlie another persons's actions in any direct sense. Yet the use of trait terms to convey our impressions of other people is so pervasive that social psychologists have treated such traits as the basic components of impressions—the elements from which our overall conception of a particular personality is constructed.

The manner in which we build an organized impression of what another person is like has occupied the attention of social psychologists for many years.

Solomon Asch (1946) expressed the importance of the person perception process this way:

> We look at a person and immediately a certain impression of his character forms itself in us . . . This remarkable capacity we possess to understand something of the character of another person, to form a conception of him as a human being, as a center of life and striving, with particular characteristics forming a distinct individuality, is a precondition of social life . . . (p. 258)

In 1943, Asch began a series of investigations to demonstrate his basic point about the immediacy with which we form an integrated, unified impression of another person based on whatever information we are given. The participants in these early studies were college students who listened to the experimenter read a list of characteristics that belonged to a particular person. They were asked to form an impression of the kind of person being described. The lists contained words such as the following: *energetic—assured—talkative—cold—ironical—inquisitive—persuasive.* After hearing the list read twice, participants were asked to write a "thumbnail sketch" of the person described by these terms. The following sketches, produced in response to the list of traits given above, are typical of the impression information process:

> He seems to be the kind of person who would make a great impression upon others at a first meeting. However, as time went by, his acquaintances would easily come to see through the mask. Underneath would be revealed his arrogance and selfishness.

Many of our impressions about others are drawn from the media. What image do you form of the person described in this article? ■

EXHIBIT 7.1

■

Profile of Ruth Bader Ginsburg

In 1960, a dean at Harvard Law School proposed one of his star students to Justice Felix Frankfurter of the Supreme Court as a law clerk. Justice Frankfurter told him that while the candidate was impressive, he wasn't ready to hire a woman and couldn't offer a job to Ruth Bader Ginsburg.

Ms. Ginsburg, who was chosen today by President Clinton for the Supreme Court, recently told that story to her law clerks to explain how she became interested in the role of women in the eyes of the law.

"She is the Thurgood Marshall of gender equality law," said Janet Benshoof, the president of the Center for Reproductive Law and Policy, repeating a common description of Judge Ginsburg. Like Justice Marshall, who shaped the legal strategy of the civil rights movement for the NAACP Legal and Educational Defense Fund before he joined the Court, Ruth Ginsburg organized the cases, found the plaintiffs and delivered the oral arguments.

Lawmakers from both parties on Capitol Hill said today that they did not foresee any major problems in Judge Ginsburg winning confirmation from the Senate Judiciary Committee.

In a speech on the Senate floor, Mr. Dole praised Mr. Clinton for making a "good choice" who "undoubtedly has the experience and the intellect to hit the ground running if confirmed."

Possibly he does not have any deep feeling. He would tend to be an opportunist. Likely to succeed in things he intends to do. He has perhaps married a wife who would help him in his purpose. He tends to be skeptical. (Asch, 1946, p. 261)

From descriptions such as these, Asch drew a number of inferences about the person perception process. First, he noted that the product is a *unified* impression. Although participants are given only a list of discrete trait terms, their own descriptions form an integrated narrative that combines the separate features into a single conception. Asch was a social psychologist who represented the *gestalt* tradition in psychology—the idea that we perceive objects and events as unified, organized, and meaningful, rather than as separate pieces of information. The **gestalt perspective** is often summed up as "the whole is greater than the sum of its parts."

Second, Asch noted that the resulting impression goes well beyond the information provided by the experimenter. References are made to motives, characteristics, and dispositions that are not directly mentioned in the original list, but are inferred from it. We are, apparently, quite capable of building a rich and elaborate personality structure from a very skeletal framework.

Asch then went on to test a number of principles of impression formation that reflected his view of the person perception process. By systematically varying the content of the lists of descriptive traits presented to respondents, he was able to demonstrate that personality impressions are strongly influenced by the context in which information is presented. In this chapter, we first describe the various principles of person perception as they were first demonstrated and interpreted by Asch within the gestalt tradition. Then, we discuss an alternative perspective on the process of person perception that developed in response to Asch's research. Finally, we compare these two models of the impression formation process as predecessors to more recent research on how we perceive other persons.

■ ■ ■ PERSON PERCEPTION: SOME BASIC PRINCIPLES

Order Effects: The Primacy of First Impressions

A recent television commercial (for an antidandruff shampoo) makes the point that "you never get a second chance to make a first impression." Common wisdom subscribes to the importance of initial impressions, and this is one area in which the results of empirical research confirm what most of us believe to be true. Asch thought that early information is especially important because we begin to form impressions right away—as soon as any information about the person becomes available. The inferences we make on the basis of the first pieces of information then color our understanding and interpretation of any new information that comes in afterward, so that the final impression is dominated by whatever came first.

To demonstrate the significance of first impressions, Asch (1946) conducted a simple experiment. He gave the same list of personality traits to different partic-

THE FAR SIDE   By GARY LARSON

ipants in different orders. Some participants were asked to form an impression of the kind of person who is *intelligent—industrious—impulsive—critical—stubborn—envious*. Others were asked their impression of a person who is *envious—stubborn—critical—impulsive—industrious—intelligent*. Although the information in these two lists is exactly the same, the descriptions that were generated did not sound like the same person at all. The person described in response to order 1 was characterized as competent and ambitious, whereas order 2 produced descriptions of an individual who was overly emotional and socially maladjusted.

These impressionistic findings were bolstered by the results of a trait checklist procedure introduced at the end of the experiment. After respondents had written their narrative sketches of the person described by the experimenter, they were given a list of eighteen pairs of opposing traits (for example, generous–ungenerous; humorous–humorless; ruthless–humane; frivolous–serious; strong–weak; dishonest–honest). From each pair of terms, the respondents were instructed to choose the one that was most consistent with the impression they had formed. Respondents were much more likely to choose favorable characteristics such as "happy," "sociable," "humorous," "strong," and "good-looking" when the stimulus traits had been presented in order 1 than when the same traits had been given in the opposite order.

The greater influence of information that comes early in a sequence is known as the **primacy effect** in impression formation. Primacy effects have been demonstrated in many person perception experiments. Anderson and Barrios (1961) replicated Asch's experiment, showing that a person described by a list that begins with positive traits and ends with negative traits is judged as more likable than a person described by the same traits in opposite order. In a more naturalistic context, Park (1986) had groups of seven students interact with each other weekly over a period of seven weeks. At the end of each session, respondents wrote verbal descriptions of their current impressions of each of the other six members of their group. Park found that whatever trait ascriptions respondents made in the first session were more likely to appear in their final impressions of that individual than traits that appeared at any later time in the series of interactions.

A series of experiments by Jones, Rock, Shaver, Goethals, and Ward (1968) found that the order in which information is received affects not only personality impressions but our judgments of another person's ability as well. In these experiments, participants were shown a folder containing the results of another individual's performance on a series of word problems. In all cases, the folder contained the person's solutions to thirty problems, fifteen of which had been scored as "correct" and fifteen as "incorrect." However, in half the cases, ten of the first fifteen solutions were "correct" answers (and ten "incorrect" answers appeared in the second half of the series). In the other half of the cases this order was reversed—the first fifteen problems seen by the judge contained ten "incorrect" solutions, whereas 10 "correct" answers did not appear until the latter half of the series. Finally, for some judges the correct and incorrect solutions were evenly distributed across both halves of the series of thirty problems.

Since judges read all thirty problems in the file folder before they were called on to make any judgment of the target person's ability or competence, they all had the same information on which to base such judgments. If anything, the performance on the last few problems in the series should have had special influence, since these were the ones that judges had seen most recently before making their assessments. (This is, in fact, what Jones and his colleagues had originally expected to find in these experiments.) Contrary to such predictions, the target who started out well early in the series and then deteriorated in performance was rated as *more* competent than a target whose correct solutions were more evenly distributed. And the target who started out badly and then improved in performance across the series was rated as *least* competent. Apparently, judges in these experiments formed an impression of the target's ability level on the basis of "early returns," and then ignored or discounted later information that contradicted these initial performance judgments.

These findings have important implications for performance evaluations in many real-life settings, such as employee evaluations on the job or how a professor might grade a paper depending on whether most of the good ideas appeared near the beginning or at the end of the essay. The tendency to base judgments about a person's ability on first impressions is quite strong. However, the results of recent experiments by Aronson & Jones (1992) indicate there are conditions under which this effect can be reversed. When an individual (such as a teacher or supervisor) observers another's performance with the goal of trying to *improve* that person's skills or abilities, then performers who start poor and end well get higher final ratings of ability than those who do well at the beginning and then decline. Apparently, when perceivers are motivated to look for improvement in ability across time, final performance counts more than early returns.

Centrality: Some Traits Are More Important Than Others

Asch also believed that some traits have more impact on the impressions we form than others. For instance, it may be more important to us to know whether a particular person is hostile or friendly than to learn whether he is tidy. When we are looking for someone to help us prepare for an important math exam, we are more likely to be influenced by information about the person's intelligence than by her sense of humor. We call this **trait centrality.**

In order to assess how much impact a particular characteristic has on our perceptions of personality, Asch looked to see what happened when one trait term in a list was replaced by its opposite. In one version of his experiments, Asch presented half the participants with the trait list *intelligent—skillful—industrious—warm—determined—practical—cautious.* The other half was given the same list except that the word "warm" in the middle was replaced by "cold." Even though only one adjective out of seven had been changed, the substitution had widespread effects on the overall impression. On the checklist evaluation, the warm person was assigned the characteristics "generous," "wise," "happy," "good-natured," "humorous," "sociable," "popular," "humane," "altruistic," and "imaginative," whereas the cold person was assigned the opposite characteristics by the majority of respondents.

In a second version of this experiment, Asch made a different substitution. Instead of "warm" or "cold" appearing in middle of the trait list, he inserted the terms "polite" or "blunt." Whether the stimulus list contained the word "polite" or "blunt" turned out to have relatively little impact on the overall impression formed or on the characteristics assigned from the trait checklist. This demonstrated that the warm–cold distinction is more *central* in our impressions of other people than characteristics such as politeness. Returning to the blind date scenario at the beginning of this chapter, consider how different Andrea might have felt if Jim had been described by Sue as a "cold fish" rather than "warm and nice."

First Impressions in the Classroom

The overall impact of the warm–cold description was demonstrated even more vividly in a "live" experiment conducted a few years after the original Asch studies (Kelley, 1950). In this experiment, trait lists similar to those presented in the Asch

EXHIBIT 7.2

■

Introduction of Guest Instructor

Mr. _____is a graduate student in the Department of Economics and Social Science here at M.I.T. He has had three semesters of teaching experience in psychology at another college. This is his first semester teaching Ec. 70. He is 26 years old, a veteran, and married. People who know him consider him to be a rather warm (cold) person, industrious, critical, practical, and determined.

From Kelley, 1950.

studies were used to create an initial expectation about a person whom participants were actually going to meet. Students in three sections of a college psychology course were introduced to a "guest lecturer" during one course period. The guest (a male accomplice of the experimenter) was someone the students had never seen before. Before his appearance in the classroom, a researcher explained to the class members that their regular instructor was out of town and that a substitute instructor would take his place. Students were told further that the department was interested in how classes react to various instructors, and that at the end of the period they would be asked to fill out some forms indicating their reaction to the guest speaker. The researcher then distributed some advance information about the upcoming speaker, in the form of a brief biographical sketch. Inserted in this sketch was the information that the instructor was considered to be either "rather warm" or "rather cold" (Exhibit 7.2).

The two versions of the biographical description were distributed randomly to different students in the class. The guest instructor then appeared and led the class in a twenty-minute discussion. During the course of the discussion, the experimenter surreptitiously recorded how much each student in the class participated in the discussion.

After the guest left, class members were asked to give their confidential impressions of the instructor, using a set of fifteen trait-rating scales (Table 7.1). Despite the fact that all students had been exposed to the same social interaction, those who had been given the prior expectation that the speaker would be "warm" evaluated him as significantly more considerate, informal, sociable, good-natured, humorous, and humane than students who had received the "cold" expectation. More important, this prior expectation also influenced their willingness to interact with the stimulus person. In the three sections of the class, 56% of the students who had the "warm" description participated in the discussion, whereas only 32% of the "cold" students took part. Participation was, in turn, related to how favorable an impression the student had of the instructor.

Kelley's experiment was replicated in another educational setting by Widmeyer and Loy (1988). In this study, a guest lecturer spoke to a large (270-student) class in physical education. Before the presentation, students were given a biographical sketch of the lecturer that described him as "warm" or "cold," as in the original experiment. Following a forty-minute lecture, students who anticipated a "warm" speaker rated the guest as a more effective teacher, as well as more sociable, more humorous, and

TABLE 7.1

■

Average Ratings of the Same Speaker by Observers in the "Warm" and "Cold" Conditions

	Average Rating	
TRAIT	COLD	WARM
Knowledgeable	4.6	3.5
Considerate	9.6	6.3
Informal	9.6	6.3
Sociable	10.4	5.6
Intelligent	5.1	4.8
Popular	7.4	4.0
Humorous	11.7	8.3
Humane	11.0	8.6

Note: 1 = most positive.
From Kelley, 1950.

Central traits are closely related to expectancy effects in person perception and social interaction: See Chapters 8 and 16.

less formal in his presentation. Together these studies offer living proof of Asch's contention that knowledge of a central personality trait such as warmth has pervasive effects on our perception and interpretation of many other characteristics of that person. Central traits apparently create *expectancies* about what the person will be like, which then influence how new information about that person is interpreted.

■ ■ ■ IMPLICIT PERSONALITY THEORY: WHAT GOES WITH WHAT?

Asch's original studies raised a number of interesting questions about the process of forming impressions. What makes some traits more central than others? Why do perceivers come to the conclusion that someone is imaginative and has a good sense of humor just because they have been described as intelligent and warm? These questions have to do with the *inferences* we make from one personality characteristic to another. By the time we are adults, we seem to have acquired a lot of assumptions about how traits fit together, about which traits are consistent with others and which are incompatible. In general, we expect intelligent people to be reliable, and we do not expect a cold person to be funny. We have, in effect, developed *implicit theories* about the structure of personality.

The term **implicit personality theory** was first introduced in a review by Bruner and Tagiuri (1954) of early research on person perception. The concept refers to evidence that the impressions we form of specific individuals are influenced by general rules we hold about the associations among personality traits.

The evaluative meaning of traits is also seen in the relationship between impression formation and interpersonal attraction: See Chapter 13.

Since the Bruner and Tagiuri review, a number of methodologies have been developed to describe and understand the nature of these implicit assumptions about traits and their relationships (Peabody & Goldberg, 1989; Schneider, 1973). The results of many such analyses have all revealed the importance of the *evaluative* meaning of trait terms as a major dimension of trait relationships. In general, traits that are evaluated as positive, favorable, or good are expected to go together, as are traits that are negative, bad, or unfavorable. Positive and negative traits are not expected to occur in combination with each other.

Evaluative Bias: The Halo Effect

The importance of evaluation as a component of trait associations helps to account for a pervasive bias in impression formation known as the **halo effect** (Cooper, 1981). Once we have learned that a person has a very positive characteristic, such as honesty, we assume that he or she has other positive traits—generosity, reliability, and so on. Further, as we learn new information about that person, we tend to interpret it in the most positive light. If we see that individual giving advice to another person, we perceive this as "helpfulness," rather than interference or "bossiness." Conversely, if initial information about a person is negative, we interpret new information in the worst possible light and reinforce our negative impression.

The halo effect can influence our perception of even seemingly objective characteristics of another person. In one experiment, Nisbett and Wilson (1977) had college students watch a videotape of a professor who spoke with a foreign accent. In one version of the tape, the professor expressed pleasant, positive attitudes toward students. In an alternate version, he expressed somewhat distant, unpleasant views. At the conclusion of the tape, students who watched the "pleasant" version rated the professor's physical appearance, nonverbal mannerisms, and accent more favorably than did students in the "unpleasant" condition.

Physical appearance factors can also create halo effects. Since in many impression formation situations the first information we receive about another person is how he or she looks, it should not be surprising that visual appearance plays an important role in first impressions. When we like what we see, we are more inclined to ascribe other favorable characteristics to that individual than when our visual impression is negative.

By far the most pervasive physical appearance effect is that associated with physical attractiveness, or beauty. Standards for beauty may vary among cultures and between historical periods, but social psychological research is consistent in demonstrating that whatever constitutes our judgment of what (or who) is beautiful also influences our evaluation of what is good (Eagly, Ashmore, Makhijani, & Kennedy, 1991).

The halo effect associated with physical attractiveness is well illustrated by the results of an experiment conducted by Dion, Berscheid, and Walster (1972). In a preliminary study, the researchers had college students rate yearbook pictures of young males and females for physical attractiveness. Based on these evaluations, twelve pictures were selected that raters agreed were in the highly attractive

The voluptuous female forms represented in the seventeenth-century paints by Rubens reflect quite different standards of female beauty than are typical of twentieth-century America. According to results of modern social psychological research on impression formation, these women should have been perceived as particularly warm, sociable, and popular. ■

range; twelve were selected that received generally unattractive ratings; and twelve were selected on the basis of receiving average attractiveness ratings.

In the second phase of the experiment, participants were given envelopes containing pictures of three females or three males—one from the attractive, one from the unattractive, and one from the average category. They were instructed to open each envelope and then rate the persons in the photographs on twenty-seven personality traits. From these ratings, an overall index of the perceived "social desirability" of the stimulus person was computed. In addition, respondents were asked to estimate the probability that the persons in the photographs would experience happiness in their personal lives and success in their careers.

The results of this experiment were striking in demonstrating the impact of physical attractiveness on impressions (see Table 7.2). Attractive individuals were rated as more positive on a wide range of socially desirable traits than were average individuals, who were rated more positively than unattractive persons. Further, attractive persons were expected to be more likely to get married, to have successful marriages, high-status occupations, and to be more happy overall than individuals of average or low attractiveness.

People like others who are physically attractive: See Chapter 13.

Expectations may become self-fulfilling prophecies: See Chapter 16.

Is there any truth to the idea that physically attractive people are also more sociable, competent, and successful? Interestingly, this may be a case where believing makes it so. If attractive individuals are *expected* to be warm and sociable, others may treat them well and as a consequence they *do* become socially skilled and happy. Since people like others who are physically attractive, expectations may become self-fulfilling prophecies. However, there is no basis for the belief that physical attractiveness and intelligence go together (Eagly et al., 1991; Feingold, 1992). Yet the expectancy that good-looking people are also intelligent persists, attesting to the influence of the implicit idea that positive traits are associated with other positive traits.

TABLE 7.2

■

Traits Attributed to Various Stimulus Others

Trait Ascription[a]	Unattractive Stimulus Person	Average Stimulus Person	Attractive Stimulus Person
Social desirability of the stimulus person's personality	56.31	62.42	65.39
Occupational status of the stimulus person	1.70	2.02	2.25
Marital competence of the stimulus person	.37	.71	1.70
Parental competence of the stimulus person	3.91	4.55	3.54
Social and professional happiness of the stimulus person	5.28	6.34	6.37
Total happiness of the stimulus person	8.83	11.60	11.60
Likelihood of marriage	1.52	1.82	2.17

[a]The higher the number, the more socially desirable, the more prestigious an occupation, etc., the stimulus person is expected to possess.
From Dion et al., 1972.

Attractive Defendants

The halo effect of physical attractiveness extends to a wide range of judgments. Essays are rated as higher in quality when accompanied by a photo of an attractive rather than an unattractive author (Landy & Sigall, 1974), and records of performance are rated as indicating higher levels of ability when attributed to a physically attractive person (Benassi, 1982). The effect even extends into the courtroom, influencing our judgments of guilt and innocence. In general, it seems that attractive defendants (both male and female) are given lighter sentences than physically unattractive defendants (Downs & Lyons, 1991; Landy and Aronson, 1969; Stewart, 1980). However, this effect can be reversed for certain types of crimes. Sigall and Ostrove (1975) found that members of a mock jury sentenced an unattractive female defendant to more years in prison than an attractive defendant when she was accused of stealing. But when the crime was one of swindling a man into making a phony investment, the beautiful defendant was sentenced more harshly. In both cases, the impression created by physical appearance seemed to extend to judgments of criminality.

Is this defendant's attractiveness likely to help or hurt her case? Research shows it depends on the charge. ■

Evaluation Isn't Everything

As pervasive as the evaluative factor is, it does not account for all trait inferences in person perception. In Asch's original study of trait centrality, the warm–cold distinction affected a large number of trait attributions. However, whether a person was described as warm or cold did not have any influence on students' ratings of his reliability, physical attractiveness, persistence, seriousness, restraint, strength, or honesty. Apparently, there are limits to the halo effect—not all positive traits are the same.

Traits also have *descriptive* meanings that influence their associations (Peabody, 1967). For instance, "cautious" and "bold" are both evaluated positively as personality characteristics, but they are not expected to belong together since they imply opposite behaviors. Both evaluative and descriptive meaning enter into our implicit theories of trait associations. The results of analyses of sixty trait terms conducted by Rosenberg, Nelson, & Vivekananthan (1968) revealed that there are two related but distinct types of good–bad evaluations. One they call the "intellectual good–bad" dimension (along which lie competence versus foolishness) and the other the "social good–bad" dimension (friendly, sociable versus unfriendly, hostile). How different traits line up on these two dimensions is depicted in Figure 7.1.

The results obtained by Rosenberg and his colleagues help explain the centrality of the warm–cold distinction in impression formation. As we can see in Figure 7.1, the traits warm and cold can be located at two relatively extreme positions along the "social desirability" axis. Traits that fall toward the right on

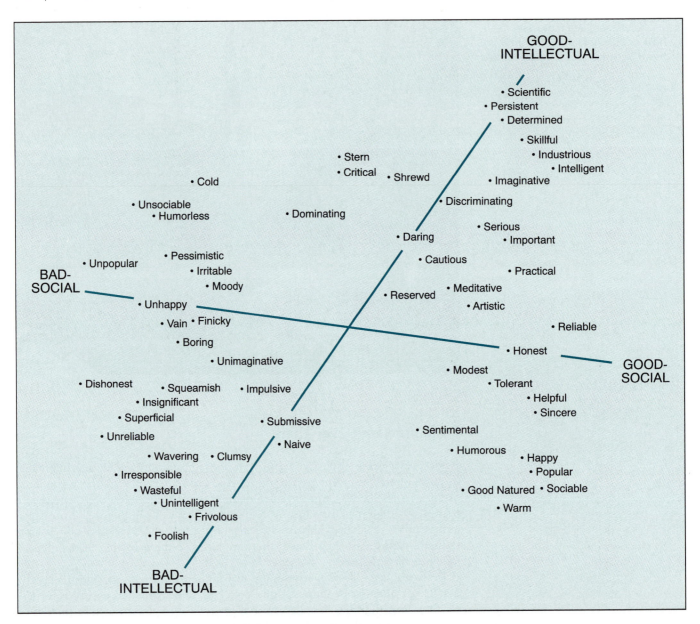

FIGURE 7.1

■

Two-dimensional configuration of 60 traits showing best-fitting axes of properties social desirability and intellectual desirability. (From S. Rosenberg, C. Nelson, and P. S. Vivekananthan, 1968.)

this dimension will be closely associated with warmth, while traits on the left are associated with coldness. Thus, knowing that a person is "warm" carries a lot of associations with other socially desirable traits. These associations, however, do not extend to judgments of intellectual competence. Traits that are high in intellectuality (such as "scientific" or "intelligent") fall toward the middle of the social good–bad dimension—they are not necessarily either warm or cold.

The two evaluative dimensions identified by Rosenberg and his colleagues were derived from sophisticated statistical techniques, but they also make a great deal of sense from a practical point of view. Our everyday social interactions—

our decisions about whom to associate with and whom to avoid—are dominated by two primary concerns. We need to know, first of all, whether other persons will be nice to us or nasty, whether we can expect them to make us *feel* good or bad. We also need to know whether others will be *useful* to us, whether they are competent and knowledgeable or stupid and foolish. Other, more subtle characteristics may enter into our evaluations as we get to know specific individuals well, but these two dimensions are of the broadest importance in our judgments of different personalities.

Further, these two dimensions of evaluation correspond to two different types of interpersonal attraction. Social desirability is related to how much we *like* another person, whereas intellectual competence is related to how much we *respect* another (Lydon, Jamieson, & Zanna, 1988). In general, we both like and respect our good friends. However, it is possible for us to separate these two forms of attraction. We may respect someone whom we do not like very much, and we may feel affection for someone whom we do not particularly respect.

■■■ SIZING OTHERS UP: HOW DO WE PUT IT ALL TOGETHER?

Asch's research on impression formation stimulated widespread interest in how we form a general, summary evaluation of a particular person. When Sue tells Andrea that Jim is a "real sweetheart," she is expressing a global positive evaluation that supercedes the specific traits or characteristics that may be attributed to Jim as an individual. Social psychologists who study impression formation have been particularly interested in the processes by which perceivers combine specific pieces of information into such a global evaluative impression.

In the years following Asch's original studies, two different models of the impression formation process were extensively tested in pursuit of an answer to this question (Figure 7.2). One was the gestalt perspective represented by Asch himself. The other was an information integration model represented most vigorously by Norman Anderson in the 1960s. We describe Anderson's model first to show how it contrasts with the Asch interpretation of the impression formation process.

Model I: Cognitive Algebra

Anderson's (1962, 1965) view of impression formation is that it is similar to a mathematical process (called **cognitive algebra**), where information contained in the component parts is combined into a summary judgment. This type of model is depicted in Figure 7.2a as a two-stage process: trait evaluation and integration. In the first stage, an *evaluative rating* is assigned to each trait that has been ascribed to the target person. In the second stage, these values are combined mathematically into a single likeability rating of the person as a whole.

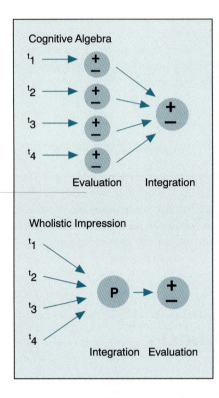

FIGURE 7.2

■

Models of Impression Formation

(a) Cognitive Algebra: Trait evaluations are combined to form an overall impression

(b) Wholistic Impression: Impression is formed first; evaluation follows

Attention-getting information leads to the formation of social stereotypes and prejudices: See Chapter 23.

To illustrate how a cognitive algebra model works, imagine that you have just met a person you describe as intelligent, practical, boring, and short. According to the principles of information integration, you first evaluate how much you like each one of these trait characteristics. Let's say that you think "intelligence" is a highly positive trait (+9 on a scale from −10 to +10), "practical" is only slightly positive (+1), and "short" and "boring" are both negatively evaluated (−3 and −5, respectively). These four values are then combined to produce your overall evaluative impression of your new acquaintance.

What mathematical rule is applied when we combine traits that differ in direction and magnitude of evaluation? According to Anderson, we can describe the combined impression as the average of the individual trait evaluations. However, this is not a simple averaging process, because some traits are seen as more important than others and therefore have greater impact on the final evaluation. Thus, the overall impression is the product of a *weighted average* of the values assigned to the individual traits, each multiplied by its degree of importance. By allowing traits to have different weights in the overall evaluation, Anderson's model can account for many of the principles of impression formation that were demonstrated in Asch's early studies. Central traits, for instance, are given extra weight because they are particularly important to our overall evaluation of another person.

The importance, or weight, assigned to a particular trait or characteristic reflects how much *attention* is paid to that information as it is received. The results of research by Anderson and others suggest that at least three factors influence the attention to trait information. One factor is the order in which information is received. We tend to pay particular attention to the first pieces of information in a sequence, while later information is attended to less well (that is, we seem to lose interest after the first few tidbits). This attention decrement can account for primacy effects in impression formation, since early information has a greater weight in the final impression. Indeed, if perceivers are forced to pay equal attention to all of the items in a list of traits, the primacy effect can be eliminated or even reversed (Anderson & Hubert, 1963).

The amount of attention we pay to particular characteristics is also affected by their direction and extremity. Negative traits seem to get more weight than positive traits. If "kind" has a +7 evaluative rating and "dishonest" has a −7 evaluation, a person who is described as both kind and dishonest is more likely to be evaluated as somewhat negative (for example, a −3 overall) rather than neutral. Similarly, a person described as moral (+10) and reserved (+2) is likely to be evaluated more positively than a simple averaging rule would predict (+8 rather than +6), because "moral" is so extremely positive that it pulls extra weight in the impression (Skowronski & Carlston, 1989).

A number of experiments have demonstrated that negative traits are generally given more weight in our overall impression than are positive traits. This is called the **negativity effect** in impression formation. Similarly, traits that have extreme evaluative meaning are given more weight than traits that are closer to neutral in value—an **extremity effect.** Susan Fiske (1980) has argued that negative and extreme characteristics receive more attention because they are novel or unusual. She demonstrated that when reading a list of traits, judges spend more time looking at negative and extreme items than at positive or neutral items, and those items that are attended to longer are also given more weight in the final impression.

Model II: Wholistic Impressions

Solomon Asch would not agree with the cognitive algebra interpretation of his findings. His original conceptualization of the impression formation process was based on the principle that the whole is greater than the sum of its parts (Asch, 1946). If personality traits are perceived and understood *in relation to each other,* then an integrated impression cannot be produced mechanistically from an evaluation of those traits considered in isolation.

Asch's view of the impression formation process is depicted in Figure 7.1b. In this model, the two stages of integration and evaluation are reversed from those in the cognitive algebra model. First, the set of traits attributed to the individual is integrated by the perceiver into a meaningful whole. Then, the perceiver assigns an evaluation to the set as a whole on the basis of this meaning.

Indirect support for Asch's conceptualization comes from research indicating that information is stored differently in memory when it is part of a unified impression than when it is not. Hamilton, Katz, and Leirer (1980) gave participants a set of sentences to read, each sentence describing a rather neutral behavior (for example, "watched a movie on TV," "took his dog out for a walk in the park"). Some participants were given explicit instructions to memorize the sentences for a later recall test. Others were told nothing about a recall test, but were instructed to think of the behaviors as describing a particular person and to form an overall impression of that person. Then all participants were asked to recall as many of the sentences as they could. Those in the impression formation condition actually recalled more of the sentences correctly than did those who had been told to memorize them. Further research has demonstrated that perceivers organize the information and remember it in a more systematic, structured way under impression formation instructions than they do under memory instructions (Hoffman, Mischel, & Baer, 1984).

A number of experiments have been done on the organization of person memory: See Chapter 8.

The Change–of–Meaning Effect.   The key to a wholistic model of impression formation is the idea that individual traits are given different meanings and values in different contexts. This change-of-meaning hypothesis has received considerable research attention, and there is convincing evidence for it. Consider, for instance, the trait "proud." Is this a positive or a negative characteristic to attribute to a person? According to results of an experiment by Hamilton and Zanna (1974), it depends on what other traits are assigned to the same person. In their study, an individual was described as proud, but also "happy and intelligent." In other cases, the individual was proud, but also "boring and rude." Judges who had been given one of these descriptions were then asked to indicate whether "proud" meant that the person was "confident" or "conceited." The meaning of the trait was more likely to be rated as confident in the first context and as conceited in the second. The same term was interpreted differently, just as Asch would have expected.

Using a different methodology, Watkins & Peynircioglu (1984) demonstrated that the same trait term takes on different meanings when embedded in different behavioral descriptions. For instance, for some participants the trait "emotional" was assigned to a person who was described as someone who "fondly embraces her friends on meeting them and sheds a little tear on leaving them." For others, "emotional" was associated with a person who "throws temper tantrums and then pleads forgiveness in a shower of tears." Later, all participants were given a test of their ability to recall the original trait word. To help them remember, they were given another word as a hint. The hint was either the word "warm" or the word "unstable." For those who had originally seen the first description, recall was easier when "warm" was the cue word rather than "unstable." For those given the second description, the reverse effect was found. Clearly, the word "emotional" had come to have different meanings in the two contexts.

Resolving Inconsistencies.   The change-of-meaning effect is particularly striking when perceivers are faced with inconsistencies in their evaluations of other persons. Research on implicit personality theory indicates that we infer personality characteristics on the basis of evaluative and descriptive consistency. Real people, however, often fail to conform to such expectations. Sometimes the descriptions we receive or convey about a particular person contain contradictions and evaluative inconsistencies. Consider the following statements: "John is intelligent and friendly but insensitive to others' feelings"; "Jill is competent but shy and insecure." Such inconsistencies challenge our ability to understand other people in an integrated way.

Almost forty years after his original series of studies, Asch conducted additional experiments to explore how perceivers resolve inconsistencies in order to form or maintain a unified impression of a stimulus person (Asch and Zukier, 1984). College students were given two-trait descriptions of a series of persons. For each pair, they were asked to imagine a person having those two attributes, write a brief description of that person, and indicate how the two traits were related.

Some of the pairs of descriptor traits were discordant in meaning (cheerful—gloomy; generous—vindictive; ambitious—lazy). By analyzing the content of the inference respondents drew from such trait pairs, Asch and Zukier identified six different strategies by which perceivers resolve apparent inconsistencies. Illustrations of these six modes of inconsistency resolution are provided in Exhibit 7.2. In this more recent work—as in his original studies—Asch again demonstrated the remarkable capacity of social perceivers to generate rich and meaningful personality structures from bare descriptions of other persons. His work has now been incorporated in newer perspectives on person perception.

■ ■ ■ SOME CONCLUDING THOUGHTS

Throughout this chapter we have focused only on the perceiver side of the impression formation process. We have ignored the issue of whether our perceptions and interpretations are accurate or true representations of the person being perceived (Funder, 1987; Zebrowitz, 1990).

There is an active and lively debate in social psychology about whether there is such a thing as "personality" at all—whether individuals do have enduring dispositions to behave in characteristic ways or whether personality concepts are simply convenient fictions, existing only in the mind of the perceiver (Jussim, 1991). As with all such questions, this one has no simple answer. On the one

EXHIBIT 7.3

■

Modes of Resolving Inconsistency: How Can A Person Be Both Cheerful and Gloomy?

1. *Segregation:* The inconsistent traits are assigned to two different personality domains. For example, a person may be *brilliant* in intellectual pursuits but *foolish* when it comes to common sense practical matters.

2. *Depth:* The two traits are seen as superficial versus deeper manifestations of the person. For example, he appears very *sociable* on the outside, but deep down he is very *lonely.*

3. *Cause–effect:* One trait is seen as causing the other in a reactive manner. For example, he is so *dependent* that he feels *hostile* toward those he depends on.

4. *Means–end:* One trait is exhibited as a means toward achieving goals related to the other. For example, a parent who is *kind* may be *strict* in order to do what is best for her children.

5. *Common source:* Both traits may be seen as arising from the same underlying personality disposition. For example, a moody person may be *cheerful* on some occasions and *gloomy* on others.

6. *Interpolation:* Some bridging assumptions are introduced to account for the inconsistency. For example, a person may be *ambitious* but appear *lazy* because he is discouraged and afraid that his ambitions will not be fulfilled.

From Asch and Zukier (1984).

hand, we have plenty of evidence of biases and distortions in the person perception process. We tend confidently to make snap judgments about the personality of other individuals on the basis of so little information that they cannot possibly be an accurate reflection of the true character of those persons. On the other hand, years of research on personality provide evidence that individuals do exhibit consistencies in behavior patterns across many situations, and these individual differences are reflected in the personality ratings given by friends and acquaintances.

We do not hope to resolve here the debate about the overall accuracy of person perception. It is certainly true that people are responsible in part for the impressions they make on others. However, we have noted the extent to which we as perceivers actively create our impressions of others. The order in which we receive information, the evaluative implications of our first impressions, and the importance of certain behaviors to ourselves all influence the judgments we make about the character of another individual. In order to make sense of the other person, we impose consistency in the face of inconsistency and form impressions of new persons on the basis of past experience with different people.

Perhaps the lesson to be learned from research on impression formation is to be wary of overconfidence in our ability to judge others accurately, especially on the basis of first impressions. The "eye of the beholder," it seems, doesn't always see clearly.

■ ■ ■ **Summary**

How we form impressions of other people has been the subject of much social psychological research since early experiments by Solomon Asch in the 1940s. In much of this research, participants are presented with a list of personality traits ascribed to a particular individual, and then form an overall evaluation of that person. From this research procedure, a number of basic principles of person perception have been identified.

Our impressions of others are influenced by primacy effects. Under most circumstances, the first things we learn about a person have more impact on our evaluations than later information. Some personality traits also have more impact than others. Characteristics such as warm–cold or intelligent–unintelligent seem to be central traits, which form the foundation of our impressions of a particular individual. Trait centrality is one aspect of implicit personality theory—our beliefs about how different person characteristics are associated with one another. One important component of implicit personality theory is a general evaluation bias—positive traits are assumed to be associated with other positive characteristics and negative traits with other negative features. This assumption leads to the halo effect in person judgments. One example of the halo effect is a physical attractiveness bias. In general, attractive individuals are assumed to have more desirable personality characteristics than less attractive persons.

Two different theoretical models have been developed to describe the processes involved in forming an impression of another person. The cognitive algebra model assumes that our overall evaluation of an individual is a mathematical integration of the evaluative ratings of each of the individual characteristics or traits associated with that person. The wholistic model assumes that we first form a global impression about what a person is like and that overall evaluation influences the meaning we ascribe to specific characteristics of the individual. According to this model, individuals are perceived as consistent "wholes." Apparent inconsistencies are resolved by constructing elaborate and meaningful personality impressions that account for individual traits.

■ ■ ■ **Suggested Readings**

1. Asch, S. E., & Zukier, H. (1984). Thinking about persons. *Journal of Personality and Social Psychology, 41,* 258–290.

2. Cooper, W. H. (1981). Ubiquitous halo. *Psychological Bulletin, 90,* 218–244.

3. Park, B. (1986). A method for studying the development of impressions of real people. *Journal of Personality and Social Psychology, 51,* 907–917.

4. Schneider, D. J. (1973). Implicit personality theory: A review. *Psychological Bulletin, 79,* 294–309.

5. Skowronski, J. J., & Carlston, D. E. (1989). Negativity and extremity biases in impression formation: A review of explanations. *Psychological Bulletin, 105,* 131–142.

6. Zebrowitz, L. A. (1990). *Social perception.* Pacific Grove, CA: Brooks/Cole.

CHAPTER 8

SOCIAL COGNITION
Impression Formation Revisited

■ Key Concepts

Social cognition
Mental representation
Schema
Script
Trait
Social stereotype
Gender stereotype
Prototype
Schema accessibility
Priming effects
Personal constructs
Self-schema
Encoding
Confirmatory bias
Assimilation
Discounting
Reconstructive memory

■ Chapter Outline

SOCIAL COGNITION AND THE "NEW LOOK"

SCHEMAS: THE STRUCTURE OF SOCIAL KNOWLEDGE
    Scripts and Roles
    Person Schemas

SCHEMA ACCESSIBILITY
    External Factors
    Internal Factors

SCHEMATIC PROCESSING
    Selective Attention and Recall
    Confirmatory Biases: Cognitive Conservatism
    Reconstructing Memory
    ■ Eyewitness Testimony

SOME CONCLUDING THOUGHTS

SUMMARY

When Ann Hopkins came up for partnership at Price Waterhouse in 1982, she looked like a shoo-in for a promotion. Of the 88 candidates—all the others were male—she had the best record at generating new business and securing multimillion-dollar contracts for the Big Eight accounting firm. Yet Hopkins's nomination was put on hold after she was evaluated by several male partners as being too "macho" and in need of a "charm school." One of them advised her to "walk more femininely, talk more femininely, wear more makeup, have her hair styled and wear jewelry." Instead she quit the firm and filed a lawsuit under Title VII of the Civil Rights Act of 1964, which forbids employment discrimination because of a person's sex . . . [In May 1989], the U.S. Supreme Court held that Price Waterhouse had based its decision in part on unlawful sexual stereotyping . . . (Time, May 15, 1989, p. 66)

The legal battle of *Hopkins v. Price Waterhouse* illustrates how a mismatch between occupational stereotypes and gender stereotypes can lead to perceiving women differently from men even when they behave similarly. When social psychologist Susan Fiske testified in the original case, she argued that evaluations of Ann Hopkins by the partners at Price Waterhouse were influenced by preconceived notions of what a woman should be like (Fiske, Bersoff, Borgida, Deaux, & Heilman, 1991). Such preconceptions bias what information is attended to and the way it is interpreted and evaluated. In her testimony, Fiske drew on the results of social psychological research known as the study of social cognition.

■■■ Social Cognition and the "New Look"

The study of social cognition extends previous research on impression formation: See Chapter 7.

Social cognition is the study of how perceivers form **mental representations** of persons and social events. Social cognition is an extension of the social psychological research on impression formation. However, social cognition draws more explicitly on a general *information-processing* framework borrowed from cognitive psychology. Information processing is the sequence of cognitive activities whereby information from the social world (data) is combined with the perceiver's knowledge (theories) to produce an interpretation, or mental representation.

Although different theorists describe the information-processing sequence in somewhat different ways (e.g., Fiske & Taylor, 1991; Hamilton, 1988; Wyer & Srull, 1986), the basic stages include the following:

■ *Attention and encoding,* the initial selection and identification of information units to be processed
■ *Elaboration,* interpretation of the new information in terms of previously existing knowledge or concepts

- *Organization,* formation of a coherent mental representation of the information as interpreted
- *Storage* of the representation in memory
- *Retrieval* from memory when relevant to a judgment or behavioral decision

Social cognition is the application of this information-processing approach to the perception of social events, social groups, and individual persons. The central feature of the social cognition perspective is the idea that our perception of new persons and events—the way we interpret and evaluate them—is largely a product of the mental representations we have developed about past experience. In the form of stored knowledge structures, the past provides the framework and the concepts that we use to make sense of the present.

Social cognition became an active area of social psychological research in the late 1970s, but had its roots in much earlier work in experimental psychology. In an influential paper entitled "On Perceptual Readiness," Bruner (1957) summarized what was then called the "new look" in the psychology of perception. Bruner contended that all perception involves categorization. Everything that is perceived is seen as a member of some category of objects or events, and takes its meaning from that categorization. Because perception is an active, interpretive process, it is influenced by the perceiver's mental "set," or readiness to apply one category system rather than another in his or her approach to a new stimulus situation. As a result, internal factors such as expectancies, needs, and values affect the outcome of perception.

Bruner and his colleagues tested these ideas with experiments on people's perception of objects, letters, and numerals, but the results of work on the "new look" have tremendous applicability in the realm of social perception as well. Like other mental representations, the impressions we form of individual persons and social groups derive in part from the information we receive about those persons and in part from the categories we use to interpret that information (Brewer, 1988; Fiske & Neuberg, 1990).

■ ■ ■ SCHEMAS: THE STRUCTURES OF SOCIAL KNOWLEDGE

As we gain experience with particular types of social situations, we develop rules for how to behave in those situations. When an individual travels by airplane for the first time, there is initial confusion about where to go in the airport, what to do with luggage, how to act toward flight attendants, and so on. With experience, the traveler learns the "rules" for checking in, boarding the plane, stowing carry-on items, ordering food and drinks, interacting with seatmates, and the like. Once acquired, these rules prove to be applicable in airports and on airplanes almost anywhere in the world.

The set of rules we develop for airplane travel illustrates how past experience becomes structured knowledge for use in processing new social information. Such knowledge structures are called schemas (Taylor & Crocker, 1981). **Schemas** are sets of rules or features that represent what we know about categories of objects or events in general.

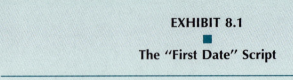

EXHIBIT 8.1

■

The "First Date" Script

Male arrives (55%). Female greets male at the door (33%). Conversation (43%). Introduce male to parents (or roommates) and leave the house (36%).

"Small talk" about common interests (33%). Go to a movie (43%). Go get something to eat or drink (23%).

Male takes female home (65%). Talk about the evening (27%). Male asks to call again (53%). Kiss (71%). Say goodnight and thank date for the evening (34%). Male returns home (25%).

Note: Parentheses = percentage of students who included item in their description of a first date.
From Pryor & Merluzzi, 1985.

Scripts and Roles

The schema for actions and events associated with particular social situations is known as a **script** (Abelson, 1981). Scripts are generalized representations of common events that tell us what to expect to find in that situation and how to expect people to behave. Scripts include *role schemas,* rules for the parts various people are expected to play in that particular setting. For instance, the role of passenger on an airplane is quite different from the role of pilot or flight attendant. Passengers, for example, are expected to stay seated with their seatbelts on for most of the flight, whereas attendants move around a great deal and serve the seated passengers. Passengers are not expected to go into the cockpit (except by special invitation). If a passenger got out of his seat while the "fasten seatbelt" sign was still lit, helped himself to a cup of coffee from the galley, and then went into the cockpit to chat with the pilot and navigator, this would be quite shocking. Such behavior would seriously violate our "airplane script." Over a lifetime, we acquire many scripts for common social situations, such as how to behave in a restaurant or what to expect on a first date (Exhibit 8.1).

Scripts not only help us to organize our behavior in new situations but they also influence our memory for events in those settings. Bower, Black, and Turner (1979) wrote a series of basic scripts (action sequences) for a number of routine situations (for example, shopping at a grocery store, attending a lecture, visiting a doctor, eating at a restaurant). They then had students read a series of short "stories," describing individuals engaging in these scripted activities. In later tests of their memory for the content of these stories, readers often inserted actions that were consistent with the script but had not actually appeared in the story. For instance, they "remembered" that the customer at the restaurant had ordered food from a menu, even though that was never actually mentioned in the story. Scripts help us to fill in details in our memory for events, even when they never actually occurred.

Person Schemas

Social cognition researchers have been particularly interested in the schemas we develop to represent our experiences with types of people and social groups. At the most general level, we have schemas representing general personality dispositions **(traits)** and broad social categories **(stereotypes);** at more specific levels, we have schemas for particular personality types **(prototypes)** and for specific individuals (including oneself). The structure and content of these schemas influence the impressions we form of people, especially on first meeting.

Implicit personality theories are based on traits and their relationships: See Chapter 7.

Traits.   Trait concepts and their relationships form the basis for implicit personality theories. Personality traits are schemas in the sense that they represent the common elements of general categories of behaviors. Behaviors that are superficially very different may all be grouped together as representations of a single trait concept. For instance, returning a lost wallet, telling the truth, and avoiding cheating on an exam are all representations of the generic trait of *honesty.*

These general trait concepts help us organize information we receive about specific behaviors of particular individuals. The influence of general trait schemas on our perception and memory for individual behavior is illustrated by experiments in person memory conducted by Cantor and Mischel (1977). In one of their studies, participants were presented with a description of a specific person. The person described was characterized either by traits associated with the general concept of *extroversion* (for example, impulsive, entertaining, friendly) or by traits associated with *introversion* (discreet, unsocial, oversensitive). Later they were given a new list of traits and asked which ones they recognized as having been presented earlier. In this test, participants gave relatively high recognition ratings to items that had not actually been presented but were closely related to the concept of an extrovert or introvert (such as boisterous or timid). As with scripts, once the target person had been classified as an introvert or extrovert, the trait schema was used to fill in memory for information about that person.

Stereotyping of social groups has a number of consequences: See Chapter 23.

Stereotypes.   In addition to categorizing behaviors in terms of personality traits, we also classify people according to broad social categories such as ethnicity, gender, and religion. The attributes that are associated with these general categories are our **social stereotypes.** The concept of stereotypes was first applied to social and political ideas by journalist Walter Lippman (1922), who characterized them as "pictures in our head" of various social groups. Categorization and stereotyping of social groups have a number of consequences, but here we are interested in stereotypes as examples of social schemas that we apply when we are processing information about a specific person. In the case of *Price Waterhouse v. Hopkins,* for instance, the federal judge concluded that the partners' decision to refuse to make Ann Hopkins a partner in the firm was influenced by social stereotyping based on sex (Fiske et al., 1991).

Much of the research on social stereotypes has been concerned with identifying the content of stereotypes that are shared by members of a culture about particular groups. In a classic study, Katz and Braly (1933) investigated the beliefs held by U.S. college students about various ethnic and nationality groups. From a long list of personality traits, students were asked to check those that were char-

TABLE 8.1

■

Gender Stereotypes: Masculine Competency and Feminine Warmth

Masculine Traits

POSITIVE	NEGATIVE
Aggressive	Uses harsh language
Independent	Blunt
Objective	Rough
Dominant	Unaware of others' feelings
Active	Sloppy
Competitive	Unexpressive
Logical	
Worldly	
Direct	
Adventurous	
Decisive	
Self-confident	
Ambitious	

Feminine Traits

POSITIVE	NEGATIVE
Talkative	Dependent
Tactful	Emotional
Gentle	Subjective
Aware of others' feelings	Submissive
Religious	Passive
Neat	Illogical
Expressive	Unworldly
	Sneaky
	Feelings easily hurt
	Indecisive
	Cries easily
	Not self-confident

From Broverman et al., 1972.

acteristic of members of each of the specified groups. Culturally shared stereotypes were defined as those traits checked by the majority of respondents in connection with a particular group. By this criterion, white stereotypes of blacks (in 1933) included the traits "superstitious," "lazy," and "happy-go-lucky," whereas the stereotype of Germans consisted of "industrious," "scientifically minded," and "stolid."

Similar methods have been applied to the specification of shared **gender stereotypes**—those characteristics on which men and women are perceived to be most different. In general, traits associated with females are related to social warmth and expressiveness, while those associated with males are related to com-

Our images of old people are subdivided into distinctive prototypes. ■

petence and power (Broverman, Vogel, Broverman, Clarkson, & Rosenkrantz, 1972) (Table 8.1).

Eagly (1987) has suggested that the content of these stereotypes is shaped by the different social roles that men and women usually play in our society. Since women are more often seen in the role of caregiver and men more often in the role of leader or administrator, the personality traits associated with gender categories are the same as those associated with different role schemas. Another source of gender stereotypes may be differences between men and women in facial features. From research on impression formation we know that "baby-faced" adults are perceived as warmer and less powerful than those with more mature faces. Since women, on average, have more babyish faces than men, Friedman and Zebrowitz (1992) argue that our common stereotypes about men and women may be derived from stereotypes of physical features.

The availability of category stereotypes may lead to hasty judgments about persons who are members of the category (Hamilton, Sherman, & Ruvolo, 1990). Once we have made a categorization, we may base further judgments and decisions on our schemas and feelings about the category itself and ignore other, more specific information that may be available in the situation (Fiske & Pavelchak, 1986). For instance, learning that an individual has AIDS leads some people to treat that individual as a homosexual, even though other information indicates that his contracting the disease had nothing to do with sexual orientation (Pryor, Reeder, & McManus, 1991).

Person Types. Social categories such as gender and ethnicity tend to be very broad. Thus, stereotypes are rather abstract. At a more specific and concrete level, we have schemas associated with particular personality types, persons who are seen to be similar in disposition, values, and habits. The mental representation of such personality types is a **prototype,** a related set of features that typifies what is distinctive about that kind of person. Prototypes represent generic concepts like "preppie," "skinhead," "women's libber" and "dirty old man." They may also represent general social roles, such as "mother," physician," and "used car salesman." Thanks to movies and television, we probably share thousands of such prototype schemas in our culture.

According to research by Cantor and Mischel (1979), person types are hierarchically organized, with general types, such as "cultured person," subdivided into more specific schemas, such as "gourmet" or "patron of the arts." Brewer, Dull, and Lui (1981) also found support for a hierarchical structure in which the broad social category of "old people" was differentiated into distinctive subtypes, such as "grandmotherly old ladies," "elder statesmen," and "senior citizens." Specific subtypes have also been identified for racial stereotypes (Devine & Baker, 1991) and occupational stereotypes, such as police (Hewstone, Hopkins, & Routh, 1992). Brewer and her colleagues also demonstrated that such subtypes are associated with *visual images,* that is, physical features and characteristics, as well as traits and behaviors. Because prototypes are concrete and rich in detail, they have a powerful organizing effect on our processing of information about new persons.

■ ■ ■ SCHEMA ACCESSIBILITY

With all of the schemas we have available to represent our past experiences with persons and social situations, how do we determine which one to apply in a new situation? After all, it would not do if we pulled out our "airplane" script when we were on our way to have dinner in a fancy restaurant (on land). The question of which schemas are actually used in processing new information is a matter of **schema accessibility,** which is determined in part by factors in the environment and in part by factors internal to the perceiver.

External Factors

Sometimes we apply a particular schema to a new situation because we have been explicitly instructed to do so. When a mother tells her children that "we are having company tonight so be on your good behavior," she is instructing them to use their "company manners" script and to characterize the visitors as "company." In most situations, however, we have to infer the appropriate schemas on our own.

Situational Cues. The reason we do not usually misapply the airplane script when we go into a restaurant is that there are plenty of cues in the situation that tell us which script is appropriate. For one thing, there is usually a sign on the building that says "Restaurant," which definitely helps to call up the correct schema. But even in the absence of clear labels, we can usually identify situations or settings based on resemblance to similar situations in the past. Even without a sign on the door, most of us could tell from situational cues alone whether we were in a doctor's office or a nightclub. Once a situation has been identified, the relevant scripts and role schemas are usually obvious.

Person Categories. Person categories, as well as situations, are often associated with distinctive cues. Clothes, such as a jogging outfit, are sometimes sufficient to make specific prototypes (such as "athlete" or "fitness nut") accessible. Some social categories, such as gender, age, and race, are associated with physical features that are visually obvious. Such categories are particularly likely to be accessed when the associated cues are made salient, or prominent, by virtue of being unusual—for example, two females in a room full of men or a solo black on an otherwise all-white work team (Taylor, 1981a). Category stereotypes also become salient when category membership corresponds to other group distinctions, for example, when all the men in an office are executives and all the women are secretaries (Oakes, Turner, & Haslam, 1991).

Internal Factors

Unambiguous cues that activate appropriate schemas are not always available in new situations. When situations are complex or uncertain, the perceiver's own expectations, needs, and values will determine what schemas are most accessible. It was these internal factors that most interested the researchers in the "new look" school (Bruner, 1957).

Recent Experience. In one experiment, Bruner and Minturn (1955) asked participants to identify symbols that were flashed briefly on a screen. One of the symbols presented was a broken capital "13". This symbol is ambiguous in that it could be perceived as either the letter "b" or the number "13." When participants had previously been exposed to a series of letters, they quickly identified this symbol as a "b," but when the previous symbols had been numbers, they were just as quick to perceive it as "13." Recent experience with letters or numbers created expectancies that "primed" the participants to use particular schemas for interpreting the new symbol.

Such **priming effects** have been demonstrated for social schema as well. In a typical priming experiment, participants are first given a nonsocial task of some kind during which they are exposed to a selected schema, such as a trait construct. In an experiment by Higgins, Rholes, and Jones (1977), for instance, the priming task was to hold certain "memory words" in mind while performing a color-naming task. The memory words were adjectives selected to represent a particular positive or negative trait concept (for example, adventurous, self-confident, independent; or reckless, conceited, aloof). In a second experiment (which they believed to be unrelated to the first task), participants took part in an impression formation study in which they were given a description of a person called Donald (Exhibit 8.2). Donald was described by a set of statements about his behaviors and attitudes. The statements were somewhat ambiguously related to the primed words. They could be interpreted in either positive or negative ways. For instance, the statement that Donald "was well aware of his ability to do many things well" could be classified as conceited or as self-confident.

The impressions that participants formed of this ambiguous Donald were strongly influenced by the content of the trait concept that had been primed in the earlier task, even though they were unaware of the connection. Those participants who had been exposed to the positive adjective set were likely to in-

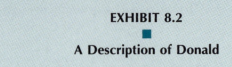

EXHIBIT 8.2

A Description of Donald

Donald spent a great deal of his time in search of what he liked to call excitement. He had already climbed Mt. McKinley, shot the Colorado rapids in a kayak, driven in a demolition derby, and piloted a jet-powered boat—without knowing very much about boats. He had risked injury, and even death, a number of times. Now he was in search of new excitement. He was thinking, perhaps, he would do some skydiving or maybe cross the Atlantic in a sailboat. By the way he acted one could readily guess that Donald was well aware of his ability to do many things well. Other than business engagements, Donald's contacts with people were rather limited. He felt he didn't really need to rely on anyone. Once Donald made up his mind to do something it was as good as done, no matter how long it might take or how difficult the going might be. Only rarely did he change his mind even when it might well have been better if he had.

Question: How would you describe Donald? Is this guy adventurous? or just plain reckless?

From Higgins, Rholes, & Jones, 1977, p. 145.

terpret Donald's actions in terms of self-confidence and adventurousness, while those who had been exposed to the negative set described Donald less positively. Further, when participants were retested fourteen days later, their memory of Donald's likeability was strongly influenced by the earlier priming. These effects of category accessibility on impression formation were replicated and extended in a series of studies by Srull and Wyer (1979, 1980), who demonstrated that traits primed on one day could influence impressions formed about individuals described twenty-four hours later.

Social categories can be made accessible through *subconscious priming*. In a number of experiments, Bargh and his colleagues (Bargh, Bond, Lombardi, & Tota, 1986; Bargh & Pietromonaco, 1982) demonstrated that primed trait adjectives can influence later impression formation even when the traits were presented subliminally. In one such experiment, participants first engaged in a task in which their assignment was to indicate by pressing a key as fast as possible every time a flash appeared on the CRT screen in front of them. Unbeknownst to the participants, the "flashes" were actually words presented so quickly that they could not be consciously perceived. Of the words subliminally presented in this way, either 0%, 20%, or 80% were related in some way to the concept of *hostility* (for example, "insult," "stab," "hate"). In a recognition test following the presentation, participants showed no conscious memory of the words presented. However, in a later impression formation experiment, their impressions of an ambiguous stimulus person were influenced by the earlier task. Those who had been presented with a large proportion of hostile words had very negative impressions of the new person. Such subliminal priming has been demonstrated for other specific traits, such as honesty and meanness, as well (Erdley & D'Agostino, 1988).

Personal Constructs.   Priming, whether conscious or unconscious, affects the temporary accessibility of stored schemas. Srull and Wyer (1980) found that primed concepts could still influence impressions formed within twenty-four hours of the priming task, but had no influence when a full week passed between priming and impression. Some schemas, however, are almost always accessible to particular individuals, whether or not they have been primed by recent experience. Zarate and Smith (1990), for instance, found that most people are very fast at classifying an individual by sex and race, and the faster the perceiver is in making a categorization by race, the more likely he or she is to use racial stereotypes in judging that individual.

These readily accessible schemas are similar to what Kelly (1955) called **personal constructs,** the traits or types that an individual characteristically uses most often in understanding and evaluating other people. A study by Higgins, King, and Mavin (1982) assessed individual differences in construct accessibility by analyzing the traits and characteristics that appeared in respondents' free descriptions of themselves and acquaintances. A concept was defined as accessible if it recurred in a particular respondent's description of several different people. Using this method, the researchers found considerable differences among perceivers in their use of trait concepts. For instance, for many individuals the concept "humorous" was highly accessible, while for others this trait never appeared in their descriptions. Similarly, "intelligent" or "friendly" are readily accessible traits for some perceivers but not for others.

The personal constructs that are most accessible to us affect how we interpret information about a new person in impression formation tasks (Bargh et al., 1986; Higgins et al, 1982). So, for example, if honesty is a highly accessible construct, we will interpret ambiguous information about a new person in terms of whether it appears to suggest honesty or dishonesty. However, if intelligence is a more important personal construct, we may interpret the same information in terms of whether the person is smart or stupid.

One of the factors that determines the chronic accessibility of person schemas is the perceiver's own self-concept. In their assessment of personal constructs, Higgins and his colleagues found considerable overlap between the terms respondents used to describe themselves and the traits they assigned to one or more of their friends (Higgins et al., 1982). Those concepts that are most central and important to individuals' perceptions of themselves have been called **self-schemas.** Traits for which perceivers are self-schematic are used for organizing and interpreting information about others as well (Markus, Smith, & Moreland, 1985).

One aspect of self-schemas that has been found to have strong influence on social cognition is gender-role orientation. Individuals who define themselves as highly masculine or feminine are *gender schematic* (Bem, 1981) and tend to divide the world into masculine and feminine categories. For these individuals, gender stereotypes are highly accessible social schemas. For instance, after viewing a videotape of a man watching a baseball game, a male who has masculinity as a central part of his self-schema will define that as a masculine activity, whereas a male who is not self-schematic for masculinity will be less likely to interpret the

Concepts central to individuals' perceptions of themselves are called self-schemas: See Chapter 11.

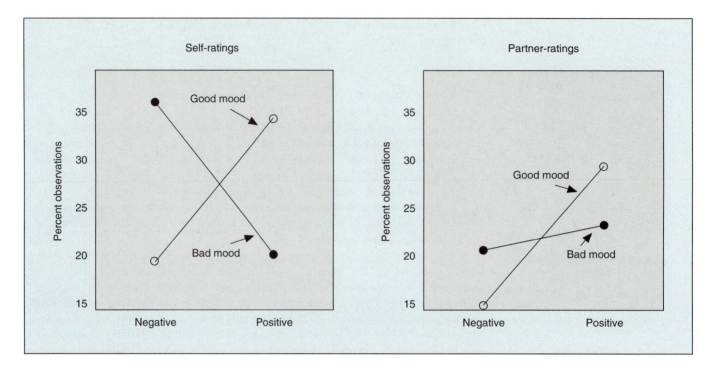

FIGURE 8.1

■

The effects of good and bad mood on the percentage of positive and negative acts identified in the social behavior of self and partner. (From Forgas, Bower, & Krantz, 1984, p. 504.)

videotape in those terms (Markus et al., 1985). These findings are consistent with the idea that our self-concept influences our perceptions of others because of its role in category accessibility.

Mood.   In addition to the more permanent personal constructs that influence our judgments of others, impressions are affected by temporary mood or arousal states. Stangor (1990), for instance, found that when participants were emotionally aroused they tended to evaluate other individuals in more extreme terms. Compared with nonaroused individuals, those who were aroused rated a slightly negative person more negatively and a slightly positive individual more positively.

Mood can apparently also prime specific trait categories that are congruent with one's current mood. Forgas and Bower (1987) created different mood states in their research participants by telling them either that they had done much "better" or much "worse" than average on a psychological test of social adjustment and personality. Following this mood manipulation, participants took part in a person perception study in which they were shown a series of descriptions of individuals and asked to make trait ratings of the persons described. The descriptions contained both positive and negative details, but the impressions formed by participants in a positive mood were consistently more favorable than the impressions of the same descriptions by those in a negative mood. Further, participants spent more time learning about mood-consistent information and were later able to recall that information better. Similar results were obtained in experiments by Erber (1991) in which mood was manipulated by exposing participants to happy or sad stories.

In a yet more dramatic demonstration of mood effects, Forgas, Bower, and Krantz (1984) induced mood states through the use of hypnosis. Participants were first videotaped during four different kinds of interactions with research confederates. One day later, they were hypnotized and instructed to recall events in their lives that would place them in either an elated or a depressed mood. Following this mood induction, they were shown the four videotapes from the previous day. As they watched the tapes, they were instructed to record each instance of positive or negative behavior performed by themselves and by their partners.

Judgments of the social interactions were strongly influenced by the individual's current mood. Those in the hypnotically induced happy state recorded significantly more positive behaviors, whereas those in the depressed state recorded significantly more negative behaviors (Figure 8.1). Studies such as these have important implications for our understanding of clinical depression. Once in a depressed mood, individuals may perpetuate their negative state by selective attention to depressive events and memories. People in a happy mood, on the other hand, do seem to view the word through rose-colored glasses.

■ ■ ■ SCHEMATIC PROCESSING

As Bruner (1957) conceived it, perception is the process of connecting new input information with stored categories. Schema accessibility is a critical part of this process because it determines which categories are activated in a new situation. The particular category that is activated then affects all subsequent steps in the information-processing sequence—what we attend to, how we interpret and organize the new information, and what we remember about it at a later time. The relationship between schema activation and schematic processing is represented in Figure 8.2.

Selective Attention and Recall

Usually, our stimulus environment is too complex and variable to pay attention to everything at the same time. Since our attention capacity is limited, we systematically "tune in" certain aspects of incoming information and ignore the rest. Only those features that are attended to (consciously or unconsciously) are *encoded,* or actively processed, and available for later recall. What we attend to is often directed by what we are looking for in the situation and what we expect to find there. These expectancies are determined by the schemas that are activated at the time.

Consistencies.   We can see an illustration of schema-driven attention in a simple experiment conducted by Brewer and Treyens (1981). They outfitted a small office with many objects and pieces of furniture, some of which were highly consistent with most people's schema for "a graduate student office" (a desk, folders, calculator, and so on) and others that were unrelated to the office schema (such as pieces of sporting equipment). Participants were brought into this office and left alone to wait there for approximately thirty-five seconds. They were then taken to another room where the experimenter gave them a test of

FIGURE 8.2

A model of schema activation and schematic processing.

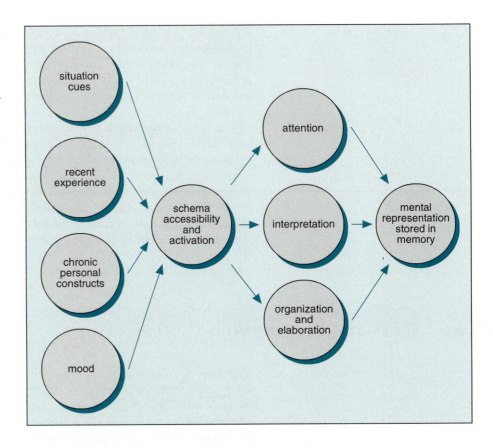

their memory for items they had just seen in the office. The probability that the students would correctly recall or recognize an item was highly related to its schema expectancy. Students also tended to "remember" seeing some items that were expected but had not actually been present in the office (such as a file cabinet).

The effects of schema-driven expectancies have been demonstrated for encoding and recall of social information as well as perception of objects. Cohen (1981), for instance, had participants view a short movie of a domestic scene in which a woman and her husband had dinner followed by an informal birthday celebration. Before seeing the film, viewers had been told that the woman was either a librarian or a waitress. Their later recognition for items of information about the woman's appearance and behavior in the movie was strongly influenced by its consistency with their prior schema. Participants who thought she was a librarian were more likely to recognize information consistent with the librarian prototype (wore glasses, played the piano) and were inaccurate in their memory for items consistent with the waitress prototype. Those who viewed the film with the waitress schema showed the opposite memory bias.

In another demonstration of expectancy effects, Rothbart, Evans, and Fulero (1979) established expectancies about a group of men. Some of the participants were told in advance that the group as a whole was considered "friendly and sociable," whereas others were told that the group was considered "intelligent and scholarly." They were then presented with information about the behaviors of fifty members of this group. Some of the behavior descriptions indicated

Would you expect this woman to be a good cook? Would you expect her to run in a marathon? ■

friendliness, some indicated intelligence, and some were not consistent with either personality construct. In a later test of recall, participants' ability to remember specific behaviors was strongly influenced by the behaviors' consistency with the prior expectancy. Behaviors consistent with the schemas that had been provided in advance were better recalled than behaviors not related to the expectancy. As with the Cohen study, schematic processing improved memory for schema-consistent information, but also reduced processing and memory for information that was not relevant to the activated schema.

Inconsistencies. Social schemas not only inform us what to expect in a new situation but they also determine what is *unexpected*. Much of the information that does not fit with our active schema is not unexpected—it is simply irrelevant. For instance, a tennis racket in a graduate student office does not fit our office expectancy, but it does not violate it either, so it tends to be ignored. However, objects or events that are incompatible with the content of our schema will be unexpected and, when they occur, are less likely to be ignored. If a police uniform was hanging in a graduate student office, it would probably provoke attention.

In their study of age-related social schemas, Brewer, Dull, and Lui (1981) found that the characteristic "hard of hearing" was not part of the "grandmotherly" prototype, even though it is not inconsistent with old age. Thus, when a grandmotherly type individual was described as being hard of hearing, this piece of information was not particularly well remembered. However, when an elderly grandmother was described as running five miles a day, this fact was very well recalled by most of the participants in the study. Such running ability is directly inconsistent with the expectancies about physical condition associated with most prototypes of the elderly. We take notice of such inconsistencies. Social categories facilitate the processing and recall of schema-relevant information, both consistent and inconsistent.

Under some circumstances, schema-inconsistent or unexpected information is remembered even better than consistent information. Hastie and Kumar (1979) gave judges a specific expectation about a target person's personality trait (such as honest). They then read a series of behaviors attributed to that person, most of which were consistent with the trait expectancy but some of which were irrelevant and a few directly inconsistent. The inconsistent behaviors were later recalled significantly better than the consistent behaviors (with irrelevant behaviors recalled least). Apparently, schema-inconsistent information not only attracts attention but it also generates extended processing and elaboration. In an attempt to explain or understand the inconsistency, we think about it in relation to other information and explanatory concepts. As a consequence, an associative network is established that makes such information easy to remember (Srull, 1981). Superior recall for inconsistent information does not occur if task demands do not allow time for elaborative processing (Bargh & Thein, 1985; Pratto & Bargh, 1991).

Confirmatory Biases: Cognitive Conservatism

The very act of using schemas to process new information helps to reinforce the original schema. This is because schema-based processing is generally biased in the direction of *confirming* prior expectations. Much of this bias occurs at the stage of interpreting the information we receive.

Interpreting Ambiguity. The priming studies reviewed earlier demonstrate that social schemas determine not only what we attend to but also how we interpret information that is otherwise ambiguous in meaning or implication. A good example of schema-based interpretation is an experiment by Darley and Gross (1983) in which college students were shown a videotape of a fourth-grade girl named Hannah. In one version of the tape, Hannah was shown in a wealthy suburban setting and described as the daughter of professionals (the "upper-class" schema condition). In another version she was depicted in a depressed urban environment, the daughter of working-class parents ("lower-class" schema). When participants were asked to predict Hannah's ability level in school based on this background data alone, they were reluctant to express any stereotyped judgments and guessed her to be average for her grade level in both conditions. However, some participants were shown an additional videotape of Hannah responding to questions in an oral achievement exam. After each response the examiner indicated whether the answer given was "right" or "wrong." The performance depicted on this second tape was ambiguous with respect to ability, since "right" and "wrong" answers were intermixed. Yet those who had previously been led to believe that Hannah was from an upper-class background evaluated this performance as indicating high ability and later remembered that Hannah had gotten most of the answers correct. Those with the lower-class schema judged the same performance as indicating low ability and recalled that Hannah missed about half the questions. Although participants would not express their schematic expectations in advance, the effects of their preconceptions showed up in their interpretation and memory of highly ambiguous information.

FIGURE 8.3

Subway scene used in rumor experiments. (From Allport & Postman, 1947.)

Interpreting new information as more consistent with a category schema than it actually is is called **assimilation.** A particularly compelling demonstration of assimilation to stereotypes was obtained in a classic study of rumor transmission by Allport and Postman (1947). In each session of the experiment, one participant was shown a picture of a scene from a subway station. In the center of the picture was a black man dressed in a suit in interaction with a white man dressed in casual clothes and holding a razor in his hand (Figure 8.3). After viewing the picture briefly, the first participant would describe it to a second person who had not seen it. The second person would then pass on the description to a third, and so on. In more than half the sessions, the description transmitted to the sixth and final participant indicated that the razor was in the hand of the black man rather than the white man, a perception consistent with prevalent cultural stereotypes but not with the actual picture.

The same effect of racial stereotypes has been demonstrated more recently in interpreting social interactions. An ambiguous act (such as shoving or poking) is more likely to be interpreted as hostile or angry when enacted by a black than by a white protagonist (Duncan, 1976; Sagar & Schofield, 1980). Assimilation effects have also been demonstrated with gender stereotypes. In job applicant evaluations, for instance, males with masculine background characteristics (for example, played on a basketball team in college) are judged to be more suitable for a masculine job (like sales manager) than female applicants with the same (masculine) characteristics. Conversely, females with feminine background characteristics are judged more suitable for a feminine job (receptionist) than males with the same profile (Glick, Zion, & Nelson, 1988).

Discounting.   Confirmatory biases often require attending to schema-consistent information and ignoring other data. However, we have also seen that information that is highly inconsistent with what we expect catches our attention and is difficult to ignore. Because it is novel or surprising, schema-inconsistent information is often processed extensively and remembered quite well. But instead of using such disconfirming information to alter our social schemas, we often find ways to explain it away. In other words, we **discount** the inconsistent data and leave our original schema intact.

An example of this belief-preserving process is seen in the results of an experiment by Lord, Ross, and Lepper (1979). Participants who either favored or opposed capital punishment were shown descriptions of two studies, one that supported the efficacy of capital punishment as a deterrent to crime and the other refuting its efficacy. Readers evaluated the study that supported their own belief as more methodologically sound and dismissed the other study as unsound. Moreover, those who had been exposed to the contradictory evidence wound up even more convinced of the validity of their original belief! In a more recent study, Echabe and Rovira (1989) found that individuals selectively remembered technical information that supported their preexisting beliefs about the causes of AIDS. But information that was contradictory to those beliefs was distorted in memory, and ended up reinforcing the prior beliefs.

Here is another example illustrating that receiving and attending to schema-inconsistent information can actually bolster the original schema or stereotype. O'Sullivan and Durso (1984) had participants listen to a tape-recorded biography of an individual who was identified by a label associated with a particular student prototype (for example, "jock," "brain," "freak"). The first two pieces of information given were attributes highly consistent with the prototype. These were followed by another trait description that was either congruent or highly incongruent with the prototype (Table 8.2).

Participants were later asked to recall as many things about the biography as they could. Recall of the initial two schema-consistent attributes was significantly better for those who had received incongruent information. In processing the inconsistency, individuals apparently recovered the earlier supportive facts and thereby strengthened memory for information that confirmed the prototype.

Discounting is often accomplished by the causal explanations we produce to account for unexpected or disconfirming events. For instance, when women perform well at a masculine task, that performance is inconsistent with expectancies based on gender stereotypes. However, if the performance can be attributed to extra effort or to "luck," then the stereotype of differential abilities is not disconfirmed. This is the pattern of attributions obtained in an experiment by Deaux and Emswiller (1974). When a woman was observed doing well on a task identified as masculine (identifying objects such as tire jacks in a hidden-object picture), her performance was attributed more to luck than the same performance by a man, which was attributed to his ability. Later studies demonstrated that the same biases operate in performance evaluations of men and women in the workplace (Heilman & Guzzo, 1978). In general, behaviors and outcomes that confirm category expectancies are more likely to be seen as caused by stable, internal factors, while disconfirming behaviors are attributed to external or unstable causes.

Discounting is often achieved by explaining away unexpected events: See Chapter 9.

TABLE 8.2

■

Illustrative Person Types

Congruent	Incongruent
TYPE: "PREPPIE"	
William wears alligator shirts and Docksiders	William wears overalls without a shirt
He is concerned about being in style	
TYPE: "JOCK"	
Bob is muscular	Bob is physically weak
He wears gym shorts to class	
TYPE: "BRAIN"	
Brad has a 4.0 GPA	Brad is vain about his appearance
He usually wears glasses	

From O'Sullivan & Durso, 1984.

We can also discount schema-inconsistent information by a mechanism called "subtyping" (Hewstone et al., 1992; Johnston & Hewstone, 1992; Weber & Crocker, 1983). When we come across individuals who do not fit a category stereotype, we may see that person as an exception to the rule who belongs to an atypical subcategory (for example, the aggressive career woman or the liberal Republican businessman). If these special prototypes are then isolated from the category as a whole, the category stereotype remains intact. Allport (1954) referred to this mental strategy as the "refencing device." When facts do not fit a preexisting schema, the exception is acknowledged but quickly fenced off from the original schema.

Reconstructing Memory

Once a social event has been processed and interpreted according to a particular schema, the judgments made at the time of encoding influence how we remember that event at a later time. Often we remember the judgment without being able to recall much about the information on which it was originally made. Thus, we *reconstruct* our memory on the basis of the impression we stored.

In an interesting study of **reconstructive memory** effects, Higgins and Rholes (1978) gave participants a lengthy behavioral description of a particular individual. They were then asked to summarize that information to another person who purportedly liked or disliked the individual being described. As expected, participants shaded their description to correspond to the audience's opinion. Later, their memory of the original information was found to be distorted in the same direction. For instance, the fact that the target had participated in three sports in high school was later remembered as "he excelled in three sports" by an individual who had earlier communicated a favorable impression.

Memory can also be reconstructed based on schemas that are introduced after the actual experience. For instance, Snyder and Uranowitz (1978) had participants read a case history of events in the life of a particular woman, describing her childhood, high school, and early career. After reading the narrative, some participants were given additional information about the woman's current life situation. Some were told that she was now married and living a heterosexual life style; others were told that she was now living a lesbian life style. A week later, participants were given a test of memory for details of the case study. The memory test consisted of thirty-six multiple choice questions, seventeen of which contained responses that were associated with the lesbian stereotype (such as "never went out with men in high school") or a heterosexual stereotype ("went steady with a boy in high school"). On these items, participants displayed a consistent memory bias, choosing those response alternatives that fit the schema they had been given.

Eyewitness Testimony

Reconstructive memory distortion has serious implications for the validity of eyewitness testimony (Loftus, 1979). In one demonstration of such effects, Loftus and Palmer (1974) showed students a film of a traffic accident depicting two cars colliding at an intersection. At the end of the film, they were asked questions about what they had seen. Among the questions was one asking how fast the cars were estimated to be traveling at the time of the accident. The wording of this question was varied, with some being asked, "How fast were the cars going when they *hit* each other?" while others were given more suggestive wording (for example, "How fast were the cars going when they *smashed into* each other?"). Those who had been given the "smashed into" wording estimated significantly faster speeds than those given the

John Demjanjuk, known as the "hangman of Treblinka," or as "Ivan the Terrible," was condemned to death by his judges in Jerusalem following a trial that lasted 14 months. When the verdict was announced, the Nazi criminal cried out, "I am innocent, God is my witness!" Later the death sentence was overturned. Many felt that testimony based on memories reconstructed from many years in the past could not be relied upon. ■

"hit" version of the question. A week later, they were also asked whether they recalled seeing any broken glass after the accident. There was no broken glass in the film, but twice as many respondents in the "smashed into" condition reported seeing it than those in the "hit" condition.

Obviously, there are limits to this type of effect. Witnesses who have seen an automobile accident are not likely to be induced to remember seeing an airplane collision. However, even subtle distortions of memory based on schematic reconstruction can have important implications, evidenced by dramatic and sometimes tragic cases of misidentification in eyewitness testimony (Loftus & Ketcham, 1991).

■ ■ ■ SOME CONCLUDING THOUGHTS

In order to understand a complex social world, we process new experiences in terms of knowledge built up from past experience. That knowledge is organized in the form of social schemas which create expectancies for the future. What we expect influences what we see, how we see it, and what we remember about it. This does not mean that we never see anything new or that our perceptions are inevitably invalid or inaccurate. Indeed, both the selection of appropriate schemas and the judgments we make are very much influenced by the data themselves. However, expectancies do alter those judgments, and every perception is something of a blend of the past and the present.

■ ■ ■ SUMMARY

Social cognition is the study of how perceivers form mental representations of persons and social events. Past experience is organized and represented in the form of social schemas, which influence how we process and understand new information and experiences. Schemas include representations of social situations (stereotypes), and person types (prototypes).

What schemas are applied in a new social situation depends on which are most accessible at that time. Schema accessibility is determined by external factors, such as the salient cues in the situation, and by factors internal to the perceiver. Recent experiences may prime particular schemas and increase the likelihood that new information will be interpreted in accord with the activated schema. Such priming effects may be subconscious. Individuals may also differ in which schemas are most accessible, depending on what personal constructs are most important to them. For instance, some individuals are gender schematic and more likely than others to process social information in terms of schemas of masculinity and femininity. Finally, temporary mood states may also influence schema accessibility in ways that alter perceptions of positive and negative events.

Schemas influence how we interpret new experiences in a number of ways. First, schemas may determine what we attend to and recall about a particular event. Information that is either consistent or inconsistent with schema-based expectations is more likely to be encoded and remembered than information that is irrelevant to the schema. Second, we use available schemas to interpret uncertain or ambiguous information. Our understanding of ambiguous events is assimilated to preexisting schematic representations. Further, information that is inconsistent or does not fit prior schemas may be discounted (treated as an exception) so that the schema is unaffected. Finally, our memory of past events may be reconstructed to fit current interpretations. Such memory reconstruction has particular significance for the validity and reliability of eyewitness testimony.

■ ■ ■ **SUGGESTED READINGS**

1. Bem, S. L. (1981). Gender schema theory: A cognitive account of sex typing. *Psychological Review, 88,* 354–364.

2. Cantor, N., & Mischel, W. (1979). Prototypes in person perception. In L. Berkowitz (Ed.), *Advances in experimental social psychology* (Vol. 12). New York: Academic Press.

3. Fiske, S. T., Bersoff, D., Borgida, E., Deaux, K., & Heilman, M. (1991). Use of sex stereotyping research in *Price Waterhouse v. Hopkins. American Psychologist, 46,* 1049–1060.

4. Fiske, S. T., & Taylor, S. E. (1991). *Social cognition.* New York: McGraw-Hill.

5. Hamilton, D. L., Sherman, S. J., & Ruvolo, C. M. (1990). Stereotype-based expectancies: Effects on information processing and social behavior. *Journal of Social Issues, 46*(2), 35–68.

6. Loftus, E. F., & Ketcham, K. (1991). *Witness for the defense.* New York: St. Martin's Press.

7. Wyer, R. S., & Srull, T. K. (1986). Human cognition in its social context. *Psychological Review, 91,* 322–359.

CHAPTER 9

ATTRIBUTION
The Social Consequences of Causal Perception

■ **Key Concepts**

Attribution theory
Internal locus
External locus
Stability
Controllability
Stigma
Self-attributions
Self-serving bias
Self-efficacy
Illusion of control

■ **Chapter Outline**

THE STRUCTURE OF PERCEIVED CAUSES
    Locus of Cause: The Internal–External Distinction
    ■ Causal Attributions and Negative Life Circumstances
    Stability of Cause: Expectations for the Future
    ■ Attributions and Success in College
    Controllability of Cause: Could it be Helped?

ATTRIBUTIONS, EMOTIONS, AND SOCIAL BEHAVIOR
    Anger: You Did It On Purpose
    Pity: You Need Help
    Manipulating Attributions: Strategies for Social Interaction

SELF-ATTRIBUTIONS: IMPLICATIONS FOR ACHIEVEMENT AND HEALTH
    Explanations for Success and Failure: Heads I Win; Tails I Don't Lose
        Depression Versus Efficacy

SOME CONCLUDING THOUGHTS

SUMMARY

Here it is Thanksgiving week, and the Los Angeles Rams are looking like the biggest turkeys in town. Coach Ray Malavasi has eliminated bad luck, biorhythms, and sunspots as the reasons why his football team has lost 9 of its last 10 games. Now he's considering the unthinkable possibilities that: (a) he has lousy players or (b) they aren't really trying. (Los Angeles Times, November 24, 1982)

While his mother and grandmother are chatting over a cup of coffee, six-year-old Billy comes racing into the living room, careens off the side wall, and crashes into an end table, causing a vase to fall on the floor and smash into bits. "Now look what you've done," screams his mother. "Go to your room at once!" "It was an accident," grandmother protests, "You can't punish him for that." "He should be punished," says mom. "He is old enough to know how to walk through a room without breaking things. He can't be allowed to get away with this sort of thing."

Bad things sometimes happen. When they do, it is rarely sufficient for us to know what happened; we want to know why it happened. Much of our understanding of social events is based on our analysis of the causes of other people's actions and their consequences. Particularly when events or outcomes are negative or unexpected, we ask ourselves why they occurred, and the reasons we come up with have a great deal to do with how we respond to those events.

There is considerable research evidence that people spontaneously engage in causal analysis of other people's behavior (Weiner, 1986). Unexpected outcomes or negative actions are particularly likely to lead to a search for causal explanation (Holtzworth-Munroe & Jacobson, 1985). More press coverage in sports columns is devoted to causal explanations of unexpected outcomes of baseball and football games than when the outcome was as predicted by pregame odds (Lau & Russell, 1980), and annual reports of corporations to their shareholders contain causal explanations mostly for business outcomes that are unfavorable and worse than expected (Bettman & Weitz, 1983).

Social psychologists are interested in the kinds of causal explanations people give for events in their lives and the effects these causal inferences have on their social behavior. The study of causal explanations in social psychology is known generally as **attribution theory.** This is not the study of actual causes of events in the scientific sense, but the study of *perceived causes*—the explanations that are generated by ordinary people in their attempt to understand their social world. In this chapter, we review theories and research on the types of causal attributions perceivers make and how these influence their reactions to another person.

Attribution theory also considers why people make particular causal judgments: See Chapter 10.

■ ■ ■ THE STRUCTURE OF PERCEIVED CAUSES

The first systematic analysis of causal thinking was presented by Fritz Heider, whose influential book *The Psychology of Interpersonal Relations* (1958) is generally regarded as the origin of attribution theory in social psychology. Heider believed that social perception is motivated by a person's need to have a coherent understanding of the world and to be able to predict and control the environment. It is for these reasons that people seek causal explanations for events, and are particularly interested in the "whys" and "wherefores" of what other people do. It is also for these reasons that causal judgments are sometimes influenced by the desire to have things make sense, to perceive the world as orderly and predictable.

Heider's analysis of implicit causal thinking made a fundamental distinction between causal factors that are located within the person **(internal locus)** and those located in the environment **(external locus).** As he put it,

> In common-sense psychology (as in scientific psychology) the result of an action is felt to depend on two sets of conditions, namely, factors within the person and factors within the environment. Naive psychology also has different terms to express the contributions of these factors. Consider the example of a person rowing a boat across a lake. . . . We say, "He is *trying* to row the boat across the lake," . . . "It is *difficult* to row the boat across the lake," "He has the *ability* to row the boat across the lake," . . . "It is sheer *luck* that he succeeded in rowing the boat across the lake." These varying descriptive statements have reference to personal factors on the one hand and to environmental factors on the other. (p. 82)

Heider further differentiated internal (person) causes into those associated with the *power* to engage in an action (ability, dispositions) and *willingness* to act (motivation, effort, intention). External contributions to actions were divided into environmental *difficulty* and the more variable factors of *opportunity* and *luck*. Weiner and his colleagues (Weiner, 1985, 1986; Weiner, Frieze, Kukla, Reed, Rest, & Rosenbaum, 1971) later used these distinctions to develop a structural analysis of perceived causes. Weiner's analysis (summarized in Table 9.1) provided a way of classifying causal explanations for events that has guided a great deal of research on attributions and their consequences.

Weiner began with Heider's primary distinction between the internal and external locus of cause. Then, Weiner noted that Heider's classification of person causes into ability and motivation and the classification of environmental causes into difficulty and luck reflect differences in stability. **Stability** of a causal explanation refers to whether it is a relatively permanent, unchanging feature of the person or environment or whether it is subject to change.

This analysis of the basic properties of different types of causes resulted in a 2 × 2 categorization scheme in which causes could be classified in terms of their locus (internal or external) and their stability (stable or unstable) (Weiner et al., 1971). *Internal, stable* causal attributions are such things as an individual's endowed physical characteristics (such as strength), abilities, or personality traits and dispositions. *Internal, unstable* causal explanations consist of changeable states such as mood, effort, or temporary disability. Among environmental factors, *external, stable* causes are enduring features of the environment like insurmountable physical barriers or social rules and regulations. Finally, *external, unstable* causal attributions are illustrated by nonrecurring events such as emergencies or chance factors such as luck.

Applying this scheme to causal explanations for achievement, Weiner and his colleagues classified alternative explanations for success and failure as (1) aptitude (internal, stable), (2) effort or exertion (internal, unstable), (3) task difficulty (external, stable), and (4) chance (external, unstable).

After working with this classification system for awhile, Weiner (1979) added a third property that could further differentiate among various types of causes. This was the dimension of **controllability**—whether the perceived cause is something that is subject to volitional control or not. Some internal states, such as laziness or sloppiness, are perceived as potentially controllable by the individual, while others, such as aptitudes and fatigue, are not. Similarly, some external causes (for example, economic conditions, teacher bias) could be subject to control, whereas others are regarded as essentially uncontrollable events (heavy traffic, weather, accidents).

The addition of this third factor produced a three-dimensional taxonomy of perceived causes that has proved to be useful across a wide variety of domains. Table 9.1 illustrates this taxonomy in terms of alternative explanations for two specific events.

By classifying causes in this three-dimensional system, we can see that causal explanations that are superficially very different may have underlying similarities. For instance, attributing a person's social success to her physical attractiveness and explaining someone's rude remark as due to his insecurity involve similar causal thinking. Both invoke causes that are internal, stable, and uncontrollable. Alternatively, attributing criminal behavior to lack of job opportunities and explaining failure as due to an unfair exam are similar in assigning causes that are external, stable, and uncontrollable. Each of the basic properties of causal explanation—locus, stability, and controllability—contributes in a special way to our interpretation of social events. In the following sections, we discuss each of the three dimensions of causal attribution, with an emphasis on their consequences for social behavior.

Locus of Cause: The Internal–External Distinction

The locus dimension has generally been regarded as the most fundamental distinction among alternative causal explanations for an event. How we respond to an event (and how we prepare ourselves for future reactions) is influenced significantly by whether we attribute the source of that event to the characteristics of some person or to the situation or environment in which it took place. Rotter (1966) identified this aspect of causal explanations as an important basis of personality differences, distinguishing between individuals who are inclined to view outcomes as controlled by internal causes and those who generally make external causal attributions. The internal–external distinction characterizes many life philosophies. The so-called Protestant ethic, for instance, incorporates the belief that success and failure are determined by forces internal to the individual.

Judgments of Success and Failure.   Our response to another person's success or failure is influenced significantly by whether we attribute the outcome

TABLE 9.1

■

A Taxonomy of Causal Attributions

Question 1: Why did Lenny do so poorly on his math exam?
Question 2: Why did Annette criticize Lenny for his poor performance?

Internal Attributions

	STABLE	UNSTABLE
CONTROLLABLE	1. Lenny is a poor student who never studies for exams	1. Lenny stayed out too late the night before the exam
	2. Annette does not think about how she hurts other people	2. Annette was trying to make Lenny feel bad
UNCONTROLLABLE	1. Lenny is a poor student with no math ability	1. Lenny was upset and made some stupid errors in the exam
	2. Annette is insecure and insensitive	2. Annette was in a bad mood

External Attributions

	STABLE	UNSTABLE
CONTROLLABLE	1. The teacher is a very tough grader	1. The wrong test was administered
	2. Annette's mother taught her to be critical	2. The teacher told Annette to evaluate Lenny's test score
UNCONTROLLABLE	1. Math is a very difficult subject	1. Lenny had an unlucky day
	2. Lenny's stupidity irritated Annette	2. Someone had just accidentally stomped on Annette's foot

to causes that are internal or external to that individual (Weiner et al., 1971). When we believe that achievement is caused by internal causes (ability and effort), we are more likely to give a person credit for successes. But we are also more likely to blame failures on the individual rather than on the task or other external circumstances. In educational settings, internal attributions work to the benefit of children who are advantaged in their early learning of basic skills. Early successes in school tasks are likely to be encouraged and rewarded by teachers who interpret them as indicators of innate ability. For children who are initially disadvantaged, however, internal attributions of inability or laziness may be misplaced.

Attitudes toward certain social
policies are related to racism in the
U.S.: See Chapter 24.

Causal Attributions and Negative Life Circumstances

Just as attitudes toward success and failure are dependent on judgments of causality, many social policy issues are influenced by our assumptions about the basic causes of negative life circumstances. Explanations of poverty and unemployment, for instance, can be classified as placing responsibility primarily either on factors internal to the individual, such as lack of motivation or poor judgment, or on factors external to the individual, such as societal conditions or general misfortune.

Such attributions are related to positions on political issues in general (Feather, 1984). Americans are somewhat more likely than Australians to give individualistic (internal) explanations for poverty, particularly those who subscribe to the Protestant ethic (Feather, 1974). In Great Britain, those who vote for the Conservative party rate individualistic causes as more important and societal causes as less important than do Labour voters in their explanations for both poverty and unemployment (Furnham, 1982a,b).

Whether we assign causes to internal or external factors has a lot to do with where we look for solutions to problems. For Americans, this difference in assignment of locus of causation sometimes leads to a conflict of values between the Protestant ethic, on the one hand, and egalitarian–humanitarian values, on the other (Katz & Hass, 1988). Feldman (1983) has shown that those who blame the relative poverty of African Americans on discrimination and other societal factors are supportive of special government programs to aid African Americans, whereas those who blame poverty on laziness or unwillingness to take advantage of job training opportunities are opposed to such programs. Basic beliefs about the causes of poverty and the work ethic may underlie contemporary forms of racism in the United States.

Stability of Cause: Expectations for the Future

Imagine that you have observed a performer on three different occasions successfully juggle six plates without missing a beat (or a plate). If you saw that individual again, would you expect him to be able to succeed at the juggling feat? Most of us would expect success based on past performance.

Now imagine that you observe someone toss a coin into the air three times in a row and all three times it comes up heads. On a fourth try, would you expect the coin to come up heads? Most people would not increase their expectation of getting a head in this situation (in fact, those subject to the so-called gambler's fallacy would expect the coin to be even less likely to come up heads again).

Why the difference? Why in one case do we generalize from past performance to the future, while in the other case we do not? The answer lies in the kind of attribution we make about the causes of the two different types of events. When someone succeeds in a task of skill, we usually attribute that outcome to *stable* attributes—the ability and skill of the performer and the nature of the task requirements. When the cause is perceived to be stable, we expect the same outcome to occur again and again. The outcome of a coin toss, however, is attributed to *unstable* environmental factors, so the conditions that produce a head on one occasion may not be expected to prevail on the next toss. Notice, however,

People who gamble often believe they have more control over the outcome of the game than they actually do. ■

how our expectations about future outcomes would change if we attributed to the juggler's successful performances to good luck and the three consecutive heads to a weighted coin.

When Do We Gamble on the Future?   Whether we perceive a task or game as depending primarily on skill (hence subject to stable causes) or luck (hence unstable) determines our aspirations and expectations for success. If a task depends on skill, we expect to succeed if we have the requisite ability and expect not to succeed if we are low in ability. Stable attributes such as ability, however, are irrelevant to expectations of success in games of chance. Nonetheless, when outcomes of a chance game go in one's favor, it is tempting to believe that such outcomes are predictable and stable.

Langer and Roth (1975) demonstrated this by having college students participate in a purely chance task of predicting the outcome of coin tosses. All participants played thirty trials, with fifteen resulting in successful predictions (wins) and fifteen losses. However, the outcomes were rigged so that for some participants the fifteen wins occurred early in the series, whereas for others the wins and losses were more evenly distributed across the thirty trials. At the end of the series, those who had experienced early wins believed they were better at successfully predicting the outcomes of coin tosses than other participants. Even though these college students knew that the coin tosses were chance events, their implicit causal explanations for initial outcomes were apparently more stable than they should have been. Research such as this sheds light on how gamblers can fool themselves into believing they can predict their outcomes in games of luck.

The stability of causal attributions enters into decision making in other arenas as well. Consider the situation in which a young man has been turned down after asking a particular young woman to the movies. Will he be likely to ask her out again? If he attributes her initial rejection to stable causes (she doesn't like me), most likely he will not. But if he makes an attribution to an unstable cause (she had an earlier commitment that night), he may be willing to try again. The past does not always predict the future.

<table>
<tr><td>

APPLYING SOCIAL PSYCHOLOGY TO EDUCATION

■ ■ ■
</td><td>

Attributions and Success in College

Wilson and Linville (1982) directly manipulated attributions of causal stability in a real-life achievement situation. They identified college freshmen who felt that their performance in their first year of college had been a failure. Some of these students were shown videotapes of interviews with more advanced students discussing their college experiences. During the course of the interviews, the students conveyed the information that school grading policies become more lenient as students progress through school, thus introducing an unstable causal explanation for poor grades in the freshman year. Students who received this information attained better grades and were actually less likely to drop out of school than students who were not exposed to the attributional manipulation. Apparently, once they had been given an unstable attribution for failure, students believed that success was still possible and were more willing to try again.
</td></tr>
</table>

Controllability of Cause: Could It Be Helped?

In the domestic situation illustrated at the beginning of this chapter, Billy's mother and grandmother were not in disagreement about whether Billy's activity level was the cause of the broken vase. What they were arguing about was the *controllability* of the cause. When grandmother says, "It was an accident," she is saying, in effect, that the action and its outcome were not under Billy's volitional control. Mother, on the other hand, believes that the cause was controllable, that Billy could have moderated his behavior and his impact on the environment.

Like stable attributions, perceiving outcomes to be controllable influences our expectations of success. In a series of ingenious experiments, Langer (1975) demonstrated that when a game has the trappings of a skill situation, participants behave as though the outcomes were controllable even though they are determined strictly by chance. For instance, in one setting participants were placed in competition with another individual (actually a confederate of the experimenter) in a card game. Each person was to draw a card from a deck of cards and, without looking at the card drawn, place a bet on whether his was the higher card. The confederate in this situation played one of two different roles. In the "dapper" condition, he was dressed in a nicely fitted sport coat and appeared confident and outgoing. In the "schnook" condition, the confederate wore a sports coat that was too small and appeared shy and awkward. Participants placed significantly higher bets on their own cards when they were playing against a "schnook" than a "dapper" competitor. Even though the opponent's personality could not have influenced the outcomes of the draw of the cards, participants apparently felt more confident, or more in control of their outcomes, when the competitor appeared incompetent (unskilled).

Controllability appears to be the most important factor that people consider when they think about the causes of events or actions (Anderson, 1991). Whether an event is attributed to controllable or uncontrollable causes influences whether we believe we could alter such events in the future. This factor is particularly important for how we react to negative events such as disasters or misfortune. If the cause of disaster is seen as stable but uncontrollable, there is little to be done but to prepare for its recurrence. However, if the cause is perceived to be controllable, we can do something to try to prevent it from happening again. Those who believe that social injustices are caused by external but controllable causes are more likely to be political activists than those who see events as basically uncontrollable.

Controllability in the Classroom.   The use of rewards and punishments in educational settings is also influenced by attributions of controllability. Weiner and Kukla (1970) compared teachers' responses to ability and effort as causal explanations for students' successes and failures on an academic exam. When students were described as making high effort (a controllable cause), teachers were more likely to reward them for good performance and to punish them less for poor performance than when effort was low. Teachers were least likely to punish failure for students with low ability (an uncontrollable cause). The finding that success is rewarded more when it is associated with high effort and failure is punished more when it is caused by lack of effort has been replicated in many cultures, including England, Germany, Brazil, India, and Iran (Weiner, 1986).

Controllability in the Courtroom.   Attributions of controllability determine the sanctions that are administered to those who commit criminal or civil offenses. While internal attributions are sufficient to establish causal responsibility, legal or moral responsibility (and punishment) often depends on whether we perceive the cause to be both internal and controllable (Fincham & Jaspars, 1980). Sanctions are stricter when failures are attributed to negligence rather than ignorance. In many jurisdictions, children are not held legally responsible for their actions because they are presumed not fully in control of their behavior or its consequences. Similarly, insanity is an internal, stable causal attribution, but its perceived uncontrollability alters our judgments of criminal responsibility and punishment.

Attributions of controllability also play a role in attitudes toward victims of crime. We do not usually view crimes such as assault and robbery as controllable by the victim, but certain behaviors—such as driving a flashy car or wearing an expensive Rolex watch—are sometimes seen as "inviting" burglary or robbery. Rape, in particular, is a crime that is often viewed as having been brought on by the victim (Borgida & Brekke, 1985), particularly if she is physically attractive (Kanekar & Hazareth, 1988). In general, we have less sympathy for crime victims if we believe they could have prevented the crime by actions under their own control.

Controllability and Social Stigma.   Our reactions to victims of crime are similar to other kinds of victimization or stigmatization. A **stigma** is any identifiable condition or feature that makes an individual subject to social rejection

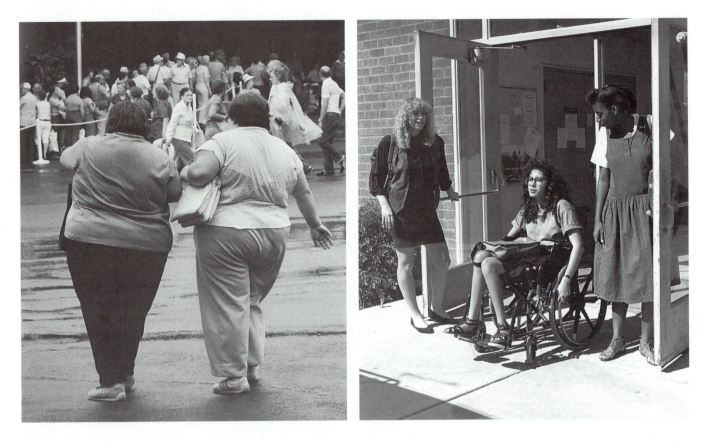

Physical handicaps and obesity are both stigmatizing conditions. But stigmatized individuals are treated differently depending on whether their condition is judged to be controllable or uncontrollable. ■

(Jones, Farino, Hastorf, Markus, Miller, & Scott, 1984). Like failure and other negative events, stigmatizing conditions such as physical and mental disabilities or aberrations give rise to causal attributions. Whether or not we attribute the stigma to causes that could be controlled by the individual is particularly influential in determining our reactions to such conditions. Among stigmatizing conditions, obesity, alcoholism, and homosexuality are generally perceived to be potentially controllable, whereas physical disabilities and mental illness and retardation are not (Weiner, 1986). Such differences in causal attribution are associated with differences in our attitudes toward those who manifest these conditions.

Which stigmas do we attribute to controllable factors and which do we perceive as uncontrollable? In one attempt to answer this question, Weiner, Perry, and Magnusson (1988) assessed college students' perceptions of individual responsibility for the onset of ten different stigmatizing conditions. They found that in general, physically based stigmas (chronic illness and disabilities) were believed to be less controllable than mental–behavioral problems (such as drug abuse). This was not universally true, however, since Vietnam War syndrome (a mental disorder) was judged to be uncontrollable (low responsibility), while acquired immune deficiency syndrome (AIDS) was perceived to be more controllable (high individual responsibility). Perceived controllability appears to be a part of shared cultural beliefs about the nature of particular stigmatizing conditions.

We may attribute the same condition to controllable causes in some cases and uncontrollable causes in others. In one study (DeJong, 1980), students believed they were about to meet another individual in a "getting acquainted" experiment. Some of the students were given a description of their acquaintance partner as an obese individual. The obesity condition was attributed either to an uncontrollable thyroid condition or to liking for food. Initial impressions of the anticipated partner were more positive when the obesity was attributed to an uncontrollable physical cause.

While a stigma that is perceived to be controllable generally leads to rejection of the stigmatized individual, uncontrollable stigma often has the opposite effect. In a laboratory experiment by Hastorf, Northcraft, and Picciotto (1979), participants observed another individual (a male experimental accomplice) work on a maze task. The accomplice was either wearing leg braces (a visible handicap) or not. The nature of the maze task was such that the physical disability should have had no relevance to success or failure. Nonetheless, participants gave much more praise to the confederate when he appeared handicapped than when he appeared nonhandicapped, although his performance was exactly the same. An uncontrollable stigma can lead to a bend-over-backwards attempt to be kind and tolerant.

■ ■ ■ ATTRIBUTIONS, EMOTIONS, AND SOCIAL BEHAVIOR

These examples of causal locus, stability, and controllability should make it clear that our attempts to explain social events are much more than intellectual exercises. According to Weiner's (1985) attribution theory, the perceived cause of an event determines the affective or *emotional* reaction we experience, which in turn determines our *motivation* to behave. In other words, causal attributions are important because they intervene between our experience of an event and a decision about how to act. Motivation is the engine that drives action, and attributions and emotions fuel that engine.

Anger: You Did It On Purpose

One of the clearest links between attributions and affect toward another person is illustrated by the emotion of anger. Anger is generated when we attribute a negative event to controllable causes internal to another person or persons (Weiner, 1985). Consider, for example, your potential reaction to having your foot stepped on by someone standing in front of you in a crowded bus. If you believe that the perpetrator was acting deliberately or carelessly (she could have controlled the action), your reaction is likely to be one of anger. On the other hand, if you realize that the individual was being uncontrollably jostled by the crowd, you are less likely to feel angry even though you may be irritated or annoyed by the incident. We do not have exactly the same reaction to pain when its cause is uncontrollable than when it is controllable. Whether we experience anger determines whether we respond to the situation with resignation or with aggression and violence (Betancourt & Blair, 1992).

The relationship between anger and aggression has been explored in depth by social psychologists: See Chapter 15.

An interesting example of the attribution–anger linkage comes from research on passengers' responses to airline flight delays (Folkes, Koletsky, & Graham,

1987). Passengers whose flights were delayed fifteen minutes or more were asked why they thought their plane was late in taking off. They were also asked whether they were angry about the delay, whether they were intending to register a complaint, and whether they would plan to fly this particular airline again in the future. The most frequent explanation by the airline for flight delays was "mechanical problems," but whether such conditions were perceived as stable and controllable predicted the degree of anger that passengers reported, which in turn predicted their intentions to complain or avoid the airline carrier in the future.

Similar effects of controllable attributions have been documented in educational settings. Brophy and Rohrkemper (1981), for instance, obtained teacher reactions to twelve vignettes describing students with classroom behavior problems. The teachers perceived some of the behaviors, such as hyperactivity and defiance, as controllable by the student, while other behaviors, such as shyness and performance anxiety, were not judged to be controllable. Teachers responded only to controllable problems with intentions to threaten or punish.

Pity: You Need Help

If we get angry when we attribute negative outcomes to controllable causes, how do we respond to others when we perceive negative events to be uncontrollable? According to Weiner's (1985) model, attributing failure and adversity to uncontrollable external or internal causes elicits our pity and intentions to help.

The link between controllability and pity was demonstrated in a study by Weiner, Graham, and Chandler (1982), who presented respondents with four different social situations involving some form of failure or problem (failure to repay a debt, committing a crime, failing an exam, needing to borrow class notes). Different versions of the stories varied according to whether the reason for the outcome was internal or external, stable or unstable, and controllable or uncontrollable. Respondents were asked to rate each story version in terms of their feelings of anger or pity in response to the situation.

The most important determinant of whether anger or pity was the dominant emotional response was the controllability of the causal explanation for the event. When the person's problem was attributable to something he or she could have controlled (for example, needing to borrow class notes because of skipping class in order to attend a party), the scenario was most likely to elicit feelings of anger; but when the same problem was caused by uncontrollable factors (needing class notes because of being out sick with the flu), the response was feelings of pity. Similar findings were obtained with ratings of controllability of stigmatizing conditions (Weiner et al., 1988). Conditions that were rated low on individual responsibility for onset were also more likely to elicit pity than conditions for which the victim was held responsible.

Other research has demonstrated a direct connection between perceived controllability of need and willingness to give help. Barnes, Ickes, and Kidd (1979), for instance, arranged for students to be telephoned by a classmate requesting to borrow their class notes. The reason given for the need was either low ability (uncontrollable) or lack of effort (controllable). The request was granted significantly more often in the uncontrollable explanation condition.

FIGURE 9.1

■

The attribution–emotion–behavior link.

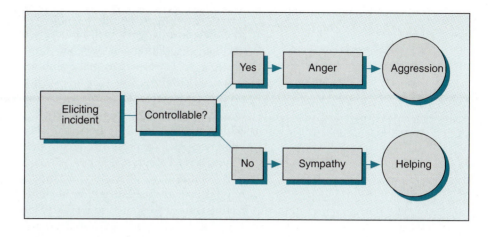

Based on these results, a number of studies have tested the full chain of causal relationships between attributions, emotion, and willingness to help (Figure 9.1). Across a wide range of helping situations and types of need, perceived controllability of the cause has been linked to whether anger or sympathy and concern is expressed for the victim, which in turn is highly correlated with willingness to give aid (Schmidt & Weiner, 1988) or to respond aggressively (Betancourt & Blair, 1992).

Manipulating Attributions: Strategies for Social Interaction

Since causal attributions influence our emotional and behavioral responses to other people, it seems reasonable that we should be concerned with how others interpret our own actions and their outcomes. One way in which we try to control the attributions that others make is the *excuses* we give when things don't go well. Weiner and his colleagues (Weiner, Amirkhan, Folkes, & Verette, 1987) asked college students to report on experiences in which they had broken some sort of social contract (for example, failed to keep a date) and to indicate the reasons they had given for the failure (whether true or false), along with actual reasons that they had not given. Excuses that were given tended to refer to external or uncontrollable factors (transportation problems, illness, other commitments); withheld explanations were primarily internal and controllable (I didn't want to go). Respondents also rated such explanations as being likely to evoke anger, compared with the explanations actually given.

Even young children display sensitivity to the emotional reactions evoked by causal explanations. Weiner and Handel (1985) asked children ages five through twelve to rate the reasons given for each of two social situations (refusing to play with someone and failing to show up at a planned meeting). Children at all ages recognized that controllable attributions would lead to anger and that internal attributions would lead to hurt feelings, and reported that they would be likely to withhold such reasons in giving excuses for the behavior.

Excuses are a direct method of attempting to control others' causal attributions, but sometimes our attributional strategies are more indirect. Jones (1989) has been interested in studying the strategies people employ to manipulate the perception of their competence and ability (stable, internal attributions). In attempting to make others see us as competent or talented, we face a dilemma. Direct strategies do not work well because self-promotion is socially unacceptable and encourages disliking and disbelief. Thus, individuals must employ more indirect strategies to get others to make ability attributions for their performance.

Jones (1989) suggests that one such strategy for inducing high-ability attributions is to deemphasize effort for past successes. Although both ability and effort may be necessary to good performance, we expect those with high ability to achieve more with less effort than those with low ability (Nicholls, 1984). By inference, then, a person reducing perceptions of effort should increase his or her perceived ability.

By withholding effort (or appearing to do so), people may increase the likelihood that their successes will be attributed to ability, while reducing the danger of having failures attributed to inability. Unfortunately, such strategies may backfire. Recall that lack of effort is also associated with more punishment for failures (and less reward for successes) than is inability. Thus, there is some question about whether people are better off being seen as high in ability (internal and stable but uncontrollable) or high in effort (internal and unstable but controllable).

■ ■ ■ SELF-ATTRIBUTIONS: IMPLICATIONS FOR ACHIEVEMENT AND HEALTH

Self-attribution affects attitudes and mental health: See Chapters 5 and 11.

Thus far, we have focused attention almost exclusively on the attributions we make for other people's actions and outcomes (or their attributions for ours). However, people are also motivated to generate causal explanations for their own outcomes. The results of such **self-attribution** processes have well-documented effects on attitudes and mental health. We touch briefly on some of these phenomena here.

Explanations for Success and Failure: Heads I Win; Tails I Don't Lose

The area in which Weiner's three-dimensional model of causal attributions has been applied most extensively is that of explanations for performance or achievement. In this domain, there is a consistent tendency for individuals to account for their own successful performance by internal factors (ability, motivation), but to explain their failures in terms of external, unstable, or uncontrollable causes (temporary incapacity, unfair tests, bad luck). In their reports to shareholders, business executives account for unfavorable outcomes in terms of external, unstable, and uncontrollable causes (market conditions, inflation, weather) more than they do for favorable outcomes (Bettman & Weitz, 1983). Following sports events, players and coaches make internal attributions for winning but are more likely to make external attributions for losses (Lau & Russell, 1980). (No wonder Rams coach Ray Malavasi was so distressed at the prospect of having to make internal causal explanations for the failures of his football team.)

In effect, we take credit for success but claim failures are not our fault. Such a pattern of attributions has been termed **self-serving bias** because of its obvious benefits for protecting self-esteem (Zuckerman, 1979). However, these attributions serve other important functions as well. When we internalize success and externalize failure, we are encouraged by our own good performance but willing to try again after a poor performance. In striving for achievement, this is an adaptive attributional tendency.

Individuals who do not exhibit self-serving attributions for success and failure tend to be at a disadvantage. Blaming oneself for poor outcomes (due, say, to inability) but attributing good outcomes to external or unstable causes discourages efforts to achieve, even in the face of past successes. There is some evidence that women tend to exhibit such attributions in areas of achievement that are traditionally masculine such as mathematics (Deaux, 1984). This may help explain why women students drop out of mathematics and science courses early in their educational careers, even when they have done well in such courses in the past. One's own past success does not predict future success if it is not attributed to stable, internal causes.

Because causal explanations for one's performance have such critical influence on future achievement, educational interventions have been developed to help individuals change self-defeating attributions. In a wide number of settings, it has been demonstrated that helping people to attribute failure to external or unstable events is successful in improving motivation and performance (Försterling, 1985). Similarly, convincing students that success is controllable and stable can improve educational achievement. In a particularly dramatic demonstration of attribution effects, Spencer and Steele (1992) showed that gender differences in performance on a difficult mathematics aptitude test could be eliminated if women students took the test believing that men and women scored equally on that particular test. Merely changing the expectation that the test would be more difficult (uncontrollable) for women significantly improved the women's actual performance.

APPLYING SOCIAL PSYCHOLOGY TO HEALTH

■ ■ ■

The illusion of control contributes to an individual's ability to maintain positive self-esteem: See Chapter 11.

Depression Versus Efficacy

The same attributional patterns that have been found to influence achievement motivation also affect our feelings of optimism or discouragement about life in general. The belief that negative events are uncontrollable and that failure is caused by internal, stable factors has been linked to hopelessness and depression (Abramson, Seligman, & Teasdale, 1978; Sweeney, Anderson, & Bailey, 1986) and with loneliness (Anderson & Riger, 1991). Those who believe that successes are internally caused and that outcomes are controllable are characterized by feelings of **self-efficacy** (Bandura, 1982) and are better able to cope with adversities (Taylor, 1983).

Indeed, in maintaining a healthy attitude toward life, it may be that a little illusion is better than too much reality. There is experimental evidence that depressed individuals are more likely to detect the fact that outcomes are being randomly determined, whereas nondepressed individuals persist in believing that the same outcomes are potentially controllable (Alloy & Abramson, 1982). This **illusion of control** may be one of many attributional biases that contribute to an individual's ability to maintain positive self-esteem and a sense of well-being (Taylor & Brown, 1988). Such effects demonstrate the potential power of causal attributions. In many ways, how we explain life has much to do with how much we enjoy it.

■ ■ ■ SOME CONCLUDING THOUGHTS

Impression formation and social cognition are based on subjective perception: See Chapters 7 and 8.

Social psychologists have long believed that we respond to other people, not simply because of what they do, but on the basis of how we perceive and interpret that behavior. The study of impression formation and social cognition reflects this fundamental assumption about the importance of subjective perception. Attribution theory has provided a systematic understanding of the processes of these subjective interpretations. Years of research on causal attributions demonstrate convincingly that our perceptions of the causes of an event intervene between our experience of the event itself and our emotional reaction to it. Probably more than any other theory in social psychology, attribution theory has found applications in all aspects of social life—from achievement in the classroom to justice in the courtroom to the maintenance of physical and mental health.

■ ■ ■ SUMMARY

Attribution theory is the study of the causal explanations people make for social events and personal experiences. Attribution theorists have investigated the basic structure of such causal explanations. Perceived causes can be distinguished in terms of three important dimensions. The locus of causality refers to whether an individual's actions or outcomes are attributed to something internal to that person (for example, dispositions or motivations) or to external factors (environmental or situational causes). Perceived causes also differ in terms of stability—whether they refer to relatively permanent, enduring factors (personal ability, social regulations) or temporary, changeable factors (personal effort, mood, or luck). Finally, causes differ in controllability. In general, individuals are held more responsible for actions and outcomes they could have controlled than for those perceived to be uncontrollable.

The causal attributions that we make about an individual's behavior have a powerful influence on our judgments about that individual and our decisions about how to respond. We react very differently to another person's failure depending on whether the failure is attributed to personal deficiencies (such as inability or lack of motivation) or external factors (discrimination, economic recession). Criminal sentences are affected by whether the cause of criminal behavior is perceived to be stable or unstable (temporary). Stigmatizing conditions, such as poverty, chronic illness, or disabilities, are treated differently depending on whether they are perceived to be controllable or uncontrollable.

According to some attribution theorists, the causal explanations we come up with mediate our emotional responses to events, which in turn influence how we behave. When negative outcomes are attributed to controllable factors, the emotional reaction is anger which promotes aggression. When negative events are attributed to uncontrollable causes, the emotional response is more likely to be that of pity or sympathy, which promotes helping.

Just as we make causal explanations for what other people do, we make attributions about our own behavior and outcomes. The nature of these self-attributions can influence how we feel about ourselves, how much we achieve, and even our physical and mental health. Of particular importance are the attributions we make about our own successes and failures. If we attribute good outcomes to internal, stable factors and bad outcomes to external or unstable factors, this is a self-serving bias which promotes a sense of efficacy and personal control. Individual differences in such self-attributions have been found to be related to differences in achievement and in depression.

■ ■ ■ **SUGGESTED READINGS**

1. Anderson, C. A., & Riger, A. L. (1991). A controllability attributional model of problems in living: Dimensional and situational interactions in the prediction of depression and loneliness. *Social Cognition, 9,* 149–181.

2. Försterling, F. (1985). Attributional retraining: A review. *Psychological Bulletin, 98,* 495–512.

3. Heider, F. (1958). *The psychology of interpersonal relations.* New York: Wiley.

4. Taylor, S. E., & Brown, J. D. (1988). Illusions and well-being: A social psychological perspective on mental health. *Psychological Bulletin, 103,* 193–210.

5. Weiner, B. (1985). An attributional theory of motivation and emotion. *Psychological Review, 92,* 548–573.

CHAPTER 10

SOCIAL INFERENCE
From Behavior to Personality

■ **Key Concepts**

Diagnosticity
Covariation principle
Consensus
Distinctiveness
Consistency
Base-rate fallacy
False consensus effect
Causal schemata
Augmentation principle
Discounting principle
Correspondent inference
Overjustification effect
Fundamental attribution error
Actor–observer bias

■ **Chapter Outline**

ATTRIBUTION AS SOCIAL INFERENCE
   The Covariation Principle
   Deviations From the Principle of Covariation
   Causal Inference from Single Observations
   Correspondent Inference Theory
   Attributions of Motivation
   ■ Undermining Intrinsic Motivation

THE PERSON ATTRIBUTION BIAS
   Person or Role?
   Why Do We Make Person Attributions?
   ■ Confession or Coercion?
   The Actor or the Observer: A Matter of Perspective

PERSON–SITUATION ATTRIBUTIONS: SIMULTANEOUS OR SEQUENTIAL?

SOME CONCLUDING THOUGHTS

SUMMARY

Emilda is ecstatic when she receives her American history term paper back with a grade of "A." Later she finds out that everyone in the class received an "A" on the term paper assignment, and her joy changes to disappointment. "If he gave everyone A's," she complains, "how can I know if my paper was really any good?"

Edward and George are discussing a mutual acquaintance named Bill. "I met Bill for the first time yesterday," says Edward, "and he is a really hostile guy. He insulted my buddy Joe all over the place." "Oh, no," George insists, "I've known Bill for years and he is usually very pleasant. Your friend Joe must have done something serious to make Bill mad."

In the preceding chapter, we discussed the kinds of causal attributions that people make for social events and the consequences those attributions have for emotions and behavior. But how do people decide what causal attributions to make? This issue is the second side to attribution theory and research. How do we determine what caused a particular action or social event? And how do our causal inferences relate to the process of forming impressions of other people?

■■■ ATTRIBUTION AS SOCIAL INFERENCE

Social inference is the process by which we draw conclusions about people from observations of their actions or behavior. The primary attributional question is whether that behavior tells us something about the *person* (internal causes) or about the *situation* (external causes). In the second vignette above, Edward and George disagree about how to interpret a particular hostile behavior by Bill. Edward concludes that the behavior was a reflection of Bill's personality. Having somewhat different information to go on, George is convinced that the actions reflected the situation in which Bill found himself, in particular the provocation by Joe.

Another way to put it is that Edward and George are disagreeing about whether the hostile behavior was **diagnostic** of the traits or states of the actor (Bill), that is, whether it revealed anything about his underlying dispositions or personality. In the first vignette at the beginning of this chapter, Emilda complains because her "A" has no diagnostic value. Since all papers received an "A," the grade does not tell her anything about the unique quality of her own paper (although it may reveal something about the disposition of the teacher who assigned the grades). In other words, she has no way of knowing whether the properties of the paper itself were the cause of the good grade.

The Covariation Principle

How do we determine whether behavior is diagnostic of (caused by) the actor's personality? According to Harold Kelley's model of attribution processes (Kelley, 1967, 1973), it is a matter of assigning cause to one of three aspects of a behavioral episode—the *person* (the actor or source of the behavior), the *entity* (the person or object in the environment that the actor is reacting to), or the *occasion* (the time and place in which the behavior takes place). In the behavioral episode "Bill insulted Joe," Bill is the person–actor, Joe is the entity, and the occasion is the context in which the insult occurred (for example, a cocktail party where everyone was drinking).

Ideally, to assign cause to one or more of these three sources we need to have information about **covariation** between the source and the behavior: We need to know whether the behavior occurs when the particular cause is present and does not occur when that cause is absent. To make such covariation judgments, we must have knowledge about more than a single behavioral episode; that is, we must ask whether the behavior occurs in the presence of other people, with other entities, or on other occasions. Figure 10.1 summarizes the information that is required to establish covariation between a behavior and its potential causes.

Establishing Covariation. Before we can attribute behavior to the *actor* (person cause), we need to consider how other people are behaving in the same situation. This is what Kelley (1967) calls **consensus** information. Consensus is high if most people are doing the same thing, in which case the actor is not uniquely associated with the behavior. On the other hand, if consensus is low (other people do not behave in this way in this situation), we are more justified in assuming covariation between the actor and the behavior.

To make an *entity* attribution, we must ask whether the actor behaves the same way toward other objects or persons. This information is what Kelley calls **distinctiveness.** If the actor does not behave the same way in the presence of other entities, distinctiveness is high, and therefore it may be justified to assume that something about the particular entity caused the actor to behave that way. Low distinctiveness means that the actor behaves in a similar way to many different objects, so the behavior cannot be attributed to this particular entity. Low distinctiveness is what caused Emilda's disappointment in her American history class. When she found out that the instructor responded with a grade of "A" to all papers, she could not attribute the good grade to the quality of her own particular term paper.

Finally, assigning cause to the *occasion* requires knowing how the particular actor has behaved at other times and places—that is, what is the **consistency** of the behavior? If the person does not usually exhibit this behavior, consistency is low and the action may be due to something about this particular occasion. However, if consistency is high (the same behavior occurs in other situations), the behavior should not be attributed to the occasion.

To return to George's and Edward's discussion about Bill's insulting behavior, Edward has made a person attribution to account for Bill's behavior. Perhaps that was because there was low consensus in the situation—Bill was the only one at the party who insulted Joe. George, on the other hand, was relying on additional covariation information. From past experience he knew that consis-

FIGURE 10.1

■

Establishing covariation: Using consensus, consistency, and distinctiveness information.

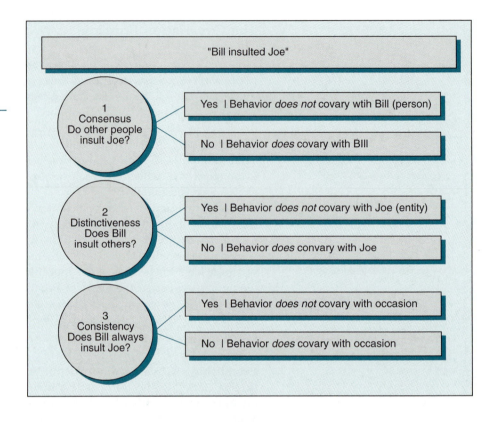

"Bill insulted Joe"

1
Consensus
Do other people insult Joe?

Yes | Behavior *does not* covary wtih Bill (person)

No | Behavior *does* covary with BIll

2
Distinctiveness
Does Bill insult others?

Yes | Behavior *does not* covary with Joe (entity)

No | Behavior *does* convary with Joe

3
Consistency
Does Bill always insult Joe?

Yes | Behavior *does not* covary with occasion

No | Behavior *does* covary with occasion

tency was low—Bill does not usually behave this way on other occasions or toward other persons. Therefore, he was willing to attribute the hostility to something in the situation—specifically to the entity, Joe. However, it might have been more appropriate to attribute it to something about the particular occasion. Perhaps Bill was unusually drunk that night. In either case, George doesn't see Bill's behavior as indicative of Bill's personal disposition.

The causal explanation that should be made for a particular social event depends on the pattern of all three types of covariation information. A person attribution is justified when consensus is low (few others behave the same way in this situation), distinctiveness is low (the person behaves this way in the presence of other objects), and consistency is high (the person behaves this way consistently in many situations). Such behaviors are diagnostic (they tell us something about the actor) because they occur uniquely in association with this person.

On the other hand, when consensus is high (everyone is responding in a similar way), distinctiveness is high (the response is only to this particular object), and consistency is high (the actor always reacts to this object in the same way), an entity attribution is called for. When consensus is high, but distinctiveness and consistency are low, it is reasonable to conclude that the behavior has something to do with the particular occasion.

Are We Intuitive Scientists?   If perceivers make causal inferences in accord with Kelley's covariation principle, they are behaving like scientists in their search for cause–effect relationships. For this reason, Kelley's theory is often referred to

TABLE 10.1

■

Covariance Information for the Behavior Episode "Ralph trips over Joan's feet while dancing"

Type of Information	HIGH	LOW
CONSENSUS	Almost everyone who dances with Joan trips over her feet	Hardly anyone else who dances with Joan trips over her feet
DISTINCTIVENESS	Ralph does not trip over other partners' feet	Ralph also trips over almost every other partner's feet
CONSISTENCY	In the past, Ralph has almost always tripped over Joan's feet	In the past, Ralph has almost never tripped over Joan's feet

From McArthur, 1972.

as the "naive scientist" model of causal attribution. But do people actually make inferences in this way? Are we intuitive scientists? The results of research on this question indicate that *when the information is made available,* perceivers do indeed make use of covariation in assigning causes for social behavior.

The first study directly testing the Kelley covariation model was conducted by McArthur (1972) using written descriptions of events as stimuli. Participants were given sixteen brief behavioral events depicting an individual actor's emotional reaction, opinion, performance, or action toward a particular stimulus (for example, "Ralph trips over Joan's feet while dancing"; "Sue is afraid of the dog"; "Henry gets a birdie on the fifth hole"). For some participants, the descriptions were given without any further information. For others, each description was followed by information about consensus (almost everyone else did the same thing or almost no one else did the same thing), distinctiveness (actor reacts the same way to other stimuli or actor almost never reacts this way to other stimuli), and consistency (actor almost always reacted this way in the past or actor almost never acted this way in the past (Table 10.1).

Following the description, participants were asked to choose among four different possible causal inferences about the event: (a) something about the person; (b) something about the stimulus (entity); (c) something about the circumstance; or (d) some combination of the preceding inferences.

McArthur's results indicated that causal attributions were influenced by the three types of covariation information. Consistency information had the most effect, with high consistency reducing circumstance attributions and increasing attributions to the person or some combination of the person and entity. Distinctiveness also had significant effects; when the actor's reaction to the object was described as different from his or her reactions to other similar entities, person attributions were reduced and entity attributions increased. Finally, knowledge about how other people acted in the same situation (consensus information) also reduced person attributions to some extent (but not as much as expected).

McArthur's methods and results have been replicated in numerous studies. Recent elaborations of Kelley's model provide even stronger evidence that people can and do use covariation information when making causal inferences (Cheng & Novick, 1990; Försterling, 1989; Hewstone & Jaspars, 1987).

Deviations From the Principle of Covariation

Although perceivers can and do make appropriate use of covariation information in their causal attributions, the studies just reviewed have revealed some systematic deviations from scientific cause–effect analyses. In particular, these deviations reflect the way in which respondents make use of consistency and consensus information.

Perceivers are biased toward a belief in others' consistency: See Chapter 7.

Other effects of expectancies of behavior based on the assumption of consistency have been noted: See Chapter 8 and 23.

Illusion of Consistency.   The impression formation research literature documents that perceivers are biased toward believing that other people are consistent. Knowledge about an actor's past behavior creates expectancies about future behaviors, based on this consistency assumption. When behavior is inconsistent with those expectations, we are more likely to make situational attributions for the new behavior than we were for the past actions.

The attributional effects of consistency were demonstrated in an experiment by Kulik (1983), who had participants watch videotapes of a male engaging in a conversation on two different occasions. For some viewers, the stimulus person behaved consistently in both tapes, either in an introverted or in an extroverted manner. For other viewers, the behaviors on the two tapes were inconsistent— one videotape demonstrated outgoing, extroverted behavior and the other exhibited introverted behavior. When the two tapes were inconsistent, behavior on the *second* video was consistently attributed to situational forces. When new behaviors are consistent with past expectations, a person attribution is confirmed. But when later behaviors are inconsistent, we make situational attributions that leave initial person attributions intact. Such attributional biases may account for the strong primacy effects in impression formation.

Failures of Consensus.   In McArthur's (1972) original study of covariation and causal attribution, she noted a tendency for individuals to ignore consensus information: Judges made person attributions for behaviors even when consensus information indicated that most other people in the situation behaved the same way as the actor. High consensus should lead perceivers to make situational or entity attributions, but instead most judges made inferences about the actor's personality. This failure to reduce person attributions in the face of high consensus has been obtained in many other research settings (Kassin, 1979).

The tendency to ignore consensus information in making causal judgments about an individual's behavior is sometimes called the **base-rate fallacy** (Kahneman & Tversky, 1973). When we make causal attributions or predictions following specific information about an individual's actions, we often fail to take into account information about how common that behavior is (Nisbett & Borgida, 1975). We can see a dramatic illustration of the base-rate fallacy in people's reactions to the behavior of participants in a well-known experiment by Stanley Milgram. Milgram (1963) found that almost 70% of participants in his experimental setting would deliver high levels of electric shock to another person under

A dramatic experiment by Milgram investigated compliance with authority: See Chapter 17.

orders from a scientific authority. Such a high rate of compliance indicates that the behavior is determined by the situation. Nonetheless, when observers are given descriptions of specific individuals from the Milgram experiment who delivered such shocks, they generally make internal person attributions for that behavior (for example, the individual is sadistic or authoritarian). Observers make such attributions even when they have been informed that the majority of participants in that situation obeyed the experimenter in delivering the shocks (Miller, Gillen, Schenker, & Radlove, 1973).

Another way in which perceivers sometimes misuse consensus information is to base their judgments of consensus on their own behavior in the situation. For instance, what do you think you would do in the following situation:

> While driving through a rural area near your home you are stopped by a county police officer who informs you that you have been clocked (with radar) at 38 miles per hour in a 25-mph zone. You believe this information to be accurate. After the policeman leaves, you inspect your citation and find that the details on the summons regarding weather, visibility, time, and location of violation are highly inaccurate. The citation informs you that you may either pay a $20 fine by mail without appearing in court or you must appear in municipal court within the next two weeks to contest the charge. (Ross, Greene, & House, 1977, p. 282)

When social psychologists gave college students at Stanford University this scenario to read, approximately half of them (46%) said they would just go ahead and pay the fine; the other half said they would contest the charge. The same students were then asked to estimate what percentage of other college students would pay the fine and what percentage would go to court. For scenarios such as these, participants consistently made high estimates of the frequency of a decision if it was the same decision they would have made in the situation. Frequency estimates were considerably lower for the choice that was different from the respondent's own decision (Ross, Greene, & House, 1977). This is known as the **false consensus effect**—a tendency for individuals to overestimate the proportion of people in the population who would think or act the same way they themselves do (Mullen, Atkins, Champion, Edwards, Hardy, Story, & Vanderklok, 1985).

Estimates based on the false consensus effect have implications for the causal attributions we make for others' decisions. When others make the same choice as we do, we assume this decision is normal (high consensus) and attributable to the entity or situation. But when others choose differently than we do, we attribute that decision to something unique about the individual. In a second study by Ross, Greene, and House (1977), students on a college campus were approached by the experimenter who asked them whether they would participate in a communications experiment. Participation meant agreeing to walk around campus for thirty minutes wearing a large sandwich-board sign that said "EAT AT JOE'S." A little more than half the students (60%) actually agreed to this request, and the remainder refused. Consistent with false consensus, however, the students' estimates of the percentage of other students who would agree was greatly influenced by their own decision (Figure 10.2). Participants in this experiment were also asked to make trait judgments about people who would comply with the request and those who would not. Students who had themselves refused to comply made strong trait inferences (person attributions) about those

FIGURE 10.2

The "false consensus" effect. Subjects' estimates of how many other students would comply with request to wear a sign. (From Ross, Greene, & House, 1977.)

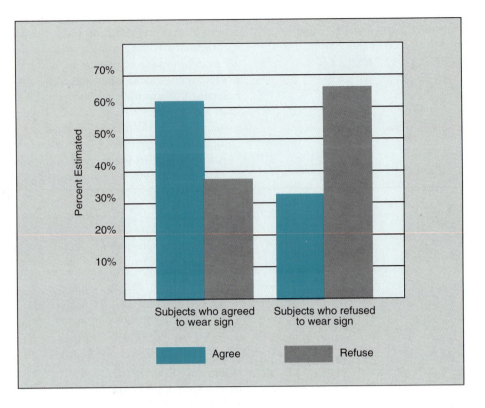

who agreed. Conversely, students who had themselves complied with the request made stronger trait judgments about those who would refuse.

In effect, our own behavior becomes a standard against which we assess the diagnosticity of others' behavior. Indeed, other experiments indicate that a person's own behavior has more impact on their causal attributions for another person's actions in the same situation than consensus information based on a large sample of cases (Hansen & Donoghue, 1977). Apparently, what we think is normal or appropriate behavior influences our causal inferences more than statistics about the actual occurrence of such behaviors in the situation.

Causal Inference From Single Observations

Use of the covariance principle in causal judgments presumes that we have relevant information about the actor, entity, and situation across *multiple* observations. Kelley (1973) realized, however, that we are often called on to make causal attributions based on a single observation of a social episode. Such one-time observations rarely offer distinctiveness or consistency information. Consensus information may be available, but we have already learned that perceivers often don't make much use of consensus in their causal judgments.

How do we go about making causal inferences when covariation data are absent? According to Kelley (1971, 1972), we rely on general rules we have learned about causal processes, which he called **causal schemata** (schemas). Kelley assumed that we evaluate the behavior *within its situational context* in order

TABLE 10.2

■

Attributing Cause: Person or Situation?

External Situation	Behavior Occurs?	Result
Facilitative	Yes	Discounting
	No	Weak person attribution
Inhibitory	Yes	Strong person attribution
	No	Discounting

to determine what possible causes of that behavior are available. We then use causal schemas to select the most likely cause or causes.

The most common causal schema assumes that either the dispositions of the person or the demands of the situation would be sufficient causes to explain a particular behavior. According to Kelley's analysis, which cause we select is determined primarily by our evaluation of the environmental forces that are operating in the situation. In many situations, certain behaviors are considered inappropriate or unusual. For instance, we know that a person is not supposed to burst out laughing at a funeral or to discuss his or her personal life at a formal dinner with strangers. When the behavior occurs despite such situational inhibitions, it leads us to make confident personal attributions about the actor. This is known as the **augmentation principle** (Kelley, 1971). The individual who laughs at a funeral is judged to be crude or insensitive; the guest who divulges intimate secrets to her dinner partner is neurotic. On the more positive side, when an individual overcomes situational barriers to accomplish something, we are more likely to credit the actor's ability and effort than if the same thing were achieved with no obstacles.

On the other hand, when we judge that the environmental forces facilitate the behavior being observed (when that behavior is normative or expected or easy), our causal attributions are more ambiguous. Because the action could reflect either the person or the situation (or both), neither cause can be assigned with confidence. This is known as the **discounting principle,** which states that the role of any particular cause in producing an effect is discounted if other plausible causes are also present (Kelley, 1973). When a rich man makes a donation to a Christmas charity while many people are watching, we do not necessarily assume he is particularly generous or kind. When the situation calls for such behavior, the action is discounted as a source of information about the actor. Table 10.2 outlines the role of perceived environmental (external) factors in determining whether person attributions are augmented or discounted.

Correspondent Inference Theory

The principles of augmentation and discounting are applied when we observe a person engaging in a particular behavior at only one point in time. Under those circumstances, we do not have covariation information to assist our causal inferences, so we rely on whatever information is present in the immediate situation. Another model of attributional processes proposed by Jones and Davis (1965) focused on this issue of how people make inferences from single observations.

Consider, for example, a situation in which we have just observed a stranger give a few coins to a homeless child. Now this certainly is a kind and generous act. But do we conclude from this one observation that the stranger is a kind and generous person? Under what conditions will observers infer that a person's actions reflect his or her personality? Jones and Davis call such personality judgments **correspondent inferences.** A correspondent inference is a person attribution where a behavior is perceived as being caused by the actor's personality dispositions (an internal, stable attribution).

According to the Jones and Davis model, correspondent inference depends on the degree of choice the actor was perceived to have, on whether the behavior is expected (typical) or not expected in the situation, and what effects the behavior has. When the behavior is perceived to be typical or required by the situation, it does not lead to correspondent inference. If our generous stranger was pressured by his girlfriend to give some coins to the child, we would be less likely to conclude that he is a kind person than if we saw him give the coins freely and spontaneously.

To take another example, suppose you observe a person open up a gift that turns out to be a hideously ugly lamp. Then she smiles at the gift giver and says, "Thank you so much. I have always admired lamps like this!" Do you immediately jump to the conclusion that the gift recipient has terrible taste in home furnishings? Not necessarily, because you realize that expressions of gratitude are expected as part of our rules of politeness, whether the recipient really likes the gift or not. This is equivalent to the discounting principle—if actions can be attributed to the situation, they tell us little about the actor's personal dispositions.

On the other hand, behavior that is not seen as required or expected does lead to inferences about the actor's dispositions. If the recipient of the ugly lamp turned to the gift giver and told him this was the most awful present she had ever received in her life, you would probably conclude that she is a rude and insensitive person. Since the behavior does not correspond to what is expected in that situation, we are more likely to perceive it as telling us something about the character of the person herself. When an action is taken despite situational pressures to do otherwise, observers are likely to make correspondent inferences from the behavior to the actor.

Some behavior is perceived as caused by an individual's personality disposition (an internal, stable attribution): See Chapter 9.

Attributions of Motivation

Another way to look at the person–situation attribution decision is in terms of attributions about the actor's motivations for behaving (Kruglanski, 1975). When behavior is not dictated by the situation, it is perceived to be *intrinsically motivated.* Behavior attributed to situational forces is *extrinsically motivated.* Intrinsically motivated behaviors are perceived to be freely chosen and predictive of future behavior in other situations. Extrinsically motivated behaviors are exhibited only when required to serve some other purpose. Attributing a person's actions to extrinsic reasons is a form of discounting.

Is this woman working on a personal project or doing a job? The same task is seen as more enjoyable if it is intrinsically rather than extrinsically motivated. ■

The distinction between intrinsic and extrinsic motivation is particularly relevant when we observe actions that take place in the presence of explicit rewards or punishments. If a child eats his peas while under threat of a spanking, we do not assume that he finds the food intrinsically enjoyable. If a person puts out effort knowing that she will receive a large bonus or lavish praise, we do not assume that she is getting intrinsic pleasure from the task. On the other hand, if there is little external reward to be expected in the situation, an intrinsic motivation for behavior is more likely.

APPLYING SOCIAL PSYCHOLOGY TO EDUCATION
■ ■ ■

People make judgments about the motivations of their own and others' behavior: See Chapter 5.

Undermining Intrinsic Motivation

We also make judgments about the intrinsic or extrinsic motivations for our own behavior, as well as for the behavior of others. This is the basis for what has been called the **overjustification effect.** When an individual receives some kind of reward, such as money or prizes, for engaging in tasks or activities that are intrinsically enjoyable, the external reward may undermine the intrinsic motivation to engage in that behavior. In effect, the presence of extrinsic reasons leads the actor to discount intrinsic reasons for the activity.

The overjustification effect was vividly demonstrated in an experiment by Lepper, Greene, and Nisbett (1973) with nursery school children. The children were taken individually from the classroom and asked to spend a few minutes drawing with felt-tip pens (a pleasurable activity). Some of the children were promised a special "good player" award (a ribbon with a prominent gold star) for doing the drawing, while others were told nothing about any award. A few days later, researchers observed all of the children during a free-play period in which the felt-tip pens were available for use. The children who had previously received no award spent twice as much time freely drawing with the pens than did children who had been given an award. The intrinsic enjoyment of the activity had apparently been reduced for the latter group of children. A similar finding was obtained in experiments by Deci (1971) in which college students were paid (or not paid) for working on interesting puzzles.

For both children and adults, the power of extrinsic rewards to undermine intrinsic motivation depends on the meaning they assign to those rewards. If people perceive the reward as the reason for engaging in the activity, intrinsic interest is reduced. However, if they interpret the reward as an unintended consequence rather than a reason for their behavior the reward does not have the same effect. In the Lepper, Greene, and Nisbett (1973) experiment, some children were given the "good player" award unexpectedly, *after* they had finished their drawings. For these children, the award had no detrimental effect on their later interest in the felt-tip pens. In this case, the children could not assume that the award had been their reason for drawing (because they did not know about it in advance), so they did not attribute the behavior to the award. Getting rewarded for good work does not always undermine intrinsic values.

■■■ THE PERSON ATTRIBUTION BIAS

Although there is often good reason for discounting people's actions as diagnostic of their personal dispositions, we do judge personality from behavior. In fact, we make such correspondent inferences far more often than we should on the basis of the attributional principles we have discussed. The tendency to make personality inferences from observations of behavior (whether warranted by the data or not) is so pervasive that it has come to be known as the **fundamental attribution error** (Ross, 1977). As social perceivers we have a strong inclination to overestimate dispositional factors as causes of behavior and to ignore or underestimate situational determinants (Jones, 1979, 1990).

One of the first demonstrations of the person attribution effect came out of a series of experiments on attribution of attitudes by Jones and Harris (1967). In these experiments, participants were asked to read essays or listen to tape-recorded speeches written by other students. Before reading or hearing the communication, the participants were told explicitly either that the speech writer had *chosen* what side of the issue to write about or that the position had been *assigned* without choice.

In the first experiment, the essays were supposedly from a political science course in which students were to write about Fidel Castro's Cuba (remember this was in the 1960s). The essay was either anti–Castro in content (the expected attitude among college students at that time) or pro–Castro (an unexpected position). Further, the essay writer had either chosen his position freely or had been assigned by the course instructor to write on that particular side of the issue. After reading the essay, participants were asked to estimate the writer's true attitude toward Castro. The resulting attitude attributions are shown in Figure 10.3.

The fact that pro–Castro speeches resulted in strong attitude attributions in the choice condition is not surprising. Freely choosing an unexpected behavior should lead to strong correspondent inferences (Jones & Davis, 1965). The same behavior in the no-choice condition, however, should have been discounted.

FIGURE 10.3

The fundamental attribution error: Attributing attitudes to others under choice and no-choice conditions.

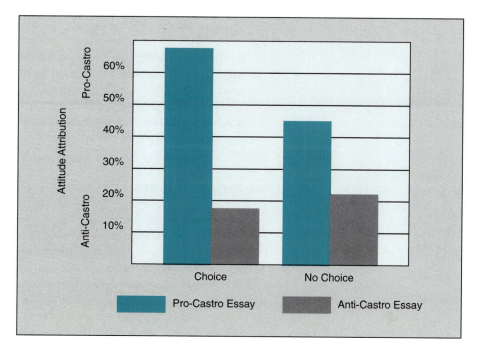

The content of the essay should not have been taken as an indication of the writer's personal attitudes since it could be accounted for fully by situational constraints. It should not have made any difference whether the essay was pro– or anti–Castro; the writer should have been assigned the same average attitude in either case. In fact, however, the different essays resulted in different attitude attributions even under no-choice conditions. This finding illustrates the fundamental attribution error.

Similar results were obtained when participants listened to speeches that were pro–Castro in a debate in which positions had been assigned or to speeches defending segregation that had been assigned as part of a psychology experiment. In all cases, the speech makers were assumed to have attitudes corresponding to the content of their speech, even when they had had no choice about the position they were presenting (Jones & Harris, 1967).

The tendency to underestimate environmental forces is so strong that it affects attributions even when perceivers themselves have been subject to the same environmental pressures. Snyder and Jones (1974) had participants write essays on positions that had been assigned to them and did not reflect their own attitudes. They then read essays that they had been prepared by other students under the same constraints. In rating these essays, respondents still tended to assign attitudes to the other students that were correspondent to the written essays, even when they knew from firsthand experience that the writers had had no choice about the content.

Ironically, situational explanations for behavior are often ignored, even when the meaning of the behavior is defined by the situation (Trope, 1986). In an experiment by Snyder and Frankel (1976), male observers watched a videotape (without sound) of a female being interviewed. Some of the observers believed they were viewing an interview dealing with sexual matters (presumably an anxiety-provoking topic), while others thought the interview was about politics.

The woman's nonverbal behavior was actually ambiguous, but she was rated as acting more upset and uncomfortable by viewers who thought she was discussing sex than by those who thought she was discussing politics (a typical context effect). Further, when observers were asked to judge the interviewee's disposition, she was rated as being a more anxious personality in the sex condition than in the politics condition! Having interpreted the actor's behavior based on the situation, perceivers then went on to make assumptions about her personality from their perceptions of her behavior.

Person or Role?

The fundamental attribution error is particularly noticeable when perceivers make inferences from single events, failing to take into account situational constraints or base-rate consensus information. However, it can also occur when we have multiple observations of the same person to base our causal attributions on. We have already mentioned the illusion of consistency that preserves many of our dispositional judgments about other people.

One reason why we see people as more consistent than they really are is that we see a particular individual repeatedly in the same situation or the same role. For instance, we know our grocery store clerk in her role as checker or our real estate agent in her salesperson role. Since people usually behave consistently when they are occupying a particular role, we have a strong tendency to think of the person as having the traits that go with that role (Ross, 1977). As teachers, we experience this all the time. Most of our students know us only in our roles as lecturer, where our behavior is constrained to be somewhat formal, controlling, and (in very large classes) unsympathetic to individual student needs. By the end of the academic term, these students often believe that we are uptight, unsympathetic personalities. Many would never recognize us by the way we behave at home or at a party.

Napolitan and Goethals (1979) demonstrated this effect experimentally in a study in which students talked with a clinical psychology graduate student who behaved in either a warm and friendly manner or in an aloof, critical way. Some of the students had been told in advance that the woman's behavior would be spontaneous. The others were told that in her role as a clinical psychologist she had been instructed to act warm and friendly (or aloof and cool). Did this make a difference to students' judgments of her personality? Evidently not. If she behaved in a warm way she was rated as a friendly person, and if she behaved in an aloof manner she was rated as less friendly, regardless of role requirements.

Why Do We Make Person Attributions?

Although evidence for a bias toward correspondent inferences came as something of a surprise to many social psychologists, it had actually been anticipated by Heider (1944, 1958) in his original presentation of attribution theory. He noted that despite the fact that events "are almost always caused by acts of persons in combination with other factors, the tendency exists to ascribe the changes entirely to persons" (1944, p. 361). To the observer, the person and his or her actions are inextricably linked; they are naturally perceived as a single unit. It is difficult not to view behavior as a reflection of the person even when we realize it is under situational control.

Language and Culture.   One explanation for the fundamental attribution error is that our individualistic culture makes us prone to person attributions because we hold individuals responsible for what they do. In a series of cross-cultural studies, Kashima and his colleagues (Kashima, Siegal, Tanaka, & Kashima, 1992) tested the idea that members of individualistic, English-speaking cultures such as the United States and Australia are more likely to believe that behaviors reflect personal attitudes, and hence are more subject to the fundamental attribution error, than are members of more communalist societies such as Japan. They found that Australian respondents did hold stronger beliefs in attitude–behavior consistency than Japanese respondents and individuals who held the consistency belief made more extreme attributions for attitude–relevant behaviors.

In another cross-cultural study, Miller (1984) asked children and adults in the United States and India to describe the causes of behaviors they had observed. Children aged eight to eleven in both cultures were fairly similar in their use of person and situational attributions, but with older groups, U.S. respondents made many more person attributions than Indian subjects. These results suggest that the emphasis on persons as causes of their own behavior is learned (or strengthened) as individuals mature within a particular culture.

The English language has an abundance of terms to describe personality traits: See Chapter 7.

The English language also promotes person attributions. We have thousands of terms to describe personality traits, but an impoverished vocabulary for describing the character of situations. Our sentence structure also places the actor as the subject (for example, "John broke the vase" rather than "The vase was broken by John"), which promotes the actor–action linkage in verbal discourse. The effect of sentence structure on causal attributions was demonstrated in an experiment by Pryor and Kriss (1977), who gave participants a series of statements to evaluate. The statements were either of the form "John likes the car" (where the person is in the salient position) or of the form "The car is liked by John" (where the object is made more salient). Respondents made more person causal attributions for sentences in the first format and more object causal attributions in the second case.

Salience.   Although there may be cultural differences in the strength of the propensity to make person rather than situation attributions for behavior, the dominant explanation for the fundamental attribution error is that it is a natural consequence of attentional processes. In actual situations or in descriptions of events, behaviors or actions tend to be more salient or conspicuous than the context (background) in which they occur. As Heider (1958) put it, "Behavior engulfs the field." Since the actor and behavior are so closely linked, our attention is automatically drawn to the person as the causal source rather than the environmental context.

The effect of visual salience was demonstrated in a series of experiments by McArthur and Post (1977). In videotapes of conversations, the behavior of actors who had been made visually conspicuous (by appearing in bright light, wearing a bold, patterned shirt, or engaging in rocking motion throughout the conversation) was assigned more to dispositional factors than that of actors who were less salient.

When one person is particularly salient in a situation, we tend to make more causal attributions to that individual. ■

What is most salient or attention-grabbing in a particular situation often depends on the perspective or orientation from which one views the event. Taylor and Fiske (1975) varied the position from which observers viewed a staged conversation between two actors. Some observers were seated behind actor 1, facing actor 2; some were facing actor 1; and some were seated midway between the two actors, not facing either one. The causal role that was assigned to the two actors was significantly affected by this seating pattern. When the observer was facing one of the actors, that actor was seen as more dominant and influential than the less salient actor.

APPLYING SOCIAL PSYCHOLOGY TO THE LAW ■ ■ ■

Confession or Coercion?

A particularly dramatic illustration of perspective effects comes from a study in which participants viewed a videotape of a suspect confessing to a crime while being interrogated by a police detective (Lassiter & Irvine, 1986). The enactment was taped from three different camera angles, focusing on the suspect, on the interrogator, or on both. Observers who saw the tape focusing on the suspect did not judge the confession to be coerced. However, those who viewed the tape with attention to the behavior of the interrogator (that is, from the suspect's point of view) were strongly aware of the interrogator's influence in the situation and more likely to judge that the confession had been coerced. These findings have particularly important implications for real-life decisions in the criminal justice system. Currently, when videotapes are made of actual confessions for the record, the camera is almost always focused on the suspect, whose actions then become the center of attention. Under these circumstances, the influence of the interrogator on the suspect's behavior is likely to be underestimated.

The Actor or the Observer: A Matter of Perspective

The effects of visual perspective take on special importance when we consider how individuals make attributions about their own behavior. There is a well-documented difference between how observers explain the behavior of another person and how that same behavior is explained by the actor him- or herself. In general, as we have noted, observers are inclined to attribute behavior to the actor's personality (the fundamental attribution error). By contrast, the actors themselves are more inclined to make causal attributions to the situation (Jones & Nisbett, 1971). This difference is particularly noticeable with negative behaviors. We are inclined to blame our own misconduct on the nature of the circumstances, even when others see it as a character flaw. However, the difference is found for positive behaviors as well. When an individual is cited for an heroic act, such as running into a burning building to save trapped children, outside observers give that individual credit for bravery and selflessness. But the hero herself is likely to say that she did it because the situation demanded it. You may consider this a case of false modesty, but situational attributions for one's own behavior are obtained for nonextraordinary, everyday actions as well, where neither modesty nor self-justification are necessary.

We can understand **actor–observer bias**—the difference in attributions—by considering the difference in perspective between the two perceivers. For the observer, it is the actor and his or her behavior that is the focus of attention. Behavior naturally seems to be *emitted* by the actor, its source. But actors themselves are rarely in a position to view their own behavior; for them what is most salient is the stimulus environment to which they are responding at the time. Behavior is *elicited* by the environment. The perspective effect was vividly demonstrated by Storms (1973), who showed individuals videotapes of themselves engaged in conversation with another student. Some saw the video from their original viewpoint (focused on the other actor), while others were shown the videotape with the camera focused on themselves (reverse perspective). Actors were then asked to make dispositional or situational attributions for their behavior during the conversation and for the behavior of the other actor. Observers who saw the video from the usual perspective exhibited the actor–observer bias (attributing their own behavior to the situation and the other's to dispositions). By contrast, those who saw the reverse perspective on the conversation reversed the attributional bias; they attributed their *own* behavior more to dispositional factors.

The actor–observer difference in perspective is particularly poignant in two-person exchanges where each person is the other's "environment." Many an argument has reached an impasse as each participant expresses competing explanations for what is going on. Actor A accuses actor B of being mean and hostile. Actor B objects, declaring, "You made me do it!" Whose perspective is correct?

■■■ PERSON–SITUATION ATTRIBUTION: SIMULTANEOUS OR SEQUENTIAL?

The evidence that perceivers are very ready to make correspondent inferences about actors' dispositions from observations of behavior has led a number of attribution theorists to modify Kelley's original model of the attributional process.

Recall that the principles of augmentation and discounting (see Table 10.2) assume that the perceiver evaluates potential person and situation causes *simultaneously,* with person attributions depending on whether the environment is judged to be facilitative or inhibitory as a causal factor.

The overwhelming evidence for the fundamental attribution error led Jones (1979) to speculate that dispositional inferences have temporal priority over situational attributions. This means that the perceiver initially makes a correspondent inference and then later adjusts that impression, more or less, as a consequence of evaluating the situation. This idea is supported by evidence that behaviors of other people are spontaneously interpreted in terms of traits (Smith & Miller, 1983; Winter & Uleman, 1984). For instance, if we hear or read the description "Mary went out of her way to greet her new neighbors," we immediately (perhaps unconsciously) define this as "friendly." Trait attributions are part of our initial comprehension or interpretation of the behavior itself, and since the behavior is closely associated with the actor, so is the trait.

Evidence for temporal priority of trait inference has led social psychologists to reconsider the nature of the attribution process. Instead of assuming that the perceiver considers person and situation causes simultaneously, attribution is viewed as a two-stage, sequential process (Gilbert, 1989; Hamilton, 1988; Trope, 1986). According to this version of attribution theory, the initial step of person attribution is effortless and spontaneous. In effect, the perceiver makes the inferential link between behavior and corresponding traits automatically. If the perceiver is occupied (engaged in a lot of other cognitive processing at the same time) or unmotivated to make any effort, the processing will stop at this point and the dispositional attribution will stick. Only if the perceiver makes the additional effort to process the event more carefully and extensively will he or she take situational factors into account. At this point the perceiver will revise dispositional attributions if situational attributions are judged to be appropriate. The difference between one-stage and two-stage models of attribution is illustrated in Figure 10.4.

An attribution experiment conducted by Gilbert, Pelham, and Krull (1988) buttresses the sequential-processing model. In this study, female students observed a series of silent videotape clips of a young woman engaged in a discussion with a stranger. In most of the clips, the woman's nonverbal behavior conveyed nervousness and anxiety. As viewers watched these tapes, they were furnished information about the situation in which the discussion took place. Half of them were told that the discussion topics were highly anxiety producing, such as talking about humiliating or embarrassing events in one's life, sexual fantasies, and personal failures. The other half of observers were told that the discussions were about relaxing topics, such as fashion trends, world travel, and great books.

While they were watching the video clips, some of the participants were kept cognitively "busy." They were given the extra task of keeping track of the specific discussion topics for later recall. Other participants were not given this extra task; they were just instructed to watch the videotape for the purpose of making personality judgments. Later, all participants were asked to make ratings of the trait anxiety of the woman on the videotape. According to the discounting principle discussed earlier, observers who were told that the video was taken under anxiety-provoking conditions should discount the anxious behavior. They should attribute less dispositional anxiety to the woman in the video than ob-

FIGURE 10.4

■

Attribution models. One-stage model: Person and situation are evaluated at the same time. Two-stage model: Person and situation evaluations are made sequentially.

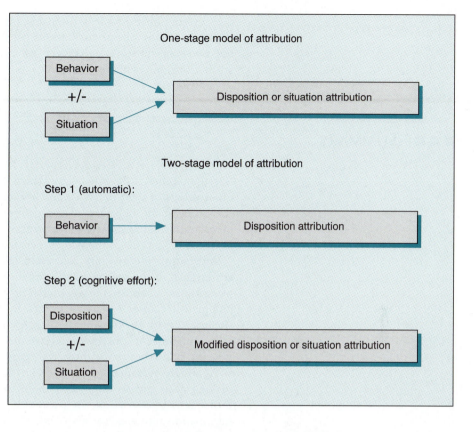

servers who had been given the relaxing situation information. This is what happened for observers who were not given any extra cognitive task. They made the appropriate situational adjustments in their ratings of the woman's disposition. When they believed the situation was relaxing, they made very high ratings of her trait anxiety, but when they believed the situation produced the anxious behavior, trait ratings were much lower.

Cognitively busy observers, however, did not make such adjustments—they rated the woman as moderately anxious regardless of the topic of discussion. Apparently, their ratings of anxiety were based directly on the evidence from the woman's behavior, because observers were not able to make the additional cognitive effort required to reevaluate the meaning of the behavior in the light of situational factors. A later study by D'Agostino and Fincher-Kiefer (1992) confirmed that willingness to make the required cognitive effort reduces the perceiver's bias toward making correspondent inferences. When individuals are motivated to understand fully the reasons for another's behavior, they can avoid the fundamental attribution error.

■■■ SOME CONCLUDING THOUGHTS

The sequential model of attribution helps explain many of the phenomena that have been identified in twenty years of attribution research. The model reconciles the evidence that people are capable of being intuitive scientists with the evidence that many of our attributions fall short of scientific validity. According to the two-stage process, perceivers can make appropriate situational and person attributions, but whether they will is a matter of time and effort.

■ ■ ■ **Summary**

Social inference is the process by which we draw conclusions about people from observations of their behavior. Such inferences depend on whether we attribute the cause of the behavior to the *person* or to the *situation*. When an action is perceived as being caused by dispositions or intentions of the person, that behavior is diagnostic of the actor's personality.

Attribution theorists are interested in why and how perceivers make causal attributions to the person or the situation. One theory holds that perceivers act like intuitive scientists, relying on the principle of covariation to make their causal judgments. Causes for social events are assigned to the person (actor) or the situation based on knowledge of consensus (how other persons behave in the same situation), distinctiveness (how the actor behaves in the presence of other objects), and consistency (how the actor behaves on other occasions).

Although evidence exists that perceivers do use covariation information in making their causal judgments, there is also evidence for deviations from the principles of covariation. In particular, perceivers often fail to take consensus information into account and make causal attributions to the actor's personality even when most other people act in the same way (the base-rate fallacy). We also use our own behavior as the basis for inferring what is normal or usual (the false consensus effect), and make dispositional attributions when others act differently than we do.

When we do not have information about how others are behaving or about past behaviors, we must rely on causal schemata to make social inferences from a single behavior. According to the augmentation principle, when an individual behaves in a way that is unexpected within the situation, we are entitled to make a personality attribution for that behavior. On the other hand, according to the discounting principle, when an individual behaves in an expected or normative manner, we should attribute that behavior to the situation and not to the person.

When an actor's behavior is perceived to be diagnostic of his or her personal dispositions, the perceiver is making a correspondent inference. Correspondent inference depends on whether the perceiver believes that the actor chose to behave the way she did. Such an inference is essentially a decision about whether the behavior was intrinsically or extrinsically motivated. According to the over-justification effect, the presence of extrinsic rewards or incentives undermines the perception of intrinsic motivation.

Although perceivers should discount behavior that is enacted under conditions of low choice, there is considerable evidence that perceivers make correspondent inferences about the actor's personality even when situational causes are present. This correspondence bias is known as the fundamental attribution error. The tendency to attribute behavior to personality may be particularly characteristic of persons raised in Western cultures. The bias is also related to the relative salience of the actor compared with the background situation or environment. Salience also accounts for the actor–observer difference in attributions. Perceivers tend to attribute other's people's behavior to their personal dispositions, but attribute their own actions to the situation.

Evidence for a bias toward making dispositional or correspondent inferences has led attribution theorists to reevaluate the social inference process. More recent models of the attribution process assume that the first step in social inference is to associate an observed behavior with a corresponding personality trait or disposition. Evaluation of the situational context comes as a second step, requiring additional cognitive effort. Although perceivers can make appropriate situational attributions, whether they do so will depend on time and motivation.

■ ■ ■ **SUGGESTED READINGS**

1. Hamilton, D. L. (1988). Causal attribution viewed from an information-processing perspective. In D. Bar-Tal & A. Kruglanski (Eds.), *The social psychology of knowledge* (pp. 359–385). Cambridge, England: Cambridge University Press.
2. Jones, E. E. (1979). The rocky road from acts to dispositions. *American Psychologist, 34,* 107–117.
3. Jones, E. E. (1990). *Interpersonal perception.* New York: W. H. Freeman.
4. Kelley, H. H. (1973). The process of causal attribution. *American Psychologist, 28,* 107–128.
5. Ross, L. (1977). The intuitive psychologist and his shortcomings: Distortions in the attribution process. In L. Berkowitz (Ed.), *Advances in experimental social psychology* (Vol. 10, pp. 173–219). New York: Academic Press.

CHAPTER 11

THE SOCIAL SELF
Self-Concept in Its Social Context

■ **Key Concepts**

Self-concept
Self-schema
Self-complexity
Possible selves
Self-esteem
Self-perception theory
Social comparison theory
Self-evaluation maintenance
Self-enhancement
Self-consistency
Self-verification

■ **Chapter Outline**

WHO AM I? THE NATURE OF THE SELF-CONCEPT
    Self-schema: The Cognitive Component
    ■ Self-complexity and the Buffering Effect
    ■ Delinquency and Self-Concept
    Self-esteem: The Evaluative Component
    Self-perception: The Behavioral Component

YOU AND ME: THE COMPARATIVE BASIS OF SELF-CONCEPT
    Social Comparison and Self-evaluation
    ■ Self-esteem in the Waiting Room
    Distinctiveness and Social Comparison
    Some Comparisons Matter More than Others
    The Ups and Downs of Social Comparison

MAINTAINING AND PROTECTING A SELF-IMAGE
    Do We Want Others to See Us As We See Ourselves?
    Cross-cultural Perspectives on the Self

SOME CONCLUDING THOUGHTS

SUMMARY

Amy's two college friends were pressuring her to come with them to this weekend's frat party. Despite their descriptions of the wild good time they would have, Amy refused to go. When asked why, she replied, "I'm just not that kind of person."

■ ■ ■

When midterm chemistry exams were returned, Kevin was chagrined to learn that he had barely pulled a "C." On the way out of class he asked his good friend Mark how he had done on the exam. Mark admitted he had really flubbed this one and received a "D." Although he didn't say so out loud, Kevin was secretly pleased. I guess I'm not so dumb, after all, he thought to himself.

■ ■ ■

When Mary stopped at the scene of an automobile accident and pulled a young child out of a burning car, she was treated as a local hero. The neighborhood paper gave her front-page coverage and everyone praised her bravery and compassion. Yet Mary seemed depressed by the whole thing. "I'm not sure I can live with this hero stuff," she told her best friend. "Everyone thinks I'm so wonderful, but they don't know the real me."

We all spend lots of time thinking about who we are or what other people think about us. The concept of self has always fascinated psychologists as well. In *The Principles of Psychology* (1890), philosopher–psychologist William James included a chapter on "Consciousness of Self" which established the study of the self as a central aspect of the emerging science of psychology. The first empirical research on the self-concept was not conducted until almost sixty years after James's classic book, but since that time thousands of studies on the subject have been published (Rosenberg, 1979).

James distinguished between two types of self-consciousness: the subjective sense of the self as an experiencing, thinking being (the "I"), and the objective or empirical self (the "me"). Social psychological research has been addressed primarily to the study of the objective self—how people think about their own actions, characteristics, or motives. Social psychologists are interested in both the structure and the content of these self-perceptions. What does Amy mean when she speaks of the "kind of person" she is? Why did Kevin feel better about himself after he learned of Mark's failure? And why didn't Mary enjoy all of the positive attention she received for her act of bravery? These are the kinds of questions we address in this chapter.

■ ■ ■ WHO AM I? THE NATURE OF THE SELF-CONCEPT

What William James referred to as the objective self is now most often labeled the **self-concept,** "the totality of the individual's thoughts and feelings having reference to himself as an object" (Rosenberg, 1979, p. 7). From this perspective, the self is a set of beliefs and attitudes, much like our attitudes toward other people or social issues, with one important exception: In the case of self-attitudes, the perceiver and the perceived are one and the same.

All belief systems include cognitive, affective, and behavioral components: See Chapter 2.

Like other belief systems, the self-concept includes cognitive, affective, and behavioral components. More than any other belief system, however, the content and organization of the self-concept has a powerful influence on individual actions and choices. There is also evidence that the way we view ourselves affects the way we view others, so the study of the self-concept plays an important part in the study of social perception in general.

Self-schema: The Cognitive Component

Recently, social psychologists working in the area of social cognition have come to think of the self-concept as a cognitive schema. **Self-schemas** are "cognitive generalizations about the self, derived from past experience, that organize and guide the processing of self-related information" (Markus, 1977, p. 64). In other words, once we have formed an impression of what we are like, that belief system acts as a sort of filter, influencing how readily we receive or accept new information about ourselves.

Schemas, or cognitive generalizations, are a useful conceptual tool in social psychology: See Chapter 8.

According to Hazel Markus (1977), the self-schema is organized around specific traits or features that we think of as most central or important to our image of ourselves. *Schematic traits* are those that we use most often when we define who we are and that have the most impact on how we feel about ourselves. Individuals differ in the traits that are most central to their self-concepts. Let us imagine, for instance, that two individuals, Madge and Lois, both have moderately high intelligence and are well organized. For Madge, her level of intelligence is of central importance to her sense of self. She is highly aware of her standing on the latest achievement test and regularly compares herself with other people to see if she is more or less intelligent than they are. But Madge rarely thinks about whether she is an organized individual. When asked, she will concede that she is well organized, but this trait is not important to her self-image. She does not use it to define herself.

Lois, on the other hand, is a community leader, very aware of her organizational talents. She spontaneously describes herself as a well-organized person, but seldom mentions her intelligence, which does not play an important role in her sense of self. Thus, although Madge and Lois are similar in the traits they would assign to themselves, they differ greatly in how those traits are organized in their respective self-concepts. According to the terminology used by Markus (1977), Madge is *schematic* with respect to intelligence and *aschematic* with respect to organization. Lois is schematic on organization and aschematic on intelligence.

Markus (1977) believed that self-schemas influence our sensitivity to information, so that we respond differently to information that is relevant or irrelevant to schematic traits. In an initial experimental test of this notion, she selected female participants according to their self-ratings on the trait dimension of independence. Women who rated themselves as moderately or highly independent and said that independence was an important aspect of their self-concept were classified as "independent schematics." Those who rated themselves on the dependent side of the scale and saw dependence as a central feature of their self-concept were classified as "dependent schematics." Women who did not consider independence or dependence as important self-descriptions were classified as "aschematics."

Selected participants were later recruited for a perception experiment in which they were shown a series of adjectives projected on a screen one at a time. Some of the adjectives were related to dependence (such as "conforming," "cautious") and others to independence ("assertive," "self-confident"). As each trait was presented, participants were instructed to press a button labeled "me" if the adjective was descriptive of themselves or to press a "not-me" button if the word was not self-descriptive. As expected, women who were schematic for independence were much faster in responding to adjectives that were associated with independence than to those related to dependence, whereas dependent schematic respondents showed the reverse response pattern. For aschematic women there was no difference in the amount of time it took to respond to independent and dependent words.

Other dimensions of self-image have also been studied, with similar results. In one experiment (Markus, Hamill, & Sentis, 1987) moderately overweight females were classified as schematic or aschematic with respect to body weight. Schematic respondents reacted much more quickly to silhouettes of a fat person than to neutral or thin silhouettes (Figure 11.1), whereas aschematic individuals showed no significant differences in speed of response to the different body shapes. In yet another study (Markus, Crane, Bernstein, & Siladi, 1982), male and female students were classified as masculine-schematic or feminine-schematic on the basis of their self-ratings on a scale of masculinity and femininity (Bem, 1974). Again, masculine schematics were much faster in responding "me" to masculine adjectives than to feminine ones, while feminine schematics showed the reverse pattern of response times. From the results of these studies, it appears that once a trait has been established as a central feature of the self-concept, individuals are more receptive to information that confirms that self-description than to information unrelated to their self-schema.

Self-complexity. Studies of the structure of self-concept lead to the question of whether each individual has a single self-schema that is active in all situations or many different self-schemas for different aspects of life. For instance, a woman who is a college professor, a mother of two young children, and a social activist may have very different conceptions of herself in these different roles. For her professional self-image, traits such as intelligence and independence may be central organizing features, but in her family role she may think of herself primarily in terms of tolerance and warmth. Yet other characteristics (for example, passionate and aggressive) may dominate her activist self-image.

FIGURE 11.1

Body silhouettes: Are you weight-schematic? (From Markus, Hamill, & Sentis, 1987, p. 58.)

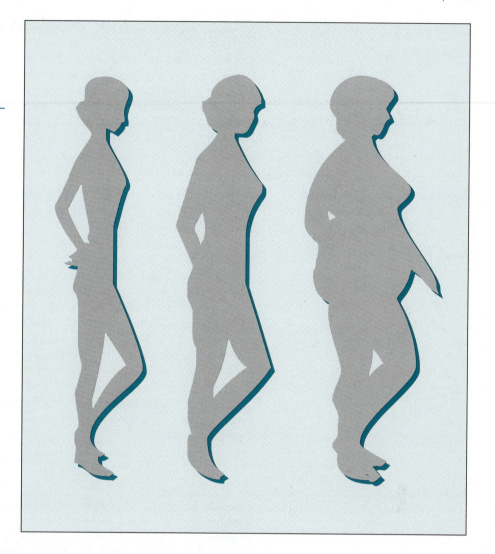

Patricia Linville (1985) has hypothesized that individuals differ in the extent to which their self-concept is differentiated into separately organized substructures. She refers to this dimension of the self-concept as **self-complexity.** Individuals who think of themselves in pretty much the same way across different situations and roles are low in self-complexity. Those who have different self-images (different central traits) for the various roles they play are said to be high in self-complexity.

Linville hypothesizes that self-complexity has important implications for a person's ability to cope with stressful events. Just how devastating a particular stressful event may be depends on how much a blow to self-image in one aspect of life spills over into other aspects. For instance, an unfortunate event such as flubbing an important exam may have negative consequences for my academic self-esteem. But what effect will that event have on my overall self-image? Will I conclude that I am a bad person? or just not quite the genius I thought I was?

Having high self-complexity (multiple, distinctive self-images) can serve as a barrier to spillover effects. For persons low in self-complexity, the effects of one negative event can spread to all aspects of the self. For those high in self-complexity, the effects of that same event will be more contained, with less devastating impact overall. Linville suggests that the buffer of self-complexity protects individuals from severe consequences of stressful life experiences.

APPLYING SOCIAL PSYCHOLOGY TO HEALTH

■ ■ ■

Self-complexity and the Buffering Effect

The buffering effect of self-complexity was demonstrated empirically in a study of 106 college students (Linville, 1987). Each student's self-complexity was assessed by a trait-sorting task (Table 11.1), along with a measure of life stresses they were experiencing at the time (such as academic stresses, financial problems, relationship difficulties, accidents). Two weeks later, the same students were retested on these measures and were also asked about psychological depression, physical symptoms, and illnesses they had during the two-week period. Consistent with the self-complexity hypothesis, students who had scored low in self-complexity showed a strong relationship between stress and physical symptoms. Those who had a high number of stressors at Time 1 were more depressed and had a greater number of physical symptoms and stress-related illnesses at Time 2. For students high in self-complexity, however, stress was not related to physical symptoms. For these students, stressful events did not generalize to their overall self-evaluation. They were apparently protected from the impact of specific stressful events and less susceptible to stress-related illness.

Possible Selves. In addition to the different self-images that we may hold of ourselves in the present, our self-concept can be extended to include the kind of persons we could imagine ourselves being in the future. Markus and Nurius (1986) refer to these images as **possible selves.** The idea of possible selves can also be traced back to James (1890):

> In each kind of self . . . men distinguish between the immediate and actual, and the remote and potential . . . Of all these wider, more potential selves, the potential social self is the most interesting . . . When for motives of honor and conscience I brave the condemnation of my own family, club, and 'set' . . . I am always inwardly strengthened in my course and steeled against the loss of my actual social self by the thought of other and better possible judges than those whose verdict goes against me now . . . This self is the true, the intimate, the ultimate, the permanent Me which I seek. (pp. 300–301)

Possible selves are not simply extensions of the way we see ourselves in the present. As indicated by the data in Table 11.2, most people can imagine themselves being quite different than they are now, in both positive and negative ways. According to Markus and Nurius, these alternative conceptions serve im-

TABLE 11.1

■

Self-Complexity as Measured by a Trait-Sorting Task: Examples of Two Subjects' Trait Sorts

Subject 1

RELATIONSHIP WITH MEN	RELATIONSHIP WITH FRIENDS	RELATIONSHIP WITH FAMILY	STUDIES	PHYSICALLY	AT PARTIES
Outgoing	Humorous	Emotional	Quiet	Individualistic	Humorous
Playful	Relaxed	Playful	Studious	Affectionate	Playful
Reflective	Assertive	Reflective	Organized	Industrious	Outgoing
Mature	Outgoing	Mature	Mature	Quiet	Sophisticated
Emotional	Mature	Assertive	Reserved	Organized	Affectionate
Assertive	Emotional	Humorous	Industrious		Competitive
Competitive	Reflective	Outgoing	Individualistic		Imaginative
Relaxed	Soft-hearted	Individualistic			Impulsive
Humorous	Not studious	Unconventional			Mature
Affectionate	Affectionate				
Soft-hearted	Individualistic				
Individualistic					
Sophisticated					

Subject 2

DORM LIFE	HOME LIFE	SCHOOL	SOCIAL LIFE	WORK (DINING HALL WORKER)	ACTIVITIES
Playful	Lazy	Reflective	Outgoing	Industrious	Imaginative
Relaxed	Emotional	Reserved	Humorous	Rebellious	Relaxed
Outgoing	Relaxed	Unorganized	Quiet	Playful	Quiet
Assertive	Humorous	Lazy	Relaxed	Outgoing	Outgoing
Competitive	Playful	Insecure	Playful	Assertive	Assertive
Affectionate	Affectionate		Insecure	Relaxed	Unorganized
Humorous	Unorganized		Impulsive		Affectionate
Soft-hearted	Soft-hearted		Not studious		Soft-hearted
Unorganized	Not studious		Conformist		
Lazy	Irresponsible				
Imaginative					
Individualistic					

From Linville, (1987), p. 667.

portant motivating functions. If we can actually "see" ourselves as successful in business, socially skilled, or a world traveler, it is easier to make the effort required to achieve those states. Similarly, if we can clearly imagine being poor, offensive, or suffering a nervous breakdown, we may take more precautions to avoid those outcomes. The ability to imagine possible future selves has strong effects on motivation and performance in the present (Ruvolo & Markus, 1992).

TABLE 11.2

■

"Possible Selves" of College Students: Percentages of Respondents Endorsing Selected Self Items

	Question	
ITEM	Does This Describe You Now?	Have You Ever Considered This a Possible Self?
Personality		
Happy	88.0	100.0
Confident	83.8	100.0
Depressed	40.2	49.6
Lazy	36.2	48.3
Life style		
Travel widely	43.6	94.0
Have lots of friends	74.6	91.2
Be destitute	4.5	19.6
Have nervous breakdown	11.1	42.7
Physical		
Sexy	51.7	73.5
In good shape	66.7	96.5
Wrinkled	12.0	41.0
Paralyzed	2.6	44.8
General abilities		
Speak well publicly	59.0	80.3
Make own decisions	93.2	99.1
Manipulate people	53.5	56.6
Cheat on taxes	9.4	17.9
Others' feelings toward you		
Powerful	33.3	75.2
Trusted	95.7	99.1
Unimportant	12.8	24.8
Offensive	24.8	32.5
Occupation		
Media personality	2.2	56.1
Owner of a business	1.4	80.3
Janitor	2.6	6.8
Prison guard	0.0	4.3

From Markus & Nurius (1987, p. 959.

Studies of the self-concept of adolescents suggest that delinquent youth lack a positive vision of "possible selves" to offset negative self-perceptions. ■

Delinquency and Self-concept

Knowing that the self-concept includes possible future selves, as well as the present self-image, gives us insights into some important differences among individuals. Oyersman and Markus (1990) conducted interviews with inner-city adolescents to assess the relationship between delinquency and self-concept. Their study included a sample of 108 nondelinquent public school students and a sample of 90 young people from group homes or a state training school for delinquent youths. In general, the delinquent and nondelinquent groups did not differ in global self-esteem or other measures of current self-image. What differentiated the groups was their conceptions of future possible selves.

Oyersman and Markus were particularly interested in the relationship between their respondents' *expected selves* (images of what they thought they could be like in the future) and their *feared selves* (possible selves that they wanted to avoid). The relationship between expected and feared selves is balanced when a positive future self is offset by a corresponding negative feared self (for example, "doing well in school" versus "not doing well in school"; "having a job" versus "being poor"). Public school students exhibited many more such balanced pairs of possible selves than did the delinquent groups. Delinquents' feared selves included negative outcomes such as "being a murderer" or "being on drugs," but they did not have expected positive selves to offset these negative images. Instead, expected selves included vague states such as "having friends," or "being happy" that did not relate directly to the feared outcomes.

The authors speculate that feared selves are more important motivators when they are paired with positive expected selves that offer a specific image, or goal, for avoiding the feared state. Thus, the critical difference between delinquent and nondelinquent youth lies in the nature of their possible selves. Delinquents cannot clearly imagine a future self that is counter to their present negative behavior and are more likely to be trapped in their current behavior patterns.

Self-esteem: The Evaluative Component

Probably the most studied aspect of self-perception is that of **self-esteem**—the individual's positive or negative feelings of personal value or self-worth. Since individual differences in self-esteem have profound effects on mental health, well-being, and interpersonal behavior, it is no wonder that this component of the self-concept has captured the attention of developmental, clinical, and personality psychologists, as well as social psychologists.

Psychologists have devised a number of different ways to measure self-esteem. Some measures are based on the individual's self-ratings along a series of evaluative trait dimensions, such as "friendly–unfriendly," "lazy–hardworking," "fair–unfair" (e.g., Julian, Bishop, & Fiedler, 1966). With such measures, overall self-esteem is calculated in terms of the total positive minus negative self-ratings that are made across all traits. Rosenberg (1979) has argued that such calculations can be misleading since they assume that all evaluative traits contribute equally to an individual's self-esteem. They do not take into account the possibility that some

TABLE 11.3

■

The Rosenberg Self-Esteem Scale

The RSE is a 10-item scale. Respondents are asked to strongly agree, agree, disagree, or strongly disagree with the following items:

(1) On the whole, I am satisfied with myself.

(2) At times I think I am no good at all.

(3) I feel that I have a number of good qualities.

(4) I am able to do things as well as most other people.

(5) I feel I do not have much to be proud of.

(6) I certainly feel useless at times.

(7) I feel that I'm a person of worth, at least on an equal plane with others.

(8) I wish I could have more respect for myself.

(9) All in all, I am inclined to feel that I am a failure.

(10) I take a positive attitude toward myself.

Source: Rosenberg (1965). Society and the adolescent self-image. Princeton, NJ: Princeton University Press.

traits or features may be more central than others to an individual's sense of self-worth. As implied by Markus's self-schema theory, an individual's self-evaluation on traits that are important to the self-concept should have more impact on overall self-esteem than less important traits. Thus, if I am schematic for intelligence and rate myself positively on the intelligence dimension, my self-esteem may be very high even though I give myself less positive ratings on sociability and athletic skill. Self-esteem is not simply the addition of one's abilities and accomplishments. It depends on the certainty and importance attached to specific self-views (Pelham & Swann, 1989).

Because individuals differ in which traits are central to self-esteem, Rosenberg argues that we should measure *global self-esteem* directly, by asking individuals how they feel about themselves generally. Items from Rosenberg's global self-esteem scale are illustrated in Table 11.3.

High global self-esteem means that one's overall self-evaluation is positive, while low self-esteem corresponds to a more negative self-image. Where does this overall evaluation come from? Many psychologists over the years have concluded that self-esteem reflects the perceived difference between an individual's *actual self-concept* (who I think I really am) and some *ideal self-image* (who I would really like to be). William James (1890) expressed the relationship this way:

$$\text{Self-esteem} = \text{success/pretensions}$$

Since James's formulation, psychologists have attempted to specify the "pretensions," or ideals against which individuals assess their actual self image.

Rosenberg (1979), for instance, differentiated desired self-concepts into *idealized images* (the "perfect" human being we would most like to be), *committed images* (the desired self that we find realistic to live up to), and *moral images* (what we feel we should or ought to be like). Similarly, Higgins (1987) has distinguished between the *ought self* (standards of what we feel we should be) and the *ideal self* (images of what we would like to be). According to his self-discrepancy theory, the ought-self and ideal-self serve as different "self-guides." The degree of discrepancy between perceptions of one's actual self and these self-guides can predict a person's emotional well-being. When an individual believes that his or her actual self differs significantly from the ideal self, the resulting emotional reaction is sadness or depression. Perceived discrepancies between the actual and ought-self, however, lead to feelings of anxiety rather than depression.

Discrepancy theories of self-esteem highlight the close relationship between the cognitive and evaluative components of the self-concept. Both actual and ideal self-images are cognitive constructs. The degree of difference between the content of one construct and the other has important affective consequences for the individual's feelings of personal value and self-worth. Thus, understanding how the content of the actual and ideal self-concepts are acquired is critical to understanding the origins of self-esteem.

Self-perception: The Behavioral Component

One source from which self-concept is built is the individual's knowledge of his or her own personal history. In a sense, we are all observers of our own behavior and actions, and we form impressions of ourselves in much the same way that we form impressions of other people—that is, based on what we do and say. Daryl Bem's (1972) influential **self-perception theory** reflects this basic idea. According to his theory, we observe our behavior and the situation in which it took place, make attributions about why the behavior occurred, and draw conclusions about our own characteristics and dispositions. In other words, we come to understand ourselves the same way we perceive and understand other people.

Other psychologists have argued that self-perception is not directly comparable to perception of others because we have knowledge of our own internal states at the time of our own actions that we do not have access to when observing other people's behavior. In forming a self-concept, individuals seem to give more weight to memories of their thoughts and feelings than to their specific actions or words. Andersen & Ross (1984) interviewed college students about various aspects of themselves and their past experiences. As part of the instructions for the interview, participants were told to limit their self-descriptions to reports of objective behavior, to reports of their thoughts and feelings, or to both.

At the end of the interview, respondents were asked to rate how satisfied they were that they had communicated a complete and accurate impression of themselves. Those who had been allowed to use descriptions of thoughts and feelings rated the interview as significantly more informative than students who had been limited to behavioral descriptions. (Interestingly, observers who listened to the taped interviews had just the opposite reactions. They believed they knew more about the person being interviewed when they heard her reporting on her actual behavior than when they listened to her reports of thoughts and feelings.)

Bem's self-perception theory describes how we form impressions of ourselves based on our behavior: See Chapter 5.

"I can't say I like the looks of that bunch."
(Drawing by Dana Fradon; © 1971 The New Yorker Magazine, Inc.)

Although this study of the subjective content of the self-concept seems to contradict Bem's behavioral self-perception theory, there is experimental evidence that people do judge their own internal states on the basis of their actions. A number of fascinating studies have been conducted demonstrating that when individuals present themselves in a certain way behaviorally, they come to think of themselves in ways that are consistent with that behavior, particularly if that behavior is public (Tice, 1992).

In one such experiment (Jones, Rhodewalt, Berglas, & Skelton, 1981), students participated in interviews where they were motivated to impress a team leader. Before being interviewed themselves, they observed a videotape of a previous interview with a successful applicant. Two different versions of the videotape were produced. In one, the applicant presented himself in a self-enhancing, boastful manner. In the other, his interview responses were modest and more self-deprecating. As expected, when it came time to be interviewed themselves, participants tended to mimic the behavior of the videotape model. Those who had seen the boastful model gave more self-enhancing answers than those who had observed the more modest applicant.

After the interviews were over, participants filled out written questionnaires that included a measure of self-esteem. The effects of the videotape on respondents' overt behavior carried over to their later self-descriptions. Those who had been influenced to act in a self-enhancing manner had higher self-esteem scores than those who had been influenced to act in a self-deprecating manner. In this case, apparently, hearing (oneself) was believing. Such feedback effects of one's own behavior on self-perception demonstrate how much the self-concept is influenced by social interactions.

■■■ YOU AND ME: THE COMPARATIVE BASIS OF SELF-CONCEPT

William James's conception of the self (and that of most psychologists since James) was highly introspective. The generally accepted idea is that we understand ourselves by looking inside and examining our own actions, thoughts, and feelings. In a highly influential paper published in 1954, social psychologist Leon Festinger challenged this view of self-understanding. According to Festinger's **theory of social comparison,** we cannot interpret our own actions and feelings without looking outward to the actions and feelings exhibited by other people.

Social comparison theory is based on the following premises:

1. Humans have a drive to evaluate their opinions and abilities; individuals need to feel confident of the correctness of their opinions and the accurate assessment of their capabilities.

2. In the absence of objective, nonsocial bases of assessment, individuals will evaluate their opinions and abilities by comparison with the opinions and abilities (performance) of others.

3. The tendency to compare oneself with another person decreases as the difference between the self and other increases; individuals will seek to compare themselves with someone close (similar) in opinions and abilities.

These assumptions have two important social psychological consequences. First, when we feel any uncertainty about who we are or what we are experiencing, we need to seek out other people for the purpose of gaining social comparison information. Our need for self-understanding becomes a major motivation for affiliating and interacting with other people, particularly similar others (Schachter, 1959). Second, the more uncertain we are, the more we are susceptible to influence from other people and how other people are responding to a situation. Social comparison is a particularly interesting form of social influence because it does not require any active intention on the part of the influencers. Through social comparison, we may be motivated to change our behavior or evaluations just by observing others' responses, in the absence of any interaction or attempt at direct influence. Thus, social comparison processes are involved in our theories of attitude change, conformity, interpersonal relations, and group process. Here, however, we limit our discussion to the effects of social comparison on self-concept.

Social comparison is an important basis for affiliation and group formation. See Chapter 22.

Social Comparison and Self-evaluation

There is much evidence that people adjust their evaluations of their own abilities in response to information about the performance of others (Brown, Novick, Lord, & Richards, 1992; Suls & Wills, 1991). The development of self-concept in children is strongly influenced by social comparisons in the school classroom (Ruble & Frey, 1987). For example, Marsh and Parker (1984) assessed the academic self-concept of children from schools that differed in their students' average ability level. Children who were surrounded by others of generally high ability tended to have lower academic self-esteem than children in schools where ability levels were generally lower. This finding matches an earlier study of college students which showed that career aspirations were more affected by peer comparisons than by quality of college. Students who earned high grades in a mediocre school had higher aspirations than students with equal performance in a more competitive school environment (Davis, 1966).

Self-esteem in the Waiting Room

A particularly dramatic demonstration of social comparison effects on self-esteem comes from a study conducted by Morse and Gergen (1970). Participants in this study were actual male job applicants, waiting for an employment interview. The researchers had arranged for another male (presumably another job applicant) to come into the same room to complete some forms while the research subject was waiting. In one condition (known as the "Mr. Clean" condition), everything about the confederate's appearance was highly socially desirable. He was dressed in a suit, well-groomed and confident looking, and equipped with an attache case, a statistics book, slide rule, and a copy of a philosophy text. In the contrasting ("Mr. Dirty") condition, the same confederate appeared in a sweatshirt and ripped trousers, wore no socks, and seemed bewildered by the whole situation. Subjects observed the stimulus person for a period of about one and a half minutes, but there was no verbal interaction between them during that time.

After the initial exposure, the actual subject was brought a series of additional forms to complete, which included a measure of global self-esteem. Those who had experienced social comparison to "Mr. Clean" scored lower on this later self-esteem measure than did those who had "Mr. Dirty" as a comparison other. Even this casual exposure to another person was apparently sufficient to have a significant impact on individuals' self-evaluation at that point in time.

Distinctiveness and Social Comparison

Not only the evaluation but also the content of one's self-concept can be affected by comparison with others. Self-descriptions often include features or traits that are particularly distinctive in the person's social environment. So, for instance, a woman chemist is most likely to think of herself in terms of her occupation when she is in the company of women who are not chemists, but to think of herself as female when she is surrounded by her male colleagues at work (McGuire & McGuire, 1988). When school children are asked to "tell us about yourself," they are most likely to mention particular physical characteristics (such as red or blond hair) if they are uncommon or atypical in their classroom. Similarly, the probability that children will mention gender as part of self-description is influenced by the sex composition of their family. A boy from a household with a female majority is more likely to specify that he is a boy than a boy from a household with equal numbers of males and females, and girls mention their gender more often when they come from male-majority households (McGuire, McGuire, & Winston, 1979). Our general sense of who we are is determined in large part by comparison and contrast with others around us.

An individual's self-concept is often built around traits or features that make that individual distinctive in his or her social environment. ■

Some Comparisons Matter More Than Others

As Festinger's principle of similarity indicates, the theory of social comparison does not assume that self-evaluations are affected by all possible comparisons with other people. Our estimates of our own ability are little affected by information about performance of others who are very distant from us on a particular dimension. So, for instance, my assessment of my skills as a basketball player are not altered when I go to a Lakers game or when I watch my five-year-old niece make attempts at shooting baskets. Comparison information has much more impact when the comparison person is similar to me on relevant attributes (Goethals & Darley, 1977). If an ability or opinion is perceived to be related to age or gender, I will evaluate my own position in comparison with someone of the same age and sex rather than with someone who differs from me on those attributes.

Close friends are particularly important comparison persons because they are likely to be similar on many relevant dimensions and are readily available for comparison. For these very reasons, individuals are likely to have mixed reactions to learning that a close friend has performed better than they did on some dimension of ability. On the one hand, a friend's success can reflect positively on oneself, raising one's own self-image by association. On the other hand, the friend's superior performance creates a negative comparison that can lower one's own self-evaluation.

Which of these opposing reactions is most likely to occur? According to Abraham Tesser's (1988) **self-evaluation maintenance** theory, it depends on whether the ability is central to the individual's own self-concept. When an ability is important or highly self-relevant, it is threatening to self-esteem when someone close to us performs well. For important skills, individuals react more negatively to a friend's good performance than they do to the same performance from a stranger. But on dimensions of low self-relevance, individuals react more positively to being outperformed by a friend than by a stranger (Tesser, Millar, & Moore, 1988). If I have no aspirations to musical genius and I have a friend who is an outstanding pianist, the better she performs, the better I will feel (by reflection). On the other hand, if I am dedicating my life to becoming a concert pianist, I will not want my friend to perform better than I do and risk the pain of negative social comparison.

The Ups and Downs of Social Comparison

Reactions to a friend's success reveal a basic conflict that individuals experience in social comparison situations. Information that another person has performed better than oneself is known as *upward comparison,* indicating the direction of difference between self and other. Knowledge that another person has performed less well than oneself is called *downward comparison.* Festinger (1954) originally hypothesized that the primary goal of social comparison is accurate self-evaluation. If accuracy is what we are after, then we should respond the same way to upward social comparisons as we do to downward comparisons. Both types of comparison help us assess more precisely where we stand on that dimension. But we do not always take good news and bad news equally well. Obviously, some other motives are operating.

In terms of effect on self-esteem, upward social comparisons are inconsistent with the need for **self-enhancement,** the desire to feel positive about ourselves and our capabilities. Indeed, when individuals are threatened with loss of self-esteem, they often seek out downward social comparisons and feel better when they can compare themselves with someone who is inferior or less advantaged (Wills, 1981). However, those who are disadvantaged do not always prefer the company of even less-advantaged others. Sometimes exposure to those who are better off than we are can inspire and motivate us to improve. Our choice of whom to compare with and our reaction to comparison information may depend on whether self-assessment, self-enhancement, or self-improvement is our primary goal (Wood, 1989).

■ ■ ■ MAINTAINING AND PROTECTING A SELF-IMAGE

The question of whether individuals are more concerned about maintaining an *accurate* self-concept or a *positive* self-concept has a long history in social psychology. In fact (like many of the ideas raised in this chapter), it can be traced back to James (1890) who distinguished between "self-seeking" and "self-estimation" as basic components of the empirical self. On the one hand, we want to believe that we are good, talented, and successful, but on the other hand, we are concerned that our self-evaluations have a basis in reality.

Sometimes, maintaining a positive self-image requires avoiding or denying negative feedback. Taylor and Brown (1988) have gone so far as to suggest that certain illusions may be adaptive for mental health and well-being. They base this conclusion on a review of evidence that individuals with high self-esteem

Most people strive to maintain a positive self-image and want others to see them that way. ■

maintain unrealistically positive self-evaluations, exaggerated feelings of control over their lives, and unwarranted optimism. For instance, most people judge themselves to be "better than average" on many positive characteristics and abilities. Since it is logically impossible for most people to be above average, at least some of these positive self-assessments are unrealistic or illusory. Similarly, most individuals judge that their chances of success and other positive future outcomes are higher than those of their peers. These overly optimistic self-views are characteristic of persons with high self-esteem. It is only individuals who are unusually low in self-esteem or moderately depressed who maintain more realistically balanced self-perceptions.

Do We Want Others to See Us as We See Ourselves?

We see the conflict between accuracy and self-enhancement most clearly when we consider how we wish other people to view us. Do we feel best when others give us only positive evaluations, or are we more gratified when others see us accurately, the way we perceive ourselves, including our faults? In social psychology this is known as the conflict between **self-enhancement** and **self-consistency,** and a long line of research suggests that both motives are involved in determining how we react to feedback about ourselves from other people (Jones, 1973; Shrauger, 1975).

For individuals with a generally positive self-image, there is relatively little conflict between self-enhancement and self-consistency. If we feel good about ourselves, positive evaluations from others are both rewarding and consistent with our self-concept. But what of individuals who have negative self-images? If I truly believe that I am not good at something, would I rather have other people believe that I am better than I think I am? Or would I prefer to have others confirm my negative self-evaluation?

That was the question posed in a classic study by Deutsch and Solomon (1959) in which self-evaluations were manipulated experimentally. In this study, participants worked in four-person teams on a series of problems designed to measure the ability to do flexible thinking. At the end of the task, they were given feedback on their individual performance, which indicated either that they had obtained the highest score on their team (individual success feedback) or that they had scored the lowest (individual failure feedback). Since participants had little previous experience with assessing their own "cognitive flexibility," the experimenter's feedback was the basis for establishing a positive or negative self-evaluation on this particular trait.

Following the performance feedback, each participant received a note, ostensibly from a fellow team member. The tone of the note was either very positive in evaluating the recipient's contribution and desirability as a team member or it was very negative. Deutsch and Solomon were interested in how participants' own self-evaluations would influence their reactions to another person who gave them favorable or unfavorable evaluations. The results of this experiment furnished evidence for both self-enhancement (preference for positive evaluations from others) and self-consistency (preference for confirmation of self-assessments). Not surprisingly, those who had a positive evaluation of their own performance reacted very positively to a note writer who confirmed their positive self-image and quite negatively to someone who gave an unfavorable evaluation. The ratings from participants in the negative self-evaluation condition, however, were more moderated. Although these individuals responded positively to the favorable note writer, they also gave positive evaluations to a negative note writer. On some ratings, those who had received the unfavorable note rated their teammate as even more likeable than those who had received a favorable evaluation (Figure 11.2).

Why would anyone prefer to hear negative rather than positive things about themselves? According to social psychologist Bill Swann, it is because we have a need for **self-verification,** which serves several important functions. Having others confirm our self-assessments (even when they are negative) contributes to a sense of certainty and predictability that fortifies confidence in our self-concept (Swann, Stein-Seroussi, & Giesler, 1992). On the more practical side, we do not want others to expect too much of us, to have to live up to images of ourselves that are beyond our aspirations. For these reasons, people behave in ways that "promote the survival of their self-conceptions" (Swann, 1987, p. 1039) and actually seek negative feedback from others that is consistent with negative self-views.

Although self-verification is an important need, it is not without painful consequences. According to Swann and his colleagues (Swann, Griffin, Predmore, & Gaines, 1987), those who have negative self-views are caught in a "cognitive–affective crossfire." Emotionally, they respond more positively to favorable eval-

FIGURE 11.2

■

Congruence versus self-enhancement in liking for evaluator. (From Deutsch & Solomon, 1959.)

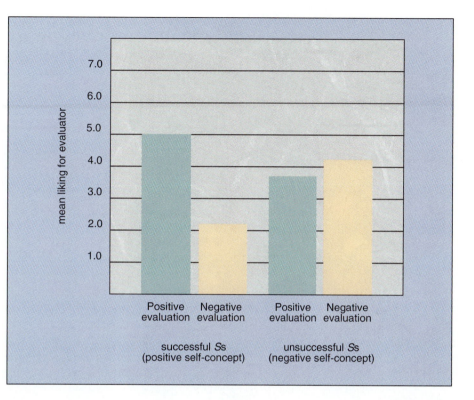

uations from others than to unfavorable ones, but cognitively they prefer feedback that confirms their negative self-assessments. Recent research on the maintenance of self-concepts suggests that even individuals with overall low self-esteem manage to reconcile the needs for self-enhancement and self-verification.

Regardless of overall self-esteem, most people have some aspects of themselves that they evaluate positively and some that they view negatively. It is possible to satisfy both motives of self-enhancement and self-verification by seeking verification of those self-views that are most positive. A series of studies by Swann, Pelham, and Krull (1989) demonstrated this is just what most people do. When given a choice of what traits to receive feedback on, a majority (both high- and low-self-esteem respondents) chose that aspect of themselves they felt most positive about. However, when feedback was given on all traits, individuals preferred favorable feedback for traits on which they had positive self-assessments and unfavorable feedback for negative self-concepts. Overall, then, people do prefer self-consistent information to inconsistent feedback, but are more likely to go out of their way to obtain feedback that is consistent with positive self-assessments.

Cross-cultural Perspectives on the Self

William James was an American philosopher, and the self-concept that he and subsequent American psychologists have studied is heavily influenced by Western culture and social thought. Western philosophy is characterized by a heavy em-

The collectivistic self-concept in Japanese culture contrasts sharply with the individualistic self-concept characteristic of Western societies. ■

phasis on the *individual* as the primary psychological entity, and the associated concept of the self focuses on characteristics that *differentiate* the individual from others in the social environment. Social psychologists with a cross-cultural perspective have pointed out that not all cultures have such an individual, differentiated concept of the self, and criticize our theories of the self as being highly culture bound (e.g., Sampson, 1988, 1989; Triandis, 1989).

Alternative perspectives on the concept of self often compare the American version of self-esteem and self-concept with that characteristic of Eastern cultures such as Japan. By contrast with the individualistic self of American psychology, the Japanese self-concept is more *relational* (Markus & Kitayama, 1991), or *collectivistic* (Triandis, Bontempo, & Villareal, 1988). Where individualistic cultures emphasize interpersonal competition, individual achievement, and independence, collectivist cultures emphasize intragroup cooperation, interdependence, and collective achievement. Thus, the Japanese self-concept is more embedded in interpersonal relationships and group memberships, and their sense of self-worth more tied to group outcomes.

Cross-cultural perspectives on the nature of self-esteem and self-image offer an important counterpoint to the individualized self-concept of American psychology. Such perspectives have created an awareness of the importance of group membership and group identity in shaping individuals' sense of self, even in Western societies.

Group identity and self-concept have been explored in detail by social psychologists: See Chapter 22.

■■■ SOME CONCLUDING THOUGHTS

William James (1890) had a number of important insights that set the agenda for much social psychological research on the nature of the self-concept. Thanks to his inspiration, we now know a great deal about how our beliefs and attitudes about ourselves are developed and sustained. From the perspective of social psychology, the important lesson from this research is that the self-concept is created and maintained through social interaction. We come to know about ourselves, in part, through comparisons with other people. And once we have established a set of beliefs about who we are, we present ourselves to others in a manner that verifies and reinforces that image of ourselves. Thus, the study of self-concept, social influence, and social interaction are closely intertwined.

■■■ SUMMARY

The self-concept is the set of beliefs and feelings that individuals hold about themselves. Like other attitudes, the self-concept includes cognitive, evaluative, and behavioral components. The cognitive component is one's self-schema, those features or attributes that are most important to an individual's perception of what he or she is like. Another aspect of the cognitive self-concept is self-complexity, the degree to which beliefs about the self are differentiated into distinct components. A third aspect of cognitions about the self involves projections into the future—images we have of possible selves, including fears, hopes, and expectations about what we could be like.

The evaluative dimension of self-concept is self-esteem, the individual's positive or negative feelings of personal value or self-worth. Self-esteem derives from the comparison between an individual's actual self-concept (what I think I am really like) and some ideal self-concept (what I think I should be like). The greater the discrepancy between actual and ideal selves, the lower or more negative the person's self-esteem.

The behavioral component of the self-concept is represented in self-perception theory, the idea that our beliefs about ourselves are based on observations of our own behavior. Such self-perceptions constitute the objective sense of self. A number of social psychological experiments have demonstrated that when individuals are induced to behave in a certain manner, their self-ratings and self-evaluations tend to become consistent with the actions they have engaged in.

Self-evaluations are also influenced by knowledge of what other people are like. The theory of social comparison holds that we form our self-images by observing the similarities and differences between ourselves and others. When an individual is exposed to other people who are highly competent or successful (upward comparisons), self-evaluation is lowered; on the other hand, exposure to less competent others (downward comparisons) can increase self-evaluations. Distinctive features or characteristics that make one different from others also are prominent in one's self-concept.

In order to maintain a positive self-evaluation, individuals might avoid comparisons with more competent individuals and reject negative information about the self. However, the need for self-enhancement is counteracted by the desire to be accurate or certain about one's self-image—the need for self-verification. Under some circumstances, individuals may prefer negative feedback that confirms their own self-perception over positive feedback that is inconsistent with their self-concept. In general, however, individuals seek to confirm positive self-images more than negative ones.

■■■ SUGGESTED READINGS

1. Berkowitz, L. (Ed.) (1988). *Advances in experimental social psychology* (Vol. 21. *Social psychological studies of the self*). San Diego: Academic Press.
2. Festinger, L. (1954). A theory of social comparison processes. *Human Relations, 7,* 117–140.
3. Higgins, E. T. (1987). Self-discrepancy: A theory relating self and affect. *Psychological Review, 94,* 319–340.
4. Markus, H., & Kitayama, S. (1991). Culture and the self: Implications for cognition, emotion, and motivation. *Psychological Review, 98,* 224–253.
5. Markus, H., & Nurius, P. (1986). Possible selves. *American Psychologist, 41,* 954–969.
6. Olson, J. M., & Zanna, M. P. (Eds.) (1990). *Self-inference processes. Ontario Symposium* (Vol. 6). Hillsdale, NJ: Erlbaum.
7. Suls, J., & Wills, T. (Eds.) (1991). *Social comparison: Contemporary theory and research.* Hillsdale, NJ: Erlbaum.
8. Taylor, S. E., & Brown, J. D. (1988). Illusion and well-being: A theory of cognitive adaptation. *Psychological Bulletin, 103,* 193–210.
9. Wood, J. V. (1989). Theory and research concerning social comparisons of personal attributes. *Psychological Bulletin, 106,* 231–248.

PART III

SOCIAL INTERACTION
Relating to Others

CHAPTER 12
Social Exchange: The Economics of Interpersonal Relationships

CHAPTER 13
Attraction and Affiliation: Choosing Our Friends and Lovers

CHAPTER 14
Bystander Intervention: People Helping People

CHAPTER 15
Aggression: People Hurting People

CHAPTER 16
Interpersonal Expectancies: The Self-fulfilling Prophesy

SOCIAL EXCHANGE
The Economics of Interpersonal Relationships

■ Key Concepts

Hedonism
Costs and rewards
Interdependence
Outcome values
Behavior (or payoff) matrix
Exchange relationship
Communal relationship
Transformation
Fate control
Mutual fate control
Behavior control
Mixed-motive game
Tragedy of the commons
Social dilemma
Prisoner's dilemma
Cooperative choice
Competitive choice

■ Chapter Outline

THE ELEMENTS OF SOCIAL EXCHANGE
    The Pivotal Concept: Interdependence
    The Nature of Outcome Values

REGULATING SOCIAL EXCHANGE: LIMITS ON PURE HEDONISM
    Types of Relationships: Communal and Exchange
    Transformations
    Social Norms

BARGAINING AND NEGOTIATION: CONTROLLING NET OUTCOMES
    Fate Control
    Behavior Control

SOCIAL DILEMMAS: INDIVIDUAL VERSUS COLLECTIVE OUTCOMES
    Tragedy of the Commons
    ■ Real-world Resource Conservation
    The Prisoners' Dilemma

SOME CONCLUDING THOUGHTS

SUMMARY

Ruby is in a quandary. She had agreed to go out with Jimmy on Saturday, but now Quentin has called. He's in town with the visiting football team, and wants to be with her after the game. Ruby has been dating Jimmy for a while. She rarely sees Quentin, who is at a university miles from hers, but she has liked him ever since high school.

■ ■ ■

Carla likes to skate, and does so every Saturday. For the last four Saturdays, however, her enjoyment has been seriously curtailed by Tommy, who is very attracted to her. Carla dislikes Tommy—a lot. On Wednesday, Carla runs into Tommy at the library and asks him to stop bothering her. Tommy is infuriated, and responds, "Forget it. I'll see you at the rink on Saturday."

■ ■ ■

Lefty and Louie have just been picked up by the police. They are being questioned in connection with the recent robbery of the First National Bank—which they committed. They have been questioned in isolation. After hours of interrogation, the district attorney offers the following deal: "Lefty, I want you to confess. If you turn state's evidence and implicate Louie, you will go free and Louie will get twenty years in the state pen. If neither of you confesses, you will each get six months for not paying your traffic tickets. If you don't confess, and Louie does, he'll go free, and you will get twenty years. If you both confess, you'll each get ten years." What will Lefty do?

■

Think about these three vignettes. There is a common theme running through each of them: the importance of **interdependence** in social relationships. In each scene, what one person does affects the feelings or outcomes of others. What determines our actions toward others is the focus of this chapter.

■ ■ ■ THE ELEMENTS OF SOCIAL EXCHANGE

Most would agree that people are motivated to maximize happiness and to minimize the costs of achieving it. This basic *hedonistic* assumption can explain a wide range of human actions. It forms the basis of **social exchange theory,** a powerful model of social interaction. The theory assumes that social life can be considered a series of transactions that are performed to obtain positive outcomes. These outcomes are provided by other people.

The foundations of social exchange theory are found in the work of Karl Marx, B. F. Skinner, and Claude Levi-Strauss. The bargaining, or exchange slant

TABLE 12.1

■

Ruby's Estimates of her Outcomes, Given Others' Reactions

Value of Specific Choice to Ruby, Given:

RUBY'S ACTION	QUENTIN'S REACTION	JIMMY'S REACTION	NET OUTCOME
Keep date with Jimmy	−50	+50	0
Lie to Jimmy, go out with Quentin	+100	−10	+90
Tell truth to Jimmy, go out with Quentin	+100	−100	0
Stay home	−10	−10	−20

that characterizes these theorists' work was made the focus of human social relationships by Homans (1958, 1974), Thibaut and Kelley (1959), and Blau (1964). All these theories share a common set of assumptions that organize, or make sense of, much social behavior. The basic assumptions of the social exchange theorists are simple and not controversial, but they generate powerful explanations about the hows and whys of human action. These assumptions are as follows:

1. We are hedonists—we seek to maximize pleasure and minimize pain and to do so at minimum *cost*.
2. Other people can be sources of pleasure or pain for us.
3. We can obtain *rewards* from others through exchange; if our actions reward others, they are likely to reward us in return.

Social exchange theorists try to quantify the gains and losses attached to specific interactions, and use the resulting quantified values to predict or explain behavior. Consider Ruby's dilemma. If she keeps her date with Jimmy, she will miss seeing Quentin. If she breaks her date, she might lose Jimmy forever. How does she decide? A social exchange theorist would quantify the likely payoffs (or outcomes) of her possible behaviors, as in Table 12.1. The behavior having the most positive outcome is most likely to be chosen. Although social exchange is a quantitatively oriented theory, its central focus is on the interdependence of behavior. Fundamental to social exchange is the idea that what one person does in an interpersonal relationship has implications for all the others in the relationship.

We do not usually assign numbers to the gains and losses we think we will incur in choosing among a set of possible actions. Social exchange theorists recognize this, but they use such values to help analyze choice situations, like the one Ruby is facing. Ruby's repertoire of possible actions are listed in Table 12.1. The numeric values represent her subjective estimates of the reward or cost associated with the outcome of each action. Note that these estimates reflect Ruby's preference for Quentin over Jimmy.

Interdependence. ■

Table 12.1 carries lots of other information about Ruby's feelings. The first row tells us that Ruby assumes Quentin will be disappointed if she does not meet him Saturday night, and his disappointment will cause her a certain degree of discomfort or unhappiness (−50). On the other hand, by not seeing Quentin, she can go out with Jimmy. This is a moderately positive outcome (+50), but not as positive as going out with Quentin (+100), as shown on the second and third rows of the table. From the second row of Table 12.1 we see that Ruby assumes that if she tells Jimmy she is sick, he will be disappointed, but not terribly so. Assuming she is not caught in the lie, Ruby could go out with Quentin and not ruin her relationship with Jimmy. This represents the most positive net outcome for her. If she tells Jimmy the truth—that she wants to go out with Quentin—her outcome will not be positive (row 3). She could avoid conflict entirely by telling both that she is not available, but this option leaves her with a negative outcome, so it is not a likely choice.

The Pivotal Concept: Interdependence

By its very name, social exchange suggests a focus on *interaction* between people. Social exchange is a theory of **interdependence.** Interdependence means that

TABLE 12.2

■

Ruby and Quentin's Behavior Matrix at Alfredo's: Possible Interaction Outcomes

Ruby's Repertory	Quentin's Repertory of Actions				
	SMILES	LAUGHS	TALKS	SPILLS DRINK	ASKS TO SPEND NIGHT
SMILES	25 20	30 25			+90 +80
LAUGHS				−40 +10	
SNEERS			−40 −40		−85 −80
YAWNS			−40 −10		

Note: Within each cell of the matrix, the number in the lower left represents the net value of the exchange for Ruby; the number in the upper right of each cell represents the net value of the exchange for Quentin.

one person's actions affect, and are affected by, what another person chooses to do. For instance, suppose Ruby decides to tell Jimmy that she cannot go out with him because she is sick. This action affects at least three people. Later on, Quentin decides he is too exhausted from the football game and cannot take Ruby out. This would change Ruby's outcomes dramatically, and maybe Jimmy's as well. In this case, Ruby's choice to lie to Jimmy would not produce a net outcome of +90. Instead, she has disappointed Jimmy slightly, and is stuck at home on Saturday night (−20). This final outcome is the product of the combination of Ruby's decision and Quentin's fatigue. Similarly, Quentin's outcome will be affected by how Ruby reacts to his decision after she lied to Jimmy. The **outcome values** of all the players in the interaction are jointly determined by the choices all the others make.

Let's suppose Ruby tells Jimmy that she is not feeling well and cannot keep their date. Later, we find Ruby and Quentin at a corner table in Alfredo's, a romantic little Italian restaurant. There is a host of behaviors Ruby and Quentin can enact in this setting, none of which would raise eyebrows. The couple could talk quietly. They could smile, laugh, or gaze pensively into each other's eyes. Quentin could reach for Ruby's hand. She could kiss him—it's that kind of place. She could smile, frown, or feign indifference. She could argue or agree with what he says, and Quentin could respond in the same manner.

Possible behaviors available to our couple and their joint values are presented in Table 12.2. This table is a **behavior matrix.** The numbers in each of the cells of the matrix represent the subjective values of the outcomes that each person would experience if that specific set of behaviors were enacted. The cells represent joint behavior combinations—what one person does affects the other and vice versa. So, for example, if Quentin smiles at Ruby, and she smiles back (or vice versa), both experience a moderately positive outcome. But suppose that Quentin says something derogatory about the football team at Ruby's school, and she takes offense, sneers, and tells him that he is a poor loser. This exchange is negative for both of them. Suppose later Quentin spills a glass of wine on himself, and Ruby, still a bit miffed, laughs at his embarrassment. This is an unpleasant experience for Quentin, but a mildly positive one for Ruby. Almost any combination of behaviors can be described in the behavior matrix, but we will not attempt to list all of them. Most of the behaviors would be intentional— talking, laughing, smiling. Social exchange assumes that interactants *choose* to engage in actions that provide the greatest benefit.

The difficulty the actors face is that neither really knows precisely how the other will respond to any given action. Thus, the choice of any particular behavior is based on the actor's estimate of the likelihood that it will result in a given outcome. Consider the cell that describes the joint behaviors in which Quentin asks Ruby to spend the night, and she smiles. This entry in the behavior matrix has the highest net values for both interactants. However, if Quentin thinks the odds are practically nonexistent that Ruby will respond in this manner, he will not risk the request.

Because some versions of social exchange theory were derived originally from research on learning and reinforcement, the general expectation is that exchanges that have proved mutually rewarding will be repeated, just as a behavior that has been reinforced will tend to be repeated. If Ruby and Quentin found the mutual exchange of smiles rewarding, they will continue this behavior. But suppose Quentin returned to Ruby's university the next week, unannounced, and was greeted with a sneer in response to his smile. He might see this as a violation of the rules they had developed at Alfredo's. He would be upset—and surprised. Why? Because patterns of exchange that had been rewarding in the past are expected to maintain their reward in future interactions—and they generally do.

The Nature of Outcome Values

The values in the behavior matrix summarize the extent to which any specific behavior exchange results in a positive or negative outcome for the actors. The values depict subjective states; what is rewarding for one person may be aversive for another. Because of the subjective nature of these net values, they are difficult to measure or to predict in advance. Despite this ambiguity, we assume that interactions that are sought out or repeated are rewarding, while those that are avoided have negative net values. The magnitude of the numbers used in the matrix are estimates of the strengths of the tendencies to engage in, or avoid, a specific exchange.

Rewards. Underlying the assignment of values is the central assumption of social exchange theory—that people seek to maximize their rewards and to minimize the costs of obtaining them. Social interactions can furnish rewards in many ways, but three stand out: First, the behavior of the other person can satisfy one or more of our motives. For example, being a very sociable young man, Quentin might not have liked the idea of spending a lonely night in a strange town. By having a date with Ruby, he was able to satisfy his desire for company. Second, a social encounter can give the actors an opportunity to perform satisfying behaviors that they could not perform alone. Suppose Quentin likes to talk about himself. He cannot brag about his performance in the football game if he is alone. He needs an audience, and Ruby provides one for him. Finally, social encounters can allow actors to enter into situations that are personally rewarding, in and of themselves. Suppose Ruby loves to show off her wardrobe. By going to the classiest restaurant in town, she has the opportunity to wear her smashing new outfit in an appropriate context and to catch the eye of every diner in the restaurant. She could have gone alone to the restaurant, dressed to kill, but this would not have proved very rewarding for her.

Costs. Social interactions carry costs. For example, if Jimmy finds out that Ruby really was not sick, he might end their relationship. Ruby would find this painful. There are other costs as well—the positive outcomes that occur in social exchanges are rarely free. People must expend effort to interact. Ruby might have had to spend hours fixing her hair, and Quentin might have had to drag himself off the trainer's table after the grueling contest. Some encounters require the expenditure of financial resources. Alfredo did not furnish dinner for nothing. Another type of expense is *opportunity cost*—the positive outcomes a person must forego because he or she is engaged in another behavior. By going out with Quentin, Ruby lost the positive outcomes she would have realized on her date with Jimmy. Quentin, on the other hand, was unable to watch the Saturday night sports highlights show, on which his outstanding performance received a rave review. The costs and rewards associated with the behaviors expressed in an exchange determine the net value each actor receives. Although it is difficult to unravel the complex web of interactions that comprises even trivial social encounters, the social exchange interpretation of interpersonal behavior offers an engaging tool for doing so.

■■■ REGULATING SOCIAL EXCHANGE: LIMITS ON PURE HEDONISM

Obviously, no social system based completely on pure hedonism could survive for long. Lasting relationships could not endure if people were concerned solely with their own outcomes, without any regard for the welfare of those with whom they interacted. Clearly, the extreme form of the social exchange model, which assumes that people are concerned only with their own outcomes, cannot be correct. A modification of the basic theory is needed. But what modifications will explain such a common feature of social life as enduring marriages or other long-term relationships? Two approaches to modifying the purely hedonistic exchange orientation have been postulated. The first of these distinguishes between two forms of relationships, communal and exchange. The other suggests that under appropriate conditions, self-sacrificial actions are transformed and experienced as hedonistic. We consider each of these approaches in turn.

Abe and Ruth have been married for fifty years. When asked the secret of their successful relationship, Ruth said, "I always try to consider Abe's feelings before doing anything." Abe merely smiled. ■

Types of Relationships: Communal and Exchange

An important modification of the unfettered social exchange model was suggested by Clark and Mills (1991), who divided interpersonal relationships into two forms, **communal** and **exchange.** The form of relationship, they argue, determines whether selfish or unselfish motives characterize social exchanges. Communal relations are formed by people who have a strong positive sentimental attachment to one another, such as committed lovers, very close friends, and family members. People in a communal relationship are deeply concerned about the welfare of the others with whom they are linked. Not only are they responsive to the needs of the significant others, they experience a positive outcome when the needs of these people are met (Clark, Mills, & Corcoran, 1989; Williamson & Clark, 1989). Why should this happen? Walster and her colleagues anticipated this question when they observed,

Communal relations are characterized by unselfish motives: See Chapter 13.

> [A] characteristic of intimate relationships . . . is that intimates, through identification with and empathy for their partners, come to define themselves as a *unit;* as *one* couple. They see themselves not merely as individuals interacting with others, but also as part of a partnership, interacting with other individuals, partnerships, and groups. (emphasis in the original) (Walster, Walster, & Berscheid, 1978, pp. 152–153)

If intimates are a unit, as Walster observes, then what is good for one member of the unit is good for the others as well. When one person benefits, all benefit. Providing a positive outcome to a loved one provides a benefit to oneself. Accordingly, participants in communal relationships do not "keep score." It would not occur to a member of a communal relationship that benefits should be returned or paid back (Clark, Mills, & Corcoran, 1989; Clark, Mills, & Powell, 1986).

The rules of the game are different in what Clark and Mills call *exchange relationships,* the focus of this chapter. Exchange relationships are not characterized by a close, intimate association. Rather, they involve the kinds of interactions that link acquaintances, business contacts, first dates, new roommates, and so on. Interactants in an exchange relationship are not particularly concerned about the welfare of one another. They are interested in maximizing their own outcomes and in **reciprocity**—if one member of the exchange provides a benefit, he or she expects to be repaid, and without undue delay (Clark et al., 1989). In exchange relationships, we are focused on our own needs, not the needs of our partner (Clark, et al., 1986). From Clark and Mills's perspective, social exchange theory is designed to explain exchange relationships, but it is not particularly useful in predicting behavior in communal relationships. Are Ruby and Quentin engaged in a communal or an exchange relationship? At this stage of the interaction, it clearly is more exchange than communal, because Ruby and Quentin are more concerned with their own outcomes than with those of their partner. This might change. With a deepening affection for each other, the relationship may become communal. Sometimes it is interesting to consider the types of relationships (communal versus exchange) in which we, ourselves, are involved.

Transformations

Another alternative to a purely hedonistic exchange orientation was advanced by Kelley and Thibaut (1978). This approach offers a means by which the hedonistic orientation of social exchange theory can be adjusted to predict actions that do not appear self-serving. This position is not antagonistic to the communal–exchange distinction of Clark and Mills; rather, it extends it. Consider a situation in which a person sacrifices his life for a perfect stranger. Obviously, relationships between strangers cannot be communal, so it is difficult to see how this sacrifice can possibly be viewed as hedonistic. Can exchange theory predict such an outcome? Kelley and Thibaut speculate that self-sacrificial actions may be hedonistic if we experience another's outcomes as our own. Thus, a positive outcome for the other person represents a reward to us as well. They termed this process a *transformation.* Even though our action might not benefit us directly—indeed, might cause us pain, even death—the other's outcome may be so important to us that it overshadows our direct experience of gain or loss. In the case of self-sacrifice for a perfect stranger, Kelley and Thibaut argue that the norm or belief on which the action is based (help people in need, always take care of children, protect old people from muggers, and the like) might be so ingrained that its maintenance, in and of itself, is the basis for transformation. We are acting because we wish to satisfy a strongly held expectation about how we should behave, not because we know and love the person in need. This approach argues that self-sacrificial actions may occur even in noncommunal relationships if social norms are sufficiently strong. Living up to social norms may in itself be hedonistic.

Social Norms

What are social norms? They are widely held rules of conduct, the definition of what is proper and expected by one's group. Norms generally do not entail legal sanctions, but we feel considerable pressure to abide by them nonetheless. In regulating hedonistic exchanges, the most relevant of all the social norms are **equity** and **equality.** The norm of equity specifies that the ratio of the rewards we reap in a relationship be proportionate to our costs or inputs and that this ratio match that of our partner in the relationship. If we give much to a social relationship, the outcome that accrues to us should reflect our contribution—it should be greater than that of a person who contributes very little. This norm puts a rein on pure exploitation, in which we attempt to realize as much as possible while contributing as little as possible.

Contrary to equity, the norm of equality specifies that everyone be rewarded equally, regardless of input. Research suggests that both equality (Allison & Messick, 1990) and equity (Harris, Messick, & Sentis, 1981; Messick & Sentis, 1979; Walster et al., 1978) guide behavior. People appear to favor equality in distributing rewards when inputs are not clear and the available rewards are small. When rewards are large and the rules defining success and failure clear, equity is favored. In general, men are prone to apply the norm of equity, while women appear to favor equality. Research by Watts, Messé, & Vallacher (1982), discussed later in this chapter, offers an interesting explanation of this apparent gender difference.

Other norms in addition to equity and equality can affect social exchanges. For example, the norm of **reciprocity** (Gouldner, 1960) specifies that we reciprocate the positive (or negative) outcomes furnished us by others. **Altruism** and **empathy** (cf. Batson, 1987; Batson & Oleson, 1991) also limit the expression of pure hedonism in social exchanges. An action is altruistic if it serves another without the requirement or expectation of reciprocation. A person who dives into a freezing lake to rescue a child probably does so without thinking about the reward the child or his parents might give. A passer-by who rushes into a burning building to save a derelict from certain death does so to save a fellow human being, not to realize some personal gain. In purely hedonistic terms, behaviors of this sort do not make sense, but they all satisfy a norm of altruism, which holds that if at all possible, we should help those in need. If the norm is ingrained in the personality of the individual, it is likely to be activated despite other considerations.

Almost all social norms impose control on unconstrained hedonism, which otherwise would put at risk any relationship formed on the basis of social exchange. Paradoxically, by controlling extreme exploitation, norms make hedonistically motivated social exchanges possible. Assuming that hedonism does play a role in determining our social relationships, it becomes important to know

How social norms are formed has been the subject of much experimental analysis: See Chapter 18.

Equity and equality are important social norms: See Chapter 13.

The norms of altruism and empathy also affect social exchanges: See Chapter 14.

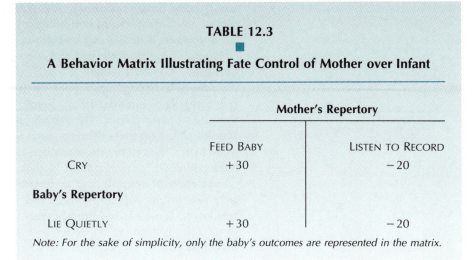

TABLE 12.3
■
A Behavior Matrix Illustrating Fate Control of Mother over Infant

	Mother's Repertory	
	FEED BABY	LISTEN TO RECORD
CRY	+30	−20
Baby's Repertory		
LIE QUIETLY	+30	−20

Note: For the sake of simplicity, only the baby's outcomes are represented in the matrix.

how we control these relationships to maximize our outcomes. Recall that through processes of transformation, maximizing our own outcomes can result in positive outcomes for others as well as ourselves.

■ ■ ■ BARGAINING AND NEGOTIATION: CONTROLLING NET OUTCOMES

If people enter into social interactions for hedonistic reasons, they should attempt to structure their encounters to maximize outcomes. Processes of social exchange are attempts to influence or control others so that their behavior falls within desired or rewarding portions of our behavior matrix. To accomplish this control requires the capability to induce the other person to act in a manner that maximizes our own rewards. Tactics people use to influence others' actions are called **control mechanisms.** They are integral to the process of social exchange, and have been discussed cogently by Kelley and Thibaut (Kelley, 1979; Kelley & Thibaut, 1978; Thibaut & Kelley, 1959).

Fate Control

The most powerful control mechanism is **fate control,** the ability to reward or punish other persons by determining their outcomes no matter what they do. For instance, parents' ability to reward or punish their infants and young children is usually much greater than the children's control over their own outcomes. Table 12.3 illustrates a situation of this kind of one-sided control. In this simplified behavior matrix, we have supplied only those values that indicate the impact of a mother's behavior on her baby. As shown, the mother can choose to feed the infant, or using her earphones, stay plugged-in to her stereo, enjoy her favorite (loud) recording, and remain oblivious to her infant's cries. Obviously, the infant would prefer being fed, but his behavior has no control over his outcomes. If he lies still or bellows, he cannot affect his mothers' behavior.

Research has documented the use of fate control as a mechanism of social exchange. A good example is available in a study in which participants played the role of a junior high school teacher who had to assign grades to students (Leventhal & Whiteside, 1973). Some "teachers" were told to assign grades on the basis of performance. Their grade allocations reflected the quality of students' actions. Other teachers were to grade in a manner that motivated their students to do better. The tactics these teachers used resulted in grades that did not directly reflect students' performances. Rather, grades varied as a consequence of the combination of aptitude and performance. For the same performance, teachers gave very bright students lower grades than students whose intellectual potential was lower. Rewards and punishments were allocated in a way designed to motivate able students to do better and less able students to continue to put out their best efforts. Under these teachers, the outcomes students experienced had little to do with their actions. Their grade was completely under the teacher's control. Within a particular scoring range, nothing the students did affected their grade. This is fate control. Most social relationships do not involve such unilateral power on the part of one of the interactants and unilateral dependence on the part of the other, but they do exist. Battered women who refuse to press charges against their husbands, abused children who never mention the pain they have suffered at the hands of parents, students treated arbitrarily by teachers—all these are examples of fate control.

More common are relationships in which the outcomes that each person in a relationship obtains are dependent on the actions of the other person. This form of interdependence is termed *mutual fate control,* and it was illustrated in our discussion of Ruby and Quentin. Given their interdependence, Ruby and Quentin each could affect the other's net outcomes. If Ruby smiled at Quentin's joke or if he complimented her on her dress, they both experienced a positive exchange. If Ruby yawned with boredom while Quentin described his exploits on the field, both suffered a loss. Under conditions of mutual fate control, what one person does affects both.

Behavior Control

Behavior control is another means by which people regulate the actions of others. It differs from fate control in that it involves the purposeful use of our own actions to affect the range of response options of others, rather than eliminating such options altogether. The second scenario at the beginning of the chapter is a good example of this type of control. In this scenario, we learn that Carla really dislikes Tommy, who has made her Saturday skating ritual something less than positive. On Wednesday morning, Carla is trying to decide whether to study for final exams or go skating on Saturday. The behavior matrix of Table 12.4 depicts the outcomes Carla thinks she will experience. Notice these values are dependent in part on Tommy's actions. If Tommy stays away, Carla will have fun skating—studying will come later. But if Tommy shows up, skating will be ruined, and her outcome will be more positive if she studies. At their chance encounter in the library, Tommy tells her that he plans to be at the rink

TABLE 12.4
■
A Behavior Matrix Illustrating Behavior Control of Tommy over Carla

	TOMMY'S REPERTORY	
	SKATE	DO SOMETHING ELSE
SKATE	−85	+75
Carla's Repertory		
STUDY	+20	+5

Note: values represent Carla's outcomes, given Tommy's actions—an example of Tommy's behavior control over Carla.

on Saturday. By this action, Tommy restricts the range of response options Carla can reasonably consider. Knowing that Tommy will be skating Saturday has clarified Carla's decision—the second column of the behavior matrix now does not exist. Tommy has behavior control over Carla because her rewards are contingent on his choice of behavior. Although he does not have the power to reward or punish Carla regardless of her behavior (fate control), he can influence her actions by stating his own future plans. In doing so, Tommy restricts Carla to a portion of the behavior matrix.

We realize that in most relationships our behaviors have consequences for others with whom we interact and vice versa. In attempting to maximize the rewards we receive from social exchanges with others, we often restrict others' range of actions so that we can experience rewarding outcomes ourselves. In this sense, most interpersonal actions can be viewed as attempts (though not always successful attempts) at behavior control.

■■■ SOCIAL DILEMMAS: INDIVIDUAL VERSUS COLLECTIVE OUTCOMES

To this point, we have presented the outcomes that actors stand to gain in any given cell of their behavior matrix. These examples might give the impression that the most favored cell of the matrix is always obvious to people. This is not so. In *mixed-motive* situations, the most positive outcome is ambiguous.

Tragedy of the Commons

A classic example of a mixed-motive situation is called the tragedy of the commons (Hardin, 1968). The situation takes its name from the traditional design of old English villages, in which the village center is devoted to a large common

TABLE 12.5

■

A Behavior Matrix Illustrating a Tragedy of the Commons

	Herder George's Repertory	
	GRAZE HERD FULLY	RESTRICT GRAZING
GRAZE HERD FULLY	−35 −35	−80 +75
Herder Pete's Repertory		
RESTRICT GRAZING	+75 −80	+30 +30

Note: Values in the upper-right of each cell represent Herder George's outcomes; the lower-left values in each cell represent Herder Pete's outcomes.

area, a pasture, on which village folks could graze their flocks. The problem inherent in such an arrangement is that if all citizens allow their animals to graze at will on the commons, the pasture will be destroyed. However, a herder who grazes only some of his animals for the good of the pasture will suffer, because his livestock will be less marketable as a result of their deprivation.

If all herders practice conservation, all are disadvantaged in the short term, but they are advantaged in the long term because the pasture is perpetuated. However, this conservative or ethical option may be undercut by cheating. By grazing one's animals fully, while others restrict theirs, a herder gains the best of both possible worlds—fat sheep and a continuing supply of green grass. A behavior matrix representing this situation, which for simplicity's sake involves only two herders, George and Pete, is presented in Table 12.5.

This illustration highlights the mixed-motive aspects of such *social dilemmas,* as they are called. Consider the effect if both herders decide to maximize their individual outcomes. In this case, both lose. They end up in the least positive cell of the matrix. On the other hand, if one acts for the common good and the other does not, then the altruist loses and the cheater prospers. Only if both herders act for the common good, to preserve the commons, can both profit.

The dilemma inherent in this matrix is that each herder *should* maximize his own outcome. No matter how the other acts, one is always better off to be self-interested. If George grazes his own flock fully, Pete is better off if he acts the same way (his outcome = −35) rather than restricting his animals (outcome = −80). And he is better off still if George acts responsibly, or cooperatively. Thus, whether Pete wishes to maximize his immediate gain or minimize his possible loss, he must graze fully. The same holds for George. The outcome of these selfish or self-protective decisions is tragic, because such actions result in an outcome whose net values to both herders are considerably less than they would have realized had both observed restraint. Short-term individual gain results in long-term collective loss—and ultimately in individual loss as well.

There are many real-world examples of social dilemmas, where choosing a rewarding individual outcome results in a negative outcome for everyone (cf. Messick & Brewer, 1983). Most people in the United States know that the country is heavily dependent on foreign oil and that a major share of the balance-of-payments deficit is related directly to energy imports. Obviously, if everyone reduced his or her consumption, the national debt would shrink (since we import so much oil to produce energy), pressures on the economy would be substantially reduced, and so on. The country could afford the kinds of social programs that would enrich the lives of all of its citizens, even the poorest. However, to do so would mean that people first would have to use less energy to heat their homes on cold days, less to cool them on hot days, drive less, be more thoughtful about conserving resources, recycle, and so on. In other words, to work for the greater good, everyone would have to make sacrifices. For many people, immediate self-interest overwhelms positive ecological attitudes. And the tragedy is, at least in the short run, that self-interested decisions do maximize immediate outcomes—while threatening future prospects.

On a more localized level, consider the dilemma of farmers who draw water from a public reservoir to irrigate their crops. Because of drought, the condition of the reservoir is perilous. The town leaders appeal to everyone to conserve. What would you do as a farmer? If you conserve, your crops will suffer and your harvest will be paltry. If you do not conserve, the reservoir might fail—but it might not if everyone else conserves. In the absence of intervention, the probable outcome is that the farmers will not heed the appeal. They do not want to devastate the town's water supply, but the other alternative spells personal disaster. With continued pressure on natural resources, examples of theses types will become increasingly commonplace. The emphasis today on recycling and conservation of natural resources is not only sensible but also recognizes the dangers implicit in exchange dilemmas whose interactants include every member of the society, not just a few.

Research on social dilemmas reveals a number of interesting, if frightening, results. We know that social dilemmas are very difficult to resolve. If a resource can be tapped by many people, it will be depleted much more rapidly than if only one person can draw from it. This suggests that if people think they can act anonymously, they might be even more self-interested than usual: If no one can know that I am personally responsible for depleting the resource, why not take as much as I desire? This phenomenon, in which people act less responsibly when they are anonymous, is called *deindividuation*. Anonymity has a consistent effect on people's actions in social dilemmas (Brewer & Kramer, 1986; Samuelson, Messick, Rutte, & Wilke, 1984). Almost inevitably, they act less responsibly. Brewer and Kramer found that people who were not personally engaged with a group experiencing a dilemma were less responsible, and more exploitative, than those who personally identified with the group. Also, Pallak and his colleagues found that people who made a public commitment to save energy were more likely to do so than those whose commitment was private (Pallak, Cook, & Sullivan, 1980).

Group membership influences our social identity: See Chapter 22.

A social dilemma of increasing concern. ■

Real-world Resource Conservation

Group incentives may be particularly effective in motivating individual conservation. Slavin, Wodarski, and Blackburn (1981) used group incentives in two field experiments which they conducted in private apartment complexes in Baltimore. The apartments used a "master meter" system, in which all electricity and water use in a building was monitored on a single meter, and the total energy cost was shared by all residents—whether they conserved or not. To increase commitment to conservation in master-metered apartments, Slavin and his colleagues invited residents to a group meeting where they discussed the need for conservation. Afterward, all residents received a letter summarizing the results of the meeting and introducing a group incentive program whereby everyone in the building would be rewarded by reductions in monthly utility bills if total electricity use was reduced by a specified amount. The incentive program was successful. It generated energy savings of 7% per month, despite the fact that users were anonymous.

Cooperating to solve resource dilemmas can also be affected by purely personal motives. Liebrand and van Run (1985) found that people who were characteristically cooperative and helpful acted more responsibly in dilemmas than did people with competitive personalities. These differences probably would be aggravated if the issue was extremely important or if the cooperative or competitive actions of others were made known. Norbert Kerr and his colleagues (e.g., Kerr & Bruun, 1983; Kerr &

MacCoun, 1985) have demonstrated a tendency of people to *free ride,* that is, to take advantage of others' actions in a group context, especially if their own unique contributions to the group product cannot be identified. Consistent with Kerr's findings, Messick and Brewer (1983) showed that people's cooperative responses in social dilemmas are hindered if they are aware of others' exploitative behaviors. These results suggest that the effects of free riders are especially troublesome in social dilemmas, because selfish actions not only frustrate cooperative intentions but also lead to an escalation of self-interested behavior by others.

Factors that influence group productivity are the focus of considerable research: See Chapter 20.

The Prisoners' Dilemma

A mixed-motive situation of an individualistic nature is the so-called *prisoners' dilemma* (Luce & Raiffa, 1957). The prototype of all prisoners' dilemmas is depicted in the third scenario that opened the chapter. Here we meet Lefty and Louie, who are in a difficult predicament, as inspection of their behavior matrix (Table 12.6) shows. Each crook's outcomes are largely dependent on the other guy. In this particular form of dilemma, two general types of choices—*cooperative* and *competitive*—are prominent. The cooperative choice in this instance is in the cell on the lower right of the behavior matrix. This cell maximizes Lefty and Louie's *joint* outcome. If there is honor among thieves—if Lefty and Louie think the other will refuse to talk—then it is in their best interest to cooperate with each other and deny everything. However, they might not trust each other. In this case, they will compete—the competitive choices are represented in the top right and lower left-hand cells of Table 12.6. In these cells, one of the crooks maximizes his outcome, but the other is severely disadvantaged. In some ways, this is the safest choice because whoever confesses avoids the most severe penalty.

TABLE 12.6

■

A Behavior Matrix Illustrating the Prisoner's Dilemma

	Louie's Repertory	
	CONFESS	KEEP QUIET
CONFESS	10 years 10 years	20 years Freedom
Lefty's Repertory		
KEEP QUIET	Freedom 20 years	6 months 6 months

Note: Values in the upper-right of each cell represent Louie's outcomes; the lower-left values in each cell represent Lefty's outcomes.

TABLE 12.7

■

A Typical Prisoner's Dilemma Payoff Matrix

	Subject 1's Repertory	
	CHOICE A₁	CHOICE B₁
CHOICE A₂	$10 $10	$25 $5
Subject 2's Repertory		
CHOICE B₂	$5 $25	$0 $0

Note: Values in the upper-right of each cell represent Subject 1's outcomes; the lower-left values in each cell represent Subject 2's outcomes.

What Lefty and Louie will do and the variables that swing their choices from cooperative to competitive and back again is a question that has attracted considerable research attention.

Typically in such research, participants are presented with a matrix of the type depicted in Table 12.7. As we see, players in this prisoners' dilemma game stand the chance of making up to $25, depending on their choice. The players' job is simply to choose either A or B. The catch is that neither knows what the other will choose. Conceptually, this matrix is similar to the dilemma Lefty and Louie face. As before, the cooperative choice maximizes the joint payoff. In this case, choice A represents cooperation. If both players choose A, they will maximize their joint payoff. The competitive choice for both players is B. If one player competes while the other cooperates, this will maximize the competitor's payoff and minimize that of the cooperator. The danger, of course, is that both players will compete. In this case, the worst possible joint outcome is obtained.

A review of many studies conducted on the prisoners' dilemma (Rapoport & Chammah, 1965) reveals that competitive choice strategies are extremely common. Whether people are playing for meaningless points or for substantial sums of money, the preponderant response is competitive rather than cooperative. This result holds even when many people will be victimized by the competitive choice (Komorita, Sweeney, & Kravitz, 1980). However, some factors do prompt people to choose cooperation, and we consider some of these in the paragraphs that follow.

Gender. Messé and his colleagues have shown that gender plays a big role in determining differences in competition and cooperation in social exchange. This work was designed to specify the factors that affected people's allocations of reward to themselves and to others. Would equity or equality rule? And would the rule be different for men and women? Messé was concerned with factors that influence people to believe they deserve more or less than their partners (Callahan-Levy & Messé, 1979; Lane & Messé, 1971, 1972; Messé, 1971; Messé & Watts, 1983; Watts, Messé, & Vallacher, 1982). Among other results, Messé's research demonstrates that gender has a strong impact on distribution rules. A common finding (Mikula, 1974) is that men generally favor a norm of equity—the more one contributes to a task or relationship, the more he expects in return. Women appear less likely than men to apply an equity norm and much less likely to act in a self-serving manner, even if equity dictates this is the appropriate behavior. For women, equality is the dominant distribution rule—women tend to furnish the same to everyone, no matter what their contribution.

To understand this difference, Watts and colleagues (1982) reviewed the reward distribution literature and found evidence suggesting that men and women characteristically have very different concerns when allocating rewards. These concerns, or motives, they hypothesized, might be the basis for variations in cooperation and competition. Considerable research has shown that men generally are *agentic*—concerned with achievement, task completion, success, and prominence. Women generally are more *communal*—concerned with interpersonal relationships, attachment, and intimacy (Bakan, 1966; Carlson, 1971). If these differences affect reward allocation, then men would appear more competitive than women. They would seek positive outcomes for themselves, while women would act more cooperatively. Such differences are not directly attributable to gender, but rather to gender-related differences in agentic–communal motives. To test these possibilities, Watts and colleagues (1982) studied men and women in a reward distribution experiment. They found the standard differences—men were more competitive and women more cooperative in the distribution of rewards. However, they also measured participants on the extent to which they were agentic or communal. Consistent with their expectations, participants who were high on agentic motives were more likely to compete to secure positive outcomes for themselves. This finding held regardless of gender. Conversely, participants high in communal motivation were more concerned with maintaining a pleasant interpersonal atmosphere. These participants were more cooperative in their distribution of rewards, again, regardless of gender. These findings suggest that the sex differences commonly obtained in mixed-motive research are attributable to differences in people's agentic or communal orientation. Since women usually are more communal, they typically are more cooperative, whereas men, who usually are more agentic, are generally more competitive.

Communication. Communication also plays a significant role in regulating cooperation or competition. The less communication, the more competition. How does it work? Kelley and Stahelski (1970) found that competitive people assume their opponent will be competitive also. Given this expectation, it makes sense to compete, as a review of Table 12.7 illustrates. But what if the competitive person's assumption is wrong? In that case, the competitive behavior based on the erroneous assumption will stimulate competition on the part of the other

Men generally favor a norm of equity in social exchange: See Chapter 13.

Expectations & self-fulfilling prophecies can have powerful effects on behavior: See Chapter 16.

person. This form of the self-fulfilling prophecy can wreak havoc in a bargaining situation. If people can communicate their intentions, such misattributions might be short-circuited and cooperation enhanced. To study this proposition, Jorgenson and Papciak (1981) investigated sixty-four four-person groups as they engaged in a commons dilemma problem. The individuals in the groups could "harvest" money from a slowly self-renewing pot. If the sum of the individual harvests was too great, the pot would be exhausted and the game would end. If participants conserved the resource, they would maximize their winnings. Participants in half the groups could converse freely with one another. The others could not. The results are clear: People who could communicate gained significantly more than those who could not. They coordinated their actions, warned others of becoming too greedy, and so on. Communication prevented misattributions and fostered cooperative responses.

Characteristics of the resource itself can facilitate or retard communication and thus affect the likelihood of cooperation or competition. Allison and his colleagues have shown that if a shared resource is easily partitioned into equal units, people typically cooperate in their distribution (e.g., Allison, McQueen, & Schaerfl, 1992). Unfortunately, many of the shared resources that are coming under increasing pressure—clean air and water and the like—are not easily partitioned, and this fosters competition rather than cooperation.

Threat. Communication also can be used to threaten one's opponent. Research on threat has produced two different sets of results. One set shows that in the prisoners' dilemma, an individual who responds to an opponent's competitive action with threat subsequently induces more cooperation. Participants who cooperate unilaterally—that is, who cooperate no matter what the other person does—typically stimulate competitive behavior on the part of the other player (Axelrod, 1984; Deutsch, Epstein, Canavan, & Gumpert, 1967). In the prisoners' dilemma, threat entails the participant's telling his or her opponent that competitive choices will be met with competition, thereby reducing everyone's net outcome. Threat, however, is a two-edged sword. Deutsch and Krauss (1960) showed that when communication is restricted, the capacity to threaten one's opponent, *whether it is used or not,* impedes cooperation. In the standard prisoners' dilemma, communication between opponents is not allowed. Because possession of a threat is integral to the prisoner's dilemma, this lack of communication helps to explain the pervasive competition common to this situation: The situation itself may bring out the worst in people because they possess the capacity to threaten, but not to negotiate.

Relationships. Prisoners' dilemma participants who know and like each other are more likely to cooperate (Harrison & McClintock, 1965; McClintock & McNeil, 1967; Swingle & Gillis, 1968). In part, this is the result of social norms, which prescribe that we cooperate with people we like. Social exchange theory suggests that a history of positive exchanges with another person, which characterizes friendships, alerts us to the possibility of further positive exchanges. Thus, we would cooperate with people we like because of our past history of positive social exchanges with them and the expectation of future rewards.

SOME CONCLUDING THOUGHTS

Social exchange theory is a rich and heavily researched approach to the study of human social interaction. It has been applied to the analysis of many important social behaviors, and as a descriptive device, as a means of focusing attention on important factors that guide our interactions, it has proved very useful. Its difficulty is that in many instances, in reducing the phenomena of interest to manageable proportions, social exchange theory simplifies issues to the point that its relevance for actual social behavior is questionable.

There have been a number of attempts to overcome this legitimate complaint. Research on social dilemmas, for example, typically involves situations of considerable complexity, and the results that have emerged from this line of research generally correspond to actual behaviors observed in real-world social dilemmas. The process of gradually getting it more and more "right" is a consistent theme in all science, and work in the social exchange tradition appears to mirror this general progression.

SUMMARY

Social exchange theory assumes that people seek to maximize pleasure and minimize costs in their social relationships. Rewards and costs are interdependent; in an exchange, each person's outcomes are affected by what the other person does. A behavior matrix summarizes the interdependent outcomes of a social exchange, defining the outcomes received by each interactant as a consequence of joint behaviors.

Social relationships can be characterized as exchange or communal. In exchange relationships, people are concerned principally with their own outcomes. In communal relationships, the other's outcomes are also of major concern. Exchange theorists refer to this orientation toward others as a transformation of outcome values. Norms, including the norms of equity, equality, and reciprocity, influence outcome values in social exchanges.

Interdependence gives people the means for influencing or controlling one another's behaviors. Under conditions of fate control, one person's behavior completely determines the outcomes another person will experience. Behavior control is a means of regulating the behavior of others through changes in one's own behavior. Fate and behavior control are the bases of bargaining and negotiation in social relationships.

Some forms of interdependence create mixed-motive situations, in which goals come into conflict. Social dilemmas are such situations. In social dilemmas, self-interest conflicts with collective (group) interests. The prisoners' dilemma is a two-person social dilemma in which people must choose between cooperative behavior (personal loss) and competitive behavior (joint loss). Research has shown that behavior in the prisoners' dilemma is influenced by gender (male and female differences in agency–communion), ability to communicate with one's partner, the presence of threat of retaliation, and the nature of the relationship that exists between the partners in the dilemma.

■ ■ ■ SUGGESTED READINGS

1. Axelrod, R. (1984). *The evolution of cooperation*. New York: Basic Books.

2. Hardin G. (1968). The tragedy of the commons. *Science, 162,* 1243–1248.

3. Kelley, H. H., & Thibaut, J. W. (1978). *Interpersonal relations: A theory of interdependence*. New York: Wiley Interscience.

4. Messick, D. M., & Brewer, M. B. (1983). Solving social dilemmas: A review. In L. Wheeler & P. Shaver (Eds.), *Review of Personality and Social Psychology* (Vol. 4, pp. 11–44). Beverly Hills, CA: Sage.

5. Rapoport, A., & Chammah, A. M. (1965). *Prisoners' Dilemma: A study of conflict and cooperation*. Ann Arbor: University of Michigan Press.

6. Stern, P. C., & Aronson, E. (Eds.). (1984). *Energy use: The human dimension*. New York: Freeman.

CHAPTER 13

ATTRACTION AND AFFILIATION
Choosing Our Friends and Lovers

■ Key Concepts

Communal relationship
Exchange relationship
Excitation transfer theory
Matching hypothesis
Proximity effect
Mere exposure hypothesis
Attitude similarity
Reciprocity
Self-disclosure
Passionate love
Companionate love
Triangular model of love
Equity theory
Investment model

■ Chapter Outline

COMMUNAL VERSUS EXCHANGE RELATIONSHIPS

FACTORS THAT INFLUENCE INITIAL ATTRACTION: HOW IT BEGINS
    Physical Attractiveness
    Does Beauty Equal Goodness?
    The Market Value of Physical Attractiveness
    Is it a Good Match? The Role of Physical Similarity

FROM ATTRACTION TO LIKING
    Physical Proximity
    ■ The Architecture of Friendship
    Attitude Similarity and Reciprocity of Positive Feelings
    Self-Disclosure

FROM LIKING TO LOVING: DIFFERENT FORMS OF CLOSENESS
    Measurement of Liking and Love
    Forms of Love
    Attachment Theory

PERSISTENCE AND DISSOLUTION OF RELATIONSHIPS
    Equity Theory
    The Investment Model
    Jealousy
    Loneliness
    ■ People as Good Medicine

SOME CONCLUDING THOUGHTS

SUMMARY

Dear Abby, I've just seen the woman of my dreams. Her name is Jenny, and she's the most perfect person I've ever encountered. Tall, blonde, and . . . well, you can imagine the rest. The problem is, I've never spoken to her. I hardly know her name. How can I get close to this woman? Abby, I've really fallen hard. I think I'm in love for the first time. Signed, Lovestruck

Grace and Coretta met for the first time when they moved into their shared dorm room at the beginning of the school year. Over time they found they had many interests and values in common and soon became good friends. By the end of their first year, they decided to remain roommates for the remainder of their time at college.

Dave is engaged to the most beautiful girl in the senior class. She's the only Homecoming queen in history of the school to be admitted to Harvard Medical School. She was voted the most popular member of the class, she's involved in lots of volunteer work on behalf of the kids of the community, she's kind and loving, and she can cook. Why is he fooling around with other women?
  a. He's crazy.
  b. Men are such pigs.
  c. See investment theory (page 272).

For many of us, nothing occupies so much of our attention as matters of attraction, friendship, and love. Why are we captivated by some people and not others? How do we choose friends? Why are others attracted to us? What makes us fall in love? How do we maintain relationships? Why do we stop loving? Social psychologists have been intrigued with these questions for years, and have discovered much of importance about intimate social relationships. In this area more than any other, social psychological researchers compete with a wide range of experts—from advice columnists and talk-show hosts to everyone's grandmother. But when it comes to understanding interpersonal relationships, common wisdom is replete with contradictory advice. Does "absence make the heart grow fonder," or is it "out of sight out of mind?" If "opposites attract," why do "birds of a feather flock together?" Clearly, this is an arena of social life in which empirical data and some theoretical framework for understanding are badly needed. In this chapter we review the approaches social psychologists have taken to studying some of the mysteries of attraction and love.

■■■ COMMUNAL VERSUS EXCHANGE RELATIONSHIPS

Before looking at factors that influence attraction, friendship, and love we must understand an important distinction in the types of relationships that can exist between two people. Based on extensive anthropological research and cross-cultural comparisons, Alan Fiske (1991) has suggested that social relationships in all human societies are built from four basic relational models, ranging from *communal sharing* at one extreme to *market pricing* at the other. This distinction is similar to the differentiation made by social psychologists Mills and Clark (1982) between two broad categories of interpersonal relationships—*communal* and *exchange*.

Communal relationships are represented by close friendship and love. In such relationships, people are deeply concerned about their partner's well-being. They give benefits or favors in response to their partner's needs or desires. **Exchange relationships** are the kinds of interactions people have in business dealings or between acquaintances (versus loved ones). In exchange relationships, there is no particular motivation to please the other person, and the welfare of the other is not a concern. If benefits are exchanged, they are exchanged with the expectation of reciprocation. In exchange relationships, we expect equity— to receive benefits comparable to those we provide. Unlike communal relationships, benefits in exchange relationships are not given for the sake of the other, but to secure benefits in return (Clark, 1984, 1986). Both forms of relationship— communal and exchange—are common, necessary, and serve useful functions in social interaction. In this chapter, we focus on communal relationships, beginning with the factors that seem to determine initial interest in establishing a personal relationship with another individual through the development and maintenance of close relationships such as friendship and love.

In exchange relationships, equity is a central concern: See Chapter 12

■■■ FACTORS THAT INFLUENCE INITIAL ATTRACTION: HOW IT BEGINS

Why are we initially attracted to one person and not to another? On what basis do we assume that we will like someone? One way to determine compatibility would be to engage in an extended discussion of likes and dislikes, cherished beliefs, attitudes, preferences, and so forth. In this way, we could tell whether a person's fundamental ideas, goals, and values correspond with ours. However, extended interactions between strangers, and the associated self-disclosures that such interactions allow, are rare and unusual. Indeed, Chaikin and Derlega (1974) found that people view self-disclosure of personal information inappropriate if it occurs between people who are not already close. Because of social constraints, therefore, we often rely on more superficial information to determine if it would be desirable to form a relationship with another person. Murstein (1970, 1976) has found that in initial interactions, people make judgments regarding the desirability of a relationship on the basis of surface features—the other's appearance, apparent indications of style and status (clothing, jewelry), and so on. Based on these rather meager signals, we decide whether to initiate a relationship.

Physical Attractiveness

The most potent and readily accessible information people use when deciding whether to pursue a relationship derives from the other's physical appearance. To evaluate others, people commonly use such features as physical attractiveness, neatness, and mode of dress. Consider the episode that began this chapter, Lovestruck's letter to Abby. Despite the fact that he never exchanged so much as a hello with Jenny, Lovestruck claims to have fallen in love with her. He has based this completely on Jenny's physical attributes, and seems willing to do almost anything to make contact with her. Can people really be influenced to such an extent by physical appearance, or is this example a mere figment of the authors' imagination? Quick review of any of a score of advice columns affirms that our letter is not off the mark. Serious readers of Abby's column will not find Lovestruck's letter unusual.

In this case, results of social psychological research confirm the importance of first impressions based on physical appearance. Let's consider one classic study of attraction in heterosexual couples. In this research, Walster, Aronson, Abrahams, and Rottman (1966) staged a dance for freshmen at the University of Minnesota. The event was advertised as a "computer dance," and students had to complete a series of measures of personality, intelligence, and social skills to qualify for it. Supposedly, this information would be used to computer-match participants with similar interests. In addition to these measures, physical attractiveness was rated surreptitiously by the investigators when students came to the box office to purchase dance tickets.

Just before the dance began, the couples were paired up, but not on the basis of similar interests. Rather, men and women were paired at random, with one exception: Men were always taller than their dates. Halfway through the dance, the organizers interrupted the festivities and asked everyone to complete a set of questionnaires. The students were to tell how much they liked their computer-matched dates, how physically attractive they found them to be, and how strongly they wanted to continue the relationship. Six months later, the investigators recontacted the students and asked how often the men had asked their partners out during that period.

Physical attractiveness had a major impact on participants' reactions to their partners. Those paired with more beautiful or handsome partners (as rated by the experimenters) were more attracted to their computer date. The greater the physical attractiveness of the other person, the more the respondent liked him or her and the greater was the desire to continue the relationship. Nothing else mattered as much as this one factor. Only physical attractiveness was systematically related to students' evaluations of their dates. No other potential determinant of attraction—personality, intelligence, or common interests—had noticeable effects.

Lest one think that this finding is limited to college students of the sixties generation, more recent studies of heterosexual dating have confirmed that physical attractiveness is the most important determinant of initial attraction for both men and women (Green, Buchanan, & Muir 1984; Sprecher, 1989). Yet despite

First impressions based on physical appearance are important: See Chapter 7.

the obvious importance of physical attractiveness in the initial phases of a potential relationship, people often report that it means very little to them. In a study in which participants evaluated factors that influenced their own dating preferences, Tesser and Brodie (1971) found that most ranked "looks" secondary to "personality" and "character." Similarly, when Miller and Rivenbark (1970) asked respondents to rate the importance of physical attractiveness at different stages in a relationship, they found this factor was never reported to be more than moderately important, even in initial encounters. Perhaps we do not like to admit that we can be swayed by physical attractiveness, but as Hatfield and Sprecher (1986) observed, although "people generally *say* looks are not too important to them . . . their actions belie their statements" (p. 119). We might hate to admit it, but looks matter.

It is possible that we are unaware of the effects of physical attractiveness on our desire to establish social relationships. Interesting research on **excitation transfer theory** (Zillman, 1983, 1984) supports this possibility. Excitation transfer theory maintains that physiological arousal can be labeled in any number of ways, and can transfer to and intensify other, unrelated emotional reactions—if people are unmindful of the origin of the arousal. In a test of this theory, White, Fishbein, and Rutstein (1981) had male participants complete a number of simple laboratory tasks, and then exercise strenuously (run in place) for either fifteen seconds or two minutes. Immediately thereafter, they watched a videotaped interview with an actress. For some participants, the actress was dressed and made up to look very attractive. For others, she was made to look very unattractive. Participants (who thought they would meet the actress at the conclusion of the study) were asked to rate her on a number of dimensions, including "romantic" attractiveness. This latter measure included ratings of "how physically attractive [she] was, how sexy, how much they would like to date her, and how much they would like to kiss her" (White et al., 1981, p. 57). Figure 13.1 shows that participants aroused physiologically by the exercise were more extreme in their evaluations: Aroused participants were more attracted to the beautiful actress and more repulsed by the unattractive actress than the nonaroused participants. However, they were unaware of any association between their level of physiological arousal and their ratings. In addition to demonstrating the interesting effects of physiological arousal on cognition, the work of White and his colleagues argues that we often are unaware of the factors that affect the intensity of our feelings.

Excitation transfer theory also has guided the study of aggression: See Chapter 15.

Does Beauty Equal Goodness?

Why are good looks so powerful a determinant of attraction? In addition to the obvious reason, that a beautiful person is esthetically pleasing, the results of considerable research suggest that we also make inferences about important internal features of others (their goodness, kindness, competence, and so on) on the basis of their physical attributes. In general, the better looking the individual—according to culturally defined standards of beauty—the more positive the personal traits inferred about him or her. What is beautiful is also expected to be good (Dion, Berscheid, & Hatfield, 1972). An analysis by Eagly, Ashmore, Makhijani, and Longo, (1991) of seventy-six attraction studies refined and reinforced this observation. These studies revealed that more attractive people were believed to have better personalities, and were viewed as more likely to succeed. Women

Does beauty = goodness? See Chapter 7.

FIGURE 13.1

Physiological arousal and romantic attraction. Note that the highly aroused participants were more extreme in their reactions to both the attractive *and* the unattractive model. (From White et al., 1981.)

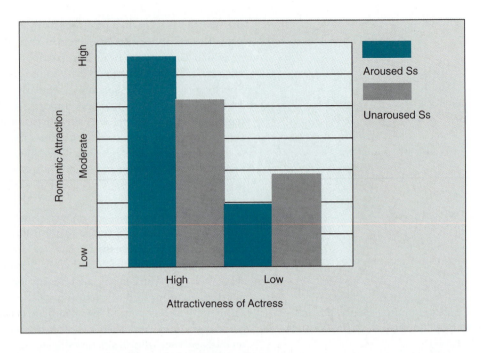

We have learned much about the effects of expectations on behavior: See Chapter 16.

as well as men tend to equate physical attractiveness with goodness, and the relationship holds at all ages, starting with infancy. For example, Karraker, Vogel, and Evans (1987) found that prettier infants were considered more sociable, competent, and the like than not-so-pretty babies, and this same bias held when the models were children, adults, or senior citizens (Johnson & Pittenger, 1984; Moore, Graziano, & Millar, 1987).

Because people expect good-looking individuals to be socially desirable, these beliefs may have a basis in fact. Many studies have shown that strong expectations are likely to be self-fulfilling. Thus, if we expect that beautiful people are sociable, kind, competent, and so on, we act in ways that confirm that expectation. In this sense, beauty might "cause" goodness—when another person is perceived to be attractive, he or she may come to behave like a beautiful person (Snyder, Tanke, & Berscheid, 1977). Reis and his colleagues have found that attractiveness is associated with the quality of social relationships; individuals who are rated as highly attractive report more satisfying and pleasurable interactions with others (Reis, Nezlek, & Wheeler, 1980; Reis, Wheeler, Spiegel, Kernis, Nezlek, & Perri, 1982). Overall, there does appear to be a positive relationship between physical attractiveness and social skills (Feingold, 1992). However, there is no evidence of any association between beauty and intelligence, mental health, or self-esteem (Eagly et al., 1991; Feingold, 1992). There is a relationship between beauty and goodness, but it is limited.

The Market Value of Physical Attractiveness

Although beautiful people may not be perfect as social partners, there are rewards to being associated with attractive people. For one thing, being friends with a highly attractive individual enhances one's own perceived attractiveness (Geiselman, Haight, & Kimata, 1984: Kernis & Wheeler, 1981). In dating relationships, men are rated more favorably when they are paired with a highly attractive woman and less favorably when accompanied by a physically unattractive woman (Sigall & Landy, 1973). When individuals are shown slides of married couples, an unattractive man paired with an attractive woman is judged to be highly intelligent, professionally successful, and wealthy (Bar-Tal & Saxe, 1976). Ratings of women, however, seem to be less affected by the attractiveness of their male partners.

This "halo" effect of female beauty may have something to do with why men put more emphasis on physical attractiveness of their partners than women do. Although physical appearance is actually an important determinant of initial attraction for both men and women, men are more likely to say that physical attractiveness is important when asked what they are looking for in a partner (Berscheid & Hatfield, 1974; Green et al., 1984; Pratto, Sidanius, & Stallworth, 1993). Women, on the other hand, give more importance to factors associated with personality and social status when describing what they desire in a mate (Buss, 1989; Buss & Schmitt, 1993; Pratto et al., 1993). For women, it may be that physical appearance is important only to the extent that it serves as a cue to a man's potential social status and earning power.

This difference between males and females in characteristics considered most important in a partner is consistent with *sociobiological* theories of mate selection. According to this perspective, based on models of biological evolution, male and female preferences in mates are determined by their respective roles in procreation and survival of offspring (Buss, 1989; Buss & Barnes, 1986; Kenrick, Sadalla, Groth, & Trost, 1990). For males, the most important factor in reproductive success is selection of females who are fertile. Physical attractiveness is important because it signifies youthfulness and health, which are associated with fertility. Females, on the other hand, have a greater investment in the long-term survival of individual offspring and require mates who will provide necessary protection and resources. Hence, women are both more selective in their preferences for a mate and more concerned with indicators of status, power, and ambition.

The sociobiological explanation of mate preferences is intriguing because it corresponds to common beliefs about sex differences in our own society and cross-culturally (Buss, 1989). Sociobiological models have been criticized, however, because they seek genetic explanations for choices that may be dictated by gender differences in economic position and power (Brewer & Caporael, 1990; Travis & Yaeger, 1991). There is already evidence that mate preference patterns are changing in the United States as the economic position of women is shifting and dual-income families are becoming the norm (South, 1991). Further, there is evidence that men's views of the "proper place" of women affects their perceptions of the importance of female attractiveness. For males with traditional sex-role attitudes, physical attractiveness plays a more crucial role in determining attraction than it does for those who reject traditionalist stereotypes (Touhy, 1979). Finally, in most surveys of mate preference, both men and women give highest ratings of importance to personality virtues such as intelligence, sympathy, and humor (Buss, 1989; Goodwin, 1990)—traits that are not directly related to reproductive success but would seem to be desirable in any close relationship.

Sometimes, matching extends even to clothing. ■

Is it a Good Match? The Role of Physical Similarity

Although physical attractiveness may have a general effect on perceived desirability of a person as a mate, the fact is that most people actually choose mates who are similar to themselves in level of physical attractiveness. This tendency has been termed the **matching hypothesis** (Berscheid, Dion, Hatfield, & Walster, 1971), and it has received reasonable empirical support. In a comprehensive test of the matching hypothesis, Murstein (1972) showed photographs of a number of men and women to judges, and asked them to rate the physical attractiveness of each. The judges were not aware that each man pictured in the photos was engaged to one of the women whose picture was also being rated. Murstein found greater similarity in the attractiveness ratings of the real couples than in ratings of couples that he had created at random from the total set of pictures. The real couples were more similar than random couples who were not engaged.

Matching on physical attractiveness also has implications for the longevity of relationships. White (1980) found that dating couples who were similar in attractiveness at the beginning of his study were more likely than couples who were not well matched to maintain their relationship six months later. In a study of the clients of a dating service, Folkes (1982) discovered that the more similar a couple in physical attractiveness, the more likely they were to progress in developing a romantic relationship—from exchanging names and phone numbers to extended conversations, dating, and so forth.

Inevitably, their affair ended: Howard worried excessively about what the pack would think, and Agnes simply ate the flowers.

In another type of matching study, Zajonc, Adelmann, Murphy, and Niedenthal (1987) asked judges to view photos of twenty-four men and twenty-four women and to guess who was married to whom. The judges did not know that two sets of photos actually had been taken of each person, the first at the beginning of their marriage, the other after twenty-five years of wedded bliss. The judges were much more accurate in matching the faces of couples after twenty-five years of marriage than they were when the same people were at the beginning of their marriage. Apparently, the faces of the long-married couples were more similar than they had been on their wedding day. We seem not only to match on attractiveness when initiating a relationship but also grow to resemble our partners as time goes by. How? Over time, it is possible that the emotional climate of a relationship would have an impact on facial structure. A couple who have been at war with each other for years probably will not have well-developed laugh lines, while close and loving partners might resemble each other because the facial muscles used to express happiness are well-developed in both. Given sufficient time, the physical (muscular) outcomes of shared emotions would express themselves in the facial appearance of the couple (Tomkins, 1962).

If people tend to prefer partners who are highly physically attractive, why is it that most of us actually select partners who are like ourselves rather than more attractive? One possibility advanced to explain matching is that individuals moderate their attraction to others depending on the probability of being rejected. The argument is based on the assumption that attractive people have great control over whom they select as partners, and hence will reject less attractive possibilities. The greater the disparity in physical attractiveness between two people, the greater the fear of rejection on the part of the less attractive person. People learn not to overstep the boundaries of their own physical attractiveness. This suggests that relationships are most likely to develop between people who are reasonably well matched—not only on physical appearance but on status, education, social class, and intelligence as well.

If fear of rejection influences attraction, then self-esteem or self-confidence also should play a role in our choice of friends and lovers. Confident people should have less fear of rejection, and therefore should be more likely to engage more attractive partners. Kiesler and Baral (1970) tested this hypothesis. In their study, male participants experienced either a success or failure experience on a judgment task. Shortly afterward, they interacted with either a beautiful or an unattractive woman. The purpose was to assess the effect of the success or failure experience on the number of advances the man made during the interaction: Did he compliment the accomplice, ask for her telephone number, ask her out on a date, and so on?

Men whose egos had been massaged by success made twice as many advances toward the beautiful woman as toward the less attractive one. The pattern for men who had experienced failure was the opposite—they made more than twice as many advances toward the less attractive woman. Evidently, the way we feel about ourselves influences the type of person we attempt to charm.

■ ■ ■ FROM ATTRACTION TO LIKING

So far we have talked about what it takes to get a relationship started. Characteristics of the other person, such as physical appearance, seem to be particularly important at early stages of acquaintance (Albright, Kenny, & Malloy, 1988). But what happens as a relationship develops over time? Theories about close relationships suggest that different factors become more important as couples progress through different stages of relationship (Murstein, 1970, 1987). Most significantly, the characteristics of each of the partners as *individuals* become less important than how they *fit together* as a pair. As we have already seen, individuals begin to make judgments about whether another person would be an appropriate match even at initial stages of attraction, and these judgments become more important over time. Understanding the nature of interpersonal fit is a large part of the study of affiliation and attraction.

Physical Proximity

Absence might make the heart grow fonder, but there is much to be said for simple geographic proximity in fostering the development of relationships

(Kerckhoff, 1974). It stands to reason that people who are so distant from each other that they never meet are unlikely to form strong bonds of friendship. But what about the opposite side of the coin? Are people who live close to each other more likely to form positive relationships than those who live at greater distances? Social psychological research clearly indicates that the answer is yes.

The Architecture of Friendship

An early investigation of the *effects of physical proximity* was conducted by Festinger, Schachter, and Back (1950), who studied the friendship patterns of MIT students residing in a housing project owned by the university. The authors determined who liked whom, and related these findings to residents' location. As shown in Figure 13.2, proximity was an important determinant of friendship: Next-door neighbors were much more likely to be friends than people who were one, two, three, or four doors away, respectively. This finding has been confirmed on numerous occasions over the years. For example, Priest and Sawyer (1967) examined friendship patterns among the residents of a 320-man dormitory at the University of Chicago. In this four-year study, dorm residents completed a questionnaire on issues of friendship choice every fall and spring. Each respondent named his best friend and the four men in the dorm whom he liked next best. Then each man was given a complete roster of dorm residents and asked to note those whom he recognized, those whom he talked to at least once a week, and those whom he liked. Priest and Sawyer analyzed the choices in terms of the actual physical distance between respondents' dorm rooms and those of all the other residents. They found results that conformed with those of Festinger and his colleagues (1950): Increased liking was associated with proximity. Of the respondents, 93% indicated they liked their roommates; 45% indicated they liked their floormates; but only 16% said they liked other

FIGURE 13.2

■

Physical proximity and likelihood of friendship. (From Festinger, Schachter, & Back, 1950). Notice the major differences in the likelihood of befriending people as a consequence of physical distance. According to Festinger and colleagues, next-door neighbors are four times more likely to be friends than people who live as few as four doors away.

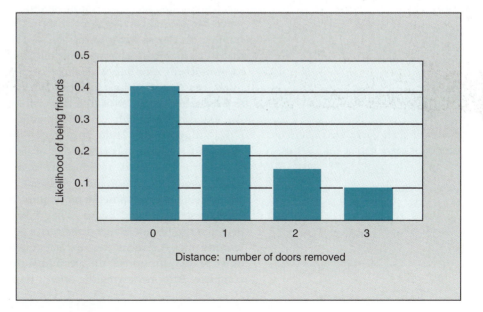

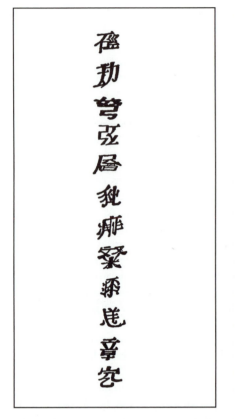

Which of these Japanese ideographs do you like best? Zajonc showed that most people prefer the one they had encountered more frequently. ■

Attitude similarity may be a cause of friendship: See Chapter 1.

dorm residents who did not reside on the same floor. This same proximity effect has been found in bomber crews (Kipnis, 1957), residential facilities for the elderly (Nahemow & Lawton, 1975), and even among those whose surnames begin with the same letter in schools that seat students alphabetically (Byrne, 1961)!

Why physical proximity itself should have such a strong effect on friendship choice is not completely apparent. At the most obvious level, the proximity–friendship relationship might occur simply because of convenience. We are more likely to encounter, and it is easier to interact with, people who are physically close to us. But there must be more to it than this. Robert Zajonc thought so, and theorized that proximity was associated with friendship because exposure causes familiarity, and we are more comfortable with the familiar than the unfamiliar. To test his **mere exposure hypothesis,** Zajonc (1968) asked judges to evaluate a set of novel ideographs. Before the evaluation, he ensured that participants saw some of the ideographs more frequently than others. As hypothesized, the more frequently seen characters were evaluated more positively than those the judges had seen infrequently. Using people as stimuli, Saegart, Swap, and Zajonc (1973) obtained a parallel result in a logistically complicated experiment that required participants to move from one experimental room to another. In the course of their migrations, some participants interacted a lot, others very infrequently. As predicted, the number of times participants encountered one another had an effect on their evaluations. Those who ran into each other frequently during the course of their travels through the experiment were more favorably disposed to one another than those who met infrequently. Apparently, familiarity does not breed contempt, but rather feelings of comfort, which lead to positive evaluations.

Attitude Similarity and Reciprocity of Positive Feelings

Similarity of attitudes also is consistently associated with friendship. Friends and lovers are more likely to agree than to disagree on important issues. There are a number of reasons why this may be so. Friendship might cause similar attitudes—that is, to maintain a harmonious relationship, people might modify their beliefs to bring them into line with those of their friends. Conversely, similar attitudes might cause relationships to form. We might be attracted to others who believe as we do, and when encountering such kindred spirits, we might befriend them. An extensive program of experimental research conducted by Donn Byrne (1971) supports this latter possibility—that attitude similarity is not merely an effect of friendship, but rather one of its causes.

In Byrne's research, respondents were asked their attitudes on a number of issues of current importance, and then were given a doctored version of an attitude scale that supposedly represented the responses another person had made. These responses were bogus. They were designed so that the correspondence between the respondent and the other person could be strictly controlled. Some respondents received scales that suggested they had little in common with the other person; for others, the attitudinal overlap with the other person was nearly complete. After reviewing the other's responses, respondents were asked whether they thought they would like the person. The higher the proportion of agreement among attitudes, the more respondents liked the person whose attitude responses they had viewed.

Why attitude similarity affects friendship choice and attraction is the topic of serious debate in social psychology. Some theorize that attitudinal agreement provides consensual validation for beliefs, which is reinforcing. Consensual information gives an individual strong evidence of the soundness of a position (Goethals, 1986a,b). The phrase "twenty million Frenchmen can't be wrong" epitomizes the folk wisdom that corresponds to the consensus-based explanation of the similarity–attraction relationship.

In addition to the consensus–social comparison explanation, research also suggests that we like those who agree with us because we assume they will like us. A study by Condon and Crano (1988) demonstrated that much of the impact of attitude similarity on friendship or affiliation is attributable to the effect of "assumed *reciprocity* of liking"—in other words, "If you like me, I'll probably like you." Condon and Crano's experiment followed the general design that Byrne (1971) used. Participants completed an attitude scale, and two days later read the (bogus) responses of another person. Similarity of the other person's attitudes was varied systematically. In addition, half the participants were told that this "other person" had seen their responses and had indicated a positive feeling for them. Others were not given any information, positive or negative about the bogus person's reaction to them (this group replicates the typical Byrne study).

All participants then were asked to indicate the extent to which they thought they would like the other person and how much they thought the other person would like them. Analysis produced some very interesting patterns. Those informed that the other person liked them reciprocated, regardless of attitude similarity or dissimilarity. When someone likes us, we tend to like them. Those who did not receive any information about the other's reaction to them were influenced by attitude similarity, as Byrne predicts. The more similar the other person's attitudes, the more attractive he or she was. However, this effect was really the result of participants' assumptions about the other person's feelings toward them. The more the other person agreed with them, the more the participants assumed that the other person would like them. It is the *assumption of liking* that dominates our reaction toward others, not attitude similarity or dissimilarity per se.

Self-Disclosure

Another element that plays an important role in the progression from attraction to friendship is the **self-disclosure** of personal or intimate information. Research suggests that self-disclosure generally advances a relationship; however, as with most things in life, timing is important. If self-disclosure is premature—if it is made while the relationship is still in an early stage, before the interactants know each other well—it is considered inappropriate and slows relational development. Self-disclosures that occur later in the relationship promote it (Chaikin & Derlega, 1974).

The association between self-disclosure and stage of relationship has been demonstrated in different cultures. Won-Doornink (1979), for instance, asked female Korean college students to choose three of their personal acquaintances to participate with them in a study. The characteristics of these three others were specified by the researcher: One was a casual acquaintance, another was a friend, and the third was their best friend. The instruction to participants was merely to engage in a conversation. Before the start of this interaction, Won-Doornink gave them a long list of topics that varied in terms of intimacy. The intimacy level of the topics for conversations chosen by the participants was directly related to the closeness of the participants. Intimate self-disclosures occurred least among casual acquaintances. Moreover, it was in such interactions that an intimate remark, if it did occur, was least likely to be reciprocated. Apparently, we have rules about what is and what is not appropriate to talk about. These rules are dependent in part on the intimacy of our relationship with our conversation partner. Self-disclosures may help to sustain close or intimate relationships, but they are inappropriate if they are made before the relationship has moved from the initial stage.

Investigating the rules of friendship, Argyle and Henderson (1984) identified a number of additional factors that appear to foster friendship formation. This work is based on a series of surveys. People were asked to generate, or to rate the importance of, behaviors they expected from friends. Among the most important behaviors expected (and without which a friendship might break down) were providing emotional support, trust and confiding in each other, defending the other in his or her absence, attempting to make the other person happy, and helping in times of need. In general, women placed greater emphasis than men on emotional support, but the basic components of communal relationships such as friendship seem to be consistent across gender and culture.

■■■ From Liking to Loving: Different Forms of Closeness

Although both friendship and love are forms of close sentimental attachment, most people believe that the two differ both quantitatively (in terms of intensity of feeling) and qualitatively. For some, the very nature of love precludes scientific investigation. But the effect of labeling our attachment to another person as "love" rather than "liking" has such profound effects that it could not be ignored as an important factor in the study of interpersonal relationships. For that reason, some social psychologists set about the task of measuring this thing called love.

Measurement of Liking and Love

Although liking and loving are distinguished by subjective interpretations of hard-to-define feelings, the distinction between these two types of emotions has important consequences for behavior, which *can* be measured in a rigorous and systematic fashion.

TABLE 13.1

■

Selected Items from Rubin's Love and Liking Scales

Love Scale Items:

1. I feel I can confide in _____ about virtually everything.

2. If I could never be with _____, I would feel miserable.

3. I feel responsible for _____'s well being.

Liking Scale Items:

1. In my opinion, _____ is an exceptionally mature person.

2. I think that _____ is one of those people who quickly wins respect.

3. I have great confidence in _____'s good judgment.

From Rubin, 1970.

Love and Liking Scales.   In the late 1960s, Zick Rubin (1970, 1973) developed two attitude scales designed to distinguish between the extent to which a person likes another and the extent to which a person loves another. Table 13.1 gives some examples of the items contained in Rubin's Love Scale and Liking Scale. As we can see, the two sets of items tap positive, but different sentiments.

Rubin (1970) administered both scales to a large sample of dating couples. He found that the two measures were related—those who reported liking their partner tended to report that they loved the partner too. Interestingly, this relationship was stronger for men than for women: If a man liked a woman, he was more likely to love her as well. Liking and loving for women was not as strongly linked; women apparently make a greater distinction between liking and love in their feelings about men. Rubin also found that the Love Scale scores of dating couples were more similar than were their responses on the Liking Scale. People in love, that is, were more in agreement on where they stood on the love measure than on the liking measure. As the Love Scale measures more intimate feelings, we would expect this pattern in people engaged in courtship.

More important, research using the Love and Liking Scales has demonstrated that scores on the measures predict different things about the nature of relationships. In a follow-up study, Rubin (1973) found that dating couples who had scored high on his Love Scale were more likely to be together six months later than were those who did not score high. Responses to the Liking Scale did not predict longevity as well as love scores. However, in the long run, love may not be as important as liking between couples. Cimbalo, Faling, and Mousaw (1976) administered Rubin's (1970) scales to a number of married couples. The sample was quite diverse: Some couples had been married less than twelve months, others for nearly twenty years. Consistent with expectations, Cimbalo and colleagues found that the longer the respondents had been married, the lower were their Love Scale scores. This is not as bleak as it first appears. Although a couple's score diminished over time, it remained high even after twenty years of marriage. In contrast, liking scores were not affected by the passage of time, remaining at the same high level regardless of length of marriage.

A study by Dermer and Pyszczynski (1978) demonstrates another important distinction between liking and loving. These investigators recruited a sample of undergraduate males, each of whom had indicated in an earlier session that he was romantically involved with someone. In the guise of an information-processing task, some of these men read a sexually arousing story, whose title—"A College Fantasy"—should provide some clues to its content. Others read material that was at best neutral—a description of the mating and courtship behavior of herring gulls. After finishing their assignment, all completed Rubin's Love and Liking Scales. Sexual arousal influenced the men's judgments of love, but not of liking. Sexually excited men reported being significantly more in love than those who read the neutral material. Liking Scale responses were not affected by the erotic content of the readings. This is further evidence that liking and loving, although similar, are influenced by different processes. Sexual arousal is more important to feelings of love than of liking, at least for males.

Relationship Closeness Inventory.   Another useful measure of the nature of relationships is the Relationship Closeness Inventory (RCI) developed by Berscheid, Snyder, and Omoto (1989). The RCI is a measure of the extent to which another person can exert an influence on our lives. Although most of the research on the RCI has focused on positive relationships, the theory behind this measure assumes that people whom we hate might also have a strong influence on us. A boss who is constantly on our case, a nasty mother-in-law or former lover—any of these people have the capability of affecting our lives in powerful ways, just as do our loved ones.

The RCI was developed to tap such influences, negative as well as positive. In constructing this measure, the investigators asked more than 500 college students to name the person they felt closest to. Most of the students felt closest to

FIGURE 13.3

■

Relationship Closeness Inventory score and duration of relationship. (From Berscheid et al., 1989.) The closer the relationship, as measured by the RCI, the greater the duration of the relationship.

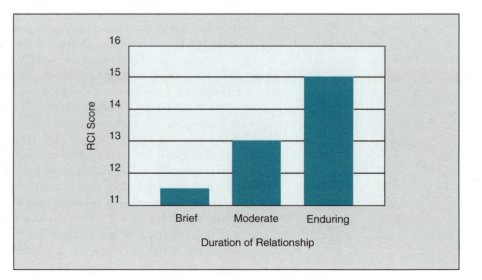

people with whom they were attached romantically. Then, all were asked a series of questions about (1) the amount of time they spent with the person they had named, (2) the number of activities they had engaged in together during the past week (activities ranged from talking on the phone with each other to having sexual relations), and (3) the extent to which the other person had an influence over their present and future activities.

Students who nominated their romantic partners felt closer to them than did those who nominated friends or family members. More interesting is that different levels of romantic involvement predicted which couples would be together at the end of nine months. As shown in Figure 13.3, Berscheid and colleagues (1989) found that the romantic partners who had the lowest scores on the RCI had the least chance of being together when the relationships were reassessed at later testing sessions, while those who had the highest scores were most likely to remain committed.

Forms of Love

In addition to differences between liking and love, social psychologists have also attempted to differentiate among different kinds of love. Walster and Walster (1978), for instance, speculated that love can take two major forms: *passionate* or *companionate*. They defined **passionate love** as "a state of intense absorption in another . . . [a longing for] complete fulfillment. A state of intense physiological arousal." In contrast, **companionate love** is defined as "the affection we feel for those with whom our lives are deeply intertwined" (p. 9). Safilios-Rothschild (1977) viewed companionate love as including friendship, closeness, and concern for the well-being of the loved one. The difference between passionate and companionate love has been compared with the difference between being *madly* in love and being *merely* in love. The distinction is important because different forms of love are associated with different types of behavioral expression. In Walster and Walster's view, a progression exists between these two forms of love. Passionate love, which typically is marked by intense sexual desire, does not last forever. As Tennov's (1979) research on more than 500 passionate lovers attests, the completion of the passionate love stage requires lovers to either progress to companionate love or dissolve the relationship.

Another interesting theory about the profusion of feelings that we define as love has been proposed by Sternberg (1986, 1988). His **triangular model of love** holds that love embodies three elements—intimacy, passion, and commitment. The way these elements combine defines the nature of the love relationship (Figure 13.4).

Intimacy is defined in Sternberg's model as extremely strong friendship, an indication of the extent to which the partners are concerned about the welfare of the other. Intimacy denotes the respect a person has for his or her loved one, the extent of mutual trust the couple possess, the degree to which they are willing to share their possessions, their most intimate self-disclosures, and themselves with the other.

Passion is the sexual attraction one feels for the other. It has to do with the physical yearning the partner induces in the other, the physical excitement a person feels in the presence of the loved one.

FIGURE 13.4

Sternberg's triangular model of love. (From Sternberg, 1988, p. 122.) The three components of the model produce a number of interesting and realistic forms of relationships.

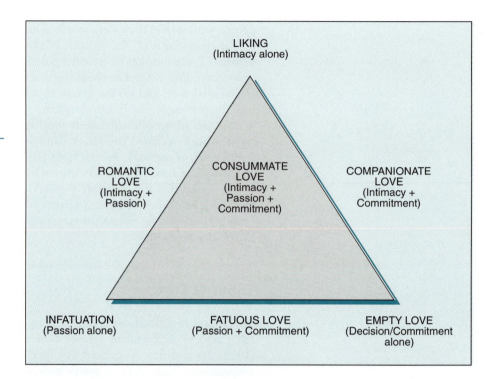

Commitment is the third component of the theory. This element implies two features: (1) the decision a person makes that he or she loves another person and (2) the individual's resolution to maintain the relationship once the decision is made to enter into it. In the model, the three components can vary in strength. Different emphasis on one or another component of the triangular system produces distinct forms of love, and it is enlightening to consider these combinations, as depicted in Figure 13.4.

Attachment Theory

Although Sternberg's model offers some intriguing analyses of the different kinds of love, it is largely a descriptive theory. It does not tell us why individuals or couples develop certain types of love attachments rather than others. Another current theory of relationships developed by Shaver and his colleagues (Hazan & Shaver, 1987; Shaver, Hazan, & Bradshaw, 1988) hypothesizes that individuals have consistent *styles* of attachment that derive from the sort of attachment they experienced as children with their parents (Ainsworth, Blehar, Waters, & Wall, 1978). As a test of this idea, Hazan and Shaver (1987) analyzed responses from more than 1,200 adults who replied to a newspaper questionnaire. Respondents were asked to choose which of three statements best described their own experience in relationships. The three descriptions (Table 13.2) were intended to represent three different attachment styles: *secure* attachments, *avoidant* attachments, and *anxious–ambivalent* attachments. The survey also contained questions about respondents' childhood relations with their parents and their beliefs about romantic love.

TABLE 13.2

■

Descriptions of Attachment Styles

1. I find it relatively easy to get close to others and am comfortable depending on them and having them depend on me. I don't often worry about being abandoned or about someone getting too close to me. **(Secure)**

2. I am somewhat uncomfortable being close to others; I find it difficult to trust them completely, difficult to allow myself to depend on them. I am nervous when anyone gets too close, and often, love partners want me to be more intimate than I feel comfortable being. **(Avoidant)**

3. I find that others are reluctant to get as close as I would like. I often worry that my partner doesn't really love me or won't want to stay with me. I want to merge completely with another person, and this desire sometimes scares people away. **(Anxious/ambivalent)**

From Hazan & Shaver, 1987.

Hazan and Shaver found that 56% of men and women respondents described their attachments as "secure." These respondents described their own romantic relationships as characterized by friendship and trust and reported warm relationships with their parents. Respondents with insecure attachment styles, on the other hand, were more pessimistic about close relationships. Those who chose "avoidant" responses reported feeling rejected by their mothers and indicated that their romantic relationships were characterized by low acceptance and high jealousy. Respondents with "anxious–ambivalent" attachment styles reported difficult relationships with their fathers and described their romantic attachments as marked by emotional extremes and frequent experiences of "love at first sight." These patterns of attachment and their relationship to childhood experiences were very similar for male and female respondents. Although survey data such as these do not provide direct information about actual childhood experiences, they do indicate some interesting consistencies between how individuals describe their adult romantic attachments and how they remember their relationships with their parents.

■■■ PERSISTENCE AND DISSOLUTION OF RELATIONSHIPS

Differences in attachment style are also associated with the longevity of relationships. Secure relationships tend to persist longer than relationships based on insecure attachment patterns. Childhood experiences may affect an individual's ability to establish a secure relationship, but social psychologists have been interested in identifying other factors that may predict how long relationships will last once established. What makes the difference between relationships that burn out quickly and dissolve and those that persist over long periods of time?

Equity Theory

One perspective on why relationships do or don't last is based on concepts drawn from **equity theory** (Messick & Cook, 1983; Walster, Walster, & Berscheid, 1978). Equity is basically a concept of fairness in which individuals expect to get benefits in proportion to the amount of effort or contribution they have made. If two people put in equivalent effort, equity dictates that they should get equivalent rewards. If one contributes more than the other, he or she should get more in return. According to equity theory, individuals will be more satisfied and happy in relationships when they feel they are receiving equitable returns than when they believe they are receiving more or less than they deserve (Walster, Walster, & Traupmann, 1978).

Equity theory holds that a relationship will persist so long as the outcomes a person experiences in it are proportional to his or her contributions to it. Thus, if one person contributes more to a relationship than his partner, but also derives more pleasure or benefits from it, he will judge it to be fair and will be willing to maintain it. Similarly, the person contributing little, but gaining less, would also find the arrangement equitable, or fair. Problems arise when relative contributions do not match outcomes. As you might expect, a person who contributes more to a relationship but derives less benefit from it feels distress and dissatisfaction. Less intuitively obvious, people who are inequitably overrewarded also are expected to find the arrangement inequitable and to withdraw from it. Emotional distress associated with inequity appears to differ for men and women. Men are most likely to feel angry and resentful when they perceive they are being underbenefitted in a relationship, but report guilt when they are overbenefitted. Women, on the other hand, are also angered by perceived inequity, but are more likely to express anger when they feel overbenefitted and to be depressed or sad when underbenefitted (Sprecher, 1986).

Perhaps because of problems with maintaining equity, unequal involvement between partners in a relationship is a strong predictor of breakup (Hill, Rubin, & Peplau, 1976). Inequity is a source of considerable tension even in established relationships. Research shows that in most marriages, women do most of the housework even when both partners work outside the home. The lack of balance in contribution is a potential source of feelings of inequity on the part of women. Such inequities can cause considerable conflict and energize other problems that otherwise might not have come to the surface.

The Investment Model

More recent models of the development of close relationships have elaborated on the concept of equity in order to understand what it takes to make relationships persist. One of the most promising of the new generation of theories is the **investment model** of relational development (Rusbult, 1980, 1983). This

The investment model of relational development is based on exchange theory: See Chapter 12.

model, based on exchange theory, is designed to predict both relational satisfaction and commitment. To judge *satisfaction,* the theory requires that we contrast the rewards a person obtains in a relationship with the costs of maintaining it. This result is compared with outcomes the person has obtained in past relationships. If the comparison is positive—that is, if rewards outweigh costs and if this outcome is at least as good as that which the individual has come to expect on the basis of past experience—he or she will be satisfied. Rewards in a relationship can range from companionship to sexual favors to the pleasure of associating with an intelligent and physically attractive partner. Costs can include financial encumbrances, time, lack of freedom, inconvenience, and the like. The model predicts greater satisfaction with a relationship as (1) rewards increase, (2) costs decrease, and (3) expectations (based on past relationships) decline.

To assess *commitment,* we first must weigh *investments,* the resources an individual puts into a relationship. Investments can range from the intangible (time spent on building the relationship) to the material (the record collection, stereo, and other objects couples sometimes accumulate). The investment model holds that the more one has invested in a relationship, the more he or she is committed to it. To estimate commitment, we first consider investments made in the relationship and the outcomes obtained in it. If investments are high and the outcomes (rewards minus costs) positive, commitment is increased. Commitment is weakened by the attractiveness of potential alternative relationships. Thus, although a person might have invested much in a relationship and judges the outcomes positively, he or she might still be less than completely committed to it if very attractive alternatives are available. The availability of such alternatives may explain Dave's otherwise puzzling behavior (recall Dave from the third scenario at the beginning of the chapter?). On the other hand, commitment might be high even in a relationship involving relatively low levels of investment and outcomes if there are no better alternatives on the horizon.

Can such a cold economic model really predict passionate relationships? Can we plug live, warm-blooded people into this theory and hope to understand anything about love? Rusbult (1983) attempted to answer these questions in a year-long longitudinal study of relationships among college students. The research assessed factors the investment model assumed to be of paramount importance: students' level of investment in a relationship, their estimates of rewards and costs, their degree of satisfaction and commitment, and their estimates of their best alternative to the relationship. Increases in rewards over the course of the study led to increases in satisfaction, as predicted. Contrary to expectations, costs had little effect on satisfaction. Commitment increased as a consequence of increases in satisfaction and investment and decreases in the quality of available alternative relationships, exactly as the model predicted. Over all, the model did well in predicting the development of satisfaction with relationships across time.

The investment model has also proved successful in predicting why some relationships persist while others break up. Simpson (1987) assembled 234 college students currently in a dating relationship. Students responded to an extensive questionnaire that tapped factors the investment model assumed to be relevant to the longevity of romantic relationships (rewards and costs, satisfaction, commitment, and alternatives). Three months later, Simpson retested the same people, and inquired whether they were still romantically involved with the person

Is the investment model only meant for economists and other logical, unemotional people? ■

they had referred to in the first session. Which measures predicted the answer to this question? Consistent with the investment model, couples who had maintained their relationship were more satisfied with their relationship and closer to each other, as assessed on the RCI. Also, they were more likely to have engaged in sex. They had been together longer (greater investment), could envision less desirable alternative partners, and thought they would have a harder time finding a better partner. All these factors fit nicely with predictions of the model.

Interestingly, many of the same factors that predict how well a relationship lasts are also associated with greater distress if and when the relationship breaks up. Those who in the first session indicated they were closer to their partners, had dated longer, and did not believe they could find a suitable alternative experienced the greatest distress at break-up. Further, women who had engaged in sex with their partner experienced greater distress at the end of the romance than those who had not. Sexual relations (and other types of commitment) appear to be a two-edged sword. They may help cement a romance, but should the relationship falter, they produce greater distress—at least for women.

Jealousy

One factor that has received considerable attention as a predictor of insecure attachment and relationship failure is *jealousy* (e.g., White & Mullen, 1990). According to Buunk and Bringle (1987), jealousy is "an aversive emotional reaction

Loneliness is not just unpleasant—it might even be dangerous to your health. ■

The ways in which we attribute causes to others' actions are the focus of considerable research: See Chapters 9 & 10.

evoked by a relationship involving one's current or former partner and a third person" (p. 124). The authors go on to note that the relationship may be real or imagined (remember Shakespeare's Othello). Jealousy threatens relationships because it arouses feelings of inequity, loss of self-esteem, and feelings that the special relationship a couple has enjoyed has been violated.

Jealousy is more likely to occur in new (and insecure) relationships, among those who feel dependent on their partner. It is likely to be stimulated by different factors in men and women. Men become jealous about their mate's sexual infidelity, whereas women are more jealous when their partner becomes emotionally involved with another (Buss, Larsen, Westen, & Semmelroth, 1992). Coping with jealousy depends on many factors, including the self-esteem of the offended partner and his or her attributions regarding the action that caused the jealous response. Actions viewed as temporary and out of character are less likely to destroy the relationship.

Loneliness

When a meaningful relationship ends, loneliness is a common, though not inevitable, outcome. Anyone who reads newspapers or watches television knows that loneliness is an important problem for a significant portion of the population. An overview of the massive research base on loneliness suggests that some people are lonely because of an inability to form close bonds with other people. For others, loneliness is attributable to the loss of an important relationship, through break-up divorce, or death (Peplau, 1985). Simpson's (1987) work suggests that when relationships become exclusive—when others are shut out of the couple's lives—the relationship's failure is especially troublesome.

It is important to understand that loneliness is a subjective feeling—it is not necessarily synonymous with being alone (Peplau & Perlman, 1982). Like jealousy, reactions to loneliness depend in large part on what attributions the individual makes about the causes of being alone. Coping strategies developed to alleviate the problems of loneliness typically focus on a combination of three. Most commonly, lonely people are encouraged (or attempt) to expand their network of social relationships. A second strategy is the attempt to change social needs (for instance, one might increase investment in career development as a primary source of self-esteem). A third is attempting to reduce the perceived importance of the deficiency (a person might become so involved in work that an unsatisfactory social life becomes less of an issue). Research in health psychology, however, suggests that avoiding close relationships as a means of coping with loneliness can be a harmful strategy.

APPLYING SOCIAL PSYCHOLOGY TO HEALTH ■ ■ ■

People as Good Medicine

Investment in close relationships can have its costs, but failing to develop close ties to others is risky also. It is generally accepted in medicine that psychosocial problems can compromise good health (Herbert & Cohen, 1993; Ruberman, 1992). In the past, most research on the social psychology of disease processes was focused on the effects of education and income. Generally, more educated and wealthier people have fewer psychosocial health problems. More recent research takes a more expansive view of potential health risk factors (e.g., Williams et al., 1992). An interesting example of this new line of research has illuminated the physical dangers of loneliness in stunning detail. In this research, Case and his colleagues (Case, Moss, Case, McDermott, & Eberly, 1992) studied people (twenty-five to seventy-five years of age) who had suffered and survived a heart attack (myocardial infarction). All 1,200 patients in the study were interviewed three to fifteen days after admission to hospital. Comprehensive medical, personal, and demographic information was collected on each patient, including evidence about their living arrangements: *Did the patient live alone, or with spouse, children, or friends?* The impact of differences on this measure was startling. Over a period of six months, patients who lived with someone else were 79% less likely than isolated patients to experience another heart attack. This finding was independent of age or marital status. Among men and women living alone, the risk of recurrent attack was greater for women. Over the course of four years, the cardiac death rate for isolated patients was 12.4% versus 5.7% for patients living with someone else. Although psychologists believe that being alone is an imperfect measure of loneliness (that is, being alone is not necessarily the equivalent of being lonely), medical evidence based on this measure strongly suggests that loneliness can pose a danger, not only to psychological health, but to physical health as well.

■ ■ ■ SOME CONCLUDING THOUGHTS

The study of attraction and affiliation, of the factors that influence our choice of friends and lovers and the longevity of our close interpersonal relationships, has occupied social psychologists from the beginning. Early research tended to limit scientific investigation to the initial stages of attraction and affiliation. Today, we are focusing on intimate or close relationships and are just beginning to learn more about these most intensely personal forms of social relations. Given the current divorce rate in most countries of the Western world, this seems to be an important line of research to pursue. We already know much about the factors that affect our attraction to others and their attraction to us, but much remains to be discovered about the factors that maintain attraction and thereby contribute to the persistence of relationships. Social psychology does not need to prove that common wisdom about these matters is wrong but to provide a scientific basis for recognizing the truths contained in that wisdom.

■ ■ ■ **SUMMARY**

Social psychologists distinguish between two forms of interpersonal relationships. Exchange relationships have to do with economic aspects of human interaction, while communal relationships are represented by close friendships and love. Research on affiliation and attraction has focused on the stages of development of close relationships—from initial attraction to long-term attachments.

Among the antecedents of attraction, physical features such as attractiveness have been found to have an important impact on the early phases of relationship development. Physical attractiveness is a strong predictor of heterosexual attraction for both men and women. According to excitation transfer theory, the sexual arousal associated with physical attraction may enhance perceived liking and romantic interest. However, males and females differ in how much importance they place on beauty as a factor in mate selection. In actuality, most individuals select partners who are similar to themselves in level of attractiveness, as predicted by the matching hypothesis.

The development of friendship and other close relationships is facilitated by physical proximity. Mere exposure to another person over an extended period of time promotes familiarity and attraction. Another important variable in the choice of friends is attitude similarity and the reciprocity of positive feelings it evokes. Self-disclosure of intimate information facilitates the transition from attraction to friendship, but premature disclosure impedes friendship development.

Liking and loving are distinguished along both qualitative and quantitative dimensions. Love has been characterized as passionate or companionate. Passionate love is a state of intense involvement, typically accompanied by strong physiological arousal. Companionate love evolves out of passionate love and is the bedrock on which most lasting relationships are built. In the triangular theory of love, three components (intimacy, passion, and commitment) combine to form different types of romantic relationships. According to attachment theory, the type of romantic relationship an individual engages in is determined in part by childhood experiences with attachment to parents.

A number of factors affect the persistence of relationships. Among the more important are considerations of equity. The investment model is a systematic attempt to assess the satisfaction obtained in a relationship as a function of the individuals' investments, their satisfaction and commitment, and their estimates of alternative relationships. When relationships falter, they falter because of a lack of intimacy and inequity in relational involvement, including experiences of jealousy. One of the outcomes of the dissolution of a relationship is loneliness. In addition to being psychologically distressing, being alone has been found to have negative implications for health.

■■■ SUGGESTED READINGS

1. Bornstein, R. F. (1989). Exposure and affect: Overview and meta-analysis of research, 1968–1987. *Psychological Bulletin, 106,* 265–289.

2. Eagly, A. H. Ashmore, R. D., Makhijani, M. G., & Longo, L. C. (1991). What is beautiful is good, but . . .: A meta-analytic review of research on the physical attractiveness stereotype. *Psychological Bulletin, 110,* 109–128.

3. Fiske, A. P. (1991). *Structures of social life.* New York: Free Press.

4. Hatfield, E., & Sprecher, S. (1986). *Mirror, mirror . . . The importance of looks in everyday life.* New York: State University of New York Press.

5. Peplau, L. A. (1985). Loneliness research: Basic concepts and findings. In G. Sarason & B. Sarason (Eds.), *Social support: Theory, research, and application.* Boston: Marinus Nijhof.

6. Simpson, J. A., & Harris, B. A. (in press). Interpersonal attraction. In A. L. Weber & J. H. Harvey (Eds.), *Perspectives in close relationships.* Boston: Allyn & Bacon.

7. Sternberg, R. J., & Barnes, M. L. (Eds.), (1988). *The psychology of love.* New Haven, CT: Yale University Press.

CHAPTER 14

BYSTANDER INTERVENTION
People Helping People

■ **Key Concepts**

Bystander intervention
Altruism
Diffusion of responsibility
Pluralistic ignorance
Misattribution (of arousal)
Image-repair hypothesis
Negative-state relief hypothesis
Empathic joy hypothesis
Empathy
Empathy–altruism model
Arousal-cost-reward model

■ **Chapter Outline**

THE MURDER OF KITTY GENOVESE

BYSTANDER INTERVENTION RESEARCH
    The Epileptic Seizure Study
    The Smoke-Filled Room
    A General Model

THE AROUSAL–COST–REWARD MODEL
    Arousal
    Normative Factors
    Nonnormative Factors

MOTIVES FOR HELPING
    Image Repair and Negative-State Relief
    The Urban Environment and Helping
    The Empathic Joy Hypothesis
    The Empathy–Altruism Model

SOME CONCLUDING THOUGHTS

SUMMARY

You are alone, walking down the aisle of your neighborhood super-market. As you approach the soft drinks section, you see—and hear—a young child crying loudly. No one else appears to be around. What do you do?

■ ■ ■

You are with your date, walking to your apartment after a late movie. Ahead of you, a poorly dressed man, probably a derelict, staggers and falls to the ground. He moans but does not move. What do you do?

■ ■ ■

You are one of a crowd of people waiting for a long-overdue bus. Having time on your hands, you scan the crowd. You count three other students, two old men, and a man in a white uniform with a stethoscope—probably a nurse or doctor. Finally, you see the bus approaching, about a half-block away. Maybe you won't be late for your final exam after all. While searching your pockets for bus fare, you notice a rider tearing down the street on his bike. He's going faster than he should, and when he turns the corner, he loses it. Bike and rider hit the curb hard. He is bleeding from a bad cut on his forehead, and his arm is bent in a very unnatural way. What do you do?

When do people help others in need? Social psychological research on this question has revealed a lot about what you might actually do in the situations described here. For example, research shows that when we are alone, as in the first scenario, we are more likely to extend help than when we are in a crowd of potential helpers. Also, we are more likely to help if we judge that our actions will not prove costly to us. So we might avoid intervening on behalf of the derelict of the second scenario—the outcome is too uncertain, the potential for unpleasantness too great. Research suggests you would be least likely to help the injured biker. Why? To give perspective on the theories and research on *bystander intervention,* we begin with a description of a real event. This sad incident engaged the emotions of people throughout the country and generated intense interest among social psychologists. It is an extreme representation of the kind of conflict—to help or not to help—that we all encounter in our day-to-day lives.

■ ■ ■ THE MURDER OF KITTY GENOVESE

In the early morning hours of a cold March day in 1963, in New York City, a young woman named Kitty Genovese was returning home after working her shift in a cafe. She parked her car at a nearby train station lot, and began to walk

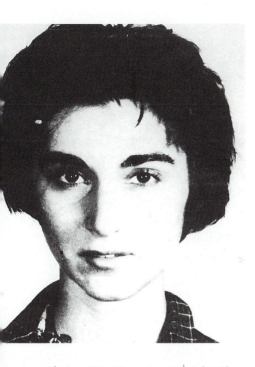

Above: Kitty Genovese. At right: The scene of her murder. (Reprinted with permission from the New York Times.)

toward her apartment. Before she got there, she was intercepted and attacked viciously by a man wielding a knife. The attacker stabbed her many times. Kitty's screams brought a response; many of the nearby residents turned on their lights, and from his window one man shouted, "Leave that girl alone." This caused the attacker to flee. However, no one came to Miss Genovese's aid, and her injuries prevented her from reaching safety. As soon as things quieted down, the assailant returned to the scene and resumed his attack. During the second attack, Kitty's screams again brought a response from her neighbors, and again the assailant fled. Once more, however, he returned to his attack as soon as the lights went out, and this time succeeded in killing his victim.

Later police investigation revealed that thirty-eight people had witnessed all or part of the thirty-five minute episode during which Miss Genovese was murdered. During that time, no one called the police. Only after she was dead did a man call, and then from a neighbor's apartment so as not to be implicated or involved. The police arrived two minutes after receiving the call. Had they been summoned immediately, Kitty Genovese might still be alive today.

The tragic death of Kitty Genovese shocked the nation and the world. In his book which explored the killing, A. M. Rosenthal, the city editor of the *New York Times,* during whose watch the story broke, voiced his dissatisfaction with the standard sociological and psychological "explanations." The usual crew of experts attributed the failure to help to apathy, to people's unwillingness to get involved, to the depersonalizing environment of New York City (Rosenthal, 1964). While all of these excuses may be partially true, none cuts to the heart of the matter. People might be apathetic, they might not want to "get involved" in police matters, New York City might be depersonalizing, but surely these factors would not generate a passivity so great as to allow a person to watch another be murdered in cold blood. Certainly *we* would never act in so callous a manner. Would we? The answer to this question may not be as comforting as we would like. On the pages that follow, we consider some of the studies and theories set in motion by the untimely death of Kitty Genovese.

■ ■ ■ BYSTANDER INTERVENTION RESEARCH

Going to the aid of another is a form of **altruism,** a selfless act on behalf of another, without regard for one's own self-interest. More than 1,000 studies on altruistic behavior were conducted in the two decades following the Genovese killing (Dovidio, 1984). They were focused on the question of why people sometimes respond effectively in emergency situations, while at other times they fail to do anything. In an inventive and provocative series of studies, John Darley and Bibb Latané attempted to come to grips with this question. They were struck by the fact that in the Genovese murder, a number of people, fully protected by the walls of their residences and in no real danger from the assassin, did not respond to the attack. Latané and Darley did not believe the witnesses simply did not care. Indeed, the evidence Rosenthal presents in his book discloses that many of the witnesses were horrified by the murder—they were far from apathetic, yet they did nothing. Why?

One of the possibilities that occurred to Darley and Latané was that the presence of many witnesses, far from helping Miss Genovese, might actually have diminished her chances of survival. They coined the term **diffusion of responsibility** to refer to the possibility that in an emergency, each witness's feelings of personal obligation might diminish as the number of witnesses increases. The greater the number of people capable of handling the problem, the less personal responsibility any specific person feels. Latané and Darley's idea holds that in an emergency in which we are the lone witness (as in the first scenario of this chapter), we will experience enormous pressure to help. If we do not, no one else will, and the outcome will be our responsibility. With many witnesses, feelings of obligation are diffused, and the consequent motivation to intervene might be so diluted that nobody does anything.

Almost by definition, emergencies are confusing. For all but those specially trained to respond, the actions one should perform in an emergency are not obvious. This confusion promotes the experience of what Latané and Darley

(1970) termed **pluralistic ignorance,** a state of uncertainty in which people use the actions of others to determine the appropriate behavior. Unfortunately, while we are intently watching a person to deduce the proper response, that person might be watching us, hoping to arrive at the same understanding. Neither of us is responding to the emergency, and thus we both might assume that inaction is the proper response: The other guy isn't doing anything, why should I?

In an emergency in which one individual is the sole witness, no one is available to serve as a model of appropriate behavior. The person alone must decide the proper response. Theoretically, pluralistic ignorance and diffusion of responsibility both reduce the likelihood of helping in situations with multiple witnesses. Contrary to the old saw, "There is safety in numbers," Latané and Darley suggest that the more numerous the potential helpers in a situation, the *less* likely it is that help will be given. Let's consider some of the research that examined these ideas.

The Epileptic Seizure Study

An early experiment of Darley and Latané (1968) demonstrated the inhibiting influence of the size of the bystander group in an emergency. In this study, respondents were brought into the laboratory and asked to talk about an issue of a personal nature. To enable them to speak freely and without embarrassment, they were assigned to individual laboratory cubicles, and communicated with one another via an intercom system. In some of the experimental conditions, only two respondents were included in the conversation; in other conditions, three took part, and in yet other conditions, five took part. In fact, only one real participant was used in any of the conditions—the others were experimental accomplices whose voices had been tape recorded.

As the interaction unfolded, respondent and accomplices spoke in turn about the problems of working and studying in the high-pressure environment of New York City, where the study took place. One of the tape-recorded accomplices hesitantly admitted that he was prone to seizures, especially when studying hard. Later in the discussion, he apparently began to experience a major problem:

> "I-er-um-I think I-I need-er-if-if could-er-er-somebody er-er-er-er-er-er-er-er give me a little-er-give me a little help here because-er-I-er-I'm-er-h-h-having a a a real problem-er-right now and I-er-if somebody could help me out it would-it would-er-er-s-s-sure be good. . . because-er-there-er-er-a cause I-er-I-uh-I've got a-a one of the-er-sei—er-er-things coming on and-and-and I could really-er-use some help so if somebody would-er-give me a little h-help-uh-er-er-er-er-c-could somebody-er-er-help-er-uh-uh-uh (choking sounds) . . . I'm gonna die-er-er-I'm . . . gonna die-er-help-er-er-seizure-er-[chokes, then quiet]." (p. 379)

Imagine your reaction in this situation. Would you rush to the aid of your fellow student, who was in such obvious distress? Wouldn't everyone? As shown in Figure 14.1a, respondents rushed to the victim's aid only *if they thought they alone knew of his distress.* In the two-person (subject and victim) groups, most people helped. When the participant thought there were two or more others present in the situation, the proportion of help given dropped steadily and precipitously.

FIGURE 14.1

■

Effects of number of bystanders on helping behavior. (From Darley & Latané, 1968.) Increasing the number of bystanders not only decreases the likelihood that someone will help in an emergency (as seen in Fig. 14.1a), but also the speed at which they respond (Fig. 14.1b).

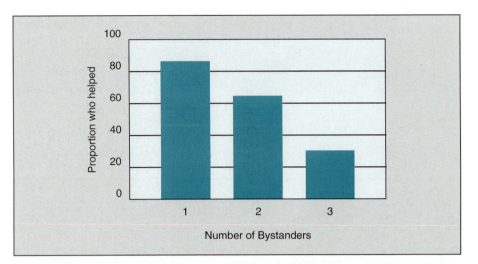

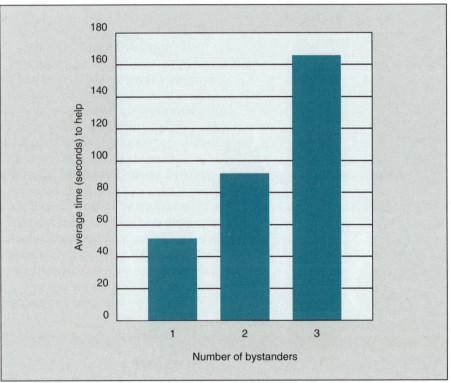

The same can be said of the time it took people to react. As shown in Figure 14.1b, participants who felt they alone were responsible for the welfare of the seizure victim responded in less than one minute; those in three-person groups took approximately one and a half minutes before offering aid; and those in five-person groups took nearly three minutes to decide to do something.

These results demonstrate the negative consequences of diffusion of responsibility. Although only the number of participants differed among the three experimental conditions, large differences in rates of helping were observed. Those who thought they were alone responded with greater frequency, and significantly more rapidly, than those who thought they were in a group. In what might have been a life-and-death situation, participants failed to respond if others were available to perform the necessary actions.

The Smoke-Filled Room

Although the epileptic seizure study compellingly demonstrated that the mere presence of others could inhibit helping, the study was not set up in such a way as to test the pluralistic ignorance component of Darley and Latané's model. Such a test was not possible because participants were studied in isolation, in an experimental cubicle, and so they could not monitor the actions of anyone else. What would have happened if others had been available? To investigate this question, Latané and Darley (1968) brought people into their laboratory and had them begin to fill out a hefty pile of attitude scales. Participants were working either in isolation or in a room with two other people. In some conditions of the study, these "others" were accomplices of the experimenter; in other conditions, all three participants were real subjects.

While participants were completing the task, the experimenters began to pump smoke into their lab room through a heating vent. This was meant to simulate a catastrophe in the making—a fire in the building. If they perceived this as an emergency, participants could react by alerting the experimenter or sounding the fire alarm. Did everyone respond this way? Not exactly. In fact, some participants persisted with the task until the room was so smoky that they could no longer read the questionnaires.

Only about 10% of those paired with the accomplices attempted to intervene. The remaining 90% simply did not react. We know that the accomplices had been trained *not* to respond to the smoke—they continued with the tests no matter what. If respondents used the accomplices' inaction as a guide, then it is understandable that they did not respond either. A more interesting result is found in the behaviors of those groups of three respondents that had no accomplices. The participants in this condition were not artificially biased by the behaviors of the purposefully inactive accomplices. But again, only about 10% of the participants sought help or attempted to sound the alarm. What did the other 90% do? They watched each other. Participants apparently concluded that since the others did not respond to the smoke pouring through the heating vent, they would not either. Most of the people in this condition stayed in the room for as long as six minutes after the smoke had begun, by which time the smoke was so thick that they could not see the questionnaires they were so determined to complete!

And what of the respondents studied in isolation? Before six minutes had elapsed, more than 75% sought help. For these participants, alone in the room, there was no one to turn to when deciding what to do. No one was available to influence their action. If they didn't sound the alarm, it wasn't going to be sounded. Under these circumstances, reactions were not influenced by pluralistic ignorance or diffusion of responsibility, and participants responded rapidly.

The results of this experiment demonstrate the impressive effects of diffusion of responsibility and pluralistic ignorance on people's behavior. Even though the participants' own lives were (apparently) in danger, many did nothing to save themselves if to do so would have required them to act in a way that appeared contrary to other people's understanding of the situation. They were more willing to risk burning than to look foolish.

A General Model

Social comparison theory is concerned with the way we use other people to help us decide upon appropriate behaviors: See Chapter 11.

The concept of pluralistic ignorance is based on Festinger's (1954) theory of social comparison, a powerful model of social behavior. The theory argues that we use other people as guides to inform our actions when we are unsure about the appropriate behavior in a given situation. In an emergency setting in which no one knows what to do, interpreting the actions (or inaction) of other people can be difficult. It is the inability to read other's actions—and their inability to read ours—that results in pluralistic ignorance. Pluralistic ignorance is more likely with strangers than friends (Latané & Rodin, 1969), because we are better able to "read" friends' versus strangers' reactions.

On the basis of their findings, Latané and Darley (1970) proposed a general model that specifies the barriers a person must cross before extending help in an emergency. This model, presented in Figure 14.2, suggests that helping responses can be short-circuited in a variety of ways, at almost any point in the help-giving process. Let's examine some of the model's implications. According to Latané and Darley, before help is given, the following barriers must be surmounted:

1. A potential helper must notice that something is wrong, that a person is in need of help; if not, no help will be given.
2. Even if the potential helper notices a problem, he or she must interpret it as one that calls for intervention. If not, no help will be given. (This barrier reflects the problem of pluralistic ignorance.)
3. Assuming that the helper passes these two steps, there remains the decision to get involved. Will the person assume responsibility for helping? Many factors drive this decision in the negative direction. (This barrier is concerned with diffusion of responsibility.)
4. Even assuming that the decision to become involved is positive, the helper must still determine the appropriate response. If the helper cannot decide on an appropriate action, intervention is unlikely. Only after all these barriers are crossed is help extended.

The Latané–Darley model is a good general roadmap of the steps people must traverse when attempting to decide to intervene on behalf of another. Today, more explicit models are available. They predict with greater precision when a person will cross the barriers outlined in the original theory. These newer models incorporate the earlier theory and research and add other factors shown to affect helping.

■ ■ ■ THE AROUSAL-COST-REWARD MODEL

One such approach is the **arousal–cost–reward model** of Piliavin, Dovidio, Gaertner, and Clark (1981, 1982). This model places heavy emphasis on the first

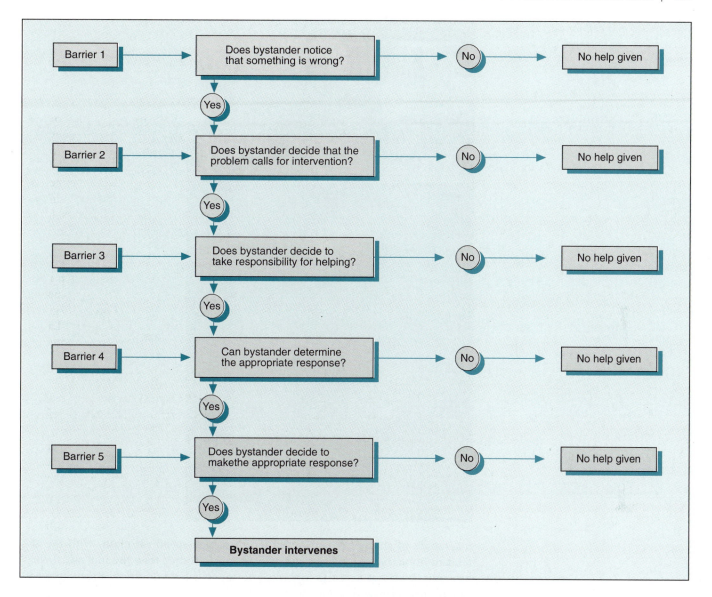

FIGURE 14.2

Barriers to helping: Decision model of bystander intervention. (From Latané & Darley, 1970.) Latané and Darley's model incorporates the concepts of pluralistic ignorance and diffusion of responsibility to help predict when a bystander will intervene, or fail to intervene, on behalf of a person in need.

and third barriers of the Latané and Darley model. The two central components of the model are *arousal* and the helper's estimate of the *costs* and *rewards* of intervening.

Arousal

The first component of the model assumes that people are aroused by the suffering and distress of others. Such arousal is unpleasant, and people actively seek ways to alleviate it. The clarity of the emergency and its severity influence the

Emergencies that call for our intervention can be extremely arousing. ■

Arousal is an important component of cognitive dissonance and aggression: See Chapters 5 and 15.

magnitude of arousal. A person witnessing a high-speed car crash, with the attendant noise, blood, and carnage, will be more aroused than the individual who hears the crash but is not in a position to see its effects, to know precisely what caused the noise, and so on.

Evidence for the importance of arousal in helping situations is clear. For example, Gaertner, Dovidio, and Johnson (1982) demonstrated that people who had witnessed an emergency and whose heart rates indicated high arousal intervened more rapidly in an emergency than did witnesses whose heart rates signified a low level of arousal. How the arousal is interpreted also is important. As discussed in the context of dissonance theory and aggression, arousal can be misinterpreted, or *misattributed,* and this has serious implications for altruistic behavior. For example, Sterling and Gaertner (1984) asked individuals to interact, via intercom, with a partner in an adjoining room. The "partner" actually was an experimental accomplice. The point of the interaction simply was to help participants form a bond with their partners. After this, participants performed varying numbers of push-ups to produce different levels of physiological arousal, and then the next interaction phase began.

About sixty seconds after exercising, participants heard their partner mutter that he had spilled a glass of water on his microphone and he was going to clean it up. They heard (tape-recorded) footsteps as their partner searched for a towel, a loud bang, and the exclamation, "This stupid ladder." Almost immediately, a tremendous crash occurred. Some participants heard nothing after this. Others heard their partner scream and then moan, "Oh, my head." These differences were meant to create different levels of ambiguity (and consequent arousal) about the nature of the emergency. For some, it was clear their partner was hurt. For others, it was not quite so obvious.

Results disclosed that when the accident was unambiguous, the physiologically aroused participants responded more quickly than unaroused participants. The exercise-aroused subjects apparently attributed their elevated physical state to the emergency, and this attribution caused them to respond rapidly. In the *ambiguous* emergency condition, however, the opposite occurred. When the emergency was not clear, physiologically aroused participants were more likely to assume that their physical state was due to exercise. This attribution reduced their motivation to intervene, because arousal was not associated with the other's need.

Arousal does not inevitably lead to helping. Many studies observed low rates of helping even in situations in which arousal was great. Clearly, arousal is not the complete answer to the puzzle. What else affects altruism? In addition to arousal, Piliavin and her colleagues suggest that the costs and rewards of helping (and failing to help) play an important role in an individual's decision to become involved in a potential emergency. In theory, when attempting to reduce the arousal associated with an emergency, the helper will choose the least costly or most rewarding method available. This explanation forms the basis of social exchange theory, a general model of interactive interpersonal behavior.

Cost factors, which have proved to have a significant influence on helping, have been defined in a variety of ways. For example, Piliavin and her colleagues found that people are less likely to help an intoxicated, as opposed to a sober, person who appears to have fallen to the floor (Piliavin et al., 1981). The researchers interpret this difference in terms of the potential risks (costs) associated with approaching a drunk person, whose reactions are difficult to predict. We might also view such reluctance as the result of a lack of sympathy for a drunk: Drunks are perceived as responsible for their own plight, and thus do not arouse much sympathy. But research also has shown that a person who is bleeding is less likely to receive assistance than one who is not. Surely we feel sympathy for a bleeding person, so why would bleeding inhibit helping? Perhaps because the costs of helping a bleeding person seem appreciably greater than those of helping the same person, in the same circumstance, who is not bleeding. Few of us are comfortable with the sight of blood, and in the age of AIDS, dealing with a person who is bleeding can be hazardous.

Considerations of costs and benefits form the basis of social exchange theory: See Chapter 12.

Costs and Rewards: Normative Factors

Most of us have learned a set of rules regarding helping. For example, most believe that children in need should be helped, that old people deserve special consideration, and so on. These socially shared expectations, or norms, are part of the social context in which we live. As Schwartz and Howard (1982) observe,

Socially shared rules, or norms, are a major focus of social influence research: See Chapter 18.

they are "backed by social sanctions and rewards" (p. 346). In other words, if we do not behave in a normatively appropriate manner, we will pay a price. The view that norms help to define social costs and rewards has been used to predict who will help and when helping will occur.

Gender. Applying a social norms perspective to gender differences in helping situations, Eagly and Crowley (1986) argued that the male role favors behavior that is heroic or chivalrous, whereas the female role fosters nurturance and caring. In most studies of helping behavior, the context is constructed in such a way that heroic intervention, rather than nurturance, is required. Accordingly, we would expect to find results that, in general, suggest that men are more helpful than women and that women receive more help than men. Eagly and Crowley's review of the results of 172 studies confirms these expectations. Men are more helpful than women, especially when intervention is dangerous (consistent with the heroic role), an audience is present (amplifying normative pressures—men *should* help people in need), and other helpers are available (amplifying competition to perform according to expectations). Does this imply that men are always more helpful than women and that women are more dependent than men? Not necessarily. In short-term encounters with strangers (which typify much of the research on helping) this appears to be true. However, in close relationships involving long-term commitment and care, it is women who generally are found to be more helpful (Otten, Penner, & Waugh, 1988).

Race or Ethnicity. An intriguing issue in research on helping concerns the effects of race or ethnicity on helping. At first glance, the literature on this topic appears contradictory (Crosby, Bromley, & Saxe, 1980). Wegner and Crano (1975), for example, showed that white subjects were more likely to help black victims than vice versa, while Gaertner and Bickman (1971) and West and his colleagues (West, Whitney, & Schnedler, 1975) showed the opposite results. A close consideration of the conflicting studies suggests a means of reconciliation. In Wegner and Crano's research, the helper was clearly visible to the person in need, who thus could monitor and respond to the individual's help or lack of help. In many of the studies that find reduced helping in cross-race situations, the victim and potential helper are not in a face-to-face relationship. In Gaertner and Bickman's experiment, for example, respondents were called on the telephone, ostensibly by a stranded (black or white) motorist who had spent his last dime in an attempt to call a service station. The caller asked the respondent to call the station for him, since he had dialed the wrong number and had no change with which to place another call. In this situation, the person in need was not in a position to monitor the respondent's compliance, and in such circumstances, requests were less likely to be honored if made by a person of a different race.

These results make sense if we assume that people in contemporary society recognize a norm that specifies that it is inappropriate to discriminate against another person because of race or ethnicity. When this antiracist norm is salient, as in face-to-face situations with innocent victims of chance events, people act in a nondiscriminatory manner. However, when the norm of nondiscrimination is not salient, when the victim cannot monitor the helper's response, when the victim "caused the problem," the likelihood of racial bias may be intensified.

Frey and Gaertner (1986) report results consistent with this reasoning. Their participants (white females) played the role of supervisor in a three-person work group. Group members worked alone. Each of the three members was given a set of Scrabble letters, and asked to form as many four-letter words as possible. One "worker" (an accomplice who was either a white or a black person) had trouble with the task. The worker's difficulty was attributed either to laziness or to the letters she was given, which made it almost impossible to perform well. To alleviate the problem, a request for help signed by either the worker or another participant (on behalf of the worker) was sent to the supervisor. The critical measure of the study was the supervisor's response to this request. Participants (supervisors) were much less likely to help if (1) the worker was black, (2) had asked for help personally, and (3) had brought the problem on herself by being lazy. If none of these conditions held, help was extended. As Frey and Gaertner observed, "The findings support the view that racial prejudice among whites is likely to be expressed in subtle, indirect, and rationalizable ways, whereas more direct and obvious expressions of prejudice are avoided. This pattern . . . seems well suited to protect a nonprejudiced, nondiscriminatory self-image among those whose racial attitudes might be best characterized as ambivalent" (p. 1087).

Discriminatory racial biases may be very subtle: See Chapter 24.

Relationship Between Helper and Victim.   Another normative factor that influences helping is the relationship between the helper and the person in need. Even a minimal personal relationship enhances the likelihood of helping. In a study by Howard and Crano (1974), for example, accomplices of the experimenters approached students seated in a library, sat down, and began to study. In some situations, after studying for a while, the accomplice asked if the participant knew the time. After a brief stay, the accomplice left, but signaled his or her intention to return by leaving books and coat at the library table. Soon, another accomplice whisked by and grabbed the books that the first had left unattended. The question of the study was the naive student's response to this theft. If the thief was not stopped immediately, the victim returned and exclaimed, "My books! What happened to my books?" Participants' helpfulness in attempting to recover the books from the thief (who had returned to the scene after divesting himself of the books and was in plain view) was affected strongly by the earlier request for the time of day. The very minimal relationship established by the victim's earlier request resulted in substantially greater levels of helping than when no prior contact had taken place.

Responsibility Assignment.   In a study similar to that of Howard and Crano's, Moriarty (1975) had his accomplices go to a beach and ask a fellow sun worshipper either to watch his radio while he took a swim or if he could borrow a match. When the "victim" left, another accomplice came by to steal his radio. Interestingly, 95% of those who had been asked to watch the radio intervened in the theft; only 20% of those who had been asked for a match did so. In light of Howard and Crano's study, it is a good bet that if Moriarty had included a no-conversation condition in his research, an intervention rate even lower than 20% would have been found. Obviously, those who had been asked to take care of the radio felt an obligation to do so. The costs for not intervening were greater in this condition than in the variation in which the conversation involved the request of a match, but even a minimal obligation makes a big difference (Quigley, Gaes, & Tedeschi, 1989).

Responsibility also can *deter* helping if another person in the emergency setting appears more able to handle it. For example, Piliavin and Piliavin (1975) staged a medical emergency in a subway car in New York City. On the trip from Harlem to the Bronx, one of the riders appeared to pass out. In some of the conditions of the study, a lab-coated accomplice who appeared to be a doctor or a medical student was present when the incident occurred. When the other subway passengers (all potential helpers) saw this doctorlike person, they would not take the first step and intervene on behalf of the person who had fainted. People who appear qualified to help are assumed responsible, and this norm-based presumption strongly reduces other people's feelings of obligation to help.

Costs and Rewards: Nonnormative Factors

Norms help us to decide when to intervene in an emergency—and when not to—but they do not completely determine our behaviors. Often, normative demands can be overcome by other factors. Time constraint, mood, and other nonnormative features can have a strong impact on our actions.

Time Constraints.   We see an interesting example of this norm-cancellation process in a study of Darley and Batson (1973), conducted with students at the Princeton Theological Seminary. The study participants had been asked to prepare a brief sermon and then to report to a laboratory in the next building. Some of the seminarians were put under considerable time pressure; others were not. As each seminarian was crossing a short alley to the next building where he was to give his sermon, he came upon a person who was "slumped in a doorway, head down, eyes closed, not moving. As the seminarian went by, the victim coughed twice and groaned, keeping his head down" (p. 104). Seminarians' reactions to the victim were observed by members of the research team, and scored as follows:

■ 0 = Apparently did not notice the victim
■ 1 = Noticed, but did not offer help
■ 2 = Did not stop, but indirectly sought to help (for example, might have informed someone that a person needed help)
■ 3 = Stopped and asked if the victim needed help
■ 4 = Stopped, took the victim inside, and left
■ 5 = Took the victim inside and stayed with him

The results of the study are summarized in Figure 14.3. As indicated, seminarians not under time pressure were willing, on average, to ask the victim if he needed help. Those in a hurry were much less likely even to offer this minimal

FIGURE 14.3

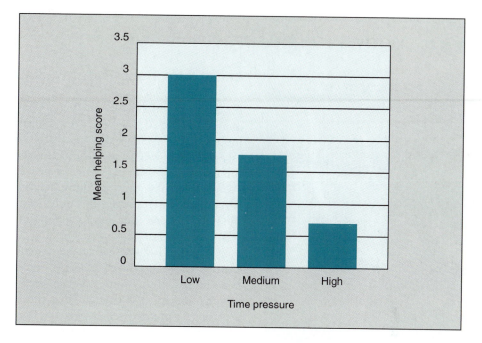

Effects of time pressure on helping. (From Darley and Batson, 1973.) The greater the time pressure, the less likely were the seminarians to help a man in obvious distress, despite the fact that they were about to give a sermon on the Good Samaritan.

assistance. Despite the fact that these men should have been attuned to the biblical requirement to "love thy neighbor as thyself," they appeared willing to pass a person obviously in need of help if they were pressed for time. This is especially surprising in light of the fact that the speech the seminarians were to deliver was drawn from the biblical parable of the Good Samaritan! Summarizing their results, Darley and Batson concluded:

> A person not in a hurry may stop and offer help to a person in distress. A person in a hurry is likely to keep going. Ironically, he is likely to keep going even if he is hurrying to speak on the parable of the Good Samaritan, thus inadvertently confirming the point of the parable. (Indeed, on several occasions, a seminary student going to give his talk on the parable of the Good Samaritan literally stepped over the victim as he hurried on his way!) (p. 107)

Mood and Helping.   Beware if results of this kind put you in a bad mood, because mood is another nonnormative factor that influences the likelihood of extending or refusing aid (Carlson, Charlin, & Miller, 1988). Research by Alice Isen and her colleagues has shown that recipients of unexpected good fortune—which causes positive mood—were considerably more helpful than others whose mood was not manipulated. For example, Isen and Levin (1972) surreptitiously deposited dimes in the change return slots of public telephones at a shopping mall. Of those people who experienced this good fortune, fourteen of sixteen later helped a female accomplice who had dropped a stack of papers in their path. Those who had not been unexpectedly rewarded were much less generous: Of this group, only one of twenty-five helped the clumsy accomplice. Clearly, feeling good has a positive effect on the likelihood of help giving.

■ ■ ■   MOTIVES FOR HELPING

Volunteers against the flood. Both image repair and negative state relief can plain this altruistic behavior. ■

Image Repair and Negative-State Relief

If positive mood enhances helping, what about feeling bad? The research on this question is mixed. In some cases, contrary to what might be expected, negative moods or bad feelings also appear to enhance the likelihood of helping. This is especially true when the bad mood is the result of a person's feeling guilty about something he or she has done. For example, when people harm another person, even accidentally, they are more helpful in later situations in which some action is required. Interestingly, this enhanced helpfulness is directed not only toward the injured victim but also to anyone in need of help. The *image-repair hypothesis* was developed to explain this finding (Cunningham, Stineberg, & Grev, 1980). This hypothesis suggests that the helpful actions performed by people who have harmed others are not necessarily directed toward undoing the harm that had been caused. If this were the case, their helping would be directed only to their victim. Instead, it is thought that the altruistic response serves the function of repairing a damaged self-image. Because we do not like to think of ourselves as mean or abusive, our self-image is jeopardized when we injure another. By helping someone—anyone—we demonstrate to ourselves that we are worthy human beings.

The image-repair hypothesis explains the results of considerable research (see Cunningham, Shaffer, Barbee, Wolff, & Kelley, 1991), but it cannot account for findings that people who merely witness an injury to another person subsequently become more helpful. Obviously, witnesses have no need to repair their self-image, so why are they more willing to help? Robert Cialdini and his colleagues (Cialdini, Darby, & Vincent, 1973; Cialdini, Kenrick & Bauman, 1982) have proposed the **negative-state relief hypothesis** to explain these kinds of results. This hypothesis argues that harming or even witnessing harm being done to another causes a negative emotional state. We are motivated to reduce these unpleasant feelings. Helping a person in need is one way of reducing negative states. As Cialdini and colleagues (1987) observe, "Saddened subjects help for egotistic reasons: to relieve sadness in themselves rather than to relieve the victim's suffering. . . . Because helping contains a rewarding component for most normally socialized adults . . . , it can be used instrumentally to restore mood" (p. 750). The hypothesis predicts that any pleasant experience that occurs between the creation of the negative state and the occasion for helping will diminish the likelihood of helping, because it reduces the need to relieve negative feelings.

To test this idea, Cialdini and his colleagues brought research participants into an experimental room that contained three large boxes of computer cards—another student's master's thesis data (Cialdini et al., 1973). The stack of boxes was rigged so that it appeared that either the participant or the experimenter had knocked them over. This was a disaster for the owner of the data, who was supposedly studying for an important exam and was not present at the time of the data spill. Carrying on with the study, participants were asked to rate a series of pictures. After five minutes of this filler activity, the experimenter left to find a credit slip with which to document the student's experimental participation.

FIGURE 14.4

■

Average number of calls volunteered as a result of negative state and reward. (From Cialdini et al., 1973.) As shown, the worse people felt, the more helpful they proved to be. Notice that those who had been placed in a negative state and then were rewarded were much less likely to help than those placed in a similar negative without subsequent reward.

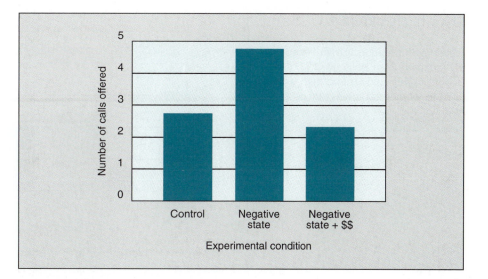

Before she left, the experimenter rewarded half the participants by paying them for their time. Since they had not expected to be paid, we can assume this payment was a happy surprise. The remaining participants were not paid.

While the experimenter was gone, an accomplice entered the lab and made the following pitch:

> Oh, Hi! Isn't Betty here? I'm in the same class she's in and she said it would be all right if I asked her subjects to help me out . . . I need some people who would be willing to call students on the phone and administer a ten-minute interview . . . I can't give you any experimental credit for doing this, but I would appreciate your help. Would you make some interview calls for me? Any number of calls up to fifteen would help.

The central measure of the study was the number of phone calls the participants pledged. Figure 14.4 summarizes these data, along with the responses of controls who did not experience the computer card explosion. As shown, those who had been reinforced after the "accident" were much less willing to assist the accomplice than were those who were still in a negative state because of the computer card mishap. In explaining their results, the researchers argued that the unanticipated reward had resolved the negative state created by the mishap, and thus their response to the request for aid resembled that of participants who had not been responsible for the mishap. The nonrewarded experimental subjects, however, were still in a negative state. They apparently resolved this state by offering help to the person in need. Consistent with this result, in a reanalysis of a number of mood-helping studies, Miller and Carlson (1990) have shown that people in a depressed state are much less likely to help than nondepressed people.

The Urban Environment and Helping

The negative-state relief hypothesis furnishes one interesting explanation for why people are motivated to help others, but findings that do not support this hy-

FIGURE 14.5

■

Percentage of helpers: Town versus city (adapted from Milgram, 1977). Clearly, in this study, more help was given to women, in towns versus the city.

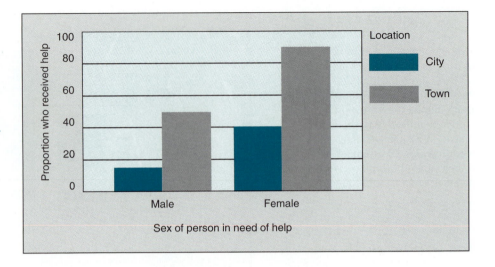

pothesis have been obtained in studies of helping in urban versus small town environments. If negative-state relief affects helping, we would expect city dwellers to be more helpful to others in need than the inhabitants of small towns, because the daily hassles of city life should induce a negative state. To relieve this state, people can do a number of things—including help giving. To test this possibility, Milgram (1977) performed an intriguing set of studies which, contrary to the expectations of the negative-state relief hypothesis, almost invariably demonstrated more helpful behavior on the part of townspeople (versus city dwellers). In one of these investigations, for example, a male or a female experimenter asked householders of a large city (Manhattan) or of small towns bordering New York if they would allow them to enter their house to use the telephone. The results of this study, presented in Figure 14.5, disclose two interesting facts. As might be expected on the basis of research discussed earlier, women were considerably more likely than men to receive assistance. However, contrary to negative-state relief expectations, city dwellers were substantiallly less likely to assist the experimenters than townsfolk.

In addition to the greater danger (costs) that might be involved in prosocial behavior in urban settings, the relative anonymity of the city also might inhibit altruism. These variables may overwhelm any negative state resulting from living in an urban environment. In an interesting test of this possibility, Zimbardo (1969) parked a car in Manhattan, near the campus of New York University. He took the license plates from the car, and propped up the hood to signify that the car was not in working order. What happened? The car was completely stripped of all moveable parts within twenty-four hours. Within three days, it was nothing more than scrap metal. When Zimbardo left a car in similar condition in the town of Palo Alto, California, he found that the only person who touched the car had done so in order to close a window that had been left open. Of course, more than anonymity differentiates Manhattan from Palo Alto, but this study gives us a provocative insight into differences that might characterize townsfolk from urbanites in their response to another in need, and suggests a host of factors that might affect the likelihood that people would come to the aid of a fellow human being.

Calvin and Hobbes   by Bill Watterson

The negative-state relief hypothesis links the internal state of the helper with the needs of the individual in distress. As such, it is an egocentrically based explanation of altruism. We help others not because of their needs, but to make ourselves feel better, to help us reestablish a good mood. The general idea that helping others is motivated by selfish concerns also characterizes other theories of altruism that lie outside the boundaries of social psychology, such as those based on evolution (Wilson, 1978).

Helping Because It Feels Good: The Empathic Joy Hypothesis

Partly in response to such egocentric explanations of helping, Smith, Keating, and Stotland (1989) developed a model of helping that assumes we enjoy other people's relief at being helped *(empathy)*. We help people, in other words, not to relieve our own distress, but rather because we are rewarded by other people's happiness. Notice that the basis of this **empathic joy hypothesis** is not entirely unselfish: We help not simply to relieve a victim's need but because the person's relief is rewarding to us. While still egocentric, this motive for helping clearly differs from ones that focus only on the helper's mood.

To test their theory, Smith and his colleagues exposed undergraduates to a videotaped interview of an unhappy young woman, a fellow student who was experiencing great difficulty adjusting to college (Smith et al., 1989). In the video, the woman expressed feelings of isolation and loneliness, and related that she was thinking of leaving the university. Similarity between participants and the woman was manipulated to create different levels of sensitivity to the woman. The researchers assumed that participants would identify more with a person similar to themselves.

Participants were given the option of videotaping advice to the student under one of two conditions: Half were told that if they gave advice to the student, they would see a video of the outcome of their help—the student would tell them if their advice was useful. The remaining respondents were led to believe they would not see the student again. They would never know if their advice had helped. The manipulation had a strong effect on people's willingness to offer advice. Consistent with the empathic joy hypothesis, participants were substantially more helpful to similar others *if* they thought they would witness the results of their advice. Similarity and empathy did not affect helping if they did not think they would be able to learn about the outcome of their suggestions. Negative-state relief cannot explain these results. If people helped only to relieve a negative state, then learning about the outcome of their advice should not have really mattered. What should matter is that they try to help. As was shown, however, this was not enough. What does explain the results is the hypothesis that we are reinforced by the positive outcomes experienced by others. People were more willing to help others like themselves if they could experience the other's outcome. If they were not to be rewarded for their help by learning of its effect, they were less willing to extend it.

The Empathy–Altruism Model

A model that has the potential to integrate both the negative-state relief and the empathic-joy hypothesis has been developed by Batson and his colleagues (e.g., Batson, 1987; Batson & Oleson, 1991). Their **empathy–altruism model,** as it is called, postulates that seeing another person in distress can stimulate two distinct reactions: *distress* and *empathy*. Distress is an unpleasant state, and the witness is motivated to reduce it. If distress is aroused by the suffering of others, it can be reduced by helping. This response, however, is egotistic, because the helper's behavior is motivated by his or her own distress, not that of the person in need. This kind of motivation is the basis of the negative-state relief hypothesis. Empathy, on the other hand, directs attention to the distress of the person in need. Empathy stimulates an altruistic response focused on reducing the distress of the other. Batson's empathy–altruism model hypothesizes that behavior can be motivated either by empathy or distress, depending on factors in the helping context.

In an interesting comparison of the empathy–altruism and negative-state relief hypotheses, Batson and his colleagues manipulated empathy and the anticipation of mood enhancement (Batson et al., 1989). All participants listened to a tape-recorded communication about a student whose parents had been killed in a car wreck. Katie Banks, the student, was trying desperately to complete college and to support her surviving brother and sister. To manipulate empathy, some participants (the low-empathy group) were to focus on the technical aspects of the communication. Others (the high-empathy group), were to try to imagine how Katie felt about the catastrophe. In addition, some of the participants anticipated that later they would see a video that would positively enhance their mood state, while others were promised a video that would cause no noticeable change in mood. Before the video was played, and after all had listened to the Katie Banks communication, the participants were asked if they would care to volunteer time helping Katie with baby-sitting, transportation, and so on. The request was made in such a manner that the experimenter would not know the participant's response.

The empathy manipulation had a powerful impact on volunteerism. As predicted by the altruism–empathy model, participants who had adopted an empathic orientation when listening to the Katie Banks story were considerably

Distress at another's plight and empathy for the person may both contribute to helping behavior. ■

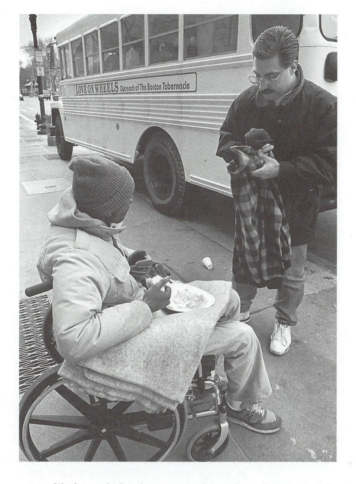

more likely to help than were those for whom empathy was not emphasized. Contrary to the expectations of the negative-state relief hypothesis, the anticipation of mood enhancement had no impact on the results. All participants were expected to be distressed at Katie's tale (and in fact they were). This negative mood state could be alleviated by helping Katie. But those promised a mood-enhancing video would not need to expend this effort to establish a positive mood—they could wait a few minutes for the video. However, the participants expecting positive mood enhancement were no less likely to volunteer than those who did not expect it. Thus, the results of the study lend more support to the empathy–altruism model than the negative-state relief hypothesis. On the other hand, in another study in the series, Batson and his colleagues showed that participants who were made sad (rather than empathic) were more likely to help than others, except if they anticipated positive mood enhancement. This finding fits the negative-state relief hypothesis.

Batson's research suggests that both empathy and negative-state relief can influence helping behavior. If the context of the helping situation fosters empathy, then altruistically motivated responses may be anticipated. If the context creates distress, but not empathy, then negative-state relief may be more likely to control actions.

■■■ SOME CONCLUDING THOUGHTS

We may not engage in helping behavior because the socially supplied information is not useful: See Chapter 18.

It is clear that the psychological meaning of altruism is not simple. We help people, or refuse to help, for a variety of reasons. Some of those reasons have to do with confusion. In some circumstances, we simply do not know what to do. In other circumstances, helping clearly is called for, but the potential costs might outweigh the rewards of our altruistic behavior. At still other times, we might help because we are in a bad mood or because we feel good when we help others.

Does it matter what factors cause us to help another person? Yes. These distinctions are critical if we are intent on understanding the features that give rise to or retard helping in a specific context. If we know which motives are most likely to be aroused, we can better develop the specific forms of appeals that will prove most effective. At times, the stakes involved in receiving help are so great that knowing the right way to request it may be a matter of life or death.

■■■ SUMMARY

Serious study of the factors that influence helping behavior, or bystander intervention, began with the untimely and unnecessary death of Kitty Genovese in New York. The work of Latané and Darley showed that thirty-eight witnesses' failure in coming to the aid of Kitty Genovese was not an aberration attributable to the apathy and depersonalization that are a part of big-city life, but the result of a set of predictable factors that are nearly as likely to operate in small towns as in big cities. Darley and Latané found that pluralistic ignorance and diffusion of responsibility could have a devastating effect on the likelihood of receiving help. In a situation in which the appropriate behavior is not obvious, as in many emergencies, people use other people to inform them of the right action to take. If others are not available, people assume responsibility for helping, and generally provide assistance if they define a situation as one calling for their intervention and if they have some idea as to the appropriate way of intervening. If others are available, people generally assume that the responsibility for intervening is shared—thus, the more witnesses, the less responsibility any specific person feels.

The arousal–cost–reward model is an attempt to specify the factors that cause people to identify a situation as one that calls for their help and that guide their decision to provide help to another. The model assumes that we are aroused by the needs of others and that we weigh the costs and rewards of helping a person in need. Widely accepted social norms help to define costs and rewards: Most of us find helping others reinforcing. Nonnormative factors such as mood and time pressure also affect the likelihood of altruistic acts.

Continuing controversies in the field concern the motivation for helping. Do we help others to alleviate a negative state (negative-state relief hypothesis), because it feels good to do so (empathic joy hypothesis), or because we are responding directly to another's need? The empathy–altruism hypothesis integrates many of these conflicting models. It holds that we can be motivated to alleviate another's suffering (1) to reduce the distress caused by witnessing it or (2) out of a sense of altruism—we help people because we can empathize with their need. Although the outcome of the process may be the same—the person in need is helped—the motives underlying the help giving and the contextual factors that activate one motive or another may be very different.

■ ■ ■ **SUGGESTED READINGS**

1. Batson, C. D. (1991). *The altruism question: Toward a social-psychological answer.* Hillsdale, NJ: Erlbaum.

2. Clark, M. S. (Ed.). (1991). *Review of Personality and Social Psychology: Altruism and Prosocial Behavior* (Vol. 12). Newbury Park, CA: Sage.

3. Dovidio, J. F., & Gaertner, S. L. (Eds.). (1986). *Prejudice, discrimination, and racism: Theory and research.* Orlando, FL: Academic Press.

4. Piliavin, J. A., & Charng, H. (1990). Altruism: A review of recent theory and research. *Annual Review of Sociology, 16,* 27–65.

5. Staub, E. (1978). *Positive social behavior and morality.* New York: Academic Press.

CHAPTER 15

AGGRESSION
People Hurting People

■ Key Concepts

Intention
Instrumental aggression
Hostile aggression
Instinctive drive to aggression
Frustration–aggression theory
Displaced aggression
Cognitive neoassociationism
Excitation transfer
Social learning theory
Erotic violence
Alcoholic disinhibition
Learned disinhibition

■ Chapter Outline

WHAT IS IT? DEFINING AGGRESSION
    Types of Aggression: Instrumental and Hostile
    Sources of Aggression: Where Does It Come From?

EXPLANATIONS BASED ON INSTINCT OR INHERITANCE
    Instinct Theories
    Inheritance Theories

EXPLANATIONS BASED ON MOTIVATION AND LEARNING
    Frustration–Aggression Theory
    Frustration–Aggression Theory: Revised Edition
    Excitation Transfer
    ■ Heat and Aggression
    Social Learning of Aggression
    Cues to Aggression

IMPORTANT SOCIAL ISSUES IN THE STUDY OF AGGRESSION
    Race and Ethnicity
    Media Aggression
    ■ Alcohol and Aggression

SOME CONCLUDING THOUGHTS

SUMMARY

The previews have just ended, and Jerry is returning to his seat at the movies. He is carrying a box of popcorn and an extra large Coke. As he squeezes down the row of seats in the darkened theater, Jerry steps on his buddy's foot. He stumbles and dumps his popcorn on Mary, sitting in the row in front, and his Coke douses Harry, Mary's date. Harry turns around and punches Jerry on the nose. Jerry falls back onto his buddy Terry, and crushes the extra-large orange soda Terry was holding on his lap. The usher rushes to the ruckus, grabs Harry in an arm lock, and roughly pushes him to the door. Mary screams at Jerry, "You clumsy oaf," and tearfully runs out. Terry goes home to change trousers. Jerry moves to a dry seat and watches the classic western The Wild Bunch.

More than 20,000 murders are committed each year in the United States (Saks, 1992), and cases of assault, mugging, robbery, and rape are almost beyond count. If you watch the evening news, read the newspaper, listen to the radio, or drive during rush hour, you will come to the inescapable conclusion that aggression is a pervasive feature of our society. Because of this, social psychologists have devoted enormous resources to the study of aggression. In this chapter, we trace some of the major explanations of aggression, and outline research that has implications for understanding what aggression is, how it is triggered, and what might be done to prevent it.

■■■ WHAT IS IT? DEFINING AGGRESSION

On the surface, defining aggression seems simple. We all know what constitutes an aggressive act. But widespread scientific agreement on a basic definition has been difficult to achieve. In an early attempt, A. H. Buss (1961) proposed that aggression be defined as any action that delivers noxious stimulation (that hurts someone). This seems like a reasonable definition until you try to apply it to actual situations. Let's consider the preceding scenario. Jerry, a notoriously clumsy guy, has tripped in a movie theater and spilled a jumbo box of popcorn on Mary, and an extra-large Coke on her date. Furthermore, he's been pushed onto his friend Terry's orange soda, which was on Terry's lap at the time. Were Jerry's actions aggressive? Most of us would not define them that way, but they satisfy Buss's definition. In each instance, Jerry delivered a noxious stimulus to another person. However, it is clear that Jerry did not intend to hurt anyone. He may be clumsy, but he's not mean. Can Jerry's behaviors be judged equal to Harry's? Is an accidental spill the aggressive equivalent of a punch on the nose? Most of us would say not.

Suppose that Jerry hit back—would that be an aggressive act or merely self-defense? Was Mary's outburst at Jerry aggressive? And what about the actions of the usher, who forcefully escorted Harry out of the theater? Questions of this type illustrate some of the complications in defining and studying aggression. Moreover, they suggest there is a missing ingredient to Buss's "noxious stimulus" definition. This missing ingredient is **intention.** If Jerry had meant to harm Mary or Harry, we would view his actions as aggressive. If he had intended no harm—he might not even have seen the couple in the dark theater—then his actions could not reasonably be defined as aggressive. Clumsy maybe, but not aggressive.

Most social psychologists today are guided by this reasoning, and define aggression as words or actions whose *intent* is to hurt another (Baron, 1977; Zillman, 1979). Interestingly, intention was viewed as an essential ingredient in one of the earliest, and still influential, theoretical analyses of aggression. Dollard, Doob, Miller, Mowrer, and Sears (1939) defined aggression as "an act whose goal . . . is injury to an organism" (p. 11). Without the intent to harm, the act is not aggressive, even though it might result in great pain and suffering. By this definition, Jerry's actions would not be defined as aggressive if he did not intend to spill his food and drink on the couple in the front row. But even if Harry missed when he swung at Jerry, his action would meet the criterion—he clearly intended harm.

In some ways, intent provides a satisfying solution to the definition problem. Accidental actions that harm someone are not defined as aggressive. However, inferring intent can lead to complications. It is difficult to know what people intend. Based on the information given, most of us would not define Jerry's actions as aggressive. However, what if we learned that Mary had just broken off her engagement with Jerry, and he was extremely jealous and upset about losing her? Would this change our definition of Jerry's actions? If it did, the change would signal a potential problem with our definition, because the same action could be categorized in different ways as a consequence of a property of the actor (intent) that we cannot really observe.

Difficulties with inferring intent are well illustrated in research by Mummendey and Otten (1989), whose participants watched one of two different films of an aggressive encounter between two adolescent boys. Some were asked to view the encounter from the perspective of the boy who initiated the aggressive interaction. Other participants viewed the encounter from the perspective of the boy who responded to the aggression. The different perspectives had a strong influence on participants' judgments of aggression, especially in one of the films, in which the initiator of the aggression was somewhat ambiguous. In this instance, participants who viewed the film from the aggressor's perspective were much less likely to believe their character started the problem. They assumed events that had transpired before the film justified the actor's behaviors, and thus the recipient of the aggression was actually responsible for the trouble. Those who viewed the film from the victim's perspective did not make this kind of attribution. They blamed the aggressor even under ambiguous circumstances. Mummendey and Otten's results suggest that inferring intent is even more difficult than it might have appeared initially, and depends, at least in part, on the perspective and expectations of the witness to the aggression.

Types of Aggression: Instrumental and Hostile

In addition to differentiating actions that are intended to hurt others from those not meant to do so, social psychologists have attempted to distinguish different

Perspective and expectancies influence how we infer motives: See Chapter 16.

Instrumental aggression is a prominent feature of Stanley Milgram's classic studies of obedience: See Chapter 17.

forms of aggression. The two major types are termed instrumental and hostile aggression (Feshbach, 1964). **Instrumental aggression** consists of actions that are intended to hurt others, but only for a specific purpose. In this case, aggression is used as a tactic to produce a desired outcome. Many parents spank their young children when they venture into the street. Are the parents delivering a noxious stimulus? There is no question of this. Do they intend to do so? Of course. So by most common definitions, spanking is an aggressive act. But do the parents intend to harm their child? Probably not. The aggressive act is calculated; it is not hostile. It is meant to impress an important lesson on the child. This is a central feature of instrumental aggression. Of course, we do not deny the reality of hostile aggression in some parents' relationships with their children. There is little doubt that much physical discipline is hostile. Such behavior is not instrumental—its major purpose is to deliver harm, not to instruct.

A good research analogue of instrumental aggression may be found in Stanley Milgram's (1974) studies of obedience. In these studies, participants playing the role of a teacher are instructed to shock a learner each time a mistake is made. The teachers are not angry with the errant learners; they deliver shocks merely to help the experimenter understand the effects of punishment on learning. The aggressive act is a tactic, not an expression of hostility or rage. Al Capone was referring to instrumental aggression when he said, "You can get more with a kind word and a gun than with a kind word alone."

Hostile aggression is the form of behavior that most of us visualize when we think about aggression. Hostile aggression is accompanied by strong emotions of anger or rage, and it is intended directly to harm or injure its target. Anyone who has ever been in a state of hostile aggression knows this state is accompanied by obvious changes in physiology: increased pulse rate, heightened blood pressure, increased blood flow to the muscles and decreased flow to the viscera (Moyer, 1976). As we see later in this chapter, the psychological origins of hostile aggression are quite distinct from those underlying instrumental aggression.

Sources of Aggression: Where Does It Come From?

We have two options when attempting to discover the source of aggression. We can look to internal causes, to factors that lie within the aggressor, or to the situational cues that provoke aggression. Theoretical analyses based on internal causes usually assume an instinctive or biological underpinning to aggression. We are aggressive because we are genetically predisposed to it (that is, we have inherited the disposition to aggress) or because of some structural abnormality (for example, brain damage, hormonal imbalance) that causes aggressive outbursts. Theories that focus on external factors—the social situations and cultural rules that promote aggression—are more likely to use motivational explanations. We aggress because someone has frustrated us or because we have learned that aggression pays in some circumstances. Both types of theories have marshalled considerable evidence, and both probably represent at least part of the truth. In the pages that follow, we discuss some of the more credible views of the sources of aggression and introduce some of the major theories of aggressive behavior.

■ ■ ■ EXPLANATIONS BASED ON INSTINCT OR INHERITANCE

Instinct Theories

Freud (1930) thought we aggress because we have an *instinctive drive* to do so: "The tendency to aggression is an innate, independent, instinctual disposition in man" (p. 102). In his introduction to psychoanalysis, Freud (1933) spoke of a death wish *(thanatos),* which is initially turned inward in a self-destructive way but that soon is directed outward, toward others. According to Freud, the death wish is the source of aggression in people. Freud viewed thanatos as a destructive force that could be controlled but never eliminated. We are always going to aggress. The expression of aggression is cathartic—that is, aggressive acts reduce the pent-up instinct to aggress and lower the likelihood of further aggression—at least for a time, until it builds up again.

A somewhat more optimistic view of aggressive instincts is offered by *ethologists,* scientists who study animals in naturalistic settings to learn more about behavior. Ethologists assume that explaining aggressive behavior in animals will help us understand aggression in people. The ethologists agree with Freud that aggression is part of our genetic make–up. For example, Konrad Lorenz (1966), a Nobel laureate and one of the world's foremost ethologists, insisted that all animals, including humans, are aggressive. However, he argued that aggression was not necessarily a bad thing. In most of the animal kingdom, it is prerequisite for survival. If an animal is to maintain its feeding and breeding territory, protect its young, and ward off rivals, it must aggress. Such aggression is adaptive; it helps the organism survive. Aggression does not occur randomly; rather, it is triggered by specific cues that release an instinctive (aggressive) response.

There are at least two problems with the ethological approach for understanding human aggression. First, we have yet to find the triggers that invariably set off aggression in people. "Innate releasing mechanisms," cues that *inevitably* give rise to aggression, have been identified for only a tiny fraction of the animal kingdom. Second, the kinds of aggression that Lorenz observed in animals involve a set of highly constrained, ritualized actions. The patterns of aggression people exhibit are characterized by their diversity. The variety of ways we humans have discovered to hurt one another does not conform to ethological expectations. This does not mean that biology plays no role in aggression, but rather that the variety of ways that aggression is expressed are not easily explained by ethological theories.

Inheritance Theories

Another approach that assumes a genetic component to aggression has been advanced by *sociobiologists,* who hold that all of our enduring forms of behavior have persisted because they help us survive (cf. Wilson, 1975; Rushton, 1988). What forms of behavior have survival value? Those that allow people to reproduce and transfer their genes to succeeding generations. Aggression surely is one such behavior. Thus, natural selection favors aggressive males, who are more

One of the many ways of expressing hostile aggression. Research suggest that males might be more prone to this form of expression than females. ■

capable of securing and defending mates. Hormonal research suggests that male sex hormones are indeed associated with aggression (Maccoby & Jacklin, 1980). So far, however, researchers have been unable to establish whether hormonal differences or variations in the socialization patterns of boys and girls are responsible for the apparent difference in aggressiveness in men and women. There are some who argue that there is no overall sex difference in aggressiveness, but rather aggression is expressed differently by men and women. In a review of eighty-six studies, Eagly and Steffen (1986) found males more willing to express physical aggression and to induce pain and injury. Females were more prone to psychological attack and verbal abuse. Both types of behavior are aggressive; they simply represent different ways of expressing it. (On the other hand, many of us would rather be yelled at than punched.)

There is substantial evidence that tendencies to aggression can be transmitted genetically. Lagerspetz (1979) demonstrated this by selectively breeding highly aggressive strains of mice. In humans, Rushton and his colleagues showed that identical (monozygotic) twins, who share the same genetic inheritance, were much more similar on ratings of aggressiveness, nurturance, altruism, and assertiveness than fraternal (dizygotic) twins (Rushton, Fulker, Neale, Nias, & Eysenck, 1986). However, although these findings support the sociobiological view, there remain many inconsistencies in this approach. For example, there are great differences in rates of aggression from society to society. If similar selection pressures exist from society to society over the course of evolution, societal differences in aggressiveness should not occur. Further, rates of aggression often differ markedly within societies over relatively short periods of time. If aggression is controlled by genetic transmission, a change in the overall rate of aggression could only happen over a long time period.

Theories based on the sociobiological approach must assume a relatively constant means of expressing aggression (that is, aggressive behaviors take the same form across a host of settings) and a relatively constant rate of aggression from group to group and from year to year. Neither of these assumptions has received much support from research. The instinct–inheritance explanations of aggression have yet to come to grips with these issues. For this reason, social psychologists, while recognizing the potential importance of biological contributions to aggression, continue to focus most of their research energies on theories that emphasize motivation and learning.

■ ■ ■ EXPLANATIONS BASED ON MOTIVATION AND LEARNING

Frustration–Aggression Theory

One of the early and still popular motivational models of aggression is **frustration–aggression theory.** This model is interesting because it connects the instinct–inheritance theories of Freud and the ethologists with the more socially oriented explanations of aggression. Devised by Dollard and his colleagues, (Dollard, Doob, Miller, Mowrer, & Sears, 1939), the central features of the original theory may be summarized as follows: (1) Frustration causes a readiness to aggress, and (2) aggression is the *inevitable* outcome of frustration (that is, the frustration–aggression sequence is built into the organism). However, (3) if the source of aggression is too powerful, aggression will be inhibited or displaced onto other targets who are less likely to retaliate. Finally, (4) aggression reduces the tension generated by frustration, and makes later aggression less likely. This cathartic outcome is similar to that proposed by Freud.

Later revisions moderated the predictions of the original theory somewhat. Neil Miller (1941), one of the authors of the original monograph, speculated that frustration could have many outcomes, only one of which was aggression. Frustration does not always cause aggression, as required in the original model. However, he still viewed aggression as the product of frustration and the link between the two was innate or instinctual. As Miller (1964) stated, it is "highly probable that . . . innate [frustration–aggression] patterns exist, that they play an important role in the development of human social behavior, and that these instinctual patterns are modifiable enough so that they tend to be disguised by learning" (p. 160). From this perspective, the theory is compatible with both the instinct- or inheritance-based theories of aggression and, because situational events (frustrations) are needed to arouse aggression, with the more socially oriented approaches (described later) as well.

Frustration.   In recounting their theory, Dollard et al. (1939) defined frustration as "an interference with the occurrence of an instigated goal-response at its proper time in the behavior sequence" (p. 7). In other words, frustration occurs when someone or something impedes our attempt to attain a desired outcome, at a specific time. Frustration evokes more aggression if the goal is important or if it blocks a goal that is near to attainment. For instance, suppose you are in the library researching a term paper. As you begin to read, a worker with a jackhammer begins to repair the street directly outside the window. The intolerable racket ruins your concentration; you cannot work. Of course, this will be frustrating, but the level of frustration will depend on a host of other factors. Suppose you cannot take the necessary book out of the library, and you need only a small amount of additional information to complete the paper. Suppose further that the paper is due the next day, that it will count for 90% of your grade, and that you have no alternative but to finish the work now. In this case, your level of frustration will be high. The racket is blocking an important goal (completing the paper) that is very close to attainment. Alternatively, suppose that you have three weeks to finish the paper, that it counts for only 5% of your grade, and that the information the book contains can be obtained in many other texts. These external circumstances will moderate your frustration considerably.

Displacement.   An important addition to the frustration–aggression theory is the possibility of **displaced aggression,** focusing our aggression on a person or thing that is not the source of our frustration. It is patently obvious that we do not always aggress against the person or thing that frustrates us. It is unlikely, for example, that you would aggress against the 6-foot 9-inch, 280 pound jackhammer operator in the library example (unless, perhaps, you are 6 feet 10 inches and 300 pounds). Yet it is clear that he/she has frustrated you. What do you do? You might scream at the librarian, or swear at the person in front of you, or write a nasty letter to the college's director of public works. Dollard and colleagues anticipated such possibilities by theorizing that unless the frustration was almost completely intolerable, we would delay our aggression and displace it onto safe targets (Dollard et al., 1939). Examples of displacement abound. When the Xerox machine breaks, many of our colleagues scream at the secretary. When the boss screams at us, we yell at our spouse or kick the cat. In such instances, aggression is displaced onto other, safer targets.

Toward whom do we displace aggression? The theory holds that we displace onto a target that is as similar as possible to the source of the frustration, while still being a safe target. Research by Berkowitz and Knurek (1967) supports this hypothesis. In their study, experimental accomplices frustrated participants, who later were given the chance to aggress against other accomplices whose first names were the same, or different from, those of the frustrator. Participants displaced higher levels of aggression onto those whose first names matched those of the frustrators.

Frustration–Aggression Theory: Revised Edition

A problem with the theory of Dollard and his colleagues arises from the fact that we know aggression can be caused by a host of factors other than frustration (Baron, 1974; 1977). In instrumental aggression, for example, aggressive behavior is only rarely the result of frustration. People aggress to gain money or control, they aggress because of martial music or rousing speeches, they aggress for all sorts of reasons that have nothing to do with frustration. This does not fit with the standard theory, which assumes all aggression to be the result of frustration. To remedy this problem, Berkowitz (1969, 1988, 1989) proposed a major theoretical revision, which he termed a cognitive neoassociationist analysis of aggression. He views frustration as one of many factors that cause aversive arousal, or negative affect (such as anger, irritability, sadness, rage). Berkowitz (1989) observed that "frustrations are aversive events and generate aggressive inclinations only to the extent that they produce negative affect. . . . [My] formulation suggests . . . that any kind of negative affect, sadness as well as depression and agitated irritability, will produce aggressive inclinations and the primitive experience of anger before the higher order processing goes into operation" (p. 71). Arousal of negative affect, whether by frustration or other means, trips a switch in us that has two responses: aggression or escape.

Which response will occur? Berkowitz suggests that it depends on our interpretation of the cause of the arousal and our memory of past events of a similar nature. If a person does something to us that we find unpleasant (causes aversive arousal), we go through an appraisal process, considering whether the action was intentional, if the punishment we received was deserved, or if the goal that was thwarted was within our grasp. In some instances, this appraisal process will result in feelings of anger toward the source of the trouble, but in others it will not. Striking examples of cognitive appraisal of negative arousal and resulting aggressive or nonaggressive responses are readily available in sports contests. In football, for example, hitting an opponent from behind is both dangerous and against the rules. If they can get up, players who are hit in this way typically respond with high degrees of aggression. However, if the source of the negative affect (in this case, anger) is a teammate, aggression usually does not erupt. Negative affect is still aroused by the contact (the player is still hurt and angry), but cognitive appraisal suppresses retaliation.

Examples of an alternative response to aversive arousal, withdrawal, also are relatively common. A person approached by a panhandler on the street can respond in a number of ways. Assuming the encounter generates unpleasant arousal, the person can give money to the beggar, verbally (or physically) aggress against him or her, or escape by moving on. The person's assessment of the situation will determine the chosen action.

Tests of some important components of Berkowitz's alternative have supported his theory. For example, Berkowitz assumes that frustration increases arousal. In research on this hypothesis, Vasta and Copitch (1981) had adults play the role of teachers. They were physically separated from the learner, and had to "teach" by signaling whether the learner had made the right response. The learner's answers were bogus; the teachers received a preprogrammed series of responses which suggested the learners were not paying any attention to them. The dependent measure of the study was the force with which the teachers hit a switch to indicate that the learner had answered. As frustration mounted—as it became more and more evident that the learners were not attending—the teachers hit the switch with increasing force. Although the switch could not affect performance, it was hit much harder when learners erred. Increased frustration caused greater arousal, if we may infer arousal from force levels.

The arousal produced by frustration can be moderated by situational appraisals, as demonstrated in a study by Moser and Levy-Leboyer (1985). In this research, people were watched as they used a pay telephone. The phone had been doctored so that it took money but otherwise did not function. When this happens, people typically yell, swear, and pound the phone. This describes the actions of some, but not all, of Moser and Levy-Leboyer's callers. For some, a set of instructions was affixed to the phone booth. They told participants where to find other pay phones, what to do if the phone did not operate properly, and so on. When this information was provided, the negative affect aroused by the inoperative telephone did not cause aggression. The original version of frustration–aggression theory would be hard put to explain variations in aggression as a consequence of the presence or absence of instructions, but the findings are in accord with Berkowitz's revised theory.

Excitation Transfer

Both the original and revised version of frustration–aggression theory assume that arousal is a necessary precondition to aggression. Zillman's (1979, 1988) **excitation transfer theory** makes a similar assumption, and complements the predictions of frustration–aggression theory. Zillman's theory is an elaboration of Schachter's (1964) earlier model of emotion. Schachter hypothesized that we interpret ambiguous physiological arousal by searching for cues in the environment that might have given rise to the physiological state. We use these environmental cues to *label* the physiological state—to identify the particular emotion we are experiencing. In a test of this hypothesis, Schachter and Singer (1962) performed a now-classic study. They gave participants epinephrine, a drug that causes physiological arousal; it boosts heart rate and induces flushing and occasional trembling. Some participants were told the drug would produce these symptoms, while others were led to believe that the drug would only cause their feet to become numb(!). After the drug took effect, participants were brought into a room with another person, ostensibly a waiting subject. After the experimenter left the room, the accomplice began acting in either a euphoric, silly way, or in an angry manner. Participants who had been *misinformed* about the arousing effects of the drug reported emotions that corresponded to those exhibited by the other person (actually an accomplice of the experimenter). Theoretically, they did so because the reason for their physiological arousal was uncertain—they did not expect to be aroused, and did not know what caused it. Therefore, they used the actions of the accomplice to label the arousal in emotional terms. Those participants who had been informed honestly about the effects of the drug were not affected by the behavior of the accomplice. Because they knew their physiological state was attributable to the drug they had ingested, they did not need his behavior to help them account for it.

Zillman (1988) has extended Schachter's theory of arousal cues by hypothesizing that the excitation (or arousal) that is evoked in one situation (from a given drug, action, or event) can transfer to later situations. As a consequence, emotional reactions in a setting might be amplified because of leftover arousal from an earlier event. Zillman suggested that such effects are most likely to occur when we are not aware of our residual arousal and when we misattribute the source of the arousal to present events rather than prior events. The effects of

Can the physiological arousal produced by jogging lead to romance? See excitation transfer theory. ■

Effects of the misattribution of arousal have been the focus of considerable research: See Chapters 5 and 13.

misattribution of arousal have been studied in a number of contexts in social psychology.

How does this work with aggressive responses? Suppose you are in a state of high physiological arousal from having run a fast mile. Shortly after finishing, while biking home, a careless driver makes a U-turn in front of you. In this circumstance, the residual physiological arousal from your running may be transferred to, or amplify, your emotional arousal (anger) induced by the driver's careless turn. You would mistakenly believe that your highly aroused internal state is attributable to your outrage at the bad driver, when in fact it is partly the result of your having run a fast mile. This misidentification of arousal, or *excitation transfer* as Zillman calls it, causes a more intense response than would have occurred had you not been physiologically aroused in the first place. Such misidentification is more likely if some time has elapsed between your running and the near accident; this facilitates your misattributing the reason for your heightened physiological state.

We find evidence for excitation transfer in aggression in an interesting experiment by Zillman, Katcher, and Milavsky (1972). In this study, participants were ostensibly paired with a subject in an adjoining lab room. They were told that they would act as teacher and the other person would be the learner. To get to know the person in the next room, participants expressed their opinions on twelve controversial issues. The learner was aware of the participant's (teacher's)

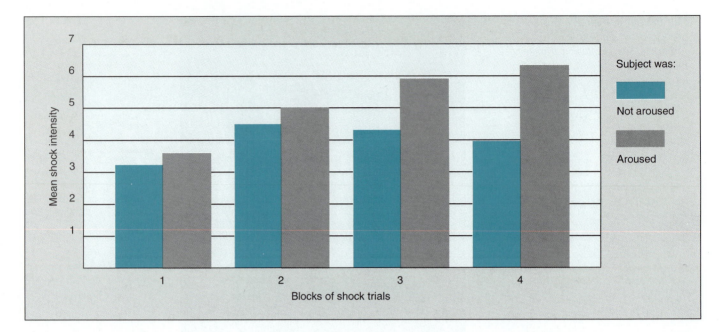

FIGURE 15.1

■

Shock Intensity Delivered to Aggressive Partners as a Function of Physiological Arousal (adapted from Zillman et al., 1972). Participants who had been punished (i.e., shocked) *and* were physiologically aroused were much more severe in their responses toward their tormentor.

responses. If he agreed, he activated a light signal. If he disagreed, he gave the participant an electric shock. The shock was really under the control of the experimenter. The study was arranged in such a way that participants in the low-instigation group received only three minor shocks and nine light flashes (indicating agreement). Those in the high-instigation condition received nine shocks of varying intensity (some painful), and only three light flashes. Afterward, half the participants in the high- and low-instigation groups engaged in a strenuous exercise session; the remaining participants sat and watched a set of boring slides.

After completing this part of the study, teacher—participants began their role. Teachers were to monitor the learner's performance and shocked him whenever he made an error. Although teachers were required to shock the learner on errors, they could vary the intensity of the shock by selecting one of ten shock buttons, which ranged on a scale from 1 (quite mild) to 10 (rather painful). Not surprisingly, teachers whose learner had shocked them frequently in the "getting acquainted" portion of the study were much more severe (gave higher levels of shock) than teachers paired with a learner who had not aggressed against them. The average shock delivered in the high-instigation condition was 4.6 on a 10-point scale; participants in the low-instigation condition delivered an average shock intensity of only 2.29. In effect, participants retaliated against partners who had been aggressive to them earlier.

Retaliation depended, however, on arousal levels. For those who had not been treated badly by their partner, physical arousal alone did not generate high levels of aggression. But arousal augmented the aggressiveness of those who had been provoked. When given the opportunity to punish the person who had provoked them, physiologically aroused participants were much more aggressive than those who had been sedentary, even though they had been equally provoked. As shown in Figure 15.1, shock intensity delivered by the physiologically aroused participants was always greater than that of the nonaroused participants, and it increased across trials. This finding is consistent with results of many experimental studies (Geen, Stonner, & Shope, 1975). Contrary to expectations based on a catharsis explanation, the results suggest that aggression may feed on itself, causing further aggression. Apparently, physiological arousal is not sufficient to amplify aggression (Zillman et al., 1972). But if the situation contains cues that suggest aggression is warranted—in this case, the justification was provided by the accomplice who had shocked the participant nine times—then the arousal generated from hard physical activity transfers to a subsequent setting and amplifies aggressive reactions.

Other forms of arousal, too, transfer to later aggressive behavior. For example, Zillman, Bryant, Cominsky, and Medoff (1981) showed males either pleasant or unpleasant erotic pornography. The unpleasant stimuli enhanced aggression, while the pleasant pornography did not. Zillman and colleagues hypothesized that scenes of bestiality and sadomasochism produced negative affect and this amplified participants' subsequent retaliatory aggression against an experimental accomplice. Pleasant erotic pornography apparently did not produce negative arousal, and it did not amplify aggression. These findings complement Berkowitz's revised model since it postulates that negative affect is a necessary component of aggressive behavior. We consider other effects of erotica on aggression later in the chapter.

APPLYING SOCIAL PSYCHOLOGY TO THE ENVIRONMENT
■ ■ ■

Heat and Aggression

We have seen that negative affect can lead to aggression. One source of negative affect that has been studied intensively is the weather. We have years and years of weather data available, along with mountains of crime statistics. When these two variables are put together, we find considerable evidence that as temperature increases, so too does public violence—riots, murders, rapes, and assaults. As shown by Anderson and Anderson (1984) in Figure 15.2, there appears to be a linear relationship between heat and aggressive crimes. The hotter it gets (up to some extreme

FIGURE 15.2
■

Heat and Aggression: Crime Ratio as a Function of Temperature (adapted from Anderson & De Neve, 1992). As the temperature rises, from a comfortable to an uncomfortable level, the rate of aggressive crime also climbs.

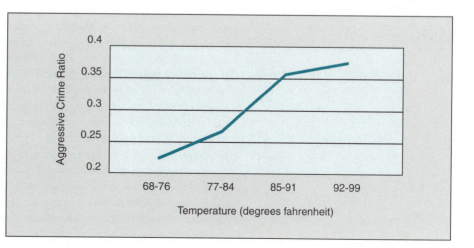

Why do almost all riots occur during the hottest days of summer?

point), the more likely it is that some form of aggressive public disorder will occur (see also Anderson & DeNeve, 1992).

Not only aggressive crimes but other aggressive actions as well are influenced by ambient temperature. In an ingenious (baseball) field study, Reifman, Larrick, and Fein (1991) found that as temperatures increased, professional baseball pitchers were more likely to hit batters. This relationship was linear—the hotter it got, the more batters were hit—and it held even after the effects of a host of other variables (such as attendance, the pitcher's general lack of control, errors, numbers of home runs hit, and so on) had been controlled.

Interestingly, laboratory research on heat and aggression usually does not correspond with the field data. In experimental research, heat and aggression are related in a very complex fashion. Baron (1972) has suggested that high heat (92°–95°F) inhibits aggression, and Baron and Bell's (1975, 1976) research supports this observation. People who had been angered were more likely to aggress against others under moderate, as opposed to extreme, ambient laboratory temperatures. Rule and her colleagues demonstrated that high ambient temperatures produced negative thoughts and arousal, which incline people to aggression (Rule, Taylor, & Dobbs, 1987). Bell and Baron (1990; Bell, 1992) also showed that high temperatures produce negative feelings, but not aggression.

What is responsible for the lack of agreement between the results of the laboratory and the natural environment? Consider the contexts in which the correlational and the experimental research have been conducted. In naturalistic settings, we expect variations in ambient temperature. The temperature on the street may be pleasant or unpleasant, but we have to live with it. An unpleasant temperature may stimulate a state of negative arousal, but we might not attribute the arousal to the temperature. Suppose, in such a state, we witness a confrontation between an impolite police officer and a minor traffic offender. We are much more likely to attribute our negative arousal to the police officer's actions than to the temperature. In other words, we would *misattribute* our discomfort and arousal.

In contrast to the naturalistic situation, ambient temperature in a laboratory is relatively constant. In the standard temperature–aggression study, however, people walk into the lab from a temperate environment and suddenly find themselves in the middle of a heat wave. This is uncomfortable, but unlike uncomfortable temperatures on the street, there is little chance that the source of discomfort will be misattributed. Under such circumstances, it is not likely that reactions to the discomfort will be displaced. It is not that negative arousal necessarily differs as a consequence of the source of the unpleasant ambient temperature (environmental versus experimenter supplied), but rather that different attributions regarding the negative state are produced. And these attributions cause the aggressive response.

Attribution plays an important role in anger and aggression: See Chapter 9.

Social Learning of Aggression

The motivational theories of Miller and Dollard, Berkowitz, and Zillman all assume a link between negative affect and aggression. These theories do well in predicting and explaining hostile aggression, but they are not particularly good at explaining instrumental aggression. The theories assume negative affect, or anger, as prerequisite to aggression, but as we know, anger often is conspicuously absent in instrumental aggression. To explain this form of aggression, we need an approach that does not assume a link between negative affect and antisocial behavior. Bandura's (1973) **theory of social learning** is such an approach. We present this theory not as an alternative to the affect-based theories of aggression, but as an auxiliary explanation—as an approach that handles forms of behavior that other models do not explain well.

A fundamental principle of the social learning approach is that all social behaviors are learned. Just as we learn to ride a bicycle or drive a car or tie our shoes, we also learn to enact or to inhibit aggressive behavior. For the social learning theorist, to understand aggression we must understand (1) the conditions under which the aggressive response was acquired, (2) the environmental factors that foster performance of the aggressive act, and (3) the circumstances that promote the maintenance or repetition of the aggressive behavior.

A classic demonstration of social learning theory in action was given by Bandura, Ross, and Ross (1963), who had nursery school children watch the behavior of an adult model in a playroom. One of the toys in the room was a large inflated Bobo doll. After playing with the other toys for a while, the model assaulted the doll, all the while uttering aggressive commentary, like "Sock him in the nose." Other children did not see the model engage in such aggressive play. When all the children were given access to the playroom, those who had observed the model mimicked her actions—they assaulted the doll while repeating, "Sock him in the nose." This imitative behavior is fascinating because the children had never performed it before, it was based solely on their observation of the actions of the model. They were not rewarded for aggression, nor was the model. Nevertheless, the children had learned a novel pattern of behavior. Apparently, aggressive behavior can be learned vicariously, without rehearsal or reward.

Are you sure about that? Among others, Berkowitz and LePage (1967) disagree. ∎

Guns don't kill people.

People kill people.

These results suggest that aggression can occur without frustration or negative affect, as a consequence of learning. Apparently, being exposed to aggressive models is sufficient to instigate aggressive behavior. If aggressive models are present in a situation, we are all the more likely to perform aggressive acts ourselves. Arms, Russell, and Sandilands (1979) observed this in their research on spectators at competitive sporting events. They found that spectators who had witnessed violent sports (hockey and wrestling) were more hostile and more willing to express aggression than those who had watched an equally competitive but nonviolent swimming meet. Observing aggression appears to be implicated in subsequent aggressive behavior; observing nonaggressive competitive behavior does not.

Cues to Aggression

Bandura's model suggests that since we learn to act aggressively, aggressive behavior will be susceptible to reinforcement or reward. Considerable research supports this expectation. For example, Bandura has shown that children are more likely to imitate aggression if the aggressive models are of the same sex and if they are rewarded for aggression (Bandura, 1965; Bandura et al., 1963). When models are punished for aggression, children are less likely to imitate them. Social learning theory also assumes that aggressive behaviors are learned in association with specific cues. Research by Berkowitz and Le Page (1967) supports this expectation. In their study, participants were angered by an accomplice and then given the chance to aggress against him by administering electric shocks. In some situations, the interaction took place in a laboratory in which a 12-gauge shotgun and a .38 caliber revolver were in plain sight. In the other condition of the experiment, the guns were replaced by badminton rackets. Angered participants were substantially more aggressive (gave higher shock intensities) when the guns were prominently displayed. Berkowitz and Le Page argue that the guns serve as learned cues that help to elicit aggression. Reflecting on his results, Berkowitz (1988) observed, "Guns not only permit violence, they can stimulate it as well. The finger pulls the trigger, but the trigger may also be pulling the finger" (p. 22).

■ ■ ■ IMPORTANT SOCIAL ISSUES IN THE STUDY OF AGGRESSION

Race and Ethnicity

Much of the violent aggression we are aware of occurs as conflict between groups that differ in race or ethnicity. The almost constant warfare in the Middle East, strife in Eastern Europe, the problems in America's cities, are all related in one way or another to ethnic conflict. We discuss issues of intergroup conflict much more extensively in later chapters, but it also is appropriate to consider race and ethnicity here as factors that serve as cues to aggression.

Race and ethnicity can be sources of great conflict: See Chapters 23–25.

Consider, for example, an important experiment of Rogers and Prentice-Dunn (1981). These experimenters used male participants, who were to help another person perform a learning task. To do so, they were to use a shock machine to encourage the learner to perform well. All the participants were white. The learner was an experimental accomplice who was white for some participants and black for others. In addition to race, the experimenters manipulated anger. This was accomplished as follows: After they had learned their role in the study, the teachers overheard the experimenter talking with the learner, explaining the experiment to him, asking him if he understood how the shock apparatus worked, how it would deliver shocks to him, and so on. In the low-anger-arousal condition, the learner simply said he understood and was ready to proceed. In the condition designed to arouse their anger, participants overheard the learner say that he hoped the teacher was not as stupid as he looked, because the equipment appeared somewhat complicated.

Did this manipulation affect the extent to which teachers shocked learners? Yes. Anger did have an effect, but the nature of the effect varied as a consequence of the learner's race. White teachers who had been insulted (and hence were angry) did not show increased retaliation against white learners. The length and intensity of shocks they delivered were not different from those of teachers who had not been angered. When the white teachers had been insulted by the black learner, however, they applied significantly higher shock levels. Interestingly, white teachers who had *not* been insulted by the black accomplice administered shocks of *significantly less intensity* than did whites paired with the noninsulting white accomplice. Rogers and Prentice-Dunn liken this latter response to reverse discrimination. Enhanced retaliation against a black accomplice occurred only when it could be justified as something other than racially motivated. A parallel pattern of results was found in an experiment using black participants (Wilson & Rogers, 1975). In this study, black participants aggressed strongly against insulting white accomplices, but were relatively unaffected by insults of black accomplices.

Frey and Gaertner (1986) explain the results of these studies. They begin with the assumption that racism exists, but that it is socially unacceptable to express it. Most people are reluctant to act in an overtly racist manner unless their actions can be framed in such a way that they appear not to be motivated by racism. However, if aggression is justified, it will be aggravated if the target is of a different race. In this way, prejudiced actions can be performed without social censure. People are constrained by social norms that inhibit cross-racial aggression, but the controls are fragile and easily overcome by insult or injury.

Media Aggression

Teaching Aggression to Children and Adults.   Along with the impact of race on aggression, another important social issue concerns the effects of displays of aggression and violence in the media, particularly television. Both Berkowitz and Bandura suggest that we can become more aggressive simply by watching aggressive TV programs. If this is so, then television may be a powerful explanation for aggression in contemporary society. Consider the fact that the average sixteen-year-old has witnessed more than 13,000 murders on television (Waters & Malamud, 1975). It is hard to believe this has no impact. If aggressive cues prompt aggression—if we can learn to be aggressive by witnessing it—then there can be little doubt that our television set is not an innocuous piece of furniture, but a source of real concern.

What does the research show? For many years there was no clear-cut answer to the question, "Does televised violence cause subsequent aggression?" The problem with much of the research on the relationship between media use and aggression is that it is correlational. In the typical study, researchers evaluate the violence of the shows people usually watch. This measure is correlated with scores of the viewer's aggressiveness. Typically, this research is performed on children, and it usually discloses a positive relationship: Greater exposure to media violence is associated with higher levels of aggression in the viewer (Huesmann, 1982). However, we cannot know from research of this kind if exposure causes aggression or if the natural aggressiveness of the viewer causes a preference for violent programs (Freedman, 1984, 1986).

Eron and his colleagues have used longitudinal data to overcome the limitations imposed by correlational data. Based on their results, they have been able to argue persuasively for a causal link between media violence and later aggression. For example, Eron, Huesmann, Lefkowitz, and Walder (1972) report a study in which they measured third-grade boys' preferences for violent or nonviolent TV programs, and determined the children's levels of aggressiveness by self-reports and ratings by peers and parents. Ten years later, Eron revisited these participants and found a significant correlation between TV preferences in third grade and later aggressiveness (Lefkowitz, Eron, Walder, & Huesmann, 1977). On the other hand, boys' aggressiveness in the third grade did not predict their preferences for violent TV ten years later. In other words, early exposure to violent media appears to affect later aggression, but early aggression has little to do with later preferences for violent TV.

A second follow-up on this same group by Huesmann and his colleagues (Huesmann, Eron, Lefkowitz, & Walder, 1984) disclosed that boys' preferences for television violence, measured when they were just eight years old, were positively related to criminal behavior twenty-two years later! Also, the seriousness of the crimes committed by this group was predictable from the amount of violent TV they watched as eight-year-olds. The results were not clear-cut for girls, probably because of the more rigid sanctions on the manner they may express aggression and the tendency for women to avoid physical violence (Eagly & Steffen, 1986). These results are striking, and they are not confined to the United States. Cross-cultural research on respondents in Australia, Finland, Israel, and Poland suggests that violent TV can predict subsequent aggression (Huesmann & Eron, 1986).

Correlation is a statistical tool that expresses the relationship between variables: See Chapter 1.

Singer and Singer (1981), using nursery school children, have corroborated Eron's and Huesmann's work. The investigators measured the relationship between children's television viewing and teachers' records of their aggressive behavior. Measures were taken four times over the course of the school year, and disclosed for boys and girls alike that aggressive behavior was strongly related to the amount of time the children spent watching action adventures on TV. In general, early viewing of violent adventure shows was related to later aggressive behavior. However, during the later phases of the study, children's aggressiveness began to predict their later preferences for violent TV. This pattern suggests that aggressive behavior, which is at least partly prompted by media violence, may cause later preference for more media violence, in a vicious circle. An escalating tolerance for violence fuels later aggressive action and promotes an appetite for more media violence. The weight of current evidence supports the position that media violence causes aggression.

Public Events and Aggression.   A line of correlational research that also suggests a connection between media violence and aggression was developed by D. P. Phillips. Phillips (1974) showed that suicides increase almost immediately after a suicide is reported in the newspaper, and the effect is stronger if the suicide receives wide coverage. Further research suggests a positive relation between televised suicides on soap operas and actual suicides (Phillips, 1982) and between heavyweight boxing matches and homicides (Phillips, 1983). Other researchers have found similar effects in the general population after hijackings (Bandura, 1973) and riots at sporting events (Dunand, 1986; Rimé & Leyens, 1988). While only suggestive, these studies indicate at a minimum that media violence bears watching—or, perhaps, not watching.

Experimental evidence on media exposure is in accord with the correlational evidence. For example, Josephson (1987) showed second- and third-grade boys one of two exciting films. One of them, a bicycle race, contained no violence. The other depicted a group of police officers revenging the death of one of their colleagues. After the film, the boys engaged in a game of floor hockey, and measures were taken of their aggressive actions (elbowing, hitting opponents with the stick, and the like). The children exposed to the violent film were more aggressive during the game *if* they had been identified by their teachers as being aggressive to begin with. Children previously identified by teachers as nonaggressive were not influenced by the violent film. With the work of Singer and Singer (1981), this result indicates that media violence may affect precisely those most susceptible to it.

Other laboratory investigations generally support the idea that media violence can cause subsequent aggression (cf. Geen, 1983). Bushman and Geen (1990) showed film clips that varied in aggressiveness. At their completion, they asked participants to write their thoughts as they viewed the film. Aggressive content of the films was strongly related to aggressive content of people's thoughts. In conjunction with the longitudinal research of Eron and Huesmann, these findings suggest that media violence can, and often does, intensify aggression. In fact, it appears that even the anticipation of media violence can intensify aggression. In an experiment by Leyens and Dunand (1991), students were recruited to rate a movie. After entering the laboratory at the Catholic University of Leuven in Belgium, the students were told the movie they were to rate had been censored by the Ministry of Culture. Some were told they would see a movie titled *Taste of Death,* obviously a violent film. Others were told they would see a film titled *Next Paradise,* which promised no violence. Before the movie was shown, participants were required to engage in a task that called for them to shock another person. Those expecting to watch the violent movie administered substantially higher shock levels to their partner than those expecting a nonviolent film. These expectations may make aggressive thoughts more accessible, paving the way for increased aggression.

Erotic Violence and Aggression. Research on media violence has recently focused on an important social problem, aggression against women, with results that are both important and disturbing. The central question is whether scenes of rape and assault of women make it more likely that women actually will become the targets of such actions. Early laboratory research showed that males who had been aroused by erotic, nonaggressive stimuli were less likely to aggress against women (Donnerstein & Barrett, 1978). However, the findings change dramatically when we consider *erotic violence,* which appears to stimulate men's aggressive reactions against women (Donnerstein, Linz, & Penrod, 1987). In a study of men's attitudes and fantasies, Malamuth (1984) demonstrated that films combining violence with explicit sexual content desensitize males to the inhumanity of rape (rape becomes more "acceptable") and stimulate more rape fantasies.

Donnerstein (1980) found that in addition to their effects on attitude, films that combine violence with eroticism heighten males' aggressive actions. Furthermore, if they had been angered before the film, men exhibited higher levels of aggression if the person who angered them was a woman. In a study by Donnerstein and Berkowitz (1981), males were angered either by a male or a female. They then watched an erotic or a violent erotic film, and were given the opportunity to retaliate against an accomplice who had angered them. Males exposed to the violent erotic stimuli were much more aggressive against females than were males exposed to the merely erotic film. When males aggressed against other males, the nature of the film did not matter. Apparently, violent erotica intensifies men's aggression toward women, but not toward men. In a second condition of the experiment, the accomplices did not anger participants prior to the films. Even in this circumstance, males who had witnessed the violent erotic film were more likely to aggress against the female accomplice than were men who had seen a neutral, or even an erotic, film. As Donnerstein (1983) observed,

> These findings . . . suggest that the aggressive responses elicited by the film were heightened by the arousal in the film itself. In addition, the disinhibitory cues present in the film (e.g., aggression is OK) acted to potentially reduce any aggressive inhibitions on the part of male subjects. (p. 150)

Violent erotica, in other words, has a twofold impact on men's aggression against women. It increases male aggression by heightening arousal, and it disinhibits heretofore repudiated actions. It appears that violent pornography is indeed dangerous for women.

Alcohol and Aggression

Review of almost any crime data reveals an impressive relation between alcohol consumption and criminal behavior. Alcohol was implicated in 64% of the 588 cases of homicide reported in a five-year period in Philadelphia (Wolfgang & Strohm, 1956). In a similar study of Chicago homicides, Voss and Hepburn (1968) discovered a 54% alcohol involvement. Of a sample of 882 persons charged with a felony, 64% were legally intoxicated when measured immediately after their arrest, and of those who had been arrested for physical violence (assault, murder, and so on), 75% were legally intoxicated (Shupe, 1954).

The data could not be more clear. Experiments focused on the alcohol–aggression relationship have "produced unequivocal evidence that alcohol facilitates the expression of physical aggression" (Taylor & Leonard, 1983, p. 82). And it appears that the greater the dose, the greater the aggression, at least up to the point when the drinker becomes incapacitated (Taylor & Gammon, 1975). The task of the scientist is not to establish a link between alcohol and aggression but to understand the process that causes the relationship.

This would seem an easy task, but as we will see, the explanation is not simple. One obvious explanation is *disinhibition;* that is, alcohol pharmacologically breaks down the inhibitions we normally maintain. This is a reasonable hypothesis, but it is not fully supported by the experimental evidence. Taylor, Gammon, and Capasso (1976) showed that participants who were intoxicated did not aggress against competitors who had made it clear that they would not instigate aggression. If alcohol disinhibited the prohibition against aggression, the intent of the competitor would not have mattered.

An alternative hypothesis is that *learned* (versus pharmacological) *disinhibition* is responsible for alcohol's effects on aggressive behavior. The presumption is that we have learned that behaviors that are normally inappropriate may be excusable when performed under the influence of alcohol. People who drink realize this and perform actions they otherwise would inhibit. Many of us have experienced learned disinhibition in action—at parties, bars, and other places where people drink too much and begin to act in uncharacteristic ways.

Learned disinhibition may help to explain the prevalence of alcohol-induced aggressive actions. It seems that alcohol produces an altered state, in which some individuals become extremely sensitive to aggression cues, real or imagined. Coupled with the learned disinhibiting effects of the substance, alcohol can foster the expression of violence which under ordinary circumstances would not occur. Alcohol not only renders the intoxicated person hypersensitive to aggressive cues but it also weakens inhibitions against aggression.

■ ■ ■ SOME CONCLUDING THOUGHTS

Aggression is both a difficult social problem and a complex psychological puzzle. After many years of intense work, we have begun to secure a grip on many of the factors that lie at the heart of this phenomenon. Much remains to be done, but theoretical treatments of aggression, including Berkowitz's revision of frustration–aggression theory, Zillman's excitation transfer approach, and Bandura's social learning model, all offer a means of explaining and integrating considerable research. Motivated, hostile aggression appears to require negative affect. An aggressive response can be intensified by residual (negative) affect that has been generated in circumstances very different from the one in which the aggressive reaction is being played out. Other situational features as well can influence the course of aggression. We can be taught that aggression is appropriate in some circumstances. Alternatively, factors that help to disinhibit social prohibitions on antisocial behavior—alcohol, crowds, riots, and aggressive cues (guns, weapons)—can intensify aggression or enhance its likelihood of occurrence. Environmental features that generate negative affect—ambient temperature, crowding, and so on—also encourage aggression. In every instance, the critical feature prompting aggression appears to be either negative affect (anger, rage) or an aspect of the situation that defeats or deflects our well-learned inhibitions against hurting people.

■ ■ ■ SUMMARY

Research on aggression has been slowed by the difficulties involved in its definition. Generally, aggression is viewed as any behavior whose intent is to deliver pain to another. Aggression, which can be either instrumental or hostile, has been examined within the theoretical context of instinct or inheritance theories, as well as learning or motivation theories. The principal instinct theories are those of Freud, the ethologists, and the sociobiologists. The most popular motivation or learning approaches are frustration–aggression theory and social learning theory. Frustration–aggression theory holds that frustration leads either to aggression against a frustrating agent or to a displacement of the aggression to a safer target. Berkowitz's revision of this theory holds that any stimulus (including frustration) that creates unpleasant arousal may cause aggression, depending on factors in the aggressor, the target, and the situation. Bandura's social learning approach assumes that aggressive behavior is a learned response, susceptible to the same laws of learning as any other behavior. Thus, behavior in the presence of cues typically associated with aggression often trigger, or disinhibit, aggressive behavior. Consistent with Berkowitz's ideas, residual physiological arousal has been shown to affect people's actions, even when they were unaware of it. Excitation transfer theory furnishes a compelling explanation of such results.

The effects of films and television on aggressive behavior have been studied at length. Early studies were not clear-cut, but the cross-cultural studies of Eron, Huesmann, and their colleagues have built a strong case for the influence of media on violent behavior. Effects of media violence against women are equivocal, but the weight of evidence now suggests that aggressive erotica can elevate violence against women by disinhibiting normative constraints against such action. Alcohol, too, disinhibits violent actions, but the precise mechanism of disinhibition is not well understood. Other environmental factors, such as heat and general discomfort, have also been implicated as potential triggers to aggressive behavior.

■ ■ ■ **SUGGESTED READINGS**

1. Berkowitz, L. (1989). Frustration-aggression hypothesis: Examination and re-formulation. *Psychological Bulletin, 106,* 59–73.

2. Berkowitz, L. (1990). On the formation and regulation of anger and aggression: A cognitive neoassociationistic analysis. *American Psychologist, 45,* 494–503.

3. Childress, S. A. (1991). Reel "rape speech": Violent pornography and the politics of harm. *Law & Society Review, 25,* 177–214.

4. Geen, R. G., & Donnerstein, E. I. (Eds.), *Aggression: Theoretical and empirical reviews* (2 vols.). New York: Academic Press.

5. Huesmann, L. R., & Eron, L. D. (Eds.). (1986). *Television and the aggressive child: A cross-national comparison.* Hillsdale, NJ: Erlbaum.

6. Mummendey, A. (1984). *Social psychology of aggression: From individual behavior to social interaction.* New York: Springer-Verlag.

7. Staub, E. (1989). *The roots of evil. The origins of genocide and other forms of group violence.* Cambridge, England: Cambridge University Press.

INTERPERSONAL EXPECTANCIES

The Self-fulfilling Prophecy

■ Key Concepts

Expectancy effects
Placebo
Blind and double blind trials
Experimenter bias
Accuracy versus expectancy
Affect–effort theory of expectancy
Teachers' expectations
Self-fulfilling prophecy
Biased information search
Innuendo effect
Self-affirmation effect

■ Chapter Outline

THE PLACEBO STUDIES
  Ancient History
  Contemporary Pharmacology

EXPERIMENTER EXPECTANCIES
  Laboratory Biases
  ■ Expectancy Effects in the Classroom
  Accuracy versus Expectancy
  The Transmission of Expectations in the Classroom

THE SELF-FULFILLING PROPHECY
  Effects of Appearance on Expectations
  Effects of Race on Expectations
  ■ Expectations on the Job
  Effects of Sex on Expectations

BIASED INFORMATION SEARCH
  "Proving" (versus Testing) One's Hypotheses
  ■ Effects of Innuendo and Leading Questions

ARE SELF-FULFILLING PROPHECIES INEVITABLY FULFILLED?
  Self-Affirmation versus the Self-Fulfilling Prophecy
  The Self-Fulfilling Prophecy and High Stakes

SOME CONCLUDING THOUGHTS

SUMMARY

Someone once described Admiral Hyman Rickover, the father of the U.S. nuclear navy, as being as agreeable as a snake. When he learned of this, Rickover was perturbed, preferring to be compared to Attila the Hun. Rickover's trips to Capitol Hill were never smooth. It seemed to Rickover that the Senate Armed Services Committee was almost always antagonistic, and he was continually forced to fight for what he knew was best for the navy, and the country.

■ ■ ■

Jim, a drug dealer, sells Joe a capsule of LSD, a powerful hallucinogenic drug, for $50. Joe takes the drug and hallucinates most of the night. Jim snickers to himself—the capsule contained only Coffeemate, and his $50 is almost pure profit.

■ ■ ■

An unfounded rumor spreads through the ranks of depositors of Happy Daze Savings and Loan. The S&L is nearly insolvent, the rumor goes, so if you want your money any time in the near future, you'd better grab it now. Depositors respond, and the run on a perfectly healthy savings institution causes it to collapse.

■

Expectations have a great effect on our beliefs and behavior: See Chapter 8.

What do these three scenarios have in common? Expectations. The expectations we hold of others and of ourselves have an enormous effect on our perceptions and evaluations. This observation has profound implications for cognitions and behavior. If we believe something about a person, our behavior will reflect this belief. In the case of Rickover, many senators felt that the admiral was feisty, hardheaded, and argumentative. As a consequence, they often took the offensive in Senate hearings, if only to forestall his attacking them. On the basis of their expectations, some senators acted negatively toward Rickover, even those who had never met him previously (Polmar, 1982).

Perhaps even more important than the effects of our expectations on our own behavior is the effect of our expectations on the behaviors of others. Senators' negative expectations of the admiral affected their actions toward him. These actions, in turn, roused Rickover's reaction to them. It was Rickover's nature never to back down from a fight. If the Senate was tough, he would be tougher. Rickover's spirited style then confirmed senators' beliefs about him!

When applied to ourselves, the expectations-affect-behavior hypothesis is easy to accept. Obviously, our expectations influence our behaviors toward others. More interesting is that these expectations can influence people to behave in ways that confirm them. This part of the expectancy loop is much less obvious. In this chapter, we describe social psychologists' attempts to establish the existence of these

Sometimes, believing treatment will work ensures that it does. ■

expectancy effects, as they are termed, and then, once established, to understand when (and how) they work, and when (and why) they don't.

■■■ THE PLACEBO STUDIES

Ancient History

Our story begins more than a century ago in Austria, where researchers became concerned that the pharmacological effect of the experimental drugs they were studying was attributable more to the suggestibility of the patients than to the inherent action of the drugs themselves. Some drugs had powerful effects in experimental trials, but failed when they were brought into the hospital or clinic. Why? Was it possible that patients' expectations about the healing power of a drug somehow influenced the disease process independent of any true drug effect? This seemed unlikely at the time, but to be on the safe side, to ensure that expectations did not affect health outcomes, *blind trials* were instituted. In a blind trial, the patient does not know whether an active drug or a *placebo* (an inert or innocuous substance) has been administered.

The blind trials did not solve the problem. At times, drugs that were successful in experimental trials still proved worthless in the field. What could account for these failures? One possibility was the researcher. Although the patients did not know whether they were taking a real drug or a placebo, the researcher did. Could the researchers inadvertently transmit expectations to their clients who in turn acted in ways to confirm them? This was deemed possible (if perhaps far-fetched), and so the double blind procedure was invented. In *double blind* research, neither patient nor physician knows whether a drug or a placebo has been administered. With this kind of design, we can be almost certain that people's expectations will not systematically bias results.

Contemporary Pharmacology

Were our pharmacological forebears overly zealous? Could the effects of a strong pharmacological agent really be induced simply on the basis of people's expectations? If I am convinced that a drug will cure me, can I cure myself by believing strongly enough? Let's consider the second scenario from the chapter's opening page, which involves Jim, a conniving drug dealer, and Joe, his hapless customer. Recall that Joe ingested a capsule of Coffeemate, thinking it was LSD, and experienced the expected hallucinogenic response. Does this scenario seem unbelievable? If it does, then the research of Reed and Witt (1965) may prove difficult to swallow. In their study, Reed and Witt administered placebos labeled LSD to their participants, who obliged by hallucinating. Believing they had ingested the real thing, the respondents experienced the reactions they had been led to believe (either through others' reports or their own past experience) the drug would induce.

At about the same time, Beecher (1966), in a double blind experiment, administered either morphine or a placebo to patients who were in pain. Neither the patients themselves nor skilled observers could distinguish the effects on the placebo group from the effects on those who actually had received the morphine: Both groups reported diminished pain. This is a compelling confirmation of the effects of expectations on behavior. If the pain-killing effects of so powerful a drug as morphine can be induced through expectancies, then it is obvious that other, more subtle but perhaps equally important, effects can be induced through expectancies as well.

■ ■ ■ EXPERIMENTER EXPECTANCIES

Laboratory Biases

The research of Reed and Witt, Beecher, and others demonstrates that expectations can influence people's reactions to drugs (or to substances they think are drugs). Expectancy effects have been demonstrated in many settings outside medicine as well. In a very important program of research, Robert Rosenthal (1966/1976) detailed the pervasive effects of **experimenter bias** expectancies on the outcomes of research. Let's begin by considering the early research of Rosenthal and Fode (1961, 1963), who conducted a laboratory exercise in which students served as experimenters. The student experimenters presented a set of ten photographs to respondents, whose task was to judge the "successfulness" of the faces depicted in the photos. Preliminary study had established that the faces were perceived by most people as more or less neutral in terms of success. However, Rosenthal told half the experimenters that the photos depicted successful people and they should expect to see relatively high successfulness ratings. The remaining experiments were told just the opposite.

Major differences in the ratings of the faces were found as a consequence of the student experimenters' expectations. Those told to expect successful ratings received successful evaluations from their respondents; those expecting low scores received low scores. The experimenters' expectation was confirmed by the respondents. Since this initial finding, the pervasive effects of experimenter expectancies have been demonstrated in scores of other highly controlled studies (Rosenthal, 1976).

As a methodological treatise, Rosenthal's work has great value: It alerts researchers to the fact that their cherished hypotheses might be confirmed simply because they are cherished. Somehow, experimenters' hopes and expectations can be transmitted to their research participants, who generally oblige by providing the answers they think the researcher wants. How this happens is something of a mystery, but current research implicates vocal tone, nonverbal behaviors, and facial expressions as the most likely media of transmittal (Burgoon, Buller, & Woodall, 1989; Harris, 1991).

APPLYING SOCIAL PSYCHOLOGY TO EDUCATION

Expectancy Effects in the Classroom

Although the importance of expectations is widely accepted in social psychology, the relevance of expectancy effects for almost every facet of social life was not recognized until Rosenthal moved his research into educational settings. In a remarkable as well as controversial experiment, Rosenthal and Jacobson (1968) obtained access to an elementary school, and tested all the children in it with a standardized measure of intelligence. The researchers misled the teachers of the school, however, telling them that the test would allow them to pinpoint children who could be expected to experience an intellectual growth spurt during the academic year. In fact, the names of 20% of the children in the school were drawn at random and identified as intellectual "bloomers." The test had nothing whatever to do with intellectual growth spurts—but teachers thought it did. The children were retested periodically over the next two years. Otherwise, nothing more was done by the researchers.

Some of the results of the study were summarized in Figure 16.1, and they are as important as they are impressive. As shown, there were meaingful differences in the

FIGURE 16.1

■

Immediate and Long-Term Expectancy Effects on IQ Scores. Teachers' expectations had a powerful effect on their students' performance on an IQ test—and the effect was evident two years later.

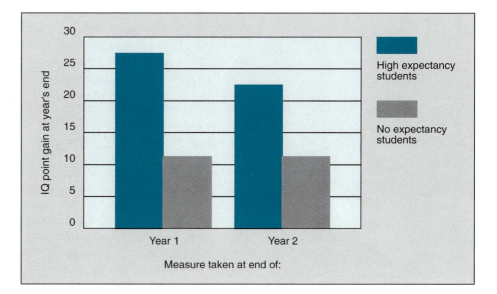

intellectual gains of the high-expectancy first-grade children over the other first-graders. On average, children expected to bloom intellectually in the first grade gained 27.4 IQ points, while the nonexpectancy controls gained only 12 points. A 15-point difference in IQ gain is striking, but even more impressive is the fact that the gains were largely maintained through the children's second year of school. Imagine what might have happened if Rosenthal and Jacobson had induced an expectation for *negative* growth!

Accuracy versus Expectancy

Although many other experimental studies of classroom teacher–student expectancy effects produced results consistent with the implications of Rosenthal and Jacobson's study, not everyone was convinced. One of the common criticisms of this line of research was that Rosenthal and Jacobson had induced teachers' expectations artificially. There remained the question of whether the expectations that researchers formed naturally, during the day-to-day workings of the classroom, would have similar effects. Accordingly, considerable research was undertaken on the issue of "naturalistic" expectations. This research focused on the question, "Do naturalistic expectations influence children's performance, or are teachers merely accurate judges of children's later performance?" (see Jussim, 1989). The distinction between *expectancy* and *accuracy* is critical, because if teachers' expectations affect, rather than reflect, academic achievement, then nonacademic factors that influence such expectations may be an important source of unjustified bias. Such bias has no place in the classroom, and if found, calls for an intensive and comprehensive program aimed at its elimination.

To resolve this issue, and to do so in a research context with real teachers and real students, Crano and Mellon (1978) studied the academic achievement of more than 5,000 British school children over their first four years of elementary school. Their data set included standardized test scores of children's achievement in English and mathematics, measures of teachers' expectations regarding their students' academic potential, and their evaluations of the children's classroom behavior. The design of the study allowed a comparison of the relative strengths of both the expectation hypothesis (Teachers' expectations cause later achievement) and the accuracy hypothesis (Children's achievements cause teachers' subsequent expectations). Results confirmed both hypotheses, but far stronger support was found for the expectation hypothesis—teachers' evaluations of their students and their probable academic accomplishments were more strongly predictive of children's later achievement than the reverse. To be sure, children's achievements did influence teachers' expectations for later success, but this relationship was by far the weaker of the two possibilities suggested by the competing expectation-versus-accuracy hypotheses.

An important feature of this study is that teachers' expectations had been formed naturally; they were not induced experimentally. As such, it supports the relevance of Rosenthal's experimental work for the rough-and-tumble natural world of the elementary classroom. Another significant finding was that expectations were not randomly distributed throughout the sample of British school children. Rather, children of lower social class were clearly disadvantaged, be-

Sex, race, attractiveness, dress, and many other factors can influence teachers' expectations of the probable academic success of their students. These expectations have been shown to have a powerful impact on students' actual achievement. ■

cause teachers were much more likely to expect them to do poorly. If teachers' expectations influence academic performance, then the potentially destructive nature of the expectation cycle becomes obvious:

■ Teachers' expectations influence children's academic performance, either positively or negatively.
■ Teachers expect less of poor children.
■ Therefore, all other things being equal, poor children will not perform as well as their more (economically) fortunate peers.
■ This pattern of performance will confirm the teachers' expectations!

In short, the children of lower social status had two strikes against them even before they came up to bat. It is little wonder that the academic achievement of elementary school children of lower socioeconomic status is inferior to that of their higher-status peers and that this achievement gap grows over the course of the school years. Unfortunately, these findings are not confined to the British Isles. The effects of poverty on the achievement gap—the ever-widening gulf between the academic performance of children of high and low socioeconomic status—are obvious in the United States as well (Baron, Tom, & Cooper, 1985; Crano, 1974; Dusek & Joseph, 1983).

Results of the sort that Rosenthal and Jacobson put forward and the implications of these findings for the educational system caused a critical firestorm in education circles. In the laboratory as well as in the schools, hundreds of studies were undertaken, and confusion reigned for a time regarding the strength, indeed, even the existence, of teacher expectancy effects. However, we are in a position to assess the literature now that the smoke has cleared, and this assessment indicates that expectancy effects are real. In a review of hundreds of studies on classroom expectancy effects, Rosenthal (1985) found that 36% produced results favoring the expectancy hypothesis. This is far from a perfect score, but it is much too large, and the issue too important, to be ignored.

The Transmission of Expectations in the Classroom

Clearly, something mediates the transmission of expectancies, but as Harris (1991) has observed, "[Although] there may be 345 studies leading to the conclusion that expectancy effects exist . . . there is very little understanding of the processes underlying them" (p. 318). We have yet to pinpoint the precise factors responsible for the transmission of expectations, but research has suggested a number of possibilities (Harris & Rosenthal, 1985).

Rosenthal (1989), for one, has developed an **affect–effort theory of expectancy.** The theory holds that a change in a *teacher's expectations* about a student's academic potential is accompanied by a change of affect: The more favorable the change in expectation, the more positive the teacher's regard for the student. Increased positive affect results in the teacher being more willing to expend effort on behalf of the student. Thus, students who induce positive expectations find themselves dealing with teachers who not only like them but also are willing to work harder to see that they learn. The reverse of the process is all too obvious. Teachers who form a negative expectation of a students' academic possibilities like them less and are less willing to work on their behalf.

The research of Crano and Mellon (1978) in the British schools supports this theory and demonstrates that a teacher's feelings about a student are crucial. The strongest expectancy effects on children's *academic* achievements were the result of teacher's ratings of the *social* or *behavioral* aspects of the children, not their views of the children's innate intellectual capabilities. Children whose teachers found them a pleasure to have in class were much more likely to score well in their academic subjects than those whose classroom behavior the teacher found objectionable. Of course, academic promise mattered to the teachers, and their evaluations of the academic potential of the students were associated with children's subsequent achievement. However, these relationships were not nearly as strong as those following from the teachers' evaluations of the social and behavioral characteristics of their students.

■ ■ ■ THE SELF-FULFILLING PROPHECY

As Rosenthal (1966) observed, expectancy effects are not novel. Although the terminology has varied over the years, research on expectations has been a part of social psychology for nearly a century (Jastro, 1900; Moll, 1898). Another name for the expectancy effect is the self-fulfilling prophecy, a term coined by Robert Merton (1948). According to Merton, a **self-fulfilling prophecy** is a two-phase process: First, an individual defines a situation incorrectly; then, his or her subsequent actions (prompted by the definition) cause the originally incorrect conception to become reality. The loan company scenario at the chapter's beginning is a classic example of a self-fulfilling prophecy. In the example, a perfectly healthy savings and loan association is brought into default because its depositors share the misconception that it is in trouble. By acting on this assumption (withdrawing their money as soon as they can), they cause the very problem they suspected, but which in the absence of their behavior would not have occurred.

How does the self-fulfilling prophecy work? Consider the following example. Suppose you were told that a person you were about to encounter in a bargaining session was a very aggressive, difficult person (remember Admiral Rickover?). Would you approach such a person differently from one whom you thought to be fair and easygoing? Would you adopt a highly cooperative stance with a person who hated you? Would you be vigilant for any sign of hostility or aggression? Jones and Panitch (1971) anticipated your answers in an interesting study. Respondents in their research played a two-person prisoners' dilemma game. They could choose to cooperate or to compete with their partner. If participants learned (falsely) that their partner did not like them, they were more likely to compete. Not surprisingly, those on the receiving end of these unjustified competitive actions readily attributed a negative attitude to their partner. What's more, they reciprocated, confirming their partner's expectations. On the other hand, if one of a pair acted cooperatively because he or she expected cooperation, the person's cooperative behavior was generally reciprocated. As you see, the self-fulfilling prophecy can produce positive as well as negative outcomes.

The prisoner's dilemma game is a widely used method in the study of decisionmaking: See Chapter 12.

Effects of Appearance on Expectations

One of the most interesting demonstrations of the self-fulfilling prophecy was a simple experiment in which male and female pairs of participants were asked to get acquainted with each other by telephone (Snyder, Tanke, & Berscheid, 1977). The college men were given a photograph of the woman with whom they were to speak. The men and the women of the study knew their conversations would be monitored. What the men did not know is that the pictures they received were not really those of the woman with whom they were to speak. Some got a picture of a very attractive woman, others of a much less attractive woman. The women themselves knew nothing of the pictures, nor did they receive pictures of their (male) phone mate.

People's appearance produces expectations of their social behaviors in others: See Chapters 7 and 13.

As had been shown in many previous studies, the photos succeeded in producing expectations about the women. The men who thought they were to talk to a beautiful woman predicted that she would be sociable, poised, with a good sense of humor, and socially adept. Those expecting to speak with the unattractive woman expected her to be unsociable, awkward, serious, and socially inept. What is more important, these "prophecies" influenced the men's behavior while on the telephone. Analyses of their conversational behavior during the interaction disclosed that men expecting a beautiful woman at the other end of the line treated her warmly, with lively humor and friendliness. If the man thought his partner was ugly, she was treated coldly, distantly, and in a very reserved manner.

These differences are striking. But there is more to the study than this. In addition to monitoring the behavior of the men, the researchers evaluated the women's behavior, and these results too are remarkable. The women (who did not know that the men had received a bogus photo) behaved in ways that confirmed the expectations of their partners! Women whose partners thought they were beautiful acted beautifully—they were more friendly, likable, and so-

Which of these two men is more likely to help an injured child? To be a better host at a party? To be a success in life? ■

Research suggests that we infer positive social traits on the basis of appearance: See Chapter 13.

Gender-based stereotypes can influence many of our most important relationships: See Chapter 23.

ciable than the women who were thought to be less attractive. The judges who made these ratings of the women's telephone conversations did not know which picture the men had received, nor were they aware of the actual physical appearance of the women whose telephone interaction they were judging. Despite this, and despite the fact that the actual appearance of the females was completely independent of the pictures that purportedly described them, the relationship held between (the photo's) attractiveness and likability. Women thought to be beautiful were also thought to be good (friendly, sociable, warm), and they fulfilled this expectation.

Does the self-fulfilling prophecy work only for men? Do women also form expectations on the basis of the physical attractiveness of the opposite sex—and do such expectations influence the target's (man's) behavior? Andersen and Bem (1981) found that both sexes are susceptible to self-fulfilling prophecies based on physical appearance. In addition, they discovered that men and women alike are more likely to fall prey to appearance-based self-fulfilling prophecies if they ascribe to gender stereotypes. Highly "feminine" women and "masculine" men were the most susceptible to the attraction-based self-fulfilling prophecy.

Research on children (Musser & Graziano, in press) has revealed a similar pattern. Children not only receive expectations but they can send them as well—even young children, as early as second grade. In Musser and Graziano's study, pairs of second- and fourth-grade school children participated in a game that called on them to make a series of decisions. One member of each pair was designated the "transmitter." The young transmitters were misinformed, however. Some thought their partner was two years older than themselves, while others thought they were two years older than their partner. When the children in the transmitter role interacted with someone they thought was a younger player, they attempted to control the interaction—and succeeded in doing so. When the other player was supposedly older, transmitters were less likely to attempt control, and the partner was more likely to do so. This pattern of differences in control and transmission suggests that the very young not only absorb but also can produce self-fulfilling prophecies.

Effects of Race on Expectations

Snyder and his colleagues forcefully demonstrated that appearance cues can have a powerful influence on expectations, which in turn can alter the behavior of both perceiver and target. Appearance can include variables other than attractiveness, and one of the most important of these is race. Word, Zanna, and Cooper (1974) investigated race-related expectancy effects in an important investigation in which participants played the role of job interviewer. The applicants were accomplices of the experimenter, and had undergone extensive training so they would all act in a standardized way. What was of interest was the behavior of the interviewers. The results showed without question that the interviewers (all of whom were white) acted very differently to job seekers as a consequence of the applicant's race. Interviewers were much more likely to interrupt black job applicants, made many more speech errors in their presence, were less intensely involved in the interview, and terminated interviews earlier than they did with white applicants.

What do these results have to do with the self-fulfilling prophecy? Let's speculate a bit. Suppose the interviewers in this study thought that black people were not as good as whites in interviews and not as qualified for the job under consideration. Suppose further that this attitude was manifested subtly in their nonverbal behaviors. Finally, suppose these subtle behavioral differences had a chilling effect on the actual performance of black job applicants. Under this set of assumptions, the interviewer's expectation of poorer performance on the part of black people would be confirmed in the interview, not because of any inherent inferiority of the black job seekers, but because the field on which the game was played was not level—the behaviors of the interviewer were not comparable across the two races.

Because of the circumstantial nature of the evidence, which only suggests that variations in interviewer behaviors caused differences in job seekers' performance, Word and his colleagues (1974) conducted a second investigation. In this study, white interviewers were trained to mimic the verbal and nonverbal interviewer actions observed in study 1. After having learned how (or how not) to act, they set about interviewing a series of participants. In some of the interactions, the interviewers adopted the general style observed when blacks had been interviewed—they were aloof, intrusive, nervous, and curt. In the other interactions, they were interested, warm, relaxed, and nonintrusive, as had been observed for white applicants. The participant job seekers (all of them white) who were interviewed under the "black" conditions were evaluated by observers as less successful, less adequate, and more nervous than those interviewed under the "white" conditions. These results are impressive because the observers were "blind"—they did not know which interviewer style was being employed. In combination, the results of the two studies by Word and his colleagues suggest that racial differences in employment interview performance are influenced as much by interviewers' behaviors as they are by the job seekers'.

Nonverbal behaviors may be cues to attitudes: See Chapter 6.

This is not a reassuring result. It suggests that even a valid test of performance can show differences as a function of race when, in reality, none exists. What's worse, the cause of the differences will be misidentified—in this case, the differences would be misattributed to the applicants and their race. As Word and his colleagues have shown, the observed differences in interview performance were really determined by differences in the behavior of the interviewers, not the interviewees. Failure to recognize the source of such differences can result in unintended, but nonetheless harmful, racism. A more complete discussion of this type of behavior is presented in a later chapter.

One of the effects of racism is discrimination: See Chapter 24.

APPLYING SOCIAL PSYCHOLOGY
TO WORK
■ ■ ■

Expectations on the Job

Expectations influence not only people's ability to land a job but their job performance as well. In a study that closely paralleled Rosenthal and Jacobson's elementary school study, King (1971) (mis)informed a welding instructor that some of his trainees showed strong aptitude; other trainees were not said to have this aptitude. Results indicated that the high-expectancy trainees were much more successful in learning welding, scored significantly better than their peers, were more prompt, and were absent from work less often. In addition, the time they needed to learn the basics of the trade was less than half that of their peers. These differences occurred despite the fact that the men did not know they had been singled out as having high aptitude for welding (which may or may not have been the case—the designations had been made at random). These "aptitude" differences were noted by the experimenter, the welding instructor, and by the high-expectancy workers' peers, who consistently nominated members of the high-expectancy group as the person they would most like to have as a coworker. This experiment demonstrates the impact of expectations even in situations that involve learning a complex skill. The teacher's expectations affected the performance and work attitudes of the high-expectancy students and those of their peers as well.

Effects of Sex on Expectations

The same kinds of results are found in self-fulfilling prophecy research on sex differences. For example, Skrypnek and Snyder (1982) had pairs of participants work on a series of tasks that were sex-typed—the tasks were either typically associated with men (fixing a light switch) or with women (icing a cake). Each participant was to divide the workload with his or her partner. They communicated via a signaling system—"I'll do task A if you do task B," and so on. Participants were physically separated, and the signaling system was used so they would not know the sex of their partner. However, one person in each pair was subtly led to believe the partner was male, others to assume the partner was female. These beliefs had a powerful impact on participants' behavior. Those thought to be male were more likely to assume masculine jobs, usually at the request of their partner. As the experiment progressed, these (mis)identified participants conformed more and more to their partner's sex-linked expectation. Thus, a female whose partner thought she really was a male would initially have the male-oriented jobs thrust on her. As the study progressed, it became more and more likely that she herself would volunteer to take on the male jobs. If a male was thought by his partner to be female, he would be urged by the partner to take on the more feminine jobs. As the experiment progressed, he would volunteer to take on these types of jobs himself. This self-fulfilling prophecy effect was observed for men and women and for male and female sex-typed jobs.

Research by Zanna and Pack (1975) and von Baeyer, Sherk, and Zanna (1981) bolsters these conclusions. Their studies demonstrate the powerful effects of perceivers' expectancies on the behaviors of the targets—especially when it counts. For example, Zanna and Pack asked females to describe themselves to an extremely attractive or extremely unattractive male partner. The women had been led to believe that the man possessed either a very traditional or a very liberated view of the ideal woman. They described themselves in ways they thought would appeal to him. When the man was very attractive, the women's self-presentation was consistent with his ideal, no matter what it was—liberated or traditional. In the unattractive partner condition, the man's preference had no effect on women's self-presentations.

■ ■ ■ BIASED INFORMATION SEARCH

"Proving" (versus Testing) One's Hypotheses

How do interpersonal expectations operate? In an experiment by Snyder and Swann (1978), participants were to interview another person, asking a series of questions about his or her likes and dislikes, activities, feelings, and the like. Some of the interviewers were told their specific task was to determine "the extent to which the target's behavior and experiences matched those of a prototypic extravert" (p. 1203). An extravert was explicitly defined as a person who was outgoing, energetic, talkative, and sociable. Others were told to assess the extent to which the target was an introvert. Introverts were defined as people who were shy, reserved, quiet, and timid.

Some participants were told explicitly that the target person was an introvert or an extravert. Other participants were told nothing of the target's personality—they simply were given one or the other description, and asked to determine whether the target was introverted or extraverted. The interviewers were given a list of twenty-six possible questions, from which they were to choose twelve. The central issue of the study was the type of questions the interviewers selected. Eleven of the twenty-six questions were the sort one would ask of an extravert ("What would you do if you wanted to liven things up at a party?" "In what situations are you most talkative?"); five questions were unrelated to personality ("What types of charity do you like to contribute to?" "What are your career goals?"); and ten questions were the type one would ask of an introvert ("What factors make it hard for you to really open up to people?" "What things do you dislike about loud parties?").

The interviewers who were informed explicitly by the experimenter that their target was an introvert or an extravert were strongly biased in their choice of

The effects of the mental pictures we hold of ourselves and others are the focus of much research: See Chapter 8.

question. The expectation they formed on the basis of the experimenter's information guided their question choice. If they thought they were paired with an extravert, interviewers consistently chose questions one would ask of an extravert. With introverted targets, they chose introvert-oriented questions. Interviewers had a schema of introverts and extraverts, and used it in choosing the questions they would ask.

More surprisingly, the same pattern was found among those who were not told in advance about the target's personality type. Remember that these interviewers were asked to determine the extent to which the target was introverted (or extraverted), but were given no indication that the target was one type of person or the other. Despite this, and the fact that either type of question would have been equally informative, the interviewers overwhelmingly used questions that would confirm their own hypotheses about what to look for in the target. When the participant was asked to decide the extent to which a person was introverted, they asked introvert-related questions and avoided the extravert-related items. If they had been asked to decide the extent to which a target was extraverted, they concentrated on extravert-oriented questions. As Snyder (1981) observed in his recapitulation of this work,

> Time and time again . . . participants planned to test their hypotheses by treating their targets as if they were the type of person they were hypothesized to be: they planned to search preferentially for behavioral evidence that would *confirm* their hypotheses. To test the hypothesis that their targets were extraverted individuals, participants were particularly likely to choose to ask precisely those questions that one typically asks of individuals already known to be extroverts . . . To test the hypothesis that their targets were introverted individuals, participants were particularly likely to choose to ask precisely those questions that one typically asks of individuals already known to be introverts. (p. 206)

Snyder and Swann stopped the experiment at this point. In this initial study, they were interested only in strategies people used to test their hypotheses, and they found that people typically adopted a confirmatory strategy. What would have happened if they had allowed the interviewers to continue, actually to ask the questions they had chosen? Would their hypotheses have been disconfirmed? After all, they were based on personality descriptions that had been assigned randomly to the target. When Snyder and Swann (1978) addressed these questions in a second study, they found that interviewers' expectations not only had a powerful influence on the questions they chose to ask, but also that their *biased information search* had a strong effect on the conclusions they ultimately formed. By biasing the information search, people obtained evidence that, to them, confirmed their hypotheses. If they asked enough introverted questions, the target appeared to be an introvert. If they concentrated on extravert-oriented questions, the targets appeared extraverted. What's more, judges who did not know the interviewers' expectations evaluated the target as the interviewers had! The process is fascinating. A person expecting to interact with an introvert asks introvert-biased questions; these questions, in turn, elicit introverted answers. Interviewers expecting to interact with extraverts ask extravert-oriented questions, and receive answers that confirm the bias. If you search in a biased fashion, you are likely to find what you are looking for.

What do you do when you want to liven-up a party? ■

APPLYING SOCIAL PSYCHOLOGY
TO THE LAW
■ ■ ■

Effects of Innuendo and Leading Questions

Research by Daniel Wegner and his associates suggests that biased information search may have very serious implications in real-world contexts (Wegner, Wentzlaff, Kerker, & Beattie, 1981). The researchers were interested in the effects of leading questions, or *innuendoes,* on people's evaluations. As part of the study, participants read the following headline:

Is Bob Talbert Linked With Mafia?

Later, they rated the subject of the headline, Bob Talbert. The ratings demonstrated that the negative association put forward in the leading question had a very serious negative effect on people's evaluations. In fact, this headline affected people's attitudes as much as the one that directly stated, "BOB TALBERT LINKED WITH MAFIA." Surprisingly, this effect held even if the source of the innuendo was not particularly credible. The *innuendo effect,* as Wegner and associates (1981) call it, is strong and ominous. In courtroom settings, their results suggest that attorneys who merely question a person's connection with an illegal activity can damage the person's credibility. It is probably for this reason that Weld and Roff (1938) found that indicting a person on a criminal charge often is enough to lead a jury to consider the person guilty.

Swann, Giuliano, and Wegner (1982) speculated that innuendo effects might occur because statements that merely associate a person with a negative activity cause observers to form impressions of the person that are consistent with the statement. Participants infer that "the recipient was the kind of person who 'deserved' the question" (p. 1032). In addition, by responding to leading questions, respondents often provide evidence that is consistent with the questions asked of them. Let's reconsider Snyder and Swann's (1978) experiment, in which interviewers asked a series of leading questions to other respondents. Questioners expecting to interact with extraverts asked questions appropriate of extraverts ("What would you do if you wanted to liven things up at a party?"). Interestingly, analysis disclosed that "whether respondents possessed the sought after attributes made little difference; overall, *respondents accepted the premises inherent in the questions 97% of the time,*" (Swann et al., 1982, p. 1033, italics added). Even introverted people who were asked an extravert-oriented question replied in a manner that indicated they accepted the premise that they were extraverted: "What would I do to liven things up at a party? Well, I would . . ." They did not say, "I don't know. I rarely go to parties, and when I do, I never try to liven things up." By accepting the premise, which is necessary to answer the (leading) question, the respondent signals that the question is not entirely off base. As Wegner et al. (1981) have shown, such acceptance leads perceivers to assume that the question is appropriate. What's more, the leading question, even if it is entirely misdirected, may have an impact on respondents' self-concepts. In an impressive series of investigations, Swann (1983, 1990; Swann, Stein-Seroussi, & McNulty, 1992) has shown that merely answering leading questions can affect the way that people view *themselves*. Thus, answering extravert-oriented questions may cause people to view themselves as extraverted.

■■■ ARE SELF-FULFILLING PROPHECIES INEVITABLY FULFILLED?

The evidence cited so far seems to suggest that people are incapable of testing interpersonal hypotheses in a rational, unbiased manner. Are unbiased interpersonal judgments beyond our capacity? Are we, in fact, prisoners of our own expectancies? The answer to these questions is Yes, sometimes—but not always. Considerable research (e.g., Darley, Fleming, Hilton, & Swann, 1988; Neuberg, 1989; Swann & Ely, 1984) has focused on the conditions under which people resist conforming to the expectancies of others and in which accuracy, rather than confirmation of expectations, characterizes behavior.

Self-Affirmation versus the Self-Fulfilling Prophecy

Swann and Ely (1984) conducted one of the original studies of resistance to expectation-induced action. The researchers did not believe that people always acted in ways that confirmed others' expectations of them, and were curious about the circumstances that would override expectancy biases. They hypothesized that people would be most resistant to others' expectations when the expectations conflicted with strongly held self-beliefs (or self-schema, to use Marcus's term). For example, suppose Jenny is a fine all-around athlete, and knows that she is. She goes out on a blind date with Tom, who has arranged to meet another couple at the local bowling alley. Tom has a low opinion of women's athletic skill in general, and expects that Jenny will have trouble keeping the ball out of the gutter most of the time. In subtle and not so subtle ways, he lets her know this. Will these expectations affect Jenny's game? Swann and Ely have shown that they will not, *if* Jenny is confident of her ability. Rather, Jenny will

Beliefs about the self, or self-schemas, have powerful effects on people's behavior: See Chapter 9.

affirm her talent. This **self-affirmation effect** counteracts Tom's biased (and potentially biasing) expectations.

On the other hand, if Tom is certain that all women are poor athletes and Jenny is uncertain of her bowling skill, her score probably will suffer because of Tom's expectations. In circumstances such as these, when the perceiver is certain of his or her belief and the target of the expectation is uncertain, the biasing effects of interpersonal expectancies have their greatest effect. Of course, this is precisely the condition that existed in most of the teacher expectancy studies reviewed earlier. Children often are uncertain of their academic abilities, especially when their self-beliefs conflict with those of their teachers. When the teacher is biased against (or in favor of) the child, such an act can have enormous consequences for the child's social and academic development.

The Self-Fulfilling Prophecy and High Stakes

In addition to self-certainty, other factors have been found to weaken the effects of expectations. One of the most obvious of these is self-interest. If people *must* be right, they often will not allow themselves to be misled by erroneous expectations. Consider an experiment conducted by Darley and his colleagues, in which participants were led to believe that the person with whom they were about to interact was not particularly good when working under pressure (Darley, Fleming, Hilton, & Swann, 1988). For some, this information was very relevant, because their task was to choose a partner for a competitive, pressure-packed game. For other participants, the information was irrelevant, because their job was merely to engage in a conversation with the person.

Participants were given a list of twenty-one questions, from which they were to choose eight to ask the target. The questions were categorized in terms of their relevance to the expectancy of "folding under pressure."

Self- or vested-interest has a powerful effect on attitudes as well: See Chapter 2.

■ Seven of the questions on the list were very relevant to the negative expectancy (for example, "Are you easily flustered?" "Have you ever blown an exam because you panicked when you noticed time running out?").
■ Seven focused on potentially negative aspects of the target that had nothing to do with the expectancy the experimenter had induced ("Do you think others would describe you as insensitive?").
■ Seven were irrelevant to the expectancy, but neutral ("Have you traveled much?" "Do you like school so far?").

As indicated in Figure 16.2, question choice was clearly influenced by the motives underlying the interaction. Those who had to choose a game partner used the questions that were relevant to the (negative) expectancy the experimenter had induced, even though it was very awkward to ask them. Those who merely had to engage in conversation avoided such questions. These "conversational" participants were more likely to pose neutral questions. All avoided the negative, irrelevant questions. This pattern of choices makes good sense, because the relevant negative expectancy questions were not particularly easy to ask (for example, "Do you tend to crumble under pressure?"), and these would be avoided, except by those who really needed the information they could supply.

After the interviewers chose a particular set of questions, they asked them in order. The experimental setup was such that interviewer and target interacted via telephone. To standardize the interaction, answers to all twenty-one questions

FIGURE 16.2

Effects of question relevance and expectancy on the type and number of questions asked of a potential partner (adapted from Darley et al., 1988). Expectations influenced the kinds of questions participants asked of their potential partner if the information was critical to success in a subsequent task.

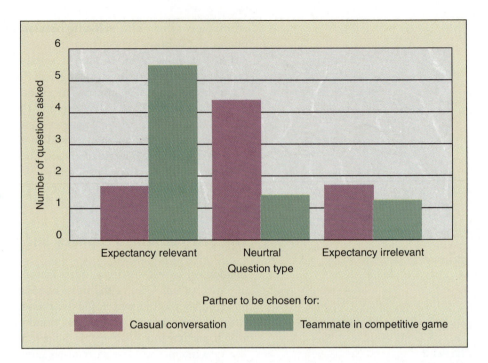

had been prerecorded and were played back, as appropriate, in response to each query. In an ingenious extension to the standard procedure, Darley and colleagues actually recorded two sets of answers. In one set, the target consistently presented himself as calm and collected, contradicting the expectation furnished by the experimenter. In the other set of answers, the target sounded mildly frantic in tone and content, confirming the experimenter's earlier description. Interviewers heard either the consistently calm or the consistently frantic answers in response to their questions.

In addition to standardizing the interaction, this setup allowed the experimenters to determine if the form and content of the answers themselves influenced participants' evaluations of the target. If the answers disconfirmed the expectation that had been induced, would the interviewers notice? And would the interviewers be affected by the relevance of their expectations? Relevance in this case is defined by the importance the interviewer attached to correctly gauging the ability of the target to act under stress. In the condition in which the subject had to choose a partner with whom to compete in a cutthroat game, the issue of composure was highly relevant.

Results bearing on the effects of relevance and the confirmatory or disconfirmatory aspect of the target's answers are presented in Figure 16.3. This figure shows that the target's answers overpowered expectations when his answers were relevant to the interviewer (that is, when the participant had to decide whether to chose the target as a partner). If the target seemed calm and composed, he was evaluated as significantly less susceptible to stress than if he seemed frantic.

On the other hand, the behavior of the target had very little effect on the evaluations of participants who did not have to choose a partner with whom to compete—those for whom the target's composure under pressure was irrelevant. In this circumstance, interviewers' evaluations were not significantly affected by the emotional tone or content of the target's answers. It was as if the interviewers in this condition of the study simply neglected to listen to their partner, and

FIGURE 16.3

■

Effects of question relevance and partner's answers on participant's evaluations of their potential partner (adapted from Darley et al., 1988). If the task was important to the participants, they listened closely to their potential partner and evaluated him on the basis of his performance. If the task was not important, participants were content to maintain their expectancy-based evaluations, even when their partner's behavior clearly disconfirmed the expectation.

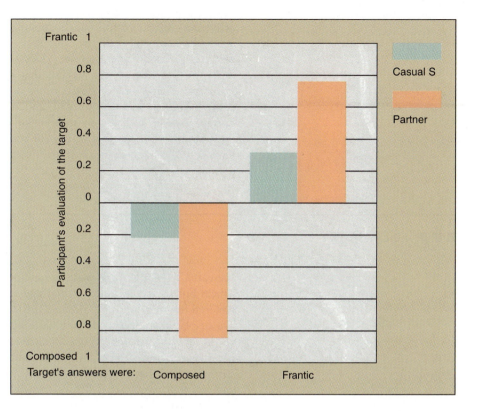

based their evaluation on the earlier-induced expectation. These results imply that our expectations do not inevitably color our perceptions and actions. When a valid reading of the situation is crucial, we can overcome the tunnel vision that prior expectancies produce.

In a study using real people as targets, rather than tape-recorded answers, Neuberg (1989) studied the behaviors of both the interviewers (for whom a negative expectancy was induced) and the targets of the expectancy, who were also experimental participants. Results indicated that the behavior of real targets was strongly influenced by the actions of the interviewer. If an interviewer held a negative expectation of a target and the target's behavior had no effect on this expectation, the targets began to behave in ways that suggested the expectation was correct. On the other hand, if the interviewer was sensitive to the target's answers, the target's behavior overwhelmed the effect of prior (negative) expectations. As Darley's research implied, Neuberg's findings demonstrate that when a person is attentive to the behaviors of another, the effects of prior expectancies can be negated.

■ ■ ■ ■   SOME CONCLUDING THOUGHTS

There is little doubt that our expectations about other people affect the ways in which we react to them. The expectations we have of others color not only our behavior but the behavior of the target of our expectations as well. Our actions provide a context within which the other person reacts. In this sense, our prophecies often are self-fulfilling. But this need not always be so. Taken together, research by Darley and associates (1988), Newberg (1989), Swann (1984), Swann & Ely (1984), and others suggests that prior expectations influence our impressions and evaluations of others most strongly when the target's self-confidence is low, accuracy is not important, and other demands of the situation intrude or distract us from forming an accurate or valid evaluation. When we are aware of the potential damage that acting on unfounded expectations or stereotypes can have, and the manner in which they operate, we are much less likely to succumb to their effects.

■■■ SUMMARY

Research has shown that our expectations influence not only our actions toward others but their actions as well. Expectancy effects in pharmacological research fostered the development of blind and double blind research procedures, and the use of placebo controls. Rosenthal extended this research into a demonstration of the effects of teachers' expectancies on children's academic performance, an issue that is the subject of considerable debate. Replication of his work has demonstrated that (1) teachers' expectancies can strongly influence children's academic performance and (2) are themselves affected by such irrelevant factors as the race, social class, and physical attractiveness of the student.

Related research on the self-fulfilling prophecy demonstrates that physical characteristics (race, sex, physical appearance) affect people's expectations about others, and these expectations color the actions of both the perceiver and the perceived. Biased information search promotes the development and operation of misguided expectancies. Through this process, people appear to search for information supportive of their beliefs, rather than for information that puts the belief to a fair test.

Expectations are not inevitably confirmed. Persons holding incorrect expectations resist their biasing effects when it is in their self-interest to obtain valid information. Similarly, people resist the biasing effects of others' expectations when the expectation conflicts with strongly held self-beliefs.

■■■ SUGGESTED READINGS

1. Harris, M. J. (1991). Controversy and cumulation: Meta-analysis and research on interpersonal expectancy effects. *Personality and Social Psychology Bulletin, 17,* 316–322.
2. Miller, D. T., & Turnbull, W. (1986). Expectancies and interpersonal processes. *Annual Review of Psychology, 37,* 233–256.
3. Rosenthal, R. (1985). From unconscious experimenter bias to teacher expectancy effects. In J. B. Dusek, V. C. Hall, & W. J. Meyer (Eds.), *Teacher expectancies* (pp. 37–65). Hillsdale, NJ: Erlbaum.
4. Swann, W. B., Jr. (1987). Identity negotiation: Where two roads meet. *Journal of Personality and Social Psychology, 53,* 1038–1051.

PART IV

SOCIAL INFLUENCE
The Psychology of Groups

CHAPTER 17
Obedience: Doing What You're Told

CHAPTER 18
Conformity and Independence: Going Along with the Crowd

CHAPTER 19
Minority Influence: When Dissidents Prevail

CHAPTER 20
Group Performance: The Effects of Working Together

CHAPTER 21
Group Decision Making: Making Choices Collectively

CHAPTER 22
Social Identity: The Group in the Individual

OBEDIENCE

Doing What You're Told

■ **Key Concepts**

Obedience
Obedience and proximity to
   victim
Obedience and personal
   responsibility
Rebellion
Generalizability
Administrative obedience
Resistance
Obedience and proximity to
   authority

■ **Chapter Outline**

MILGRAM'S RESEARCH PROGRAM
   The Basic Paradigm
   Variations on the Theme

OBJECTIONS TO THE PROGRAM OF RESEARCH
   Ethics
   Generalizability
   ■ The Obedient Nurse

ADMINISTRATIVE OBEDIENCE
   Distinguishing Features
   Extending the Series
   ■ Using Real Managers
   How Does It Happen? The Postexperimental Questionnaire

FORCES FOR COMPLIANCE OR RESISTANCE

SOME CONCLUDING COMMENTS

SUMMARY

Forward the Light Brigade!
Was there a man dismay'd?
Not tho' the soldier knew
Someone had blunder'd:
Their's not to make reply
Their's not to reason why.
Their's but to do and die.
—Alfred, Lord Tennyson (1842)

■ ■ ■

A madman decides that the Jews are a good scapegoat for his country's political and economic troubles, and decides to eradicate them. He becomes chancellor of Germany, and after a decade of mounting terror and violence, he gives the extermination order. Thousands bend to the task of carrying out the leader's wishes. Not all who work on the campaign of genocide hate Jews and agree with the order, yet few attempt to subvert Hitler's Final Solution. Obedience to authority is paramount, and six million perish. Years later, Adolph Eichmann, a central figure in the extermination campaign, is brought to the bar of justice. His defense? "I was not responsible. I was only doing my job." A superior officer gave him an order. As a good soldier he carried it out.

■

The story told in Tennyson's poem is as old as warfare—the incompetent general orders his troops into a position that can only result in their destruction. Everyone from the captain to the lowliest private knows that the outcome of his foolish order will be disaster, yet the captain obeys, his men follow, and many perish.

Fighters on both sides of the struggle in the former Yugoslavia have been accused of atrocities. Are these men responsible, or are their military superiors, who gave the orders, ultimately accountable for their subordinates' actions? ■

The Charge of the Light Brigade is a perfect example of obedience taken to the extreme.

With such vivid examples in our recent history, you might assume that the study of blind obedience has been a high priority for social psychology. Obedience has been studied from the early days of the discipline (Adorno, Frankel-Brunswik, Levinson, & Sanford, 1950), and is being investigated with increased scrutiny today (e.g., Kelman & Hamilton, 1989; Staub, 1989). However, systematic investigation of obedience developed in social psychology only after Stanley Milgram's remarkable studies in the 1960s. Milgram's research on obedience, the reaction to his investigations, and the research stimulated by the ensuing controversy are the focus of this chapter. If nothing else, we hope to show the destructive potential of mindless obedience, how it is created, and how it can be overcome.

■ ■ ■ MILGRAM'S RESEARCH PROGRAM

Obedience can mean different things to different people, but since Milgram's work, it has taken on special significance for social psychologists. In social psychology, *obedience* refers to a person's willingness to conform to the demands of an authority, even if those demands violate the person's sense of what is right. In most research contexts, the authority requires a participant to deliberately harm another person. This demand conflicts with participants' moral values. The way people resolve this conflict is the central issue.

The study of obedience is controversial. Many feel that researchers should not place people in such conflicts. Psychologists raised powerful ethical objections to Milgram's research when it was first published (e.g., Baumrind, 1964; Orne, 1962; Orne & Holland, 1968; Patten, 1977). More than a quarter-century has passed since his studies, yet Milgram's work still excites debate. To find out what triggers these reactions, let's examine his work. We do so with three tasks in mind: (1) to find out what he did; (2) to decide whether the research was worth doing, considering the risks it posed; and (3) to judge whether Milgram's research aided social psychologists' quest for new knowledge.

The Basic Paradigm

When Milgram began his research, he wanted to understand the things that caused people to follow the demands of authorities, even if those demands resulted in direct harm to other people. Milgram's central question can be summarized as follows: "Will a person hurt another simply because he or she is ordered to do so?" The relevance of this issue could not be greater. The Nazi atrocities of World War II, the My Lai massacre in Vietnam, the slaughter of innocent people in the former nation of Yugoslavia, and other, similar outrages come to mind when we think about Milgram's research. Such connections help to explain the intensity of interest and debate that surrounds his work.

To study obedience in a controlled environment, Milgram (1963, 1965, 1974) devised a set of experimental arrangements that were meant to enhance the experimenter's authority. Participants entered a laboratory filled with high-tech electronic gadgets. The experimenter wore a white lab coat. He was friendly, but very serious. His every action stressed the importance of the study.

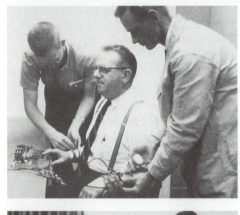

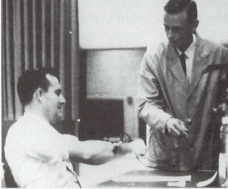

Two participants served in each research session. They were to play the role of either teacher or learner. The teacher read a list of words to the learner and the learner had to memorize them. But there was a bit more to it than this. The experimenter explained that the study was designed to see if punishment aided learning. Accordingly, the teacher had to administer an electric shock to the learner, in increasing voltages, each time the learner made a mistake.

As you might have guessed, the game was rigged. The participant was always the teacher. The experimenter's accomplice always played the role of learner, a man in his mid-fifties, polite, balding, and affable. He seemed concerned about the study and appeared a bit apprehensive about being shocked.

The apparatus used in (apparently) administering shock was the formidable-looking device shown at left. To simplify the teacher's job, the front panel of this "shock generator" was laid out in a neat progression of increasingly severe shock levels from 15 volts to 450 volts, with labeled gradations running from "slight shock" to "danger, severe shock" and, most ominously, "XXX"!

When he described the task, Milgram demonstrated the shock generator to the teachers, and even administered a 45-volt sample shock to give them an idea of how it felt. Milgram also escorted teachers into the learner's room, separate from the teacher's, where he strapped the learner to a chair and placed electrodes on his arm. As this was being done, the learner requested reassurance that the shocks would not be dangerous, because he suffered heart problems. The experimenter reassured him, and the learning task began.

The central question of the study was very simple: How much shock was the teacher willing to administer before refusing to continue. It should be noted that teachers in this study participated for pay, but the payment was given before the task was begun, and they were assured they could keep the money ($4.50) regardless of the course of the experiment.

The course of the teacher–learner interaction was carefully arranged. At first, the learner performed well. No shocks were called for, and it looked as if the study would be a pleasant romp in the laboratory. Then the learner made a mistake, and the teacher was required to deliver a 15-volt shock. This is a very minor shock, but still it meant administering pain to another person. Worse was yet to come, however. The errors began to pile up, and the required shock level moved rapidly and alarmingly from "slight" to "moderate" to "intense"—and beyond. In addition to making mistakes, the learner began to complain about the pain of the shocks. In reality, he never experienced any shocks. His responses were tape recorded and played back to the teacher, so that all teachers in the study were exposed to a constant set of stimuli. A complete listing of the learner's prerecorded remarks is presented in Table 17.1. As shown, at 75 volts, the learner groaned; at 150 volts, he complained and asked to be released from the study; at 180 volts, he yelled that he could not stand the pain; at 270 volts, the teacher heard an anguished scream; and at 330 volts and beyond, there was an ominous silence—the learner either would not or could not respond further.

At some point in this scenario, almost all subjects tried to stop the study. The experimenter always responded, "Please continue," to their initial requests to end it. If they persisted, the experimenter responded, "Go on," or "The experiment requires that you continue," or "It is absolutely essential that you continue," or, in the case of extremely strong resistance, "You have no other choice—you must go on."

What proportion of the participant sample was willing to do so? Yale University undergraduates were given a detailed description of the study and asked

The pictures at left illustrate Milgrams's experiment. Shown here are the "shock generator," the "learner" being strapped into his chair, and a subject being directed to administer a severe shock and a subject refusing to go on. Despite their objections, most of the subjects obeyed the experimenter. ■

TABLE 17.1
■
The Learner's Script (From Milgram, 1974)

Voltage	Remark
75	Ugh!
90	Ugh!
105	Ugh! (loudly)
120	Ugh! Hey this really hurts.
135	Ugh!
150	Ugh! Experimenter! That's all. Get me out of here. I told you I had heart trouble. My heart's starting to bother me now. Get me out of here, please. My heart's starting to bother me. I refuse to go on. Let me out.
165	Ugh! Let me out!
180	Ugh! I can't stand the pain. Let me out of here!
195	Ugh! Let me out of here. Let me out of here. My heart's bothering me. Let me out of here! You have no right to keep me here! Let me out! Let me out of here! Let me out! Let me out of here! My heart's bothering me. Let me out! Let me out!
210	Ugh! Experimenter! Get me out of here. I've had enough. I won't be in the experiment any more.
225	Ugh!
240	Ugh!
255	Ugh! Get me out of here!
270	(Screaming) Let me out of here. Let me out of here. Let me out of here. Let me out. Do you hear? Let me out of here!
285	(Scream)
300	(Screaming) I absolutely refuse to answer any more. Get me out of here. You can't hold me here. Get me out. Get me out of here.
315	(Intense scream) I told you I refuse to answer. I'm no longer part of this experiment.
330	(Intense scream) Let me out of here. Let me out. My heart's bothering me. Let me out, I tell you. Let me out of here. Let me out of here. You have no right to hold me here. Let me out! Let me out! Let me out of here! Let me out! Let me out!
330+	(The learner made no sounds after the 330-volt level.)

to estimate the proportion of people whom they thought would be willing to carry the study to the end of the shock series. They estimated approximately 3% of the participants would obey the experimenter. A group of psychiatrists asked the same question gave approximately the same answer.

Both groups were very badly mistaken. Fully 65% of the participants (twenty-six of forty) in the experiment described here continued to administer increasingly higher voltages of electric shock *all the way to the end* of the shock series, despite the fact that the learner by then had ceased to respond. For all they knew,

TABLE 17.2

■

**Levels at Which Subject–Teachers Defected
(Adapted from Milgram, 1974)**

Voltage	Number of Defectors	Percentage	Cumulative Percentage
300	5	12.5	12.5
315	4	10.0	22.5
330	2	5.0	27.5
345	1	2.5	30.0
360–435	2	5.0	35.0
450	26[a]	65.0	100.0

[a]*These subjects carried on to the end of the shock series. They were obedient to the bitter end.*

the learner could have been lying dead or severely injured in the next room as a direct consequence of their actions. A breakdown of the distribution of participants who quit and the shock levels at which they defected is presented in Table 17.2. As can be seen, 35% of the sample refused to continue to the end of the shock scale. This is little consolation, however, because not a single person quit before reaching the 300-volt level, the point at which the learner refused or was unable to respond.

How could the participants act in such a cruel and inhuman fashion? Were they specially selected from a population of sadists, child beaters, skinheads, and neo–nazis? Were they chosen for their special susceptibility to the siren song of authority? Had they been trained to obey orders at all costs? Did they enjoy hurting people? The one common answer to all of these questions is No. The men used in this study were a relatively average lot from New Haven, Connecticut, who had answered a newspaper ad to participate in scientific research at Yale University. They ranged in age from twenty to fifty years; 20% were professionals, 40% had white-collar jobs, and 40% were unskilled laborers. They matched the demographic characteristics of the population at large.

College students should take no comfort from the fact that this sample did not consist of the typical college sophomore. When students were employed in subsequent research, the results were no different. Later studies conducted outside New Haven, without the Yale University identification, resulted in slightly weaker, but essentially similar, findings. Likewise, when women were used as subjects, the same level of destructive obedience was found (Milgram, 1974). The basic findings seem to hold without regard to the age, gender, or level of education of the subjects.

A key to understanding the high levels of obedience Milgram found in this and many of his later studies (described in the next section) lies in his clever use of concessions. Initially, he asked very little of his participants. A 15-volt shock really is not painful, and participants knew it. Even though most of them would never deliberately hurt someone, they were willing to administer 15 volts to contribute to the study, to science. Then they had to administer a 30-volt shock. This too does not involve much, if any, pain, so they obeyed. And so on. The

The Branch Davidian catastrophe in Waco, Texas, reinforces the relevance of Milgram's work to contemporary affairs. ■

The foot-in-the-door technique is one of many forms of social influence studied in social psychology: See Chapter 18.

participants were induced to make a series of small concessions. None of the concessions was great, but before long, they were administering dangerous levels of shock. Inducing small concessions is an effective method of producing obedience or compliance. It was a tactic widely employed by the Chinese and North Koreans in brainwashing American prisoners of war in the 1950s (Schein, 1961). In a later chapter we describe studies that suggest that inducing people to do a small service (say, displaying a small sticker that says, "Drive Safely") will make them much more willing to accede to a much larger service later. This "foot-in-the-door" effect, as it is so aptly termed, is a well-known and widely used tactic of salespersons, politicians, and con artists. Milgram was a master of the phenomenon. He used it in all his obedience studies. He never asked much of his participants—but before long, many of them were giving a great deal more than they should have.

Variations on the Theme

Milgram conducted twenty variations of his basic research paradigm, and some of these deserve consideration because they had a major impact on participants' willingness to shock another person into senselessness. According to Miller (1986), these variations help set the boundaries on Milgram's work, and help us to understand the behavior that at least initially appears so extraordinary.

Physical Proximity.   A factor that had a strong impact on obedience rates was the physical proximity of the teacher and learner. When Milgram placed them in the same room, the level of obedience dropped to 40%. And when the setup demanded that the teacher force the hand of the learner onto an electric grid, only 30% of the teachers were willing to follow the experimenter's demands completely. This still seems an extraordinary proportion, but it is substantially less than the 65% found in the "standard" context.

Personal Responsibility.   Another variable that matters greatly is personal responsibility. Milgram's participants often asked, "Who is responsible for the well-being of the learner?" In response to questions of this sort, the teachers always were told that the experimenter was responsible. Even though it was they who were administering the painful, possibly fatal shocks, many teachers were willing to continue with the experiment once they had obtained the experimenter's assurance that he, not they, was responsible.

Why is the specification (perhaps we should say the misspecification) of responsibility so important? To answer this question, Tilker (1970) designed an experiment that mimicked Milgram's, with a few important exceptions: Tilker's study involved the interaction of three, rather than two, participants. Confederates played the roles of both teacher and learner; the naive participant's role was that of an observer. This change was made so that responsibility for any harm coming to the learner could be explicitly controlled. In one condition of the study, the subject–observer was told that he had complete responsibility for the conduct of the study and for the well-being of the learner. In a second condition, responsibility was mixed: The teacher and observer were to share responsibility. In the third condition, the observer was told the teacher had complete responsibility.

These variations had an impact on the likelihood that the observer would terminate the experiment. All participants who were assigned complete responsibility terminated the experiment as soon as the learner expressed any negative reaction to the shocks. In the other conditions, the participants were much less likely to try to terminate the study. Why? Because they were not responsible for its outcome.

Rebellion.   In a variation on the theme of responsibility, Milgram (1974) conducted a study in which the naive participant acted as teacher in concert with two others. These other "teachers" were experimental accomplices, who rebelled and refused to go on with the study soon after the learner began to complain about the shocks. The experimenter demanded that the naive participant continue in their absence, but under these circumstances—all responsibility now lay on the shoulders of the subject—only 10% obeyed. Specification of personal responsibility has a major impact on people's willingness to blindly obey orders. What's more, the presence of rebellious models helps others resist authority. We return to this observation later in the chapter.

▪▪▪ OBJECTIONS TO THE PROGRAM OF RESEARCH

Ethics

There is little question that Milgram's results were startling. But were they worth the price? Consider Milgram's (1963) early description of one his subjects:

I watched a mature and initially poised businessman enter the laboratory smiling and confident. Within 20 minutes he was reduced to a twitching, stuttering wreck, who was rapidly approaching a point of nervous collapse. (p. 376)

In a later description, Milgram (1965) observed:

With numbing regularity good people were seen to knuckle under the demands of authority and perform actions that were callous and severe. Men who are in everyday life responsible and decent were seduced by the trappings of authority, by the control of their perceptions, and by the uncritical acceptance of the experimenter's definition of the situation, into performing harsh acts. . . . The results, as seen and felt in the laboratory, are to this author disturbing. They raise the possibility that human nature, or—more specifically—the kind of character produced in American democratic society, cannot be counted on to insulate its citizens from brutality and inhumane treatment at the direction of malevolent authority. A substantial proportion of people do what they are told to do, irrespective of the content of the act and without limitations of conscience, so long as they perceive that the command comes from a legitimate authority. (pp. 74–75)

These descriptions were profoundly disturbing to many psychologists, not only because of Milgram's observations on human nature but also because he had deliberately placed his participants under extreme stress. Even after seeing the effects of such stress, he continued to perform studies of this kind. Many did not believe he had the right to do this and responded accordingly.

Baumrind (1964), for example, attacked Milgram on the grounds of both ethics and *generalizability*. In the first place, Baumrind argued, Milgram had no right to put participants into a situation in which they were reduced, in Milgram's own words, to "twitching, stuttering wreck[s]." Participants were not warned in advance that the study had any such risks. They were lied to, made to think the other participant was a naive subject like themselves and that they had seriously injured him. Baumrind argued that people's sense of their own worth must have been affected by this experience, and this was not justifiable.

In his defense, Milgram (1964) responded that he had carefully debriefed participants at the completion of the study, and had included a friendly reconciliation between teacher and learner. Furthermore, he had conducted mail follow-up research on his participants, sending them a description of the study and its results and soliciting their reactions to it. Defiant and obedient participants alike said they were glad to have participated. Nearly 85% of the sample indicated a willingness to participant in further experiments of the type Milgram had conducted. If these people were severely damaged by the experience, Milgram argued, why would they be willing to participate again in his research.

Strictly speaking, Milgram avoided answering Baumrind's criticisms, which concluded that his research could not be justified. Milgram argued that much was learned at little cost (though he could not have known this at the time of his research). Yes, participants were deceived, they did think they had injured another person, and their actions might have been stressful and caused them to think less highly of themselves. But even if all this were true, Milgram argued, the stress and adjustment in self-concept were transitory, as evidenced by the follow-up data. His defense? The importance of the research justified its cost. Who is right? Ultimately, who wins this debate depends on the beliefs and values of the evaluator.

Today this argument is largely irrelevant. As a result of the furor that Milgram's studies caused, strong procedures have been established to protect research participants from excesses of researchers. In the United States, all university-related research must be examined in advance by an independent review board. These boards, which can be exacting, are charged with protecting research participants. Milgram's studies probably could not be conducted in most North American universities today—they would not pass muster.

Generalizability

A second objection raised to Milgram's studies concerns their generalizability. Critics felt his research setting was so artificial that his findings would not generalize to the world outside the laboratory. Orne and his colleagues (Orne, 1962; Orne & Holland, 1968) argued that Milgram obtained high rates of obedience for two reasons. First, his study was associated with prestigious Yale University. Second, participants did not really believe that permanent injury would come to the learner. Milgram effectively answered the first of these criticisms by removing his study from the Yale campus and conducting research in a seedy section of Bridgeport, Connecticut. Although his obedience rates were not as great as at Yale, they were still remarkable. Milgram filmed a series of his experimental sessions to answer the question, "Did participants believe they were injuring another?" (see *Obedience*, by Stanley Milgram, 1965, distributed by the New York University Film Library). If ever a picture were worth a thousand words, this one is. Anyone watching this film cannot doubt that teachers thought they were harming the learner. They were nervous and upset; some were shaking or laughing semihysterically. The film is not fun to watch, but it leaves little doubt about the power of Milgram's research. Still, evidence such as this is not systematic, nor necessarily valid. What does research in real-world settings suggest, when obeying or disobeying orders clearly matters? When the chips are down, will people blindly follow the dictates of authority? The studies that follow suggest they will.

APPLYING SOCIAL PSYCHOLOGY TO HEALTH
■ ■ ■

The Obedient Nurse

Is blind obedience relevant to our everyday lives? Let's consider a pair of important studies. The first of these was conducted by Hofling and associates (Hofling, Brotzman, Dalrymple, Graves, & Pierce, 1966). In this research, nurses were ordered by doctors to administer a drug to a patient. The order was given via telephone, by a doctor with whom the nurse was not acquainted. The drug was not commonly used in the hospital. The dosage the doctor prescribed was double the maximum listed on the drug's package. Did the nurses obey this potentially life-threatening order? The frightening answer: Twenty-one of the twenty-two nurses who unwittingly served as participants in this study were ready to administer the prescription, at the dosage the doctor requested. Later research by Rank and Jacobson (1977) showed that when nurses were familiar with the medicine they were to administer and were free to consult with their peers, a much lower obedience rate (two of eighteen) was found. This is an improvement over the ratio of Hofling and associates. Even so,

11% is an unacceptable proportion of health workers willing to follow orders despite their potentially disastrous outcome. Is obedience relevant? At a minimum, these studies suggest it is, especially if you are ever a hospital patient.

■■■ ADMINISTRATIVE OBEDIENCE

Despite results of this type, Milgram's critics maintained their belief that his findings were largely attributable to the unreal features of the experimental context he had constructed. They insisted that his participants did not really believe anything serious could happen to the learner. Their apparent willingness to injure another person was merely a manifestation of this faith in the experimenter. Although the research of Hofling and associates (1966) and Rank and Jacobson (1977) just described indicates otherwise, these investigations do not mimic the essential features of Milgram's research paradigm. Thus, the issue remained unresolved. Critics argued that to decide the validity of Milgram's findings, studies were required that (1) carefully replicated the main features of his research, (2) posed the dilemma to hurt or to obey realistically, so that people knew that by obeying they would definitely damage another person, and (3) were engineered so that participants clearly understood *they* were responsible for whatever damage occurred.

Two investigators from the Netherlands, Wim Meeus and Quentin Raaijmakers, met these requirements in an important program of research on *administrative obedience*. This research was conducted to learn if the extreme acquiescence found in Milgram's studies was due to the experimental arrangements he employed or whether obedience was a true social phenomenon with which we must reckon. They constructed a research environment that resembled Milgram's in important ways. The study differed from Milgram's in terms of the particular form of damage people were asked to inflict, but it echoed the critical conflict between acquiescence to authority and compassion for one's peers. By changing the form of the punishment, Meeus and Raaijmakers (1986, 1987) created a situation in which the participants had no doubt that their actions were real, that they were having a strong and damaging effect on another person, and that they, the participants, were responsible for these effects. By assuring these impressions, the experimenters hoped to confirm or offset the criticisms that have clouded interpretation of Milgram's work.

Distinguishing Features

To Meeus and Raaijmakers, two critical features distinguished their studies from Milgram's

■ The participants administered psychological–administrative violence, rather than physical violence, to the victim. This kind of violence is a more common means of enforcing authority in modern Western societies than the physical violence that characterized Milgram's work.

■ The participants knew before beginning the study that they could cause the victim to suffer permanent harm (Meeus & Raaijmakers, 1987).

These distinguishing features made the research more applicable to the real world and answered Milgram's critics. The studies promised to provide information that not only allowed a better estimate of the worth of Milgram's work but also reflected the extent to which obedience occurs in real settings, when the stakes really matter.

As with Milgram's work, the cast of characters in Meeus and Raaijmakers's studies included an experimenter and two research participants, one of whom was an accomplice. The accomplice reported to the laboratory to take a test to determine his suitability for a job he said he badly needed. Unemployment in the Netherlands was high, and the applicant was unemployed. The other participant was a naive subject (24 such participants were used in this study). It was made clear to the participant that if the applicant was successful in his interview test, he would be given a job; if unsuccessful, he would remain unemployed.

In the initial phase of the study, the experimenter secured the applicant's permission to allow the test to be administered orally. He assured him that the interview was part of a study he was conducting and that it would not influence his chances on the test. The participant knew this was less than completely candid, but the applicant (apparently) did not, and agreed to the arrangement.

The participants' task was to play the role of the interview administrator. They had been coached in advance by the experimenter to make a series of negative remarks about the applicant's answers, to denigrate his personality, and to disrupt his performance. The experimenter admitted this disruption could cause the interviewee to blow his chances for the job. Furthermore, he explained that ability to perform under stress was irrelevant to the job under consideration. The disruptive remarks had nothing to do with the applicant's suitability. Still, the experimenter said he wanted the stress induction procedure to be followed because he was interested in the relationship between stress and achievement. The negative remarks were scripted—participants only had to read them. They were instructed to follow the script even if the applicant objected. These instructions set the stage for the dilemma between participants' value of scientific research and their compassion for another person in desperate need of a job.

Over the course of the interaction, the script called for the interviewer to make 15 increasingly demeaning remarks about the applicant's performance. The experimenter called these "stress remarks," so the participant could not possibly confuse their function. On the initial questions, no extraneous remarks were made. The applicant's performance showed he was clearly qualified for the job. After the applicant had sailed through the first eight questions, the interviewer began to intervene with derogatory comments. For example, after one answer, the interviewer observed, "If you continue like this, you will fail the test." To a later answer the interviewer remarked, "This job is much too difficult for you according to the test." The interviewer made these remarks despite the fact that the applicant had answered the questions correctly, and the interviewer knew this.

Because of these remarks, the applicant's stress level appeared to rise markedly, and his promising performance began to deteriorate. It was clear that if the interviewer's disruptive remarks continued, the applicant would fail and lose the job he so badly needed. As the interview progressed, the applicant repeatedly asked the interviewer to stop interrupting, and at a point midway through, he revoked his consent to the oral test. These reactions were meant to resemble the objections of Milgram's learner when he began to receive strong shocks.

Like Milgram's, Meeus and Raaijmakers's critical measure was simple: It was the number of participants who proceeded to the end of the stress remark series—the proportion who were willing to read all 15 of the demeaning remarks despite the strong objections of the applicant. The outcome was remarkable. Although participants believed their actions were ruining the chances of a perfectly qualified individual for a job he desperately needed, twenty-two of twenty-four continued to the very end of the stress remarks series. One of the interviewers stopped after 11 remarks, when the damage already had been done; only one participant quit (after 3 remarks) in time for the applicant to salvage his chances. On average, participants made 14.3 of the 15 possible stress remarks.

Extending the Series

It is difficult to imagine results that could better complement Milgram's, but Meeus and Raaijmakers did not stop here. Like Milgram, they continued to explore obedience in a series of studies. In one of these, participants were allowed to make as many or as few of the stress remarks as they wished. They were given the stress-inducing script of the first study, but were not required to follow it. Under these conditions, the average number of stress remarks delivered was 6.9, and not one of the fifteen interviewers continued to the end of the series. In conjunction with the main study, these findings suggest that the interviewers did not enjoy demeaning the interviewee. When given the opportunity to pull back, they did so.

In yet another variation, Meeus and Raaijmakers attempted to determine if the presence or absence of the experimenter mattered (the effect of proximity to authority). This study mimics one of Milgram's, in which the experimenter left the room and communicated with the teacher via telephone. In Milgram's study, absence of the experimenter diminished obedience rates considerably, from the standard 65% to 20%. In one condition of the Meeus–Raaijmakers extension, the experimenter left the room after instructing the subject. No surveillance could take place in this condition, and the experimenter could not urge the interviewer to persist. In this circumstance, only 36% of the participants delivered all 15 stress remarks.

APPLYING SOCIAL PSYCHOLOGY TO THE WORK FORCE
■ ■ ■

Using Real Managers

To test the real-world applicability of their study, the researchers employed a sample of personnel managers as participants. They reasoned that these people would know the importance of a job in Holland's precarious economy. Further, they were committed to the fair treatment of all applicants and were expected to do their best for them. The researchers expected the personnel managers to resist requests to treat applicants unethically. They were wrong. Nearly all (fourteen of fifteen) of the personnel managers delivered all 15 stress remarks, and the lone dissenter delivered 10 of 15. Their professional qualifications did not insulate the managers from the obedience demands of the experiment.

How Does It Happen? The Postexperimental Questionnaire

Meeus and Raaijmakers administered a comprehensive questionnaire at the completion of each of their studies in order to learn something about the thoughts and feelings their participants experienced during the interaction with the applicant. The information they obtained furnishes interesting insights into the justifications the interviewers used to explain their actions. These results help us to understand people's apparently blind compliance with the arbitrary demands of an authority. The findings also address some of the criticisms of Milgram's earlier work, and in almost every instance support his conclusions.

First, the questionnaire data show that participants believed they were damaging the applicant. They did not, as some of Milgram's critics contended, assume that no real harm would come to the applicant as a result of their actions. Participants felt that the candidate was well-qualified for the job, and would have passed the test were it not for their interference. They were very uncomfortable in their role, and most indicated they had considered terminating the experiment—but as we know, very few did. Nonetheless, it is clear that the interviewers did not enjoy ruining the applicant's chances. Most said they had a hard time making the stress remarks and were very tense during the interaction.

Participants believed the experimenter was unfair, but they also expressed a high regard for him! These results illuminate the fundamental obedience conflict between a strong regard for the experimenter (in a sense, a personification of science) and their feelings of solidarity with a fellow human being, the job applicant. Participants' evaluation of the experiment itself were consistent with this ambivalent response: They rated the experiment important and interesting while at the same time judging it irresponsible.

In light of all this ambivalence, we might wonder why most participants persisted in behavior that they knew was damaging to one of their peers. Why did not a reasonable fraction of them refuse to cooperate? The answer to this question is found in their *attributions of responsibility*. Participants felt that the experimenter, not they, were responsible for the harm done to the job seeker. In fact, they considered themselves no more responsible than the applicant himself for the harm done (to the applicant!). Put another way, in their judgment, the victim was as responsible as the harm doer. Although the logic of this position is contorted, it is not unique. Remember Eichmann's defense. The man responsible for setting up the machinery used to murder millions of innocent people claimed that he was merely following someone else's orders. If anyone was to blame, it was the person who gave the order, not he. Destructive obedience occurs because people are willing to lay responsibility for its consequences onto the authority who demands it.

The "blame-the-victim" effect deflects responsibility for an action from the perpetrator to the receiver: See Chapter 10.

The Meeus and Raaijmakers research series strongly supports the earlier research of Milgram. In a setting that was realistic, had real-world consequences, and was obviously involving, people proved willing to destroy another person's chances for a necessary job simply because they were told to do so. The findings are not comforting but they are strong, and they clearly replicate Milgram's.

One rebel can encourage others to rebellion against authority. This one man was able to stop a convoy of tanks in the abortive revolution in Peking, China, 1989. ■

■ ■ ■ FORCES FOR COMPLIANCE OR RESISTANCE

Is there nothing to be done? Will authority always exert so powerful an influence on behavior? Not necessarily. A final study by the Dutch researchers suggests that a lack of social support was a major reason behind participants' acquiescence. In almost every situation, participants were alone when deciding what to do. They could not consult with friends or advisers. A host of factors that impel participants to obedience are built into this experimental context. What would happen if this were not so—if participants could consult with peers before deciding to continue or rebel? Would they display *resistance?* To study this question, the researchers paired individual participants with two accomplices. All three were to administer the stressful interview. The stage was set. After the applicant began to complain, the accomplices turned on the experimenter and refused to continue. The experimenter demanded that the naive participant carry on without them. At issue was whether the participant obeyed. Consistent with the results of Milgram's "three teacher" study, in which two accomplices refused to continue (and almost all participants followed their lead), Meeus and Raaijmakers found only three of nineteen participants willing to continue on their own after the "rebellion." Support for the more humane position, provided by the accomplices who refused to carry on with the study, was sufficient to bolster their resolve to terminate the experiment. This result suggests that blind obedience is most likely when a person is isolated from social support and least likely when it is available. Just as did Hofling and associates in their hospital study, Meeus and Raaijmakers demonstrated the importance of social support for resisting the trap of blind, destructive obedience. Janis has shown how isolation and a lack of

The phenomenon of "groupthink" may lead good people to make bad decisions: See Chapter 21.

Asch's work set the tone for much research on social influence: See Chapter 18.

Minority opinion can have clear effects on behavior: See Chapter 19.

social support can cause responsible people to make disastrously irresponsible decisions. We discuss his research on "groupthink" in a later chapter.

Research by Gamson and his colleagues demonstrates that social support can offset authority-based pressures (Gamson, Fireman, & Rytina, 1982). In this study, *groups* of participants were put under illegitimate pressure to obey. Over the course of their extended interaction, individual participants voiced their discontent with the research. The rebellious remarks began when the authority was not present, but as discontent grew, objections became more vocal and more public. Ultimately, almost all refused to comply with the wishes of the authority. At least in part, the presence of more than one person in the setting helped to defuse the authority's power. The work of Asch bears out this observation. In one of his important investigations, Asch (1951) showed that a unanimous majority had considerable influence on the judgments of a naive participant. However, if only one member of the majority dissented, the power of the majority was broken.

■ ■ ■ SOME CONCLUDING COMMENTS

Research on obedience helps to explain why military organizations and totalitarian social systems place such extraordinary stress on complete conformity to all orders. The defection of only a few can cause a widespread breakdown of authority. The revolutionary political changes that occurred in communist Eastern Europe during the last days of the 1980s fit well with this view. So long as the great mass of people could be kept in line, the political system endured. When enough people finally said, "No more," the entire structure collapsed in short order. Obedience is an important element of social psychological inquiry. Although the work in this field has been largely undertaken in the laboratory, its implications could not be more practical. We need to know why people will sometimes violate their most sacred beliefs when an authority tells them to do so. And we need to know when they will refuse to do so. If Milgram and those who followed him have illuminated this question—and there is considerable evidence that they have—then social psychology has made an important contribution to the society in which we live.

■ ■ ■ SUMMARY

Milgram's work on obedience is important and disturbing. It suggests that people can be induced to bend their strongly held moral principles to satisfy the demands of authority. Research that followed Milgram's original investigations suggests that his results are more generalizable than his critics claim. This says nothing about the critics' other objection to Milgram's work, namely, that he should not have put people under the stress and pressure they experienced in his studies. Ethically, Milgram's research is troubling. On the other hand, much of importance was learned. How one weighs the good against the bad is in part a personal decision, but science appears now to learn in a direction of Milgram's claim that his findings justified the risk. Even so, these studies probably could not be performed today.

Recent work on administrative violence complements Milgram's, and demonstrates the power of authority figures even when subjects are convinced that their actions are doing great harm to the welfare of another. If ever a set of studies validated another, Meeus and Raaijmakers' validates Milgram's. Their research also extends Milgram's by showing that the social support of one's peers can offset the tendency toward blind obedience. However, the flip side of this observation also should be kept in mind: If all are acquiescing to authority, independent action based on one's own cherished beliefs becomes difficult, if not impossible.

■ ■ ■ SUGGESTED READINGS

1. Kelman, H. C., & Hamilton, V. L. (1989). *Crimes of obedience: Toward a social psychology of authority and responsibility*. New Haven, CT: Yale University Press.
2. Meeus, W. H. J., & Raaijmakers, Q. A. W. (1987). Administrative obedience as a social phenomenon. In W. Doise & S. Moscovici (Eds.), *Current issues in European social psychology* (Vol. 2, pp. 183–230). Cambridge, England: Cambridge University Press, and Paris: Editions de la Maison des Sciences de l'Homme.
3. Milgram, S. (1974). *Obedience to authority*. New York: Harper & Row.
4. Miller, A. G. (1986). *The obedience experiments: A case study of controversy in social science*. New York: Praeger.
5. Staub, E. (1989). *The roots of evil: The origins of genocide and other group violence*. New York: Cambridge University Press.

CHAPTER 18

CONFORMITY AND INDEPENDENCE

Going Along with the Crowd

■ **Key Concepts**

Norm
Autokinetic effect (illusion)
Informational social influence
Normative social influence
Public compliance, or conformity
Private acceptance, or conversion
Stimulus ambiguity
Perception of expertise
Foot-in-the-door effect
Door-in-the-face effect
Reciprocal concessions
Perceptual contrast
Low ball technique
Commitment
Anticonformity
Independence

■ **Chapter Outline**

SHERIF'S AUTOKINETIC ILLUSIONS
    Study 1: Isolated Respondents
    Study 2: Paired Respondents
    Study 3: Conflicting Response Norms

A DIFFERENT PERSPECTIVE: ASCH'S LINES
    The Standard Paradigm
    Extensions
    Sherif and Asch: Are the Implications of Their Research Contradictory?
    Some Theoretical Distinctions

CONTEXTUAL AND PERSONAL VARIABLES THAT AFFECT SOCIAL INFLUENCE
    Ambiguity or Task Difficulty
    Gender
    Other's Expertise
    Individual Differences

COMPLIANCE-GAINING STRATEGIES
    The Foot-in-the-Door
    The Door-in-the-Face
    The Low-Ball Technique
    ■ The Low Ball and Conservation

RESISTANCE TO SOCIAL INFLUENCE
    Anticonformity
    Independence

SOME CONCLUDING THOUGHTS

SUMMARY

After a high-speed car chase through the streets of Los Angeles, Rodney King, a black man, is stopped and beaten by four white policemen. Other officers watch. Only one of the policemen attempts to stop the beating, and even he appears to have taken part in it initially. What caused these officers to act in this way?

JJ is taking her fourth-grade arithmetic final. She has just added a long string of numbers and reached a sum of 474. She glances at Brian, the class's math whiz, and sees that he has recorded 574. JJ changes her answer to 574.

Son: "Dad, I want to go camping. Can I borrow the car for the next two weeks?"
Dad: "Are you nuts?"
Son: "OK, then can I use it on my date tonight?"
Dad: "Sure—now you're being reasonable."

Asking for far more than we expect, so that our actual wish seems more reasonable than it would otherwise, is a tactic people use to get their way. We all have used this maneuver in one form or another, and it probably has been used on us as well. Such actions are forms of behavior we label *social influence*. Although they appear to differ markedly, all three of the preceding scenarios depict examples of social influence. In them, one or more people have changed their behavior as a consequence of the words or actions of others. As these scenarios show, social influence can operate in a variety of ways. In the Rodney King incident, we know from sworn testimony that at least one police officer felt obliged to join in the beating because to refuse would have invited the ridicule of his fellow officers. A different sort of social influence is at work in the arithmetic test scenario. In this instance, JJ is not being pressured by Brian in any way, but Brian obviously has affected JJ's actions. In the dad and son scene, the son has made an outrageous request. He knows it will not be granted, but that is not his aim. When he poses his second request, the one he really cares about, it seems so much more reasonable that dad complies. In this chapter, we explore theories and research on social influence and the variety of ways it works. This information will not only allow you to be more socially influential but also to be more aware when tactics of social influence are being applied to you.

■ ■ ■ SHERIF'S AUTOKINETIC ILLUSIONS

Sherif's research on norm formation is a classic contribution to social psychology: See Chapter 1.

We begin with the work of Muzafer Sherif. Sherif was concerned with the manner in which norms are formed. A **norm** is a rule of conduct, commonly agreed on (implicitly or explicitly) and adopted by a specific group. Norms are not prescriptive for all people in all places at all times, but are held by a given group of individuals at a particular time. For example, on most beaches in the United States today, it is *normative* (or normal) that women wear tops on their swimming suits; on the French Riviera, such dress is nonnormative. The dress norm differs from place to place and from time to time. Sherif wanted to understand the social processes that govern the ways such rules of conduct are formed and how they affect behavior.

Study 1: Isolated Respondents

To study norm formation, Sherif (1935) creatively made use of a little-understood perceptual illusion, the *autokinetic effect*. The autokinetic effect works this way: If you fix your gaze for a minute or so on a small pinpoint of light in an otherwise totally darkened room, the light will appear to move. The perception of movement occurs even though the light is stationary. The autokinetic effect is a compelling illusion—if you try it yourself, the light will seem to move even though you know it is fixed. In his studies, Sherif (1936) asked judges, tested individually, to fixate on the light and estimate the distance it traveled. Each made a series of distance judgments. Of course, no one knew the light was stationary. Reviewing his data, Sherif noticed an interesting and consistent pattern. On the initial judgments, everyone's estimates were extremely variable. For example, a person's first judgment might be 6 inches, the next 24 inches, the next 1 inch, and so on. However, after a relatively few trials, variability decreased, and the judge's estimates began to converge around a given value. This value differed from judge to judge, but the pattern was consistent: High initial variability of estimates soon faded, and an individual's judgments settled on a narrow range of values.

Figure 18.1 depicts this general pattern, with data from three hypothetical participants. Judgmental differences among them are obvious—but don't miss the similarities. Initial judgments are extremely variable; however, the variability soon diminishes, and the responses of each participant narrow down to a relatively tight range. The average values of these ranges differ from person to person, and this set the stage for Sherif's (1936) speculations about the nature of norm formation. He reasoned that his individual respondents had formed an implicit rule for interpreting the light's movement, and they applied this rule with ever greater consistency with each judgment. This rule formation process is intriguing because it occurs in the context of a complete illusion.

Study 2: Paired Respondents

To this point, there is nothing inherently social in the study just described—judges were studied individually, no interaction took place between people, and

FIGURE 18.1

◼

Autokinetic Estimates of 3 Independent Respondents Over 15 Trials. Notice the high initial variability of each respondent. Over trials, the variability of the estimates diminishes dramatically.

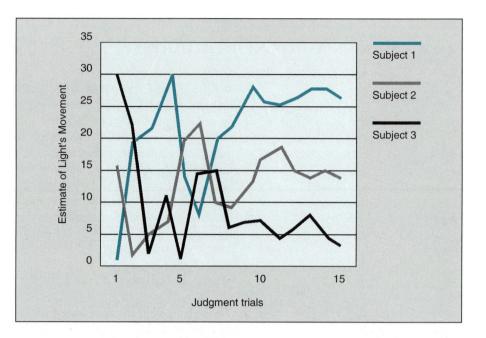

so on. But the first study laid the foundation for Sherif's later studies of norm formation and social influence. In study 2, Sherif (1936) required *pairs* of naive participants to make their autokinetic judgments, one after the other, on each trial. The response patterns of the individual participants resemble the response records of those studied in isolation, with one crucial difference—the judgments of the paired respondents *converge* over the judgment trials. Although both (paired) judges start with highly variable responses, their judgments soon appear to merge. It is as if they had come to an unspoken agreement about the length of the light's movement. Apparently, a response rule (a norm) shared by the interacting judges develops over the course of interaction.

What is the best explanation of the convergence of paired judges' estimates? Did respondents really see what they reported? The convergence of judgments suggests one of two possibilities: Either (1) judges were combining the information of the other's estimates with their own to form the best estimate, or (2) they were simply going along with their partner to avoid confrontation. Sherif favored the first alternative, which supports a considerably more positive view of human behavior than the second (Campbell, 1990).

Informational Social Influence. This first interpretation corresponds to what Jones and Gerard (1967) label **informational social influence,** a process by which people use the information provided by others to facilitate their understanding of ambiguous stimuli and to assist them when forming judgments. Informational social influence may explain the results of Sherif's paired judgment research (study 2), as follows: Participants combined their estimates with their partners' to arrive at a shared, *interdependent* interpretation of the stimulus. Over the judgment series, they learned to weigh their own perceptions and the reports of their partner to zero-in on the "reality" of the light's movement. This learned judgment rule is a social norm, which persists and guides later judgments. This explanation depicts people as rational decision makers who use all the data at their disposal (including the judgments of others) to come to the best possible judgment.

The police involved in the Rodney King beating may have been responding to the established norm that one always backs-up a fellow police officer. ■

Normative Social Influence.   An alternative explanation of Sherif's second study is based on **normative social influence,** which suggests that to avoid confrontation and maintain equanimity, judges had simply gone along with their partners. They had not used their partner's information to enhance accuracy; they had just accepted the other's responses, no matter what. The normative social influence interpretation sees people as compliant and wishy-washy, willing to agree to incorrect views about the nature of reality to avoid unpleasantness or remain in good standing in a group. From this perspective, Sherif's judges converged because they were afraid to deviate from the responses of the other member of their groups. Returning to one of the earlier scenarios, we can characterize the actions of some of the police officers in the Rodney King affair as the outcome of normative social influence. If an officer had failed to go along with the group, he would have been taunted, ostracized, or worse. There was strong normative pressure for all to join in the beating. Rather than risk confrontation, ridicule, or ostracism, some officers acted in ways they knew were wrong.

Study 3: Conflicting Response Norms

Which of these two forms of social influence—normative or informational—characterizes Sherif's findings? From the data at hand, we can only guess, and Sherif knew this. So he conducted a third study, and its results strongly support an informational social influence interpretation. The initial stage of study 3 is identical to that of study 2. Pairs of judges are brought together to make autokinetic estimates; they respond in tandem, as before. Consistent with the earlier study, respondents' estimates converge. Unlike study 2, however, the investigation does not end at this point. Instead, the judges report to Sherif's laboratory a few days after the initial session and make another series of estimates. At this second session, judges are paired with partners with whom they have not interacted previously.

What was Sherif's purpose in mixing up the groups in the second session? Consider again the competing explanations of study 2. If participants had really learned a norm, which they believed was accurate, they would be expected to use it in the second session. However, the norms of the newly paired participants would be different, because people coming from different initial judgment contexts would have formed different norms. Thus, disagreements in reported perceptions would be expected in the second session if *informational* social influence was responsible for the results of the first session. So, if a norm (a relatively enduring rule of conduct) had been formed in the first phase of the study, disagreement would characterize interactions in the second phase.

However, suppose the convergence of the first session was the result of participants' unwillingness to risk disapproval by making estimates too discrepant from those of their partners. In this case, the results of the second part of study 3 would display considerable convergence between paired respondents' estimates. If *normative* social influence is the correct explanation of the results of Sherif's studies, rapid convergence of estimates should characterize judgments in phase 2.

The results of study 3 support the informational social influence explanation. In the first phase, participants' responses resembled those of the judges of study 2: In both investigations, estimates converged. In the second phase of study 3, when respondents from different groups were paired, a very different pattern was obtained. Unlike the phase 1 results, estimates did not converge in the second phase. It is as if a subject, having learned a response norm in the first phase of the study, was unwilling to deviate from it when paired with a person whose response norm was different. If the convergence of estimates found in the first phase had been the result of normative social influence, participants would not have maintained their characteristic response level. The findings support Sherif's "rational man" orientation, and suggest that we *do* weigh available information when attempting to optimize judgments.

■■■ A DIFFERENT PERSPECTIVE: ASCH'S LINES

The Standard Paradigm

We find a different perspective on social influence in the work of Solomon Asch (1951, 1956). As with Sherif's studies, groups of people were brought together in Asch's laboratory to make a series of simple perceptual judgments (Asch, 1951, 1956). However, a very different kind of judgment task was implemented. All these studies take the same general form: Participants view a stimulus line and a set of three comparison lines. Their job is to judge which of the three comparison lines matches the stimulus. Figure 18.2 presents a typical stimulus set. Notice how easy the judgment is. Asch's task was far from perceptually or intellectually challenging. Figure 18.2 is not exaggerated. When people were studied individually and asked to match stimulus and comparison lines, they were correct 98% of the time.

FIGURE 18.2

■

Examples of Asch's Judgment Stimuli: Direction to Respondent was to Match Stimulus Line with a Comparison Line. Unlike Sherif's very difficult judgment,
Asch's task involved a very simple discrimination. This difference might be responsible for the different results these researchers obtained.

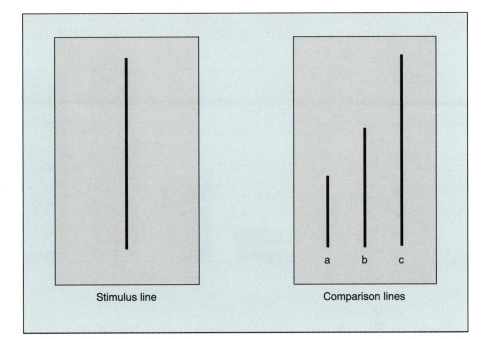

Stimulus line   Comparison lines

In Asch's studies, respondents usually made twelve such judgments. They made these judgments in a group, but the game was rigged. Only one person in each group was truly naive. The others were accomplices, employed by Asch to act as real participants. In the original version of the study, judges responded aloud, in fixed order, on every judgment trial. The naive judge always responded in either the last or next-to-last position. On prespecified trials the accomplices unanimously chose one of the *incorrect* alternatives. Over a dozen trials, they unanimously made incorrect estimates on six of them.

Asch's purpose was to see whether the incorrect majority would have any influence on the naive subjects. Because the correct answer is so obvious, he expected that naive participants would not be swayed by social influence (Campbell, 1990). Asch was wrong. Contrary to expectations, more than 75% of all naive judges agreed at least once with the confederates. Put another way, about one-third of all influence attempts were successful, despite the fact that the correct answer was so transparently obvious. This is conformity.

Extensions

Asch discovered some interesting facts when he probed this phenomenon further. For example, task difficulty makes a difference. More conformity was evident when the three comparison lines were similar in length, making the judgment more difficult (Asch, 1952). In other studies, Asch (1951) systematically varied the number of experimental accomplices he employed, from one to fifteen. Increasing the number of accomplices increased conformity, but only up to a point—and that point was reached rather early (Figure 18.3). A big jump in conformity was found when the number rose from one to two and from two to three; going beyond three or four accomplices made little difference. Fifteen accomplices were no more influential than three in inducing conformity.

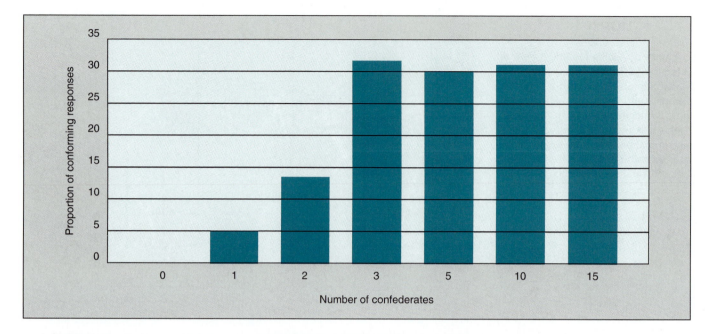

Minorities can have a powerful effect on j dgments and actions: See Chapter 19.

FIGURE 18.3

■

The Effect of Number of Experimental Accomplices on Respondent Conformity in a Judgment Task. Notice that going beyond 3–4 accomplices in Asch's line judgment task had little effect on the rate of compliance.

Stone (1967) hypothesized that if the task was made more difficult, more accomplices would induce even greater conformity. He supported this hypothesis in an experiment that made use of Sherif's autokinetic illusion—a stimulus context considerably more ambiguous than Asch's. (In fact, there is no "correct" judgment in the autokinetic situation.) Stone's study resembled Sherif's study 3, but in Stone's rendition, judges first formed autokinetic norms either alone or with one or three other judges. They returned to the laboratory the next day to make another series of estimates with people who had participated earlier with different partners. Stone found that participants who formed norms with three others were most resistant to their new response mates' information, whereas those from the one-person group were least resistant. Apparently, the greater the consensus about a norm, the stronger it is (cf. Harkins & Petty, 1983, 1987).

In another extension, Asch found that he could obliterate all social influence by including a lone dissenter among the accomplices. With even one dissenter in the ranks, conformity to the majority was destroyed, even if the majority consisted of fourteen other people all making the same (incorrect) judgment. Subsequent research by Allen and his colleagues (Allen, 1965, 1975; Allen & Wilder, 1980) has replicated and extended this result. It suggests that dissenters are effective because they destroy the apparent consensus of the majority, encouraging the judge to develop alternatives to the incorrect response.

Sherif and Asch: Are the Implications of Their Research Contradictory?

Contradictory views of human nature are suggested by the research of Sherif and Asch. Sherif's research supports the view that people are rational decision makers, who use all the data available to them to come to a valid judgment. Asch's

"Well, heck! If all you smart cookies agree, who am I to dissent?"

(Drawing by Handlesman; © 1972 The New Yorker Magazine, Inc.)

Dissent can be a factor in resisting social influence: See Chapter 17.

research appears to sustain the view that people are acquiescent, unwilling to stand up for what they clearly see is right. Which view is correct? An important issue in comparing Sherif and Asch is the validity, or truthfulness, of their research participants. Did their respondents really see what they reported seeing, or were they merely going along with their partners to minimize confrontation and embarrassment? If participants were truthfully reporting what they saw, then it is reasonable to assume that their responses would not change drastically when the influence source was no longer physically present and could not observe their judgments. The response norms they had formed would persist. However, if they were merely going along with the accomplice(s), their future judgments would not be similar to those produced in the accomplice's presence.

In Sherif's case, evidence shows that participants really saw what they said they saw. Judges in the second part of study 3 continued to respond as they had in the first phase, despite the fact that (1) the person with whom they had originally responded was no longer present, and (2) their answers were inconsistent with those of their new partner. It is more difficult to judge the validity of participants' responses in Asch's studies, because his studies never included a session in which judges and accomplices were separated and allowed to respond anonymously. In some of his studies, however, judges did respond privately (in writing), and in this circumstance compliance rates were reduced substantially. From this result, we may conclude that judges who complied in Asch's studies probably were not reporting their true perceptions.

If this conclusion is correct, then it may be that Sherif and Asch were studying different phenomena, which might occur under different circumstances, with different outcomes. Sherif was concerned with people's reactions under conditions of great ambiguity. In such circumstances, it may be that informational social influence takes precedence. He found that such influence had a lasting impact on people's perceptions and behaviors.

In Asch's research, the judgment task was quite unambiguous. In this case, normative social influence appeared to operate. This form of influence, which caused immediate compliance, probably had little carryover to later situations.

Both Sherif and Asch found that we are conforming. But we conform for different reasons, and these reasons have implications for the duration of conformity.

Some Theoretical Distinctions

To highlight the difference between Sherif's and Asch's results, Festinger (1953) suggested that a distinction be made between *public compliance* with a source of influence, and the *private acceptance* of the source's message. In Festinger's view, public compliance, or **conformity** as it also is called, is nothing more than acquiescence to the apparent wishes of the influence source, without any real acceptance of the source's position. Public compliance occurs because a source of influence has power or control over the fate or resources of the other (cf. Thibaut & Kelley, 1959), and can monitor actions to ensure that the desired behavior is enacted. People are motivated to maintain consistency with the influence source (be it an individual or a group) because of the source's power to reward and punish. In the case of conformity to a group's norms, the motivation includes the desire to maintain membership. Public compliance, or conformity, means people bringing their public behavior (but not necessarily their beliefs) in line with the demands of the influence source.

Private acceptance, or **conversion,** as it also is called, involves the internalization of the influence source's position. Conversion occurs when characteristics of the influence source suggest that the response is valid (Kelman, 1958). Recall the chapter-opening scenario in which JJ changes her answer on the arithmetic test so that it is the same as Brian's. Why did she do this? Because Brian was right so often in the past. Brian did not attempt to influence JJ—he did not even know that JJ was reading his exam. He was influential because JJ had internalized the belief that Brian was a math whiz, and she accepted Brian's answer as correct.

The distinction between public compliance and private acceptance is important for predicting the persistence of effects. A person who advocates a position

A source of influence may have power or control over the fate or resources of the other: See Chapter 12.

Susan is influencing Joan even though she does not know that Joan is copying from her work. ■

solely in response to normative social pressure will cease to do so when the pressure is removed or when the influence source is unable to monitor his or her behavior. But if people advocate a position because they believe it to be valid, they will continue to advocate it even when the agent of influence is no longer present and has no ability to determine whether the sought-for actions are being performed. This latter group has internalized, or privately accepted, the information given, and will act accordingly in future interactions.

From this perspective, it is apparent that Sherif and Asch were concerned with different aspects of social influence. Sherif's work focused on conversion, or private acceptance. In his study of norm formation, he was interested in judgments that were socially influenced and that persisted, even in the effective absence of the original influence source. Asch's work on the other hand, looked at public compliance. He did not investigate the persistence of the startling effects he produced, but rather the factors that gave rise to or diminished them.

■■■ CONTEXTUAL AND PERSONAL VARIABLES THAT AFFECT SOCIAL INFLUENCE

Ambiguity and Task Difficulty

Stimulus ambiguity and task difficulty have been studied extensively in research on conformity. The conclusion is that the more ambiguous or difficult the task, the more susceptible are people to social influence; that is, the more weight they accord social information relative to their own perceptions (Allen & Crutchfield, 1963; Endler, 1965). When Asch (1952) reduced the differences between his comparison lines, making the judges' task more difficult, he found greater susceptibility to social influence. Similarly, judges who are highly competent or certain of their ability are likely to place great weight on their own perceptions. As a result, they are less susceptible to social influence (Endler, 1965, 1966).

Gender

For many years, it was widely accepted that women were more susceptible than men to social influence. In the early literature on social influence, generalizations of this type were commonplace (e.g., Allen & Crutchfield, 1963; Reitan & Shaw, 1964; Whittaker, 1963). However, close inspection of the studies on which this generalization was based reveals that many of the experimental tasks employed in establishing the gender-difference findings were sex-typed in favor of males; that is, the experiments employed tasks on which men might reasonably be expected to enjoy an advantage relative to women. Under these circumstances, it is reasonable that women would conform to men and that men would reject women's advice. But suppose we were to use an experimental task in which no gender-linked advantage was apparent or in which everyone agreed that women were generally better qualified than men. Would a sex difference arise under these circumstances? The answer to this question is clear: Sex differences disappear when gender conveys no superior status on the experimental task (Endler, 1965). When women are accorded superior status by virtue of gender-related qualifications, the usual relationship is reversed (Karabenick, 1983; McGuire, 1985).

In an interesting investigation of this issue, Cacioppo and Petty (1980) asked men and women to view pictures of stimuli on which earlier testing had indicated major differences between men and women in knowledge and familiarity. The stimuli were pictures of either tackles made in a football game or women's fashions. On the back of each set of pictures were four written comments (evaluations provided by other judges), rating the quality of the tackle or the fashion represented in the picture. Judges were to indicate the extent to which they agreed with the comments. Findings indicated that men were considerably more susceptible to observations about women's fashions, and women were more easily persuaded about the quality of tackles in a football contest. On topics of which we know little, it is sensible to accept socially supplied information.

The results of Cacioppo and Petty and of many other studies like this one suggest that previous findings of gender-related differences in susceptibility to social influence are a consequence of variations in people's perceptions of expertise, not gender. These findings are in substantial agreement with the impressive program of research and reviews of sex differences in influence that Alice Eagly and her associates have performed (Eagly, 1978, 1983; Eagly & Carli, 1981; Eagly, Wood, & Fishbaugh, 1981). In light of their results, the following observations appear in order:

■ Sex differences in past research can be attributed to the nature of the experimental tasks that were employed.
■ Neither males nor females enjoy a natural advantage in social influence contexts.
■ Past evidence for sex differences was probably a result of participants' attributions of others' (confederates') competence.

Other's Expertise

All of the factors discussed earlier can be distilled into a single underlying cause that appears responsible for informational social influence. This cause is the *perception of expertise,* or competence. If people feel themselves to be competent at a task, by virtue of gender, past success, or low task difficulty, they will be more resistant to social influence than if they have experienced a history of failure, perceive themselves incompetent, and so on. If a person is paired with another who is expert at the task under consideration, the expert's judgments will be accorded greater weight relative to self-perceptions. Such expert influence will be especially significant in contexts in which the task is difficult, the judgment ambiguous, or in which the naive judge has little self-confidence or prior experience.

A test of these conclusions was conducted in a study in which judges in a novel (and difficult) perceptual judgment situation were informed that their partner (an accomplice of the experimenter) had already participated in a similar study, and had proved either notably skilled or notably unskilled at it (Crano, 1970). Consistent with expectations, judges paired with the competent confederate were more strongly influenced by his or her judgments than those paired with an apparently incompetent one. This result held regardless of the gender of accomplice or participant.

Another result of this experiment also deserves mention. The study was conducted in two phases: In the first, judges made a series of estimates in concert with the (competent or incompetent) confederate; in the second phase, the confederate was removed and judges were asked to make another series of estimates of stimuli identical to those they had judged. This two-phase experiment was meant to parallel Sherif's general approach, to allow a determination of the extent to which the influence induced in the presence of the confederates persisted in their absence. The results revealed that judges influenced by the expert continued to respond in the second phase as if the expert were still present and monitoring their responses. In Sherif's terms, the judges had formed a response norm in the initial phase of the study and maintained the norm when the social pressures under which it had been formed were no longer operative.

Judges paired with the nonexpert accomplice also were influenced somewhat by his or her estimates (relative to controls, who responded alone), but this influence dissipated on the accomplice's removal. The perception of expertise apparently operates in two ways: If respondents think they are competent at the task, they will be resistant to influence; however, information supplied by one more competent than oneself will encourage conversion or private acceptance. In this circumstance, social influence effects will persist even after the influence source is removed.

Individual Differences

Are there stable and reliable differences among people in susceptibility to social influence? Are some people characteristically more likely to weigh the perceptions of others more (or less) heavily than their own? Are some people characteristically anticonformist, others compliant, others less obviously one or another type? It seems obvious that such differences exist. We all know people who are so hardheaded they cannot be convinced of anything and others who can be persuaded to accept almost any point of view. In general, research shows that people who have a positive view of themselves, a strong desire to appear unique, and relatively little concern with the opinions of others will weigh their own perceptions more heavily than socially supplied information (e.g., Hancock & Sorrentino, 1980; Hogg & Abrams, 1990; Maslach, Santee, & Wade, 1987; 1974; Rhodes & Wood, 1992; Snyder & Fromkin, 1980). On the other hand, people who lack confidence, who are unsure of their own worth or of their position in the group, will be more ready to make use of socially supplied information. Hancock and Sorrentino (1980), for example, found that people who had received little support from other group members, and as such were unsure of group members' feelings toward them, were more likely to knuckle under to the group's position. From earlier research, we would expect this effect to be particularly strong if group membership is viewed as particularly desirable or attractive (Brehm & Festinger, 1957). Group cohesiveness and the desire to identify with the group appear to foster public acceptance of socially supplied (group-sanctioned) information.

■■■ COMPLIANCE-GAINING STRATEGIES

Real-world applications of social influence principles have taken many forms. Some are focused strictly on techniques for inducing compliance, with or without private acceptance. Three of the most interesting of these are the foot-in-the-door, the door-in-the-face, and the low-ball technique. Although these applications differ in many ways, they all induce people to act in ways that at least originally appear to be contrary to their beliefs or their self-interest. We should all be acquainted with these tactics if for no other reason than their widespread use (Cialdini, 1988). It would be unusual to find anyone reading this book who has not been influenced by, or who has not used, at least one of these compliance-gaining strategies.

Maintaining group cohesion sometimes requires acceptance of group-sanctioned beliefs: See Chapter 19 and 22.

The Foot-in-the-Door

When people do a minor favor for someone, they are more susceptible to later requests of greater magnitude, even requests that they otherwise might refuse. Enhanced susceptibility to influence as a consequence of having done a prior favor is called the **foot-in-the-door effect.** The effect was first demonstrated experimentally by Freedman and Fraser (1966), who went door to door in residential neighborhoods and asked people to display a 3-inch-square sign that said "BE A SAFE DRIVER." Almost everyone complied with this trivial request. Two weeks later, a different person returned to the same neighborhoods and asked homeowners if they would display in their front yards a large sign that read DRIVE CAREFULLY. A photo of the sign suggested that once in place, it would obscure the entire front of the house; what's more, it was poorly lettered and very unattractive. Only 17% of the householders who had *not* been contacted initially complied with the request. The compliance figure was 76% among those who had agreed to display the 3 × 3-inch "BE A SAFE DRIVER" sign two weeks earlier! This difference is extraordinary, as is the absolute magnitude of compliance in this prior-favor condition.

Almost no one refused to display this sign. Having agreed to this, people were more susceptible to a much more bothersome request. ■

How are these remarkable findings explained? One possibility is that those who had agreed to the initial request had a special interest in safe driving. They had complied initially because they were concerned about auto safety. When contacted later, they naturally were more compliant than the population at large to a request related to safe driving. Two features of Freedman and Fraser's study argue against this self-selection interpretation: (1) The initial request was so minor that almost nobody refused, and thus it is unlikely that only those who were ultraconcerned about safe driving selected themselves into the initially acquiescent group. (2) Even more important, the experimenters conducted a variation of the study in which the initial request required homeowners to sign a petition to "keep California beautiful." These people too proved more acquiescent to the request to display the ugly safe driving sign! Why?

Freedman and Fraser proposed that people changed their opinions about themselves as a consequence of their initial act. They came to think of themselves as altruists, as the kind of people willing to go out of their way to act on their beliefs. They had formed the impression of themselves as helpful and socially

Bem's self-perception theory states that we update our attitudes on the basis of our most recent relevant behaviors: See Chapter 5.

responsible, and when the later (and larger) request was made, they responded accordingly. This explanation draws from Bem's (1972) self-perception theory, which holds that we update our attitudes (even our self-attitudes) on the basis of our most recent relevant behaviors. Thus, if we behave altruistically, even in a very minor way, we will think of ourselves as altruistic. Considerable research following Freedman and Fraser's study has replicated its results (see Crano & Sivacek, 1982; Dillard, Hunter, & Burgoon, 1984). The foot-in-the-door phenomenon suggests that even the most trivial acts can affect susceptibility to subsequent influence.

The Door-in-the-Face

The **door-in-the-face effect** is almost the mirror image of the foot-in-the-door. This strategy involves asking for a very major favor or concession, which is almost inevitably refused. Then a more modest request is advanced. The idea here is that the target is more likely to grant the second request after having refused the first. Cialdini and his colleagues (Cialdini, Vincent, Lewis, Catalan, Wheeler, & Darby, 1975) confirmed this expectation in a study in which college students were approached on campus and asked to donate their time to a worthy cause. In one condition of the study, they were asked to act as chaperons for a group of juvenile delinquents on a two-hour trip to the zoo. Only 17% of the subjects agreed to do so. However, another group was first asked if they would volunteer two hours of their time each week for two years (!) as unpaid counselors at the county juvenile detention center. All refused. When these students then were asked to chaperon the juvenile delinquents, 50% agreed. These differences (50% versus 17%) in compliance rates are striking; they suggest the power of the door-in-the-face technique.

How does it work? Cialdini his and colleagues (1975) suggest a *reciprocal concessions* explanation. The context of the door-in-the-face resembles one of negotiation: "Will you do X? No? O.K., how about Y?" In negotiations, when one side concedes a point, the other is expected to reciprocate, and thus the second (lesser) request is more likely to be granted. A second explanation is *perceptual contrast* (Miller, Seligman, Clark, & Bush, 1976). Because it is so much smaller than the first request, the second appears even smaller than it would if it had been presented in isolation, and thus is more readily accepted.

Neither the reciprocal concessions nor the perceptual contrast explanation of the door-in-the-face phenomenon have been confirmed unambiguously. Both offer plausible explanations of this interesting tactic of persuasion, and both can explain "dad's" responses to his son's request to borrow the car in the chapter's second scenario.

The Low-Ball Technique

The low ball is a common (if unethical) sales tactic, in which people are first induced to commit to purchase an item for an unrealistically low price. Before the deal is completed, the "mistaken" price is discovered, the purchase denied, and a higher price substituted. In the absence of the low ball, people will not agree to the higher price. However, given their initial commitment, people are much more susceptible to the revised (and considerably larger) price. Cialdini and his colleagues, (Cialdini, Cacioppo, Bassett, & Miller, 1978) demonstrated the low-ball technique in a simple study: Students were called and asked to volunteer to serve as experimental participants. Of the number called, 56% agreed. After committing themselves to the study, they were told that the study was to be run at 7 A.M., and were given the opportunity to withdraw their commitment. Not a single student withdrew, and 95% of them actually appeared at the appointed time for the experiment! However, when students were told of the time of the experiment in advance of their commitment, only 24% were willing to participate. The low ball made a major difference (56% versus 24%) in compliance rates.

The persistence of low-ball-induced commitment was demonstrated in an interesting research series by Joule and his colleagues (Joule, 1987; Joule & Beauvois, 1987). Participants, all smokers, agreed to serve for a very modest incentive in a study of concentration. After agreeing, they were told that the study required them to abstain from smoking for eighteen hours. More than 90% of the participants agreed to serve despite this requirement and despite the fact that the experimenter announced that their modest incentive was to be reduced considerably. Participants had committed themselves, and apparently were determined to make good on their commitment. Even more impressive were participants' responses to Joule's request that they take part in another study weeks later. More than 90% of the original group was willing to volunteer again! Their commitment to the study carried over into the future.

The Low Ball and Conservation

In a study with important societal implications, Pallak, Cook, and Sullivan (1980) used the low-ball technique to encourage energy conservation. In this study, experimenters visited people's homes and gave them information about the ways they could cut energy consumption. Some consumers were promised that if they reduced their energy usage, their names would appear in the local paper and they would be lauded for their public-spiritedness

Those who merely received the energy tips (without the promise of favorable publicity) agreed to save energy, but did no better than a comparison group that had not been visited by the experimenters. The people promised the favorable public notice, however, cut their consumption markedly, by more than 12%. Then the experimenters withdrew the original offer from the favorable-publicity group. They returned and apologized, saying they were unable to keep their promise. The participants would not be written up in the paper. Did this stifle their energy conservation? On the contrary—their energy consumption following the broken promise was even lower (by 15%) than when they were working under the impression that the promise would be kept. Why? The promise of free publicity fostered people's *commitment* to conservation. This commitment caused people to engage in behaviors that they found rewarding (they received lower bills, felt better about conserving energy, about being more environmentally conscious, and so on). This reinforcement caused the behaviors to persist even when the promise that caused them initially (favorable publicity) was withdrawn. The low ball depends on people committing themselves to a product or behavior and coming to enjoy (or anticipating the enjoyment of) the outcome of the commitment.

■ ■ ■ RESISTANCE TO SOCIAL INFLUENCE

Anticonformity

To this point, we have concentrated on factors that promote social influence. But this is only a part of the story. We also need to consider variables that sustain people's resistance to influence. Research focused on people's propensity to resist has distinguished two forms of resistance, *anticonformity* and *independence* (Nail, 1986; Willis, 1972; Willis & Levine, 1976). Anticonformists accept socially supplied information, but their public behavior suggests the opposite. Behaviorally, the anticonformist uses socially supplied information as a reference point from which to deviate publicly. Such a person characteristically opposes the group, even though he or she may privately agree with it. In a perverse sort of way, the anticonformist is as dependent on social information as the conformist.

A powerful example of anticonformity is seen in a fascinating experiment by Frager (1970). In this study, college students in Japan were placed in an Asch–type social influence setting. More than one-third of the participants gave incorrect responses on trials on which the confederate majority provided the objectively (and obviously) correct answer! To maintain independence from the influence group, these participants resisted accepting socially supplied information despite the fact that it agreed with their own perceptions. When a subsample of this anticonformist group was tested a year later on the same stimuli, alone, their accuracy was greater than 95%. This suggests that the anticonformists did not simply have bad eyesight—it could not have improved that much over the intervening year. Rather, they based their responses in the first session not on what they saw but on what the others apparently did not see.

Independence

In contrast to the anticonformist, the independent individual is not swayed one way or another by the information supplied by external sources. Such people place the greatest weight on their own perceptions and past experience and relatively little on socially supplied information. Unlike the anticonformist, the independent individual does not need social inputs to help direct his or her perceptions and behaviors: To these people, socially supplied information is simply irrelevant.

Paul Nail (1986; Nail & Van Leeuwen, in press) has discussed the distinction between anticonformist and independent people in useful reviews summarizing the range of reactions that can be expected in response to social influence. His ideas are valuable because they offer a framework within which to conceptualize

TABLE 18.1
■
Forms of Response to Social Influence

		Private Acceptance	
		YES	NO
Public Acceptance	YES	Conversion	Compliance
	NO	Anticonformity	Independence

anticonformity and independence, as well as conformity and compliance. Nail holds that it is important to know not only the individual's public reaction (acceptance or rejection) to socially supplied information but also the extent to which the person privately accepts the information. Knowing both of these reactions allows us to categorize the behavior in one of four classes. A summary of his model, using the terminology in this chapter, is presented in Table 18.1. Public acceptance of social information coupled with private acceptance is defined as conversion. Public acceptance without private acceptance is compliance. The importance of this distinction is that conversion persists in the absence of the pressures under which it was induced; compliance is transitory, dependent on the pressures of the moment and the ability of the source of the pressure to monitor behavior.

Public rejection of social information coupled with its private acceptance is anticonformity. Such a response is unusual and noteworthy, but it does occur, as the research of Frager (1970) and others (e.g., Baer, Hinkle, Smith, & Fenton, 1980) shows. Public *and* private dismissal of socially supplied information defines independence, where the individual marches to the beat of his or her own drummer.

Clearly, the context in which social information is made available has a powerful effect on the particular form of response that occurs. For example, independence is least likely in novel, difficult situations in which the guidance offered by prior experience is minimal and judges' confidence in their own perceptions is low. The more ambiguous or difficult the context, the more people will depend on sources external to themselves. Independence and anticonformity are most probable when the actor has considerable experience in the context in which a judgment is to be made and the judgment is relatively concrete or unambiguous. Both situational and personal factors can prompt independence or anticonformity.

■■■ SOME CONCLUDING THOUGHTS

Study of conformity is an important feature of the social psychological landscape. Understanding the factors that foster conformity, conversion, independence, and

The study of obedience, and of attitude change, owes much to research on conformity: See Chapters 2–4, and 17.

anticonformity is critical to understanding why people behave the way they do. The complexity of this issue is well represented in the combined work of Sherif and Asch. Both ostensibly studied the same phenomenon, but as was shown, the implications of their work are very different. Research on conformity is a foundation for the important research of Milgram, and has laid the groundwork for the study of attitude change.

Social psychologists have accumulated a vast store of information over the sixty years that they have studied social influence. Campbell (1961) describes an interesting method to organize and distill this knowledge. He suggests that we consider the available sources of information when thinking about social influence. These sources can be reduced to three general categories: (1) past experience, (2) one's own direct perceptual inputs, and (3) socially supplied information. Most social influence introduces a conflict between one's own perceptual inputs and socially supplied information. The issue is the extent to which people weigh their own perceptual inputs against socially supplied information in deciding on a judgment or course of action. The more disproportionate the reliance on external information, the greater the social influence. Greater dependence on one's own perceptions suggests resistance to conformity or conversion. Ultimately, all research on social influence is directed to discovering variables that induce disproportionate over- or underweighing of socially supplied information (see Crano, 1975; Nail & van Leeuwen, in press, for an elaboration of this point).

■ ■ ■ SUMMARY

We have learned much about the process of social influence since Sherif's pioneering investigations in the 1930s. His autokinetic studies suggested that people use socially supplied information to guide their present and future judgment processes. Asch demonstrated that social pressure could influence people's verbal reports of their perceptions. Unlike Sherif, Asch did not investigate the persistence of these reported perceptions in the absence of surveillance, and hence the veracity of his subjects' reports is open to question. This lack of specificity stimulated attempts to understand the contexts in which social influence had the most lasting effects. Festinger distinguished between public compliance with a source of influence, and the private acceptance (conversion) of the source's information. Later theoretical work distinguished among compliance, conversion, and two other potential reactions to social influence, independence and anticonformity.

Empirical research suggests that people's feelings of self-efficacy, or competence, will have a powerful effect on the extent to which they weigh socially supplied information relative to their own perceptions. The more competent people feel themselves to be, the less weight they assign to information external to themselves. Similarly, the more competent the source of information, the greater its influence. The more difficult the judgment context, the more likely people are to rely on others when deciding on a course of action or forming a judgment. People differ in the extent to which they are willing to entertain information that is external to their own beliefs and perceptions.

Many different tactics of social influence have been developed. Some of the most interesting of these are the foot-in-the-door, the low ball, and the door-in-the-face techniques. The first two of these appear to require commitment to a particular outcome. Commitment creates the conditions for further compliance or concessions. The door-in-the-face is the result of reciprocal concessions ("I'll back down on my initial request, if you're willing to concede to my scaled-down version") or contrast (a moderate request following a larger one is perceived as being more modest than it would have in the absence of the larger request).

■■■ SUGGESTED READINGS

1. Cialdini, R. B. (1988). *Influence: Science and practice* (2nd ed.). Glenview, IL: Scott, Foresman.

2. Dillard, J. P., Hunter, J. E., & Burgoon, M. (1984). Sequential-request persuasive strategies: Meta analysis of the foot-in-the-door and the door-in-the-face. *Human Communication Research, 10,* 461–488.

3. Hogg, M. A., & Abrams, D. (1990). *Social identifications: A social psychology of intergroup relations and group processes.* London: Routledge.

4. Nail, P. R., & Van Leeuwen, M. D. (1993). An analysis and restructuring of the diamond model of social responses. *Personality and Social Psychology Bulletin, 19,* 106–116.

CHAPTER 19

MINORITY INFLUENCE
When Dissidents Prevail

■ **Key Concepts**

Symmetric versus asymmetric influence
Two-process theory
Social comparison
Behavioral style
Consistency
Blue–green studies
Rigidity
Compliance versus conversion
Direct versus indirect influence
Convergent and divergent thought
Diffusion of influence
In-group (or single) minorities
Out-group (or double) minorities

■ **Chapter Outline**

AN ALTERNATIVE VIEW
  Symmetry versus Asymmetry
  Modes of Influence
  Rigidity, Consistency, and Originality
  ■ Fighting Pollution
  Direct versus Indirect Influence

EXTENSIONS OF THE MINORITY INFLUENCE EFFECT
  Convergent and Divergent Thought
  Diffusion of Influence Effects

SOME UNRESOLVED ISSUES
  Who or What is a Minority?
  One Process or Two?

SOME CONCLUDING THOUGHTS

SUMMARY

Most major animal research facilities resemble fortresses, with heavy locked doors, alarms, and tight security. Scientists who use animals in their research must take elaborate and costly precautions to ensure their well-being. At least in part, this is attributable to a small group of committed and persistent animal-rights activists, who have shown they will not tolerate mistreatment of animals. Their behavior not only has affected legislation regarding the way in which animals must be fed, housed, and treated but also the ways scientists do research. Although nobody advocates mistreatment of animals, many reasonable people consider the extreme animal-rights activists misguided. To stop all animal research, which some have proposed, would retard scientific research on birth defects, AIDS, cancer, and many other life-limiting diseases. What is not in dispute, however, is that a small number of committed people have produced major changes.

■ ■ ■

Asch's studies of social influence examined the effect of majority opinion on individual judgments: See Chapter 18.

How do minorities have such effects as those just noted? We offer some insights into the process of minority influence on the pages that follow.

Social psychology's preoccupation with social influence is intense and long-standing. Usually, such research examines the manner in which the *majority* imposes its will on a *minority* (cf. Levine, 1980; Levine & Russo, 1987). In Asch's classic studies, a naive participant is exposed to the phony perceptual judgments of as many as fifteen experimental accomplices. The research looks at the extent to which a group—the majority—influences an individual's responses (Asch 1951, 1955, 1956). But this is only half the story. Looking only at the response of a dependent minority to the pressure of a powerful majority neglects the possibility of the minority's influencing the majority. Obviously, social influence is a two-way street.

How many people were concerned enough about saving dolphins that they worked to force tuna fishing fleets to use special nets for catching tuna that would not also trap and kill dolphins? Probably very few. Yet, this minority position prevailed and changed the practices of companies, even though the change had considerable cost. ■

From left to right: Galileo, Freud, and Einstein. Minorities who revolutionized Western science and society. ■

Throughout history, we see many examples of powerless minority groups— or individuals—who have converted the majority to their way of thinking. Galileo, Darwin, Freud, Marx, Einstein, the early Christians—all minority voices at one point, had profound effects on their world and ours, even though they were in no position to force anyone to listen to them. From the standard perspective, which views conformity as a response to social pressure, it is difficult to explain how these minorities could have had any impact.

■ ■ ■ AN ALTERNATIVE VIEW

Is something wrong with the classical influence model? Obviously, answered Serge Moscovici, who criticized the standard approach to studying conformity. He proposed a model describing the possibility that the minority could influence the majority, and laid out the conditions under which this would be most likely (cf. Moscovici, 1974, 1976, 1980, 1985; Moscovici, Lage, & Naffrechoux, 1969). Because Moscovici has had such a strong impact on contemporary studies of social influence, we examine his views in detail.

Symmetry versus Asymmetry

To Moscovici, the classical approach seemed unbalanced. It assumed an *asymmetric* relationship in which the minority could be the target, but never the source of influence, and the majority could be the source, but never the influence target. The standard operating procedures of the conformity experiment did not afford the minority the opportunity to persuade the majority of anything. Even a cursory review of history reveals this is not the way the world works—at least not always. To counter the standard orientation, Moscovici proposed a *symmetric* relationship, whereby minority and majority each have the power to confront and influence the other (a **two-process theory**). Further, and more controversially, he insisted that influence processes will differ depending on whether the majority or minority is the source of influence. Both could influence each other, but the manner in which minorities influence the majority is not the same as the way in which the majority works its will on the minority. Their tactics are different, as are people's underlying thought processes that occur in response to majority or minority pressure.

Moscovici based his assumptions on his views of the ways minorities operate in the real world. We consider these assumptions and review the research evidence for and against them. Can minorities influence the majority, and if so, does the process differ from that in majority influence?

Modes of Influence

Moscovici assumed that the majority is concerned primarily with social control—with maintaining the status quo and assuring that people behave in ways consistent with the group's norms and values. The majority can bring the weight of considerable social pressure to bear when attempting to push its position. People respond to pressure from the majority by comparing their present attitude or behavior with that recommended by the majority. Through this **social comparison** process, people learn where they are in relation to the "party line." Often, the pressure of the majority is so great that people change their *public behavior* so as to approximate the majority position *(compliance)*. This avoids conflict with the majority, since the individual appears to be in harmony with the majority norm. However, the process often does not result in any fundamental change in actual beliefs. Although people outwardly comply with the majority's requirements, they maintain their original attitudes. Thus, when group pressure or surveillance is relaxed, behavior and expressed attitudes return to the original (prepressured) position.

Minorities cannot bring the same kind of social pressure to bear as majorities do when promoting their positions. A minority cannot coerce the majority. Indeed, minorities often are outwardly rejected, for even to be seen as agreeing with a minority is not a pleasant prospect for many. People resist agreeing with a minority because they fear that agreement might suggest a connection they would rather avoid (Mugny, Kaiser, Papastamou, & Perez, 1984).

This does not mean that minorities cannot cause change. A minority transgresses group norms by suggesting alternative ways of acting or thinking. As a consequence, Moscovici argues, the minority causes cognitive conflict merely by making its position known. This conflict prompts people to reexamine their beliefs and actions. Such examination may result in attitude and behavior change, but generally the change is not immediate. Not only do people not want to be seen agreeing with a minority but also they do not want to think of themselves as doing so, because such agreement threatens the self-concept. Still, the conflict precipitated by the minority forces people to think about its message at some level. When the threat of identification with the minority is removed—for example, when the minority source has left the scene—its position may be adopted.

According to Moscovici, two forces operate in minority influence. The first promotes the immediate overt *rejection* of the (minority) source. The second force becomes evident after some time has passed, when the influence target mulls

Social influence may result in either public compliance or real change: See Chapter 18.

Drawing by Booth; (c) 1977 The New Yorker Magazine, Inc.

over the minority's position and compares it with the majority's. In some cases, the logic of the minority's brief will be recognized and accepted. Thus, the temporal course of belief or behavior change in response to social influence is hypothesized to be different for minority and majority influence sources. With a majority influence source, we expect to see immediate behavioral change in

The majority promotes compliance; the minority promotes conversion: See Chapter 18.

the recommended direction (compliance), but a later reversion to the original position, because behavior change is not accompanied by a change of belief. In the case of minority influence, we expect to see immediate rejection of the source's position, with a delayed change of belief and behavior in the direction advocated. Two different motives are responsible for these varying patterns of belief and behavior change. The majority promotes *compliance;* the minority promotes *conversion.*

Rigidity, Consistency and Originality

When are minorities persuasive? Moscovici and Mugny (1983) theorized that the manner in which the minority presents its case—its *behavioral style,* to use their term—is crucial. A behavioral style is a general strategy of influence. Any number of behavioral styles can be employed by a persuasive source. For example, a minority source might adopt the facade of fairness by emphasizing its quest, not for advantage, but for equitable treatment: "We're only asking for what is right." It might present itself as being intellectually and morally superior: "If you really understood this issue, if your heart was in the right place, you would agree with us." It might attempt to convey the image of helpfulness— "I'm only suggesting this for your own good." Of all the behavioral styles that can be adopted, however, research suggests that the most effective is *consistency.* It is not what the minority says, so much as the consistency with which it hammers away at its position.

Moscovici and Mugny (1983) indicate that a minority group (or a representative of the minority) that is consistent in advancing its position stands a reasonable chance of prevailing. Inconsistent minorities are certain to fail. In an early experimental demonstration of the necessity for minority consistency modeled on Asch's classic studies, Moscovici and his associates (1969) brought together six individuals in an apparently simple perceptual judgment task. Their job was to judge the colors of slides flashed onto a screen. All the slides were obviously and unambiguously blue. However, in one of the experimental conditions, two of the six participants responded "green" on every trial. These two were experimental accomplices. The naive subjects complied with the accomplices on 8% of the judgments. Eight percent might not seem like much until we consider that participants who responded without accomplices *always* said blue when judging the slides.

To emphasize the importance of minority consistency, Moscovici and colleagues ran a second condition in their study (the *blue–green studies*). In this variation, the accomplices responded "green" on only two-thirds of the trials and "blue" on the remainder. In this circumstance, the minority had no effect on the judgments of the naive majority participants. From this pattern of findings, Moscovici deduced that the minority is effective only when it is consistent— when it never wavers from its position.

Moscovici and Lage (1978) repeated this study with two variations. In one condition, participants discussed the concept of "originality" before beginning the judging task; in the other, the experimenter stressed the importance of this quality. The proportion of green (minority-influenced) responses in these two conditions was 13% and 30%, respectively. Apparently, merely making the concept of originality salient (or *priming* originality) enhances susceptibility to minority influence.

FIGURE 19.1

Effects of rigidity or consistency on minority influence (adapted from Nemeth et al., 1974). The minority was an effective influence source of its message was viewed as consistent, but not rigid.

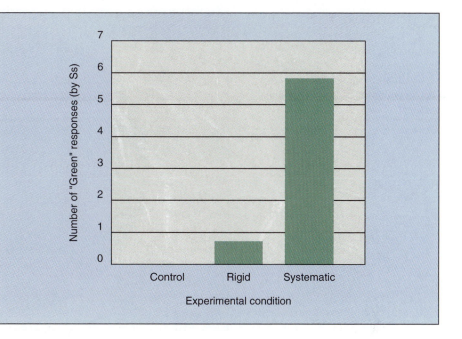

Although consistency is essential, it must be distinguished from *rigidity*. If, by dint of its absolute consistency, the minority is perceived is rigid, it will have little persuasive impact. There is a fine line between rigidity and consistency, but research by Nemeth, Swedlund, and Kanki (1974) suggests that the line can be drawn. In their research, they presented twenty-eight blue slides to participants, who were tested in groups of six. Although all the slides were unambiguously blue, half were considerably brighter than the others. In one-third of the groups, the two accomplices gave the green response when the slide was bright; for the remaining trials, they said blue. In another third of the groups, the rule was reversed—the accomplices responded green to the dull slides and blue to the bright ones. In the remaining groups, the accomplices responded green to half the slides and blue to the remaining slides, but their responses were not related to any physical characteristic (such as brightness) of the slides.

These experimental variations were meant to suggest either rigidity or consistency. If accomplices' reported judgments were related to the physical features of the slides (brightness), the reports were thought to suggest consistency. If they were unrelated to the slides' physical features, the judgments were thought to suggest rigidity.

Did these variations matter? The results illustrated in Figure 19.1 suggest that they did. As shown, control group participants, who responded without an accomplice, always judged the slides to be blue. Thus, any deviation from a 100% blue response may be taken as evidence of social influence. Figure 19.1 also shows that a substantial portion of the experimental participants reported that some of the slides were green. These misjudgments, clearly the result of social influence, occurred when the reports of the minority accomplices were related to objective features of the slides—that is, when the accomplices' reports were consistent (but not rigid). When accomplices' reports were *consistently* associated with the slides' brightness, such that the bright (or the dull) slides were *always* judged green, the naive judges responded green more than 20% of the time. When accomplices' reports were rigid (that is, consistent, but not based on any

Priming a specific attitude or belief can have a powerful effect on subsequent judgments: See Chapter 8.

FIGURE 19.2

■

Focus on this blue circle for approximately 30 seconds. Then shift your focus to a blank wall or page. What is the color of the afterimage you see?

physical feature of the object of judgment), they had very little effect on participants' judgments. These findings suggest that although consistency is necessary, there must be some basis for it.

APPLYING SOCIAL PSYCHOLOGY TO THE ENVIRONMENT

■ ■ ■

Fighting Pollution

These results suggest that people will be more influenced by minorities that appear flexible, rather than rigid, in their position. Mugny and his colleagues explored this possibility in an interesting study on ecology and industrial pollution (Mugny, Rillet,

TABLE 19.1

■

Slogans used to Create Flexible and Rigid Persuasive Messages

Rigid Slogans	Flexible Slogans
Factories that do not abide by the standards should be closed down!	The automobile industry should be required to equip all vehicles with emission controls!
We should immediately prohibit industries from manufacturing detergents!	The manufacture of detergents should be regulated!
Air polluting industries should be banned!	Polluting industries should be fined!

From Mugny & Perez, 1991.

& Papastamou, 1981). They created two persuasive messages that argued against pollution. The messages were attributed to an "ecologically oriented, political fringe minority group." The two messages were identical except for three phrases contained in the body of the communication. As shown in Table 19.1, the flexible message contained three slogans that were much more moderate than those of the rigid message. Results showed that people's attitudes were considerably more influenced by the flexible communication. In an interesting sidelight to this study, some participants read instructions that placed a high value on originality, while others were induced to think about the negative aspects of deviance. Depending on one's perspective, either of these terms might characterize the minority's message. Mugny found that subjects primed to value originality were more likely to accept either message. This suggests that minorities will be most successful when the context of their message encourages originality or openness to new ideas.

Direct versus Indirect Influence

The results of both the Moscovici and the Nemeth "blue–green" studies demonstrate clearly that minority sources can affect the judgments of naive respondents. But does this impact persist, does it represent a genuine change of perceptions, or is it merely a temporary (and sometimes rather minor) verbal change in response to the apparently confident minority? Moscovici himself admitted (cf. Moscovici & Lage, 1976) that the early studies did not answer these questions. To pursue this further, Moscovici and Personnaz (1980) extended the blue–green research design in some ingenious ways. In the new approach, the experimenters showed pairs of judges (one of whom was an accomplice) slides that were unambiguously and invariably blue. In the study's first phase, all judges responded silently, in writing, noting the color they perceived on each slide presentation. After fifteen silent judgments, the experimenter collected the written responses and gave the judges information regarding the typical response. Half the judges were told that 81.8% of a representative sample of the population perceived the slides as blue, whereas the remaining 18.2% of the population saw the slides as green. The remaining half of the sample was told the opposite—that 18.2% had seen the slides as blue, while the remaining 81.8% had judged them as green.

An interactive judgment task then began; (blue) slides were flashed onto a screen, and the judge and accomplice reported their perceptions aloud. For all fifteen slides, the accomplice always said green. For some participants, the accomplice's report was a minority response, since they had been told earlier that only 18.2% of the population perceived the slides as green. For the remaining participants, who had been told that 81.8% of the population perceived the color as green, the accomplice's was a majority response.

After the fifteen public judgments, a new response mode was introduced. Judges viewed another set of (blue) slides and wrote the color they saw. In addition, through the use of a color wheel (which contained the entire color spectrum, from red to violet), they indicated the color of the *afterimage* they perceived after the slide was removed (Figure 19.2). Both responses were silent and thus not accessible to the accomplice.

The results of this study (and of others like it—Personnaz, 1981; Personnaz & Guillon, 1985) are as interesting as they are controversial (Doms & Van Aver-

FIGURE 19.3

∎

Focus on this green circle for approximately 30 seconds. Then shift your focus to a blank wall or page. What is the color of the afterimage you see?

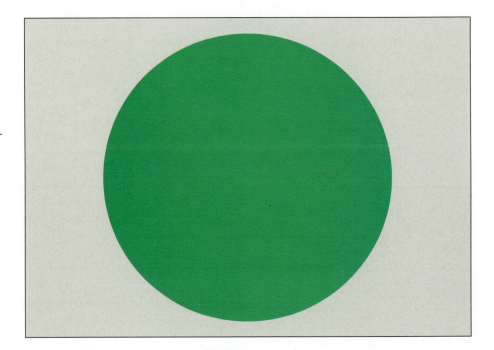

maet, 1980; Sorrentino, King, & Leo, 1980). First, very little influence was evident in any public response session. Despite the fact that some participants were told that more than 80% of a representative sample perceived the slide as green and that their partner sided with the majority, judges' public responses were unaffected. With very few exceptions, they reported the blue slides as being blue.

However, judges' private responses in the last phase of the experiment differed substantially from their public disclosures. Again, on the color-naming task, there was little evidence of majority or minority influence. Everyone wrote "blue" when the slides were flashed on the screen. In Moscovici's terms, there was no **direct influence** on judgments; that is, the judges were not swayed by the information specific to a given color judgment. However, the visual afterimages reported by judges were strongly affected by the minority or majority status of the accomplice with whom they had been paired, suggesting **indirect influence.** Those paired with the majority accomplice reported orange afterimages, and orange is the complement of blue. This is reasonable: Their public responses were "blue," and the afterimages they reported after each slide were the complement of this color. This suggests that in the interactive judgment session, the participants were reporting what they saw.

What is surprising in this study is that the participants paired with the minority accomplice reported afterimages that corresponded to having been exposed to *green* slides. The afterimages they reported were red, and red is the complement of green, not blue. Despite the fact that they continued to report seeing blue slides, the afterimage data suggests they had been influenced. Their afterimages were complementary to green, the color the accomplice reported seeing. Because the judges were unwilling to acknowledge any direct influence, either to the accomplice or to themselves, they continued to respond "blue." On a measure that they did not consciously control, an *indirect* measure of influence, the impact of the minority appeared.

■■■ EXTENSIONS OF THE MINORITY INFLUENCE EFFECT

Convergent and Divergent Thought

If (direct and indirect) minority influence is possible, it is important to understand how the process works. Research by Charlan Nemeth has made significant contributions in this area that help us understand the manner that minority dissent affects people's thoughts. Nemeth (1986) believes that people respond differently to disagreement, depending on the majority or minority status of the source of conflict. She has argued that finding oneself at odds with the majority is stressful, because we generally assume that the majority is correct. Under such circumstances, we focus our attention on the majority's position, and usually adopt the majority's rules of evidence when deciding the truth of a position. In deciding between the majority's view and our own, we reduce our consideration of possible courses of action to two—comply with or resist the majority. Coupled with the tendency to adopt the majority's rules of evidence, this drastic reduction in alternatives increases the likelihood that we will overtly adopt the majority's position. By framing the decision process in terms of only two possibilities **(convergent thinking)** we create a dilemma for ourselves. If we maintain our original position, we must out of necessity reject the majority. For most, this is a difficult step.

When we are confronted with minority dissent, Nemeth argues, our first reaction is disapproval and dismissal. A one-shot minority argument thus has little hope of succeeding. However, if the minority is consistent and persistent, we are forced to come to grips with its position. In such a circumstance, we reappraise the issue. We do not necessarily adopt the minority's perspective in our process of reappraisal, but rather open ourselves to a host of possible alternatives (only one of which has been put forward by the minority). Nemeth terms this opening-up process **divergent thinking.** Thinking divergently, we might adopt the minority view, we might stick with our established position, or we might decide on one of the many alternative possibilities that we have not thought of before, but have now generated.

Many of us have experienced this form of influence. It seems especially common in work groups. The group has settled on a particular way of doing things, and has done so for a long time. When someone objects to the standard operating procedure, he or she is usually rejected—"We have always done it this way. Why change now?" The initial effect of the minority voice may appear minimal, but it might cause other members of the (majority) group to reconsider its procedures and to think of other ways the job might be done. Although they might not accept the minority worker's advice, the majority may modify its way of doing things because the advice prompted consideration of a wide variety of options.

Nemeth's interest is not with the particular position that ultimately is adopted but rather on the thought processes stimulated by dissent. In a study of these processes, Nemeth and Kwan (1987) presented unusual strings of six letters (such as tNOWap) to participants, and asked them to write the first three-letter word they saw. Studied in groups of four, participants almost always listed the word formed by the capital letters read from left to right (in this case, NOW). After completing five letter strings, judgments were collected and reviewed by the experimenters, who informed the naive respondents that either three (a majority) or one (a minority) of the participants had listed the word formed by the reverse sequencing of the capitals (in the case of the example, WON, rather than NOW). Then, all were exposed to a new set of letter strings, and instructed to form all the combinations they could during each string's fifteen-second exposure.

Participants told that the majority had used a backward spelling strategy tended to form backward combinations to the exclusion of other combinations. Thus, for the word tNOWap, they formed words like paW, paN, pOt, and so on. Those exposed to the minority, however, used backward (pat), forward (Nap), and mixed sequencing (apt), detecting substantially more words. Nemeth argued that participants who thought the majority had used a backward processing strategy had simply adopted the strategy wholesale, without thinking much about it, and used it throughout the entire experiment. This strategy diminished their overall performance.

People in conflict with the minority gave evidence of divergent thinking, as hypothesized. They used all the available strategies—forward, backward, and mixed processing. Because of this, they were able to form more word combinations. While previous research suggests that minorities can influence people's attitudes, Nemeth's work suggests that they do so by changing the ways people process information (Nemeth, Mayseless, Sherman, & Brown, 1990). To sum up, it appears that minority dissent can influence the way we think about issues in fundamental ways.

Diffusion of Influence Effects

If minorities induce divergent thinking, as Nemeth and others (e.g. Maass, West, & Cialdini, 1987) claim, then other, related aspects of minority influence may be expected to occur as time passes. The emphasis on the passage of time is important, because the mulling over of the minority's message, an outcome of the divergent thinking process, takes time. Accordingly, effects of a minority's (direct and indirect) influence should be most obvious after time has passed. In a comprehensive summary of the time-related aspects of minority influence, Perez and Mugny (1990) suggest that the minority's message may not only have an influence (albeit a delayed one) on people's attitudes and behavior but also that this influence might spread to other, related issues as well. The *diffusion* of minority influence to related realms of cognition is thought to be the result of divergent thinking.

To illustrate, in Perez and Mugny's (1987) study, 165 Spanish high school girls read a message strongly in favor of voluntary abortion. This position was contrary to Spanish law and to the attitudes of the participants as well. The message was attributed either to a speaker of minority or majority status. After reading the message, participants expressed their attitudes toward both voluntary abortion *and* birth control. The results of the study indicated that the proabortion message was most successful when the source was in the majority group. However, this direct influence had little indirect impact—it did not influence participants' attitudes toward contraception. The opposite pattern occurred when a minority speaker was the source of the proabortion message. In this case, the speaker had little impact on participants' attitudes toward abortion, the communication topic. However, the indirect influence of the message was evident in changed attitudes toward birth control. These results suggest that minority influence can spread beyond the boundaries of the targeted topic to related issues.

■ ■ ■ SOME UNRESOLVED ISSUES

Who or What is a Minority?

The definition of minority has never been a major concern of researchers interested in this form of social influence. Perhaps the definition seems obvious. However, failure to pay attention to this issue may have retarded progress. Two general approaches characterize research in this field. In one approach, minorities are viewed in simple numeric terms. If 51% of the population is X, and 49% is Y, then Y is in the minority. In much of the research on minority influence, this numeric criterion has been used to define majority or minority status: The minority is some fraction of the total group. This approach has the advantage of convenience. It is easy to tell people that 88%—or 12%—of some group perceives a slide as green or blue or feels a certain way about an issue. The numeric definition of minority depends on differences in beliefs or perceptions between one group and another.

This form of definition, however, misses some important features of the real world of minority groups. When we think of a minority, many of us envision an oppressed, underprivileged, and distinguishable outgroup—not only numerically infrequent but also inferior in one way or another. Often, that is, a stigma is assigned to minority status, whether that status refers to race, religion, nationality, or any of a host of other distinguishing features. Few studies of minority influence use stigmatized groups to represent the minority. This may be a problem, for although being "different" does not inevitably result in discrimination (Mummendey & Schreiber, 1983; Mummendey et al., in press), discrimination based on difference occurs with sufficient frequency to raise concern that the effects found in the field of minority influence may depend on the manner in which minority is defined—as a numeric entity or a stigmatized subgroup.

In much research on minority influence, it is tacitly assumed that research participants identify with (belong to) the majority. Under some circumstances, however, participants may identify with the minority. In the early research, participants' self-perceptions of identity were not controlled or measured. Failure to control this factor makes it difficult to interpret results. In some situations, the minority was not only a minority but an *in-group* as well (a group with whom the participant identified). When differences occur in such studies, it is difficult to determine if they are attributable to the minority status of the source or to similarities in group status of the source and target. In other settings, participants probably do not identify with the minority (the minority is an *out-group*). Here again, if majority–minority differences occur, it is impossible to know whether they are attributable to group size or to differences in response to in-groups versus out-groups. Recent work in minority influence has begun to come to grips with this issue (Clark & Maass, 1988; Martin, 1988a,b; Mugny & Perez, 1991). It appears that out-group minorities (or **double minorities,** as they are sometimes termed) are most likely to be discriminated against and least likely to

Prejudice and discrimination against stigmatized majorities are salient research topics in social psychology: See Chapters 23 and 24.

succeed in attempts at social influence. Double or out-group minorities have ideas or characteristics that set them apart and, in addition, are not members of the group they are attempting to influence. Single (or in-group) minorities are members of the group they are attempting to persuade. Their position differs from that of the majority of their own group. A member of the National Security Council is an in-group minority if his or her ideas conflict with those of the other council members. An out-group minority in this instance would be the head of state from another country, whose ideas are contrary to the council's. In most circumstances, the in-group minority has a much greater chance of prevailing on the majority than the out-group minority.

One Process or Two?

Throughout this chapter, we have assumed that minorities and majorities use different tactics and activate different thought processes when they wield influence. From this perspective, majority influence is dependent on pressure and force and the target's dependency on the majority. Finding themselves in disagreement with the majority motivates people to compare themselves with the position put forward and to determine whether their own view or that of the majority is correct. If the pressure is sufficient, the comparison process will prompt people to bring their overt behavior into line with the majority's. However, this change is not necessarily accompanied by changes in belief, and so it may be temporary. Conversely, the minority is initially dismissed, but its message, presented consistently and persistently, causes people to rethink the issue. They entertain a host of divergent options, settle on one of them, and experience real personal change.

Not everyone is convinced that these different processes actually occur (e.g., Tanford & Penrod, 1984; Turner, Hogg, Oakes, Reicher, & Wetherell, 1987). For example, there is considerable evidence that majority influence does persist sometimes. It is not easy for the standard theory of minority influence to account for such persistence. In a comprehensive review of this issue, Kruglanski and Mackie (1990) found that evidence for the two-process interpretation is weak. Although they could not state without reservation that identical processes characterize both majority and minority influence, it is their contention that evidence for different processes is not compelling.

Where process differences do appear, Kruglanski and Mackie suggest they might be a result of incidental features that are related, but not identical, to minority status. For example, minorities might be effective in some circumstances because their position is so different from mainstream beliefs that people notice their message and admire their courage in pushing their ideas. Under these conditions, it is not minority status that causes influence but the appearance of sincerity or commitment. Although the attribution of sincerity may typically be made of the minority group member who is willing to speak up for an unpopular cause, a majority representative who is perceived as sincere may be equally effective. We know from considerable earlier research that information sources who appear committed to their position are more persuasive than those who have ulterior motives (cf. Hovland et al., 1953; Koeske & Crano, 1968; Petty &

Caioppo, 1986). So it may be that it is not minority status that matters but a feature usually associated with minority status.

■■■ SOME CONCLUDING THOUGHTS

There is little doubt that minorities can change majority belief and actions. History is filled with examples. And there is also little doubt that most social influence research has concentrated on majority influence. This imbalance began to be redressed with the pioneering work of Moscovici and his colleagues. Today we know a lot about the ways minorities operate—how they succeed and why they sometimes fail in getting their message across. Whether the processes by which majorities and minorities impart influence are the same remains an open question. Similarly, the precise factors that cause a minority to have greater or lesser impact are still being explored. Despite these uncertainties, it is fair to say that the study of minority influence effects has reinvigorated social influence research in general. Today we are concerned with the manner in which minorities affect others; we no longer question whether they can do so.

■■■ SUMMARY

According to Moscovici, influence is transmitted asymmetrically in the traditional (majority-centered) social influence model: The majority can persuade, and the minority can be persuaded. He argued for a symmetric orientation, in which each group can influence the other. The majority brings the weight of social pressure to bear when advancing its position. People at odds with the position compare their beliefs with the majority's (social comparison), and attempt to bring their overt behavior into line with that recommended. Minorities cannot bring strong social pressure to bear, but their mere existence causes cognitive conflict. Reaction to this conflict usually entails immediate overt rejection; however, over time, the minority may prevail if it presents its position with consistency, especially in contexts in which originality is salient.

Minorities appear to stimulate diverse ways of thinking about issues. Over time, this divergent thought may facilitate adoption of the minority's position. Even when the minority's appeal is not adopted, attitudes consistent with its position may diffuse to other, related, issues. Such indirect influence can have a powerful impact on attitudes associated with the targeted belief (the direct influence target).

Although considerable research has demonstrated the power of minorities to persuade, controversy remains. Moscovici's two-process model is not universally accepted. For some, identical processes characterize influence by minority and majority. The definition of minority also remains unsettled, with distinctions now made between single and double minorities. Despite these unresolved issues, much progress has been made, and research on minority influence is flourishing.

■ ■ ■ SUGGESTED READINGS

1. Kruglanski, A. W., & Mackie, D. M. (1990). Majority and minority influence: A judgmental process analysis. In W. Stroebe & M. Hewstone (Eds.), *European review of social psychology* (Vol. 1, pp 229–261). London: Wiley.

2. Levine, J. M., & Russo, E. M. (1987). Majority and minority influence. In C. Hendrick (Ed.), *Review of personality and social psychology: Group processes* (Vol. 8). Newbury Park, CA: Sage.

3. Maass, A., West, S. G., & Cialdini, R. B. (1987). Minority influence and conversion. In C. Hendrick (Ed.), *Review of personality and social psychology* (Vol. 8). Beverly Hills, CA: Sage.

4. Moscovici, S. (1985). Innovation and minority influence. In G. Lindzey & E. Aronson (Eds.), *The handbook of social psychology,* 3rd ed. (Vol. 2, pp. 347–412). New York: Random House.

5. Mugny, G., & Perez, J. A. (1991). *The social psychology of minority influence.* Cambridge, England: Cambridge University Press, and Paris: Editions de la Maison des Sciences de l'Homme.

6. Nemeth, C. J. (1986). Differential contributions of majority and minority influence. *Psychology Review, 93,* 1–10.

CHAPTER 20

GROUP PERFORMANCE
The Effects of Working Together

■ Key Concepts

Social loafing
Social facilitation
Social inhibition
Evaluation apprehension
Cohesion
Free riding
Optimizing tasks
Maximizing tasks
Additive tasks
Conjunctive tasks
Disjunctive tasks
Motivation loss
Process loss

■ Chapter Outline

WHY PEOPLE WORK IN GROUP SETTINGS

SOCIAL FACILITATION: THE PRESENCE OF OTHERS
    General Arousal
    Evaluation Apprehension
    Distraction

INTERACTIVE GROUPS: WORKING TOGETHER
    Participant Characteristics
    Commitment and Cohesion
    ■ Work-group Norms
    Participant Behavior
    Task Demands
    ■ Does Pay Distribution Matter?

SOME CONCLUDING THOUGHTS

SUMMARY

Two heads are better than one.
Many hands make light work.
Too many cooks spoil the broth.

■ ■ ■

Suppose you are acquainted with five other students in your social psychology course. One day, early in the term, you happen to find yourselves talking together after class. During this conversation, one person suggests that it might be a good idea to form a study group in order to learn the course material more effectively. Five of you immediately see the wisdom in this suggestion and make plans to meet the next night for a planning session; the lone holdout declines, saying she always does better when she studies alone.

Do people accomplish more when they work together in groups or when they work individually? The familiar sayings and the anecdote at the chapter opening illustrate conflicting ideas about such collective endeavors. On the one hand, group work permits people to pool their efforts and talents in order to get a job done more efficiently or effectively. On the other hand, groups require coordination and cooperation, without which group members may actually interfere with each others' ability to get the job done right.

Since working in groups represents a major aspect of social life, social psychologists have long been interested in the study of group productivity (see Shaw, 1932). As with many questions about human social behavior, there is no simple answer to the riddle of group productivity. As we will see, the products of persons working together in group settings can be better or worse than, or even no different from, those of individuals working separately. The only realistic answer to any query about group productivity is "It depends." But what does it depend on? Answering this question is the focus of this chapter.

■ ■ ■ WHY PEOPLE WORK IN GROUP SETTINGS

We use the term *group setting* to refer to social gatherings in which accomplishing some task—getting a job done or achieving some common goal—is the primary focus (Zander, 1985). This distinguishes task-oriented situations from the many other types of social settings in which people can, and do, interact, such as family gatherings, recreational groups, and conventions.

One of the questions of interest is why and when individuals choose to work in group settings rather than individually. Why, for instance, did some members

Although many groups are formed for purely social reasons, people often get together in groups to accomplish a task. ■

of your social psychology class decide to join their fellow students and form the study group? Evidence indicates that people do so because they believe they will be better off working with others than working alone, that working in a group context increases their chances of task success.

In one study on this issue, Vancouver and Ilgen (1989) gave students a list of six tasks that they might later be asked to perform. A brief description accompanied each potential work assignment, so that participants could get a sense of the sorts of skills and effort that each job entailed. The participants first responded to a questionnaire that measured their estimate of how successful they would be at performing each task. Then they were told that some of them would work as individuals on a task assigned to them, whereas others would work on that same task collectively.

Participants were then allowed to express a preference for work settings—to choose, for each task, whether they wanted to work on it by themselves or in collaboration with others. Vancouver and Ilgen's results were very consistent with the notion that people join groups to promote positive outcomes for themselves. Students strongly preferred to work alone on tasks on which they thought they could do well, but strongly preferred to work collectively on tasks about which they felt little confidence of success.

Moreover, there is evidence that persons expect to have an easier time succeeding at a task if they work at it with others. Numerous studies have shown that people often expend less effort on a task if they work on it collectively. For example, Latané, Williams, and Harkins (1979) asked participants to perform a simple but effortful task—to shout as loudly as they could—under different social conditions. Sometimes participants shouted as individuals, sometimes they shared this task with one other person, and sometimes they worked with three or five others. (In actuality, each participant was alone in a soundproof chamber, where the volume of his vocal output could be assessed individually.)

Results of this experiment in group productivity indicated that collective output exceeded the typical performance of individuals working alone. However,

FIGURE 20.1

The social-loafing effect: Comparison of actual output of 2- 4- and 6-person groups to possible output of individuals alone. (From Latané et al., 1979.)

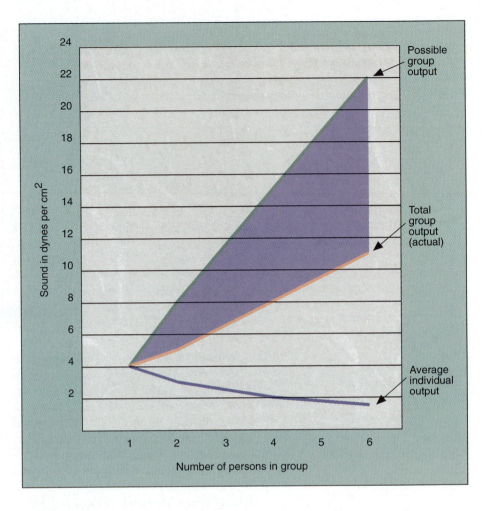

in the group settings each member put out less volume than individuals who were working alone. As a consequence, the total group output was less than it could have been if all members had performed as well in the group setting as they did as individuals. Moreover, the difference between effort expended working alone and in a group setting increased with increasing group size; that is, participants worked even less hard in the six-person setting than they did in pairs (Figure 20.1). This relaxation of effort when tasks are shared has been dubbed **social loafing.** (Although the term carries somewhat negative implications, it should be pointed out that the effort reduction associated with group settings is not necessarily bad for achievement of group goals. Some tasks, such as moving a very heavy piece of furniture, could not be accomplished by individual effort alone, but can be achieved by several individuals working together, even if each does not put out maximum effort.)

These findings suggest that group settings promote expectations of shared burdens and thus the belief that less effort is needed for task accomplishment. In other words, people work in groups because they expect that they will be more likely to succeed *and* that they can do so with less individual effort. We turn now to the question of whether group productivity does indeed meet these expectations.

In games like tug-of-war everyone participates, but no one knows how much effort is being expended by any one player. Group activities such as this sometimes produce "social loafing." ∎

∎∎∎ SOCIAL FACILITATION: THE PRESENCE OF OTHERS

There is considerable evidence that individuals do work better and more efficiently in group settings than when they are alone. In fact, the mere presence of other people may enhance performance, even when those people are not working together on a task.

One of the earliest studies that might be called a social psychology experiment was conducted by Norman Triplett (1898) to test the idea that motor performance is enhanced by the presence of coactors. Triplett had been struck by the well-known finding that cyclists attain higher speeds when they are being paced or racing in competition with other cyclists than when racing alone. Triplett believed this enhanced performance occurred because the "presence of another rider is a stimulus to the racer in arousing the competitive instinct . . . the means of releasing or freeing nervous energy for him that he cannot of himself release . . ." (p. 516).

Triplett designed a laboratory experiment to test these effects on motor performance. The apparatus he used consisted of two fishing reels arranged side by side; the participant's task was simply to reel string as fast as possible. Forty children were tested under two performance conditions—working alone or working in competitive pairs. About half of the participants in the experiment performed better (reeled faster) when they were in the group situation than when they were alone, as Triplett had expected. Of the other half, some performed the same in both settings, but some actually performed worse when they were paired with others. Triplett's study showed that the presence of others working on the same task can enhance individual performance, but not in all cases.

Since Triplett's classic experiment, much research has demonstrated that persons perform differently when working in a social context than when working alone, even when the others present are not working on the same task. Many of these studies (e.g., Carment, 1970; Dashiell, 1930; Travis, 1925) obtained the social facilitation effects that originally inspired Triplett. **Social facilitation** refers to the finding that individuals perform better in the presence of others than when working alone. In contrast, other studies (e.g., Burwitz & Newell, 1972; Martens & Landers, 1972; Travis, 1928) found evidence of **social inhibition**—performers did worse in the presence of others. And to complicate matters even further, still other studies (e.g., Allport, 1920; Markus, 1978; Pessin, 1933; Sanna & Shotland, 1990) have obtained a mixed pattern—participants did better when performing in the company of others under some conditions, but did worse under other conditions.

For many years, these mixed results puzzled social psychologists. In 1965, Robert Zajonc made an important observation that helped resolve the mystery. He noted that, in social situations, people tend to perform better when their task is simple or well learned—something they could successfully accomplish with relative ease—but tend to do more poorly when the task is complicated or new—something that is difficult for them to perform. Zajonc's observation was very consistent with the procedures and findings of the many investigations of social facilitation–inhibition. For instance, in a study by Markus (1978), participants were asked to perform a variety of simple, everyday tasks—put on a pair of shoes, don a coat, and so on. Sometimes they did so in the usual manner (for example, put on their own shoes); sometimes they did so in an unusual way (put on a coat that fastened in the back rather than the front). Results showed that the presence of others enhanced performance when a well-learned behavior was required, but it hurt performance when the necessary actions were unusual.

Why should the presence of others enhance performance of easy tasks but detract from performance of difficult tasks? A number of social scientists, including Zajonc, have proposed different explanations for this phenomenon. Three of these explanations—general arousal, evaluation concerns, and distraction—have received the most attention and empirical support.

General Arousal

In a theory similar to Triplett's original idea, Zajonc (1965, 1980) has proposed that the mere presence of others *arouses* performers, that is, increases their energy, makes them more alert, more motivated, and so forth. Moreover, for many years psychologists have known that there is a complicated relationship between arousal and performance (Yerkes & Dodson, 1908). Among other things, heightened general arousal increases the inclination to express well-learned ("dominant") responses. Based on this research, Zajonc reasoned that the arousing presence of others should enhance performance of easy tasks, where the dominant response is in fact the correct one; but it should decrease performance of difficult tasks, where the dominant response interferes with the production of necessary behaviors.

Arousal is also known to have a curvilinear relationship to performance (Figure 20.2). When arousal is initially very low, increases in level of arousal have a facilitating effect: The more aroused we are, the better we are likely to perform. However, after a point, we can become overly aroused: Additional increases in arousal then lowers performance.

FIGURE 20.2

■

The arousal–performance relationship: At very low levels of arousal, individuals are not motivated to perform well. As arousal increases, performance improves, up to a point at which higher arousal begins to interfere with ability to perform well, especially on complex tasks.

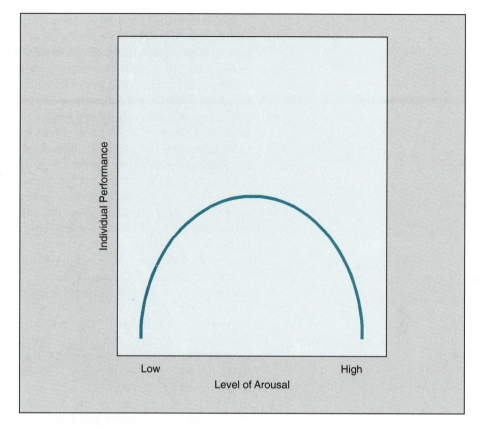

In a series of studies, Baumeister and his colleagues (e.g., Baumeister, 1985; Baumeister & Showers, 1986) have demonstrated that this curvilinear effect of arousal is related to social facilitation–inhibition. Results of competitive sporting events, for instance, show that under most circumstances, sports teams tend to perform better before a friendly audience ("the home team advantage"), but when the contest is particularly important and pressure is high (such as a championship game), the presence of the home crowd actually lowers success rates.

Evaluation Apprehension

Nicholas Cottrell (1972) offered an explanation for social facilitation–inhibition that differs somewhat from Zajonc's. Cottrell proposed that not all forms of arousal create facilitation or inhibition effects on performance. In social situations, performance is affected by a particular kind of arousal, which Cottrell labeled evaluation apprehension. **Evaluation apprehension** is anxiety created by an individual's concerns about being judged or evaluated by others. Concerns about what others will think about us can produce either social facilitation or inhibition effects. On the one hand, it can motivate increased effort and improve performance (Jackson & Williams, 1985), but on the other hand, it can increase the tendency to express dominant responses that may interfere with good performance on complex tasks (Cohen, 1979).

Research has yielded evidence to support Cottrell's position. For example, studies (e.g., Cottrell, Wack, Sekerak, & Rittle, 1968; Martens & Landers, 1972) have shown that social facilitation–inhibition is greatly diminished when the others who are present cannot, or clearly are not interested in, evaluating the worker's performance (for example, when they are busy attending to other things and not paying attention to the performer). Also, expectations about the outcomes of evaluation can either enhance or inhibit performance. Geen (1979) and Sanna and Shotland (1990) found that for performers who expected to fail at a task, the presence of a potentially evaluative audience hurt performance, whereas it enhanced performance for those who expected to do well.

An interesting new line of research compares the effect of presence of another person with the presence of some other living being such as a pet dog. The presence of another individual—even a close personal friend—has been found to increase arousal and interfere with performance on a stressful task such as doing arithmetic problems. However, the presence of the subject's own pet during task performance actually decreased indicators of stress and improved performance (Allen, Blascovich, Tomaka, & Kelsey, 1991). Apparently, only other humans can evoke evaluation anxiety, whereas familiar pets have the power to reduce stress.

Evaluation apprehension can account for many of the effects of the presence of others on task performance that have been obtained in research with human subjects. Evaluation apprehension does not account so well for the fact that social facilitation and inhibition effects have also been observed in nonhuman species (Clayton, 1978). Experiments with several subhuman species, including cockroaches, have demonstrated that performance of simple behaviors (such as running speed) is enhanced when other members of the species are present in the situation, but that performance of more difficult behaviors may be depressed. These animal behavior studies support Zajonc's position that arousal is generated by the mere presence of others, even when no performance evaluation is expected.

Distraction

Robert S. Baron (1986) has proposed yet a different mechanism for understanding social facilitation and inhibition, which differs substantially from the arousal-based explanations of either Zajonc or Cottrell. Baron has argued that the presence of others is potentially *distracting*—thinking about the interpersonal situation can take our minds off the task at hand. This creates a situation of divided attention that will affect performance *depending on how much concentrated attention is required*. When a task is routine or boring, distraction can actually increase attention and effort and enhance performance. However, with complex or difficult tasks, distraction is likely to interfere with effective performance.

In a series of studies, Baron and his collaborators have demonstrated that distraction is a viable explanation for social facilitation–inhibition (e.g., Groff, Baron, & Moore, 1983; Sanders, 1981; Sanders & Baron, 1975; Sanders, Baron, & Moore, 1978). Their work has shown that (a) the presence of other people does indeed prove distracting in work situations, and (b) nonsocial distractions (such as music) can enhance or hurt performance in the same manner that the presence of others can. Many students may have experienced the mixed effects of distractors when doing homework. When homework assignments involve routine or repetitive tasks, working in front of the TV or with loud music blaring may actually facilitate getting the work done. But the same distractions may prove fatal when the homework requires more concentration.

Taken together, the large number of studies of social facilitation–inhibition suggests that all three processes—general arousal, evaluation concerns, and distraction—can affect task performance in group situations. The presence of others can arouse us for a number of reasons, but heightened concern about being evaluated is likely to be a frequent and potent basis for such feelings. Moreover, it is likely that arousal of any sort, if it is strong enough, will enhance or detract from performance, depending on what we have to do to accomplish the task. And it very well could be that evaluation concerns, or strong arousal of any sort, is distracting to us. Overall, then, it appears that the three explanations are not incompatible. They merely emphasize different aspects of the same general phenomenon—how the presence of others can impinge on our thoughts and feelings in ways that affect our ability to perform a task successfully.

■ ■ ■ INTERACTIVE GROUPS: WORKING TOGETHER

Obviously, the impact on performance of working in a group setting is a consequence of many more factors than just the mere presence of co-workers. When individuals actually work together on a common project or task, social interaction and coordination of effects contribute to the final outcome. Under interactive conditions, characteristics of the group members, the nature of the task, and the situation in which the work is conducted all influence the level of group performance.

Participant Characteristics

People bring a variety of personal characteristics—personality traits, motives, beliefs, and so forth—with them to all their social encounters (cf. Aronoff & Wilson, 1985). Moreover, a large body of empirical work has demonstrated that these personal factors can influence how successful group members are at achieving task success. In reviewing this literature, we focus on three major categories of personal variables: personality characteristics, gender, and personal beliefs.

Personality characteristics. For some time, many psychologists were particularly interested in identifying those aspects of the human personality that had the greatest impact on group processes in general. Although there appear to be no simple relationships between individual characteristics and the outcome of group interaction, such work did provide some useful insights into relationships between personality and group productivity. For example, such diverse personality variables as sociability (Bouchard, 1969), need for prominence (Shaw & Harkey, 1976), self-control, and emotional stability (Haythorn, 1953) have all been found to be positively related to group performance.

Of greater significance are the studies that have investigated the relationship between personality and group productivity from a more interactive perspective (Aronoff & Wilson, 1985; Endler & Magnusson, 1976.) From this point of view, effects of personality characteristics do not operate in isolation from other aspects of the group setting. Rather, the personality characteristics of individual group members must be considered in context of the rest of the group—including the compatibility with personal characteristics of other group members—to predict group performance.

In an experiment illustrating this interactionist perspective, Smelser (1961) asked males to work together in pairs on a railroad-scheduling task (employing actual, working model trains). Members of a team had to coordinate their efforts to allow two different trains to use some common track to get to different destinations. Performance was measured in terms of how many complete trips a team could execute in a fixed period of time.

Smelser had teams work in two different role settings. In one condition, one team member was assigned to the role of "dispatcher," who had to plan and organize the schedule that both he and his teammate would carry out. In the other role assignment condition, the two team members worked as peers in the planning and implementation of the task. Unbeknown to them, participants had been selected on the basis of their level of dominance—the characteristic inclination to take charge and tell others what to do—as measured by a previously administered personality inventory. High- and low-dominant subjects were scheduled to participate so that all combinations of personality and role assignments could be examined.

Results indicated that the most productive groups were those in which a high-dominant subject was the dispatcher and a low-dominant subject was his (subservient) teammate (Figure 20.3). In contrast, the least productive groups were those in which the reverse was true—when a low-dominant dispatcher had a high-dominant teammate. Other combinations of dominance scores and role assignments generated intermediate levels of productivity. Clearly, it is the extent to which participants' personality characteristics mesh with other aspects of the group setting that affects productivity, more than the personality characteristics considered in isolation.

Sex Composition. Just as personality characteristics of group members must be considered in interaction with group structure, the gender of group members combines with task requirements to influence overall group performance. The majority of experimental studies on group performance are conducted with groups in which all of the members are the same sex. Thus, gender effects on productivity are usually investigated by comparing the performance of all-male groups with that of all-female groups on the same task.

In a review of some fifty-two studies of this type, Wood (1987) found that, on average, male groups tended to outperform female groups. However, this result must be qualified in two important ways. First, the tasks used in most of these studies were ones on which males performing individually tend to outperform females working individually. The superior performance of male groups may reflect a bias toward use of tasks (such as motor performance or quantitative analyses) on which males are generally more skilled or practiced than females.

Second, the nature of the requirements for performing well on the group task makes a difference in the relative performance of male and female groups. Groups

FIGURE 20.3

Group productivity as a function of role assignment. (From Smelser, 1961.)

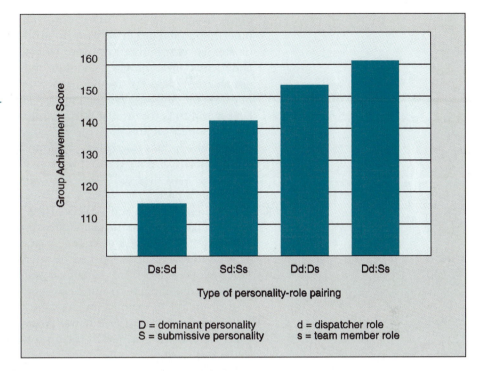

composed of males generally outperform female groups when the group activity is highly *task focused,* that is, when members need to work individually to produce as much or as fast as possible (such as amount of purely motor activity or generating lists of possible solutions to a problem). However, when the group activity requires cooperation and coordination, female groups tend to perform as well or better than male groups.

Finally, those studies that have used mixed-sex groups have generally found that such groups outperform both all-male and all-female groups (Wood, 1987). There is evidence that the complementarity of male and female roles contributes to group productivity. Social expectations may also be operating here. Some research indicates that males are willing to work harder on a task when their partner is female rather than another male, in part because they believe that males are supposed to contribute more to joint efforts than are females (Kerr & MacCoun, 1985).

Personal Beliefs.   Effects of gender roles on group performance illustrate that participants in group settings bring with them beliefs and expectations about how they and their fellow group members should act. Research—particularly studies by Norbert Kerr and his colleagues (e.g., Kerr & Bruun, 1983; Messé, Kerr, & Sattler, 1992)—has demonstrated that these beliefs can have a substantial impact on group productivity. One study (Messé et al., 1992) examined the idea that persons in group settings who were invested with a superior status (such as "boss," "manager," or "supervisor") would believe themselves to be privileged. As such, these individuals would not work as hard on an unpleasant task that they shared with others.

To test this hypothesis, the researchers had male participants perform a simple but strenuous task in two-person teams. In some groups, one member was randomly assigned to be a "supervisor." This person was told that he would have other responsibilities in addition to working on the task along with his subordinate. To ensure that data were usable, for each work trial he had to read a code letter off a computer monitor and record it on a special sheet. In other groups, this additional (coding) task was also given to one of the participants, but now the job was described in low-status terms—something that a lowly log keeper had to perform. In a third condition, workers were not given any special titles or additional jobs; they merely worked on the task as peers. Results showed that beliefs—in this case beliefs about privilege—affected group performance. To the detriment of their team's productivity, nominal supervisors worked significantly less hard than did either log keepers (who had exactly the same jobs as they did) or peers.

Research by Karau and Williams (1990) also demonstrates how beliefs—in this case, beliefs about the meaningfulness of the task and one's importance to its completion—can have a positive impact on performance in groups. In this study, pairs of undergraduates worked on a task. Some worked as individuals, while others worked as a team. Moreover, some participants were led to believe the task was unimportant—it was being used because it was convenient, but it had no real utility. In contrast, others were led to believe that the task was meaningful, that performance on it was related to cognitive abilities. Finally, participants were led to believe that their co-worker was either very good or very bad at the task.

Participants in the team condition who believed they were working on a meaningful task with an incompetent co-worker actually worked harder than the typical worker in the individual condition. In contrast, team members in all the other conditions tended to work less hard than individual workers. The

Group cohesion is a sense of unity and camaraderie among group mnembers. ■

findings of these and other studies suggest that a wide variety of beliefs—including performance norms, which are discussed in the next section—can have either positive or negative consequences for group productivity.

Commitment and Cohesion

Commitment of group members reflects a belief that the group is a worthwhile, valuable enterprise, one worth participating in, nurturing, and maintaining (Moreland & Levine, 1988). Such beliefs are usually accompanied by positive feelings of attraction to the group and to fellow group members. Thus, commitment is closely related to the concept of group **cohesion**—"a feeling of group unity, camaraderie, and esprit de corps" (Forsyth, 1990, p. 83). Commitment is the attitude of the individual group member toward the group and its activities, whereas cohesion is a characteristic of the group as a whole—the shared beliefs of the group members (Hogg, 1992).

Research has indicated that a variety of factors influence the level of commitment that members have to their group. For example, variables such as task success (Anderson, 1974; Blanchard, Weigel, & Cook, 1975), clear task procedures (Anderson, 1975), effective leadership (Schaible & Jacobs, 1975), and attitude similarity (Terborg, Castore, & DeNinno, 1976) have all been found to affect members' positive beliefs and feelings about their group situation. In general, these findings suggest that commitment (and thus cohesion) is a consequence of how rewarding participants find their experiences in the group to be.

APPLYING SOCIAL PSYCHOLOGY
TO WORK
■ ■ ■

Work-group Norms

Although it seems clear that there is a close relationship between group cohesion and positive feelings about membership in a group, the question remains, is there any relationship between commitment–cohesion and group performance? Many investigations have explored this issue, but the answer they have given is far from simple. Some studies have yielded evidence of a positive relationship between favorable feelings toward the group and productivity, but other investigations generated only marginal or mixed support for this hypothesis (Mudrack, 1989; Stogdill, 1972).

The picture becomes somewhat clearer when we consider a field study by Seashore (1954), which surveyed factory workers' commitment to their group and productivity. The results of Seashore's survey did not indicate that groups with high commitment and cohesion were always highly productive. Instead, he found that cohesion was associated with *homogeneity* of performance; that is, workers in highly cohesive groups tended to match each other's performance level (so all performed poorly, moderately, or well), whereas in low-cohesive groups, individual performances were much more diverse.

These results suggest that members of cohesive groups tend to be more conforming to one another and hence are more productive only when they have accepted a norm that advocates high productivity. Since it is likely that such norms are often held in group settings, not surprisingly, studies often (but not always) have found a

Assembly line employees often develop work norms as a group. Working faster than group standards is punished as "rate busting." ■

positive relationship between commitment–cohesion and group performance. However, when work groups do not value high performance (as in factories where antimanagement attitudes prevail), then high group cohesion may lead to lower productivity.

Participant Behavior

In group settings, participants work and behave in a social fishbowl where they are both the observers and the observed. As such, groups provide members with many opportunities to use the activities of others as clues to how they should act. Such clues can take one (or both) of two forms: (1) Information about each others' task behavior can give participants a basis for deciding how much work they themselves should perform. (2) Participants' actions can be explicit or implied evaluations of the work that other members perform. In many ways, these two factors resemble the distinction between "informational" and "normative" sources for conformity. In either case, the group situation means that participants' behaviors influence and are influenced by how other members behave.

The distinction between informational and normative sources for conformity *discussed in Chapter 18 is similar to that for group behaviors in work situations.*

Performance Information Effects. A straightforward hypothesis about the impact of participants' work behavior on one another's performance would predict that everyone would tend to model everyone else and thus all perform at a similar level. Recall from our earlier discussion that Seashore (1954) found the members of highly cohesive work groups tended to match each other's productivity, and other studies of experimental groups have also demonstrated performance modeling effects (e.g., Jackson & Harkins, 1985; Kerr, 1983).

However, other evidence indicates that participants in group settings sometimes use the work behaviors of their colleagues as a basis for performing more or less well than those around them do. At the beginning of this chapter, we discussed evidence that individuals work in groups because they believe they can get more accomplished with less effort by working with others rather than alone. If other participants in a group are performing at a high level, there is less need to work so hard oneself. In many cases, group members will lower their efforts to achieve task success when they see that a co-worker is willing to carry the load. Instead of matching the co-worker's level of productivity, they tend to "free ride" (Kerr, 1983; Kerr & Bruun, 1981; 1983).

Free riding (working less hard when others are present to put out the effort) is closely related to the social-loafing effect discussed earlier. It is most likely to occur when individuals do not feel that their own personal efforts are essential to the group's success. People are less likely to free ride if they believe their efforts are essential to task success—and they will work even harder than their co-workers when the task is particularly important (Kerr & Bruun, 1983; Karau & Williams, 1990).

Evaluation Effects. As we noted earlier, concerns about what others think of our performance is one of the likely explanations for social facilitation–inhibition effects. Thinking that others might evaluate us can arouse or distract us such that we perform better on easy tasks but worse on difficult tasks. Harkins (1987; Harkins & Szymanski, 1987) has proposed that such evaluation concerns operate in the same way to affect collective productivity in group settings.

Harkins's argument offers another explanation for social-loafing effects in group settings. He believes that social loafing will occur only when the nature of the group situation reduces evaluation concerns, as when individual performances (typically on rather simple tasks) are pooled and thus cannot be evaluated. In such cases, the bigger the pool—the greater the number of persons contributing to the common product—the harder it is to evaluate any single piece of work, and the more effort loss occurs.

To understand how social loafing works according to Harkins, consider the difference between two sports events—a relay race and a tug-of-war. In the relay, each individual's performance contributes to the final team outcome and that contribution is monitored on an individual level—we know how fast each team member ran in his or her leg of the race. With the tug-of-war, individual efforts also determine the team success, but individual contributions cannot be assessed separately. No one knows exactly how hard each member of the team actually pulled on the rope. In conditions such as these, where individual effort is not identifiable, social loafing is most likely to occur.

Findings from a number of studies support Harkins's analysis of social-loafing effects. For instance, research consistently has found that informing participants in group settings that their individual output can be monitored greatly reduces the tendency to loaf (e.g., Hardy & Latané, 1986; Kerr & Bruun, 1981; Williams, Harkins, & Latané, 1981). Participants who expect to be able to perform well work harder within a group when they believe their performance can be evaluated (Sanna, 1992). A study by Harkins (1987) showed that group members whose performances were pooled worked less hard and expressed little if any concern about evaluation. Moreover, individuals who worked alone, but were led to believe their productivity could not be evaluated, showed similar tendencies to loaf.

While raising evaluation concerns can eliminate social loafing or effort loss in group contexts, it does not always enhance group performance. Jackson and

Williams (1985) found that evaluation concerns enhanced group productivity on a simple task—a typical social facilitation effect—but interfered with group productivity on a complex task—a typical social inhibition effect.

Taken together, this body of research suggests that people tend to work less hard in group settings when they feel the group gives them a place to hide, that is, when their output cannot be monitored. On the other hand, people tend to work harder in group settings when they feel that the social situation provides others (such as their coworkers) with an opportunity to evaluate what they do. Whether increased effort also leads to increased performance and productivity depends in part on the nature of the task that the group has to accomplish.

Task Demands

The personal characteristics and behavior of other group members are important features of group settings. A number of contextual factors, such as the structure of communication and role relationships, have also proved to be very important determinants of group productivity (e.g., Guetzkow, 1968; Leavitt, 1951; Shaw, 1954). Of all these factors, however, probably the most important single influence on group process and outcome is the nature of the task that the group has to perform. Task characteristics affect how all other factors operate and combine to determine the final group product.

More than twenty years ago, Ivan Steiner (1972) made a sophisticated and comprehensive analysis of tasks in group settings that remains a source of understanding and insight to this day. Steiner noted that how well groups perform is dependent in large part on how well equipped they are to meet task demands. These demands are a consequence of three structural dimensions:

1. **Task divisibility**—the extent to which everyone has to engage in the same activity, as would be the case for a unitary task such as loading a heavy piano onto a moving truck, versus working on subtasks, as would be the case for designing and building a piano.

2. **Task goal**—the extent to which task success is measured in terms of quality of output *(optimizing tasks),* as in writing a jointly authored report, versus quantity *(maximizing tasks),* as in many production or selling tasks.

3. **Combinational procedure**—the manner in which individual effort is combined to yield a group product. A number of such procedures are possible. For example, tasks can be *additive,* where group performance is the sum of individual output, as in the case of needing to generate as many unusual, creative uses for a common object (for example, an empty beer bottle) as you can. In contrast, tasks can be *conjunctive,* where every group member must do her or his part for the group to finish its work, as when all members of a relay team must successfully complete their leg of the race and pass the baton; or tasks can be *disjunctive,* where only one member has to succeed for the group to succeed, as is true when a number of students are working together to solve a tricky math problem.

In Steiner's view, group performance is determined by the extent to which the group has the appropriate tools to meet task demands. Here, "tools" refer primarily to human resources (the number of persons, as well as their skills, motivation, and so forth), nonhuman resources (such as material, equipment, and time), and a procedure that effectively coordinates use of the resources that are available. Within this framework, Steiner emphasized two critical determinants of group productivity: member motivation to succeed at the task and the coordination procedure. He believed that actual group performance will approach optimal group performance (for a given set of resources) to the extent that (a) members are maximally motivated to succeed, and (b) they can coordinate their efforts with little waste, interference, or redundancy.

Performance suffers from **motivation loss** (or effort loss) to the extent that concerns with productivity are less than they could be. For instance, research has shown that persons social loaf substantially more when performing group tasks of low intrinsic interest than when they are enjoying what they are doing (e.g., Brickner, Harkins, & Ostrom, 1986; Zaccaro, 1984).

Performance also suffers what Steiner called **process loss,** when coordination procedures are less than satisfactory for the task demands confronting the group. A number of studies have shown that groups do better when they have, or can quickly develop, a procedure that allows them to coordinate their activities and pool their resources in a reasonable manner (e.g., Anderson, 1961; Laughlin, 1980; Stasser, Kerr, & Davis, 1980; Wilson, Aronoff, & Messé, 1975).

APPLYING SOCIAL PSYCHOLOGY TO WORK
■ ■ ■

The effect of pay distribution rules such as equity and equality is an aspect of social exchange theory: See Chapter 12.

Does Pay Distribution Matter?

The important point from Steiner's perspective is that task demands interact with other features in the group situation to determine overall productivity. To illustrate, let's consider one experimental study in which task structure was combined with distribution of payment for performance. In this research (Vallacher, Messé, & Fullerton, 1987), participants worked in pairs on a jigsaw puzzle task for pay. Each member had his or her own subset of pieces to put in the puzzle, but success was possible only by seeing the pieces that the co-worker had managed to place correctly.

Pairs were assigned to one of two conditions of combinational procedures: For some, group success was defined as that point in the session where one member had correctly placed all her or his pieces in the puzzle—a *disjunctive* task demand. For

FIGURE 20.4
■

Performance as a function of task demands (disjunctive–conjunctive) and pay scheme (equity–equality). (From Vallacher et al., 1987).

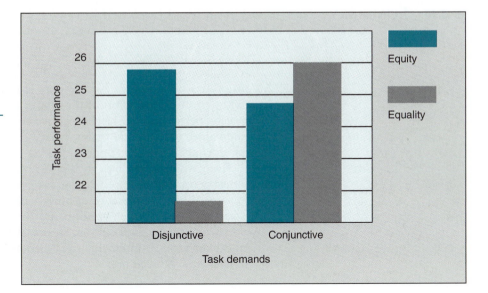

others, group success was defined as that point at which both members had correctly placed all their pieces—a *conjunctive* task demand. Moreover, some pairs in each condition were told that the team's earnings (determined by how quickly they had met the criterion of success) would be divided *equally,* whereas other pairs were informed that their earnings would be divided *equitably,* so that the better one worker did compared with the other, the greater that person's share would be.

Results indicated that task demands determined the effect of pay scheme on group performance. When pairs worked on the puzzle as a conjunctive task, pay scheme did not matter. However, when the puzzle was cast as a disjunctive task, pairs were much more productive when pay was to be distributed equitably than when it was to be divided equally (Figure 20.4). In this last condition, the less able worker tended to free ride on the efforts of the co-worker. In this study, as in others, task demands were a key to understanding what factors improved group performance.

■■■ SOME CONCLUDING THOUGHTS

As we said earlier, the answer to the question of whether groups do indeed perform better than individuals is "It depends." It depends on the characteristics of the group members, their commitment to group goals, the structure of the group, and the nature of the task demands. In addition, it is important to note that social groups do more than perform tasks. Groups are important sources of social influence, interpersonal support, social identity, and self-evaluation. Because working in groups engages all of the processes of social interaction, group productivity is much more than the sum total of individual task performance.

■■■ SUMMARY

Task group settings are situations in which individuals interact in order to accomplish a task or achieve some common goal. Individuals often choose to work in groups because they believe they are more likely to succeed, and to do so with less individual effort, if they work together rather than alone. Much social psychological research has been directed to determining under what conditions individuals in groups do perform more effectively and efficiently than they would as individuals working alone.

Even when individuals are not working together on a task, the presence of other persons in the situation tends to have an effect on individual task performance. When the presence of others enhances performance, the effect is one of social facilitation; when performance deteriorates in group settings, the effect is social inhibition. Explanations for social facilitation and inhibition include the effects of arousal, evaluation apprehension, and distraction on performance of simple and complex tasks.

When individuals actually work together in order to accomplish a task, performance is further complicated by the need for social interaction and coordination of efforts. The success of interacting groups depends on the combined effects of personality characteristics and beliefs of the group members and characteristics of the group situation. One important factor is the degree of commitment that members have to the group and its goals, which determines group cohesion. Another factor is the mutual influence that group members' behavior has on one another. Under some circumstances, group members exhibit social loafing—they put out less effort when other group members are available to get the work done. Social loafing is less likely to occur when interest in the group task is high and when individual efforts can be evaluated by other group members.

Probably the single most important determinant of group productivity is the nature of the task that the group has to perform. Steiner has analyzed the structure of group tasks in terms of three important dimensions—task divisibility, task goal, and the combinational procedure by which member performance is combined to determine success. Steiner argues that the nature of the task interacts with all other aspects of the group setting to determine group performance.

■ ■ ■ **SUGGESTED READINGS**

1. Forsyth, D. R. (1990). *Group dynamics,* 2nd ed. pacific Grove, CA: Brooks/Cole.

2. Harkins, S. G., & Szymanski, K. (1987). Social loafing and social facilitation: New wine in old bottles. In C. Hendrick (Ed.), *Group processes and intergroup relations* (pp. 167–188). Newbury Park, CA: Sage.

3. Sanders, G. S. (1981). Driven by distraction: An integrative review of social facilitation theory and research. *Journal of Experimental Social Psychology, 17,* 227–251.

4. Steiner, I. D. (1972). *Group process and productivity.* New York: Academic Press.

5. Wood, W. (1987). A meta-analytic review of sex differences in group performance. *Psychological Bulletin, 102,* 53–71.

6. Worchel, S., Wood, W., & Simpson, J. (1992). *Group process and productivity.* Newbury Park, CA: Sage.

CHAPTER 21

GROUP DECISION MAKING
Making Choices Collectively

■ **Key Concepts**

Group dynamics
Orientation
Social decision scheme
Plurality
Majority rule
Consensus formation
Task solution certainty
Group polarization
Normative social influence
Informational social influence
Groupthink

■ **Chapter Outline**

EXPERIMENTAL STUDIES OF GROUP DECISION MAKING
    The Group Decision-making Process
    ■ The Use of Decision Schemas

INDIVIDUAL PREFERENCES AND COLLECTIVE DECISIONS
    Decision Making in Juries
    Task Solution Certainty: Can We Tell If We're Right?
    Group Polarization

THREATS TO THE QUALITY OF GROUP DECISIONS
    ■ THE PSYCHOLOGY OF GROUPTHINK

SOME CONCLUDING THOUGHTS

SUMMARY

One day you find yourself serving on a jury. You and eleven other jurors have just heard a civil case in which an automobile accident victim is suing the driver of the other car for damages to person and property. During the trial, you learn that the defendant has already been convicted of reckless driving in a separate criminal trial—so there is no disputing his guilt. What you and the other members of the jury must decide is how much money to award the plaintiff for her trauma and loss. As the trial draws to a close, you decide in your own mind that the plaintiff should receive a sizable amount as compensation, and the figure $50,000 pops into your head. Now you are sitting around a table in the jury room, about to deliberate this issue. As you soon learn from the ensuing discussion, your idea to award the plaintiff $50,000 is about average for the group; everyone agrees that a large payment is called for, but there is some initial dispute about what constitutes "large." Four of your colleagues are advocating a much bigger award, but at least six jurors state they had individually concluded that amounts less than $50,000 seemed right. After much discussion, you settle on an award in the amount of $75,000.

Jury decision making represents just one of many settings in which decisions are made collectively, by a group of people. For example, group decisions are made in the context of family units, business management groups, committees, and policy-making groups. In our society, both the legal and political systems are dominated by group decision-making bodies—juries, legislatures, cabinets, and judicial panels, such as the Supreme Court. Understanding the process and outcomes of collective decision making has wide application to important social issues.

EXPERIMENTAL STUDIES OF GROUP DECISION MAKING

Much of the social psychological knowledge about group decisions comes from laboratory studies of **group dynamics** (Cartwright & Zander, 1968). Typically in these studies, a group of three to six individuals (usually previously unacquainted and usually male) are assembled in a laboratory and given a specified problem to solve or decision to make. Then, without further instruction as to how to proceed, they are let loose to work out a mutually agreed-on solution or decision by process of discussion and information exchange.

Over the last forty years, this laboratory paradigm has been used to study three types of questions about collective decision making:

1. *Process*—what do groups of people do while they are engaged in making group decisions or choices?

Juries are important examples of group decision making. ■

2. *Context*—what factors determine the decision that is reached?
3. *Quality*—how good a decision does the group come to?

The Group Decision-making Process

In the late 1940s and early 50s, Robert F. Bales and his associates (e.g., Bales, 1950a, b, 1953; Bales & Strodtbeck, 1951) conducted observations of numerous laboratory groups to determine whether consistent patterns of behavior regularly occur when group members discuss issues and make decisions.

Typically, Bales and his collaborators assembled groups of between two and ten undergraduate males, and paid them to discuss a set of "human relations" problems. Each group met four different times over a period of weeks to talk about work situations in which an administrator was having some trouble with his workers, while at the same time his own superior was pressuring him to accomplish some difficult task. Each time, group members first were given a summary of a particular case to read; then the group was asked to discuss why the persons in the scenario were behaving as they were and to decide what the administrator should do about the situation. The group's deliberations were unobtrusively observed by trained coders who systematically categorized the behaviors that group members engaged in during the course of discussions.

The data collected from observing these encounters suggested that group process is typified by three phases of deliberation. In the initial phase—what Bales called *orientation*—group members concentrate on reaching a common view of both the problem before them and the procedures to use to solve it. At some point in the discussion, the emphasis changes and group members begin to concentrate on proposing and considering possible solutions—the *evaluation* phase. Finally, as one particular choice gains popularity in the group, members once again shift their focus in an attempt to move toward a group decision. Bales called this final stage the *control* phase.

Since Bales's pioneering work, other social scientists have developed similar perspectives on the processes of group decision making (e.g., Forsyth, 1990). Different theorists use somewhat different terminology to refer to the stages of group decision making, but three phases—orientation, discussion, decision—appear to be common to all analyses of the group decision-making process, and we focus on these here.

Orientation.   Initially, members must identify an issue that is to be resolved, a problem that needs solving, a disagreement that has to be addressed, a matter in need of a conclusion, and so forth. In other words, they must realize that something needs deciding. In addition, this stage also is characterized by some initial choices about how to approach the problem—the procedure to be used to try to reach a decision.

Research indicates that groups seldom engage in explicit discussions about procedures for coming to a decision (Hackman & Morris, 1975; Varela, 1971), although in every group there has to be at least some tacit consensus on this issue or the process could not go forward. There is evidence that explicitly attending to procedural issues during the orientation stage promotes better decisions (e.g., Hackman, Brousseau, & Weiss, 1976; Hirokawa, 1980). In Hirokawa's study, participant groups were asked to make some decisions about a hypothetical emergency—a crash landing that left astronauts stranded on the moon. Groups had to decide what supplies and resources would be most useful for the victims to have with them to survive this mishap.

Groups were evaluated by comparing their decisions with the recommendations of actual experts on such matters. Hirokawa then examined a number of group process variables to see if any were related to decision quality. Results showed that the one variable that best distinguished groups who did well on this problem from groups who did poorly was planning time: Members of successful groups talked more about strategies for decision making than did their less successful counterparts.

Discussion.   As the focus of decision making becomes increasingly clear, group members move into the next stage of the process, in which they actually present and discuss issue-relevant information. In this stage, members identify possible choices and seek information that helps them to evaluate the quality of these alternatives. Also during this stage, members will discuss possibilities for implementing their collective decision and evaluating its consequences.

Patrick Laughlin has extensively investigated the discussion stage of group decision making (e.g., Laughlin, 1980, 1988; Laughlin & Futoran, 1985; Laughlin & Shippy, 1983). Laughlin observed that in this part of the process, members initially try to formulate one or more working hypotheses, which then serve as the basis for subsequent information exchange, expressions of personal opinions, and evaluation of available relevant evidence.

Other work has shown that the extent of discussion is a very important determinant of decision quality. Studies have demonstrated, for instance, that the sheer amount of discussion per se—without even considering the content or

FIGURE 21.1

■

The Group Decision-Making Process. In the process of reaching a decision, small groups consistently go through three phases of deliberation, beginning with a general orientation to the problem and process, through discussion of alternative solutions, to a final stage of decision selection. How much agreement is required to reach a final group decision depends on the social decision scheme that is adopted by that group.

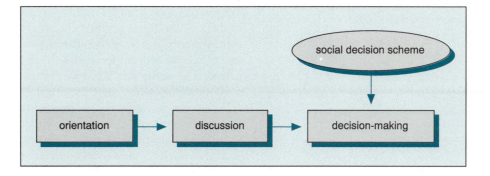

quality of what is being said—relates positively to the value of the decisions that are made (Harper & Askling, 1980; Katz & Tushman, 1979; Lanzetta & Roby, 1960; Laughlin, 1988). In general, more discussion generates better decisions.

Of course, the content of the discussion matters as well, as Laughlin (1988) has also demonstrated. He found that better choices were associated with more time spent on evidence evaluation relative to hypothesis generation. The best decisions are made when group members not only come up with multiple ideas but also take the time to evaluate each one thoroughly. As we shall see, this requirement for quality decision making is not always met in many group decision contexts.

Decision Making.   At some point, if a sufficient number of members believe they have achieved a reasonable basis for coming to a conclusion, the group will enter the third stage in the process. This is the point at which participants actively attempt to make some collective decision. Sometimes external forces—such as a deadline, an impending critical event, or the like—impose a degree of urgency on the group's proceedings, so that members feel compelled to stop deliberating and start deciding.

Once the decision-making stage is reached, the group members must share some social decision scheme if they are to reach agreement about a collective choice. **Social decision schemes** are the rules or procedures by which members combine their individual preferences to generate a collective decision for the group (Davis, 1973, 1982). Decision rules include procedures such as *voting* (where members state their individual preferences, and the alternative that has enough support to satisfy a "win rule", a *plurality* or *majority,* becomes the group decision), *averaging* (where members calculate some midpoint among the range of preferences expressed), *delegating* (where some individual group member or subgroup is given authority to decide for the group as a whole), and *consensus formation* (where discussion continues until everyone agrees on a particular decision). Figure 21.1 illustrates the three stages of the group decision process.

The Use of Decision Schemes

The social decision scheme applied by a particular group may be either explicit or implicit. A research study by Chan (1991) illustrates implicit social decision schemes. Chan observed real-life groups in which hospital personnel (administrators, staff doctors, nurses) were brought together to discuss the features that were most important to them when deciding what wheelchairs to purchase for their institution. Features such as the reputation of the manufacturer for building a quality product, durability, ease of movement, and so forth were all dimensions on which wheelchairs could be judged. The group was asked to identify the one feature that the members collectively thought was the most important.

Before people met in their groups, they were asked individually to state what feature they personally thought was the most important. As you might expect, there were some differences of opinion across types of staff as to what feature counted most. For instance, nurses tended to favor ease of movement, whereas administrators tended to think the reputation of the manufacturer was paramount. When the personnel got together, however, it was most often the case that the collective decision endorsed ease of movement as the most important criterion for purchasing wheelchairs—the choice that the nurses tended to favor. Why? Apparently, the groups used a social decision scheme in which the opinion of the people with the most hands-on experience with the product in question had the most weight in determining the groups' collective preference.

In some group settings, the decision scheme is made explicit. For example, it is often the case that juries, when trying to reach a verdict, will formally poll their members to determine the distribution of individual verdicts; and they will continue to do so until all members vote the same or it is clear that they are hopelessly deadlocked.

Research suggests that no one decision scheme is unconditionally preferred to any other; it depends on the type of decision to be made (Wood, 1984). For example, Kaplan & Miller (1987) found that group members preferred a scheme that uses unanimity when the decision concerned delicate, subjective issues (such as moral dilemmas), but preferred a majority-wins scheme when the decision involved more objective matters (solving intellectual problems).

▪▪▪ INDIVIDUAL PREFERENCES AND COLLECTIVE DECISIONS

Although the processes that groups go through in trying to reach decisions tend to be similar from group to group, the actual decisions made by different groups vary widely. A variety of personal, interpersonal, and situational variables affect collective choice, including personality traits and sex roles (Fleischer & Chertkoff, 1986; Magargee, 1969), social status (Torrence, 1966), group size (Kerr & MacCoun, 1985), and the decision rule applied (Miller, 1985). However, in the attempt to identify the factors that underlie the decision made by particular groups, by far the most attention has been paid to the relationship between initial individual preferences and group outcomes (cf. Baron, Kerr, & Miller, 1992; Forsyth, 1990).

Decision Making in Juries

A great deal of work in the social psychology of groups has examined how individual choices or preferences are ultimately combined to produce a group decision. James Davis, for example, has been conducting a program of research on group decision making for about twenty years that has yielded considerable information on the influence of members' individual choices on the group outcome (Davis, 1982). Much of this work has taken place in the context of simulated jury decision making (e.g., Davis, 1980; Kerr & MacCoun, 1985; Stasser, Kerr, & Bray, 1982).

Juries are particularly appropriate settings in which to study the link between individual ideas and collective decisions. Consider a juror's typical experience. First, she or he sits with the rest of the jury and observes the events that transpire in the courtroom. At this stage, the juror is basically functioning as an individual, weighing evidence, thinking of questions, coming to conclusions, and so on. It is only when both sides have rested their cases that the jurors begin to function as a group with the task of reaching a verdict or judgment. Thus, most jurors come into that group situation with an initial idea or preference about what the final decision should be. By ascertaining these individual preferences in advance and then observing the jury's verdict, researchers can identify the underlying social decision scheme that the jury has used.

In their research on such decision schemes, Davis and his colleagues have studied the outcomes of the deliberations of groups of undergraduates who play the role of jurors in a mock trial. In one case, 80% of the individual jurors initially sided with the defendant. In any given jury, it is likely that most of the jurors will be inclined toward acquittal. There are a few groups, however, in which individuals favoring conviction comprise the majority, and some in which both positions are equally represented. By observing the decisions made by such mock juries, the researchers addressed the following question: What is the minimal number of jurors of the same mind (either for acquittal or for conviction) needed for the jury to reach a verdict rather than becoming hopelessly deadlocked (or "hung," as deadlocked juries are termed in the legal profession)?

As it turned out, a specific scheme described very well the outcomes of these juries. If a two-thirds majority agreed initially, a verdict was reached; otherwise, the jury was deadlocked. That is, before deliberations began, at least eight of the twelve persons on the jury had to hold the same idea about the defendant's fate if the group was likely to ever agree on a verdict; any less than this number, and the group would very likely end up as a hung jury. Of course, groups in other situations might use other social decision schemes. The point of this study is that it is possible to assess systematic relationships between the distribution of initial positions held by group members and the nature of the decision they will ultimately reach.

Task Solution Certainty: Can We Tell If We're Right?

Other work by Davis and his colleagues (e.g., Davis, Hoppe, & Hornseth, 1968; Davis, Hornik, & Hornseth, 1970; Davis, Kerr, Sussman, & Rissman, 1974) has identified one particularly important determinant of decision schemes—the extent to which a clearly valid decision can be reached. This aspect of decision making is referred to as **task solution certainty.** In a trial situation, jurors typically are faced with a very complex task. They must evaluate evidence and testimony that often are contradictory. They must attempt to use that evidence as a basis for reaching a judgment. And they must employ a fixed standard of certainty (for example, "beyond a reasonable doubt"; "by a preponderance of the evidence") when doing so. An individual juror might hold some initial sense of the correct verdict, but still not be entirely confident that this position is correct. Typically, then, the jurors' task is one of moderate solution certainty.

Other tasks—for instance, deciding what number to bet on in a dice game—are simpler, but they also allow much less confidence in the validity of one's judgment about what to do. A roll of the dice is a chance event; any one person's guess about the outcome of the roll is as good as any other's. Realistically, then, solution certainty should be very low for this type of task. Still other tasks—for example, taking a multiple-choice examination on social psychology—tend to promote a much greater sense of solution certainty. In these situations, there is some basis for determining whether a proposed answer is correct or not.

Davis and his colleagues have demonstrated that when groups are faced with tasks for which there is very low solution certainty, members tend to adopt a decision scheme where any one participant's ideas are as likely to be adopted by the group as any other's (Davis et al., 1970; Johnson & Davis, 1972). However, as decision certainty increases to a moderate level, groups tend to use a plurality scheme, where whichever solution has the largest number of supporters wins (Davis et al., 1968). When solution certainty increases still further to become moderately high, groups adopt some type of majority scheme (say, two-thirds or else deadlocked) when trying to reach a collective decision (Davis et al., 1974).

Laughlin has extended these findings by demonstrating that for tasks with very high solution certainty—typically problems for which the answer, once it is revealed, is readily recognized as correct—groups tend to adopt some type of "truth wins" decision scheme (e.g., Laughlin & Adamopoulos, 1980, 1982). In these situations, members tend to discuss possible answers, but reach a decision rapidly as soon as one group member poses the correct solution.

Group Polarization

To this point, we have been considering group situations in which members initially hold a variety of ideas about the matter in question. However, it sometimes is the case that members basically share a common idea and differ only with regard to the extremity of their position. The jury example at the beginning of this chapter is one such case. Recall that in this situation you and your fellow jurors all agree that the plaintiff should prevail—that she should receive some substantial monetary compensation for the damage and suffering the defendant caused her. But the question is, exactly how much compensation? The group members' individual ideas about the appropriate payment vary widely. What amount will the group decide on?

The result in this case—a rather high figure proposed by the more extreme members of the jury—corresponds to findings from a large body of work in the

TABLE 21.1

■

The Group Polarization Effect

Distribution of Initial Individual Judgments	Average (Mean) Judgment	Group Decision
Juror 1: $10,000		
Juror 2: $25,000		
Juror 3: $25,000		
Juror 4: $29,000		
Juror 5: $30,000		
Juror 6: $40,000		
Juror 7: $50,000		
Juror 8: $50,000	$57,000	
Juror 9: $75,000		$75,000
Juror 10: $100,000		
Juror 11: $100,000		
Juror 12: $150,000		

social psychology of groups. In group decision making, extreme positions tend to prevail; that is, when group members initially agree in general but differ in specific positions, the decision reached by the group is more extreme than the average of the initial preferences of its individual members (Dion, Baron, & Miller, 1970; Isenberg, 1986; Myers, 1982; Myers & Lamm, 1976). Social psychologists have termed this phenomenon **group polarization,** because the collective choice tends to be pulled away from the average toward an extreme pole of possible choices (Table 21.1).

The polarization effect was first demonstrated in studies by Stoner (1961) that involved decisions about a series of life-choice dilemmas. Participants were given a set of hypothetical scenarios in which an individual was faced with making an important life decision. One option available in each case was a "safe" choice, where the outcomes would be relatively certain and secure but only of moderate utility. The other option was a "risky" one, where high payoffs were possible but not certain. The participant's task was to make a rating from 1 to 10 as to how high the odds of success should be before the individual ought to take the risky choice. (Choosing high odds meant minimizing risk, while recommending low odds represented higher risk taking.)

Individuals in the Stoner study first made their risk assessments alone. Then they were assigned to small groups and asked to discuss each of the problems and reach a group consensus of how much risk they should advocate. For every choice problem, the group consensus turned out to be *more extreme* than the average of the judgments made individually. In most cases, the group decision favored greater risk than the individual judgements (an effect that came to be known as the "shift-to-risk" phenomenon). But for some problems, the group consensus was consistently in the direction of greater cautiousness.

In groups, people often take greater risks than they would as individuals. ■

Since Stoner's research on risk decisions, the tendency of a group decision to polarize (to be more extreme than the average) has been demonstrated for a variety of topics, in numerous countries, in both laboratory and field settings (Doise, 1969; Lamm & Myers, 1978; Mackie, 1986; Myers & Bishop, 1970; Moscovici & Zavalloni, 1969; Pruitt, 1971; Runyan, 1974; Wallach, Kogan, & Bem, 1962). It occurs when people in groups discuss their positions on social issues, as well as their assessments of risk and other judgments. There is little if any controversy over the existence of the polarization phenomenon. But there is less agreement about why this phenomenon occurs. Researchers have generated support for a number of potential explanations for group polarization, including social decision rules and normative and informational sources of social influence.

Social Decision Schemes. Earlier, we reviewed evidence that suggests that group members tend to adopt a plurality or majority social decision scheme when the issue in question is of low or moderate solution certainty. Much of the research on group polarization, in fact, has employed issues of this type. The choice decisions that Stoner (1961) used are typical of the problems that have been used in these studies. There is no objective criterion of how much to risk, so decision certainty is only moderate at best. Other studies involve discussion of attitude issues such as the advisability of a nuclear weapons freeze as discussion topics (e.g., Mackie, 1986). Positions on such issues are matters of opinion, with little if any basis in physical reality. Similarly, determining how much money is enough to give an accident victim adequate compensation also seems to require a great deal of subjective estimation, based on personal views, values, and so on.

Since decision problems of moderate solution certainty tend to promote the use of plurality as a decision rule, we would speculate that group polarization occurs in part because, initially, there often is a plurality (if not majority) of group members who favor an outcome that is more extreme than the average for the entire group. In searching for a decision scheme, the group tends to move in the direction of the judgment that has the largest number of adherents, even though this deviates from the average judgment (Kerr, Davis, Meek, & Rissman, 1975; Zuber, Crott, & Werner, 1992).

While evidence indicates that social decision schemes play a role in group polarization, it is unlikely that these processes are the whole story. Other forces also operate to affect group polarization, including the same social psychological processes that underlie social influence and group conformity in general.

Group polarization is affected by, among other factors, social influence and group conformity: See Chapter 18 and 19.

Normative Social Influence.   In trying to explain group polarization in risk-taking decisions, Brown (1965) speculated that in our culture, we tend to see taking moderate chances as an appropriate strategy for situations of risk for gain (such as playing the stock market, career advancement, and so on). Clearly, there is no objective basis for this belief, but it appears to be a part of our culture (Stoner, 1968). Moreover, the concept of "moderate risk" is not defined very precisely, so we have only vague ideas about translating this cultural norm into specific judgments. To do so, it is likely that we will turn to the judgments of relevant others as a reference point for our own decision. Furthermore, our concerns with making a good impression (Tedeschi, 1981) enhance this tendency to behave as others do when making collective decisions, particularly when those others are advocating socially valued positions.

Research has yielded considerable support for the hypothesis that *normative social influence* underlies group polarization (e.g., Laughlin & Earley, 1982; Runyan, 1974; Sanders & Baron, 1977). An experiment by Mackie (1986), for instance, demonstrated that polarization depends on whether discussants share a common group identity. In this study, participants listened to a tape recording of a set of people expressing their views on a particular issue. The persons on the tape were described either as unrelated individuals or as members of a group to which the participant also belonged. Mackie found that the participants' own attitudes on the issue in question become more extreme (that is, polarized) when they heard the views of group members than when they heard those of individuals. Being exposed to discussion was not enough to polarize attitudes unless the group had normative influence on the participant.

Informational Social Influence.   Normative social influence on polarization has been found to be strongest when the topic in question involves values and preferences (Laughlin & Earley, 1982) or when the issue being discussed is rather general and vague (Boster & Hale, 1989). By contrast, when group discussion centers on matters requiring facts and intellectual analysis, there is evidence that group polarization is most affected by compelling, logical arguments (Laughlin & Earley, 1982). In these circumstances, *informational social influence,* rather than normative influence, underlies group decision making (Kaplan & Miller, 1983).

Burnstein and Vinokur (Burnstein, 1982; Burnstein & Vinokur, 1973, 1975, 1977; Vinokur & Burnstein, 1974) have extensively studied the combined effects of information salience and quality as the source of group polarization. In general, group members tend to shift their position on an issue to be more consistent with the strongest and most compelling arguments that are presented during discussion. In many cases, these are arguments in favor of extreme positions.

Thus, polarization following group discussion may be accounted for by the greater persuasiveness of arguments representing one extreme side of the issue. (The effects of informational influence imply that if two extreme positions are both represented in group discussion, the group will split into two polarized factions, and that is what has been observed to happen in such cases.)

In summary, it seems clear that group polarization is such a pervasive outcome of group discussion precisely because it is caused by many aspects of group process. Decision uncertainty, social comparison, normative values, and informational influences all conspire to favor extreme positions over less extreme alternatives when individuals get together to make a collective decision.

■■■ THREATS TO THE QUALITY OF GROUP DECISIONS

As the work on group polarization indicates, social psychologists are concerned with both the basic mechanisms of group decision making and the quality of the decisions that are made. Of particular concern is understanding when and why groups make very poor decisions. Research has revealed that at every stage of the decision-making process, forces act to decrease the quality of collective choices. During the *orientation* stage, group members usually do not take sufficient time to organize themselves and their agenda (Hackman & Morris, 1975; Varela, 1971). The outcomes of the *discussion* stage are compromised by incomplete, biased information exchange (Stasser & Titus, 1985, 1987). Finally, the particular social decision scheme that groups use during the *decision-making* stage can interfere with optimal decision making (Stasson, Kameda, Parks, Zimmerman, & Davis, 1991).

APPLYING SOCIAL PSYCHOLOGY TO POLITICS

■■■

The Psychology of Groupthink

Irving Janis conducted what is probably the most comprehensive review of the forces that interfere with high-quality decision making (Janis, 1982, 1983, 1989). Janis first became intrigued by this problem when he read historical accounts of the Bay of Pigs fiasco—a major U.S. foreign policy blunder that occurred during John F. Kennedy's presidency. In April 1961, a small band of Cuban exiles, under the sponsorship of the United States, launched an invasion of their homeland at the Bay of Pigs. The plan, developed by the CIA, was to train a squad of commandos and give them the means to launch an amphibious assault on Cuba. The expectation was that once these troops established a beachhead, they would serve as the nucleus for a popular uprising by which the Cuban people would overthrow the communist regime of Fidel Castro.

As it turned out, events did not unfold as expected. The Cuban military forces easily repelled the invasion, the Cuban people did not rise up against their leader, and the attempt was an embarrassing failure. In retrospect, it was easy to see why the invasion was likely to fail. Why, then, did President Kennedy and his cadre of high-powered advisers not see the major flaws in the plan (underestimating Castro's

President John F. Kennedy and his cabinet during the Cuban missile crisis in 1962. Political decision making under crisis conditions may promote what Irving Janis described as "groupthink." ■

popular appeal; thinking that a small band of troops could successfully overcome massive, well-trained armed forces; and so forth)?

Janis studied the details of the group decision processes that led to this and other government blunders (like Watergate and the escalation of the Vietnam war), as well as group decisions on a less grand scale (such as those made by airplane crews). From his examination of these situations, Janis developed ideas about a destructive psychological force that he termed **groupthink.**

Janis (1982, 1983) concluded that faulty decision making occurs primarily as a consequence of a distorted cognitive style (groupthink) that prevents group members from evaluating evidence, supporting ideas, and making decisions in a careful, rational manner. In Janis's view, groupthink is generated by specific conditions and is expressed in specific symptoms.

Bases of Groupthink. Janis identified a number of factors in group settings that he thought were the likely determinants of groupthink. Strong *cohesiveness* is one such determinant. Cohesiveness involves a sense of comraderie and the belief that the group is special and worthwhile. Strong cohesiveness can create an atmosphere in which harmony and good feeling take precedence over critical thinking and expressions of dissent. Similarly, *isolation* is a potential problem. When a group has limited input from outside sources, the information and options it considers are likely to be incomplete and biased. Also, a closed *leadership style,* in which the leader tends to be autocratic and forceful in presenting her or his preferences, leads to groupthink. Finally, *decision pressure* contributes to faulty group process. A sense of urgency to come to a decision (partly to leave

Cohesiveness, an important factor in group productivity, is also one factor in groupthink: See Chapter 20.

FIGURE 21.2

■

The Elements of Groupthink. Janis's (1982) theory of group decision making outlines the factors that give rise to a "groupthink" orientation and the consequences for the process and outcomes of group discussion.

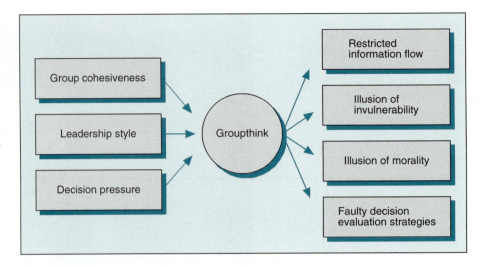

time for bolstering and rationalizing the choice that is made) minimizes time spent in important orientation and discussion activities. Figure 21.2 depicts these elements of groupthink.

Symptoms of Groupthink. Janis speculated that groupthink shows itself in a variety of symptoms. First, a number of factors operate to restrict the flow of information and ideas among members: (1) *pressure* from others to maintain the "party line"; (2) *self-censorship* (avoiding expression of deviant opinions) as a consequence of concerns with maintaining a positive image in the minds of fellow group members; and (3) the presence of *mindguards*—members who take it on themselves to prevent the intrusion into group discussions of ideas and information they think would be disruptive. All three factors limit the information that members have available to consider, with the consequence that a group decision is based on incomplete information and inadequate review of potential options. They also lead members to perceive more unanimity of views than actually exists. Thus, the faulty option that becomes the group's choice benefits from support in (illusory) social reality.

Second, members engaging in groupthink harbor certain illusions about their group and about relevant outside groups and entities. Group members often believe their group is highly competent, infallible, powerful, and effective—they share an *illusion of invulnerability*. Similarly, they also view their cause as just, guided by the highest ideals, on God's side, and so forth, all expressions of the *illusion of morality*. Conversely, members may share a perception of relevant outsiders as weak, evil, and easily beaten, contributing to the belief that one's own side will prevail.

Finally, groups whose members are affected by groupthink manifest many signs of faulty decision-making strategies. For instance, groups can become so involved in the details of a plan that they overlook the basic goals they are seeking to accomplish. As a result, a series of smaller decisions are made without consideration of their overall consequences. The tragic involvement of the United States in Vietnam—characterized by a series of small increases in commitment, which over time led to a massive U.S. presence—is but one example of how this faulty strategy can lead to poor outcomes.

Research Evidence for Groupthink. Research conducted to assess the validity of Janis's ideas has generally supported his perspective (Courtright, 1978; Flowers, 1977; Hensley & Griffin, 1986; Herek, Janis, & Huth, 1987; Moorhead & Montanari, 1986; Tetlock, 1979). One study (Herek et al., 1987), for example, examined a variety of international problems that the U.S. government faced, and analyzed the content of the group deliberations that preceded relevant policy decisions. Results showed that the larger the number of groupthink symptoms observed in the predecision deliberations, the lower the quality the decisions were judged to be.

Discussion groups studied in the social psychological laboratory have also been found to exhibit symptoms of groupthink, particularly when the groups have high cohesion and share a sense of common social identity (Turner, Pratkanis, Probasco, & Leve, 1992). Cohesive groups sometimes make poor decisions because they are more concerned with protecting a positive image of their group than with the validity of the ideas they are relying on. Social identity is a powerful force for conformity to group norms.

Based on a systematic review of results of groupthink research, McCauley (1989) concluded that Janis may have overestimated the importance of distorted thinking and cognitive biases as the basis of groupthink, and underestimated the importance of compliance in generating flawed collective decisions. Conforming to a group decision does not always mean the individual agrees with that judgment. Compliance is going along with the group even when one is not personally convinced. Some members might really know better, but do not express their contrary views; instead, they merely acquiesce to the group's choice. It is their actions that are faulty not necessarily their thought processes.

In sum, it appears that groups can come to poor decisions because conditions exist that (1) promote faulty thinking in group members, and (2) inhibit some members who really know better from dissenting. Both of these conditions can be alleviated by structuring group discussion in ways that promote expression of competing ideas and openness to input from outside (Janis, 1989).

Social identity is a force for conformity to group norms: See Chapter 22.

Compliance rather than conformity may be active in groupthink: See Chapter 18.

■■■ SOME CONCLUDING THOUGHTS

In this chapter, we reviewed the major processes that operate when groups make decisions. It is clear from this material that the people engaged in this enterprise (all of us at one time or another) often do so without paying adequate attention to procedures that would promote better choices. Instead, people in groups are easily influenced by social psychological processes (biased information exchange, groupthink, compliance pressures) that work against quality decisions. Perhaps by understanding these biasing influences, we can hope to alter the course of decision-making processes in families, committees, juries, and policy-making bodies to promote expression and evaluation of multiple points of view before decisions are reached.

■■■ **SUMMARY**

There are many social situations in which groups of individuals discuss problems and reach decisions collectively. Social psychological research has been directed toward understanding both the process and outcome of such group decision making. Early research on group dynamics was particularly interested in the process of discussion and information exchange that takes place when groups try to reach a decision. Analyses of experimental groups suggest that group process goes through at least three stages—orientation, discussion, and decision. The amount of time spent in the first two stages has considerable influence on the quality of decisions reached in the last stage.

In order to reach a decision, groups must adopt an implicit or explicit social decision scheme, a rule or procedure for combining individual choices or preferences to generate a collective choice. The nature of decision schemes has been studied most extensively in the context of jury decision making. One determinant of the type of decision rule adopted is the task solution certainty, the extent to which the decision involves highly subjective or objective bases of validity.

A well-documented finding of research on group decision making is the group polarization phenomenon. In general, a decision reached as the result of group discussion is more extreme, or polarized, than the average judgment or opinion of the individuals who comprise the group. Polarization is apparently the product of specific social decision schemes, as well as the normative and informational social influences that operate during group discussion.

Polarization is related to the quality of group decision making. Many studies of experimental and natural groups indicate many factors may contribute to poor decision outcomes in group settings. Irving Janis concluded that faulty decision making results from a particular cognitive style—groupthink—that characterizes the decision-making processes of cohesive groups. Groupthink is most likely to occur when groups are operating with a sense of urgency. It has been studied most widely in political decision-making contexts.

■■■ **SUGGESTED READINGS**

1. Baron, R. S., Kerr, N. L., & Miller, N. (1992). *Group process, group decision, group action.* Belmont, CA: Brooks/Cole.
2. Dion, K. L., Baron, R. S., & Miller, N. (1970). Why do groups make riskier decisions than individuals? In L. Berkowitz (Ed.), *Advances in experimental social psychology* (Vol. 5, pp. 306–377). New York: Academic Press.
3. Forsyth, D. R. (1990). *Group dynamics,* 2nd ed. Pacific Grove, CA: Brooks/Cole.
4. Janis, I. L. (1982). *Victims of groupthink,* 2nd ed. Boston: Houghton Mifflin.
5. Janis, I. L. (1989). *Crucial decisions: Leadership in policymaking and crisis management.* New York: Free Press.
6. Myers, D. G., & Lamm, H. (1976). The group polarization phenomenon. *Psychological Bulletin, 83,* 602–627.
7. Paulus, P. B. (Ed.). (1983). *Basic group processes.* New York: Springer-Verlag.

CHAPTER 22

SOCIAL IDENTITY
The Group in the Individual

■ **Key Concepts**

In-group
Ethnocentrism
Reference group
Social comparison theory
Social identity theory
Personal identity
Basking in reflected glory (BIRG)
Positive distinctiveness
Disidentification
Relative deprivation
Fraternal deprivation

■ **Chapter Outline**

IN-GROUP LOYALTY AND ETHNOCENTRISM
   Changing Groups or Individuals
   ■ Changing Sexual Behavior
   Membership Groups and Reference Groups

WHY DO IN-GROUPS MATTER?
   Social Comparison: The Search for Consensus
   Social Identity: Groups and the Sense of Self
   The Importance of Distinctiveness
   The Need for Outgroups
   The Importance of Positive Identity
   Minority Self-esteem

FROM SOCIAL IDENTITY TO SOCIAL CHANGE
   Relative Deprivation: When Is Inequality Unfair?
   ■ Response to Injustice—Acceptance versus Collective Action

SOME CONCLUDING THOUGHTS

SUMMARY

On November 18, 1978, more than 900 men, women, and children committed suicide at the encampment of Jonestown in Guyana. Told that their group was under seige, members of the Reverend Jim Jones's People's Temple lined up to receive glasses of red Kool-Aid laced with cyanide. All drank the liquid as they were told, and almost all died within thirty minutes.

■■■

Students Sacrifice Selves to Protect Caste Privilege: In India, scores of middle-class youths have committed suicide to protest government policies opening more jobs to the poor.
—Los Angeles Times, *October 20, 1990*

■■■

". . . I'm willing to die for my colors . . ."
—*"Colors" (Ice-T)*

The dramatic suicides of members of the Jonestown cult and of Indian teenagers illustrate the extremes to which individuals will go on behalf of the groups to which they belong. Fortunately, most of our group memberships do not demand this level of self-sacrifice, but many of the things we do make sense only if they

Jonestown in Guyana, November 1978. ■

are understood as expressions of our identification with a group. Many of our day-to-day choices about what to wear, how to spend leisure time, and what political positions to espouse are influenced by a desire to symbolize or represent our important group memberships.

We are all members of many different types of groups, ranging from small, face-to-face groupings of family and friends to large social categories such as gender, religion, and nationality. For social psychologists, a group is any collection of individuals who recognize that they have something in common—a shared identity. For any individual, the social world is divided into *in-groups* (social categories of which he or she is a member) and *out-groups* (social categories to which he or she does not belong). The relationship between in-groups and out-groups is an area of social psychological study that is covered extensively in Chapters 24 and 25. The present chapter is devoted to research and theory about the relationship between individuals and their in-groups.

■■■ IN-GROUP LOYALTY AND ETHNOCENTRISM

An area of social psychological study is the relationship between in-groups and out-groups. See Chapters 24 and 25.

The psychological meaning of group membership does not seem to be restricted by group size or direct interaction with fellow group members. For some people, national citizenship or social class has as much influence on their behavior as their own immediate family. In-group membership is more than mere cognitive classification; there is emotional significance attached to the social category. Attachment to in-groups and preference for in-groups over out-groups may be a universal characteristic of human social life. Sumner (1906) coined the term **ethnocentrism** to refer to this social psychological phenomenon:

> . . . a differentiation arises between ourselves, the we-group, or in-group, and everybody else, or the others-groups, out-groups. The insiders in a we-group are in a relation of peace, order, law, government, and industry, to each other . . . Ethnocentrism is the technical name for this view of things in which one's own group is the center of everything, and all others are scaled and rated with reference to it . . . Each group nourishes its own pride and vanity, boasts itself superior, exalts its own divinities, and looks with contempt on outsiders . . . (pp. 12–13).

Such group loyalties are apparently acquired early in life. By age six or seven, for instance, children exhibit strong preference for their own nationality, even before the concept of "nation" has been fully understood (Tajfel, Nemeth, Jahoda, Campbell, & Johnson, 1970). And elementary school children show clear evidence of social distance norms—preferring relationships with members of their own social groups and avoiding close personal contact with children of other gender, race, or social class (e.g., Brewer, Ho, Lee, & Miller, 1987).

Changing Groups or Individuals

Kurt Lewin, a major early figure in social psychology, was convinced that people will often do things for the sake of their groups that they could not be convinced to do as individuals. He demonstrated this point with an interesting series of experiments on changing food habits during World War II (Lewin, 1947). During a time when providing for the needs of troops abroad was producing food shortages at home, the goal of the research was to increase housewives' willingness to serve organ meats (such as kidneys, sweetbreads, and beef hearts) as part of regular family meals.

Under the auspices of meetings of Red Cross volunteer groups, some women were exposed to an illustrated lecture about the vitamin and mineral value of these meats and linking the problem of nutrition with the war effort. The lecture included interesting graphics and information on how to prepare the foods, and at the end copies of recipes for "delicious dishes" were distributed to all members of the audience. In other group sessions, women were exposed to the same information, but in the context of a group discussion. Without any direct salesmanship, the women were led into a discussion about how housewives like themselves could overcome their aversion to serving these foods for the sake of nutrition and the war effort. At the end of the meeting, the women were asked to indicate by a show of hands who was willing to try one of these meats during the next week.

A follow-up survey a week or so later revealed that only 3% of the women who had heard the lecture reported serving one of the meats, but 32% of the women who had participated in group discussion did so. Lewin attributed the effectiveness of group-based change to the explicit group norms that were established during discussion and group decision making and the unwillingness of individuals to depart too far from group standards once they had been set. In the absence of group consensus, information alone had little impact.

APPLYING SOCIAL PSYCHOLOGY TO HEALTH
■ ■ ■

Changing Sexual Behavior

The lesson of Lewin's classic experiment has been learned again more recently with efforts to influence individuals to change their sexual practices to reduce risk of contracting AIDS. A number of studies of the effectiveness of information campaigns suggest that gay community norms play a major role in AIDS prevention behavior among gay men. Gay men who belong to communities that support changes in sexual behavior have shown dramatic reductions in high-risk practices and lowered risk for HIV infection across time (Stall, Coates, & Hoff, 1988). Without community support, however, information about the dangers of AIDS may have little effect when delivered to individuals (Fisher, 1988). As with Lewin's earlier research, changes in individual behavior seem to be dependent on group commitment and support.

Membership Groups and Reference Groups

Individuals can be classified as members of many social groups, but not all ingroups have equal importance or impact on individual behavior. For this reason, social psychologists draw a distinction between *membership groups* and *reference*

Bennington College, where Theodore Newcomb conducted his study of reference groups in 1930's.

Newcomb's study of values and attitudes examined the influence of reference groups: See Chapter 1.

groups. Whereas membership groups include any in which a person is recognized by others as belonging, reference groups are those groups that an individual wants to be accepted by and uses as a basis for self-evaluation (Kelley, 1952).

A classic study of the influence of reference groups on individuals' personal values and attitudes is the study conducted by Theodore Newcomb (1943) at Bennington College. At the time Newcomb began his study in 1935, Bennington had a 50-member faculty and a student body of approximately 250. For the most part, the students came from wealthy, privileged family backgrounds and arrived on campus with generally conservative political viewpoints and values. The faculty and staff, on the other hand, held more liberal attitudes associated with the New Deal politics of the time, and liberal positions were widely espoused in the college community.

Over a four-year period, Newcomb studied the political and economic attitudes of Bennington students as they progressed through college. At regular intervals, he measured their attitudes toward issues such as welfare, progressive taxation, labor unions, and economic planning. What he found was a consistent change in student values from the time they entered Bennington until their senior year (Figure 22.1). On average, the students became less conservative in their political and economic attitudes the longer they were at Bennington College. Further, the values acquired in the college community had lasting impact. A follow-up study of Bennington graduates twenty-five years later revealed that they were still less conservative in 1960 than most women of their age and social–economic status (Newcomb, Koenig, Flacks, & Warwick, 1967).

But not all Bennington students exhibited strong changes toward liberal values. Those who became most liberal in their attitudes also tended to be the most active in college life, most popular, and most likely to be identified as leaders. A minority of students retained conservative attitudes throughout their college years, and these women tended to be less involved in college activities, less

FIGURE 22.1

■

Changes in political attitudes of Bennington College students: 1935–1939. (From Newcomb, 1943)

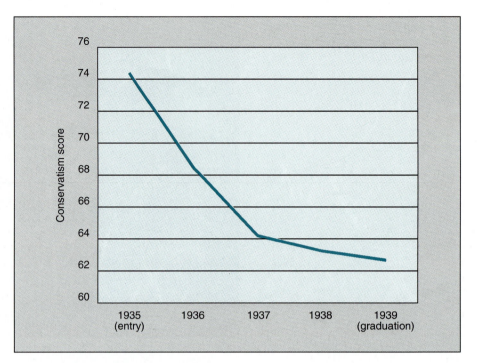

popular, and most likely to retain strong ties to family or off-campus social groups. In other words, just being a member of the college community and exposed to the liberal atmosphere of Bennington College did not inevitably lead to attitude change. What mattered was whether or not the college became an important reference group for the individual student. Those whose reference groups were elsewhere did not identify with the college and also resisted its norms and values.

■■■ WHY DO IN-GROUPS MATTER?

In order to be "good" group members, people often have to sacrifice personal preferences and individuality. Why are group ties so important to individuals? It is clear that belonging to groups provides many benefits to group members, but it also entails costs and obligations. Psychologists and social scientists have generated many theories about why people are willing to pay the price of group membership. We focus in this chapter on two theories that have had the most impact in social psychology—*social comparison theory* and *social identity theory*.

Social Comparison: The Search for Consensus

Festinger's theory of social comparison helps explain how attitudes and self-concept are formed: See Chapter 11.

Leon Festinger's (1954) theory of social comparison was developed to explain how groups influence individual attitudes. Before publishing the formal theory of social comparison, Festinger (1950) put forth an earlier version of the theory which focused on the processes of communication and consensus formation in small groups. His purpose in this earlier paper was to explain why members of groups tend to be so similar in attitudes, values, and behavior.

A basic premise of Festinger's explanation is the idea that people need a sense of subjective validity for their beliefs about themselves and the world around them. Much of our knowledge or understanding about the world we live in does not come from direct personal experience. We may come to learn that ice is cold and walls are solid by direct contact with these objects, but knowledge about what is right or true—especially our knowledge about social groups and social behaviors—often has no such objective referent. In order to achieve a sense of validation of such beliefs, people engage in "social reality testing." Beliefs are seen as valid or appropriate when they are shared by similar others, that is, by members of appropriate reference groups. The more uncertain an individual is about the correctness of a belief or attitude, the more important it becomes to find consensual support for that belief. Similarity to reference groups induces stability and confidence in one's own perceptions.

This need for social reality creates an interesting dynamic relationship between group membership and social influence. First, individuals seek similar others to confirm or validate their beliefs, but once similar others have been identified, beliefs become dependent on agreement with those persons. As a consequence, group members engage in mutual influence in order to maintain subjective validity of their beliefs and values. Any discrepancy between one's own opinion and those of the reference group produces uncertainty and openness to change.

The effect of uncertainty on seeking the company of similar others was first demonstrated experimentally in another classic study by Schachter (1959). In this experiment, female students arrived at the research laboratory and learned that their participation would involve receiving a series of electric shocks. In one experimental condition, the participant was greeted by a researcher who introduced himself as "Dr. Zilstein" and explained that the shocks would be very mild, "more like a tickle than anything unpleasant." In the alternative experimental condition, the same "Dr. Zilstein" appeared with a stethoscope displayed prominently in his white jacket pocket and surrounded by elaborate electrical equipment. Far from reassuring participants, he warned them that "the shocks will be quite painful but, of course, they will do no permanent damage" (p. 13).

What Schachter was trying to do with these experimental variations was to induce different levels of fear and uncertainty in the research participants. Those who were given reassurances about the nature of the upcoming electric shock were assumed to be in a state of low uncertainty and little fear. Those who had been led to anticipate something more severe were assumed to be in a state of relatively high fear and uncertainty about what would happen to them.

At this point in the experiment, the researcher explained to the student that it would take about ten minutes to set up the laboratory equipment, and during that time she could wait in another room. Each participant was given a choice between waiting alone in a separate waiting room or in a classroom down the hall "with some of the other girls here" who were participating in the same experiment. Once the student had indicated her preference between waiting alone or with other participants, she was pleasantly surprised to find out that the experiment was over (no shocks were ever actually delivered). The whole thing had been set up to find out whether individuals in this situation would seek affiliation with others in the same boat.

Schachter (1959) studied the effect of uncertainty on seeking the company of similar others: See Chapter 1.

FIGURE 22.2

■

Choosing company or isolation as a function of fear. Percentage of women in Schachter's experiment who preferred to wait with others or stay alone under high and low fear conditions. (Data from Schachter, 1959)

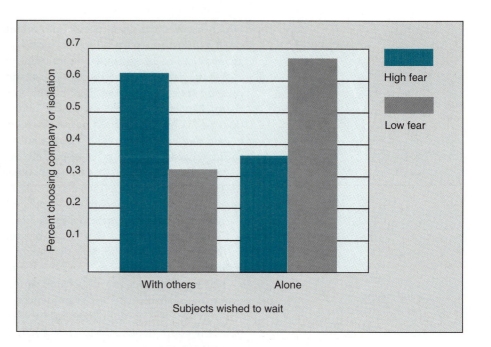

As expected on the basis of Festinger's social comparison theory, women in the high-fear–uncertainty condition showed more desire to be with others than did those in the low-fear condition. Out of thirty-two participants in the high-fear condition, twenty expressed a clear preference to wait with others, whereas only ten out of thirty in the low-fear condition had such a preference (Figure 22.2).

Schachter believed that uncertainty led to the need to be with others, but only with others who were similar to themselves, facing the same situation. This was demonstrated in a later version of the experiment in which participants, after being put through the high-fear condition, were again given a choice between waiting alone or with others down the hall. But this time, the others were not participants in the experiment but students waiting for an exam. With that option, *none* of the research participants chose to wait with others. Apparently, affiliation to reduce uncertainty is selective—only the in-group will do.

Uncertainty not only leads individuals to seek out the company of others of their own kind but also increases susceptibility to influence. In an experiment that combined Schachter's fear-arousal manipulation with an Asch–type conformity study, Darley (1966) demonstrated that individuals who were anticipating electric shock were more likely to conform to other people's judgments on a perceptual task.

In the Darley experiment, during the period in which participants thought they were waiting for the electric shock procedure, they took part in a "hearing acuity test." For this phase of the experiment, the participant listened to a series of tape recordings and counted the number of clicks that occurred during each segment. The respondent gave her estimate of the number after hearing the judgments made by three other individuals, who were actually confederates of the experimenter. For twelve of the eighteen judgments, all three confederates gave an objectively wrong answer. Participants who had been placed in the high-

Asch's (1950) experiment demonstrated that even simple perceptual judgments can be influenced by social conformity in groups: See Chapter 18.

fear (electric shock) condition were more likely to conform to this false majority judgment than were participants who were not anticipating shocks. As in the original Schachter experiment, this conformity effect was particularly strong when the participant believed that the other three people were also going to receive the shocks.

Agreeing with members of one's in-group apparently increases certainty and subjective validity of beliefs and attitudes. Finding out that others disagree reduces certainty—but only if those others are in-group members. Learning that out-groupers do not share our opinions or values does not shake our confidence in the correctness of those beliefs (Orive, 1988). On many issues of values and preferences, we expect to agree with in-group members but not necessarily with everyone. Only in-groupers count as sources of validation, at least for subjective judgments (Gorenflo & Crano, 1989).

Social Identity: Groups and the Sense of Self

Apart from providing support for our views of social reality, the groups we belong to play a very important role in defining who we are and establishing a sense of identity. Gordon Allport (1954) recognized this close relationship between group membership and the self when he wrote:

> Nor do we need to postulate a "consciousness of kind" to explain why people adhere to their own families, clans, ethnic groups. The self could not be itself without them . . . attachment to one's own being is basic to human life . . . and along with this beloved self go all of the person's basic memberships . . . (p. 30)

Clothing and hairstyles often signal distinctive group identities. ■

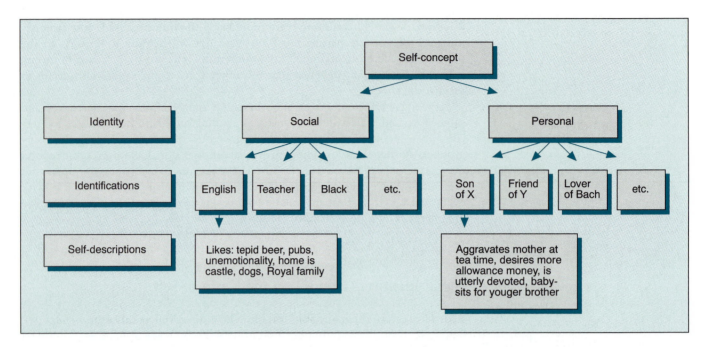

FIGURE 22.3

■

Personal identities and social identities. (From M. A. Hogg, & D. Abrams, (1988), *Social identifications,* London: Routledge, p. 24.)

More recently, this idea has been elaborated in the *theory of social identity* developed by Henri Tajfel and John Turner (Tajfel, 1978, 1979, 1981; Turner, 1985). This theory draws a fundamental distinction between personal identity and social identity as different aspects of an individual's self-concept. **Personal identity** refers to those idiosyncratic self-descriptions that differentiate the individual from other members of his or her social groups, that is, the things that make a person unique. **Social identity,** on the other hand, refers to "that part of an individual's self-concept which derives from his knowledge of his membership of a social group (or groups) together with the value and emotional significance attached to that membership" (Tajfel, 1978, p. 63).

Although self-esteem is usually defined as one's personal self-evaluation, people also have a "collective self-esteem" which reflects pride in their group memberships (Luhtanen & Crocker, 1992). As Hogg and Abrams (1988) put it, "People derive their identity (their sense of self, their self-concept) in great part from the social categories to which they belong. The group is thus in the individual . . ." (p. 19). Figure 22.3 illustrates social versus personal identity.

Personal and social identity represent different levels of self-categorization (Turner, Hogg, Oakes, Reicher, & Wetherell, 1987). How individuals see themselves and behave at any one time will depend on which particular personal or social identification is salient. When an individual shifts from personal to social identity, his or her self-concept becomes *depersonalized* and the self is defined in terms of shared characteristics of the in-group. As one viewer of the 1993 Tournament of Roses parade put it, "For an instant, all the pain, the problems and the hatred around the city were swept away . . . It was like I wasn't an individual but a part of a whole group" (*Los Angeles Times,* January 2, 1993, p. 1).

When a particular group identity is salient, individuals also adapt their behavior to conform to characteristics that are typical of the in-group. They seek to behave in ways that fit the distinctive characteristics of that group. The processes of self-categorization and social identification can help account for a wide range of group behaviors, including formation of group norms, conformity, group polarization, and crowd behavior (Turner et al., 1987; Turner, 1991). Figure 22.4 describes the process leading from in-group formation to group behavior, according to Social Identity Theory.

Gender Identity. An experiment by Hogg and Turner (1987) on gender identity illustrates how social identity affects perceptions of the self. In this study, male and female college students participated in a discussion under one of two conditions. In the personal identity condition, the discussion was between two people of the same sex and the two discussants represented different sides of the issue. In the social identity condition, the discussion was among four people—two males and two females—and the sexes differed on the issue. Following the social interaction, participants in the condition where sex identity was salient characterized themselves as more typical of their sex and attributed more masculine or feminine traits to themselves than in the personal identity condition. (Interestingly, participation in the sex-salient discussion condition lowered self-esteem for women, but raised self-esteem among the male participants.)

This experiment demonstrates that salient social identities can alter how we think about ourselves and also, potentially, how we actually behave. For instance, when a woman's female identity is not particularly salient, she may think of herself in terms of personal traits that are not relevant to masculinity or femininity, such as organized, neat, and politically conservative. Under these circumstances, her social and political behaviors may be dictated by these personal characteristics (she cleans up after her adolescent son and votes for a Republican congressman). When her female identity is made salient, however, this same woman may think about herself in terms of characteristics that make her more like other women and distinct from most men—nurturant and dependent. Under these circumstances, her behaviors may change to be consistent with this alternative self-image (she ignores conservative policies and votes for a social welfare program).

The Importance of Distinctiveness

In a complex social world, individuals have many possible social identities available to them. Which identity is adopted at any one time will depend on which group distinctions are salient in the social context. Social categories are defined in contrast to one another. As Tajfel (1979) put it, we are what we are because *they* are not what we are. Individuals adopt social identities that are distinctive and exclusive within a particular context (Brewer, 1991).

The shifting nature of in-group categorizations in different social contexts is charmingly illustrated by a passage from H. G. Wells (1905), *A Modern Utopia*. Describing a certain botanist, Wells writes:

> He has a strong feeling for systematic botanists as against plant physiologists, whom he regards as lewd and evil scoundrels in this relation; but he has a strong feeling for all botanists and indeed all biologists, as against physicists, and those who profess the exact sciences, all of whom he regards as dull, mechanical, ugly-minded scoundrels in this relation; but he has a strong feeling for all who profess what he calls Science, as against psychologists, sociologists, philosophers, and literary men, whom

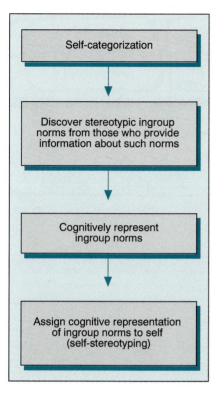

FIGURE 22.4

■

A model of the relationship between in-group formation and conformity to group norms. (From Hogg, & Abrams, 1988, p. 172.)

he regards as wild, foolish, immoral scoundrels in this relation; but he has a strong feeling for all educated men as against the working man, whom he regards as a cheating, lying, loafing, drunken, thievish, dirty scoundrel in this relation; but as soon as the working man is comprehended together with these others, as *Englishmen* . . . (p. 322)

Wells's insightful description of levels of social identity was confirmed experimentally in a study by Abrams and Hogg (1988). Students from Dundee, Scotland, listened to recordings of two speakers with different accents. In one version, a speaker from another Scottish town (Glasgow) was paired with a Dundee (hometown) speaker. In another version, the same Glasgow accent was paired with a speaker with an English accent. In the first condition, where the Glasgow speaker was classified as an out-group member, he received much lower ratings from Dundee students than the same speaker in the second context, where he was classified as an in-group member (Scottish as opposed to English). (Presumably, the speaker with the English accent could also have achieved in-group status if he had been paired with another speaker with a German or Russian accent.)

The Need for Out-groups. The effect of social context on group identification raises the question of whether in-group loyalty depends on the presence of a specific out-group. There is no doubt that salience of in-group identity is enhanced when a contrasting out-group is also made salient. Wilder and Shapiro (1984) conducted an experiment with students at Rutgers University in which participants worked in a booth with a pennant of some kind displayed prominently on the wall. The pennant was symbolic of in-group identity (Rutgers University), a relevant out-group (Princeton University), or an irrelevant group (the New York Yankees).

The participants' first task in the experiment was to read a list of fifty words. Later they were given a word recognition test in which they were shown a new list of words and asked to circle those that had been seen previously. The recognition test list included ten words associated with Rutgers (in-group words), some of which had not been in the original list. Participants circled more in-group words (showed more false recognition) when they were in a booth with *either* a Rutgers or a Princeton pennant than in the Yankees-pennant condition.

Wilder and Shapiro's results indicate that the presence of an out-group cue enhances in-group awareness. But they also indicate that in-group cues alone

These men are clearly identifying with their team. Are they "basking in reflected glory?" ■

have a similar effect. This was also demonstrated in a field experiment with members of fifth-grade handball teams (Rehm, Steinleitner, & Lilli, 1987). The children on one team were given bright orange shirts to wear, as a symbol of team identity. Members of the opposing team wore their own shirts, which varied in shape and color. Thus, for the "orange team," the in-group was made salient and distinctive, while the out-group was less distinct. For members of the opposing team, it was the out-group that was more distinctive in this setting. Observations of the subsequent games revealed that the children on the orange-shirt team played much more aggressively (were more concerned that their own team won) than those on the nondistinct team. The distinctiveness of the in-group apparently had more effect on level of identification with the team than did out-group distinctiveness.

The Importance of Positive Identity

Context is not the only factor that influences the strength of social identification with particular in-groups. People also seek group identifications that contribute to enhancing their positive self-esteem. When our group does well, we often take personal pride in the group's achievements even when we had nothing to do with attaining them. Robet Cialdini and his colleagues (Cialdini, Borden, Thorne, Walker, Freeman, & Sloan, 1976) labeled this effect "basking in re-flected glory" (BIRG). They demonstrated this aspect of social identity in a clever field study conducted at seven different university campuses across the country during the college football season. On Monday mornings, following regular football games, members of Cialdini's research team went around their respective campuses counting the number of school sweatshirts that were being worn. They found that the number of sweatshirts was significantly higher when the school's team had won the football game on the previous Saturday than when their team had lost. In fact, the larger the margin of victory in favor of the school's team, the more sweatshirts were displayed.

Identification with one's team can have important effects on personal self-concept as well. One experiment found that after sports fans watched a live basketball game, their estimates of their own skills were influenced by the outcome of the game. When their team was successful, fans predicted they would perform better in a later experimental task than when their team had lost (Hirt, Zillman, Erikson, & Kennedy, 1992).

Social identity theory also recognizes the role of group identification in achieving positive self-esteem. An individual's sense of self-worth is enhanced when his or her in-group has **positive distinctiveness**—when the in-group can be perceived as better than relevant out-groups on some important attributes. In general, individuals identify more strongly with groups that are successful and have high status, particularly when the high-status group is a distinctive minority (Ellemers, Van Doosje, Van Knippenberg, & Wilke, 1992). But the relationship between social identity and self-esteem works two ways. Individuals are more likely to identify with groups that are positively valued, but they also seek positive valuation of groups with which they identify. Enhancement of the in-group is as much a consequence of social identity as a cause.

Some research even indicates that social identity with a group may be increased when the group is threatened or stigmatized. Results of an experiment by Turner and his colleagues (Turner et al., 1984) demonstrated that when individuals are committed to group membership, in-group defeat produces even higher levels of in-group preference than in-group success. Comstock (1991) has argued that the formation of gay and lesbian social identities in the United States has been largely in response to discrimination and oppression. Despite the fact that most gay men and lesbian women could avoid being identified in terms of their sexual orientation if they chose, the numbers who openly identify themselves as homosexual has increased since the 1950s, at the same time that political, verbal, and physical attacks on this group have increased. This appears to be a spiraling process, whereby oppression is met by stronger identification and greater oppression, leading to the current situation in which gays and lesbians constitute a politically active minority with strong group pride.

Minority Self-esteem

The role of group identification in maintaining individual self-esteem is of particular interest in the case of disadvantaged social groups, such as ethnic minorities. One might expect that members of such groups would suffer from low self-esteem. The effects of stigmatization and negative expectancies from the majority and of negative social comparisons could make it very difficult for members of disadvantaged social categories to achieve or maintain positive self-esteem. Yet many studies of self-esteem among African-Americans and other minority groups have not confirmed that low self-esteem is widespread in these populations. On the contrary, average self-esteem is often quite high (Crocker & Major, 1989; Cross, 1985; Rosenberg, 1979).

Stigmatization and negative expectancies affect minority groups: See Chapters 16 and 23.

Negative social comparisons usually affect individual self-esteem: See Chapter 11.

How do disadvantaged and stigmatized minorities maintain self-esteem in the face of discrimination and prejudice? One possibility is that they deny (at least psychologically) their group identity. This is suggested by the results of a classic study of racial identity among African-American children conducted in the 1940s (Clark & Clark, 1947). Using a projective technique to assess perceptions of racial groups, the Clarks asked African-American school children to choose among a set of four dolls in response to a series of questions. The dolls were identical except for coloring: Two of the dolls were white with blond hair, and two were brown with black hair. The children (who ranged in age from three to seven years old) were asked to pick the doll 'that you like best to play with . . . ," "that is a nice doll . . . ," and "that looks like you."

Of the 253 African-American children who participated in the Clarks' study, 33% chose a white doll rather than a brown doll in response to the request to pick a doll that "looks like you." More significantly, 67% selected a white doll as "nice" and 59% preferred a white doll to a brown doll as the one they liked best to play with. A majority of the African-American children showed an evaluative bias in favor of the out-group over the in-group, even though almost all of the children were able to identify correctly which dolls were "white" and which were "colored."

The findings from the doll preference studies led social psychologists at that time to conclude that racial identity does not provide for positive self-esteem among African-Americans and that personal esteem may have to be achieved at the cost of **disidentification** with their social group. A poignant example is the seven-year-old African-American boy who told the researcher in the Clarks' study that he is actually white but "I look brown because I got a suntan in the summer" (p. 178).

In contrast to the disidentification hypothesis, more recent social psychological theory and research suggests that self-esteem of minority-group members may be enhanced by embracing rather than denying their social identity. Identification with the in-group may serve as a buffer between the individual and the negative effects of social prejudice and discrimination. Crocker and Major (1989) propose three different ways in which identification with a stigmatized group may actually be used to protect a positive self-concept. Two of these use selective social comparison. First, as we have already mentioned, individuals tend to compare themselves primarily with other members of their own in-groups. By restricting their frame of reference to the in-group, members of disadvantaged groups may avoid negative comparisons with the more privileged majority.

In-group social comparison is facilitated by physical isolation or segregation of in-group and out-group. In an integrated social context, comparisons between groups may be more difficult to avoid. In these settings, minority-group members may adopt a second strategy for preserving positive distinctiveness by rejecting the values of the society that place their group at a disadvantage and instead emphasizing attributes or abilities at which their own group excels. In the workplace, for instance, women tend to value high pay and opportunity for promotion less than men do, and place greater value on security and interpersonal relationships—areas where women are not so disadvantaged. In studies of sports teams, it is found that losing teams tend to see their opponents as playing dirty, emphasizing their own good sportsmanship by comparison (Lalonde, 1992). Group members also tend to exaggerate differences when they favor the in-group, but underestimate differences that favor the out-group (Brewer, 1979).

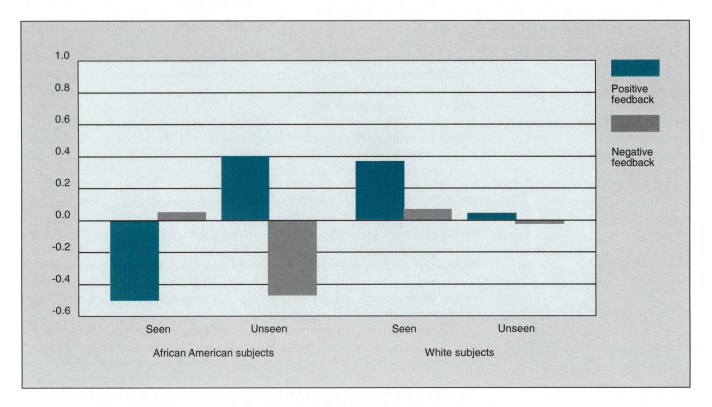

FIGURE 22.5

Changes in self-esteem following positive or negative feedback. When minority subjects knew they could be seen by their evaluator, feedback was apparently attributed to racial biases rather than to personal attributes. (From Crocker et al., 1991, p. 225.)

A third way in which members of stigmatized groups may preserve self-esteem is to attribute negative experiences to prejudice against the group as a whole. Loss of a job can be devastating to self-esteem, but if it is seen as the result of discrimination against one's group, the individual may be less likely to experience the loss as a personal failure.

The self-protective effect of attributing negative feedback to prejudice was demonstrated in a study that experimentally manipulated perceptions of prejudice (Crocker, Voelkl, Testa, & Major, 1991). In this experiment, female participants wrote an essay that was then critically reviewed by a male evaluator. Earlier in the experiment, the women had received an opinion questionnaire supposedly completed by the male reviewer, which revealed that he either was or was not generally prejudiced against women. Women who received a negative evaluation from a *nonprejudiced* reviewer suffered more negative affect and loss of self-esteem than those who received the same negative feedback from someone who was clearly prejudiced against their sex in general.

In a second experiment, similar attribution effects were found with black subjects and white evaluators. In this case, black students received either positive or negative evaluations from a white who either could see them or could not see them. The researchers reasoned that when blacks knew that the evaluator could see them, they could attribute their evaluations to racial prejudice, but when they could not be seen, this attribution would be difficult to make. Consistent with that assumption, participants showed lowered self-esteem in response to negative feedback only when their evaluator could not seem them (Figure 22.5).

Interestingly, a parallel effect was also obtained for positive evaluations. When a black subject received positive feedback from a white evaluator who could not see that he was black, it had more positive effect on his self-esteem than when he could be seen by the evaluator. Apparently, positive evaluations can also be attributed to race rather than personal characteristics. While such attributions protect the individual from negative evaluations, they also, unfortunately, reduce the benefit of positive feedback.

■ ■ ■ FROM SOCIAL IDENTITY TO SOCIAL CHANGE

Group identification among members of disadvantaged or low-status social groups raises interesting questions about how individuals view the position of their own groups within society as a whole. Social identity researchers have long been interested in the issue of why some members of low-status groups seem to accept the status system that puts their group at a disadvantage, whereas others perceive status differentials as unfair and seek to change the system on which they are based.

Relative Deprivation: When Is Inequality Unfair?

A great deal of research on social justice supports the idea that individuals' feelings of being deprived or disadvantaged are based on the comparisons they make rather than the absolute value of their own condition. This principle is dramatically illustrated by the case of young members of the upper castes of India cited at the beginning of this chapter. By any objective standards, the Brahmin, Kshatriya, and Vaishya castes were doing quite well, even in the face of government economic reforms designed to benefit the disadvantaged castes. Yet the perception that their own caste was losing position relative to the lower castes created a sense of comparative disadvantage that was sufficient to motivate dramatic protest against the reforms.

Feelings of resentment and the sense of injustice that arise from perceiving that one has less than one deserves (compared with others) is called **relative deprivation.** The concept of relative deprivation was developed by social scientists during World War II to explain some paradoxical findings that emerged in the study of morale among American soldiers (Stouffer, Suchman, DeVinney, Star, & Williams, 1949). Researchers found, for instance, that soldiers in air force units, where rates of promotion were quite high, had *more* complaints about the promotion system than soldiers in the military police, where promotions were few and far between. Equally surprising, they found that African-American soldiers who were stationed in the southern United States (where overt discrimination based on race was very visible) had *higher* morale than African-American soldiers stationed in the less racist northern states. Stouffer and his colleagues explained these anomalous results in terms of different standards of comparison used by soldiers in different units. Compared with peers who were advancing at a rapid rate, air force soldiers who had not yet been promoted felt deprived, even though their objective chances of promotion were higher than those of soldiers in other units. Similarly, the high morale of African-American soldiers stationed in the South may have derived from comparisons with African-American civilians who fared very poorly. African-American soldiers in the North, on the other hand, may have felt deprived relative to civilian African-Americans in that region who were earning higher wages in war-related factory jobs.

Members of disadvantaged groups in general may not feel deprived or aggrieved if they compare themselves with similarly disadvantaged others. Women professionals, for instance, tend to feel satisfied with their jobs, despite lower pay and status, as long as they compare their outcomes with those of other female colleagues and not with male colleagues (Zanna, Crosby, & Loewenstein, 1987). Since individuals do tend to limit their interpersonal social comparisons to members of their own in-groups, does this mean that women and other economically and politically disadvantaged groups never resent their position relative to men or higher status groups? The answer to that question rests on an important distinction between the experience of relative deprivation at the personal level and what Runciman (1966) called fraternal deprivation. **Fraternal deprivation** arises from comparisons between the outcomes of one's in-group as a whole and those of more advantaged groups. Whereas personal deprivation depends on interpersonal comparisons with similar others, fraternal deprivation is based on intergroup comparisons between dissimilar groups.

Feelings of personal deprivation and fraternal deprivation are not necessarily closely connected. Indeed, it is frequently found that members of disadvantaged groups perceive that their group is discriminated against, but report that they personally have not experienced any discrimination (Crosby, 1982; Taylor, Wright, Moghaddam, & Lalonde, 1990). Feelings of personal relative deprivation may make individuals feel resentful and unhappy, but they rarely lead to collective action. It is those who are most concerned about differences between in-group and out-group who are likely to participate in efforts to change the social system. Among African-Americans, for instance, perception of fraternal deprivation is much more important than personal deprivation as a predictor of support for the civil rights movement and participation in riots (Vanneman & Pettigrew, 1972; Walker & Pettigrew, 1984). Similarly, French-speaking Canadians are much more likely to support the Quebec nationalist movement if they perceive that French Canadians as a whole are disadvantaged economically compared with English-speaking Canadians. Relative deprivation at the personal level, however, had no relation to nationalist attitudes (Guimond & Dubé-Simard, 1983).

APPLYING SOCIAL PSYCHOLOGY TO POLITICS
■ ■ ■

Response to Injustice—Acceptance versus Collective Action

The perception that one's in-group is being treated unjustly appears to be an important factor in social activism, but it is not the whole story. Historically, many disadvantaged groups seem to learn to live with inequities rather than protest on behalf of their group. In an experimental study of perceived injustice, Martin, Brickman, and Murray (1984) presented female participants with descriptions of a fictitious company in which salary levels for men and women sales managers were different. They found that the greater the discrepancy between male and female salaries, the greater the feelings of collective relative deprivation among the women participants. However, this was not sufficient to motivate collective action. Only some of the women who perceived the injustice thought they would be willing to engage in actions such as work slowdowns or protest meetings.

According to social identity theory, an individual's response to status differences between in-group and out-group will depend on whether their belief system focuses on *social mobility* or *social change* (Tajfel & Turner, 1986; Taylor & McKirnen, 1984). Social mobility refers to a belief that the status system is flexible and permeable. This means that individuals can hope to move upward in the status hierarchy, even if they start out in a low-status group. As long as individuals believe they can dissociate from their social group and improve their own personal lot, they have little motivation to change the system. Personal identity is more important than social identity for achieving positive status.

On the other hand, when individuals believe that the status system is inflexible and that movement between groups is blocked, then their own opportunities for positive identity are tied to their group membership. Under these circumstances, social identity dominates over personal identity, and individuals are motivated to engage in collective efforts to change their in-group's power and status position. These predictions were borne out in an experimental study by Wright, Taylor, and Moghaddam (1990), in which participants were rejected from entrance in a high-status advantaged group because of a quota that had been placed on entry to the group. Even when the quota was very small, most students preferred to respond to this situation through individual actions such as requesting reconsideration or individual protest. Only when the high-status group was completely closed (a quota of 0%) did participants show a strong interest in collective protest.

■ ■ ■ SOME CONCLUDING THOUGHTS

Social identity theory furnishes us with a link between the social systems studied by sociologists, economists, and political scientists and the psychology of the individual that is of most interest to social psychologists. Individuals participate in the larger society through their social group memberships, and much of individual social behavior can be understood by knowing the social groups with which the person identifies. When an individual identifies with a larger collective, the values, successes, and failures of that group become part of that person's self-concept. As the title of this chapter suggests, not only do individuals exist within groups but also, in a psychological sense, groups exist in individuals.

■ ■ ■ SUMMARY

Individual acts of self-sacrifice demonstrate the importance of group loyalty in human behavior. Ethnocentrism is the general term for loyalty to one's own groups (in-groups) and the tendency to prefer in-groups over out-groups. A distinction is made between membership groups (all those to which a particular individual belongs) and reference groups (those that the individual actively identifies with).

The two major theories of group identification are social comparison theory and social identity theory. Social comparison theory emphasizes the individual's need for knowledge and certainty as the primary basis for group identification. Social identity theory emphasizes the need for self-categorization and positive distinctiveness as the bases of group identification. Minority-group members face a conflict between social identity and the search for positive distinctiveness. Sometimes this conflict is resolved by disidentification from the social group. Alternatively, stigmatized groups may adopt a sense of group pride that buffers self-esteem of individual group members.

Members of disadvantaged social groups experience relative deprivation—the sense of injustice that arises from getting less than one deserves in comparison with others. Fraternal deprivation refers to feelings of relative deprivation on behalf of one's in-group as a whole. Fraternal deprivation is an important factor in motivating social activism and the formation of collective movements. Social identity provides a critical link between the psychology of the individual and the larger societal context in which individuals function.

■ ■ ■ SUGGESTED READINGS

1. Brewer, M. B. (1991). The social self: On being the same and different at the same time. *Personality and Social Psychology Bulletin, 17,* 475–482.

2. Crocker, J., & Major, B. (1989). Social stigma and self-esteem: The self-protective properties of stigma. *Psychological Review, 96,* 608–630.

3. Crosby, F. (1982). *Relative deprivation and working women.* New York: Oxford University Press.

4. Festinger, L. (1950). Informal social communication. *Psychological Review, 57,* 271–282.

5. Hogg, M. A., & Abrams, D. (1988). *Social identifications.* London: Routledge.

6. Newcomb, T. M. (1943). *Personality and social change.* New York: Dryden Press.

7. Tajfel, H., & Turner, J. C. (1986). The social identity theory of intergroup relations. In S. Worchel & W. Austin (Eds.), *Psychology of intergroup relations* (pp. 7–24). Chicago: Nelson-Hall.

8. Turner, J. C., Hogg, M., Oakes, P., Reicher, S., & Wetherell, M. (1987). *Rediscovering the social group: A self-categorization theory.* Oxford: Basil Blackwell.

PART V

INTERGROUP RELATIONS
The Psychology of Conflict

CHAPTER 23
Intergroup Attitudes: Prejudice and Stereotypes

CHAPTER 24
Discrimination: The Behavioral Consequences of Prejudice

CHAPTER 25
Intergroup Relations: Conflict or Cooperation?

INTERGROUP ATTITUDES
Prejudice and Stereotypes

■ Key Concepts

Stereotypes
Prejudice
Category accentuation
Illusory correlation
In-group bias
Ethnocentrism
Out-group homogeneity
Authoritarian personality
Displaced aggression
Belief congruence theory
Social-role theory

■ Chapter Outline

ATTITUDES TOWARD SOCIAL GROUPS: COGNITION AND EMOTION
    Stereotypes: The Content of Category Schemas
    Prejudice: The Emotional Side of Intergroup Perception
    The Relationship Between Stereotypes and Prejudice

CATEGORIZATION: THE COGNITIVE BASIS OF STEREOTYPES AND PREJUDICE
    Accentuation: Enhancing Category Distinctions
    Learning Stereotypes: Illusory Correlations
    In-group–Out-group Categorization
    ■ Cross-racial Recognition and the Eyewitness

OTHER CONTRIBUTING FACTORS: PERSONALITY AND SOCIETY
    Personality Factors
    Social Learning Factors
    Unconscious Prejudice
    ■ Overcoming the Habit of Prejudice

SOME CONCLUDING THOUGHTS

SUMMARY

You've got to be taught to be afraid
Of people whose eyes are oddly made
Or people whose skin is a diff'rent shade
You've got to be carefully taught.

You've got to be taught before it's too late
Before you are six or seven or eight
To hate all the people your relatives hate
You've got to be carefully taught.

—Rogers and Hammerstein, South Pacific

■ ■ ■

A basic fact of social life is that we divide people into categories that distinguish one kind of person from another. Gender, ethnic origin, age, physical stature, political and religious beliefs, and many other features categorize us in more or less meaningful ways. Social categories are far more than statistical conveniences. The categories to which individuals are assigned shape their lives and the nature of their interpersonal relationships.

In an earlier chapter, we discuss how social category schemas influence the way we process information about persons who happen to be members of the category. In the present chapter, we consider in more detail what social psychologists know about the structure and content of such group schemas and about their origins. Much of the work that has been done in this area in the past thirty years stems from an influential book written by Gordon Allport in 1954, entitled *The Nature of Prejudice*. Throughout this chapter, we refer to ideas and issues raised in that book. We begin with a discussion of the nature of stereotypes and prejudice and the relationship between them. In later sections of the chapter, we examine factors that contribute to the creation and maintenance of prejudice and stereotypes.

Social category schemas influence information processing: See Chapter 8.

■ ■ ■ ATTITUDES TOWARD SOCIAL GROUPS: COGNITION AND EMOTION

Social attitudes have cognitive, affective, and behavioral components: See Chapter 2.

Social attitudes can be described in terms of cognitive (knowledge), affective (feeling), and behavioral components. Attitudes toward specific social groups can be decomposed into cognitive and affective components (Esses, Haddock, & Zanna, 1993; Stangor, Sullivan, & Ford, 1991). When applied to social groups, the cognitive content of attitudes is referred to as **stereotypes** and the affective–emotional component as **prejudice.**

Stereotypes: The Content of Category Schemas

Stereotypes are generalized beliefs about the characteristics and behaviors of a group taken as a whole. Sometimes stereotypes are conceptualized as the image

TABLE 23.1

■

National Stereotypes in the United States

Following are the four characteristics most frequently assigned to ten nationalities by U.S. college students in 1933. How many of these stereotypes do you think would still be held today?

Germans	**Italians**
scientific-minded	artistic
industrious	impulsive
stolid	passionate
intelligent	quick-tempered

Irish	**English**
pugnacious	sportsmanlike
quick-tempered	conventional
witty	conservative
honest	intelligent

Chinese	**Japanese**
superstitious	intelligent
sly	industrious
conservative	progressive
loyal to family ties	shrewd

Negroes	**Jews**
superstitious	shrewd
lazy	mercenary
happy-go-lucky	industrious
ignorant	grasping

Americans	**Turks**
industrious	cruel
intelligent	very religious
materialistic	treacherous
ambitious	sensual

From Katz & Braly, 1933.

we have of a *typical* group member. The classic study of national stereotypes by Katz and Braly (1933) asked college students to check those traits "most typical" of members of particular racial and ethnic groups. Using this methodology, the researchers found that Germans were characterized as scientific and industrious, Turks as cruel and religious, and Jews as shrewd and mercenary (Table 23.1).

Similar methods have been applied to the study of gender stereotypes. More recent research has combined assessment of the content of national stereotypes and of gender stereotypes, with interesting results. Descriptions of the "typical"

Discrimination is the behavioral consequence of stereotypes and prejudice: See Chapter 24.

member of a particular nationality turn out to be quite similar to stereotypes of the typical *male* of that nationality. However, when respondents are asked to describe the typical *female* of the same nationality, feminine stereotypes tend to intrude into the national stereotype. For instance, Russians (and Russian men) are characterized by U.S. college students as "competitive," "conforming," "traditional," "scientific," and "industrious." Russian women, too, are described as "conforming" and "traditional," but they also are stereotyped as "devoted to others" and "emotional," traits that do not appear in the national stereotype by itself (Eagly & Kite, 1987).

Another way to think about stereotypes is that they are traits that are perceived to be more *common,* or frequent, among members of a particular social category than among others (Brigham, 1971). Having two legs may be a feature typical of members of a particular social group, but it is not likely to be a component of the group stereotype. This feature does not distinguish members of that group from members of almost all other human groups. In a recent study of national and ethnic stereotypes, Jonas and Hewstone (1986) found that ratings of the typicality of a trait and estimates of its relative frequency in a social group were highly related. Stereotypes are apparently characteristics that are considered both typical of members of a social group and more common to that group than to others.

Gender stereotypes are one of several kinds of social category schemas: See Chapter 8.

Prejudice: The Emotional Side of Intergroup Perceptions

In terms of definition and cognitive process, stereotypes are not unlike schemas of other natural categories such as objects, actions, and situations. We have a concept of the typical elementary school teacher in the same sense that we have a concept of the typical apple, or the typical baseball game. What most distinguishes social category schemas from others is the emotional content associated with our perceptions of social groups (Stangor, Sullivan, & Ford, 1991). Social schemas are rarely neutral. Both the content of the beliefs we have about category characteristics and the emotional reactions we have toward category labels are usually positively or negatively charged.

Technically, prejudice refers to either positive or negative affective reactions toward a group as a whole. It is possible to be favorably disposed toward some groups and antagonistic toward others. However, the term is more commonly used to refer to negative evaluations of groups other than one's own. Most social psychological research on prejudice and its consequences has focused on the more narrow definition of prejudice as negative affect directed toward all members of a specific social category.

The Relationship Between Stereotypes and Prejudice

Stereotypes are often viewed as the beliefs that support prejudicial attitudes. However, the relationship between the cognitive and the emotional components of group schemas is not always so simple. For one thing, the content of stereotypes, even of hated groups, is not entirely negative. Even racially prejudiced individuals tend to believe that African Americans are "athletic" and "musical," traits that may be considered neutral or even positive. In a methodological examination of the relationship between prejudicial attitudes and stereotyping, Brigham (1971) found that the degree to which stereotypic traits were attributed to a social group was only moderately correlated with negative attitudes toward that group.

Further, the same beliefs can be viewed in both positive and negative ways. In the 1930s, Americans believed that Germans were stolid and orderly. After the outbreak of World War II, these same characteristics were seen as being cold and compulsive. Clearly, the emotional tone of the schema was influenced by the nature of the historical relationship between the two nations, but the content of the beliefs came from other sources.

Although stereotypes and prejudice are not identical, the processes of categorization and schema formation that give rise to stereotypes also provide the cognitive underpinnings for prejudice. The two are closely linked, both theoretically and empirically, and it is usually considered appropriate to study them together (Bar-Tal, Graumann, Kruglanski, & Stroebe, 1989).

■ ■ ■ CATEGORIZATION: THE COGNITIVE BASIS OF STEREOTYPES AND PREJUDICE

Allport (1954) explicitly recognized that both stereotypes and prejudice have their roots in the cognitive processes associated with categorization. Categories, he recognized, are necessary for organizing and making sense of the social and physical environment. Social categories become problematic, however, because of what he called the "principle of least effort," the tendency to rely on oversimplified generalizations and to resist information that complicates our categorical distinctions. Allport's ideas clearly anticipated the results of later research on confirmatory biases.

Accentuation: Enhancing Category Distinctions

Confirmatory biases help maintain stereotypes: See Chapter 8.

The role of categorization processes in social perception was also emphasized by Henri Tajfel (1969). Tajfel's theory of **category accentuation** helped to explain the formation and maintenance of social stereotypes. Accentuation is a process of assimilation and contrast that occurs whenever we group objects into separate categories. Once such a categorization has been imposed, our subjective judgments of the objects are changed. We tend to judge items within the same category as more similar (assimilation), and items from different categories as more dissimilar (contrast), than they actually are. The result is an increase in perceived homogeneity within categories and distinctiveness between categories.

A concrete demonstration of category accentuation was furnished in a judgment experiment by Tajfel and Wilkes (1963). The stimuli in that experiment were eight lines, varying in length from 16.2 cm to 22.9 cm (Figure 23.1). For some judges, the lines were presented without labels. For others, the four shorter lines were labeled with the letter A and the four longer lines were labeled B.

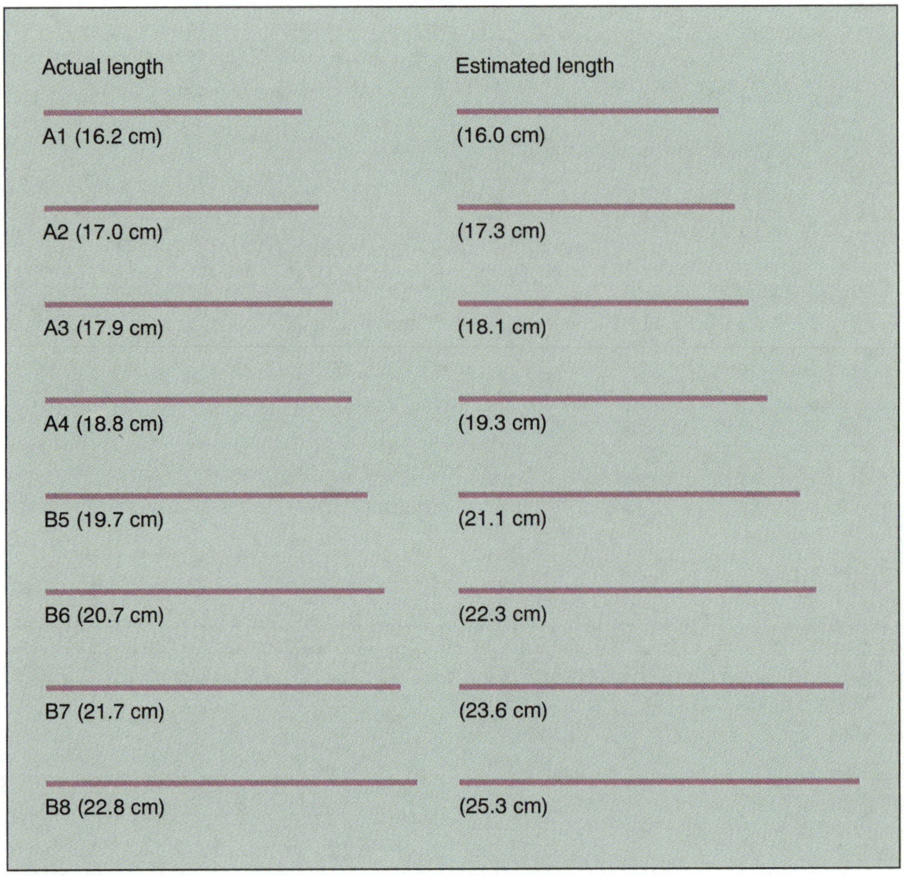

FIGURE 23.1

■

Judgments of length of lines: assimilation and contrast. (From Tajfel & Wilkes, 1963.) When subjects were asked to estimate the lengths of these lines, lines labeled "B" were systematically overestimated relative to lines labeled "A."

Actual length	Estimated length
A1 (16.2 cm)	(16.0 cm)
A2 (17.0 cm)	(17.3 cm)
A3 (17.9 cm)	(18.1 cm)
A4 (18.8 cm)	(19.3 cm)
B5 (19.7 cm)	(21.1 cm)
B6 (20.7 cm)	(22.3 cm)
B7 (21.7 cm)	(23.6 cm)
B8 (22.8 cm)	(25.3 cm)

Judges were shown the lines, one at a time in random order, and asked to estimate the length of each. The average estimates produced by judges in the categorization (label) condition is also shown in Figure 23.1. Compared with those in the no–label condition, these judges exaggerated the difference in length between lines labeled A and lines labeled B. This effect was particularly marked for the two lines at the boundary of the categories. The difference between the perceived length of the longest line in category A and the shortest line in category B was much greater than the actual difference between the two lines. As a result, the perceived distinctiveness of the two categories was accentuated. Similar effects are obtained when people judge heights of men and women (Biernat, Manis, & Nelson, 1991). On average, men are taller than women, but this difference is exaggerated when judges make estimates of the heights of individual males and females.

By the same process, members of a social group are perceived to have similar attitudes and to be different from members of other groups, even when the group assignments have been arbitrary (Wilder, 1981). In general, the more salient category distinctions are, the less we notice individual differences within categories and the more we see each group as a single, homogenous unit. Once categories have been formed, we are biased toward information that enhances the differences between categories and less attentive to information about similarities between members of different categories (Krueger, Rothbart, & Sriram, 1989). These effects of categorization are now widely recognized as the psychological foundation for social stereotyping and intergroup prejudice (Hamilton & Trolier, 1986; Taylor, 1981a; Wilder, 1986).

Learning Stereotypes: Illusory Correlations

Stereotypes may be acquired in many different ways, but one important source of stereotype content may be an association between a social category and particularly distinctive members of that category. Distinctive cases often influence our perception of whole groups of people. In one experiment, for instance, students were shown fifty slides, each stating the height of a particular man. Ten of the men in the group were over 6 feet tall. For half of the participants, these ten were described as slightly over 6 feet (for example, 6'4"); for the other half, these ten were substantially taller than 6 feet (6'11"). When asked later to estimate how many in the set had been over 6 feet tall, participants who had seen the moderately tall cases overestimated by about 5%, but students who had seen the extremely tall cases overestimated their frequency by 50% (Rothbart, Fulero, Jensen, Howard, & Birrell, 1978). In a second experiment, participants were shown brief descriptions of the behaviors of another fifty men, ten of whom had committed a crime. For some participants these crimes were nonviolent (like forgery); for others they were violent crimes (such as rape). Again, judges overestimated the frequency of crimes in the group as a whole much more when they had been exposed to the distinctive, extreme types of cases.

Similar processes operate in real-world stereotypes. Because of the salience of some highly visible African-American sports figures, we tend to overestimate the proportion of African Americans who are athletic. Because cases of welfare fraud receive much media attention, the public image of welfare recipients is dominated by these cases rather than the actual facts about welfare families (Cook & Curtin, 1987).

When we learn an association between a group and its particularly distinctive members, this is **illusory correlation.** The perceived association is illusory because it occurs under conditions in which there is actually no relationship between group membership and the distinctive characteristic. Illusory correlation is best illustrated by the results of an experiment by Hamilton and Gifford (1976), who presented research participants with a series of thirty-nine sentences, each describing a behavior by a particular person. The person was identified by a first name and membership in one of two groups ("group A" or "group B"), followed by a specific behavior (for example, "Paul, a member of group A, cleaned up the house before company came").

In the set of stimuli presented by Hamilton and Gifford, there were twenty-six people identified as members of group A and only thirteen members of group B. Thus, group A was twice as frequent as group B, which was a more distinctive minority. Further, the behaviors described were either desirable actions (such as, "did volunteer work for a political cause") or undesirable ones ("made another person uncomfortable by a sarcastic remark"). Desirable behaviors were more frequent than undesirable behaviors, but the two types of be-

TABLE 23.2

■

Illusory Correlation: Perceiving Distinctive Pairings

Information Presented to Subjects (actual frequencies)

	GROUP A	GROUP B
DESIRABLE BEHAVIORS	18	9
UNDESIRABLE BEHAVIORS	8	4

Remembered Information (mean estimated frequencies)

	Group A	Group B
DESIRABLE BEHAVIORS	17.1	7.3
UNDESIRABLE BEHAVIORS	8.9	5.7

From Hamilton & Gifford, 1976.

havior were distributed proportionately between groups A and B (Table 23.2). The sentences were presented to participants in random order. After they had read the whole set, participants were asked to estimate how many desirable and undesirable behaviors had been performed by members of group A and how many by members of group B.

In the statements that had been presented, the frequencies of group A's desirable and undesirable behaviors were both double those of group B. Thus, there was no actual relationship between group membership and desirability: Within each group, desirable behaviors occurred two-thirds of the time and undesirable behaviors one-third. However, membership in group B and performance of undesirable behaviors were both *distinctive* because they were relatively infrequent. In the recall test, judges overestimated the frequency of undesirable behaviors by minority-group members (the co-occurrence of two distinctive events) (see Table 23.2). Because of this overestimation, the proportion of negative behaviors was perceived to be proportionally higher among members of group B than of group A—an illusory correlation. Consistent with this perceived association, judges gave group B more unfavorable evaluations than group A on a series of trait ratings. A few distinctive cases gave rise to a negative stereotype.

In-group–Out-group Categorization

Although categorization per se affects social perception, it does not account for either the content or the emotional significance attached to social categories and category stereotypes. To understand more fully the nature of stereotyping and prejudice, we have to recognize the special role of self-involvement in social categories.

Social categories include a fundamental distinction between groups that one belongs to *(in-groups)* and groups that do not include oneself *(out-groups)*. For categories based on gender, there is *my* gender and the other gender; for categories based on ethnicity, there is *my* ethnic group and other ethnic groups; for occupational categories, there is the occupation to which *I* belong and other occupations, and so on. Any basis for categorizing people also includes making an important distinction between "us" and "them," which has powerful emotional consequences (Perdue, Dovidio, Gurtman, & Tyler, 1990). Here, we consider how categorization affects intergroup attitudes.

Category distinctions are important for self-identification: See Chapter 22.

In-group Bias. Probably the most fundamental process associated with in-group–out-group distinctions is the tendency to favor one's own group over others *(in-group bias)*. In the case of social groups, the cognitive bias to accentuate differences between categories is enhanced when the in-group can be evaluated positively and the out-group negatively (Brewer, 1979). In other words, we are more likely to exaggerate the difference between groups on traits where the in-group is regarded as superior to out-groups.

Researchers have studied in-group bias using artificially created groups: See Chapter 24.

The general belief that one's own group is good and morally correct while out-groups are immoral and bad is the basis for **ethnocentrism.** Ethnocentrism has been studied most extensively in connection with intergroup relations among nationalities and ethnic communities (LeVine & Campbell, 1972). However, the tendency to evaluate in-groups more positively than out-groups applies to other social categories as well. Even when individuals are divided arbitrarily into distinct groups, they evaluate their own group products more favorably than those of out-groups and attribute more competence and trustworthiness to in-group members (Brewer, 1979). Table 23.3 lists some elements of ethnocentrism.

In-group bias also affects our memory and attributions for the behaviors of individual in-group and out-group members. Howard and Rothbart (1980) divided participants into two categories by telling half that they were "underestimators" and half that they were "overestimators." Consistent with the in-group bias effect, these assignments (which were actually quite meaningless) generated expectancies on the part of participants about category attributes. Members of the overestimator category thought overestimators in general would have more positive characteristics than underestimators. Those assigned to the underestimator category showed the opposite expectancy.

TABLE 23.3
■
Elements of Ethnocentric Perception

"WE" are:	"THEY" are:
virtuous and superior	contemptible and immoral
strong	weak
cooperative and trustworthy	untrustworthy and uncooperative
dutiful, obedient	disobedient
loyal	treacherous

All participants were then presented with forty-eight self-descriptive statements from individuals who were identified as overestimators and underestimators. For each category, sixteen of the statements described positive behaviors and eight depicted negative characteristics. In a later recognition test, participants were more accurate in remembering negative information about members of the out-group category than in remembering negative behaviors by in-group members. Memory for information that fit in-group bias was superior to memory for information that was inconsistent with that bias.

Behaviors that are inconsistent with in-group bias are also more likely to be *discounted* through causal attribution processes. When a member of our own group behaves in a positive or desirable manner, we are likely to attribute that behavior to internal, stable characteristics (to positive personality dispositions). Undesirable behaviors by an in-group member are more often discounted, attributed to external or unstable factors (for example, he was just having a bad

Large masses of people are perceived as a single, homogenous group. ◼

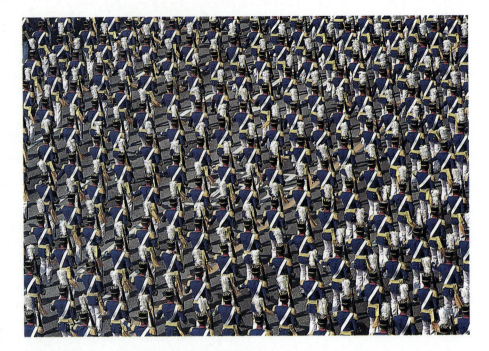

day). Just the opposite attribution bias is applied to out-group members: Desirable behaviors are externally attributed and undesirable ones are internal (Hewstone, 1990). Pettigrew (1979) refers to this bias as "the ultimate attribution error" because it permits us to maintain favorable images of the in-group and unfavorable stereotypes of the out-group even in the face of the contradictory behavior.

In-group bias also leads us to discount information that comes from an out-group member. In an experiment by Mackie, Worth, and Asuncion (1990), participants listened to a persuasive message that was sent by a member of an out-group or by a member of their in-group. When the communication was from a fellow in-group member, participants paid close attention to its content. If the message was a strong one, they were persuaded by it, but if it was a weak argument, they did not accept it. However, when the same information came from an out-grouper, participants were generally unpersuaded no matter what the content of the message was. Out-group messages were apparently dismissed out of hand.

Out-group Homogeneity. We have already referred to the fact that categorization results in perceptions of similarity among category members. However, this tendency to homogenize social categories is also subject to a form of in-group bias. In general, out-group categories are perceived to be more homogeneous than are in-group categories. The perception that all members of a category are alike is readily applied to out-groups, but we are more sensitive to individual differences among members of our own in-groups. As with other forms of information, we seem to pay more attention to variability of in-groups than of out-groups.

Perceived homogeneity is assessed by asking judges how much members of a group are expected to vary on specific traits or dimensions. In many different

Attribution refers to the perceived causes of social events or behavior. See Chapter 10.

contexts, these estimates prove to be smaller for judgments of out-group categories than for in-group categories (Mullen & Hu, 1989; Park & Judd, 1990; Park & Rothbart, 1982; Quattrone, 1986). Perceivers are also more likely to notice and remember distinguishing characteristics of members of their own in-group, but fail to recall differentiating information about out-group members (Park & Rothbart, 1982; Park, Judd, & Ryan, 1991).

<table>
<tr><td>

APPLYING PSYCHOLOGY TO THE LAW

■ ■ ■

</td><td>

Cross-racial Recognition and the Eyewitness

One manifestation of the out-group homogeneity bias is evident in research on *cross-racial identification*. Numerous studies of people's ability to recognize faces have demonstrated that both black and white respondents show in-group bias in correct recognition of black and white faces (Brigham & Malpass, 1985). In these studies, participants are typically shown a series of photographs of faces of black and white target persons. They are later presented with a much larger set of photographs and asked to pick out the ones they had seen previously. In this task, white respondents are more accurate in their recognition of white target faces and more likely to misidentify black faces they had not actually seen before. Black respondents are similarly more accurate in their recognition of black target faces, although the cross-racial bias is generally greater for whites than for blacks (Anthony, Copper, & Mullen, 1992).

Own-race recognition bias has also been demonstrated in real-life interactions. In one study, for instance, black and white store clerks interacted with a black and a white research confederate who posed as customers. A short while later, the clerk was asked to identify each of the two confederates from a lineup of photographs. They were consistently better at correctly recognizing customers of their own race than they were at identifying members of the out-group (Brigham, Maass, Snyder, & Spaulding, 1982). These recognition biases result from less sensitivity to differences among out-group faces and a greater tendency to perceive a range of different faces as quite similar.

</td></tr>
</table>

■ ■ ■ OTHER CONTRIBUTING FACTORS: PERSONALITY AND SOCIETY

In recent years, social psychological research on intergroup relations has been dominated by a search for the cognitive underpinnings of prejudice and stereotypes. However, even the most devoted of social cognition theorists recognize that cognitive factors alone are not sufficient to account for the extreme emotions sometimes associated with group perceptions or for the wide individual differences that exist in expressions of prejudice and stereotyping. Other research traditions within social psychology have focused on personality and socialization as the major factors for understanding prejudice at the individual level.

Personality Factors

Allport (1954) believed that some individuals are more predisposed to prejudicial attitudes than others. The "prejudiced personality" is likely to exhibit generalized hatred toward all out-groups. In support of this position, Allport cited an early study by Hartley (1946) in which attitudes toward members of different nations and ethnic groups were assessed. In addition to thirty-two familiar groups, the survey included the names of three fictitious ethnic groups (such as the "Daniereans"). Attitudes expressed toward these nonexistent groups were highly correlated with attitudes toward real groups. Respondents who were generally negative about known out-groups were also prejudiced against these new groups.

The Authoritarian Personality.   Probably the most well-known theory of the prejudiced personality was developed in the 1940s by a group of Berkeley psychologists interested in explaining the extreme anti–Semitism exhibited by Germans during World War II (Adorno, Frenkel-Brunswik, Levinson, & Sanford, 1950). According to the theory of the **authoritarian personality,** prejudice against Jews and other minorities is one manifestation of a general system of political beliefs that stems from punitive and domineering childrearing practices. Unable to express resentment directly against powerful authority figures, the child develops ego-defensive beliefs that include rigid conservatism, respect for status and tradition, intolerance, and projection of unacceptable beliefs onto out-groups who are both hated and feared.

As a theory that emphasizes psychodynamic rather than social causes of prejudice, the authoritarian personality has not had a central position in social psychological research. The original research on which the measurement of the authoritarian personality was based has been extensively criticized on methodological grounds. However, more recent work using new measures of authoritarian attitudes demonstrates that this is still an important dimension of individual differences in political beliefs and social values (Altenmeyer, 1988).

One theory of aggressive behavior holds that aggression is caused by experiences of frustration. See Chapter 15.

Frustration and Displaced Aggression.   Another psychodynamic theory that has influenced social psychological research is the *scapegoat* theory of prejudice derived from the frustration–aggression hypothesis. Allport (1954) devoted considerable attention to the idea that minority out-groups serve as scapegoats, or targets for displaced, pent-up aggression. When people's needs for economic or personal security are frustrated, they are generally unable to direct aggression toward the actual source of frustration, so they target instead groups that are helpless or stigmatized.

A classic experiment by Miller and Bugelski (1948) demonstrated the relationship between frustration and prejudice. College students working at a summer camp were assessed on their attitudes toward Japanese and Mexicans. Some time later, some of the students were forced to give up a free evening at a local theater in order to stay at the camp and take a series of tedious tests. Attitudes toward Mexicans and Japanese were then reassessed. Compared with the group who did not experience the frustration experience, those forced to give up their evening displayed increased prejudice at the second testing. Although the frustration had been imposed by the students' own group, the resulting aggression found its expression against out-groups.

Self-esteem. Closely related to frustration-based explanations of the origin of prejudice are theories that place the source in individual needs for personal status and self-esteem. Since self-esteem is often based on comparison between oneself and others, one function of prejudice and in-group bias is that it allows even individuals with a generally negative self-concept to feel they are better than someone else.

Self-esteem may be based on comparison between oneself and others: See Chapter 11.

The self-esteem theory is supported by results of research indicating that when personal self-esteem has been threatened, individuals express more in-group bias. Cialdini & Richardson (1980), for instance, found that college students who had been told they performed poorly on a test of creativity rated their own university more highly and a rival university more negatively than did students who had been given more positive feedback. In a different experimental context, Meindl & Lerner (1984) manipulated participants' self-esteem temporarily by rigging an accident. At the beginning of the experimental session, the researcher asked the participant to retrieve a missing chair from the office next door. The chair was arranged in such a way that when the participant moved it, a large stack of computer cards spilled in disarray on the floor—computer cards that contained essential data from a graduate student's dissertation research. On discovering the "accident," the experimenter instructed the participant to just leave the room as it was, "rather than cause more damage."

Following this incident, the participants (who were all English-speaking Canadians) took part in an attitude survey in which they were instructed to respond as members of the English-speaking majority in Canada. The survey included a series of questions on the "Quebec issue," in which respondents were asked to express their agreement or disagreement with various attitudes toward French-speaking Canada. Participants who had just experienced the esteem-lowering accident expressed significantly more negative attitudes toward their French-speaking countrymen than did those who had not had such an experience, supporting the hypothesis that out-group derogation may serve to mend self-esteem.

Intergroup discrimination may be used to enhance self-esteem: See Chapters 22 and 24.

Belief Dissimilarity. One final theory of the relationship between individual needs and prejudice views prejudice as a defense of personal belief systems. According to **belief congruence theory** (Rokeach, 1960), the knowledge that others do not share important beliefs and values is both cognitively unpleasant and threatening. Out-groups are rejected because they are perceived to hold beliefs that are dissimilar to one's own. A large number of studies of interpersonal attraction have demonstrated that belief dissimilarity is more important than category membership alone in acceptance or rejection of individual group members (Insko, Nacoste, & Moe, 1983).

Stereotypes of out-groups include beliefs about the attitudes and values that members of the out-group hold. Beliefs that the out-group holds values that are incongruent with the values most important to one's own group is associated with the intensity of antagonism toward that out-group (Schwartz & Struch, 1989). The affective response to belief dissimilarity provides the emotional fuel that converts group differences into out-group rejection and hostility.

Social Learning Factors

Although individuals differ in degree of prejudice expressed toward out-groups in general, there is also a great deal of shared prejudice within any social group. Stereotypes are socially shared perceptions that are acquired in the process of socialization in the same way that we learn other cultural values and norms (Gardner, 1993). Recent experiments conducted on college campuses demonstrate that expression of racist or antiracist opinions is very much influenced by the normative influences in the environment (Blanchard, Lilly, & Vaughn, 1991). Allport (1954) went so far as to estimate that "about half of all prejudiced attitudes are based only on the need to conform to custom, to let well enough alone, to maintain the cultural pattern" (p. 286).

Pettigrew (1986) has long been a proponent of the view that prejudice results primarily from conformity to group norms and rules. During the 1950s, he conducted a series of studies of whites from South Africa and in the American South that demonstrated that those who conformed most to prevailing social norms were also most prejudiced against blacks. South African students who were born there or identified with the Nationalist Party exhibited more antiblack prejudice and stereotypes than other South Africans (Pettigrew, 1958). Similarly, among adults in the American South (but not in the North), church attenders and political party members were more intolerant of blacks than other southerners (Pettigrew, 1959). Apparently, in societies were prejudice is the norm, those who are most involved in the culture and its traditions are also most prejudiced.

Media Effects. There is considerable evidence that racial, ethnic, and gender stereotypes and attitudes are acquired quite early in life (e.g., Katz, 1976; Lambert & Klineberg, 1967). Culturally shared stereotypes and intergroup attitudes are transmitted through parents, schools, peer groups, and the mass media. Social psychologists have been particularly interested in how ethnic and gender groups are represented in books, newspapers, television, and movies, to assess how our social stereotypes are shaped by these media portrayals.

In the 1960s and 70s, African Americans were consistently underrepresented in both written and visual media. In 1967, only 4% of TV commercials included African-American actors, and of those that did, 80% depicted them in stereotypic roles such as maids or cooks (Johnson, Sears, & McConahay, 1971). Ten years later, the representation of African Americans in television broadcasting had increased considerably. Results of an analysis of the 1977–78 seasons of prime time TV revealed that African Americans appeared in 20% of commercials, 52% of situation comedies, and 59% of drama programs (Weigel, Loomis, & Soja, 1980). Moreover, most of these appearances portrayed equal status cross-racial interactions. Nonetheless, the appearances of African Americans tended to be much briefer than those of white actors, and cross-racial interactions were generally infrequent (less than 4% of program time) and formal rather than intimate. Media portrayals continued to reflect the nature of black–white relations typical of the society at large.

The representation of women in TV and advertising is even more dramatic in its perpetuation of gender stereotypes and expectations. The content of books, newspaper stories, and television programming reveals that males are portrayed in a wide variety of activities and settings, whereas females tend to be restricted

Typically, photographs of men feature their faces, while photographs of women feature more of the body. This concept is referred to as "faceism." ■

to family roles and domestic settings. In television commercials, for instance, men are cast in the role of experts or narrators most of the time; women are almost always product users or consumers (Bretl & Cantor, 1988). Experimental research has demonstrated that exposure to commercials that depict women in traditional rather than nontraditional roles negatively affects women viewers' self-confidence and independence of judgment in later tasks (Jennings, Gies, & Brown, 1980).

An analysis of photographs from various news media revealed a particularly interesting form of gender discrimination. Inspection of 1,750 photographs of people in magazines and newspapers revealed that approximately two-thirds of the vertical dimension of photos of males was devoted to the face, whereas less than half of the average female photo was of the face (Archer, Iritani, Kimes, & Barios, 1983). This difference in prominence of the face was labeled "faceism" by Archer and his colleagues, who found the same bias in classic artwork and in student drawings. More than an oddity, this differential facial prominence has consequences for social perception. When judges were asked to evaluate target photos of both males and females, those pictured with high facial prominence were perceived to be more intelligent and ambitious!

Stereotypes and Social Roles.   Many of the biases revealed in media portrayals of women and minorities have to do with the roles or activities they are typically cast into. One theory of social category stereotypes holds that the content of stereotypes is determined largely by the social roles with which particular social groups have come to be associated. For instance, many features of the U.S. stereotype of African Americans can be traced to their historical position as slaves. Similarly, the traditional division of labor between males and females has led to a situation in which men are more likely to be employed full time in managerial

Some prejudices are expressed overtly. But many prejudices operate at an unconscious level. ■

positions, while women are more likely to work at home or at part-time, low-status jobs. Differences associated with these economic roles are incorporated in gender stereotypes: Men are "naturally" dominant; women are nurturant (Eagly, 1987).

According to **social-role theory,** behaviors and characteristics that are exhibited in carrying out a particular social or economic role eventually come to be seen as *dispositions* attributed to the members of the social group who have been assigned that role (LeVine & Campbell, 1972). This effect was demonstrated experimentally in a study by Hoffman and Hurst (1990) in which college students read about a hypothetical society on a distant planet. The society was composed of two different groups—the "Orinthians" and the "Ackmians." Participants were also told that the species on this planet did not have different sexes, so that any individual could mate with any other and reproduce. Participants were then given descriptions of fifteen individual Orinthians and fifteen Ackmians, each described by a social role (city worker or child raiser) and three personality traits. The social roles were differently distributed so that twelve of the fifteen members of one group were child raisers and twelve of the fifteen members of the other group were city workers. The personality traits, however, were distributed equally across members of both groups.

After reading the individual descriptions, participants were asked a series of questions about their impressions of the two social groups. In ratings of the Ackmians in general and the Orinthians in general, average personality trait assessments tended to correspond to the social roles that had been assigned to the two groups. The group that had more child-raiser members was described as having more communal traits (such as affectionate, emotional, gentle) and fewer agentic traits (such as independent, self-confident, competitive) than the other group. Participants tended to assume that members of the two groups had different personality dispositions corresponding to different social roles, despite the fact that the actual personality descriptions did not differ. Further, the category stereotypes were generalized to individual category members even when they did not occupy the typical social role. An Ackmian city worker was rated as more gentle and emotional than an Orinthian city worker if other Ackmians were primarily child raisers.

Unconscious Prejudice

The impact of widely shared stereotypes and intergroup attitudes may be so pervasive that we adopt them without conscious awareness. Higgins and King (1981) argue that gender stereotypes are highly accessible social schemas, activated automatically when we are not thinking about it. Similarly, Bem (1970, 1987) has described sex-role expectancies as an "unconscious ideology " (Table 23.4).

Racial and ethnic stereotypes may also be activated automatically, without conscious intent. In one experiment, it was found that presenting the labels "black" or "white" facilitated speed of response to words that were associated with the respective group stereotypes (Dovidio, Evans, & Tyler, 1986). After being given the label, participants were presented with a trait word (for example,

Some stereotypes are so prevalent that they are accepted unconsciously. ■

EXHIBIT 23.1

■

A Modern Marriage

Here is one young man's description of his marriage:

My wife and I met at Cornell and married right after graduation. I turned down a good job offer in Oregon and accepted a less desirable position in New York City where my wife would have more opportunities to look for work in her specialty. Because she recently found a good position, her salary easily covers the cost of child care for our two-year-old. My wife and I share the household tasks equally. For example, she cooks the meals, but I do the laundry for her and help her with many of her other household tasks.

Now let's try the same description with the genders reversed:

My *husband* and I met at Cornell and married right after graduation. I turned down a good job offer in Oregon and accepted a less desirable position in New York City where my *husband* would have more opportunities to look for work in *his* specialty. Because *he* recently found a good position, *his* salary easily covers the cost of child care for our two-year-old. My *husband* and I share the household tasks equally. For example, *he* cooks the meals, but I do the laundry for *him* and help *him* with many of *his* other household tasks.

Does the first description seem more natural? Why?

(From Bem, 1987, p. 11.)

---

stubborn) and required to respond as quickly as possible whether the trait was "ever true" of members of the category. Following the label "black," responses were much faster for traits (particularly negative traits) associated with the black stereotype (such as lazy) than for nonstereotypic words (such as ambitious).

In a dramatic demonstration of unconscious priming effects, Devine (1989) presented white respondents with words in a subliminal perception task. The words were displayed outside the foveal visual field so that participants were unaware that any words had been presented. For some respondents, 80% of the words were terms associated with the cultural stereotype of African Americans (for example, black, poor, athletic); for the remaining participants only 20% of the words were stereotype related. After the priming task, all participants were given a paragraph to read, describing a person named Donald. The paragraph contained a number of behaviors that were ambiguous with respect to hostility or aggressiveness (for example, refusing to pay his rent until his apartment is repainted). Respondents in the 80% condition were more likely to form an impression of Donald as a hostile individual than were those in the 20% condition. Apparently, the unconscious activation of the black stereotype also activated the concept of hostility (an element of the black stereotype), even though Donald had no association with the category of blacks and hostility had never appeared in the list of subliminally presented words.

Devine (1989) interpreted her results to indicate that even nonprejudiced individuals in our society have well-formed racial stereotypes. Although these stereotypes may be overridden in consciously expressed attitudes and beliefs, they were still available at a preconscious level. Just how much these preconscious associations influence our social perceptions and behaviors is an intriguing question.

APPLYING PSYCHOLOGY TO SOCIAL ISSUES

■ ■ ■

Overcoming the Habit of Prejudice

Prejudice and stereotypes are like well-established habits of thinking that are difficult to overcome. Even people who reject prejudicial beliefs at the conscious level reveal prejudice on measures that are not subject to conscious control. Does this mean that expression of nonprejudiced attitudes is hypocritical? Not necessarily, according to Devine and her colleagues, who believe that what is important is whether individuals recognize the internal conflict between nonprejudiced beliefs and lingering stereotypic thoughts and feelings (Devine, Monteith, Zuwerink, & Elliott, 1991). Allport (1954) argued that feelings of guilt and self-criticism arise when one is aware of discrepancies between one's actual reactions and beliefs about how one should respond. Recognizing the conflict, and feeling guilty about it (what Devine calls "prejudice with compunction") is the first step toward efforts to reduce the prejudice habit.

Some support for the idea that automatic prejudices can be overcome by conscious effort comes from research by social psychologist Ellen Langer on what she calls "mindfulness" (Langer, 1989). Mindfulness refers to making thoughtful, considered responses to social situations in place of mindless, more-or-less automatic responses. In one experimental application of her ideas, Langer and her colleagues (Langer, Bashner, & Chanowitz, 1985) trained sixth-grade students to make more mindful responses to handicapped individuals. Over a period of four days, the children were shown a series of photographs of individuals with different handicaps (one confined to a wheelchair, one blind, one deaf, one with a missing arm). In the experimental (mindfulness-training) condition, the children were asked to respond to complex questions about the person depicted in each photograph (for example, think of four different reasons why the person might be good at his or her profession and four reasons why he or she might be bad at it). In the control condition, children saw the same slides but were asked simple questions that did not require much extensive thought or conscious processing (for example, think of one reason why the person would be good or bad at their profession).

Following the training period, all the children were given measures assessing avoidance and discrimination against handicapped others. Children in the mindfulness-training condition were significantly more willing to interact socially with a handicapped child, and showed less indiscriminate prejudice against children with various disabilities. According to Langer, the children had learned to be more discriminating and hence less prejudiced. Similar results have been obtained with college students, demonstrating that stereotyping can be reduced when perceivers are motivated to pay attention to individuating information about category members (Fiske & von Hendy, 1992).

■ ■ ■ Some Concluding Thoughts

Let's reconsider the words of the Rogers and Hammerstein song with which this chapter started. Is it true that we have to be "carefully taught" to despise groups that are strange or different from our own? Is prejudice learned, or does it come naturally?

The social psychological research on the cognitive bases of intergroup perception certainly suggests that stereotyping and prejudice do not require much learning. Formation of group stereotypes appears to be a normal consequence of categorization processes, and in-group bias follows readily from categorizations that divide the social world into "us" and "them." Both the cognitive and motivational biases associated with in-group–out-group distinctions are seemingly universal.

On the other hand, both the content and the emotional significance of social categories are the product of considerable learning. Not all category distinctions are imbued with social meaning (consider, for example, the distinction between people with blue eyes and people with brown eyes). And even meaningful social categories do not always arouse strong hatred or hostility. (Librarians and physicians are clearly distinct social groups, but they rarely consider killing each other.) Clearly, we do have to learn the social and emotional meaning that is attached to the many ways in which we categorize people into social groups. As Tajfel (1969) put it, "The process of categorization provides the mold which gives shape to intergroup attitudes, and the assimilation of social values and norms provides their content" (p. 91).

■ ■ ■ Summary

Like other social attitudes, prejudice has both cognitive and emotional components. The cognitive component of intergroup attitudes is represented by the content and structure of social stereotypes, or beliefs about what characteristics are typical of members of a particular social group in comparison with other groups. Apart from specific beliefs, prejudice also includes affective or emotional responses to particular social groups.

Although stereotypes and prejudice are not identical, both derive from basic cognitive processes of social categorization and category accentuation. Once people have been grouped into social categories, there is a strong tendency to overestimate the similarity among members within categories and to exaggerate differences between categories. Stereotypes may be acquired through association between a category and particularly distinctive members. Illusory correlation refers to the overestimation of the frequency of distinctive characteristics within a social category.

Social categorization has a special property in that some categories include oneself while other categories do not. Thus, social categories can be divided into in-groups (those that include oneself) and out-groups (those that do not). This involvement of the self gives rise to systematic biases in the content of social stereotypes and the affect associated with social categories. The most pervasive form of in-group bias is ethnocentrism, the tendency to believe that in-group characteristics are more positive than out-group characteristics and to interpret group differences in ways that favor the in-group over out-groups. Another cognitive bias is the out-group homogeneity effect, the tendency to perceive out-group members as all alike, even though we are aware of individual differences and diversity within our in-groups.

Although social psychologists have been particularly interested in the cognitive processes underlying prejudice and stereotypes, social psychological research has also been directed to personality and societal factors that give rise to prejudice and discrimination. Psychodynamic theories of prejudice are represented in research on the authoritarian personality, which focuses on the ego-defensive functions of out-group hostility. At the individual level, prejudice is also fueled by frustration and displaced aggression, by the need to maintain self-esteem through derogation of out-groups, and by perceived dissimilarities in fundamental beliefs and social values. At the societal level, intergroup prejudices are the product of social norms, represented in the media, and social roles associated with specific social categories.

Of particular interest is recent research demonstrating a distinction between conscious and unconscious prejudice. Although prejudicial beliefs may be rejected at the conscious level, well-learned social stereotypes are still operative at a preconscious level, which influences perceptions and feelings outside conscious control. When prejudices are well learned, it takes conscious effort and attention to overcome their effects.

■■■ SUGGESTED READINGS

1. Allport, G. W. (1954). *The nature of prejudice.* Reading, MA: Addison-Wesley.
2. Bar-Tal, D., Graumann, C., Kruglanski, A., & Stroebe, W. (Eds.). (1989). *Stereotyping and prejudice: Changing conceptions.* New York: Springer-Verlag.
3. Biernat, M., Manis, M., & Nelson, T. (1991). Stereotypes and standards of judgment. *Journal of Personality and Social Psychology, 60,* 485–499.
4. Devine, P. G. (1989). Stereotypes and prejudice: Their automatic and controlled components. *Journal of Personality and Social Psychology, 56,* 5–18.
5. Eagly, A. H., & Kite, M. E. (1987). Are stereotypes of nationalities applied to both men and women? *Journal of Personality and Social Psychology, 53,* 451–462.
6. Zanna, M. P., & Olson, J. M. (Eds.). (1993). *The psychology of prejudice. The Ontario Symposium (Vol 7).* Hillsdale, NJ: Erlbaum.

CHAPTER 24

DISCRIMINATION
The Behavioral Consequences of Prejudice

■ Key Concepts

Minimal intergroup situation
Social identity theory
Positive distinctiveness
Collective self-esteem
Social distance
Aversive racism
Reverse discrimination
Symbolic racism
Realistic group conflict theory
Fraternal deprivation

■ Chapter Outline

DISCRIMINATION IN THE MINIMAL INTERGROUP SITUATION
    Discrimination and Rules of Fairness
    Social Identity and Self-esteem

INTERPERSONAL DISCRIMINATION
    Social Distance
    Nonverbal Behavior, Anxiety, and Ambivalence

INSTITUTIONALIZED DISCRIMINATION: RACISM AND SEXISM
    The Role of Political Ideologies: Symbolic Racism
    ■ Reactions to Political Change

SOME CONCLUDING THOUGHTS

SUMMARY

Annette is seeing her high school counselor about planning for her future career. When asked about her abilities and interests, Annette says she is doing well in mathematics and enjoys that subject. "Well," the counselor tells her, "if you like math, then maybe you should consider being an accountant. Accounting is a good career for a woman these days."

■ ■ ■

A defendant who murdered a white person is eleven times more likely to be given a death sentence than when the victim was black.
                                            —The New York Review, *March 3, 1988*

■

In 1970, high school boys in Bristol, England, took part in a series of social psychological experiments that changed dramatically the future of research on intergroup relations. The experiments, conducted by Henri Tajfel and his colleagues (Tajfel, 1970; Tajfel, Billig, Bundy, & Flament, 1971), consisted of two phases. In the first phase, eight boys from the same high school were brought together in a lecture room and told they would be participating in a study of visual judgment. A series of forty slides consisting of large clusters of dots were then flashed on a screen briefly, and subjects wrote down their estimates of the number of dots that appeared in each cluster. Their judgments were collected and taken away for scoring. The researcher then explained that some people consistently overestimate the number of dots in this judgment task, while others consistently underestimate the actual number.

While the dot estimates were being "scored," the boys were taken into separate rooms for the second phase of the experiment. At this point, they were each assigned a code number (to keep their personal identity unknown to others in the session) and then told whether their total number of guesses in the dot estimation task had been among the four highest in the session (the overestimators) or among the four lowest (underestimators). In actuality, these assignments were made randomly. The dot estimation task was used simply to divide the eight participants into two distinctive categories on an arbitrary basis.

The second phase of the experiment consisted of a different decision task in which participants assigned monetary rewards or penalties to other participants in the session. Every participant was given a booklet containing eighteen pages of allocation matrices. On each page of the booklet was a matrix consisting of a series of number pairs, as illustrated in Figure 24.1. The pairs represented alternative allocations of points (worth money), with the upper number going to the person whose group label and code number was indicated on the top row and the bottom number going to another person whose label and code were attached to the bottom row. Each page of the booklet consisted of such a set of choices for a different pair of recipients.

Now let us consider the decision process of participants in these experiments when they were called on to allocate points on behalf of two other individuals.

To Person X	18	17	16	15	14	13	12	11	10	9	8	7	6	5
To Person Y	5	6	7	8	9	10	11	12	13	14	15	16	17	18

FIGURE 24.1

■

Allocation matrix. (From Tajfel, 1970, p. 97.)

What could be the basis for such a decision? Keep in mind that the decision never involved the decision maker directly (the code numbers always referred to two participants other than the decision maker himself), and he did not know the identity of the two recipients except by code number. Under such circumstances it is generally assumed that the fairest decision rule is to allocate each recipient as close to an equal number of points as possible. In the case of the choice matrix in Figure 24.1, this would mean selecting one of the options that assigned 12 points to one and 11 to the other (choice 7 or 8).

When making allocations for individuals who belonged to the same category (that is, both were labeled overestimators or both underestimators), participants did tend to choose the most equal point distribution. However, Tajfel and his colleagues were particularly interested in what would happen in those cases when the two target individuals belonged to different categories (one overestimator and one underestimator). In this case, one of the targets would be identified as belonging to the same category as that of the decision maker (an *in-group* member), while the other would be identified as an *out-group* member. Under these circumstances, category membership did make a difference in allocation decisions. Decision makers consistently deviated from the point of maximum fairness in order to assign more points to the member of their own in-group. In the first experiment, twenty-six out of thirty-two participants gave more points to in-group targets than to out-group targets. Rarely did they go so far as to allocate the maximum possible to the in-grouper and the minimum to the out-grouper, but they did deviate significantly from an equal distribution. In the matrix in Figure 24.1, for instance, participants allocated an average of 13 points to in-group targets and only 10 to out-group targets.

■ ■ ■ **DISCRIMINATION IN THE MINIMAL INTERGROUP SITUATION**

The behavior of the decision makers in the Tajfel experiments illustrates *intergroup discrimination*. Fellow participants were treated differently by the decision makers *on the basis of their group membership alone*. Apparently, allocators felt justified in making decisions that discriminated in favor of in-group members and against out-group members, even though they did not know anything about the individuals personally. Since 1970, this finding has been replicated in many experiments using different types of allocation matrices and different bases of group categorization (Brewer, 1979).

The results of the original Tajfel experiments surprised social psychologists because social discrimination was exhibited on such an arbitrary basis. The experimental procedures use what is called a **minimal intergroup situation.** Participants are classified into separate categories that have no prior meaning (before coming to the research setting, students had never heard of "overestimators" and "underestimators"). Further, category members are unknown to one another. There is no group interaction, no history of intergroup conflict, and participants have no self-interest in the allocations they make. Yet they make decisions that discriminate in favor of members of one category over the other.

Before the publication of these experiments, most social psychologists had assumed that such discrimination was the result of existing prejudice and hostility that developed over time in the course of intergroup relations. Now we know that intergroup discrimination can be produced by mere categorization into separate groups, in the absence of any history of intergroup contact or conflict. This discovery not only had a profound effect on theories of intergroup behavior but it also had important methodological implications. It became clear that important intergroup processes could be studied in the laboratory under experimentally controlled conditions. This greatly enhanced social psychologists' ability to test theories about the processes underlying intergroup discrimination.

Discrimination and the Rules of Fairness

The most surprising result of the Tajfel experiments is that participants were willing to allocate rewards in a way that favored one individual (an in-group member) over another (an out-group member) without any apparent justification for the inequality. The fact that point allocations in the minimal intergroup situation deviate from equal distribution suggests that in-group–out-group distinctions alter concepts of what is fair or just (Messé, Hymes, & MacCoun, 1986; Platow, McClintock, & Liebrand, 1990).

The rule of equity is one basis for making fair distributions: See Chapter 12.

Equality as a rule of fairness assumes that individuals are the same in all relevant respects and hence deserve the same outcomes. Other rules of fairness take individual differences into account in determining outcome distributions. The rule of *equity,* for instance, holds that individuals should receive outcomes proportional to their inputs. Those who contribute more in terms of abilities or efforts should also receive more, according to the principle of equity. One explanation for the presence of in-group favoritism in the minimal intergroup situation is that participants assume that members of their own group are higher in ability or aptitude than members of the out-group (an interesting form of in-group bias in its own right). Differences in competence provide one justification for awarding somewhat more points to some individuals than others. When groups actually do differ in status or power, the tendency to discriminate in favor of the in-group is especially strong for members of the higher status or dominant group (Sachdev & Bourhis, 1991).

To test the influence of equity considerations in intergroup allocations, some experiments have given participants explicit information about individual differences in performance or contribution at the time allocations are made (Ancok & Chertkoff, 1983; Ng, 1984). Participants are first divided into two categories

FIGURE 24.2

Allocation of monetary reward on the basis of production. This figure shows how much more money was allocated to a more productive worker than to a less productive co-worker. Note that the differential reward is much greater when an in-group member was the high producer. When the in-group produced less than the out-group, subjects preferred an equal distribution of pay, instead of a distribution based on equity. (From Ng, 1984.)

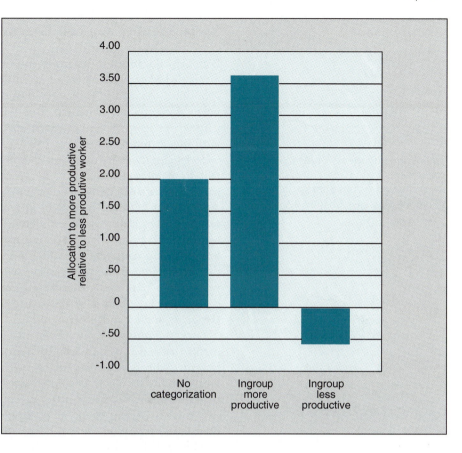

and then take part in a task that earns money for the group as a whole. At the end of the experiment, they are given the opportunity to distribute part of the earnings between two other members of the group. According to information given about individual contributions to the group task, one of these members was more productive than the other. When category identity of the two members is not known, participants typically make an allocation in line with equity principles—the more productive member is allocated somewhat more points than the less productive member. When the two group members belong to different social categories, however, the allocation rule is altered (Figure 24.2). If the more productive individual also happens to be a member of the decision maker's own in-group, even more is allocated to that individual. The principle of equity is used as a justification for enhancing the in-group member's outcomes.

But what happens if the in-group member is less productive than the out-group member? Does the rule of equity still apply? Apparently not, because in this case participants tend to make close to equal allocations between the productive out-group member and the less productive in-group member. Which rule of fairness is applied seems to be influenced by category membership. If equity can be applied to the benefit of an in-group member, rewards are distributed differentially. However, if equity does not work to the in-group's benefit, allocators shift to an equality distribution rule. In-group bias apparently precedes selection of rules of fairness.

Social Identity and Self-Esteem

Biases in allocations to in-group and out-group members are very similar to the biases that have been observed when individuals make allocations to themselves. Allocators use equity principles more often when it benefits themselves than when they are not benefited. But when self-interest is not at stake, why do participants seem to care so much about what in-group members get compared with out-group members?

Social identity theory holds that individuals gain a sense of self-esteem in part from their social group memberships: See Chapter 22.

Social identity theory maintains that individuals gain their sense of self-esteem in part from identification with the social groups to which they belong. When a particular social identity is salient, individuals are motivated to achieve *positive distinctiveness* between their own group and relevant out-groups: They prefer to see their own group as both different from and better than other groups. This form of intergroup comparison enhances their own self-esteem. By treating fellow in-group members favorably, individuals contribute to the positive value of that group identity in comparison with out-groups. Individuals who have experienced a temporary setback to personal self-esteem are particularly likely to discriminate on behalf of their in-group in the minimal intergroup situation (Hogg & Sunderland, 1991).

Social identity as a motive for in-group bias has been confirmed by experiments that have measured self-esteem in the minimal intergroup situation. Participants who have been categorized and are then given the opportunity to allocate points to in-group and out-group members score higher in self-esteem than individuals who are categorized but do not have any opportunity to exhibit in-group favoritism (Lemyre & Smith, 1985; Oakes & Turner, 1980). Even though the allocations do not benefit the person directly, having the opportunity to benefit fellow in-group members at the expense of out-group members apparently does have implications for the individual's own feelings of self-worth. The contribution to self-evaluation derived from group membership has been labeled **collective self-esteem** (Luhtanen & Crocker, 1992). Individuals with a strong sense of collective self-esteem are particularly likely to react to threats to their in-group status by discriminating against out-groups (Crocker & Luhtanen, 1990).

■ ■ ■ INTERPERSONAL DISCRIMINATION

Intergroup discrimination is altering one's behavior on the basis of the category membership of a person: See Chapter 16.

The in-group favoritism exhibited in the minimal intergroup situation is a relatively impersonal form of discrimination in that it takes place without any face-to-face interaction between the decision maker and the targets of the decision. Points are allocated on the basis of group membership identification alone, without knowing who the individuals being affected are. Other forms of discriminatory behavior are exhibited in the course of interpersonal interactions. Any time we alter our social behavior because we are aware of the category membership of the person we are interacting with, we are exhibiting a form of intergroup discrimination.

Social discrimination based on category membership should be distinguished from differential treatment of individuals based on roles or position in society. In the classroom setting, teachers are treated differently from students, as are doctors and patients, employers and employees. Social categories and social roles often become closely associated within a given social system. But here we are talking about discriminatory behavior directed toward an individual based on his or her membership in a particular social category alone, in the absence of role or status differences.

Social categories and social roles often become associated in forming stereotypes: See Chapter 23.

Social Distance

Social behaviors differ in terms of the degree of intimacy they imply. In our society, for instance, working in the same office or riding on the same bus are relatively impersonal, nonintimate social relationships. Belonging to the same social club, sharing meals, and engaging in personal self-disclosure are progressively more intimate forms of interaction. The concept of *social distance* refers to the level of intimacy of social interaction that individuals find acceptable between themselves and members of particular social categories.

The development of measures of social distance was initiated by the publication in 1933 of the Bogardus Social Distance Scale, used to assess the degree of prejudice toward various racial and ethnic groups in the United States (Bogardus, 1933). The scale consists of a series of items ordered according to degree of intimacy (Table 24.1). For each target group, individuals indicate what items they find acceptable in terms of contact with members of that group. The most intimate form of behavior tolerated indicates the degree of social distance at which that group is held. High social distance is indicated when groups are rejected from any but the most impersonal contact (for example, as visitors to the country). Acceptance of more personal contact (as neighbors or "chums") means low social distance.

Years of research with the social distance scale in many countries indicates that variations in social distance based on class or ethnicity are common to all societies (Sherif & Sherif, 1953). Orderings of social groups within a society on social distance scales tend to be consistent and stable for relatively long periods of time.

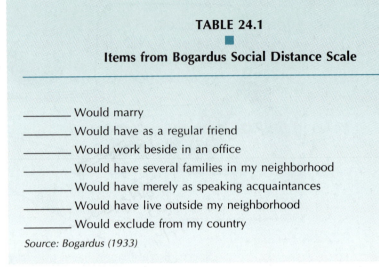

TABLE 24.1

■

Items from Bogardus Social Distance Scale

_____ Would marry

_____ Would have as a regular friend

_____ Would work beside in an office

_____ Would have several families in my neighborhood

_____ Would have merely as speaking acquaintances

_____ Would have live outside my neighborhood

_____ Would exclude from my country

Source: Bogardus (1933)

Clearly, social distance preferences are part of the cultural norms that govern interactions among members of different groups within a community.

High social distance toward a particular social group means avoidance of any form of direct personal interaction. Until recently, in the United States, southern whites avoided social contact with blacks through laws excluding blacks from white schools, eating establishments, and sections of public buses. (Apartheid laws in South Africa supported even more extreme forms of interracial social distance.) Today, moderately intimate social contact between blacks and whites is accepted, but more intimate relations such as marriage are still disapproved.

Social distance norms tend to preserve status differences between social groups (Sidanius, 1993). Even when members of lower-status groups admire those with higher status, both dominant and subordinate groups tend to avoid and disapprove of intimate relationships with the out-group (Schwarzwald, Amir, & Crain, 1992). Intergroup discrimination shows up in the formation of close, interpersonal relationships even when it is not evident in other forms of bias.

Nonverbal Behavior, Anxiety, and Ambivalence

Although social contact between racial and ethnic groups is now widely promoted in many settings, the social interactions that take place are not always smooth. Discomfort associated with intergroup contact affects the nature of social behavior in many subtle ways. Anticipation of interaction with members of out-groups arouses anxiety and fear of rejection (Stephan & Stephan, 1985). When contact does occur, feelings of anxiety are expressed in self-consciousness, stilted nonverbal behavior, emotional reactivity, and limited duration of contact.

Differences in nonverbal behaviors have been demonstrated in a number of studies of social interactions between white participants and a black or white confederate (Crosby, Bromley, & Saxe, 1980). Hendricks and Bootzin (1976), for instance, found that white females chose to sit farther away when interacting with a black rather than a white partner. When spatial distance was determined

Members of different racial and ethnic groups often maintain high levels of social distance. ■

Certain nonverbal behaviors create self-fulfilling prophecies in interracial interactions: See Chapter 16.

by instructions from the experimenter, the degree of discomfort reported by participants following the interaction was related to closeness when the partner was black, but not when he or she was white. In the context of a job interview, Word, Zanna, and Cooper (1974) found that white interviewers sat farther away, made more speech errors, and terminated the interview sooner when the applicant was black rather than white.

Some social psychologists contend that the uneasiness and discomfort that individuals experience during intergroup contact stems from a deep ambivalence about their own prejudiced attitudes. In a society that promotes egalitarian values, negative feelings toward out-groups (particularly minority out-groups) are unacceptable and a source of inner conflict. The nature of such value conflict is well illustrated in the following case study of anti-Semitism reported by Allport (1954):

> I have no contacts with Jews except at school, where I avoid them as much as possible. . . . What I dislike most is the way they always seem to stick together. They are clannish and when one moves into a neighborhood, they all move in. I do not hate individuals because some of the nicest people I know are Jewish. I have met and enjoyed the company of Jewish girls, but sometimes when I see a group of them quibbling over something, my temper flares. I hate to see any group maltreated for their religious beliefs. It is not their beliefs I condemn. I just don't like the way they behave. Of course I know that all men are created equal and that no one is really better than anyone else. (p. 327)

In the case of black–white relationships, this value conflict takes the form of what is called *aversive racism* (Gaertner & Dovidio, 1986). Whites who hold antiprejudicial values do not accept racist beliefs at a conscious cognitive level, but may still experience negative emotional reactions toward blacks. In order to escape feelings of conflict, whites may prefer to avoid contact with blacks or to

Interracial dating and marriage represent the reduction of social distance between groups. ■

keep any contacts short and impersonal. These aversive feelings produce social behaviors that are more subtle than overt hostility, but are nonetheless discriminatory.

Helping and Hurting.   Unintended intergroup discrimination emerges in many forms of interpersonal behavior. Discrimination based on racial identity has been demonstrated in field experiments on spontaneous helping (Crosby, Bromley, & Saxe, 1980). Most of these experiments have observed white subjects' discrimination toward black confederates, but some studies have demonstrated discrimination on the part of blacks as well. Wegner and Crano (1975), for instance, observed responses to a black or white confederate who dropped a large batch of computer cards while walking across a university campus. In this situation, whites who observed the event were equally likely to stop and help either a black or a white confederate, but blacks were more likely to help if the victim was black rather than white.

The behavior of white respondents in cross-racial interactions depends on the nature of the situation. When the need for help is clear and unambiguous, whites often respond in ways that consciously avoid any racist bias. However, when the situation is more ambiguous, individuals often resolve ambiguity by relying on social prejudices. In emergency situations, for instance, it is not always clear whether one should intervene or try to help. The presence of other bystanders

The ambiguity of a situation affects a person's willingness to intervene in an emergency: See Chapter 14.

in such situations makes the decision more ambiguous (Latané & Darley, 1970). If others do not seem to be helping, the individual may feel that intervention is inappropriate. In such ambiguous circumstances, the group identity of the person needing help becomes a factor.

In one experiment, conducted by Gaertner and Dovidio (1977), participants overheard a potential emergency through an intercom system. The students (who were all white females) believed they were participating in an experiment on ESP. Each participant sat in a cubicle with no contact with other participants except by intercom. One person was assigned the role of "receiver," while another was given the role of "sender." The receiver was shown a photograph of the sender, who was either a black or a white female. In one version of the experiment, the receiver believed she was the only one participating with the sender, while in another condition she believed she was one of three receivers present in the session.

At the beginning of each trial in the experiment, the sender (actually a tape recording prepared by the experimenters) signaled her readiness to begin "sending," and the receivers indicated their guess as to the symbol she was transmitting. On the seventeenth trial, the sender was heard getting up to fix a stack of chairs in her cubicle. There was a crashing noise, with the sound of the sender screaming that the chairs were falling on her, followed by silence. The dependent variable of the study was whether the receiver got up and left her cubicle to help the person in distress in the other booth.

When participants believed they were alone in the situation, the race of the victim made no significant difference. Approximately 90% of the receivers in this condition got up and went out to help either a black or a white participant. However, when they believed there were other persons present in the situation, the victim's race had a large effect on helping. In this condition, 75% of participants reacted to help a white victim, but only 38% responded to a black victim. When other people are present in a potential emergency situation, the need for help becomes more ambiguous. It is under these conditions that subtle racial biases became apparent.

Similar evidence of subtle racial biases has also been demonstrated in experimental studies of aggression. Rogers and Prentice-Dunn (1981) had white participants administer a series of electric shocks to another participant in the guise of a biofeedback study. The other person was either a black or a white confederate who behaved in a prearranged manner—either very friendly toward the real participant or in an insulting and unfriendly manner. The number of shocks to be delivered was determined by the experimenter, but the person who delivered it was given responsibility for adjusting the level of shock as seemed appropriate. The level of shock intensity selected by the participant was the measure of aggression.

When the confederate had acted in a friendly manner, the level of shock delivered to the black confederate was actually somewhat lower than that selected for the white confederate. But in response to unfriendly behavior, the differential was reversed and the black confederate received significantly higher shock levels than did the white. Under conditions promoting low aggression, participants exhibited no racial prejudice, but when the situation furnished an excuse for justified aggression, this was expressed more intensely toward black targets.

Experimental studies of aggression often involve decisions about delivering electric shocks to another person: See Chapter 15.

Reverse Discrimination.   The finding that the friendly black confederate in the Rogers and Prentice-Dunn experiment received less shock than the white confederate is a case of discrimination in favor of an out-group, also known as *reverse discrimination*. When participants know their responses are being videore-corded, they deliver less intense shocks to a black target than to a white target, even though they give more shock to blacks than whites under anonymous conditions (Donnerstein & Donnerstein, 1973). The more a behavior is recognized as discriminatory, the more a member of an egalitarian society will bend over backwards not to exhibit such behavior toward a minority-group member (Dutton, 1973).

Reverse discrimination is produced by the same internal value conflict that produces ambivalence and aversive racism. When individuals who wish to believe they are unprejudiced are made aware of discriminatory behavior, they deliberately avoid it, sometimes demonstrating reverse discrimination in the process. This is well illustrated by the results of a study by Dutton and Lake (1973), in which white students who rated themselves as not racially prejudiced took part in what they believed to be an experiment on autonomic responses. In the course of the experiment, galvanic skin response (GSR) and pulse rate of the participant was allegedly monitored as they watched a series of slides of social scenes, which included some scenes of interracial interactions. Feedback on their autonomic response was given to participants as they viewed each slide, presumably an indication of the degree of negative arousal they experienced in response to each. For half the participants, the false feedback given in response to the interracial scenes was neutral, indicating no negative arousal. But for the remaining viewers, the feedback indicated they were experiencing high arousal, suggesting they had unconscious racial prejudice.

When participants had completed this experiment, the researchers arranged that they would be approached as they left the laboratory by a black or white panhandler who requested spare change for food. Participants' response to this request was significantly affected by the race of the confederate and the feedback they had just received (Figure 24.3). Those who had received neutral feedback about their responses to interracial scenes were somewhat more likely to help and to give more money to a white than a black panhandler. But when students had been threatened by evidence of their own prejudice, their reactions were reversed and they gave significantly more to the black than to the white confederate. Discriminatory behavior is clearly subject to voluntary control when individuals are acutely aware of their own actions.

▪▪▪ INSTITUTIONALIZED DISCRIMINATION: RACISM AND SEXISM

Discriminatory interpersonal behavior is embedded in a larger social context of intergroup discrimination (Jones, 1972). The cumulative effects of differential responding to individuals on the basis of category membership can mean large differences in opportunities and outcomes for those groups as a whole. Consider, for example, Annette's interaction with her high school counselor at the begin-

FIGURE 24.3

∎

Effect of threat to nonprejudiced self-image on contributions to a panhandler. White students were more likely to give money to a black panhandler if they had just participated in an experiment where they learned they may hold unconscious racial prejudice. (From Dutton & Lake, 1973.)

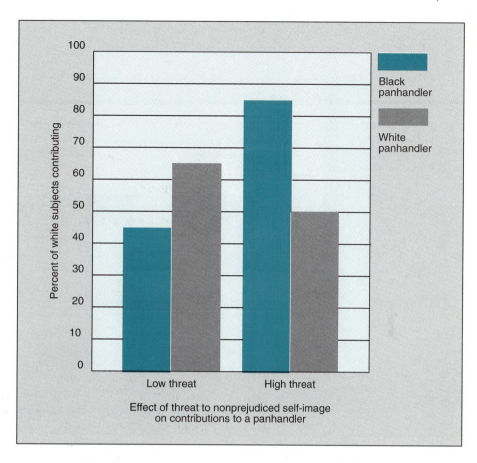

Effect of threat to nonprejudiced self-image on contributions to a panhandler

ning of this chapter. With Annette's interest in mathematics, why does the counselor suggest a career in accounting rather than physics or engineering? Surely this advice is discriminatory, in the sense that it would not be the same as the advice given to a male student with the same academic record and interests. The cumulative effect of advice such as this is to limit the career options offered to women in our society. Similarly, the cumulative effect of judges making decisions about appropriate sentencing that are subtly influenced by racial biases produces large discrepancies in outcomes within the criminal justice system for black and white defendants.

The collective effects of discrimination may not always be experienced consciously at the individual level. Interestingly, despite the well-documented differences between men and women in job opportunities and wages, most women in the work force deny feeling personally discriminated against in their own employment situation (Crosby, 1982; Crosby, Fufall, Snyder, O'Connell, & Whalen, 1989). Yet experiments have demonstrated that sex discrimination in employment selection and advancement is widespread. Levinson (1975), for instance, had male and female students respond by phone to job ads that had been placed in the local newspaper. Some of the jobs were traditionally masculine (such as management trainee or bus driver), whereas others were traditionally feminine (such as receptionist or dental assistant). Despite identical qualifications,

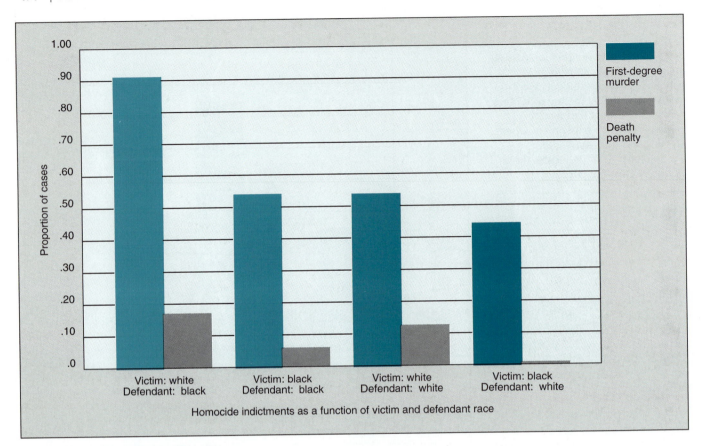

Homocide indictments as a function of victim and defendant race

FIGURE 24.4

Homicide indictments as a function of victim and defendant race. The probability of conviction of first degree murder and a death penalty sentence is significantly increased for cases involving a black defendant and a white victim. (From Radelet, 1981.)

male callers were more often encouraged to apply when responding to masculine jobs and females for feminine jobs. Similarly, a more recent study by Glick, Zion, and Nelson (1988) demonstrated that resumés with female names were less likely to be selected for interviews for a masculine job (sales manager) than the same resumé with a male name, even when the resumé contained information indicating that the applicant had engaged in "masculine" activities (for example, captain of a varsity basketball team). Conversely, male applicants with feminine traits were less likely to be selected for feminine-typed jobs than female applicants with the same attributes.

Experimental studies also reveal discrimination in the application of criminal justice that may be difficult to detect in individual cases. In one field experiment, for instance, a shoplifting was staged in view of white shoppers. The crime was much more likely to be reported by witnesses when the shoplifter was black rather than white (Dertke, Penner, & Ulrich, 1974). As indicated by the statistics cited at the chapter opening, the criminal justice system also seems to operate differently depending on whether the victim is white or black. In one study, for instance, Radelet (1981) examined all homicide indictment cases in twenty counties of Florida in 1976–77. He found that the probability that the crime would be prosecuted as a first-degree murder case was significantly higher when the victim was white, particularly when the defendant was black, and the probability of the death sentence was also significantly higher in these cases (Figure 24.4).

Malcolm X was a highly visible representative of Black Activism in the 1960's. ■

Advantage-justifying ideology affects members of disadvantaged groups: See Chapter 22.

The Protestant Ethic holds that individuals are responsible for their own fate: See Chapter 9.

The Role of Political Ideologies: Symbolic Racism

Overt racial prejudice in the United States has decreased considerably over the last fifty years. In surveys of ethnic stereotypes and beliefs, white respondents are much less likely today to endorse negative beliefs about blacks or to approve of discriminatory laws and policies (Dovidio & Gaertner, 1986; Karlins, Coffman, & Walters, 1969: Schuman, Steeh, & Bobo, 1985). Yet statistics on employment, wages, housing, and political representation still reveal large differences between black and white citizens of this country. The fact that discrimination in economic and political realms continues despite changed attitudes has led some social psychologists to speculate that racism in our society has not disappeared but has taken different, more disguised forms.

Indirect expressions of racial prejudice are variously referred to as "modern racism" (McConahay, 1986) or **symbolic racism** (Kinder & Sears, 1981; Sears, 1988). According to these theories, underlying racial prejudices are expressed in positions on race-relevant political issues such as affirmative action, busing, social welfare spending, and election of black candidates for political office. According to Sears (1988), there is nothing new about these forms of indirect racism, since they reflect long-standing political ideologies that have always supported anti-black policies in the United States.

The idea that political ideologies and values support intergroup discrimination is represented in many social psychological theories, including **realistic group conflict** theories of intergroup relations (Bobo, 1983). Conflict theory holds that hostility between groups is caused by direct competition for scarce, valuable resources. These resources may be economic goods such as land and money or psychological resources such as status and power. According to this view, prejudice and social distance are "products of interaction between groups in which vital interests, goals, values of the group come into conflict" (Sherif & Sherif, 1953; p. 114).

When one group gains advantage over another in the competition for resources and status, the members of that group develop ideologies that justify the advantage in order to make it acceptable to both groups. Prejudicial attitudes and the content of stereotypes help to rationalize existing social structures such as status differences based on sex and ethnicity (Allport, 1954; Hacker, 1951; Sidanius, Pratto, Martin, & Stallworth, 1991). As socially shared belief systems, prejudice and stereotypes are part of the values and ideologies that legitimate status, power, and other social inequalities (Tajfel, 1981).

Most societies are characterized by marked inequalities and status differences among groups, and political beliefs and values tend to justify and preserve those inequalities (Sidanius, 1993). Katz and Hass (1988) argue that in contemporary American society, there is an inherent value conflict between egalitarian–humanitarian values and existing inequalities, which are justified ideologically by the values embodied in the Protestant ethic. They found that endorsement of beliefs associated with the Protestant ethic is correlated with antiblack attitudes.

Ideological factors become particularly important when the legitimacy of status differences is threatened or challenged in the course of social change. These are the conditions that promote feelings of **fraternal deprivation,** the perception that one's in-group is being disadvantaged relative to its former position (Runciman, 1966). Even when individuals themselves are not suffering any loss of economic position or prestige, they may feel deprived because their *group's* position is being lowered. Vanneman and Pettigrew (1972), for instance, found that hostility toward blacks by working-class whites was related to their resentment about the political and economic gains being made by blacks as a group, even if those gains had no direct effect on their personal welfare. Experimental studies have also demonstrated that when the position of high-status groups is threatened, discrimination against low-status out-groups is increased (Ng & Cram, 1988).

Tajfel (1981) was also interested in the response of advantaged social groups when the basis for their advantaged position becomes insecure. He predicted that under these circumstances, members of high-status groups would seek to increase the psychological and social distinctions between their group and others in attempts to preserve the status quo. Ironically, threats to the legitimacy of existing discrimination have the effect of increasing discrimination on the part of advantaged groups.

<table>
<tr><td>

APPLYING SOCIAL PSYCHOLOGY
TO POLITICS

■ ■ ■

</td><td>

Reactions to Political Change

Tajfel's analysis of the response of high-status groups to social change is supported by research on white reactions to black political movements in the United States (Bobo, 1988). The results of national surveys taken from 1964 to 1980 indicated that whites were consistently more negative than blacks toward the civil rights movement across that time period. Further, the perception of the movement changed in different ways for black and white survey respondents. During the 1960–68 period, when civil rights activism was particularly high, 70–80% of white respondents thought that civil rights were being pushed "too fast" and that the movement was "too violent." During this same time, only 10–20% of blacks thought that civil rights were moving too fast. In the next decade, from 1970 to 1980, when militant activism had moderated, perceptions changed somewhat among both groups. Of whites, 60% in 1970 and only 40% in 1980 thought things were moving too fast, whereas 30–45% of blacks in this period felt the civil rights movement had slowed too much with too little progress made. As the threat of rapid change waned, whites' tolerance for civil rights ideology increased, but only when the relative status of blacks politically and economically was still quite low. Figure 24.5 illustrates these changes.

</td></tr>
</table>

■ ■ ■ SOME CONCLUDING THOUGHTS

The study of discrimination and prejudice goes well beyond the domain of social psychology. As a social issue, institutionalized discrimination is studied by sociologists, political scientists, and social philosophers, as well as psychologists. In this chapter, we have tried to represent the unique contribution of social psychologists to this interdisciplinary effort. Social psychologists are particularly interested in discrimination as it is manifested in interpersonal behavior between individuals representing different social categories. Thus, they have studied how

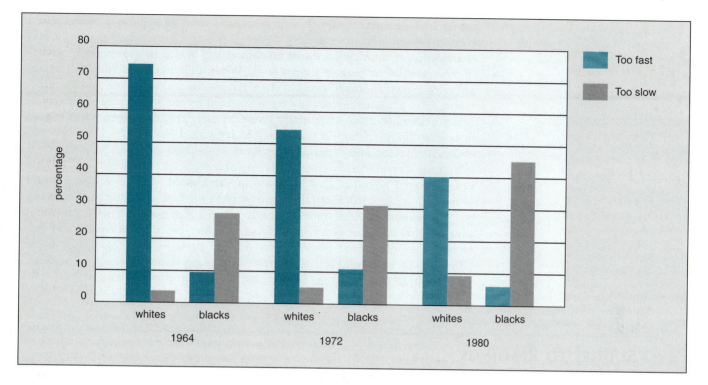

FIGURE 24.5

∎

Responses to the question of whether the civil rights push was too fast or too slow, 1964–1980. (From Bobo, 1988.)

discrimination is exhibited in social interactions and in decision-making contexts such as reward allocations, job interviews, and jury verdicts. Clearly, not all forms of discrimination can be reduced to the consequences of behavior at this individual or interpersonal level, but interpersonal discrimination is one major contributor to social injustice.

∎∎∎ **SUMMARY**

The results of a series of studies by Tajfel (1970) increased social psychologists' interest in the experimental study of intergoup discrimination. Tajfel demonstrated that even in a minimal intergroup situation (where individuals have no contact with other group members), participants will engage in discriminatory behaviors that benefit a fellow in-group member over a member of an out-group. Such discrimination indicates that in-group–out-group distinctions alter individuals' conceptualizations of what is fair and just. When social identity is salient, favoritism toward in-group members serves to achieve positive distinctiveness between in-group and out-group in the interest of collective self-esteem.

Discrimination based on category membership is evidenced in many forms of interpersonal social interaction. Individuals maintain social distance between their in-group and out-groups by avoiding intimate relationships outside their own group. Intergroup contact is marked by nonverbal signs of discomfort and anxiety even when verbal behavior is positive. This conflict between antiprejudicial attitudes and discriminatory behavior leads to a form of avoidance of interracial contact known as aversive racism.

Evidence of unintended discrimination is also found in experimental studies of interpersonal helping and aggression. When individuals are not consciously aware of the racial implications of their actions, decisions to help another individual or to respond aggressively are influenced by the victim's race. However, when whites are made consciously aware of their prejudice, they often engage in reverse discrimination in responding to individual blacks.

Discriminatory interpersonal behavior is embedded in a societal context of intergroup discrimination, particularly racism and sexism. Although overt expressions of racial prejudice have declined in the United States over the last fifty years, indirect forms of racial discrimination are evident in political attitudes and policy preferences. Such indirect forms of prejudice reflect what some social psychologists call symbolic racism. Discriminatory practices and inequality between social groups are supported by shared beliefs and ideologies that justify differences in status and power. Threats to existing status relationships between groups arouse realistic group conflict and resistance to social change.

■ ■ ■ **SUGGESTED READINGS**

1. Bobo, L. (1983). Attitudes toward the black political movement: Trends, meaning, and effects of racial policy preferences. *Social Psychology Quarterly, 51,* 287–302.

2. Crosby, F., Bromley, S., & Saxe, L. (1980). Recent unobtrusive studies of black and white discrimination and prejudice: A literature review. *Psychological Bulletin, 87,* 546–563.

3. Dovidio, J. F., & Gaertner, S. L. (Eds.). (1986). *Prejudice, discrimination and racism: Theory and research.* New York: Academic Press.

4. Jones, J. M. (1972). *Prejudice and racism.* Reading MA: Addison-Wesley.

5. Katz, P., & Taylor, D. (Eds.). (1988). *Eliminating racism: Profiles in controversy.* New York: Plenum Press.

CHAPTER 25

INTERGROUP RELATIONS
Conflict or Cooperation?

■ **Key Concepts**

Superordinate goals
Prisoner's dilemma
Mirror image
Contact hypothesis
Cooperative interdependence
Status equality
Personalization

■ **Chapter Outline**

ROBBERS CAVE: A CLASSIC EXPERIMENT IN INTERGROUP RELATIONS
    The Lessons of Robbers Cave
    ■ Missiles versus Factories
    Intergroup Competitiveness: Cause or Consequence?

IGNORANCE AND MISPERCEPTION IN INTERGROUP RELATIONS
    ■ The Image of the Enemy

INTERGROUP CONTACT: THE SOCIAL PSYCHOLOGY OF DESEGREGATION
    The Role of Social Science in Desegregation
    Contact Experiments: Defining the Limits

SOME CONCLUDING THOUGHTS

SUMMARY

"Serbian Planes Violate "No-Fly Zone" in Bombing of Bosnia Village"

■ ■ ■

"Fifteen-Year-Old Boy Shot to Death During
Gang Fighting in Los Angeles"

■ ■ ■

"Twelve Arrested as Anti-Abortion and Pro-Choice Activists Clash
at Family Planning Clinic in New York City"

■

These headlines, taken from one day's news stories, are just a few of the many instances of intergroup conflict and violence that confront us daily. In our home-towns, the nation, and the world, conflict among members of opposing groups is so common as to be almost expected. The conflict is not always violent, of course. Some battles are fought in the political arena, the law courts, or the economic marketplace. But group behavior is so often characterized by hostility that the study of intergroup relations may often seem to be the same as the study of intergroup conflict.

Social psychologists have long been intrigued (and distressed) by the frequency with which group differences breed intergroup hostility. The study of stereotypes, prejudice, and in-group bias helps us to understand the psychological foundation for intergroup conflict. In this chapter, we turn our attention to structural factors that contribute to the initiation and maintenance of conflict between groups, with the hope of gaining an understanding of how such conflict might be reduced.

Stereotypes, prejudice, and ethnocentrism are the psychological underpinnings of intergroup conflict: See Chapters 22, 23, 24.

■ ■ ■ ROBBERS CAVE: A CLASSIC EXPERIMENT IN INTERGROUP RELATIONS

In the summer of 1954, twenty-two eleven-year-old boys arrived by bus at a campsite in Robbers Cave, Oklahoma, to participate in a three-week summer camp session. The boys, all from white, middle-class backgrounds, were unaware that their camping experience would be part of a series of field studies conducted by social psychologist Muzafer Sherif and his colleagues to test theory of inter-group conflict and conflict reduction (Sherif, 1966; Sherif, Harvey, White, Hood, & Sherif, 1961).

Before beginning the summer camp session, the boys (who were all previously unacquainted) were arbitrarily divided into two subgroups. The two groups arrived at the camp on separate buses and were settled into cabins at a considerable distance from each other. For the first week of the session, contact between the two groups was prevented. During this time, the members of each group engaged

Interaction between groups is often characterized by conflict and violence. ■

in cooperative activities that contributed to group formation. To further the development of group identity, the boys were encouraged to adopt a group name. One group chose to call themselves the "Rattlers"; the other became the "Eagles."

When contact between the two groups did occur, beginning in the second week, it was under conditions of intergroup *competition,* primarily in the form of competitive sports events. But the hostilities that ensued extended well beyond the playing field. After being defeated in one game, for instance, the Eagles burned a banner left behind by the Rattlers. The next morning, the Rattlers seized an Eagles flag, and from that point on raids on each other's campsites were frequent, along with name calling and fist fights. Conversations and the content of posters drawn by group members documented highly derogatory images of the other group. By the end of this stage, cohesiveness within groups had increased, but both groups expressed strong preferences not to have any further contact with the other group, even if it meant foregoing pleasant activities such as movies if members of the other group were to be present.

At this point, the researchers had succeeded in demonstrating that groups with no cultural, physical, or status differences between them, composed of boys selected for good psychological adjustment and sociability, could become warring factions based on the presence of competing group interests alone. The competition that had been introduced was a "zero-sum" situation—one group's win was always the other group's loss. Once the groups had experienced this form of competition on the playing field, they continued to define all further intergroup interactions in zero-sum terms.

Having created two rival groups with hostile attitudes and negative images of each other, the researchers' final task was to find conditions that would reduce the intensity of intergroup conflict. As an initial step toward conflict reduction, the groups were brought into contact with each other under conditions that were pleasant but involved no objective competition. These events included things like a common banquet, Fourth of July fireworks, and movies. Instead of reducing conflict, these events simply served as opportunities for mutual name calling and attack. The common meals, for instance, were marked by shoving and contests over which group would be first in line for food. So much food and paper was thrown around that the meals became known as "garbage wars."

After demonstrating the failure of contact alone to reduce intergroup hostility, the researchers then introduced a new feature into the situation—the presence of *superordinate goals*. The general idea was that if incompatible group goals (competition) produced hostility, then common goals should reduce it. Superordinate goals were defined as important needs shared by members of both groups that could be met only by mutual cooperation. Common goals were created by facing the Rattlers and Eagles with several urgent situations that required cooperative effort.

One such situation was the breakdown of the water supply system to the camp. The flow of water, which came through pipes from a tank about a mile away, was interrupted, and the boys from both groups had to work together to locate the source of the problem. On a second occasion, a truck that was needed to fetch food supplies to a camp picnic refused to start, and all of the boys had to join in a coordinated effort to pull the truck by rope until it started. Yet a third opportunity arose when members of both groups had a particular movie high on their list of preferences for viewing at the camp. They were told that the movie was too expensive to acquire and both groups wound up contributing money in order to rent it.

None of these incidents alone was sufficient to eliminate the strong intergroup hostilities, but the cumulative effect of the series of joint activities did have a significant influence. During the final week of the camp session, name calling and shoving in meal lines had stopped and some friendships were formed across group lines. On the last day, the Rattlers and the Eagles elected to ride home together on the same bus rather than take separate buses (and even stopped along the way for shared refreshments, purchased by one group's remaining prize money).

Realistic group conflict is one basis for intergroup discrimination: See Chapter 24.

The Lessons of Robbers Cave

Sherif and his colleagues set out to demonstrate a number of points about the nature of intergroup relations in their summer camp experiments. Their work was conducted within the framework of realistic group conflict theory, which holds that the nature of group relations is determined by the perceived relationship between in-group and out-group interests. When one group can attain its goals (for resources, status, or power) only at the expense of another group, intergroup conflict is the inevitable consequence. Conflict can be reduced only by the acceptance of shared, superordinate goals in place of competing interests.

Most social psychologists accept the idea that competition over scarce economic or social resources heightens intergroup differences and hostility. Experimental studies in the laboratory confirm Sherif's findings that placing groups in competition increases in-group bias and discrimination (Brewer, 1979), as well

The Prisoner's Dilemma refers to decision situations in which cooperative and competitive goals are in conflict: See Chapter 12.

as anxiety and negative affect toward the out-group (Wilder & Shapiro, 1989). In real life, perceived incompatibility of goals is clearly a component of conflict between labor and management in industry, among political groups within nations, and among nations in the global scene. Much of this conflict has the characteristics of the *prisoner's dilemma:* A cooperative solution that would benefit both sides may be available, but if each side expects the other to pursue its own advantage, the result is competition that leads to the disadvantage of both.

APPLYING SOCIAL PSYCHOLOGY TO POLITICS

Missiles versus Factories

The arms race between the United States and the U.S.S.R. from 1950 to 1990 has been characterized as a prisoner's dilemma game on a large scale. To study the way people make decisions in such dilemmas, social psychologists have devised experimental games that simulate the arms race in the laboratory (Pilisuk, 1984). In one such game, two players each begin with five "missiles." Over the course of five moves, they each have the opportunity to convert any of these missiles into factories (that is, to disarm). These decisions are made secretly, but at the end of five trials, the payoffs to each of the players are determined by the number of missiles each has at that point, according to the payoff matrix illustrated in Figure 25.1.

FIGURE 25.1

Payoff Matrix for Experimental Arms Race. In this experiment, players had to decide whether to invest in "missiles" or "factories." Both players are better off if neither one buys missiles. But if one player has more missiles than the other, the player with most missiles wins (from Pilisuk, 1984).

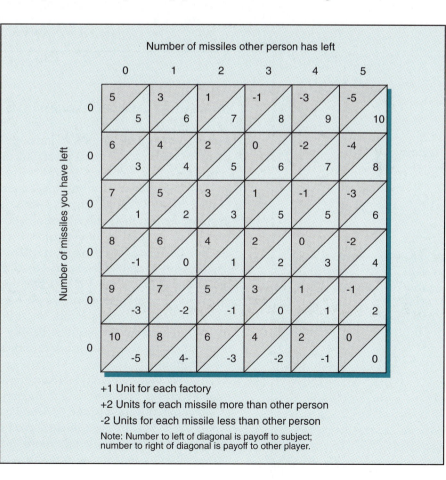

The nature of this payoff structure is such that each player is better off if he or she winds up with *more* missiles than the other player. For instance, if the other person ends with two missiles, you are better off if you have three missiles rather than two (even though you also have fewer factories). However, if both players pursue this competitive strategy, they both wind up with nothing (the lower right cell of the matrix), whereas they each could have won 5 points if they had both disarmed completely (zero missiles each). In studies using this experimental game, Pilisuk found that players wound up with an average of three missiles at the end of the series of five moves. As a result, they both won far fewer points (2 points each) than they could have had with a mutual disarmament strategy (5 points each). Further, if players were given the opportunity to initiate a "surprise attack" after one five-trial sequence, fully one-third of the time at least one player took the attack option *even if there was virtually no chance of success from such an attack.* Apparently, out of fear of the opponent, many players chose a preemptive attack rather than risk falling behind in the arms race. The college student participants in Pilisuk's arm's race experiment behaved very much like the boys of Sherif's summer camp:

> One group adopted a strategy to deter the other from future raids on its cabin. They collected green apples "just in case," to be prepared. The other group promptly began collecting apples themselves, and these also were hoarded against eventuality of attack. Although expressly forbidden by the research staff and actually prevented on one occasion, the upper crust of one group succeeded in carrying out a raid when both groups had what they considered ample supplies of apples. (Sherif, 1966, p. 119)

Intergroup Competitiveness: Cause or Consequence?

Although objective conflicts of interest certainly play an important role in intergroup relations, some social psychologists argue that competition is not the sole basis for conflict between groups. In some instances, in fact, competition may be the consequence of in-group–out-group differentiation rather than its cause (Tajfel, 1978; Tajfel & Turner, 1986). Minimal intergroup experiments clearly demonstrate that in-group favoritism and discrimination against out-group members occur as soon as individuals are classified into distinct categories, in the absence of preexisting conflict of interests. According to social identity theory, this happens because positive in-group identity is attained through comparisons with the out-group. As Tajfel (1981) put it, "The characteristics of one's group as a whole . . . achieve most of their significance in relation to perceived differences from other groups and the value connotations of these differences" (p. 258). The need for positive identity creates a kind of "social competition" between groups that is the product (rather than the cause) of in-group–out-group categorization.

The idea that competition results from group formation is further supported by experiments demonstrating a discontinuity between interpersonal and intergroup competitiveness (Insko & Schopler, 1987; Insko, Schopler, Hoyle, Dardis, & Graetz, 1990). In experimental games, decisions made by groups of two or three members are consistently more comeptitive and less cooperative than decisions made by individuals in the same circumstances. For instance, more com-

Experiments on intergroup relations sometimes involve minimal groups created in the laboratory: See Chapter 24.

Social identity theory helps explain ethnocentrism and intergroup discrimination: See Chapters 22, 24.

petitive choices are made when prisoner's dilemma games are played between two pairs of individuals rather than two single individuals (McCallum, Harring, Gilmore, Drenan, Chase, Insko, & Thibaut, 1985). Also, bargaining decisions made by group consensus are more competitive than decisions made by individuals even when those individuals are choosing on behalf of groups (Insko et al., 1987). Since the objective conflict of interest does not change when the situation is intergroup rather than interpersonal, these experiments suggest that group membership enhances competitive motivation. People in groups seem to act under greater fear that another group will try to take advantage of them (Insko et al., 1990). Thus, the potential for conflict is apparently greater in intergroup situations than in interpersonal ones.

■■■ IGNORANCE AND MISPERCEPTION IN INTERGROUP RELATIONS

The competitive atmosphere that characterizes intergroup relations is a breeding ground for mistrust and misperception. The relationship between competitiveness and social perception was cleverly demonstrated in a laboratory experiment reported by Cooper and Fazio (1986). Participants, who were in groups of three to six individuals, viewed a videotape of a team of two people engaging in a communication task. In one condition, participants believed they were taking part in a person perception experiment and were instructed merely to observe the dyad, or pair. In another condition, participants were told they themselves would be assigned to pairs who would later compete against the team in the videotape for a cash prize.

During the course of the videotape, the members of the videotaped team requested a time-out, which was responded to reluctantly by the experimenter since time-outs were not part of the rules of the task. At this point, the members of the dyad in the video had a brief discussion and then resumed the task. The nature and purpose of their request for a time-out was left ambiguous. After viewing this videotape, participants in the person perception condition tended to interpret the request for time-out in a neutral way, assuming it was for the purpose of asking clarifying questions or going to the bathroom. For observers in the future competition condition, however, the request took on more sinister implications. Most participants in this condition assumed the purpose was to cheat or gain some unfair advantage in the task. When they evaluated the video team at the end of the experiment, these judges rated them as significantly less honest than did participants in the person perception condition. Apparently, the same ambiguous behavior was deemed to be more suspicious and dishonest when the team on the videotape was a competitive out-group.

APPLYING SOCIAL PSYCHOLOGY
TO POLITICS
■■■

The Image of the Enemy

Distrust and misattributions of intent are also characteristic of social perception at the international level (Jervis, 1976; Silverstein, 1989; White, 1970, 1977). Nations in conflict tend to perceive each other in remarkably predictable ways. When psychologist Urie Bronfenbrenner returned from a trip to the Soviet Union in 1960, he reported his observations drawn from conversations with Russian citizens (Bronfenbrenner, 1961). As he talked with people about U.S.–Soviet relations he found that "the Russians' distorted picture of us was curiously similar to our view of them—a *mirror image*" (p. 46). The view of the enemy's aggressive intent is mirrored

---

TABLE 25.1

■

"The Mirror Image": U.S. and U.S.S.R. Version

The American View	The Soviet View
Russia is a warmonger bent on imposing its system on the rest of the world. Witness Czechoslovakia, Berlin, Hungary, and now Cuba and the Congo. The Soviet Union consistently blocks Western proposals for disarmament by refusing necessary inspection controls.	America is the warmonger imposing its power rest of the world. Witness American intervention in 1918 and after World War II with troops and bases on every border of the U.S.S.R. America has repeatedly rejected Soviet disarmament proposals while demanding the right to inspect within Soviet territory.
Communists, who form but a small proportion of Russia's population, control the government and exploit the society and its resources in their own interest.	A capitalistic–militaristic clique controls the American government and its media of communication and exploits the society and its resources.
In spite of the propaganda, the Soviet people are not really behind their government. Most of them would prefer to live under our system of government if they only could.	Unlike their government, the bulk of the American people want peace and disapprove of American aggression. If the American people were allowed to become acquainted with our system of communism, they would choose it as their form of government.
The Soviets do not keep promises and they do not mean what they say. Their talk of peace is but a propaganda maneuver.	The Americans do not keep promises and they do not mean what they say. They have no intention of disarming.
Soviet demands on such crucial problems as disarmament, Berlin, and unification are completely unrealistic. Disarmament without adequate inspection is meaningless. In pursuit of their irresponsible policies the Soviets do not hesitate to run the risk of war itself.	The American position on such crucial problems as disarmament, East Germany, and China is completely unrealistic. They demand to know our secrets before they disarm. In pursuit of their irresponsible policies the Americans do not hesitate to run the risk of war itself.

From Bronfenbrenner, 1966, pp. 46–48.

in each group's image of the other (Table 25.1). This image is also characterized by what White (1970) calls the "blacktop illusion," the idea that it is the political leaders of the enemy nation who are evil and aggressive and that the ordinary citizen would actually be in favor of us if they were not deluded and controlled by their leaders.

The perception that "we" are peaceful and cooperative while "they" are aggressive and competitive is characteristic of conflict in arenas other than international politics. Thomas and Pondy (1977), for instance, documented similar attributions in a study of business executives. When asked to describe a recent conflict they had been involved in, 74% characterized their own intentions and behavior as cooperative, whereas only 12% believed the other party was also cooperative, and 73% judged the other to be competitive and unreasonable. In other words, within a conflict situation, each individual thinks the other is the source of the competition and conflict. (Anyone who has helped counsel friends through an impending divorce will know what this means.)

One problem with the attribution of competitive intent to others is that such expectations tend to be self-fulfilling. When we act to defend ourselves against the expected aggression, our competitive actions confirm the out-group's expectations of our own intent and elicit competition in return (Kelley & Stahelski, 1970). Each side behaves in a way that reinforces the other's misperceptions. Breaking the cycle of distrust sometimes requires extraordinary efforts, but it can work, as illustrated in Exhibit 25.1.

Expectations often create a self-fulfilling prophecy: See Chapter 16.

EXHIBIT 25.1
■
GRIT: Graduated and Reciprocated Initiatives in Tension-reduction

---

In 1959, social psychologist Charles Osgood suggested that the suspicion and distrust between the Soviet Union and the United States was so great that if one of the countries were to disarm totally, it would probably be interpreted by the other side as some kind of trickery. To reduce that tension, Osgood (1959, 1962) proposed "an arms race in reverse." Briefly, the GRIT strategy involves unilateral initiatives to reduce tension. One party takes deescalatory steps without requiring prior commitment from the other, *assuming that these acts will eventually be reciprocated.*

In a real-world demonstration of GRIT, U.S. President John Kennedy announced on June 10, 1963, a unilateral peace initiative halting all atmospheric nuclear testing. The next day in the United Nations, the Soviet Union removed its objection to sending observers to war-torn Yemen, and the United States removed its objection to restoration of full status to the Hungarian delegation to the U.N. On June 15, Khrushchev reciprocated with a welcoming speech and announced that the production of strategic bombers was halted. In another five days, the Soviet Union agreed in Geneva to the hot line that had been proposed by the United States, and in August the test-ban treaty was agreed to after having been stalled for a long time.

From "The Kennedy Experiment," Etzioni, 1967.

■■■ INTERGROUP CONTACT: THE SOCIAL PSYCHOLOGY OF DESEGREGATION

Misperceptions and distrust between groups in conflict are also fed by lack of contact between members of the opposing groups. Hostile groups tend to maintain high social distance, avoiding interactions with out-group members. Mutual avoidance precludes opportunities for acquiring information that might disconfirm perceptions of the others' motives and character and promotes *autistic hostility* (Newcomb, 1947). The nature of autistic hostility is well illustrated in this parable from Allport (1954):

> See that man over there?
> Yes.
> Well, I hate him.
> But you don't know him.
> That's why I hate him. (p. 265)

According to Allport, this exchange captures the reasoning behind the so-called **contact hypothesis** of intergroup relations. If ignorance and unfamiliarity promote hostility, then opportunities for personal contact between members of opposing groups should reduce hostility by increasing mutual knowledge and acquaintance. Of course, social scientists were not so naive as to believe that physical proximity alone is sufficient to eliminate intergroup conflict. The results of Sherif's summer camp experiments demonstrated clearly that contact could provide opportunity for the escalation of conflict as much as for its reduction. The contact hypothesis has been carefully qualified to specify the *conditions* under which intergroup contact should promote positive relations (Amir, 1969).

These conditions were most recently summarized by Cook (1985). According to his review, contact can produce favorable attitudes when (1) the situation promotes *equal status* interactions between members of the social groups; (2) the interaction encourages behaviors that *disconfirm stereotypes* that the groups hold of each other; (3) the situation involves *cooperative interdependence* among members of both groups; (4) the situation has high "acquaintance potential," promoting *intimate contact* between participants; and (5) the *social norms* in the situation are perceived as favoring intergroup acceptance.

One way to understand the conditions associated with the contact hypothesis is to think of them as an application of the principles of *dissonance theory*. Dissonance theory suggests that an effective way to change people's attitudes is to first change their behavior. Avoidance and social distance from members of specific groups are forms of negative social behavior that are consistent with hostile attitudes and distrust. If individuals with such negative attitudes find themselves in situations in which they engage in positive social interactions with members of the despised group, their behavior is inconsistent with their attitudes toward the group as a whole. It is just this sort of inconsistency that dissonance theory predicts will result in changes of attitudes to justify the new behavior. However, contact alone does not guarantee that positive interactions will occur. The contact situation must be structured in a way that promotes positive social behavior without coercion if dissonance-induced attitude change is to take place.

Dissonance theory links attitude change to initial behavior change: See Chapter 5.

Clearly, many contact situations do not meet all or most of the qualifying conditions for the contact effect. Superficial contacts in formal settings, for instance, or contacts between employers and servants would not be expected to have any favorable effects on intergroup attitudes; nor would forced contact in situations where local authorities clearly do not support the contact effort. Indeed, research indicates that contact under these circumstances does little to alter prevailing social stereotypes or intergroup hostility.

The Role of Social Science in Desegregation

When the U.S. Supreme Court agreed to review the case of *Brown v. Board of Education of Topeka* in 1953, it had among the documents in the case a paper entitled "The Effects of Segregation and the Consequences of Desegregation: A Social Science Statement" (1953), which was submitted as an appendix to the plaintiff's legal briefs. The statement had been drafted by social psychologists Isidor Chein, Kenneth B. Clark, and Stuart Cook, and was signed by thirty-two social scientists, including anthropologists, psychologists, and sociologists who were experts in race relations.

At the time, seventeen states in the United States either required or permitted local school districts to provide segregated schooling for black and white children. Until 1953, the U.S. Supreme Court had accepted the notion that "separate but equal" facilities for school children of different races did not violate Fourteenth Amendment rights to equal protection under the law. The *Brown* case challenged that notion. The social science statement focused on psychological and social research documenting the negative effects of legally sanctioned segregation on the self-esteem of black children and the perpetuation of prejudice and negative stereotypes. The statement also made some recommendations regarding the potentially positive effects of desegregation. It cited field research on desegregation in public housing, employment, and military units to support the conclusion that *under the right conditions* desegregation could promote positive intergroup relations and reduce unfavorable attitudes (e.g., Deutsch & Collins, 1951).

When the Supreme Court rendered its decision in the case in 1954, it reversed the "separate but equal" doctrine and ruled that segregated schooling was unconstitutional. We have only indirect evidence that the social science statement influenced this opinion, but some of the wording justifying the decision resembles arguments presented in the Statement (Cook, 1984) (Exhibit 25.2). Through the *Brown* case, social scientists became intimately concerned in promoting interracial contact through school desegregation and, later, in studying its effects.

School Desegregation: The Record. Since the historic 1954 Supreme Court ruling, school desegregation in the United States has had a controversial history. The original case dealt with de jure segregation, where segregated schools were mandated by law, often requiring that black children be bused from their own neighborhoods in order to attend segregated black schools at a distance. Since then the courts have also ruled against de facto (actual but not legally mandated) segregation of neighborhood schools, sometimes requiring busing

EXHIBIT 25.2

■

From the 1954 Supreme Court Decision on School Segregation

To separate them from others of similar age and qualifications solely because of their race generates a feeling of inferiority as to their status in the community that may affect their hearts and minds in a way unlikely ever to be undone. . . . Segregation of white and colored children in public schools has a detrimental effect upon the colored children. The impact is greater when it has the sanction of the law; for the policy of separating the races is usually interpreted as denoting the inferiority of the Negro group. A sense of inferiority affects the motivation of a child to learn. Segregation with the sanction of law, therefore, has a tendency to retard the educational and mental development of Negro children and to deprive them of some of the benefits they would receive in a racially integrated school system. Whatever may have been the extent of psychological knowledge at the time of *Plessy v. Ferguson,* this finding is amply supported by modern authority.

Brown v. Board of Education, 1954, p. 494

programs in order to desegregate schools within and across districts. As a consequence, the effects of desegregation in school settings have been tested under a great variety of favorable and unfavorable circumstances.

What is the effect of school desegregation on intergroup relations? Reviews of field studies in the United States and elsewhere reveal that the answer is "mixed" (Cook, 1984; Miller & Brewer, 1984; Stephan, 1986). Studies in some settings have documented positive racial attitudes under desegregation. The most notable long-term effect is increased likelihood that blacks from desegregated schools will enroll in integrated colleges, live in integrated neighborhoods, and work in integrated employment settings (Braddock, 1985). On the other hand, many studies have found that white prejudice against blacks increased following desegregation or showed no improvement. In addition, observational studies have documented the phenomenon of "resegregation," whereby blacks and whites in racially mixed schools rarely interact, either because of student preferences in friendship choices (Schofield & Sagar, 1977) or because of teaching practices that track children into racially homogeneous groupings (Epstein, 1985). Research in both the United States and Israel indicates that tracking on the basis of academic abilities seriously undermines the immediate and long-term positive influences of desegregated schooling (Schofield, 1979; Schwarzwald & Cohen, 1982).

The fact that school desegregation did not have uniformly positive effects on intergroup relations has led some to criticize the validity of the 1953 social science statement (e.g., Gerard, 1983). Defenders, however, point out that the statement was directed primarily at the negative effects of legally mandated segregation that existed at the time, and could not have been expected to anticipate all of the forms of mandated desegregation that later developed (Cook, 1984). Further, the statement was very careful in specifying the conditions under which desegregation could be expected to be successful. The results of thirty years of field and laboratory experiments on intergroup contact have clearly validated the importance of those qualifying conditions.

Contact Experiments: Defining the Limits

The full version of the contact hypothesis reflected the outcomes of early experience with intergroup contact in natural settings. One aspect of the hypothesis *(cooperative interdependence)* was systematically tested in the Robbers Cave experiment, and since then many of the other features of the contact hypothesis have been tested in controlled experiments. The results of those experiments have both confirmed and expanded the list of factors that are critical to the effectiveness of contact in promoting positive intergroup relations.

Amount of Contact.   Most successful integration efforts have contact over an extended period of time or multiple cooperative interactions. In the Robbers Cave study, a single cooperative incident did not do much to alter intergroup hostility, but several such experiences did make a difference. Some of the first laboratory experiments on interracial contact found that it took intensive interactions between prejudiced whites and a black coworker over a twenty-day period to attain significant reductions in prejudicial attitudes toward that coworker (Cook, 1985). Laboratory experiments with artificially created groups have also found that reduction of in-group bias is a function of the frequency and duration of intergroup interaction (Wilder & Thompson, 1980; Worchel, Andreoli, & Folger, 1977).

The number of independent contacts with different members of the out-group also has a significant effect on intergroup perceptions. It takes exposure to many diverse group members to break down stereotypes and perceived homogeneity of out-groups (Linville, Salovey, & Fischer, 1989; Weber & Crocker, 1983). In an experiment with young children, Katz and Zalk (1978) found that exposing white children to multiple black faces reduced prejudice more than face-to-face contact with two specific black children. In general, a variety of contact experiences produces more generalized change than experiences that are limited to a few group members or a single interaction setting.

Cooperation.   Sherif's demonstration that intergroup conflict is reduced in the presence of superordinate goals requiring cooperative effort has been replicated in a wide variety of settings. Blake and Mouton (1986) report experiments with 150 groups of executives from industrial organizations, with results that parallel those of the Robbers Cave study. In each experiment, a phase of intergroup competition was followed by a series of cooperative tasks that reduced the negative effects of the earlier competitiveness. Effective cooperation requires at least two important conditions of interdependence: shared goals (if one gains, we all gain) and shared effort (we must work together in order to achieve our goals).

APPLYING SOCIAL PSYCHOLOGY TO EDUCATION
■ ■ ■

Probably the most extensive application of Sherif's findings has been the implementation of cooperative learning programs in desegregated classrooms. In cooperative learning exercises, children work through lessons or assignments in small groups, teaching each other as they go along. A number of different methods of cooperative learning strategies have been devised, but all incorporate basic principles of the contact hypothesis (Slavin, 1985). One form of cooperative learning is the "jigsaw" technique, which was developed by social psychologist Eliot Aronson and has been studied in ethnically mixed elementary school classrooms in Texas and California (Aronson, Blaney, Stephan, Sikes, & Snapp, 1978; Aronson & Gonzalez, 1988). In the jigsaw method, children are assigned to six-member groups that are academically and ethnically diverse. The material for a particular unit (for example, a geography lesson) is divided into six parts, and each child is given an opportunity to become an "expert" on one section of the unit. In effect, each group member is given one piece of the puzzle. It is then that child's responsibility to teach what he or she knows to the other members of the group so they all can do well on later tests of the material. The idea is to create an environment in which each child has something to gain by learning from each of the others, in a form of positive interdependence. This is in stark contrast to the usual competitive atmosphere in classrooms where children score points by performing at the expense of classmates.

Reviews of the effectiveness of implementing cooperative learning strategies such as jigsaw indicate that group learning is associated with increases in liking for class-

Cooperative learning promotes intergroup contact in the classroom. ■

mates, increased cross-ethnic interactions, and generalized reduction in ethnic prejudice (Johnson & Johnson, 1981; Sharan, 1980; Slavin, 1985). The success of cooperative learning methods have been acclaimed as one of the most important contributions of social psychology principles to education. As Slavin (1985) put it, "Thirty years after Allport laid out the basic principles, we finally have practical, proven methods for implementing contact theory in the desegregated classroom. These methods are effective for increasing student achievement as well as improving intergroup relations" (p. 60).

Status Equality. An important qualification for the effectiveness of cooperative contact as a method of improving intergroup relations is that the conditions promote equal-status interaction among the participants. In many racially and ethnically mixed settings this is not so easily achieved, since participants come into the situation with preexisting status differences based on group membership. Even if there are no formal status differentials within the cooperative setting, ethnic identity may serve as a generalized cue for expectations of differences in ability and competence. As a consequence, members of higher-status groups may be unwilling to learn from or be influenced by members of lower-status groups, and their expectations of lesser competence may be reinforced (Cohen, 1982, 1984). Under these conditions, the relative positions of members of the cooperative work group are not truly equal. Cooperation may be undermined when the contributions of the two groups are not well balanced (Garza & Santos, 1991).

Cooperative learning strategies attempt to override status expectancies by furnishing group members with specialized knowledge that makes each member critical to the group's success. But attempts to compensate for initial status disadvantages must strike a delicate balance. We discuss in an earlier chapter how advantaged or high-status groups may react to direct threats to in-group status differences. However, even though status compensation may be regarded as unfair, it may be a necessary step toward successful intergroup contact, as was demonstrated in an important laboratory experiment by Norvell and Worchel (1981). In the initial phases of this experiment, participants were arbitrarily divided into two groups who then competed on a series of tasks. In one condition, no information was given on who won the competition, but in the other condition, one group was consistently announced as the winner. This manipulation served to establish a history of status differences between the two groups.

In the second phase of the experiment, the two groups were brought together to work on a cooperative task. In some cases, one of the groups was given a special advantage—extra information that would help in the cooperative endeavor. In other cases, no special information was conveyed to either group. The effect of this special status advantage on intergroup attitudes following cooperation varied depending on the nature of initial group differences. If the groups had previously been equal, the special information created a status imbalance that reduced intergroup attraction compared with the no-advantage condition. However, when the two groups were different in status, cooperation did not improve intergroup attraction *unless* the initially low-status group had the special advantage. The special information served to compensate for status ine-

High-status groups may react negatively to threats to in-group status differences: See Chapter 24.

FIGURE 25.2

Effects of Status Inequality on Liking for Out-group Members Following Cooperative Interaction. Liking for out-group members was increased when a previously disadvantaged group was given a compensatory advantage. This positive effect occurred even though the differential advantage was perceived as "unfair." (From Norvell & Worchel, 1981.)

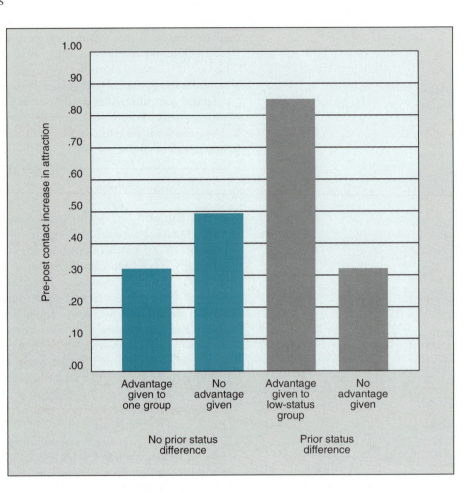

qualities and improved intergroup relations even though the advantage was perceived as "unfair" in all conditions (figure 25.2).

The results of this experiment have interesting implications for policies concerning affirmative action for disadvantaged groups. Such policies are often regarded as unfair because they violate principles of procedural justice (Barnes-Nacoste, 1992). But in the long run, such policies may improve intergroup relations because they satisfy desires for *distributive justice* (equal or equitable outcomes for members of all groups) and promote conditions for equal-status contact.

Salience. In-group bias is most difficult to overcome when in-group–out-group distinctions are highly salient. In situations where visual cues or status differences make participants continually aware of category membership, contact is not likely to break down prior prejudices or stereotypes (Brewer & Miller, 1984; Worchel, 1986). When category identity is salient, all of the cognitive biases we discuss in other chapters of this text conspire to preserve and maintain category differences and negative expectations about the out-group. Even if the contact itself is pleasant and free of conflict, it is not likely to have any lasting effects on intergroup attitudes.

Cognitive biases operate to perpetuate stereotypes and prejudice: See Chapters 8, 10, 11, 23.

One reason that superordinate goals are effective in reducing intergroup hostility is that they minimize attention to category differences by creating a new inclusive group identity. When such a superordinate category is made salient, group members are more likely to think of themselves as one unit, rather than two separate groups. Original in-group–out-group distinctions become less salient when both groups are included in a new in-group that encompasses previously separate groups. When that happens, in-group favoritism is extended to the whole collective (Gaertner, Mann, Murrell, & Dovidio, 1989; Gaertner, Mann, Dovidio, Murrell, & Pomare, 1990).

Personalization. The salience of intergroup distinctions is also reduced if the contact situation promotes opportunities to get to know out-group members as individuals. Attending to personal characteristics of group members not only provides the opportunity to disconfirm category stereotypes but it also breaks down the monolithic perception of the out-group as a homogeneous unit (Wilder, 1978). The importance of personalized relations with out-group members is supported by results of laboratory experiments with artificially created social categories (Miller, Brewer, & Edwards, 1985). In one such experiment, participants first established in-group identities as "overestimators" or "underestimators" based on their performance in a dot estimation task. Then four-person teams were composed of two members of the overestimator category and two underestimators. The teams engaged in a cooperative problem-solving task in which they had to discuss an issue until they reached consensus on a common solution.

During the cooperative interaction phase of the experiment, some groups were encouraged to be highly task oriented, to focus their attention on the quality of their solution to the problem. In other groups, participants were encouraged to socialize and get to know one another as individuals. Following the cooperative experience, participants in the task-focused teams still exhibited in-group bias in their evaluations of in-group and out-group members, but those in the more personalized groups showed significantly less in-group bias (Bettencourt, Brewer, Croak, & Miller, 1992).

Personalization of out-group members can alter intergroup stereotypes, but highly personalized relationships do not always reduce prejudice. Critics of the contact hypothesis point out that positive interpersonal experiences do not necessarily generalize to attitudes toward the group as a whole (Hewstone & Brown, 1986). Wilder (1986) states that two elements have to be established for intergroup contact to be considered a success. First, the individual has to establish positive connections to individual members of the out-group. Second, those associations have to be extended to the out-group category itself.

■ ■ ■　SOME CONCLUDING THOUGHTS

Experimental studies have demonstrated that positive experiences with a single out-group member do not readily generalize to the group as a whole unless the individual is viewed as a typical category member (Desforges, Lord, Ramsey,

Mason, Van Leeuwen, West, & Lepper, 1991; Wilder, 1984). It is all too easy to define one's friend as an exception to the rule and dissociate him or her from the out-group category (Rothbart & John, 1985). Personalized contact can be expected to alter intergroup attitudes only when it includes multiple group members and many occasions. This points out the importance of considering the elements of the contact situation in combination. For the most part, experimental research has focused on one aspect of the contact environment at a time, successively demonstrating the importance of each to the effectiveness of the contact experience. But the component parts are best considered as a whole. We have already seen that intergroup cooperation that is highly task focused does not have the same effect as more personalized cooperative interaction, and personalization interacts with the number and frequency of contact experiences. Reducing intergroup conflict does not come easily. Establishing mutual tolerance and trust between groups requires interventions that combine social psychological processes at the individual, interpersonal, and group levels.

■ ■ ■   SUMMARY

Much more than interpersonal relationships, intergroup relations seem to be characterized by conflict and competition. Social psychologists have long been interested in studying the sources of such intergroup conflict and the conditions required to reduce it. Much of the experimental research on intergroup relations stems from a classic field study by Sherif (1954) conducted at a summer camp in Oklahoma. Sherif found that arbitrarily dividing the boys attending the camp into two separate competing groups quickly produced intergroup rivalry, antagonism, and hostility. Once conflict was generated, it could be reduced only by introduction of superordinate goals, which required that members of both groups work together to achieve a common purpose.

Sherif's experiment was designed around the idea that antagonism between groups is derived from competition or conflicting goals. More recent work has suggested, however, that intergroup antagonism may cause competitiveness rather than the other way around. When individuals are divided into distinct groups or social categories, group members tend to seek competitive advantage for their in-group over out-groups, which in turn promotes mutual distrust and suspicion between groups.

Since distrust is often based on ignorance and unfamiliarity with members of out-groups, social psychologists have assumed that intergroup hostilities can be reduced by increasing opportunities for personal contact between members of opposing groups. Known as the contact hypothesis, this assumption contributed to policies promoting racial desegregation of schools in the United States. Results of studies of the outcomes of school desegregation and findings from social psychological experiments in laboratory settings have confirmed that contact is effective in reducing intergroup hostility only under specified conditions. Changes in intergroup attitudes and behavior occur only when members of groups interact under conditions that promote *extensive, cooperative, equal-status,* and *personalized* contact.

■ ■ ■ **SELECTED READINGS**

1. Cook, S. W. (1985). Experimenting on social issues: The case of school desegregation. *American Psychologist, 40,* 452–460.

2. Hewstone, M., & Brown, R. (Eds.). (1986). *Contact and conflict in intergroup encounters.* Oxford, England: Basil Blackwell.

3. Miller, N., & Brewer, M. B. (Eds.). (1984). *Groups in contact: The psychology of desegregation.* New York: Academic Press.

4. Silverstein, B. (1989). Enemy images: The psychology of U.S. attitudes and cognitions regarding the Soviet Union. *American Psychologist, 44,* 903–913.

5. Worchel, S., & Austin, W. (Eds.). (1986). *Psychology of intergroup relations.* Chicago: Nelson-Hall.

Accessibility
Extent to which an attitude impinges on our consciousness

Accuracy versus expectancy
Issue of whether beliefs and presumptions affect the behavior and performance of others, or whether they correctly reflect the actual behavior and performance of others.

Administrative obedience
Conforming to institutional rules, procedures, and roles which result in psychological harm to another.

Affect-effort theory of expectancy
Theory of teacher expectations which holds that a teacher's beliefs about a student's academic potential influences liking for the student, which in turn influences the teacher's willingness to help the student.

Alcohol disinhibition
Lowering of the normal restraints on behavior as a result of intoxication.

Altruism
Selfless acts of helping without regard for one's self-interest.

Anticonformity
Behavior referenced to the norms of a group, but which is directly opposed to the group.

Arousal-cost-reward model
Theory of helping behavior which sees helping as a function of emotional arousal and assessment of the costs and rewards of helping.

Assimilation
Information within the latitude of acceptance is perceived as more similar to one's own attitude than it really is, and no defenses are made against it.

Attitude-behavior consistency
The issue of whether our actions follow from our beliefs.

Attitude similarity
Having beliefs and opinions in common with another person increases attraction.

Attitudes = evaluations
Defining attitudes in terms of "good-bad" responses to an attitude object.

Autokinetic effect (illusion)
A perceptual illusion in which a stationary pinpoint of light in a darkened room appears to move.

Aversive consequences
Negative outcomes of behavior which may be a necessary condition to trigger dissonance according to revised versions of dissonance theory.

Behavior control
Use of purposeful action to affect the range of response options of other persons.

Behavior (payoff) matrix
Table showing the subjective values of outcomes for different behavioral choices for each person in an social exchange relationship.

Behavioral style
The specific behaviors through which minorities influence majorities.

Biased information search
Seeking information from others which confirms prior impressions or expectations.

Blind and double blind trials
Conditions in which neither the recipients nor the experimenters know whether an active treatment or placebo has been applied.

Bystander intervention
The extent to which people are willing to give help to another person in need.

Central processing route
Processing persuasive messages by thinking, analyzing and assessing the logic and quality of information.

Cognitive dissonance
Unpleasant motivational state caused by inconsistency between attitudes, values and beliefs or between our cognitions and our actions.

Cognitive neoassociationism
Revision of the frustration-aggression theory which expands the potential instigators of aggression to include any negative effect or emotion and argues that our response to negative affect (aggression or escape) depends on our interpretation of the cause of the arousal.

Commitment
A pledge, promise or feeling of obligation to a position or course of action.

Communal relationship
Close relationship in which people are concerned about the welfare of others.

Companionate love
Affection we feel for those with whom our lives are deeply intertwined which includes friendship, closeness and concern of the other's well-being.

Competitive choice
Choices which maximize one person's outcomes, but disadvantage the other.

Compliance versus conversion
Issue of whether a social influence has a temporary effect on public behavior or a more long term effect on internalized beliefs.

Conclusion drawing
Persuasive message which ends with a definite main point.

Consistency
The most important behavioral style of minorities shown to influence majorities.

Contrast (or boomerang) effect
In the study of attitude change, information falling into one's latitude of rejection is perceived as more dissimilar to one's own attitude than it actually is and counter arguments are generated.

Convergent and divergent thinking
Distinction between the influence of majorities in limiting our options and the influence of minorities in opening up our options.

Cooperative choice
Choices which maximize outcomes for both individuals.

Costs and rewards
Assumption of social exchange theory that we evaluate relationships according to the gains and losses that they bring to us.

Counterargumentation
Internal debate caused by information which raises questions about the validity of our attitudes and offers an alternative position.

Diffusion of influence
The spread of minority influence to other related areas of thinking and attitudes.

Diffusion of responsibility
The diminished sense of personal responsibility felt by individuals as the number of witnesses to a situation in which help might be given increases.

Direct experience
Events which we personally live through—"see with our own eyes." Increases attitude-behavior consistency.

Direct versus indirect influence
Moscovici's description of research findings in which public behaviors are unaffected by majority or minority influence, but private responses, not under conscious control, show the impact of minority influence.

Displaced aggression
Focusing our aggression on a person or thing that is not the source of our frustration.

Distraction
Factor which causes a lowered ability to process, analyze and formulate counterarguments to a persuasive message.

Door-in-the-face effect
Enhanced susceptibility to accept a second modest request or concession after having first refused a major request.

Efficiency and sufficiency principles
Principles governing the use of systematic or heuristic information processing which state that people will use the least effortful means of processing information as long as they have confidence in the validity of the outcome.

Effort justification
A type of dissonance research in which people work hard to obtain a particular outcome. High effort is associated with approbation of the work or outcome.

Elaboration likelihood model
(ELM) Describes factors influencing how people will process a persuasive message; specifically, whether they think about the contents of the message or attend to peripheral cues surrounding the delivery of the message.

Empathetic joy hypothesis
Theory of helping behavior stating that we are motivated to help others because we are rewarded by others' happiness.

Empathy
Response to seeing a person in distress which focuses on reducing the distress of the other.

Empathy-altruism hypothesis
Theory of helping behavior stating that harm to another stimulates distress or altruism in a potential helper.

Equity theory
Conception of fairness in relationships in which individuals expect to receive benefits in proportion to the contribution they have made.

Erotic violence
Aggression which combines sexual arousal and hostility.

Exchange relationship.
A non-intimate relationship in which people are primarily concerned with maximizing their own outcomes.

Excitation transfer theory
A theory maintaining that physiological arousal can be labelled in different ways and carried over to intensify other unrelated emotional reactions.

Expectancy effects
The effects of our beliefs, perceptions and presumptions on our own and others' behavior.

Experimenter bias
The effects of researchers' expectations on the responses of study participants.

Expertise
Knowledge and credentials of a source of information.

Extremity
Factor affecting attitude-behavior consistency. Reflects the polarity of the attitude—the degree to which it differs from neutrality or indifference.

Facial electromyogram (EMG)
Measure of electrical activity in the facial muscles.

Fate control
The ability to reward or punish others by controlling outcomes no what the person does.

Foot-in-the-door effect
Enhanced susceptibility to influence as a consequence of having done a prior favor.

Free choice
A type of dissonance research in which people pick alternatives which vary in their similarity and desirability.

Frustration-aggression theory
Model of aggression arguing that blocked goals produce an inevitable readiness to aggress.

Galvanic skin response (GSR)
Measure of general arousal based on the conductivity of the skin.

Generality/specificity of attitudes & behavior
Explanation of the attitude-behavior link which considers the relationship at different levels of interpretation and focus.

Generalizability
Extent to which research findings are widely applicable or valid outside the laboratory, in the "real world."

Hedonism
An assumption of social exchange theory that we seek to maximize pleasure and minimize pain at minimal cost.

Heuristic processing
Use of simpler, quicker and easier decision rules to process attitude-relevant information.

Heuristic-systematic model
Model specifying two ways people may process attitude-relevant information; intentional effort to judge the truth of a message or reliance based on simpler processing and processing shortcuts.

Hostile aggression
Behavior intended to harm or injure accompanied by strong emotions of anger or rage.

Hypocrisy
An alternative view of dissonance research based on people's attempt to maintain a positive self-image when they are induced to act at odds with their beliefs.

Image-repair hypothesis
Helping behavior, occurring after a person has caused harm to another, that is motivated by a need to offset a negative self-image rather than undo the harm done.

Impression management
An alternative explanation for dissonance research based on people's conscious efforts to look good to others; to appear consistent in attitudes and behavior whether they actually are or not.

In-group (or single) minorities
Minorities with whom people identify.

Independence
Behavior which is not influenced by the group, but is based on an individual's own perceptions and experience.

Informational social influence
The use of information provided by others in understanding ambiguous situations and in forming judgments.

Innuendo effect
The negative influence of leading questions and negative associations on people's evaluations of others.

Inoculation hypothesis
Increase in the resistance of an attitude to persuasion after being exposed to a weak persuasive argument.

Instinctive drive to aggression
Freud's conception of an innate disposition or motivation for aggression.

Instrumental aggression
An action intended to hurt others to produce a desired outcome.

Insufficient justification
A type of dissonance research, in which people are induced to act contrary to their beliefs and cannot undo or easily explain their behavior.

Intelligence, self-esteem & persuability
Audience characteristics investigated by attitude researchers for their role in the effects of a persuasive message.

Intention
Factor affecting the attitude-behavior link which focuses on people's motives and expectations.

Interdependence
One person's actions affect and are affected by what another person does.

Investment model
Model based on exchange theory designed to describe the determinants of relational satisfaction and commitment in terms of costs, rewards and contributions to the relationship.

Involvement
How much we care about and are actively involved with an attitude.

Knowledge
How much we know about an attitude object. Increases attitude accessibility.

Latitude of acceptance
The range of positions that people perceive as similar to their own and therefore consider true.

Latitude of rejection
The range of positions that people perceive as unacceptable or untrue.

Learned disinhibition
Lowered restraints on behavior that are acquired responses to alcohol intoxication.

Likert scale
Attitude rating scale emphasizing the evaluative component of attitude statements.

Low ball technique
Sales tactic in which people commit to a purchase at an unrealistically low price, the "mistaken" price is discovered, the purchase denied and a higher price is substituted.

Matching hypothesis
A tendency for people to choose mates who are similar to themselves in level of physical attractiveness, education, wealth, etc.

Mere exposure hypothesis
Explanation for the effects of physical closeness which holds that proximity increases familiarity and familiarity increases comfort and positive evaluations.

Mere thought
Thought alone increases the extremity of evaluations of an attitude object.

Misattribution
A manipulation in dissonance research in which people are led to a false interpretation of their internal physiological state, which subsequently affects their attitudes and evaluations.

Misattribution (of arousal)
The misinterpretation of the source of emotional arousal.

Mixed-motive game
Situation in which the most positive outcome is ambiguous and dependent on the interdependent actions of two or more people.

Mood and persuasion
Research finding that happy peoples' attitudes are easier to change.

Mutual fate control
Outcomes of each person in a relationship are dependent on the actions of the other person.

Need for cognition
Motivation to engage in effortful thought in analyzing information.

Negative-state relief model
Theory of helping behavior arguing that harming or witnessing harm to another causes an unpleasant emotional reaction and that people are motivated to reduce or eliminate this reaction.

Norm
A rule of conduct commonly agreed upon and adopted by a specific group.

Normative social influence
Acquiescence to others to avoid conflict and to maintain group equanimity.

Obedience
A persons' willingness to conform to the demands of an authority.

Obedience and personal responsibility
Decreased conformity to authority as a result of personal responsibility for negative actions.

Obedience and proximity to authority
Conformity to authority increases as closeness to authority in-

creases and isolation from social support for nonconformity increases.

One-sided versus two-sided message
Research concerned with whether a persuasive message is more effective if one or both sides of the issue are presented.

Out-group (or double) minorities
Minorities with whom people do not identify.

Outcome values
Subjective value of behavioral choices for each participant in a social exchange relationship.

Passionate love
A state of intense absorption in another person coupled with high physiological arousal.

Perception of expertise
Feeling of individual competence as a task. Shown to affect the extent of informational social influence.

Perceptual contrast
Explanation for the door-in-the-face effect based on the perceived difference in size of the first as opposed to the second request.

Peripheral processing route
Processing persuasive messages by attending to factors irrelevant to the content or logical merit of the information, such as the expertise or attractiveness of the message source.

Placebo
An inert or innocuous substance.

Pluralistic ignorance
A state of uncertainty in which people look to others' actions to determine appropriate action.

Postdecision regret
Uncertainty and second-guessing that follows a decision.

Prisoner's dilemma
Mixed motive situation in which one person's outcomes are dependent on another person's choices and vice versa, and each person does not know what choices the other will make.

Private acceptance or conversion
Internalization of the influence source's position.

Proximity effect
Increased liking is associated with physical closeness.

Public compliance or conformity
Acquiescence to an influence source without acceptance of the source's position.

Rebellion
Decreased conformity to authority when others refuse to conform.

Reciprocal concessions
Explanation for the door-in-the-face-effect based on the notion that people feel obligated to concede to others after others have conceded to them.

Reciprocity
Explanation for the effect of attitude similarity in which we assume that people who agree with us will like us.

Resistance
Refusal or opposition to conform to the demands of an authority. Increases as social support for such opposition increases.

Reverse incentive effect
Favorable evaluation of a task for which a comparatively low reward was received.

Rigidity
Absolute consistency in behavior which undermines minority influence.

Role playing
Technique in which people act out a position with which they might disagree.

Self-affirmation
An alternative explanation for dissonance research focusing on people's need to protect their self-concept from threats and to re-establish their integrity.

Self-affirmation effect
Tendency to assert beliefs and abilities which are strongly and confidently held even when the expectations of others challenges those beliefs and abilities.

Self-disclosure
The degree to which we reveal ourselves to others.

Self-fulfilling prophecy
Defining a situation incorrectly and then subsequent action consistent with this definition becomes reality.

Self-perception
An alternative to dissonance theory proposed by Bem, which argues that we infer our own and others' attitudes from observable behavior.

Semantic-differential scale
Attitude measurement technique using scales bounded by antonym pairs.

Sleeper effect
The dissipation, over time, of source-based attitude change.

Social comparison
Process by which people respond to majority influence by examining their present attitude or behavior in relation to the majority's position.

Social dilemma
Situation in which choosing a rewarding individual outcome results in a negative outcome for everyone.

Social judgement theory
Theory of attitude change which holds that the effects of a persuasive message depend on people's ego involvement with the issue.

Social learning theory
A view of social behavior emphasizing the conditions under which the behavior was acquired, environmental factors that control its expression and conditions under which it is maintained.

Source credibility
The expertise and trustworthiness of an information source.

Stimulus ambiguity
The level of clarity of the judgement task. Shown in research to affect peoples' susceptibility to social influence.

Symmetric versus asymmetric influence
Relationship of minorities and majorities specifying which may be the target and which the source of social influence.

Systematic processing
Effortful, intentional and motivated processing of attitude-relevant information to assess its truth.

Teacher's expectations
Beliefs teachers have about the academic potential of individual students.

Thurstone scale
One of the earliest measurement instruments for assessing attitudes which asks respondents to pick statements which best summarize their feelings towards a topic.

Tragedy of the commons
Social dilemma in which short-term individual gain conflicts with the long term good of a larger group as illustrated by the classic example of English villagers' use of limited grazing land.

Transformation
Process by which the hedonistic orientation of exchange relationships may be adjusted to include self-sacrificial actions when social norms are very strong.

Triangular model of love
Theory of love based on three elements: intimacy, passion and commitment.

Trustworthiness
Manipulative intent and self-interest of a source of information.

Two-process theory
Symmetric influence model which holds that both the minority and majority have the power to influence the other, but through different means.

Unobtrusive measures
Indirect measures in which attitudes are inferred from behavior.

Vested interest
The extent to which an issue is associated with one's well-being.

■■■ REFERENCES

Abelson, R. P., Aronson, E., McGuire, W. J., Newcomb, T. M., Rosenberg, M. J., & Tannenbaum, P. (Eds). (1968). *Theories of cognitive consistency: A sourcebook.* Chicago: Rand-McNally.

Abelson, R. P. (1981). Psychological status of the script concept. *American Psychologist, 36,* 715–729.

Abramson, L., Seligman, M., & Teasdale, J. (1978). Learned helplessness in humans: Critique and reformulation. *Journal of Abnormal Psychology, 87,* 49–74.

Abrams, D., & Hogg, M. A. (1988). Language attitudes, frames of reference, and social identity: A Scottish dimension. *Journal of Language and Social Psychology, 6,* 201–213.

Adorno, T. W., Frankel-Brunswik, E., Levinson, D. J., & Sanford, R. N. (1950). *The authoritarian personality.* New York: Harper & Row.

Ainsworth, M., Blehar, M., Waters, E., & Wall, S. (1978). *Patterns of attachment: A psychological study of the strange situation.* Hillsdale, NJ: Erlbaum.

Ajzen, I., & Fishbein, M. (1980). *Understanding attitudes and predicting social behavior.* Englewood Cliffs, NJ: Prentice-Hall.

Ajzen, I. (1985). From intentions to actions: A theory of planned behavior. In J. Kuhl & J. Beckman (Eds)., *Action control: From cognitions to behavior* (pp. 11–39). Heidelberg: Springer.

Albright, L., Kenny, D. A., & Malloy, T. E. (1988). Consensus in personality judgments at zero acquaintance. *Journal of Personality and Social Psychology, 55,* 387–395.

Allen, K. M., Blascovich, J., Tomaka, J., & Kelsey, R. M. (1991). Presence of Human Friends and Pet Dogs as Moderators of Autonomic Responses to Stress in Women. *Journal of Personality and Social Psychology.* March 1991, 582–589.

Allen, M., & Stiff, J. (1989). Testing three models for the sleeper effect. *Western Journal of Speech Communication, 53,* 411–426.

Allen, V. L., & Crutchfield, R. S. (1963). Generalization of experimentally reinforced conformity. *Journal of Abnormal and Social Psychology, 67,* 326–333.

Allen, V. L., & Wilder, D. A. (1980). Impact of group consensus and social support on stimulus meaning. Mediation of conformity by cognitive restructuring. *Journal of Personality and Social Psychology, 39,* 1116–1125.

Allen, V. L. (1965). Situational factors in conformity. In L. Berkowitz (Ed.), *Advances in experimental social psychology* (Vol. 2, pp. 133–175). New York: Academic Press.

Allen, V. L. (1975). Social support for non-conformity. In L. Berkowitz (Ed.), *Advances in experimental social psychology* (Vol. 8, pp. 1–43). New York: Academic Press.

Alley, T. R. (1988). *Social and applied aspects of perceiving faces.* Hillsdale, NJ: Erlbaum.

Allison, S. T., McQueen, L. R., & Schaerfl, L. M. (1992). Social decision making processes and the equal partitionment of shared resources. *Journal of Experimental Social Psychology, 28,* 23–42.

Allison, S. T., & Messick, D. M. (1990). Social decision heuristics in the use of shared resources. *Journal of Behavioral Decision Making, 3,* 195–204.

Alloy, L. R., & Abramson, L. (1982). Learned helplessness, depression, and the illusion of control. *Journal of Personality and Social Psychology, 42,* 1114–1126.

Allport, F. H. (1920). The influence of the group upon association and thought. *Journal of Experimental Psychology, 3,* 159–182.

Allport, G. W., & Odbert, H. S. (1936). Trait names: A psycholexical study. *Psychological Monographs, 47*(1, Whole No. 211).

Allport, G. W., & Postman, L. J. (1947). *The psychology of rumor.* New York: Holt.

Allport, G. W. (1935). Attitudes. In C. Murchison (Ed.), *Handbook of social psychology* (Vol. 2). Worchester, MA: Clark University Press.

Allport, G. W. (1985). The historical background of social psychology. In G. Lindzey & E. Aronson (Eds.), *Handbook of social psychology* (Vol. 1, 3rd ed., pp. 1–46). New York: Random House.

Allport, G. W. (1954). *The nature of prejudice.* Reading, MA: Addison-Wesley.

Altenmeyer, B. (1988). *Enemies of freedom: Understanding right-wing authoritarianism.* San Francisco: Jossey-Bass.

American Psychological Association Committee for the Protection of Human Participants in Research (1982). *Ethical principles in the conduct of research with human participants.* Washington, DC: American Psychological Association.

Amir, Y. (1969). Contact hypothesis in ethnic relations. *Psychological Bulletin, 71,* 319–342.

Ancok, D., & Chertkoff, J. M. (1983). Effects of group membership, relative performance, and self-interest on the division of outcomes. *Journal of Personality and Social Psychology, 45,* 1256–1262.

Andersen, S. L., & Ross, L. (1984). Self-knowledge and social inference: I. The impact of cognitive/affective and behavioral data. *Journal of Personality and Social Psychology, 46,* 280–293.

Andersen, S., & Bem, S. L. (1981). Sex typing and androgyny in dyadic interaction. *Journal of Personality and Social Psychology, 41,* 74–86.

Anderson, A. B. (1975). Combined effects of interpersonal attraction and goal-path clarity on the cohesiveness of task oriented groups. *Journal of Personality and Social Psychology, 31,* 68–75.

Anderson, A. B. (1974). *Toward a more complex model of group cohesion: The interactive effects of success-failure, participation opportunity, intrinsic interest, and pay condition.* Unpublished doctoral dissertation, Michigan State University, East Lansing, MI.

Anderson, C. A., & Riger, A. L. (1991). A controllability attributional model of problems in living: Dimensional and situational interactions in the prediction of depression and loneliness. *Social Cognition, 9,* 149–181.

Anderson, C. A. (1991). How people think about causes: Examination of the typical phenomenal organization of attributions for success and failure. *Social Cognition, 9,* 295–329.

Anderson, C., & Anderson, D. (1984). Ambient temperature and violent crime: Tests of the linear and curvilinear hypotheses. *Journal of Personality and Social Psychology, 46,* 91–97.

Anderson, C., & DeNeve, K. M. (1992). Temperature, aggression, and the negative affect escape model. *Psychological Bulletin, 111,* 347–351.

Anderson, N. H., & Barrios, A. A. (1961). Primacy effects in personality impression formation. *Journal of Abnormal and Social Psychology, 63,* 346–350.

Anderson, N. H., & Hubert, S. (1963). Effects of concomitant verbal recall on order effects in personality impression formation. *Journal of Verbal Learning and Verbal Behavior, 2,* 379–391.

Anderson, N. H. (1962). Application of an additive model to impression formation. *Science, 138,* 817–818.

Anderson, N. H. (1965). Averaging versus adding as a stimulus-combination rule in impression formation. *Journal of Experimental Psychology, 70,* 394–400.

Anderson, N. H. (1961). Group performance in an anagram task. *Journal of Social Psychology, 55,* 67–75.

Anthony, T., Copper, C., & Mullen, B. (1992). Cross-racial identification: A social cognitive integration. *Personality and Social Psychology Bulletin, 18,* 296–301.

Apple, W., Streeter, L. A., & Krauss, R. M. (1979). Effects of pitch and speech rate on personal attributions. *Journal of Personality and Social Psychology, 37,* 715–727.

Archer, D., Iritani, B., Kimes, D., & Barios, M. (1983). Face-ism: Five studies of sex differences in facial prominence. *Journal of Personality and Social Psychology, 45,* 725–735.

Argyle, M., & Henderson, M. (1984). The rules of friendship. *Journal of Social and Personal Relationships, 1,* 211–237.

Arms, R. L., Russell, G. W., & Sandilands, M. L. (1979). Effects on the hostility of spectators of viewing aggressive sports. *Social Psychology Quarterly, 42,* 275–279.

Aronoff, J., & Wilson, J. P. (1985). *Personality in the social process.* Hillsdale, NJ: Erlbaum.

Aronson, E., Blaney, N., Stephan, C., Sikes, J., & Snapp, M. (1978). *The jigsaw classroom.* Beverly Hills, CA: Sage.

Aronson, E., Brewer, M. B., & Carlsmith, J. M. (1985). Experimentation in social psychology. In G. Lindzey & E. Aronson (Eds.), *Handbook of social psychology* (Vol. 1, 3rd ed., pp. 441–486). New York: Random House.

Aronson, E., Fried, C., & Stone, J. (1991). Overcoming denial and increasing the intention to use condoms through the induction of hypocrisy. *American Journal of Public Health, 81,* 1636–1638.

Aronson, E. (in press). The return of the repressed: Dissonance theory makes a comeback. *Psychological Inquiry.*

Aronson, E., & Gonzalez, A. (1988). Desegregation, jigsaw, and the Mexican-American experience. In P. Katz & D. Taylor (Eds.), *Eliminating racism: Profiles in controversy* (pp. 301–314). New York: Plenum Press.

Aronson, E., & Mills, J. (1959). The effects of severity of initiation on liking for a group. *Journal of Abnormal and Social Psychology, 59,* 177–181.

Aronson, J., & Jones, E. E. (1992). Inferring abilities after influencing performance. *Journal of Experimental Social Psychology, 28,* 277–299.

Asch, S. E., & Zukier, H. (1984). Thinking about persons. *Journal of Personality and Social Psychology, 46,* 1230–1240.

Asch, S. E. (1951). Effects of group pressure upon the modification and distortion of judgment. In H. Guetzkow (Ed.), *Groups, leadership, and men.* Pittsburgh: Carnegie Press.

Asch, S. E. (1946). Forming impressions of personality. *Journal of Abnormal and Social Psychology, 41,* 258–290.

Asch, S. E. (1955). Opinions and social pressure. *Scientific American, 193,* 31–35.

Asch, S. E. (1956). Studies of independence and conformity: I. A minority of one against a unanimous majority. *Psychological Monographs, 70* (9).

Asch, S. E. (1952). *Social psychology.* New York: Prentice-Hall.

Axelrod, R. (1984). *The evolution of cooperation.* New York: Basic Books.

Axsom, D., & Cooper, J. (1985). Cognitive dissonance and psychotherapy. The role of effort justification in inducing weight loss. *Journal of Personality and Social Psychology, 21,* 149–160.

Axsom, D. (1989). Dissonance and behavior change in psychotherapy. *Journal of Experimental Social Psychology, 25,* 234–252.

Baer, R., Hinkle, S., Smith, K., & Fenton, M. (1980). Reactance as a function of actual versus projected autonomy. *Journal of Personality and Social Psychology, 38,* 416–422.

Bagby, R. M., Parker, J. D. A., & Bury, A. (1990). A comparative citation analysis of attribution theory and the theory of cognitive dissonance. *Personality and Social Psychology Bulletin, 16,* 274–283.

Bakan, D. (1966). *The duality of human existence.* Chicago: Rand-McNally.

Bales, R. F., & Strodtbeck, F. L. (1951). Phases in group problem solving. *Journal of Abnormal and Social Psychology, 46,* 485–495.

Bales, R. F. (1950a). A set of categories for the analysis of small group interaction. *American Sociological Review, 15,* 257–263.

Bales, R. F. (1950b). *Interaction process analysis: A method for the study of small groups.* Cambridge, MA: Addison-Wesley.

Bales, R. F. (1953). The equilibrium problem in small groups. In T. Parsons, R. F. Bales, & E. A. Shils (Eds.), *Working papers in the theory of action* (pp. 111–161). Glencoe, IL: Free Press.

Bandura, A., Ross, D., & Ross, S. A. (1963). Imitation of film-mediated aggressive models. *Journal of Abnormal and Social Psychology, 66,* 3–11.

Bandura, A. (1965). Influences of models' reinforcement contingencies on the acquisition of imitative responses. *Journal of Personality and Social Psychology, 1,* 589–593.

Bandura, A. (1982). Self-efficacy: Mechanism in human agency. *American Psychologist, 37,* 122–147.

Bandura, A. (1973). *Aggression: A social learning analysis.* Englewood Cliffs, NJ: Prentice-Hall.

Bargh, J. A., Bond, R., Lombardi, W., & Tota, M. (1986). The additive nature of chronic and temporary sources of construct accessibility. *Journal of Personality and Social Psychology, 50,* 869–878.

Bargh, J. A., & Pietromonaco, P. (1982). Automatic information processing and social perception: The influence of trait information presented outside of conscious awareness on impression formation. *Journal of Personality and Social Psychology, 43,* 437–449.

Bargh, J. A., & Thein, R. D. (1985). Individual construct accessibility, person memory, and the recall-judgment link: The case of information overload. *Journal of Personality and Social Psychology, 49,* 1129–1146.

Barnes-Nacoste, R. (1992). About the psychology of affirmative action: Putting the science back in. Presentation at the annual meeting of the American Psychological Society. San Diego, CA.

Barnes, R., Ickes, W., & Kidd, R. (1979). Effects of perceived intentionality and stability of another's dependency on helping behavior. *Personality and Social Psychology Bulletin, 5,* 367–372.

Baron, R. A., & Bell, P. A. (1975). Aggression and heat: Mediating effects of prior provocation and exposure to an aggressive model. *Journal of Personality and Social Psychology, 31,* 825–832.

Baron, R. A., & Bell, P. A. (1976). Aggression and heat: The influence of ambient temperature, negative affect, and a cooling drink on physical aggression. *Journal of Personality and Social Psychology, 33,* 245–255.

Baron, R. A. (1972). Aggression as a function of ambient temperature and prior anger arousal. *Journal of Personality and Social Psychology, 21,* 183–189.

Baron, R. A. (1974). Aggression as a function of victim's pain cues, level of prior anger arousal, and exposure to an aggressive model. *Journal of Personality and Social Psychology, 29,* 117–124.

Baron, R. A. (1977). *Human aggression.* New York: Plenum Press.

Baron, R. M., Tom, D. Y. H., & Cooper, H. M. (1985). Social class, race, and teacher expectations. In J. B. Dusek, (Ed.), *Teacher expectancies.* Hillsdale, NJ: Erlbaum.

Baron, R. S., Kerr, N. L., & Miller, N. (1992). *Group process, group decision, group action.* Belmont, CA: Brooks/Cole.

Baron, R. S. (1986). Distraction-conflict theory: Progress and problems. In L. Berkowitz (Ed.), *Advances in experimental social psychology* (Vol. 19, pp. 1–40). New York: Academic Press.

Bar-Tal, D., Graumann, C., Kruglanski, A., & Stroebe, W. (Eds.). (1989). *Stereotyping and prejudice: Changing conceptions.* New York: Springer-Verlag.

Bar-Tal, D., & Saxe, L. (1976). Perceptions of similarly and dissimilarly attractive couples and individuals. *Journal of Personality and Social Psychology, 33,* 722–781.

Bassili, J. N., & Fletcher, J. F. (in press). Response-time measurement in survey research: A method for CATI and a new look at non-attitudes. *Public Opinion Quarterly.*

Bassili, J. N. (1979). Emotion recognition: The role of facial movement and the relative importance of upper and lower areas of the face. *Journal of Personality and Social Psychology, 37,* 2049–2058.

Batson, C. D., Batson, J. G., Griffit, C. A., Barrientos, S., Brandt, J. R., Sprengelmeyer, P., & Bayly, M. J. (1989). Negative-state relief and the empathy-altruism hypothesis. *Journal of Personality and Social Psychology, 56,* 922–933.

Batson, C. D., & Oleson, K. C. (1991). Current status of the empathy-altruism hypothesis. In M. S. Clark (Ed.), *Review of personality and social psychology: Altruism and prosocial behavior* (Vol. 12). Beverly Hills, CA: Sage.

Batson, C. D. (1987). Prosocial motivation: Is it ever truly altruistic? In L. Berkowitz (Ed.), *Advances in experimental social psychology* (Vol. 20, pp. 65–122). Orlando, FL: Academic Press.

Baumeister, R. F., & Showers, C. J. (1986). A review of paradoxical performance effects: Choking under pressure in sports and mental tests. *European Journal of Social Psychology, 16,* 361–383.

Baumeister, R. F., & Tice, D. M. (1984). Role of self-presentation and choice in cognitive dissonance under forced compliance: Necessary or sufficient causes? *Journal of Personality and Social Psychology, 46,* 5–13.

Baumeister, R. F. (1985). The championship choke. *Psychology Today, 19,* 48–52.

Baumgardner, M. H., Leippe, M. R., Ronis, D. L., & Greenwald, A. G. (1983). In search of reliable persuasion effects: II. Associative interference and persistence of persuasion in a message-dense environment. *Journal of Personality and Social Psychology, 45,* 524–537.

Baumrind, D. (1964). Some thoughts on ethics of research: After reading Milgram's "Behavioral study of obedience." *American Psychologist, 19,* 421–423.

Beecher, H. K. (1966). Pain: One mystery solved. *Science, 151,* 840–841.

Belch, G. E., Belch, M. A., & Villareal, A. (1987). Effects of advertising communications: Review of research. *Research in Marketing, 9,* 59–117.

Bell, P. A., & Baron, R. A. (1990). Affect and aggression. In B. S. Moore & A. M. Isen (Eds.), *Affect and social behavior* (pp. 64–88). Cambridge, England: Cambridge University Press, and Paris: Editions de la Maison des Sciences de l'Homme.

Bell, P. A., & Baron, R. A. (1976). Aggression and heat: The mediating role of negative affect. *Journal of Applied Social Psychology, 6,* 18–30.

Bell, P. A. (1992). In defense of the negative affect escape model of heat and aggression. *Psychological Bulletin, 111,* 342–346.

Bem, D. J., & Allen, A. (1974). On predicting some of the people some of the time: The search for cross-situational consistencies in behavior. *Psychological Review, 81,* 506–520.

Bem, D. J. (1965). An experimental analysis of self-persuasion. *Journal of Experimental Social Psychology, 1,* 199–218.

Bem, D. J. (1972). Self-perception theory. In L. Berkowitz (Ed.), *Advances in experimental social psychology* (Vol. 6). New York: Academic Press.

Bem, D. J. (1967). Self-perception: An alternative interpretation of cognitive dissonance phenomena. *Psychological Review, 74,* 183–200.

Bem, D. J. (1970). *Beliefs, attitudes and human affairs.* Belmont, CA: Brooks/Cole.

Bem, D. (1987). A consumer's guide to dual-career marriages. *IRL Report, 25*(1), 10–12.

Bem, S. L. (1981). Gender schema theory: A cognitive account of sex typing. *Psychological Review, 88,* 354–364.

Bem, S. L. (1974). The measurement of psychological androgyny. *Journal of Consulting and Clinical Psychology, 42,* 155–162.

Benassi, M. A. (1982). Effects of order of presentation, primacy, and physical attractiveness on attributions of ability. *Journal of Personality and Social Psychology, 43,* 48–58.

Berkowitz L. (1990). On the formation and regulation of anger and aggression: A cognitive neoassociationistic analysis. *American Psychologist, 45,* 494–503.

Berkowitz, L., & Devine, P. G. (1989). Research traditions, analysis, and synthesis in social psychologifcal theories: The case of dissonance theory. *Personality and Social Psychology Bulletin, 15,* 493–507.

Berkowitz, L., & Knurek, D. (1967). Label-mediated hostility generalization. *Journal of Personality and Social Psychology, 5,* 364–368.

Berkowitz, L., & LePage, A. (1967). Weapons as aggression-eliciting stimuli. *Journal of Personality and Social Psychology, 11,* 202–207.

Berkowitz, L. (1968, September). Impulse, aggression, and the gun. *Psychology Today,* pp. 18–22.

Berkowitz, L. (1988). Frustrations, appraisals, and aversively stimulated aggression. *Aggressive Behavior, 14,* 3–11.

Berkowitz, L. (1969). The frustration-aggression hypothesis revisited. In L. Berkowitz (Ed.), *Roots of aggression: A re-examination of the frustration-aggression hypothesis.* New York: Atherton.

Berkowitz, L. (1989). Frustration-aggression hypothesis: Examination and reformulation. *Psychological Bulletin, 106,* 59–73.

Berry, D. S., & McArthur, L. Z. (1986). Perceiving character in faces: The impact of age-related craniofacial changes on social perception. *Psychological Bulletin, 100,* 3–18.

Berry, D. S., & Zebrowitz-McArthur, L. (1988). What's in a face? Facial maturity and the attribution of legal responsibility. *Personality and Social Psychology Bulletin, 14,* 23–33.

Berscheid, E., Dion, K., Hatfield (Walster), E., & Walster, G. W. (1971). Physical attractiveness and dating choice: A test of the matching hypothesis. *Journal of Experimental Social Psychology, 7,* 173–189.

Berscheid, E., Snyder, M., & Omoto, A. M. (1989). The Relationship Closeness Inventory: Assessing the closeness of interpersonal relationships. *Journal of Personality and Social Psychology, 57,* 792–807.

Berscheid, E., & Hatfield (Walster), E. (1974). Physical attractiveness. In L. Berkowitz (Ed.), *Advances in experimental social psychology* (Vol. 7). New York: Academic Press.

Betancourt, H., & Blair, I. (1992). A cognition (attribution)–emotion model of violence in conflict situations. *Personality and Social Psychology Bulletin, 18,* 343–350.

Bettencourt, B. A., Brewer, M. B., Croak, M. R., & Miller, N. (1992). Cooperation and reduction of intergroup bias: The role of reward structure and social orientation. *Journal of Experimental Social Psychology, 28,* 301–319.

Bettman, J. R., & Weitz, B. A. (1983). Attributions in the boardroom: Causal reasoning in corporate annual reports. *Administrative Science Quarterly, 28,* 165–183.

Biernat, M., Manis, M., & Nelson, T. (1991). Stereotypes and standards of judgment. *Journal of Personality and Social Psychology, 60,* 485–499.

Bither, S. W., Dolich, I. J., & Nell, E. B. (1971). The application of attitude immunization techniques in marketing. *Journal of Marketing Research, 8,* 56–61.

Blake, R. R., & Mouton, J. S. (1986). From theory to practice in interface problem solving. In S. Worchel & W. Austin (Eds.), *Psychology of intergroup relations* (pp. 67–82). Chicago: Nelson-Hall.

Blanchard, F., Lilly, T., & Vaughn, L. (1991). Reducing the expression of racial prejudice. *Psychological Science, 2,* 101–105.

Blanchard, F. A., Weigel, R. H., & Cook, S. W. (1975). The effect of relative competence of group members upon interpersonal attraction in co-operating interracial groups. *Journal of Personality and Social Psychology, 32,* 1020–1030.

Blau, P. M. (1964). *Exchange and power in social life.* New York: Wiley.

Bless, H., Bohner, G., & Schwarz, F. (1990). Mood and persuasion: A cognitive response analysis. *Personality and Social Psychology Bulletin, 16,* 331–345.

Bobo, L. (1988). Attitudes toward the black political movement: Trends, meaning, and effects of racial policy preferences. *Social Psychology Quarterly, 51,* 287–302.

Bobo, L. (1983). Whites' opposition to busing: Symbolic racism or realistic group conflict? *Journal of Personality and Social Psychology, 45,* 1196–1210.

Bogardus, E. S. (1933). A social distance scale. *Sociology and Social Research, 17,* 265–271.

Bohner, G., Crow, K., Erb, H. P., & Schwarz, N. (1992). Affect and persuasion: Mood effects on the processing of message content and context cues and on subsequent behaviour. *European Journal of Social Psychology, 22,* 511–530.

Borgida, E., & Brekke, N. (1985). Psychological research on rape trials. In A. Burgess (Ed.), *Rape and sexual assault: A research handbook* (pp. 313–342). New York: Garland.

Boster, F. J., & Hale, J. L. (1989). Response scale ambiguity as a moderator of choice shift. *Communication Research,* 532–551.

Bouchard, T. J., Jr., (1969). Personality, problem-solving procedure and performance in small groups. *Journal of Applied Psychology, 53,* 1–29.

Bower, G. H., Black, J. B., & Turner, T. J. (1979). Scripts in memory for text. *Cognitive Psychology, 11,* 177–220.

Braddock, J. H. (1985). School desegregation and black assimilation. *Journal of Social Issues, 41*(3), 9–22.

Breckler, S. J., & Wiggins, E. C. (1989). On defining attitude and attitude theory: Once more with feeling. In A. R. Pratkanis, S. J. Breckler, & A. G. Greenwald (Eds.), *Attitude structure and function* (pp. 407–427). Hillsdale, NJ: Erlbaum.

Breckler, S. J., & Wiggins, E. C. (1991). Cognitive responses in persuasion: Affective and evaluative domains. *Journal of Experimental Social Psychology, 27,* 180–200.

Brehm, J. W., & Cohen, A. (1962). *Explorations in cognitive dissonance.* New York: Wiley.

Brehm, J. W., & Festinger, L. (1957). Pressures toward uniformity of performance in groups. *Human Relations, 10,* 85–89.

Brehm, J. (1956). Post-decision changes in desirability of alternatives. *Journal of Abnormal and Social Psychology, 52,* 384–389.

Bretl, D. J., & Cantor, J. (1988). The portrayal of men and women in U. S. television commercials: A recent content analysis and trends over 15 years. *Sex Roles, 18,* 595–609.

Brewer, M. B., Dull, V. T., & Lui, L. (1981). Perceptions of the elderly: Stereotypes as prototypes. *Journal of Personality and Social Psychology, 48,* 89–102.

Brewer, M. B., Ho, H-K., Lee, J-Y., & Miller, N. (1987). Social identity and social distance among Hong Kong school children. *Personality and Social Psychology Bulletin, 13,* 156–165.

Brewer, M. B., & Caporael, L. R. (1990). Selfish genes versus selfish people: Sociobiology as origin myth. *Motivation and Emotion, 14,* 237–243.

Brewer, M. B., & Kramer, R. M. (1986). Choice behavior in social dilemmas: Effects of social identity, group size, and decision framing. *Journal of Personality and Social Psychology, 50,* 543–549.

Brewer, M. B., & Miller, N. (1984). Beyond the contact hypothesis: Theoretical perspectives on desegregation. In N. Miller & M. Brewer (Eds.), *Groups in contact: The psychology of desegregation* (pp. 281–302). New York: Academic Press.

Brewer, M. B. (1988). A dual process model of impression formation. In T. Srull & R. Wyer (Eds.), *Advances in social cognition* (Vol. 1, pp. 1–36). Hillsdale, NJ: Erlbaum.

Brewer, M. B. (1979). In-group bias in the minimal intergroup situation: A cognitive-motivational analysis. *Psychological Bulletin, 86,* 307–324.

Brewer, M. B. (1991). The social self: On being the same and different at the same time. *Personality and Social Psychology Bulletin, 17,* 475–482.

Brewer, W. F., & Treyens, J. C. (1981). Role of schemata in memory for places. *Cognitive Psychology, 13,* 207–230.

Brickner, M. A., Harkins, S. G., & Ostrom, T. M. (1986). Effects of personal involvement: Thought-provoking implications for social loafing. *Journal of Personality and Social Psychology, 51,* 763–770.

Brigham, J. C., Maass, A., Snyder, L., & Spaulding, K. (1982). The accuracy of eyewitness identifications in a field setting. *Journal of Personality and Social Psychology, 42,* 673–681.

Brigham, J. C., & Malpass, R. S. (1985). The role of experience and contact in the recognition of faces of own- and other-race persons. *Journal of Social Issues, 41*(3), 139–155.

Brigham, J. C. (1971). Ethnic stereotypes. *Psychological Bulletin, 76,* 15–38.

Bronfenbrenner, U. (1961). The mirror image in Soviet-American relations: A social psychologist's report. *Journal of Social Issues, 17*(3), 45–56.

Brophy, J. E., Rohrkemper, M. M. (1981). The influence of problem ownership on teachers' perceptions of and strategies for coping with problem students. *Journal of Educational Psychology, 73,* 295–311.

Broverman, I., Vogel, S., Broverman, D., Clarkson, F., & Rosenkrantz, P. (1972). Sex role stereotypes: A current appraisal. *Journal of Social Issues, 28,* 59–78.

Brown, J. D., Novick, N., Lord, K., & Richards, J. (1992). When Gulliver travels: Social context, psychological closeness, and self-appraisals. *Journal of Personality and Social Psychology, 62,* 717–727.

Brown, R. (1965). *Social psychology.* New York: Free Press.

Brown v. Board of Education of Topeka, 347 U.S. 483 (1954).

"The effect of segregation and the consequences of desegregation: A social science statement." Appendix to appellants' briefs: *Brown v. Board of Education of Topeka* (1953). *Minnesota Law Review,* 37 427–439.

Bruner, J. S., & Minturn, A. L. (1955). Perceptual identification and perceptual organization. *Journal of General Psychology, 53,* 21–28.

Bruner, J. S., & Tagiuri, R. (1954). The perception of people. In G. Lindsey (Ed.), *Handbook of social psychology* (Vol. 2). Cambridge, MA: Addison-Wesley.

Bruner, J. S. (1957). On perceptual readiness. *Psychological Review, 64,* 123–152.

Burgoon, J. K., Buller, D. B., & Woodall, W. G. (1989). *Nonverbal communication: The unspoken dialogue.* New York: Harper & Row.

Burgoon, M., & Miller, G. R. (1971). Prior attitude and language intensity as predictors of message style and attitude change following counterattitudinal advocacy. *Journal of Personality and Social Psychology, 20,* 246–253.

Burnstein, E., & Vinokur, A. (1977). Persuasive arguments and social comparison as determinants of attitude polarization. *Journal of Experimental Social Psychology, 13,* 315–332.

Burnstein, E., & Vinokur, A. (1973). Testing two classes of theories about group-induced shifts in individual choices. *Journal of Experimental Social Psychology, 9,* 123–137.

Burnstein, E., & Vinokur, A. (1975). What a person thinks upon learning that he has chosen differently from others. Nice evidence for the persuasive-arguments explanation of choice shifts. *Journal of Experimental Social Psychology, 11,* 412–426.

Burnstein, E. (1982). Persuasion as argument processing. In H. Brandstatter, J. H. Davis, & G. Stocker-Kreichgauer (Eds.), *Group decision making* (pp. 103–124). London: Academic Press.

Burwitz, L., & Newell, K. M. (1972). The effects of mere presence of coactors on learning a motor skill. *Journal of Motor Behavior, 4,* 99–102.

Bushman, B. J., & Geen, R. G. (1990). Role of cognitive-emotional mediators and individual differences in the effects of media violence on aggression. *Journal of Personality and Social Psychology, 58,* 156–163.

Buss, A. H. (1961). *The psychology of aggression.* New York: Wiley.

Buss, D. M., Larsen, R. J., Westen, D., & Semmelroth, J. (1992). Sex differences in jealousy: Evolution, physiology, and psychology. *Psychological Science, 3,* 251–255.

Buss, D. M., & Barnes, M. (1986). Preferences in human mate selection. *Journal of Personality and Social Psychology, 50,* 559–570.

Buss, D. M., & Schmitt, D. P. (1993). Sexual strategies theory: An evolutionary perspective on human mating. *Psychological Review, 100,* 204–232.

Buss, D. M. (1989). Sex differences in human mate preferences: Evolutionary hypotheses tested in 37 cultures. *Behavioral and Brain Sciences, 12,* 1–14.

Buunk, B., & Bringle, R. G. (1987). Jealousy in love relationships. In D. Perlman & S. Duck (Eds.), *Intimate relationships: Development, dynamics, and deterioration.* Newbury Park, CA: Sage.

Byrne, D., & Nelson, D. (1965). Attraction as a linear function of proportion of positive reinforcements. *Journal of Personality and Social Psychology, 1,* 659–663.

Byrne, D. (1961). The influence of propinquity and opportunities for interaction on classroom relationships. *Human Relations, 14,* 63–70.

Byrne, D. (1971). *The attraction paradigm.* New York: Academic Press.

Cacioppo, J. T., Petty, R. E., Kao, C. F., & Rodriguez, R. (1986). Central and peripheral routes to persuasion: An individual difference perspective. *Journal of Personality and Social Psychology, 51,* 1032–1042.

Cacioppo, J. T., & Petty, R. E. (1980). Sex differences in influenceability: Toward specifying the underlying processes. *Personality and Social Psychology Bulletin, 6,* 651–656.

Cacioppo, J. T., & Petty, R. E. (1982). The need for cognition. *Journal of Personality and Social Psychology, 42,* 116–131.

Cacioppo, J. T., & Tassinary, L. G. (Eds.) (1990). *Principles of psychophysiology: Physical, social, and inferential elements.* Cambridge, England: Cambridge University Press.

Calder, B. J., & Ross, M. (1973). *Attitudes and behavior.* Morristown, NJ: General Learning Press.

Callahan-Levy, C., & Messé, L. A. (1979). Sex differences in the allocation of pay. *Journal of Personality and Social Psychology, 37,* 379–394.

Campbell, D. T., & Stanley, J. C. (1966). *Experimental and quasi-experimental designs for research.* Chicago: Rand McNally.

Campbell, D. T. (1990). Asch's moral epistemology for socially shared knowledge. In I. Rock (Ed.), *The legacy of Solomon Asch: Essays in cognition and social psychology.* Hillsdale, NJ: Erlbaum.

Campbell, D. T. (1961). Conformity in psychology's theories of acquired behavioral dispositions. In I. A. Berg & B. M. Bass (Eds.), *Conformity and deviation.* New York: Harper.

Cantor, N., & Mischel, W. (1979). Prototypes in person perception. In L. Berkowitz (Ed.), *Advances in experimental social psychology* (Vol. 12). New York: Academic Press.

Cantor, N., & Mischel, W. (1977). Traits as prototypes: Effects on recognition memory. *Journal of Personality and Social Psychology, 35,* 38–48.

Cantril, H. (1940). *The invasion from Mars: A study in the psychology of panic.* Princeton, NJ: Princeton University Press.

Carlson, M., Charlin, V., & Miller, N. (1988). Positive mood and helping behavior: A test of six hypotheses. *Journal of Personality and Social Psychology, 55,* 211–229.

Carlson, R. (1971). Sex differences in ego functioning: Exploratory studies of agency and communion. *Journal of Consulting and Clinical Psychology, 37,* 267–277.

Carment, D. W. (1970). Rate of simple motor responding as a function of coaction, competition, and sex of the participants. *Psychonomic Science, 19,* 340–341.

Cartwright, D., & Zander, A. (Eds.). (1968). *Group dynamics: Research and theory* (3rd ed.). New York: Harper & Row.

Case, R. B., Moss, A. J., Case, N., McDermott, M., & Eberly, S. (1992). Living alone after myocardial infarction: Impact on prognosis. *Journal of the American Medical Association, 267,* 515–519.

Chaiken, S., Axsom, D., Yates, S. M., Wilson, D., Hicks, A., & Liberman, A. (1988). *Heuristic processing of persuasive messages: The role of temporary and chronic sources of accessibility.* Unpublished ms., New York University.

Chaiken, S., Liberman, A., & Eagly, A. H. (1989). Heuristic and systematic processing within and beyond the persuasion context. In J. S. Uleman & J. A. Bargh (Eds.), *Unintended thought.* New York: Guilford Press.

Chaiken, S., & Yates, S. (1985). Affective-cognitive consistency and thought induced polarization. *Journal of Personality and Social Psychology, 49,* 1470–1481.

Chaiken, S. (1980). Heuristic versus systematic information processing and the use of source versus message cues in persuasion. *Journal of Personality and Social Psychology, 39,* 752–766.

Chaiken, S. (1986). Physical appearance and social influence. In C. P. Herman, M. P. Zanna, & E. T. Higgins (Eds.), *Physical appearance, stigma, and social behavior: The Ontario Symposium* (Vol. 3, pp. 143–177), Hillsdale, NJ: Erlbaum.

Chaiken, S. (1987). The heuristic model of persuasion. In M. P. Zanna, J. M. Olson, & C. P. Herman (Eds.), *Social Influence: The Ontario Symposium* (Vol. 5, pp. 3–39). Hillsdale, NJ: Erlbaum.

Chaikin, A. L., & Derlega, V. J. (1974). Liking for the norm-breaker in self-disclosure. *Journal of Personality, 42,* 112–129.

Chan, G. (1991). A comparison of focus groups and survey questionnaires in market research. Paper presented at the Michigan Undergraduate Psychology Conference, Albion, MI.

Cheng, P. W., & Novick, L. R. (1990). A probabilistic contrast model of causal induction. *Journal of Personality and Social Psychology, 58,* 545–567.

Cialdini, R. B., Borden, R., Thorne, A., Walker, M., Freeman, S., & Sloan, L. (1976). Basking in reflected glory: Three (football) field studies. *Journal of Personality and Social Psychology, 34,* 366–375.

Cialdini, R. B., Ciacioppo, J. T., Bassett, R., & Miller, J. A. (1978). Lowball procedure for producing compliance: Commitment then cost. *Journal of Personality and Social Psychology, 36,* 463–476.

Cialdini, R. B., Darby, B. K., & Vincent, J. E. (1973). Transgression and altruism: A case for hedonism. *Journal of Experimental Social Psychology, 9,* 502–516.

Cialdini, R. B., Kenrick, D. T., & Baumann, D. J. (1982). Effects of mood on prosocial behavior in children and adults. In N. Eisenberg (Ed.), *The development of prosocial behavior* (pp. 339–359). Orlando, FL: Academic Press.

Cialdini, R. B., Schaller, M., Houlihan, D., Arps, K., Fultz, J., & Beaman, A. L. (1987). Empathy-based helping: Is it selflessly or selfishly motivated. *Journal of Personality and Social Psychology, 52,* 749–758.

Cialdini, R. B., Vincent, J. E., Lewis, S. K., Catalan, J., Wheeler, D., & Darbey, B. L. (1975). Reciprocal concessions procedure for inducing compliance: The door-in-the-face technique. *Journal of Personality and Social Psychology, 31,* 206–215.

Cialdini, R. B., & Richardson, K. D. (1980). Two indirect tactics of image management: Basking and blasting. *Journal of Personality and Social Psychology, 39,* 406–415.

Cialdini, R. B. (1988). *Influence: Science and practice* (2nd ed.). Glenview, IL: Scott, Foresman.

Cimbalo, R. S., Faling, V., & Mousaw, P. (1976). The course of love: A cross-sectional design. *Psychological Reports, 38,* 1292–1294.

Clark, K. B., & Clark, M. P. (1947). Racial identification and preference in Negro children. In T. M. Newcomb & E. Hartley (Eds.), *Readings in social psychology* (pp. 169–178). New York: Holt.

Clark, M. S., Mills, J., & Corcoran, (1989). Keeping track of the needs and inputs of friends and strangers. *Personality and Social Psychology Bulletin, 15,* 533–542.

Clark, M. S., Mills, J., & Powell, M. (1986). Keeping track of needs in communal and exchange relationships. *Journal of Personality and Social Psychology, 51,* 333–338.

Clark, M. S., & Mills, J. (1979). Interpersonal attraction in exchange and communal relationships. *Journal of Personality and Social Psychology, 37,* 12–24.

Clark, M. S., & Mills, J. (1991). Reactions to and willingness to express emotion in communal and exchange relationships. *Journal of Experimental Social Psychology, 27,* 324–336.

Clark, M. S. (1986). Evidence for the effectiveness of manipulations of communal and exchange relationships. *Personality and Social Psychology Bulletin, 12,* 414–425.

Clark, M. S. (1984). Record-keeping in two types of relationships. *Journal of Personality and Social Psychology, 47,* 549–557.

Clark, R. D., III, & Maass, A. (1988). Social categorization in minority influence: The case of homosexuality. *European Journal of Social Psychology, 18,* 347–364.

Clayton, D. A. (1978). Socially facilitated behavior. *Quarterly Review of Biology, 53,* 373–392.

Cohen, A. R. (1962). A dissonance analysis of the boomerang effect. *Journal of Personality, 30,* 75–88.

Cohen, C. E. (1981). Person categories and social perception: Testing some boundaries of the processing effects of prior knowledge. *Journal of Personality and Social Psychology, 40,* 441–452.

Cohen, E. G. (1982). Expectation states and interracial interaction in school settings. *Annual Review of Sociology, 8,* 209–235.

Cohen, E. G. (1984). The desegregated school: Problems in status power and interethnic climate. In N. Miller & M. Brewer (Eds.), *Groups in contact: The psychology of desegregation* (pp. 77–96). New York: Academic Press.

Cohen, J. L. (1979). Social facilitation: Increased evaluation apprehension through permanency of record. *Motivation and emotion, 3,* 19–33.

Collins, B. E. (1970). *Social psychology.* Reading, MA: Addison-Wesley.

Comstock, G. D. (1991). *Violence against lesbians and gay men.* Columbia University Press.

Condon, J. W., & Crano, W. D. (1988). Implied evaluation and the relationship between similarity and interpersonal attraction. *Journal of Personality and Social Psychology, 54,* 789–797.

Cook, S. W. (1985). Experimenting on social issues: The case of school desegregation. *American Psychologist, 40,* 452–460.

Cook, S. W. (1984). The 1954 Social Science statement and school desegregation: A reply to Gerard. *American Psychologist, 39,* 819–832.

Cook, T. D., & Curtin, T. R. (1987). The mainstream and the underclass: Why are the differences so salient and the similarities so unobtrusive? In J. Masters & W. Smith (Eds.), *Social comparison, social justice, and relative deprivation: Theoretical, empirical and policy perspectives.* Hillsdale, NJ: Erlbaum.

Cook, T. D., & Flay, B. R. (1978). The temporal persistence of experimentally induced attitude change: An evaluative review. In L. Berkowitz (Ed.), *Advances in experimental social psychology* (Vol. 11). New York: Academic Press.

Cooper, J., Zanna, M. P., & Goethals, G. R. (1974). Mistreatment of an esteemed other as a consequence affecting dissonance reduction. *Journal of Experimental Social Psychology, 10,* 224–233.

Cooper, J., Zanna, M. P., & Taves, P. A. (1978). Arousal as a necessary condition for attitude change following induced compliance. *Journal of Personality and Social Psychology, 36,* 1101–1106.

Cooper, J., & Fazio, R. H. (1984). A new look at dissonance theory. In L. Berkowitz (Ed.), *Advances in experimental social psychology* (Vol. 17, pp. 229–266). Orlando, FL: Academic Press.

Cooper, J., & Fazio, R. H. (1989). Research traditions, analysis, and synthesis: Building a faulty case around misinterpreted theory. *Personality and Social Psychology Bulletin, 15,* 519–529.

Cooper, J., & Fazio, R. H. (1986). The formation and persistence of attitudes that support intergroup conflict. In S. Worchel & W. Austin (Eds.), *Psychology of intergroup relations* (pp. 183–195). Chicago: Nelson-Hall.

Cooper, J., & Worchel, S. (1970). Role of undesired consequences in arousing cognitive dissonance. *Journal of Personality and Social Psychology, 16,* 199–206.

Cooper, W. H. (1981). Ubiquitous halo. *Psychological Bulletin, 90,* 218–244.

Cottrell, N., Wack, D., Sekerak, G., & Rittle, R. (1968). Social facilitation of dominant responses by the presence of an audience and the mere presence of others. *Journal of Personality and Social Psychology, 9,* 245–250.

Cottrell, N. (1972). Social facilitation. In C. McClintock (Ed.), *Experimental social psychology* (pp. 185–236). New York: Holt, Rinehart, & Winston.

Courtright, J. A. (1978). A laboratory investigation of groupthink. *Communication Monographs, 43,* 229–246.

Craig, K. D., & Patrick, C. J. (1985). Facial expression during induced pain. *Journal of Personality and Social Psychology, 48,* 1080–1091.

Crano, W. D. (in press). Components of vested interest and their impact on attitude-behavior consistency. In R. E. Petty and J. Krosnick (Eds.), *Attitude strength: Antecedents and consequences.* Hillsdale, NJ: Erlbaum.

Crano, W. D., & Brewer, M. B. (1986). *Principles and methods of social research.* Boston: Allyn & Bacon.

Crano, W. D., & Mellon, P. M. (1978). Causal influence of teachers' expectations on children's academic performance: A cross-lagged panel analysis. *Journal of Educational Psychology, 70,* 39–49.

Crano, W. D., & Messé, L. A. (1982). *Social psychology: Principles and themes of interpersonal behavior.* Homewood, IL: Dorsey.

Crano, W. D., & Messé, L. A. (1970). When *does* dissonance fail? The time dimension in attitude measurement. *Journal of Personality, 38,* 493–508.

Crano, W. D., & Sivacek, J. (1982). Social reinforcement, self-attribution, and foot-in-the-door phenomenon. *Social Cognition, 1,* 110–125.

Crano, W. D. (1974). Causal analyses of the effects of socioeconomic status and initial intellectual endowment on patterns of cognitive development and academic achievement. In H. R. Green (Ed.), *The aptitude-achievement distinction.* New York: McGraw-Hill.

Crano, W. D. (1970). Effects of sex, response order, and expertise in conformity: A dispositional approach. *Sociometry, 33,* 239–252.

Crano, W. D. (1975). *Conformity behavior: A social psychological analysis.* Homewood, IL: Learning Systems Press.

Crocker, J., Voelkl, K., Testa, M., & Major, B. (1991). Social stigma: The affective consequences of attributional ambiguity. *Journal of Personality and Social Psychology, 60,* 218–228.

Crocker, J., & Luhtanen, R. (1990). Collective self-esteem and ingroup bias. *Journal of Personality and Social Psychology, 58,* 60–67.

Crocker, J., & Major, B. (1989). Social stigma and self-esteem: The self-protective properties of stigma. *Psychological Review, 96,* 608–630.

Crosby, F., Bromley, S., & Saxe, L. (1980). Recent unobtrusive studies of black and white discrimination and prejudice: A literature review. *Psychological Bulletin, 87,* 546–563.

Crosby, F., Fufall, A., Snyder, R., O'Connell, M., & Whalen, P. (1989). The denial of personal disadvantage among you, me, and all the other ostriches. In M. Crawford & M. Gentry (Eds.), *Gender and thought* (pp. 79–99). New York: Springer-Verlag.

Crosby, F. (1982). *Relative deprivation and working women.* New York: Oxford University Press.

Cross, W. E. (1985). Black identity: Rediscovering the distinction between personal identity and reference group orientation. In M. Spencer, G. Brookins, & W. Allen (Eds.), *Beginnings: The social and affective development of black children* (pp. 155–171). Hillsdale, NJ: Erlbaum.

Croyle, R., & Cooper, J. (1983). Dissonance arousal: Physiological evidence. *Journal of Personality and Social Psychology, 45,* 782–791.

Cunningham, M. R., Shaffer, D. R., Barbee, P. L., & Kelley, D. J. (1990). Separate processes in the relation of elation and depression to helping: Social versus personal concerns. *Journal of Experimental Social Psychology, 26,* 13–33.

Cunningham, M. R., Steinberg, J., & Grev, R. (1980). Wanting to and having to help: Separate motivations for positive mood and guilt-induced helping. *Journal of Personality and Social Psychology, 38,* 181–192.

Darley, J. M., Fleming, J. H., Hilton, J. L., & Swann, W. B., Jr. (1988). Dispelling negative expectancies: The impact of interaction goals and target characteristics on the expectancy confirmation process. *Journal of Experimental Social Psychology, 24,* 19–36.

Darley, J. M., & Batson, C. D. (1973). "From Jerusalem to Jericho": A study of situational and dispositional variables in helping behavior. *Journal of Personality and Social Psychology, 27,* 100–108.

Darley, J. M., & Gross, P. H. (1983). A hypothesis-confirming bias in labeling effects. *Journal of Personality and Social Psychology, 44,* 20–33.

Darley, J. M., & Latané, B. (1968). Bystander intervention in emergencies: Diffusion of responsibility. *Journal of Personality and Social Psychology, 8,* 377–383.

Darley, J. M. (1966). Fear and social comparison as determinants of conformity behavior. *Journal of Personality and Social Psychology, 4,* 73–78.

Darwin, C. (1872). *The expression of emotion in man and animals.* London: Murray.

Dashiell, J. F. (1930). An experimental analysis of some group effects. *Journal of Abnormal and Social Psychology, 25,* 190–199.

Davis, J. A. (1966). The campus as a frog pond: An application of the theory of relative deprivation to career decisions of college men. *American Journal of Sociology, 72,* 17–31.

Davis, J. H., Hoppe, R. A., & Hornseth, J. P. (1968). Risk-taking: Task, response pattern and grouping. *Organizational Behavior and Human Performance, 3,* 124–142.

Davis, J. H., Hornik, J. A., & Hornseth, J. P. (1970). Group decision schemes and strategy preferences in a sequential response task. *Journal of Personality and Social Psychology, 15,* 397–408.

Davis, J. H., Kerr, N. L., Sussman, M., & Rissman, A. K. (1974). Social decision schemes under risk. *Journal of Personality and Social Psychology, 30,* 248–271.

Davis, J. H. (1980). Group decision and procedural justice. In M. Fishbein (Ed.), *Progress in social psychology.* Hillsdale, NJ: Erlbaum.

Davis, J. H. (1973). Group decision and social interaction: A theory of social decision schemes. *Psychological Review, 80,* 97–125.

Davis, J. H. (1982). Social interaction as a combinational process in group decision. In H. Brandstatter, J. H. Davis, & G. Stocker-Kreichgauer (Eds.), *Group decision making* (pp. 27–58). London: Academic Press.

Davitz, J. R. (1964). *The communication of emotional meaning.* New York: McGraw-Hill.

Dawes, R. M., & Smith, T. L. (1985). Attitude and opinion measurement. In G. Lindzey & E. Aronson (Eds.), *The handbook of social psychology* (3rd ed., Vol. 1, pp. 509–566). New York: Random House.

Dawson, M. E., Schell, A. M., & Filion, D. L. (1990). The electrodermal system. In J. T. Cacioppo & L. G. Tassinary (Eds.), *Principles of psychophysiology: Physical, social, and inferential elements.* Cambridge, England: Cambridge University Press.

Deaux, K., & Emswiller, T. (1974). Explanations for successful performance on sex-linked tasks: What is skill for the male is luck for the female. *Journal of Personality and Social Psychology, 29,* 80–85.

Deaux, K. (1984). From individual differences to social categories: Analysis of a decade's research on gender. *American Psychologist, 39,* 105–116.

DeBono, K. G., & Harnish, R. J. (1988). Source expertise, source attractiveness, and the processing of persuasive information: A functional approach. *Journal of Personality and Social Psychology, 55,* 541–546.

DeBono, K. G., & Telesca, C. (1990). The influence of source physical attractiveness on advertising effectiveness: A functional perspective. *Journal of Applied Social Psychology, 20,* 1383–1395.

Deci, E. L. (1971). Effects of externally mediated rewards on intrinsic motivation. *Journal of Personality and Social Psychology, 18,* 105–115.

Deforges, D., Lord, C., Ramsey, S., Mason, J., Van Leeuwen, M., West, S., & Lepper, M. (1991). Effects of structured cooperative contact on changing negative attitudes toward stigmatized social groups. *Journal of Personality and Social Psychology, 60,* 531–544.

DeJong, W. (1980). The stigma of obesity: The consequences of naive assumptions concerning the causes of physical deviance. *Journal of Health and Social Behavior, 21,* 75–87.

Dermer, M., & Pyszczynski, T. A. (1978). Effects of erotica upon men's loving and liking responses for women they love. *Journal of Personality and Social Psychology, 36,* 1302–1309.

Dertke, M., Penner, L., & Ulrich, K. (1974). Observer's reporting of shoplifting as a function of thief's race and sex. *Journal of Social Psychology, 94,* 213–221.

Deutsch, M., Epstein, Y., Canavan, P., & Gumpert, P. (1967). Strategies of inducing cooperation. *Journal of Conflict Resolution, 11,* 345–360.

Deutsch, M., & Collins, M. E. (1951). *Interracial housing: A psychological evaluation of a social experiment.* Minneapolis: University of Minnesota Press.

Deutsch, M., & Krauss, R. M. (1960). The effect of threat upon interpersonal bargaining. *Journal of Abnormal and Social Psychology, 61,* 181–189.

Deutsch, M., & Solomon, L. (1959). Reactions to evaluations by others as influenced by self-evaluations. *Sociometry, 22,* 92–113.

Devine, P. G., Monteith, M. J., Zuwerink, J. R., & Elliot, A. M. (1991). Prejudice with and without compunction. *Journal of Personality and Social Psychology, 60,* 817–830.

Devine, P. G., & Baker, S. M. (1991). Measurement of racial stereotype subtyping. *Personality and Social Psychology Bulletin, 17,* 44–50.

Devine, P. G. (1989). Stereotypes and prejudice: Their automatic and controlled components. *Journal of Personality and Social Psychology, 56,* 5–18.

Dillard, J. P., Hunter, J. E., & Burgoon, M. (1984). Sequential-request persuasive strategies: Meta analysis of the foot-in-the-door and the door-in-the-face. *Human Communication Research, 10,* 461–488.

Dion, K. K., Berscheid, E., & Hatfield (Walster), E. (1972). What is beautiful is good. *Journal of Personality and Social Psychology, 24,* 285–290.

Dion, K. L., Baron, R. S., & Miller, N. (1970). Why do groups make riskier decisions than individuals? In L. Berkowitz (Ed.), *Advances in experimental social psychology* (Vol. 5, p. 306–377). New York: Academic Press.

Dion, K., Berscheid, E., & Walster, E. (1972). What is beautiful is good. *Journal of Personality and Social Psychology, 24,* 285–290.

Doise, W. (1969). Intergroup relations and polarization of individual and collective judgments. *Journal of Personality and Social Psychology, 12,* 136–143.

Doise, W. (1986). *Levels of explanation in social psychology.* Cambridge, England: Cambridge University Press.

Dollard, J., Doob, L. W., Miller, N. E., Mowrer, O. H., & Sears, R. R. (1939). *Frustration and aggression.* New Haven, CT: Yale University Press.

Doll, J., & Ajzen, I. (1992). Accessibility and stability of predictors in the theory of planned behavior. *Journal of Personality and Social Psychology, 63,* 754–765.

Doms, M., & van Avermaet, E. (1980). Majority influence, minority influence and conversion behavior: A replication. *Journal of Experimental Social Psychology, 16,* 283–292.

Donnerstein, E. I., & Berkowitz, L. (1981). Victim reactions in aggressive erotic films as a factor in violence against women. *Journal of Personality and Social Psychology, 41,* 710–724.

Donnerstein, E., Linz, D., & Penrod, S. (1987). *The question of pornography.* London: Free Press.

Donnerstein, E., & Barrett, G. (1978). Effects of erotic stimuli on male aggression toward females. *Journal of Personality and Social Psychology, 36,* 180–188.

Donnerstein, E., & Donnerstein, M. (1973). Variables in interracial aggression: Potential in-group censure. *Journal of Personality and Social Psychology, 27,* 143–150.

Donnerstein, E. (1980). Aggressive erotica and violence against women. *Journal of Personality and Social Psychology, 39,* 267–277.

Donnerstein, E. (1983). Erotica and human aggression. In R. G. Geen & E. Donnerstein (Eds.), *Aggression: Theoretical and empirical reviews* (Vol. 1). New York: Academic Press.

Dovidio, J. F., & Gaertner, S. L. (1986). *Prejudice, discrimination and racism: Theory and research.* New York: Academic Press.

Dovidio, J. F. (1984). Helping behavior and altruism: An empirical and conceptual overview. In L. Berkowitz (Ed.), *Advances in experimental social psychology* (Vol. 17, pp. 361–427). New York: Academic Press.

Dovidio, J., Evans, N., & Tyler, R. (1986). Racial stereotypes: The contents of their cognitive representation. *Journal of Experimental Social Psychology, 22,* 22–37.

Downing, J. W., & Judd, C. M. (in press). Effects of repeated attitude expressions on response latency and extremity. *Journal of Personality and Social Psychology.*

Downs, A. C., & Lyons, P. M. (1991). Natural observations of the links between attractiveness and initial legal judgments. *Personality and Social Psychology Bulletin, 17,* 541–547.

Dunand, M. A. (1986). Violence et panique dans le stade football de Bruxelles en 1985: Approache psychosociale des evenements [Violence and panic in the Brussels football stadium in 1985: A psychosocial approach to these remarkable events]. *Cahiers de Psychologie Cognitive, 6,* 235–266.

Duncan, B. L. (1976). Differential social perception and attribution of intergroup violence: Testing the lower limits of stereotyping of blacks. *Journal of Personality and Social Psychology, 34,* 590–598.

Dusek, J. B., & Joseph, G. (1983). The bases of teacher expectancies: A meta-analysis. *Journal of Educational Psychology, 75,* 327–346.

Dutton, D. G., & Lake, R. A. (1973). Threat of own prejudice and reverse discrimination in interracial situations. *Journal of Personality and Social Psychology, 28,* 94–100.

Dutton, D. G. (1973). Reverse discrimination: The relationship of amount of perceived discrimination toward a minority group on the behavior of majority group members. *Canadian Journal of Behavioural Sciences, 5,* 34–45.

D'Agostino, P., & Fincher-Kiefer, R. (1992). Need for cognition and the correspondence bias. *Social Cognition, 10,* 151–163.

Eagly, A. H., Ashmore, R. D., Makhijani, M. G., & Longo, L. C. (1991). What is beautiful is good, but . . .: A meta-analytic review of research on the physical attractiveness stereotype. *Psychological Bulletin, 110,* 109–128.

Eagly, A. H., Wood, W. W., & Fishbaugh, L. (1981). Sex differences in conformity: Surveillance by the group as a determinant of male nonconformity. *Journal of Personality and Social Psychology, 40,* 384–394.

Eagly, A. H., & Carli, L. L. (1981). Sex of researchers and sex-typed communications as determinants of sex differences in influenceability: A meta analysis of social influence studies. *Psychological Bulletin, 90,* 1–20.

Eagly, A. H., & Chaiken, S. (1984). Cognitive theories in persuasion. In L. Berkowitz (Ed.), *Advances in experimental social psychology* (Vol. 17, pp. 267–359). New York: Academic Press.

Eagly, A. H., & Crowley, M. (1986). Gender and helping behavior: A meta-analytic review of the social psychological literature. *Psychological Bulletin, 100,* 283–308.

Eagly, A. H., & Kite, M. E. (1987). Are stereotypes of nationalities applied to both men and women? *Journal of Personality and Social Psychology, 53,* 451–462.

Eagly, A. H., & Steffen, V. J. (1986). Gender and aggressive behavior: A meta-analytic review of the social psychological literature. *Psychological Bulletin, 100,* 309–330.

Eagly, A. H. (1983). Gender and social influence: A social psychological analysis. *American Psychologist, 38,* 971–981.

Eagly, A. H. (1978). Sex differences in influenceability. *Psychological Bulletin, 85,* 86–116.

Eagly, A. H. (1987). *Sex differences in social behavior: A social role interpretation.* Hillsdale, NJ: Erlbaum.

Echabe, A. E., & Rovira, D. P. (1989). Social representations and memory: The case of AIDS. *European Journal of Social Psychology, 19,* 543–551.

Eisenberg, N., & Lennon, R. (1983). Sex differences in empathy and related capacities. *Psychological Bulletin, 10,* 345–357.

Ekman, P. (Ed.). (1973). *Darwin and facial expression.* New York: Academic Press.

Ekman, P., Friesen, W. V., O'Sullivan, M., Chan, A., Diacoyanni-Tarlatzis, I., Heider, K., Krause, R., LeCompte, W., Pitcairn, T., Ricci-Bitti, P., Scherer, K., Tomita, M., & Tzavaras, A. (1987). Universals and cultural differences in the judgments of facial expressions of emotion. *Journal of Personality and Social Psychology, 53,* 712–717.

Ekman, P., Friesen, W. V., & Scherer, K. (1976). Body movements and voice pitch in deception interaction. *Semiotica, 16,* 23–27.

Ekman, P., & Friesen, W. V. (1971). Constants across cultures in the face and emotion. *Journal of Personality and Social Psychology, 17,* 124–129.

Ekman, P., & Friesen, W. V. (1974). Detecting deception from the body or face. *Journal of Personality and Social Psychology, 29,* 288–298.

Ekman, P., & Friesen, W. V. (1978). *Facial Action Coding System: A technique for the measurement of facial movement.* Palo Alto, CA: Consulting Psychologists Press.

Ekman, P. (1972). Universals and cultural differences in facial expression of emotions. In J. Cole (Ed.), *Nebraska Symposium on Motivation* (Vol. 19, pp. 207–282). Lincoln: University of Nebraska Press.

Ekman, P. (1982). *Emotion in the human face.* Cambridge, England: Cambridge University Press.

Ellemers, N., Van Doosje, B., Van Knippenberg, A. & Wilke, H. (1992). Status protection in high status minority groups. *European Journal of Social Psychology, 22,* 123–140.

Endler, N. S., & Magnusson, D. (Eds.). (1976). *Interactional psychology and personality.* Washington, D.C.: Hemisphere.

Endler, N. S. (1966). Conformity as a function of different reinforcement schedules. *Journal of Personality and Social Psychology, 4,* 175–180.

Endler, N. S. (1960). Social conformity in perception of the autokinetic effect. *Journal of Abnormal and Social Psychology, 61,* 489–490.

Endler, N. S. (1965). The effects of verbal reinforcement on conformity and deviant behavior. *Journal of Social Psychology, 66,* 147–154.

Epstein, J. L. (1985). After the bus arrives: Resegregation in desegregated schools. *Journal of Social Issues, 41*(3), 23–43.

Erber, R. (1991). Affective and semantic priming: Effects of mood on category accessibility and inference. *Journal of Experimental Social Psychology, 27,* 480–498.

Erdley, C. A., & D'Agostino, P. R. (1988). Cognitive and affective components of automatic priming effects. *Journal of Personality and Social Psychology, 54,* 741–747.

Eron, L. D., Huesman, R., Lefkowitz, M. M., & Walder, L. O. (1972). Does television violence cause aggression? *American Psychologist, 27,* 253–263.

Esses, V. M., Haddock, G., & Zanna, M. P. (1993). Values, stereotypes, and emotions as determinants of intergroup attitudes. In D. Mackie & D. Hamilton (Eds.), *Affect, cognition and stereotyping: Interactive processes in group perception* (pp. 137–166). New York: Academic Press.

Etzioni, A. (1967). The Kennedy experiment. *Western Political Quarterly, 20,* 361–380.

Exline, R. V. (1972). Visual interaction: The glances of power and preference. In J. Cole (Ed.), *Nebraska Symposium on Motivation* (Vol. 19). Lincoln: University of Nebraska Press.

Fazio, R. H., Powell, M. C., & Williams, C. J. (1989). The role of attitude accessibility in the attitude to behavior process. *Journal of Consumer Research, 16,* 280–288.

Fazio, R. H., Zanna, M. P., & Cooper, J. (1977). Dissonance and self-perception: An integrative view of each theory's proper domain of application. *Journal of Experimental Social Psychology, 13,* 464–479.

Fazio, R. H., & Williams, C. J. (1986). Attitude accessibility as a moderator of the attitude-perception and attitude-behavior relations. *Journal of Personality and Social Psychology, 51,* 505–514.

Fazio, R. H., & Zanna, M. P. (1981). Direct experience in attitude-behavior consistency. In L. Berkowitz (Ed.), *Advances in experimental social psychology* (Vol. 14). New York: Academic Press.

Fazio, R. H. (1990). Multiple processes by which attitudes guide behavior: The MODE model as an integrative framework. In M. P. Zanna (Ed.), *Advances in experimental social psychology* (Vol. 23. pp. 75–109). New York: Academic Press.

Feather, N. (1974). Explanations of poverty in Australian and American samples. The person, society and fate? *Australian Journal of Psychology, 26,* 199–216.

Feather, N. (1984). Protestant ethic, conservatism, and values. *Journal of Personality and Social Psychology, 46,* 1132–1141.

Feingold, A. (1992). Good-looking people are not what we think. *Psychological Bulletin, 111,* 304–341.

Feingold, P. C., & Knapp, M. L. (1977). Anti-drug commercials. *Journal of Communication, 27,* 20–28.

Feldman, S. (1983). Economic individualism and American public opinion. *American Politics Quarterly, 11,* 3–30.

Ferris, C. B., & Wicklund, R. A. (1974). An experiment on importance of freedom and prior demonstration. In R. A. Wicklund (Ed.), *Freedom and reactance.* Hillsdale, NJ: Erlbaum.

Feshbach, S. (1964). The function of aggression and the regulation of aggressive drive. *Psychological Review, 71,* 257–272.

Festinger, L., Schachter, S. S., & Back, K. (1950). *Social pressures in informal groups: A study of human factors in housing.* New York: Harper & Row.

Festinger, L., & Carlsmith, J. M. (1959). Cognitive consequences of forced compliance. *Journal of Abnormal and Social Psychology, 58,* 203–211.

Festinger, L. (1953). An analysis of compliance behavior. In M. Sherif and M. O. Wilson (Eds.), *Group relations at the crossroads*. New York: Harper.

Festinger, L. (1954). A theory of social comparison processes. *Human Relations, 7*, 117–140.

Festinger, L. (1950). Informal social communication. *Psychological Review, 57*, 271–282.

Festinger, L. (1957). *A theory of cognitive dissonance*. Stanford, CA: Stanford University Press.

Fincham, F. D., & Jaspars, J. M. (1980). Attribution of responsibility: From man the scientist to man as lawyer. In L. Berkowitz (Ed.), *Advances in experimental social psychology* (Vol. 13, pp. 82–139). New York: Academic Press.

Fishbein, M., & Ajzen, I. (1981). Acceptance, yielding, and impact: Cognitive processes in persuasion. In R. E. Petty, T. M. Ostrom, & T. C. Brock (Eds.), *Cognitive responses in persuasion* (pp. 339–359). Hillsdale, NJ: Erlbaum.

Fishbein, M., & Ajzen, I. (1975). *Belief, attitude, intention and behavior: An introduction to theory and research*. Reading, MA: Addison-Wesley.

Fisher, J. D. (1988). Possible effects of reference group-based social influence on AIDS-risk behavior and AIDS prevention. *American Psychologist, 43*, 914–920.

Fiske, A. P. (1991). *Structures of social life*. New York: Free Press.

Fiske, S. T., Bersoff, D., Borgida, E., Deaux, K., & Heilman, M. (1991). Use of sex stereotyping research in *Price Waterhouse v. Hopkins. American Psychologist, 46*, 1049–1060.

Fiske, S. T., Von Hendy, H. M. (1992). Personality feedback and situational norms can control stereotyping processes. *Journal of Personality and Social Psychology, 62*, 577–596.

Fiske, S. T., & Neuberg, S. L. (1990). A continuum of impression formation, from category-based to individuating processes: Influences of information and motivation on attention and interpretation. In M. Zanna (Ed.), *Advances in experimental social psychology* (Vol. 23, pp. 1–74). San Diego: Academic Press.

Fiske, S. T., & Pavelchak, M. A. (1986). Category-based versus piecemeal-based affective responses: Developments in schema-triggered affect. In R. M. Sorrentino & E. T. Higgins (Eds.), *Handbook of motivation and cognition: Foundations of social behavior* (pp. 167–203). New York: Guilford Press.

Fiske, S. T., & Taylor, S. E. (1991). *Social cognition*. New York: McGraw-Hill.

Fiske, S. T. (1980). Attention and weight in person perception: The impact of negative and extreme behavior. *Journal of Personality and Social Psychology, 38*, 889–906.

Fleischer, R. A., & Chertkoff, J. M. (1986). Effects of dominance and sex role expectations on leader selection in dyadic work groups. *Journal of Personality and Social Psychology, 50*, 94–99.

Flowers, M. L. (1977). A laboratory test of some implications of Janis' groupthink hypothesis. *Journal of Personality and Social Psychology, 35*, 888–896.

Folkes, V. S. (1982). Forming relationships and the matching hypothesis. *Personality and Social Psychology Bulletin, 8*, 631–636.

Folkes, V., Koletsky, S., & Graham, J. (1987). A field study of causal inferences and consumer reaction: The view from the airport. *Journal of Consumer Research, 13*, 534–539.

Forgas, J. P., Bower, G. H., & Krantz, S. E. (1984). The influence of mood on perceptions of social interactions. *Journal of Experimental Social Psychology, 20*, 497–513.

Forgas, J. P., & Bower, G. H. (1987). Mood effects on person-perception judgments. *Journal of Personality and Social Psychology, 53*, 53–60.

Forsyth, D. R. (1990). *Group dynamics* (2nd ed.). Pacific Grove, CA: Brooks/Cole.

Frager, R. (1970). Conformity and anti-conformity in Japan. *Journal of Personality and Social Psychology, 15*, 103–210.

Freedman, J. H., & Fraser, S. (1966). Compliance without pressure: The FITD technique. *Journal of Personality and Social Psychology, 4*, 195–202.

Freedman, J. L., Cunningham, J. A., & Krismer, K. (1992). Inferred values and the reverse-incentive effect in induced compliance. *Journal of Personality and Social Psychology, 62*, 357–368.

Freedman, J. L. (1984). Effect of television violence on aggressiveness. *Psychological Bulletin, 96*, 227–246.

Freedman, J. L. (1986). Television violence and aggression. *Psychological Bulletin, 100*, 372–378.

Frenkel, O. J., & Doob, A. N. (1976). Post-decision dissonance at the polling booth. *Canadian Journal of Behavioral Science, 8*, 347–350.

Freud, S. (1930). *Civilization and its discontents*. London: Hogarth Press.

Freud, S. (1933). *New introductory lectures on psycho-analysis*. New York: Norton.

Frey, D. L., & Gaertner, S. L. (1986). Helping and the avoidance of inappropriate interracial behavior: A strategy that perpetuates a nonprejudiced self-image. *Journal of Personality and Social Psychology, 50*, 1083–1090.

Friedman, H., & Zebrowitz, L. A. (1992). The contribution of typical sex differences in facial maturity to sex role stereotypes. *Personality and Social Psychology Bulletin, 18*, 430–438.

Frijda, N. H. (1988). The laws of emotion. *American Psychologist, 43*, 349–358.

Funder, D. C. (1987). Errors and mistakes: Evaluating the accuracy of social judgment. *Psychological Bulletin, 101*, 75–90.

Furnham, A. (1982a). Why are the poor always with us? Explanations for poverty in Britain. *British Journal of Social Psychology, 21*, 311–322.

Furnham, A. (1982b). Explanations for unemployment in Britain. *European Journal of Social Psychology, 12*, 335–352.

Försterling, F. (1985). Attributional retraining: A review. *Psychological Bulletin, 98*, 495–512.

Försterling, F. (1989). Models of covariation and attribution: How do they relate to the analogy of analysis of variance? *Journal of Personality and Social Psychology, 57*, 615–625.

Gaertner, S. L., Dovidio, J. F., & Johnson, G. (1982). Race of victim, nonresponsive bystanders, and helping behavior. *Journal of Social Psychology, 117*, 69–77.

Gaertner, S. L., Mann, J., Dovidio, J., Murell, A., & Pomare, M. (1990). How does cooperation reduce intergroup bias? *Journal of Personality and Social Psychology, 59*, 692–704.

Gaertner, S. L., Mann, J., Murrell, A., & Dovidio, J. (1989). Reducing intergroup bias: The benefits of recategorization. *Journal of Personality and Social Psychology, 57*, 239–249.

Gaertner, S. L., & Bickman, L. (1971). Effects of race on the elicitation of helping behavior: The wrong number technique. *Journal of Personality and Social Psychology, 20*, 218–222.

Gaertner, S. L., & Dovidio, J. F. (1977). The subtlety of white racism, arousal, and helping behavior. *Journal of Personality and Social Psychology, 35,* 691–707.

Gaertner, S. L., & Dovidio, J. F. (1986). The aversive form of racism. In J. Dovidio & S. Gaertner (Eds.), *Prejudice, discrimination and racism* (pp. 61–89). New York: Academic Press.

Gamson, W. A., Fireman, B., & Rytina, S. (1982). *Encounters with unjust authority.* Homewood, IL: Dorsey.

Gardner, R. C. (1993). Stereotypes as consensual beliefs. In M. Zanna & J. Olson (Eds.), *The psychology of prejudice. The Ontario Symposium* (Vol. 7). Hillsdale, NJ: Erlbaum.

Garza, R. T., & Santos, S. J. (1991). Ingroup/outgroup balance and interdependent interethnic behavior. *Journal of Experimental Social Psychology, 27,* 124–137.

Geen, R. G., Stonner, D., & Shope, G. L. (1975). The facilitation of aggression by aggression: Evidence against the catharsis hypothesis. *Journal of Personality and Social Psychology, 31,* 721–726.

Geen, R. G. (1983). Aggression and television violence. In R. G. Geen & E. I. Donnerstein (Eds.), *Aggression: Theoretical and empirical reviews* (Vol. 2, pp. 103–125). New York: Academic Press.

Geen, R. G. (1979). Effects of being observed on learning following success and failure experiences. *Motivation and Emotion, 4,* 355–371.

Geiselman, R., Haight, N., & Kimata, L. (1984). Context effects in the perceived physical attractiveness of faces. *Journal of Experimental Social Psychology, 20,* 409–424.

Geller, E. S. (1975). Increasing desired waste disposals with instructions. *Man-Environment Systems, 5,* 125–128.

Gerard, H. B., & Mathewson, G. C. (1966). The effects of severity of initiation on liking for a group: A replication. *Journal of Experimental Social Psychology, 2,* 278–287.

Gerard, H. B. (1983). School desegregation: The social science role. *American Psychologist, 38,* 869–877.

Gibson, J. J. (1979). *The ecological approach to visual perception.* Boston: Houghton Mifflin.

Gilbert, D. T., Pelham, B. W., & Krull, D. S. (1988). On cognitive busyness: When person perceivers meet persons perceived. *Journal of Personality and Social Psychology, 54,* 733–740.

Gilbert, D. T. (1989). Thinking lightly about others: Automatic components of the social inference process. In J. Uleman & J. Bargh (Eds.), *Unintended thought: Limits of awareness, intention, and control* (pp. 189–211). New York: Guilford Press.

Gillig, P. M., & Greenwald, A. G. (1974). Is it time to lay the sleeper effect to rest? *Journal of Personality and Social Psychology, 29,* 132–139.

Ginosar, Z., & Trope, Y. (1980). The effects of base rates and individuating information on judgments about another person. *Journal of Experimental Social Psychology, 16,* 228–242.

Glick, P., Zion, C., & Nelson, C. (1988). What mediates sex discrimination in hiring decisions? *Journal of Personality and Social Psychology, 55,* 178–186.

Goethals, A. R. (1986a). Fabricating and ignoring social reality: Self-serving estimates of consensus. In J. Olson, C. P. Herman, & M. P. Zanna (Eds.), *Ontario symposium on social cognition IV.* Hillsdale, NJ: Erlbaum.

Goethals, A. R. (1986b). Social comparison theory: Psychology from the lost and found. *Personality and Social Psychology Bulletin, 12,* 261–278.

Goethals, G. R., & Darley, J. M. (1977). Social comparison theory: An attributional approach. In J. Suls & R. Miller (Eds.), *Social comparison processes: Theoretical and empirical perspectives* (pp. 259–278). Washington, DC: Hemisphere.

Goldberg, C. (1975). Conformity to majority type as a function of task and acceptance of sex-related stereotypes. *Journal of Psychology, 89,* 25–37.

Goodwin, R. (1990). Sex differences among partner preferences: Are the sexes really very similar? *Sex Roles, 23,* 501–513.

Gorenflo, D. W., & Crano, W. D. (1989). Judgmental subjectivity/objectivity and locus of choice in social comparison. *Journal of Personality and Social Psychology, 57,* 605–614.

Gouldner, A. (1960). The norm of reciprocity: A preliminary statement. *American Sociological Review, 25,* 161–178.

Grayson, B., & Stein, M. I. (1981). Attracting assault: Victims' nonverbal cues. *Journal of Communication, 31,* 68–75.

Green, S. K., Buchanan, D. R., & Muir, S. K. (1984). Winners, losers, and choosers: A field investigation of dating initiation. *Personality and Social Psychology Bulletin, 10,* 502–511.

Groff, B. D., Baron, R. S., & Moore, D. L. (1983). Distraction, attentional conflict, and drivelike behavior. *Journal of Experimental Social Psychology, 19,* 359–380.

Gruder, C. L., Cook, T. D., Hennigan, K. M., Flay, B. R., Alessi, C., & Halamaj, J. (1978). Empirical tests of the absolute sleeper effect predicted from the discounting cue hypothesis. *Journal of Personality and Social Psychology, 36,* 1061–1074.

Guetzkow, H. (1968). Differentiation of roles in task-oriented groups. In D. Cartwright & A. Zander (Eds.), *Group dynamics: Research and theory,* (3rd ed., pp. 512–526). New York: Harper & Row.

Guimond, S., & Dube-Simard, L. (1983). Relative deprivation theory and the Quebec Nationalist Movement: The cognition-emotion distinction and the personal-group deprivation issue. *Journal of Personality and Social Psychology, 44,* 526–535.

Hacker, H. M. (1951). Women as a minority group. *Social Forces, 30,* 60–69.

Hackman, J. R., Brousseau, K. R., & Weiss, J. A. (1976). The interaction of task design and group performance strategies in determining group effectiveness. *Organizational Behavior and Human Performance, 16,* 350–365.

Hackman, J. R., & Morris, C. G. (1975). Group tasks, group interaction process, and group performance effectiveness: A review and proposed integration. In L. Berkowitz (Ed.), *Advances in experimental social psychology* (Vol. 8, pp. 47–99). New York: Academic Press.

Hall, E. T. (1966). *The hidden dimension.* Garden City, NY: Doubleday.

Hall, J. A. (1984). *Nonverbal sex differences.* Baltimore: Johns Hopkins University Press.

Hamilton, D. L., Katz, L. B., & Leirer, V. O. (1980). Cognitive representation of personality impressions: Organizational processes in first impression formation. *Journal of Personality and Social Psychology, 39,* 1050–1063.

Hamilton, D. L., Sherman, S. J., & Ruvolo, C. M. (1990). Stereotype-based expectancies: Effects on information processing and social behavior. *Journal of Social Issues, 46*(2), 35–68.

Hamilton, D. L., & Gifford, R. K. (1976). Illusory correlation in interpersonal perception: A cognitive basis of stereotypic judgments. *Journal of Experimental Social Psychology, 12,* 392–407.

Hamilton, D. L., & Trolier, T. K. (1986). Stereotypes and stereotyping: An overview of the cognitive approach. In J. Dovidio & S. Gaertner (Eds.), *Prejudice, discrimination, and racism* (pp. 127–164). New York: Academic Press.

Hamilton, D. L., & Zanna, M. P. (1974). Context effects in impression formation: Changes in connotative meaning. *Journal of Personality and Social Psychology, 29,* 649–654.

Hamilton, D. L. (1988). Causal attribution viewed from an information-processing perspective. In D. Bar-Tal & A. Kruglanski (Eds.), *The social psychology of knowledge* (pp. 359–386). Cambridge, England: Cambridge University Press.

Hancock, R. D., & Sorrentino, R. M. (1980). The effects of expected future interaction and prior group support on the conformity process. *Journal of Personality and Social Psychology, 16,* 261–370.

Hansen, C. H., & Hansen, R. D. (1988). Finding the face in the crowd: An anger superiority effect. *Journal of Personality and Social Psychology, 54,* 917–924.

Hansen, R. D., & Donoghue, J. (1977). The power of consensus: Information derived from one's own and other's behavior. *Journal of Personality and Social Psychology, 35,* 294–302.

Hardin, G. (1968). The tragedy of the commons. *Science, 162,* 1243–1248.

Hardy, C., & Latané, B. (1986). Social loafing on a cheering task. *Social Science, 71,* 165–172.

Harkins, S. G., & Petty, R. E. (1987). Information utility and the multiple source effect. *Journal of Personality and Social Psychology, 52,* 260–268.

Harkins, S. G., & Petty, R. E. (1983). Social context effects in persuasion: The effects of multiple sources and multiple targets. In P. Paulhus (Ed.), *Basic group processes* (pp. 149–175). New York: Springer-Verlag.

Harkins, S. G., & Szymanski, K. (1987). Social loafing and social facilitation: New wine in old bottles. In C. Hendrick (Ed.), *Group processes and intergroup relations* (pp. 167–188). Newbury Park, CA: Sage.

Harkins, S. (1987). Social loafing and social facilitation. *Journal of Experimental Social Psychology, 23,* 1–18.

Harper, N. L., & Askling, L. R. (1980). Group communication and quality of task solution in a media production organization. *Communication Monographs, 47,* 77–100.

Harrison, A. A., & McClintock, C. G. (1965). Previous experience within the dyad and cooperative game behavior. *Journal of Personality and Social Psychology, 1,* 671–675.

Harris, M. J., & Rosenthal, R. (1985). The mediation of interpersonal expectancy effects: 31 meta-analyses. *Psychological Bulletin, 97,* 363–386.

Harris, M. J. (1991). Controversy and cumulation: Meta-analysis and research on interpersonal expectancy effects. *Personality and Social Psychology Bulletin, 17,* 316–322.

Harris, R. J., Messick, D. M., & Sentis, K. P. (1981). Proportionality, linearity, and parameter constancy. Messick and Sentis reconsidered. *Journal of Experimental Social Psychology, 17,* 210–225.

Hartley, E. L. (1946). *Problems in prejudice.* New York: Kings Crown Press.

Hass, R. G. (1981). Effects of source characteristics on cognitive responses in persuasion. In R. E. Petty, T. M. Ostrom, & T. C. Brock (Eds.), *Cognitive responses in persuasion* (pp. 141–172). Hillsdale, NJ: Erlbaum.

Hastie, R., & Kumar, P. (1979). Person memory: Personality traits as organizing principles in memory for behaviors. *Journal of Personality and Social Psychology, 37,* 25–38.

Hastorf, A., Northcraft, G., & Picciotto, S. (1979). Helping the handicapped: How realistic is the performance feedback received by the physically handicapped? *Personality and Social Psychology Bulletin, 5,* 373–376.

Hatfield, E., & Sprecher, S. (1986). *Mirror, mirror . . . The importance of looks in everyday life.* New York: State University of New York Press.

Hatfield, E., & Walster, G. W. (1978). *A new look at love.* Reading, MA: Addison-Wesley.

Hatfield, E. (1988). Passionate and companionate love. In R. J. Sternberg & M. L. Barnes (Eds.), *The psychology of love* (pp. 191–217). New Haven, CT: Yale University Press.

Haythorn, W. (1953). The influence of individual members on the characteristics of small groups. *Journal of Abnormal and Social Psychology, 48,* 276–284.

Hazan, C., & Shaver, P. (1987). Romantic love conceptualized as an attachment process. *Journal of Personality and Social Psychology, 52,* 511–524.

Heider, F. (1944). Social perception and phenomenal causality. *Psychological Review, 51,* 358–374.

Heider, F. (1958). *The psychology of interpersonal relations.* New York: Wiley.

Heilman, M. E., & Guzzo, R. A. (1978). The perceived cause of work success as a mediator of sex discrimination in organizations. *Organizational Behavior and Human Performance, 21,* 356–357.

Hendricks, M., & Bootzin, R. (1976). Race and sex as stimuli for negative affect and physical avoidance. *Journal of Social Psychology, 98,* 111–120.

Henley, N. M. (1977). *Body politics.* Englewood Cliffs, NJ: Prentice-Hall.

Hensley, T. R., & Griffin, G. W. (1986). Victims of groupthink: The Kent State University Board of Trustees and the 1977 gymnasium controversy. *Journal of Conflict Resolution, 30,* 497–531.

Herbert, T. B., & Cohen, S. (1993). Depression and immunity: A meta-analytic review. *Psychological Bulletin, 113,* 472–486.

Herek, G., Janis, I. L., & Huth, P. (1987). Decisionmaking during international crises: Is quality of process related to outcome? *Journal of Conflict Resolution, 31,* 203–226.

Hewstone, M., Hopkins, N., & Routh, D. (1992). Cognitive models of stereotype change: (1) Generalization and subtyping in young people's views of the police. *European Journal of Social Psychology, 22,* 219–234.

Hewstone, M., & Brown, R. (1986). Contact is not enough: An intergroup perspective on the 'contact hypothesis.' In M. Hewstone & R. Brown (Eds.), *Contact and conflict in intergroup encounters* (pp. 1–44). Oxford, England: Basil Blackwell.

Hewstone, M., & Jaspars, J. (1987). Covariation and causal attribution: A logical model of the intuitive analysis of variance. *Journal of Personality and Social Psychology, 53,* 663–672.

Hewstone, M. (1990). The "ultimate attribution error?" A review of the literature of intergroup causal attribution. *European Journal of Social Psychology, 20,* 311–336.

Higgins, E. T., King, G. A., & Mavin, G. H. (1982). Individual construct accessibility and subjective impressions and recall. *Journal of Personality and Social Psychology, 43,* 35–47.

Higgins, E. T., Rholes, W. S., & Jones, C. R. (1977). Category accessibility and impression formation. *Journal of Experimental Social Psychology, 13,* 141–154.

Higgins, E. T., & King, G. (1981). Accessibility of social constructs: Information-processing consequences of individual and contextual variability. In N. Cantor & J. Kihlstrom (Eds.), *Personality and social interaction* (pp. 69–121). Hillsdale, NJ: Erlbaum.

Higgins, E. T., & Rholes, W. S. (1978). "Saying is believing": Effects of message modification on memory and liking for the person described. *Journal of Experimental Social Psychology, 14,* 363–378.

Higgins, E. T., & Stangor, C. (1988). Context-driven social judgment and memory: When "behavior engulfs the field" in reconstructive memory. In D. Bar-Tal & A. Kruglanski (Eds.), *The social psychology of knowledge* (pp. 262–298). Cambridge, England: Cambridge University Press.

Higgins, E. T. (1987). Self-discrepancy: A theory relating self and affect. *Psychological Review, 94,* 319–340.

Hill, C. T., Rubin, Z., & Peplau, L. A. (1976). Break-ups before marriage: The end of 103 affairs. *Journal of Social Issues, 32,* 147–167.

Hirokaowa, R. Y. (1980). A comparative analysis of communication patterns within effective and ineffective decision-making groups. *Communication Monographs, 47,* 312–321.

Hirt, E., Zillmann, D., Erickson, G., & Kennedy, C. (1992). Costs and benefits of allegiance: Changes in fans' self-ascribed competencies after team victory versus defeat. *Journal of Personality and Social Psychology, 63,* 724–738.

Hoffman, C., Mischel, W., & Baer, J. (1984). Language and person cognition: Effects of communicative set on trait attribution. *Journal of Personality and Social Psychology, 46,* 1029–1043.

Hoffman, C., & Hurst, N. (1990). Gender stereotypes: Perception or rationalization? *Journal of Personality and Social Psychology, 58,* 197–208.

Hofling, C. K., Brotzman, E., Dalrymple, S., Graves, N., & Pierce, C. M. (1966). An experimental study in nurse-physician relationships. *Journal of Nervous and Mental Disease, 143,* 171–180.

Hogg, M. A., & Abrams, D. (1988). *Social identifications: A social psychology of intergroup relations and group processes.* London: Routledge.

Hogg, M. A., & Sunderland, J. (1991). Self-esteem and intergroup discrimination in the minimal group paradigm. *British Journal of Social Psychology, 30,* 51–62.

Hogg, M. A., & Turner, J. C. (1987). Intergroup behaviour, self-stereotyping and the salience of social categories. *British Journal of Social Psychology, 26,* 325–340.

Hogg, M. A. (1992). *The social psychology of group cohesiveness: From attraction to social identity.* London: Harvester-Wheatsheaf.

Holman, R. H. (1986). Advertising and emotionality. In R. A. Peterson, W. D. Hoyer, & W. R. WIlson (Eds.), *The role of affect in consumer behavior* (pp. 119–140). Lexington, MA: Lexington Books.

Holtzworth-Munroe, A., & Jacobson, N. S. (1985). Causal attributions of marital couples: When do they search for causes? What do they conclude when they do? *Journal of Personality and Social Psychology, 48,* 1398–1412.

Homans, G. C. (1958). Social behavior as exchange. *American Journal of Sociology, 63,* 597–606.

Homans, G. C. (1974). *Social behavior: Its elementary forms* (Rev. ed.). New York: Harcourt Brace Jovanovich.

Hovland, C. I., Janis, I. L., & Kelley, H. H. (1953). *Communication and persuasion.* New Haven, CT: Yale University Press.

Hovland, C. I., Lumsdaine, A., & Sheffield, F. (1949). *Experiments on mass communications* (Studies in social psychology in World War II, Vol. 3, published by the Social Science Research Council, 226). Princeton, NJ: Princeton University Press.

Hovland, C. I., & Mandell, W. (1952). An experimental comparison of conclusion-drawing by the communicator and by the audience. *Journal of Abnormal and Social Psychology, 47,* 581–588.

Hovland, C. I., & Weiss, W. (1951). The influence of source credibility on communication effectiveness. *Public Opinion Quarterly, 15,* 635–650.

Howard, J. W., & Rothbart, M. (1980). Social categorization and memory for in-group and out-group behavior. *Journal of Personality and Social Psychology, 38,* 301–310.

Howard, W., & Crano, W. D. (1974). Effects of sex, conversation, location, and size of observer group on bystander intervention in a high risk situation. *Sociometry, 37,* 491–507.

Huesmann, L. R., Eron, L. D., Lefkowitz, M. M., & Walder, L. O. (1984). Stability of aggression over time and generations. *Developmental Psychology, 20,* 746–775.

Huesmann, L. R., & Eron, L. D. (Eds.). (1986). *Television and the aggressive child: A cross-national comparison.* Hillsdale, NJ: Erlbaum.

Huesmann, L. R. (1982). Television violence and aggressive behavior. In D. Pearl & L. Bouthilet (Eds.), *Television and behavior: Ten years of scientific progress and implications for the 80's.* Washington, D.C.: U.S. Government Printing Office.

Insko, C. A., Arkoff, A., & Insko, V. M. (1965). Effects of high and low fear-arousing communications upon opinions toward smoking. *Journal of Experimental Social Psychology, 1,* 256–266.

Insko, C. A., Pinkley, R., Hoyle, R., Dalton, B., Hong, G., Slim, R., Landry, P., Holton, B., Ruffin, P., & Thibaut, J. (1987). Individual versus group discontinuity: The role of intergroup contact. *Journal of Experimental Social Psychology, 23,* 250–267.

Insko, C. A., Schopler, J., Hoyle, R., Dardis, G., & Graetz, K. (1990). Individual-group discontinuity as a function of fear and greed. *Journal of Personality and Social Psychology, 58,* 68–79.

Insko, C. A., & Schopler, J. (1987). Categorization, competition, and collectivity. In C. Hendrick (Ed.), *Review of personality and social psychology* (Vol. 8, pp. 213–251). Beverly Hills, CA: Sage.

Insko, C., Nacoste, R., & Moe, J. (1983). Belief congruence and racial discrimination: Review of the evidence and critical evaluation. *European Journal of Social Psychology, 13,* 153–174.

Isenberg, D. J. (1986). Group polarization: A critical review and meta-analysis. *Journal of Personality and Social Psychology, 50,* 1141–1151.

Isen, A. M., & Levin, P. F. (1972). Effect of feeling good on helping: Cookies and kindness. *Journal of Personality and Social Psychology, 21,* 384–388.

Isen, A. M. (1987). Positive affect, cognitive processes, and social behavior. In L. Berkowitz (Ed.), *Advances in Experimental Social Psychology* (Vol. 20). New York: Academic Press.

Isen, A. M. (1970). Success, failure, attention, and reaction to others: The warm glow of success. *Journal of Personality and Social Psychology, 15,* 294–301.

Izard, C. E. (1977). *Human emotions.* New York: Plenum Press.

Jackson, J. M., & Harkins, S. G. (1985). Equity in effort: An explanation of the social loafing effect. *Journal of Personality and Social Psychology, 49,* 1199–1206.

Jackson, J., & Williams, K. (1985). Social loafing on difficult tasks: Working collectively can improve performance. *Journal of Personality and Social Psychology, 49,* 937–942.

James, W. (1890/1981). *The principles of psychology* (Vols. 1, 2). Cambridge, MA: Harvard University Press.

Janis, I. L., Kaye, D., & Kirschner, P. (1965). Facilitating effects of "eating while reading" on responsiveness to persuasive communications. *Journal of Personality and Social Psychology, 1,* 181–186.

Janis, I. L., & Feshbach, S. (1953). Effects of fear-arousing communications. *Journal of Abnormal and Social Psychology, 48,* 78–92.

Janis, I. L., & Hovland, C. I. (Eds.). (1959). *Personality and persuasibility.* New Haven, CT: Yale University Press.

Janis, I. L., & Mann, L. (1965). Effectiveness of emotional role-playing in modifying smoking habits and attitudes. *Journal of Experimental Research in Personality, 1,* 84–90.

Janis, I. L., & Terwilliger, R. (1962). An experimental study of psychological resistances to fear-arousing communications. *Journal of Abnormal and Social Psychology, 65,* 403–410.

Janis, I. L. (1983). Groupthink. In H. H. Blumberg, A. P. Hare, V. Kent, & M. F. Davis (Eds.), *Small groups and social interaction* (Vol. 2, pp. 39–46). Chichester, England: Wiley.

Janis, I. L. (1989). *Crucial decisions: Leadership in policymaking and crisis management.* New York: Free Press.

Janis, I. L. (1982). *Victims of groupthink* (2nd ed.). Boston: Houghton Mifflin.

Jastro, J. (1900). *Fact and fable in psychology.* Boston: Houghton Mifflin.

Jennings (Walstedt), J., Geis, F., & Brown, V. (1980). Influence of television commercials on women's self-confidence and independent judgment. *Journal of Personality and Social Psychology, 38,* 203–210.

Jervis, R. (1976). *Perception and misperception in international politics.* Princeton, NJ: Princeton University Press.

Johnson, C. E., & Davis, J. H. (1972). An equiprobability model of risk taking. *Organizational Behavior and Human Performance, 8,* 159–175.

Johnson, D. F., & Pittenger, J. B. (1984). Attribution, the attractiveness stereotype, and the elderly. *Developmental Psychology, 20,* 1168–1172.

Johnson, D. W., & Johnson, R. T. (1981). Effects of cooperative and individualistic learning experiences on interethnic interaction. *Journal of Educational Psychology, 73,* 444–449.

Johnson, P. B., Sears, D. O., & McConahay, J. B. (1971). Black invisibility, the press, and the Los Angeles riot. *American Journal of Sociology, 76,* 698–721.

Johnston, L., & Hewstone, M. (1992). Cognitive models of stereotype change: 3. Subtyping and the perceived typicality of disconfirming group members. *Journal of Experimental Social Psychology, 28,* 360–386.

Jonas, K., & Hewstone, M. (1986). The assessment of national stereotypes: A methodological study. *Journal of Social Psychology, 126,* 745–754.

Jones, E. E., Farino, A., Hastorf, A., Markus, H., Miller, D., & Scott, R. (1984). *Social stigma.* New York: Freeman.

Jones, E. E., Rhodewalt, F., Berglas, S., & Skelton, J. (1981). Effects of strategic self-presentation on subsequent self-esteem. *Journal of Personality and Social Psychology, 41,* 407–421.

Jones, E. E., Rock, L., Shaver, K., Goethals, G., & Ward, L. (1968). Pattern of performance and ability attribution: An unexpected primacy effect. *Journal of Personality and Social Psychology, 10,* 317–340.

Jones, E. E., & Davis, K. E. (1965). A theory of correspondent inferences: From acts to dispositions. In L. Berkowitz (Ed.), *Advances in experimental social psychology* (Vol. 2). New York: Academic Press.

Jones, E. E., & Gerard, H. B. (1967). *Foundations of social psychology.* New York: Wiley.

Jones, E. E., & Harris, V. A. (1967). The attribution of attitudes. *Journal of Experimental Social Psychology, 3,* 1–24.

Jones, E. E., & Nisbett, R. E. (1971). *The actor and the observer: Divergent perceptions of the causes of behavior.* Morristown, NJ: General Learning Press.

Jones, E. E. (1989). The framing of competence. *Personality and Social Psychology Bulletin, 15,* 477–492.

Jones, E. E. (1979). The rocky road from acts to dispositions. *American Psychologist, 34,* 107–117.

Jones, E. E. (1990). *Interpersonal perception.* New York: W. H. Freeman.

Jones, J. M. (1972). *Prejudice and racism.* Reading, MA: Addison-Wesley.

Jones, R. A., & Brehm, J. W. (1970). Persuasiveness of one and two-sided communications as a function of awareness that there are two sides. *Journal of Experimental Social Psychology, 6,* 47–56.

Jones, S.C., & Panitch, D. (1971). The self-fulfilling prophecy and interpersonal attraction. *Journal of Experimental Social Psychology, 7,* 356–366.

Jones, S. (1973). Self- and interpersonal evaluations: Esteem theories versus consistency theories. *Psychological Bulletin, 79,* 185–199.

Jorgenson, D. O., & Papciak, A. S. (1981). The effects of communication, resource feedback, and identifiability on behavior in simulated commons. *Journal of Experimental Social Psychology, 17,* 373–385.

Josephson, W. D. (1987). Television violence and children's aggression: Testing the priming, social script, and disinhibition prediction. *Journal of Personality and Social Psychology, 53,* 882–890.

Joule, R. V., & Beauvois, J. L. (1987). *Petite traite de manipulation a l'usage des honnetes gens.* Grenoble: Presses Universitaires de Grenoble.

Joule, R. V. (1987). Tobacco deprivation: The foot-in-the-door technique versus the low-ball technique. *Journal of Social Psychology, 17,* 361–365.

Julian, J., Bishop, D., & Fiedler, F. (1966). Quasi-therapeutic effects of intergroup competition. *Journal of Personality and Social Psychology, 3,* 321–327.

Jussim, L. (1991). Social perception and social reality: A reflection-construction model. *Psychological Review, 98,* 54–73.

Jussim, L. (1989). Teacher expectations: Self-fulfilling prophecies, perceptual biases, and accuracy. *Journal of Personality and Social Psychology, 57,* 469–480.

Kahle, L. R., & Beatty, S. E. (1987). Cognitive consequences of legislating postpurchase behavior: Growing up with the bottle bill. *Journal of Applied Social Psychology, 17,* 828–843.

Kahneman, D., & Tversky, A. (1973). On the psychology of prediction. *Psychological Review, 80,* 237–251.

Kalgren, C. A., & Wood, W. (1986). Access to attitude-relevant information in memory as a determinant of attitude-behavior consistency. *Journal of Experimental Social Psychology, 22,* 328–338.

Kanekar, S., & Nazareth, A. (1988). Attributed rape victim's fault as a function of her attractiveness, physical hurt, and emotional disturbance. *Social Behaviour, 3,* 37–40.

Kaplan, M. F., & Miller, C. E. (1983). Group discussion and judgment. In P. B. Paulus (Ed.), *Basic group processes* (pp. 65–94). New York: Springer-Verlag.

Kaplan, M. F., & Miller, C. E. (1987). Group decision making and normative versus informational influence: Effects of type of issue and assigned decision rule. *Journal of Personal and Social Psychology, 53,* 306–313.

Karabenick, S. A. (1983). Sex-relevance of content and influenceability. *Personality and Social Psychology Bulletin, 9,* 243–252.

Karau, S. J., & Williams, K. D. (1990). Social compensation: The effects of coworker ability and task meaningfulness. Paper presented at the meeting of the Midwestern Psychological Association, Chicago, IL.

Karlins, M., Coffman, T., & Walters, G. (1969). On the fading of social stereotypes: Studies in three generations of college students. *Journal of Personality and Social Psychology, 13,* 1–16.

Karraker, K. H., Vogel, D. A., & Evans, S. (1987, August). *Responses of students and pregnant women to newborn physical attractiveness.* Paper presented at the meeting of the American Psychological Association, New York.

Kashima, Y., Seigal, M., Tanaka, K., & Kashima, E. (1992). Do people believe behaviours are consistent with attitudes? Towards a cultural psychology of attribution processes. *British Journal of Social Psychology, 31,* 111–124.

Kassin, S. (1979). Consensus information, prediction, and causal attribution: A review of the literature and issues. *Journal of Personality and Social Psychology, 37,* 1966–1981.

Katz, D., & Braly, K. W. (1933). Racial stereotypes of 100 college students. *Journal of Abnormal and Social Psychology, 28,* 280–290.

Katz, I., & Hass, R. G. (1988). Racial ambivalence and American value conflict: Correlational and priming studies of dual cognitive structures. *Journal of Personality and Social Psychology, 55,* 893–905.

Katz, P. A., & Zalk, S. R. (1978). Modification of children's racial attitudes. *Developmental Psychology, 14,* 447–461.

Katz, P. A. (1976). The acquisition of racial attitudes in children. In P. Katz (Ed.), *Towards the elimination of racism* (pp. 125–154). New York: Pergamon Press.

Katz, R., & Tushman, M. (1979). Communication patterns, project performance, and task characteristics: An empirical evaluation and integration in an R & D setting. *Organization Behavior and Group Performance, 23,* 139–162.

Keating, C., Mazur, A., & Segall, M. (1981). A cross-cultural exploration of physiognomic traits of dominance and happiness. *Ethology and Sociobiology, 2,* 41–48.

Kelley, H. H., & Stahelski, A. J. (1970). The social interaction basis of co-operators' and competitors' beliefs about others. *Journal of Personality and Social Psychology, 16,* 66–91.

Kelley, H. H., & Stahelski, A. J. (1970). Errors in perception of intentions in a mixed-motive game. *Journal of Experimental Social Psychology, 6,* 379–400.

Kelley, H. H., & Thibaut, J. W. (1978). *Interpersonal relations: A theory of interdependence.* New York: Wiley Interscience.

Kelley, H. H. (1967). Attribution theory in social psychology. In D. Levine (Ed.), *Nebraska symposium on motivation* (Vol. 15, pp. 192–241). Lincoln: University of Nebraska Press.

Kelley, H. H. (1973). The process of causal attribution. *American Psychologist, 28,* 107–128.

Kelley, H. H. (1950). The warm–cold variable in first impressions of persons. *Journal of Personality, 18,* 431–439.

Kelley, H. H. (1952). Two functions of reference groups. In G. Swanson, T. Newcomb, & E. Hartley (Eds.), *Readings in social psychology* (pp. 410–414). New York: Holt.

Kelley, H. H. (1971). *Attribution in social interaction.* Morristown, NJ: General Learning Press.

Kelley, H. H. (1972). *Causal schemata and the attribution process.* Morristown, NJ: General Learning Press.

Kelley, H. H. (1979). *Personal relationships.* Hillsdale, NJ: Erlbaum.

Kelly, G. A. (1955). *The psychology of personal constructs.* New York: W. W. Norton.

Kelman, H. C., & Hamilton, V. L. (1989). *Crimes of obedience: Toward a social psychology of authority and responsibility.* New Haven, CT: Yale University Press.

Kelman, H. C., & Hovland, C. I. (1953). "Reinstatement" of the communicator in delayed measurement of opinion change. *Journal of Abnormal and Social Psychology, 48,* 326–335.

Kelman, H. C. (1958). Compliance, identification, and internalization: Three processes of attitude change. *Journal of Conflict Resolution, 2,* 51–60.

Kenrick, D., Sadalla, E., Groth, G., & Trost, M. (1990). Evolution, traits, and the stages of human courtship: Qualifying the parental investment model. *Journal of Personality, 58,* 97–116.

Kerckhoff, A. C. (1974). The social context of interpersonal attraction. In T. Huston (Ed.), *Foundations of interpersonal attraction.* New York: Academic Press.

Kernis, M. H., & Wheeler, L. (1981). Beautiful friends and ugly strangers: Radiation and contrast effects in perceptions of same-sex pairs. *Personality and Social Psychology Bulletin, 7,* 617–620.

Kerr, N. L., Davis, J. H., Meek, D., & Rissman, A. K. (1975). Group position as a function of member attitudes: Choice shift effects from the perspective of social decision scheme theory. *Journal of Personality and Social Psychology, 35,* 574–593.

Kerr, N. L., & Bruun, S. E. (1983). Dispensability of member effort and group motivation losses: Free-rider effects. *Journal of Personality and Social Psychology, 44,* 78–94.

Kerr, N. L., & Bruun, S. E. (1983). Dispensibility of member effort and group motivation losses: Free-rider effects. *Journal of Personality and Social Psychology, 44,* 78–94.

Kerr, N. L., & Bruun, S. E. (1981). Ringelmann revisited: Alternative explanations for social loafing. *Personality and Social Psychology Bulletin, 7,* 224–231.

Kerr, N. L., & MacCoun, R. J. (1985). Role expectations and social dilemmas: Sex roles and task motivation in groups. *Journal of Personality and Social Psychology, 49,* 1547–1556.

Kerr, N. L., & MacCoun, R. J. (1985). The effects of jury size and polling method on the product of jury deliberation. *Journal of Personality and Social Psychology, 48,* 349–363.

Kerr, N. L. (1983). Motivation losses in small groups: A social dilemma analysis. *Journal of Personality and Social Psychology, 45,* 819–828.

Kiesler, S. B., & Baral, R. L. (1970). The search for the romantic partner: The effects of self-esteem and physical attractiveness on romantic behavior. In K. Gergen & D. Marlow (Eds.), *Personality and social behavior.* Reading, MA: Addison-Wesley.

Kinder, D. R., & Sears, D. O. (1981). Prejudice and politics: Symbolic racism versus racial threats to the good life. *Journal of Personality and Social Psychology, 40,* 414–431.

King, A. S. (1971). Self-fulfilling prophecies in training the hard-core: Supervisors' expectancies and the underprivileged and workers' performance. *Social Science Quarterly, 52,* 369–378.

Kipnis, D. M. (1957). Interaction between members of bomber crews as a determinant of sociometric choice. *Human Relations, 10,* 263–270.

Knox, R. E., & Inkster, J. A. (1968). Post-decision dissonance at post time. *Journal of Personality and Social Psychology, 8,* 319–323.

Koeske, G., & Crano, W. D. (1968). The effect of congruous and incongruous source-statement combinations on the judged credibility of a communication. *Journal of Experimental Social Psychology, 4,* 384–399.

Kogan, N., & Wallach, M. (1964). *Risk-taking: A study in cognition and personality*. New York: Holt, Rinehart, & Winston.

Komorita, S. S., Sweeney, J., & Kravitz, D. A. (1980). Cooperative choice in the N-person dilemma situation. *Journal of Personality and Social Psychology, 38*, 504–516.

Kozlowski, L. T., & Cutting, J. E. (1977). Recognizing the sex of a walker from a dynamic point-light display. *Perception and Psychophysics, 21*, 575–580.

Kramer, R. M., & Brewer, M. B. (1984). Effects of group identity on resource use in a simulated commons dilemma. *Journal of Personality and Social Psychology, 46*, 1044–1057.

Kraut, R. E., & Johnston, R. E. (1979). Social and emotional messages of smiling: An ethological approach. *Journal of Personality and Social Psychology, 37*, 1539–1553.

Krueger, J., Rothbart, M., & Sriram, N. (1989). Category learning and change: Differences in sensitivity to information that enhances or reduces intercategory distinctions. *Journal of Personality and Social Psychology, 56*, 866–875.

Kruglanski, A. W., & Mackie, D. M. (1990). Majority and minority influence: A judgmental process analysis. In W. Stroebe & M. Hewstone (Eds.), *European review of social psychology* (Vol. 1, pp. 229–261). London: Wiley.

Kruglanski, A. W. (1975). The endogenous–exogenous partition in attribution theory. *Psychological Review, 82*, 387–406.

Kulik, J. A. (1983). Confirmatory attribution and the perpetuation of social beliefs. *Journal of Personality and Social Psychology, 44*, 1171–1181.

Lagerspetz, K. (1979). Modification of aggressiveness in mice. In S. Feshbach & A. Fraczek (Eds.), *Aggression and behavior change* (pp. 66–82). New York: Praeger.

Laird, J. D. (1984). The real role of facial response in the experience of emotion: A reply to Tourangeau and Ellsworth and others. *Journal of Personality and Social Psychology, 47*, 909–917.

Lalonde, R. N. (1992). The dynamics of group differentiation in the face of defeat. *Personality and Social Psychology Bulletin, 18*, 336–342.

Lambert, W. E., & Klineberg, O. (1967). *Children's view of foreign peoples*. New York: Appleton-Century-Crofts.

Lamm, H., & Myers, D. G. (1978). Group-induced polarization of attitudes and behavior. In L. Berkowitz (Ed.), *Advances in experimental social psychology* (Vol. 11, pp. 145–195). New York: Academic Press.

Landy, D., & Aronson, E. (1969). The influence of the character of the criminal and his victim on the decisions of simulated jurors. *Journal of Experimental Social Psychology, 5*, 141–152.

Landy, D., & Sigall, H. (1974). Beauty is talent: Task evaluation as a function of the performer's physical attractiveness. *Journal of Personality and Social Psychology, 29*, 299–304.

Lane, I. L., & Messé, L. A. (1971). Equity and the distribution of rewards. *Journal of Personality and Social Psychology, 20*, 1–17.

Lane, I. L., & Messé, L. A. (1972). The distribution of insufficient, sufficient, and oversufficient rewards: A clarification of equity theory. *Journal of Personality and Social Psychology, 21*, 228–233.

Langer, E. J., & Roth, J. (1975). Heads I win, tails it's chance: The illusion of control as a function of the sequence of outcomes in a purely chance task. *Journal of Personality and Social Psychology, 32*, 951–955.

Langer, E. J. (1975). The illusion of control. *Journal of Personality and Social Psychology 32*, 311–328.

Langer, E., Bashner, R., & Chanowitz, B. (1985). Decreasing prejudice by increasing discrimination. *Journal of Personality and Social Psychology, 49*, 113–120.

Langer, E. (1989). *Mindfulness*. New York: Addison-Wesley.

Lanzetta, J. T., & Roby, T. B. (1960). The relationship between certain group process variables and group problem-solving efficiency. *Journal of Social Psychology, 52*, 135–148.

Lanzetta, J., Cartwright-Smith, J., & Kleck, R. (1976). Effects of nonverbal dissimulation on emotional experience and autonomic arousal. *Journal of Personality and Social Psychology, 33*, 359–370.

LaPiere, R. T. (1934). Attitudes vs. actions. *Social Forces, 13*, 230–237.

Lassiter, G. D., & Irvine, A. A. (1986). Videotaped confessions: The impact of camera point of view on judgments of coercion. *Journal of Applied Social Psychology, 16*, 268–276.

Lasswell, H. D. (1948). The structure and function of communication in society. In L. Bryson (Ed.), *Communication of ideas*. New York: Harper & Row.

Latane, B., & Darley, J. M. (1970). *The unresponsive bystander: Why doesn't he help?* New York: Appleton-Century-Crofts.

Latané, B., Williams, K., & Harkins, S. (1979). Many hands make light the work: The causes and consequences of social loafing. *Journal of Personality and Social Psychology, 37*, 822–832.

Latané, B., & Darley, J. M. (1968). Group inhibition of bystander intervention. *Journal of Personality and Social Psychology, 10*, 215–221.

Latané, B., & Rodin, J. (1969). A lady in distress: Inhibiting effects of friends and strangers on bystander intervention. *Journal of Experimental Social Psychology, 5*, 189–202.

Laughlin, P. R., & Adamopoulos, J. (1982). Social decision schemes on intellective tasks. In H. Brandstatter, J. H. Davis, & G. Stocker-Kreichgauer (Eds.), *Group decision making* (pp. 80–94). London: Academic Press.

Laughlin, P. R., & Adamopoulos, J. (1980). Social combination processes and individual learning for six-person cooperative groups on an intellective task. *Journal of Personality and Social Psychology, 38*, 941–947.

Laughlin, P. R., & Earley, P. C. (1982). Social combination models, persuasive arguments theory, social comparison theory, and choice shift. *Journal of Personality and Social Psychology, 42*, 273–280.

Laughlin, P. R., & Futoran, G. C. (1985). Collective induction: Social combination and sequential transition. *Journal of Personality and Social Psychology, 48*, 608–613.

Laughlin, P. R., & Shippy, T. A. (1983). Collective induction. *Journal of Personality and Social Psychology, 45*, 94–100.

Laughlin, P. R. (1988). Collective induction: Group performance, social combination processes, and mutual majority and minority influence. *Journal of Personality and Social Psychology, 54*, 254–267.

Laughlin, P. R. (1980). Social combination processes of cooperative problem solving groups on verbal intellective tasks. In M. Fishbein (Ed.), *Progress in social psychology* (pp. 127–155). Hillsdale, NJ: Erlbaum.

Lau, R. R., & Russell, D. (1980). Attributions in the sports pages. *Journal of Personality and Social Psychology, 39*, 29–38.

Leavitt, H. J. (1951). Some effects of certain communication patterns on group performance. *Journal of Abnormal and Social Psychology, 46*, 38–50.

LeBon, G. (1896). *The crowd: A study of the popular mind*. London: Ernest Benn.

Lefkowitz, M. M., Eron, L. D., Walder, L. O., & Huesmann, L. R. (1977). *Growing up to be violent*. New York: Pergamon Press.

Leippe, M. R., & Elkin, R. A. (1987). When motives clash: Issue involvement and response involvement as determinants of persuasion. *Journal of Personality and Social Psychology, 52,* 269–279.

Lemyre, L., & Smith, P. M. (1985). Intergroup discrimination and self-esteem in the minimal group paradigm. *Journal of Personality and Social Psychology, 49,* 660–670.

Leone, C., Taylor, L. W., & Adams, K. C. (1991). Self-generated attitude change: Some effects of thought, dogmatism, and reality constraints. *Personality and Individual Differences, 12,* 233–240.

Lepper, M., Greene, D., & Nisbett, R. E. (1973). Undermining children's intrinsic interest with extrinsic reward: A test of the "overjustification" hypothesis. *Journal of Personality and Social Psychology, 28,* 129–137.

LeVine, R. A., & Campbell, D. T. (1972). *Ethnocentrism: Theories of conflict, ethnic attitudes and group behavior*. New York: Wiley.

Leventhal, G. S., & Whiteside, H. D. (1973). Equity and the use of reward to elicit high performance. *Journal of Personality and Social Psychology, 25,* 75–83.

Leventhal, H. (1974). Attitudes: Their nature, growth, and change. In C. Nemeth (Ed.), *Social psychology: Classic and contemporary integrations*. Chicago: Rand-McNally.

Leventhal, H. (1970). Finding and theory in the study of fear communications. In L. Berkowitz (Ed.), *Advances in experimental social psychology* (Vol. 5). New York: Academic Press.

Levine, J. M., Russo, E. M. (1987). Majority and minority influence. In C. Hendrick (Ed.), *Review of personality and social psychology: Group processes* (Vol. 8). Newbury Park, CA: Sage.

Levine, J. M. (1980). Reaction to opinion deviance in small groups. In P. B. Paulus (Ed.), *Psychology of group influence* (pp. 375–429). Hillsdale, NJ: Erlbaum.

Levinson, R. M. (1975). Sex discrimination and employment practices: An experiment with unconventional job inquiries. *Social Problems, 22,* 533–543.

Lewin, K. (1947). Group decision and social change. In T. M. Newcomb & E. Hartley (Eds.), *Readings in social psychology* (pp. 330–344). New York: Holt.

Leyens, J.-P., & Dunand, M. (1991). Priming aggressive thoughts: The effect of the anticipation of a violent movie upon the aggressive behavior of the spectators. *European Journal of Social Psychology, 21,* 507–516.

Liberman, A., & Chaiken, S. (in press). Value conflict and thought-induced attitude change. *Journal of Experimental Social Psychology*.

Liebrand, W. B. G., & van Run, G. J. (1985). The effects of social motives on behavior in social dilemmas in two cultures. *Journal of Experimental Social Psychology, 21,* 86–102.

Likert, R. (1932). A technique for the measurement of attitudes. *Archives of Psychology, 140,* 1–55 (whole number).

Linder, D., & Worchel, S. (1970). Opinion change as a result of effortfully drawing a counterattitudinal conclusion. *Journal of Experimental Psychology, 6,* 432–448.

Linville, P. W., Salovey, P., & Fischer, G. W. (1989). Perceived distributions of the characteristics of in-group and out-group members: Empirical evidence and a computer simulation. *Journal of Personality and Social Psychology, 57,* 165–188.

Linville, P. W. (1985). Self-complexity and affective extremity: Don't put all your eggs in one cognitive basket. *Social Cognition, 3,* 94–120.

Linville, P. W. (1987). Self-complexity as a cognitive buffer against stress-related illness and depression. *Journal of Personality and Social Psychology, 52,* 663–676.

Lippman, W. (1922). *Public opinion*. New York: Harcourt Brace.

Loftus, E. F., & Ketcham, K. (1991). *Witness for the defense*. New York: St. Martin's Press.

Loftus, E. F., & Palmer, J. C. (1974). Reconstruction of automobile destruction: An example of the interaction between language and memory. *Journal of Verbal Learning and Verbal Behavior, 13,* 585–589.

Loftus, E. F. (1979). *Eyewitness testimony*. Cambridge, MA: Harvard University Press.

Lord, C. G., Ross, L., & Lepper, M. (1979). Biased assimilation and attitude polarization: The effects of prior theories on subsequently considered evidence. *Journal of Personality and Social Psychology, 37,* 2098–2109.

Lord, C. G. (1989). The "disappearance" of dissonance in an age of relativism. *Personality and Social Psychology Bulletin, 15,* 513–518.

Lorenz, K. (1966). *On aggression*. New York: Harcourt, Brace, & World.

Luce, R. D., & Raiffa, H. (1957). *Games and decisions*. New York: Wiley.

Luhtanen, R., & Crocker, J. (1992). A collective self-esteem scale: Self-evaluation of one's social identity. *Personality and Social Psychology Bulletin, 18,* 302–318.

Lydon, J. E., Jamieson, D. W., & Zanna, M. P. (1988). Interpersonal similarity and the social and intellectual dimensions of first impressions. *Social Cognition, 6,* 269–286.

Lykken, D. T. (1981). *A tremor in the blood. Uses and abuses of the lie detector*. New York: McGraw-Hill.

Maass, A., West, S. G., & Cialdini, R. B. (1987). Minority influence and conversion. In C. Hendrick (Ed.), *Review of personality and social psychology* (Vol. 8). Beverly Hills, CA: Sage.

Maccoby, E. E., & Jacklin, C. N. (1980). Sex differences in aggression: A rejoinder and reprise. *Child Development, 51,* 964–980.

Mackie, D. M., & Worth, L. T. (1989). Processing deficits and the mediation of positive affect in persuasion. *Journal of Personality and Social Psychology, 57,* 27–40.

Mackie, D. M., & Worth, L. T. (1990). "Feeling good, but not thinking straight": The impact of positive mood on persuasion. In J. T. Forgas (Ed.), *Affect and social judgments* (pp. 201–220). Oxford: Pergamon Press.

Mackie, D. M. (1986). Social identification effects in group polarization. *Journal of Personality and Social Psychology, 50,* 720–728.

Mackie, D., Worth, L., & Asuncion, A. (1990). Processing of persuasive in-group messages. *Journal of Personality and Social Psychology, 58,* 812–822.

Madden, T. J., Ellen, P. S., & Ajzen, I. (1992). A comparison of the theory of planned behavior and the theory of reasoned action. *Personality and Social Psychology Bulletin, 18,* 3–9.

Maheswaran, D., & Chaiken, S. (in press). Heuristic processing can enhance systematic processing: The effect of consensus information and message valence on persuasion. *Journal of Personality and Social Psychology*.

Malamuth, N. M. (1984). Aggression against women: Cultural and individual causes. In N. M. Malamuth & E. I. Donnerstein (Eds.), *Pornography and sexual aggression*. Orlando, FL: Academic Press.

Mann, L., & Janis, I. L. (1968). A follow-up on the long-term effects of emotional role-playing. *Journal of Personality and Social Psychology, 8,* 3393–42.

Markus, H., Crane, M., Bernstein, S., & Siladi, M. (1982). Self-schemas and gender. *Journal of Personality and Social Psychology, 42,* 38–50.

Markus, H., Hamill, R., & Sentis, K. (1987). Thinking fat: Self-schemas for body weight and the processing of weight relevant information. *Journal of Applied Social Psychology, 17,* 50–71.

Markus, H., Smith, J., & Moreland, R. (1985). Role of the self-concept in the perception of others. *Journal of Personality and Social Psychology, 49,* 1494–1512.

Markus, H., & Kitayama, S. (1991). Culture and the self: Implications for cognition, emotion, and motivation. *Psychological Review, 98,* 224–253.

Markus, H., & Nurius, P. (1986). Possible selves. *American Psychologist, 41,* 954–969.

Markus, H. (1977). Self-schemata and processing information about the self. *Journal of Personality and Social Psychology, 35,* 63–78.

Markus, H. (1978). The effect of mere presence on social facilitation: An unobtrusive test. *Journal of Experimental Social Psychology, 14,* 389–397.

Marsh, H. W., & Parker, J. W. (1984). Determinants of student self-concepts: Is it better to be a relatively large fish in a small pond even if you don't learn to swim as well? *Journal of Personality and Social Psychology, 47,* 213–231.

Martens, R., & Landers, D. M. (1972). Evaluation potential as a determinant of coaction effects. *Journal of Experimental Social Psychology, 8,* 347–359.

Martin, J. P., Brickman, P., & Murray, A. (1984). Moral outrage and pragmatism: Explanations for collective action. *Journal of Experimental Social Psychology, 20,* 484–496.

Martin, L., Harlow, T., & Strack, F. (1992). The role of bodily sensations in the evaluation of social events. *Personality and Social Psychology Bulletin, 18,* 412–419.

Martin, R. (1988a). Ingroup and outgroup minorities: Differential impact upon public and private responses. *European Journal of Social Psychology, 18,* 39–52.

Martin, R. (1988b). Minority influence and "trivial" social categorization. *European Journal of Social Psychology, 18,* 465–470.

Maslach, C., Santee, R. T., & Wade, C. (1987). Individuation, gender role, and dissent: Personality mediators of situational forces. *Journal of Personality and Social Psychology, 53,* 1088–1093.

McArthur, L. A. (1972). The how and what of why: Some determinants and consequences of causal attribution. *Journal of Personality and Social Psychology, 22,* 171–193.

McArthur, L. Z., & Baron, R. M. (1983). Toward an ecological theory of social perception. *Psychological Review, 90,* 215–238.

McArthur, L. Z., & Berry, D. S. (1987). Cross-cultural consensus in perceptions of babyfaced adults. *Journal of Cross-cultural Psychology, 18,* 165–192.

McArthur, L. Z., & Post, D. L. (1977). Figural emphasis and person perception. *Journal of Experimental Social Psychology, 13,* 520–535.

McCallum, D., Harring, K., Gilmore, R., Drenan, S., Chase, J., Insko, C. A., & Thibaut, J. (1985). Competition between groups and between individuals. *Journal of Experimental Social Psychology, 21,* 301–320.

McCane, T. R., & Anderson, J. A. (1987). Emotional responding following experimental manipulation of facial electromyographic activity. *Journal of Personality and Social Psychology, 52,* 759–768.

McCauley, C. (1989). The nature of social influence in groupthink: Compliance and internalization. *Journal of Personality and Social Psychology, 57,* 250–260.

McClintock, C. G., & McNeil, S. P. (1967). Prior dyadic experience and monetary reward as determinants of cooperative and competitive game behavior. *Journal of Personality and Social Psychology, 5,* 282–294.

McConahay, J. B. (1986). Modern racism, ambivalence, and the modern racism scale. In J. Dovidio & S. Gaertner (Eds.), *Prejudice, discrimination and racism* (pp. 91–125). New York: Academic Press.

McDougall, W. (1908). *An introduction to social psychology.* London: Methuen.

McGee, M. G., & Snyder, M. (1975). Attribution and behavior: Two field studies. *Journal of Personality and Social Psychology, 32,* 185–190.

McGuire, W. J., McGuire, C. V., & Winston, W. (1979). Effects of household sex composition on the salience of one's gender in the spontaneous self-concept. *Journal of Experimental Social Psychology, 15,* 77–90.

McGuire, W. J., & McGuire, C. V. (1988). Content and process in the experience of self. In L. Berkowitz (Ed.), *Advances in experimental social psychology* (Vol. 21, pp. 97–144). San Diego: Academic Press.

McGuire, W. J., & Papageorgis, D. (1961). The relative efficacy of various types of prior belief-defense in producing immunity from persuasion. *Journal of Abnormal and Social Psychology, 62,* 327–337.

McGuire, W. J. (1985) Attitudes and attitude change. In G. Lindzey & E. Aronson (Eds.), *The handbook of social psychology* (3rd ed., Vol. 2, pp. 233–346). New York: Random House.

McGuire, W. J. (1985). Attitudes and attitude change. In G. Lindzey & E. Aronson (Eds.), *Handbook of social psychology* (3rd ed., Vol. 2), pp. 233–346. New York: Random House.

McGuire, W. J. (1964). Inducing resistance to persuasion. In L. Berkowitz (Ed.)., *Advances in experimental social psychology* (Vol. 1, pp. 192–229). New York: Academic Press.

McGuire, W. J. (1969). The nature of attitudes and attitude change. In G. Lindzey & E. Aronson (Eds.), *The handbook of social psychology.* (2nd ed., Vol. 3). Reading MA: Addison-Wesley.

Meeus, W. H. J., & Raaijmakers, Q. A. W. (1987). Administrative obedience as a social phenomenon. In W. Doise & S. Moscovici (Eds.), *Current issues in European social psychology* (Vol. 2, p. 183–230). Cambridge, England: Cambridge University Press, and Paris: Editions de la Maison des Sciences de l'Homme.

Meeus, W. H. J., & Raaijmakers, Q. A. W. (1986). Administrative obedience: Carrying out orders to use psychological administrative violence. *European Journal of Social Psychology, 16,* 311–324.

Megargee, E. I. (1969). Influence of sex roles on the manifestation of leadership. *Journal of Applied Psychology, 53,* 377–382.

Mehrabian, A. (1972). *Nonverbal communication.* Chicago: Aldine-Atherton.

Meichenbaum, D. H., & Deffenbacher, J. L. (1988). Stress inoculation training. *The Counseling Psychologist, 16,* 69–90.

Meichenbaum, D. H. (1985). *Stress inoculation training.* New York: Pergamon Press.

Meindl, J. R., & Lerner, M. J. (1984). Exacerbation of extreme responses to an out-group. *Journal of Personality and Social Psychology, 47,* 71–84.

Merton, R. K. (1948). The self-fulfilling prophecy. *Antioch Review, 8,* 193–210.

Messe, L., Hymes, R., & MacCoun, R. (1986). Group categorization and distributive justice decisions. In Bierhoff et al. (Eds.), *Justice and social relations* (pp. 227–248). New York: Plenum Press.

Messick, D. M., Wilke, H., Brewer, M. B., Kramer, R. M., Zemke, P. E., & Lui, L. (1983). Individual adaptation and structural change as solutions to social dilemmas. *Journal of Personality and Social Psychology, 44,* 294–309.

Messick, D. M., & Brewer, M. B. (1983). Solving social dilemmas: A review. In L. Wheeler & P. Shaver (Eds.), *Review of personality and social psychology* (Vol. 4, pp. 11–44). Beverly Hills, CA: Sage.

Messick, D. M., & Cook, K. S. (Eds.) (1983). *Equity theory: Psychological and sociological perspectives*. New York: Praeger.

Messick, D. M., & Sentis, K. P. (1979). Fairness and preference. *Journal of Experimental Social Psychology, 15,* 418–434.

Messé, L. A., Kerr, N. L., & Sattler, D. N. (1992). "But some animals are more equal than others": The supervisor as a privileged status in group contexts. In S. Worchel, W. Wood, & J. Simpson (Eds.), *Group process and productivity* (pp. 203–223). Newbury Park, CA: Sage.

Messé, L. A., & Watts, B. L. (1983). Complex nature of the sense of fairness: Internal standards and social comparison as bases for reward evaluations. *Journal of Personality and Social Psychology, 45,* 84–93.

Messé, L. A. (1971). Equity in bilateral bargaining. *Journal of Personality and Social Psychology, 17,* 287–291.

Mikula, G. (1974). Nationality, performance, and sex as determinants of reward allocation. *Journal of Personality and Social Psychology, 29,* 435–445.

Milgram, S. (1963). Behavioral study of obedience. *Journal of Abnormal and Social Psychology, 67,* 371–378.

Milgram, S. (1964). Issues in the study of obedience: A reply to Baumrind. *American Psychologist, 19,* 848–852.

Milgram, S. (1965). Some conditions of obedience and disobedience to authority. *Human Relations, 18,* 57–76.

Milgram. S. (1974). *Obedience to authority*. New York: Harper & Row.

Milgram, S. (1977). *The individual in a social world*. Reading, MA: Addison-Wesley.

Millar, M. G., & Tesser, A. (1989). The effects of affective-cognitive consistency and thought on the attitude-behavior relation. *Journal of Experimental Social Psychology, 25,* 189–202.

Miller, A. G. (1986). *The obedience experiments: A case study of controversy in social science*. New York: Praeger.

Miller, A., Gillen, B., Schenker, C., & Radlove, S. (1973). Perception of obedience to authority. *Proceedings of the 81st Annual Convention of the American Psychological Association, 8,* 127–128.

Miller, C. E. (1985). Group decision making under majority and unanimity decision rules. *Social Psychology Quarterly, 48,* 51–60.

Miller, H. L., & Rivenbark, W. H., III (1970). Sexual differences in physical attractiveness as a determinant of heterosexual liking. *Psychological Reports, 27,* 701–702.

Miller, J. G. (1984). Culture and the development of everyday social explanation. *Journal of Personality and Social Psychology, 46,* 961–978.

Miller, M. D., & Burgoon, M. (1979). The relationship between violations of expectations and the induction of resistance to persuasion. *Human Communication Research, 5,* 301–313.

Miller, N. E., & Bugelski, R. (1948). Minor studies of aggression: II. The influence of frustrations imposed by the in-group on attitudes expressed toward out-groups. *Journal of Psychology, 25,* 437–442.

Miller, N. E. (1964). Some implications of modern behavior therapy for personality change and psychotherapy. In P. Worchel & D. Byrne (Eds.), *Personality change*. New York: Wiley.

Miller, N. E. (1941). The frustration-aggression hypothesis. *Psychological Review, 48,* 337–342.

Miller, N., Brewer, M. B., & Edwards, K. (1985). Cooperative interaction in desegregated settings: A laboratory analogue. *Journal of Social Issues, 41*(3), 63–79.

Miller, N., & Brewer, M. B. (Eds.). (1984). *Groups in contact: The psychology of desegregation*. New York: Academic Press.

Miller, N., & Carlson, M. (1990). Valid theory-testing meta-analyses further question the negative state relief model of helping. *Psychological Bulletin, 107,* 215–226.

Miller, R. L., Seligman, C., Clark, N. T., & Bush, M. (1976). Perceptual contrast versus reciprocal concession as mediators of induced compliance. *Canadian Journal of Behavioural Science, 8,* 401–409.

Mills, J., & Clark, M. S. (1982). Communal and exchange relationships. In L. Wheeler (Ed.), *Review of personality and social psychology*. Beverly Hills, CA: Sage.

Moll, A. (1898). *Hypnotism*. (4th ed.). New York: Scribners.

Montepare, J. M., & McArthur, L. Z. (1988). Impressions of people created by age-related qualities of their gaits. *Journal of Personality and Social Psychology, 55,* 547–556.

Moore, J. S., Graziano, W. G., & Millar, M. G. (1987). Physical attractiveness, sex role orientation, and the evaluation of adults and children. *Personality and Social Psychology Bulletin, 13,* 95–102.

Moorhead, G., & Montanari, J. R. (1986). An empirical investigation of the groupthink phenomenon. *Human Relations, 39,* 399–410.

Moreland, R. L., & Levine, J. M. (1988). Group dynamics over time: Development and socialization in small groups. In J. E. McGrath (Ed.), *The social psychology of time* (pp. 151–181). Newbury Park, CA: Sage.

Moriarity, T. (1975). Crime, commitment, and the responsive bystander: Two field experiments. *Journal of Personality and Social Psychology, 31,* 370–376.

Morse, S., & Gergen, K. (1970). Social comparison, self-consistency, and the concept of self. *Journal of Personality and Social Psychology, 16,* 148–156.

Moscovici, S., Lage, E., & Naffrechoux, M. (1969). Influence of a consistent minority on the responses of a majority in a color perception task. *Sociometry, 32,* 365–380.

Moscovici, S., & Lage, E. (1976). Studies in social influence III: Majority versus minority influence in a group. *European Journal of Social Psychology, 6,* 349–365.

Moscovici, S., & Lage, E. (1978). Studies in social influence IV: Minority influence in a context of original judgments. *European Journal of Social Psychology, 8,* 349–365.

Moscovici, S., & Mugny, G. (1983). Minority influence. In P. B. Paulus (Ed.), *Basic group processes* (pp. 41–64). New York: Springer-Verlag.

Moscovici, S., & Personnaz, B. (1980). Studies in social influence V: Minority influence and conversion behavior in a perceptual task. *Journal of Experimental Social Psychology, 16,* 270–282.

Moscovici, S., & Zavalloni, M. (1969). The group as a polarizer of attitudes. *Journal of Personality and Social Psychology, 12,* 125–135.

Moscovici, S. (1985). Innovation and minority influence. In G. Lindzey & E. Aronson (Eds.), *The handbook of social psychology* (3rd ed., Vol. 2, pp. 347–412). New York: Random House.

Moscovici, S. (1974). Social influence I: Conformity and social control. In C. Nemeth (Ed.), *Social psychology: Classic and contemporary integrations* (pp. 179–216). Chicago: Rand-McNally.

Moscovici, S. (1980). Toward a theory of conversion behavior. In L. Berkowitz (Ed.), *Advances in experimental social psychology* (Vol. 13, pp. 2209–2239). New York: Academic Press.

Moscovici, S. (1976). *Social influence and social change*. New York: Academic Press.

Moser, G., & Levy-Leboyer, C. (1985). Inadequate environment and situation control: Is a malfunctioning phone always an occasion for aggression?

Environment and Behavior, 17, 520–533.

Moyer, K. E. (1976). *The psychobiology of aggression.* New York: Harper & Row.

Mudrack, P. E. (1989). Group cohesiveness and productivity: A closer look. *Human Relations, 42,* 771–785.

Mugny, G., Kaiser, C., Papastamou, S., & Perez, J. A. (1984). Intergroup relations identification, and social influence. *British Journal of Social Psychology, 23,* 317–322.

Mugny, G., Rillet, D., & Papastamou, S. (1981). Influence minoritaire et identification social dans des contextes d'originalité et de déviance. *Revue Suisse de Psychologie, 40,* 314–332.

Mugny, G., & Perez, J. A. (1991). *The social psychology of minority influence.* Cambridge: Cambridge University Press, and Paris: Editions de la Maison des Sciences de l'Homme.

Mullen, B., Atkins, J., Champion, D., Edwards, C., Hardy, D., Story, J., & Vanderklok, M. (1985). The false consensus effect: A meta-analysis of 115 hypothesis tests. *Journal of Experimental Social Psychology, 21,* 262–283.

Mullen, B., & Hu, L. (1989). Perceptions of ingroup and outgroup variability: A meta-analytic integration. *Basic and Applied Social Psychology, 10,* 233–252.

Mummendey, A., Simon, B., Dietze, C., Grunert, M., Haeger, G., Lettgen, S., & Schaferhoff, S. (1992). Categorization is not enough: Intergroup discrimination in negative resource allocation. *Journal of Experimental Social Psychology, 28,* 125–144.

Mummendey, A., & Otten, S. (1989). Perspective-specific differences in the segmentation and evaluation of aggressive interaction sequences. *European Journal of Social Psychology, 19,* 23–40.

Mummendey, A., & Schreiber, H. J. (1983). Better or just different? Positive social identity by discrimination against, or by differentiation from outgroups. *European Journal of Social Psychology, 13,* 389–397.

Murstein, B. I. (1987). A clarification and extension of the SVR theory of dyadic pairing. *Journal of Marriage and the Family, 49,* 929–933.

Murstein, B. I. (1972). Physical attractiveness and marital choice. *Journal of Personality and Social Psychology, 22,* 8–12.

Murstein, B. I. (1970). Stimulus-value-role: A theory of marital choice. *Journal of Marriage and the Family, 32,* 465–481.

Murstein, B. I. (1976). *Who will marry whom? Theories and research in marital choice.* New York: Springer.

Musser, L. M., & Graziano, W. G. (in press). Behavioral confirmation in children's interactions with peers. *Basic and Applied Social Psychology.*

Myers, D. G., & Bishop, G. D. (1970). Discussion effects on racial attitudes. *Science, 169,* 778–779.

Myers, D. G., & Lamm, H. (1976). The group polarization phenomenon. *Psychological Bulletin, 83* 602–627.

Myers, D. G. (1982). Polarizing effects of social interaction. In H. Brandstatter, J. H. Davis, & G. Stocker-Kreichgauer (Eds.), *Group decision making* (pp. 125–161). London: Academic Press.

Nahemow, L., & Lawton, M. P. (1975). Similarity and propinquity in friendship formation. *Journal of Personality and Social Psychology, 32,* 205–213.

Nail, P. R., & Van Leeuwen, M. D. (in press). An analysis and restructuring

of the diamond model of social response. *Personality and Social Psychology Bulletin.*

Nail, P. R. (1986). Toward an integration of some models and theories of social response. *Psychological Bulletin, 100,* 190–206.

Napolitan, D. A., & Goethals, G. R. (1979). The attribution of friendliness. *Journal of Experimental Social Psychology, 15,* 105–113.

Nemeth, C. J., Mayseless, O., Sherman, J., & Brown, Y. (1990). Exposure to dissent and recall of information. *Journal of Personality and Social Psychology, 58,* 429–437.

Nemeth, C. J., Swedlund, M., & Kanki, B. (1974). Patterning of the minority's responses and their influence on the majority. *European Journal of Social Psychology, 4,* 53–64.

Nemeth, C. J., & Kwan, J. (1987). Minority influence, divergent thinking, and detection of correct solutions. *Journal of Applied Social Psychology, 17,* 786–797.

Nemeth, C. J. (1986). Differential contributions of majority and minority influence. *Psychological Review, 93,* 1–10.

Neuberg, S. L. (1989). The goal of forming accurate impressions during social interactions: Attenuating the impact of negative expectancies. *Journal of Personality and Social Psychology, 56,* 374–386.

Newcomb, T. M., Koenig, K., Flacks, R., & Warwick, D. (1967). *Persistence and change: Bennington College and its students after 25 years.* New York: Wiley.

Newcomb, T. M. (1947). Autistic hostility and social reality. *Human Relations, 1,* 69–86.

Newcomb, T. M. (1943). *Personality and social change.* New York: Dryden Press.

Newcomb, T. M. (1961). *The acquaintance process.* New York: Holt, Rinehart, & Winston.

Ng, S. H., & Cram, F. (1988). Intergroup bias by defensive and offensive groups in majority and minority conditions. *Journal of Personality and Social Psychology, 55,* 749–757.

Ng, S. H. (1984). Equity and social categorization effects on intergroup allocation of rewards. *British Journal of Social Psychology, 23,* 165–172.

Nicholls, J. G. (1984). Achievement motivation: Conceptions of ability, subjective experience, task choice, and performance. *Psychological Review, 91,* 328–346.

Nisbett, R. E., & Borgida, E. (1975). Attribution and the psychology of prediction. *Journal of Personality and Social Psychology, 32,* 932–943.

Nisbett, R. E., & Wilson, T. D. (1977). The halo effect: Evidence for unconscious alteration of judgments. *Journal of Personality and Social Psychology, 35,* 250–256.

Norvell, N., & Worchel, S. (1981). A re-examination of the relation between equal status contact and intergroup attraction. *Journal of Personality and Social Psychology, 41,* 902–908.

Oakes, P. J., Turner, J. C., & Haslam, S. A. (1991). Perceiving people as group members: The role of fit in the salience of social categorizations. *British Journal of Social Psychology 30,* 125–144.

Oakes, P. J., & Turner, J. C. (1980). Social categorization and intergroup behaviour: Does minimal intergroup discrimination make social identity more positive? *European Journal of Social Psychology, 10,* 295–301.

Orive, R. (1988). Social projection and social comparison of opinions. *Journal of Personality and Social Psychology, 54,* 953–964.

Orne, M. T., & Holland, T. T. (1968). On the ecological validity of laboratory deceptions. *International Journal of Psychiatry, 6,* 282–293.

Orne, M. T. (1962). On the social psychology of the psychological experiment: With particular reference to demand characteristics and their implications. *American Psychologist, 17,* 776–783.

Orr, S. P., & Lanzetta, J. T. (1980). Facial expression of emotion as conditioned stimuli for human autonomic responses. *Journal of Personality and Social Psychology, 38,* 278–282.

Osgood, C. E., Suci, & Tannenbaum, P. (1957/1978). *The measurement of meaning.* Urbana: University of Illinois Press.

Osgood, C. E. (1959). Suggestions for winning the real war with communism. *Journal of Conflict Resolution, 3,* 295–325.

Osgood, C. E. (1962). *An alternative to war or surrender.* Urbana: University of Illinois Press.

Otten, C. A., Penner, L. A., & Waugh, G. (1988). That's what friends are for: The determinants of psychological helping. *Journal of Social and Clinical Psychology, 7,* 34–41.

Oyersman, D., & Markus, H. (1990). Possible selves and delinquency. *Journal of Personality and Social Psychology, 59,* 112–125.

O'Sullivan, C. S., & Durso, F. T. (1984). Effect of schema-incongruent information on memory for stereotypical attributes. *Journal of Personality and Social Psychology, 47,* 55–70.

Pallak, M. S., Cook, D. A., & Sullivan, J. J. (1980). Commitment and energy conservation. In L. Bickman (Ed.), *Applied social psychology annual* (Vol. 1). Beverly Hills, CA: Sage.

Park, B., Judd, C. M., & Ryan, C. (1991). Social categorization and the representation of variability information. In W. Stroebe & M. Hewstone (Eds.), *European Review of Social Psychology* (Vol. 2, pp. 211–245). Chichester, England: John Wiley.

Park, B., & Judd, C. M. (1990). Measures and models of perceived group variability. *Journal of Personality and Social Psychology, 59,* 173–191.

Park, B., & Rothbart, M. (1982). Perception of out-group homogeneity and levels of social categorization: Memory for the subordinate attributes of in-group and out-group members. *Journal of Personality and Social Psychology, 42,* 1051–1068.

Park, B. (1986). A method for studying the development of impressions of real people. *Journal of Personality and Social Psychology, 51,* 907–917.

Patel, A. S., & Gordon, J. E. (1960). Some personal and situational determinants of yielding to influence. *Journal of Abnormal and Social Psychology, 61,* 411–418.

Patten, S. C. (1977). Milgram's shocking experiments. *Philosophy, 52,* 423–440.

Patterson, M. L. (1983). *Nonverbal behavior: A functional perspective.* New York: Springer-Verlag.

Peabody, D., & Goldberg, L. R. (1989). Some determinants of factor structures from personality-trait descriptors. *Journal of Personality and Social Psychology, 57,* 552–567.

Peabody, D. (1967). Trait inferences: Evaluative and descriptive aspects. *Journal of Personality and Social Psychology Monographs, 7* (Whole No. 644).

Pelham, B. W., & Swann, W. B. (1989). From self-conceptions to self-worth: On the sources and structure of global self-esteem. *Journal of Personality and Social Psychology, 57,* 672–680.

Peplau, L. A., & Perlman, D. (1982). *Loneliness: A sourcebook of current theory, research, and therapy.* New York: Wiley.

Peplau, L. A. (1985). Loneliness research: Basic concepts and findings. In G. & B. Sarason (Eds.), *Social support: Theory, research, and application.* Boston: Marinus Nijhof.

Perdue, C., Dovidio, J., Gurtman, M., & Tyler, R. (1990). Us and them: Social categorization and the process of intergroup bias. *Journal of Personality and Social Psychology, 59,* 475–486.

Perez, J. A., & Mugny, G. (1990). Minority influence: Manifest discrimination and latent influence. In D. Abrams & M. Hogg (Eds.), *Social identity theory: Constructive and critical advances.* London: Harvester Wheatsheaf.

Perez, J. A., & Mugny, G. (1987). Paradoxical effects of categorization in minority influence: When being an outgroup is an advantage. *European Journal of Social Psychology, 17,* 157–169.

Personnaz, B., & Guillon, M. (1985). Conflict and Conversion. In S. Moscovici, G. Mugny, & E. van Avermaet (Eds.), *Perspectives on minority influence.* Cambridge, England: Cambridge University Press.

Personnaz, B. (1981). Study in social influence using the spectrometer method. Dynamics of the phenomenon of conversion and covertness in perceptual responses. *European Journal of Social Psychology, 11,* 431–438.

Pessin, J. (1933). The comparative effects of social and mechanical stimulation on memorizing. *American Journal of Psychology, 45,* 263–270.

Peterson, P. D., & Koulack, D. (1969). Attitude change as a function of latitudes of acceptance and rejection. *Journal of Personality and Social Psychology, 11,* 309–311.

Pettigrew, T. F. (1958). Personality and sociocultural factors in intergroup attitudes: A cross-national comparison. *Journal of Conflict Resolution, 2,* 29–42.

Pettigrew, T. F. (1959). Regional differences in anti-Negro prejudice. *Journal of Abnormal and Social Psychology, 59,* 28–36.

Pettigrew, T. F. (1979). The ultimate attribution error: Extending Allport's cognitive analysis of prejudice. *Personality and Social Psychology Bulletin, 5,* 461–476.

Pettigrew, T. F. (1986). *Modern racism: American black-white relations since the 1960s.* Cambridge, MA: Harvard University Press.

Petty, R. E., Cacioppo, J. T., & Haugtvedt, C. P. (1992). Ego-involvement and persuasion: An appreciative look at the Sherifs' contribution to the study of self-relevance and attitude change. In D. Granberg & G. Sarup (Eds.), *Social judgment and intergroup relations: Essays in honor of Muzafer Sherif* (pp. 147–175). New York: Springer-Verlag.

Petty, R. E., Harkins, S. G., & Williams, K. K. (1980). The effects of group diffusion of cognitive effort on attitudes: An information processing view. *Journal of Personality and Social Psychology, 38,* 81–92.

Petty, R. E., Wells, G. L., & Brock, T. C. (1976). Distraction can enhance or reduce yielding to persuasion. *Journal of Personality and Social Psychology, 34,* 874–884.

Petty, R. E., & Cacioppo, J. T. (1986a). *Communication and persuasion: Central and peripheral routes to attitude change.* New York: Springer-Verlag.

Petty, R. E., & Cacioppo, J. T. (1986b). The elaboration likelihood model of persuasion. In L. Berkowitz (Ed.), *Advances in experimental social psychology* (Vol. 19, pp. 123–205). New York: Academic Press.

Petty, R. E., & Cacioppo, J. T. (1990). Involvement and persuasion: Tradition versus integration. *Psychological Bulletin, 107,* 367–375.

Petty, R. E., & Cacioppo, J. T. (1986). *Communication and persuasion: Central and peripheral routes to attitude change.* New York: Springer-Verlag.

Petty, R. E., & Cacioppo, J. T. (1981). *Attitudes and persuasion: Classic and contemporary approaches.* Dubuque, IA: Wm. C. Brown.

Phillips, D. P. (1982). The impact of fictional television stories on US adult fatalities: New evidence on the effect of the mass media on violence. *American Journal of Sociology, 87,* 1340–1359.

Phillips, D. P. (1983). The impact of mass media violence on US homicides. *American Sociological Review, 48,* 560–568.

Phillips, D. P. (1974). The influence of suggestion on suicide: Substantive and theoretical implications of the Werther effect. *American Sociological Review, 39,* 334–354.

Piliavin, J. A., Dovidio, J. F., Gaertner, S. L., & Clark, R. D., III. (1982). Responsive bystanders: The process of intervention. In V. J. Derlega & J. Grzelak (Eds.), *Cooperation and helping behavior: Theories and research.* New York: Academic Press.

Piliavin, J. A., Dovidio, J. F., Gaertner, S. L., & Clark, R. D., III. (1981). *Emergency intervention.* New York: Academic Press.

Piliavin, J. A., & Piliavin, I. M. (1975). The effect of blood on reactions to a victim. *Journal of Personality and Social Psychology, 32,* 429–438.

Pilisuk, M. (1984). Experimenting with the arms race. *Journal of Conflict Resolution, 28,* 296–315.

Platow, M. J., McClintock, C. G., & Liebrand, W. G. (1990). Predicting intergroup fairness and ingroup bias in the minimal group paradigm. *European Journal of Social Psychology, 20,* 221–239.

Polmar, N. (1982). *Rickover.* New York: Simon & Schuster.

Pratkanis, A. R., Greenwald, A. G., Leippe, M. R., & Baumgardner, M. H. (1988). In search of reliable persuasion effects: III. The sleeper effect is dead. Long live the sleeper effect. *Journal of Personality and Social Psychology, 54,* 203–218.

Pratto, F., Sidanius, J., & Stallworth, L. (1993). Sexual selection and the sexual and ethnic basis of social hierarchy. In L. Ellis (Ed.), *Social stratification and socioeconomic inequality* (Vol. 1, pp. 111–137). Westport, CT: Praeger.

Pratto, F., & Bargh, J. A. (1991). Stereotyping based on apparently individuating information: Trait and global components of sex stereotypes under attention overload. *Journal of Experimental Social Psychology, 27,* 26–47.

Priest, R., & Sawyer, J. (1967). Proximity and peership: Bases of balance in interpersonal attraction. *American Journal of Sociology, 72,* 633–649.

Pruitt, D. G. (1971). Choice shifts in group discussion: An introductory review. *Journal of Personality and Social Psychology, 20,* 339–360.

Pryor, J. B., Reeder, G. P., & McManus, J. A. (1991. Fear and loathing in the workplace: Reactions to AIDS-infected co-workers. *Personality and Social Psychology Bulletin, 17,* 133–139.

Pryor, J. B., & Kriss, M. (1977). The cognitive dynamics of salience in the attribution process. *Journal of Personality and Social Psychology, 35,* 49–55.

Pryor, J. B., & Merluzzi, T. V. (1985). The role of expertise in processing social interaction scripts. *Journal of Experimental Social Psychology, 21,* 362–379.

Quattrone, G. A. (1986). On the perception of a group's variability. in S. Worchel & W. Austin (Eds.), *Psychology of intergroup relations* (pp. 25–48). Chicago: Nelson-Hall.

Quigley, B., Gaes, G. G., & Tedeschi, J. T. (1989). Does asking make a difference? Effects of initiator, possible gain, and risk on attributed altruism. *Journal of Social Psychology, 129,* 259–267.

Radelet, M. (1981). Racial characteristics and the imposition of the death penalty. *American Sociological Review, 46,* 918–927.

Rank, S. G., & Jacobson, C. K. (1977). Hospital nurses' compliance with medication overdose orders: A failure to replicate. *Journal of Health and Social Behavior, 18,* 188–193.

Rapoport, A., & Chammah, A. M. (1965). *Prisoners' Dilemma: A study of conflict and cooperation.* Ann Arbor: University of Michigan Press.

Raskin, D. C. (1986). The polygraph in 1986: Scientific, professional, and legal issues surrounding application and acceptance of polygraph evidence. *Utah Law Review, 29–74.*

Razran, G. H. S. (1940). Conditioned response changes in rating and appraising socio-political slogans. *Psychological Bulletin, 37,* 481.

Reed, C. F., & Witt, P. N. (1965). Factors contributing to unexpected reactions in two human drug-placebo experiments. *Confina Psychiatrica, 8,* 57–68.

Regan, D. T., & Fazio, R. (1977). On the consistency between attitudes and behavior: Look to the method of attitude formation. *Journal of Experimental Social Psychology, 13,* 28–45.

Rehm, J., Steinleitner, J., & Lilli, W. (1987). Wearing uniforms and aggression: A field experiment. *European Journal of Social Psychology, 17,* 357–360.

Reifman, A. S., Larrick, R. P., & Fein, S. (1991). Temper and temperature on the diamond: The heat-aggression relationship in major league baseball. *Personality and Social Psychology Bulletin, 17,* 580–585.

Reis, H., Nezlek, J., & Wheeler, L. (1980). Physical attractiveness in social interaction. *Journal of Personality and Social Psychology, 38,* 604–617.

Reis, H., Wheeler, L., Spiegel, N., Kernis, M., Nezlek, J., & Perri, M. (1982). Physical attractiveness in social interaction II: Why does appearance affect social experience? *Journal of Personality and Social Psychology, 43,* 979–996.

Reitan, H. T., & Shaw, M. E. (1964). Group membership, sex-composition of the group and conformity behavior. *Journal of Social Psychology, 64,* 45–51.

Rhine, R. J., & Severance, L. J. (1970). Ego-involvement, discrepancy, source credibility, and attitude change. *Journal of Personality and Social Psychology, 16,* 175–190.

Rhodes, N., & Wood, W. (1992). Self-esteem and intelligence affect influenceability: The mediating role of message reception. *Psychological Bulletin, 111,* 156–171.

Riggio, R. E., & Friedman, H. S. (1986). Impression formation: The role of expressive behavior. *Journal of Personality and Social Psychology, 50,* 421–427.

Riggio, R. E. (1986). Assessment of basic social skills. *Journal of Personality and Social Psychology, 51,* 649–660.

Rime, B., & Leyens, J.-P. (1988). Violence dans les stades: La response des psychologues [Violence in the stadiums: The response of psychologists]. *La Recherche, 19,* 528–531.

Robinson, J., & McArthur, L. Z. (1982). Impact of salient vocal qualities on causal attribution for a speaker's behavior. *Journal of Personality and Social Psychology, 43,* 236–247.

Rogers, R. W., & Prentice-Dunn, S. (1981). Deindividuation and anger-mediated interracial aggression: Unmasking regressive racism. *Journal of Personality and Social Psychology, 41,* 63–73.

Rogers, R. W., & Prentice-Dunn, S. (1981). Deindividuation and anger-mediated interracial aggression: Unmasking regressive racism. *Journal of Personality and Social Psychology, 41,* 63–73.

Rokeach, M. (1960). *The open and closed mind.* New York: Basic Books.

Rosenberg, M. (1979). *Conceiving the self.* New York: Basic Books.

Rosenberg, M. (1965). *Society and the adolescent self-image.* Princeton, NJ: Princeton University Press.

Rosenberg, S., Nelson, C., & Vivekananthan, P. S. (1968). A multidimensional approach to the structure of personality impressions. *Journal of Personality and Social Psychology, 9,* 283–294.

Rosenthal, A. M. (1964). *Thirty-eight witnesses.* New York: McGraw-Hill.

Rosenthal, R., Hall, J. A., DiMatteo, M. R., Rogers, P., & Archer, D. (1979). *Sensitivity to nonverbal communication.* Baltimore: Johns Hopkins University Press.

Rosenthal, R., & Fode, K. L. (1961). The problem of experimenter outcome-bias. In D. P. Ray (Ed.), *Series research in social psychology, Symposia studies series, No. 8.* Washington: National Institute of Social and Behavioral Science.

Rosenthal, R., & Fode, K. L. (1963). Three experiments in experimenter bias. *Psychological Reports, 12,* 491–511.

Rosenthal, R., & Jacobson, L. (1968). *Pygmalion in the classroom.* New York: Holt, Rinehart & Winston.

Rosenthal, R. (1985). From unconscious experimenter bias to teacher expectancy effects. In J. B. Dusek, V. C., Hall, & W. J. Meyer (Eds.), *Teacher expectancies* (pp. 37–65). Hillsdale, NJ: Erlbaum.

Rosenthal, R. (1989). The affect effort theory of the mediation of interpersonal expectation effects. Donald T. Campbell Award Address, American Psychological Association, New Orleans.

Rosenthal, R. (1966). *Experimenter effects in behavioral research.* New York: Appleton, Century, Crofts.

Rosenthal, R. (1976). *Experimenter effects in behavioral research* (Enl. ed.). New York: Irvington Publishers/Halsted Press.

Ross, E. A. (1908). *Social psychology: An outline and source book.* New York: Macmillan.

Ross, L., Greene, D., & House, P. (1977). The false consensus phenomenon: An attributional bias in self-perception and social-perception processes. *Journal of Experimental Social Psychology, 13,* 279–301.

Ross, L. (1977). The intuitive psychologist and his shortcomings: Distortions in the attribution process. In L. Berkowitz (Ed.), *Advances in experimental social psychology* (Vol. 10, pp. 173–219). New York: Academic Press.

Rothbart, M., Evans, M., & Fulero, S. (1979). Recall for confirming events: Memory processes and the maintenance of social stereotypes. *Journal of Personality and Social Psychology, 15,* 343–355.

Rothbart, M., Fulero, S., Jensen, C., Howard, J., & Birrell, P. (1978). From individual to group impressions: Availability heuristics in stereotype formation. *Journal of Experimental and Social Psychology, 14,* 237–255.

Rothbart, M., & John, O. P. (1985). Social categorization and behavioral episodes: A cognitive analysis of the effects of intergroup contact. *Journal of Social Issues, 41*(3), 81–104.

Rotter, J. B. (1966). Generalized expectancies for internal versus external control of reinforcement. *Psychological Monographs, 80,* 1–28.

Ruberman, W. (1992). Psychosocial influences on mortality of patients with coronary heart disease. *Journal of the American Medical Association, 267,* 559–560.

Rubin Z. (1970). Measurement of romantic love. *Journal of Personality and Social Psychology, 16,* 265–273.

Rubin, Z. (1973). *Liking and loving: An invitation to social psychology.* New York: Holt, Rinehart & Winston.

Ruble, D. N., & Frey, K. S. (1987). Social comparison and self-evaluation in the classroom: Developmental changes in knowledge and function. In J. Masters & W. Smith (Eds.), *Social comparison, social justice, and relative deprivation* (pp. 81–104). Hillsdale, NJ: Erlbaum.

Rule, B. G., Taylor, B. R., & Dobbs, A. R. (1987). Priming effects of heat on aggressive thoughts. *Social Cognition, 5,* 131–143.

Runciman, W. C. (1966). *Relative deprivation and social justice: A study of attitudes to social inequality in twentieth century England.* Berkeley, CA: University of California Press.

Runyan, D. L. (1974). The group risky-shift effect as a function of emotional bonds, actual consequences, and extent of responsibility. *Journal of Personality and Social Psychology, 29,* 670–676.

Rusbult, C. E. (1983). A longitudinal test of the investment model: The development (and deterioration) of satisfaction and commitment in heterosexual involvements. *Journal of Personality and Social Psychology, 45,* 101–117.

Rusbult, C. E. (1980). Commitment and satisfaction in romantic associations: A test of the investment model. *Journal of Experimental Social Psychology, 16,* 172–186.

Rushton, J. P., Fulker, D. W., Neale, M. C., Nias, D. K. B., & Eysenok, H. J. (1986). The heritability of individual differences. *Journal of Personality and Social Psychology, 50,* 1192–1198.

Rushton, J. P. (1988). Epigenetic rules in moral development: Distal-proximal approaches to altruism and aggression. *Aggressive Behavior, 9,* 35–50.

Russell, J. A., & Bullock, M. (1985). Multidimensional scaling of emotional facial expressions: Similarity from preschoolers to adults. *Journal of Personality and Social Psychology, 48,* 1290–1298.

Ruvolo, A., & Markus, H. (1992). Possible selves and performance: The power of self-relevant imagery. *Social Cognition, 10,* 95–124.

Sachdev, I., & Bourhis, R. Y. (1991). Power and status differentials in minority and majority group relations. *European Journal of Social Psychology, 21,* 1–24.

Sadler, O., & Tesser, A. (1973). Some effects of salience and time upon interpersonal hostility and attraction. *Sociometry, 36,* 99–112.

Saegart, S. C., Swap, W. C., & Zajonc, R. B. (1973). Exposure, context, and interpersonal attraction *Journal of Personality and Social Psychology, 25,* 234–242.

Safilios-Rothschild, C. (1977). *Love, sex, and sex roles.* Englewood Cliffs, NJ: Prentice-Hall.

Sagar, H. A., & Schofield, J. W. (1980). Racial and behavioral cues in black and white children's perceptions of ambiguously aggressive acts. *Journal of Personality and Social Psychology, 39,* 590–598.

Saks, M. J. (1992). Obedience versus disobedience to legitimate versus illegitimate authorities issuing good versus evil directives. *Psychological Science, 3*, 221–223.

Sampson, E. E. (1989). The challenge of social change for psychology: Globalization and psychology's theory of the person. *American Psychologist, 44*, 914–921.

Sampson, E. E. (1988). The debate on individualism: Indigenous psychologies of the individual and their role in personal and societal functioning. *American Psychologist, 43*, 15–22.

Samuelson, C. D., Messick, D. M., Rutte, C. G., & Wilke, H. (1984). Individual and structural solutions to resource dilemmas in two cultures. *Journal of Personality and Social Psychology, 47*, 94–104.

Sanbonmatsu, D. M., Kardes, F. R., & Sansone, C. (in press). Remembering less and knowing more: The effects of time of judgment on inferences about unknown attributes. *Journal of Personality and Social Psychology.*

Sanders, G. S., Baron, R. S., & Moore, D. L. (1978). Distraction and social comparison as mediators of social facilitation effects. *Journal of Experimental Social Psychology, 14*, 291–303.

Sanders, G. S., & Baron, R. S. (1977). Is social comparison irrelevant for producing choice shifts? *Journal of Experimental Social Psychology, 13*, 303–314.

Sanders, G. S., & Baron, R. S. (1975). The motivating effects of distraction on task performance. *Journal of Personality and Social Psychology, 32*, 956–963.

Sanders, G. S. (1981). Driven by distraction: An integrative review of social facilitation theory and research. *Journal of Experimental Social Psychology, 17*, 227–251.

Sanna, L. J., & Shotland, R. L. (1990). Valence of anticipated evaluation and social facilitation. *Journal of Experimental Social Psychology, 26*, 82–92.

Sanna, L. J. (1992). Self-efficacy theory: Implications for social facilitation and social loafing. *Journal of Personality and Social Psychology, 62*, 774–786.

Saxe, L., Dougherty, D., & Cross, T. (1985). The validity of polygraph testing: Scientific analysis and public controversy. *American Psychologist, 40*, 355–366.

Schachter, S. (1964). The interaction of cognitive and physiological determinants of emotional state. In L. Berkowitz (Ed.), *Advances in experimental social psychology* (Vol. 1). New York: Academic Press.

Schachter, S. (1959). *The psychology of affiliation: Experimental studies of the sources of gregariousness.* Stanford, CA: Stanford University Press.

Schacter, S., & Singer, J. (1962). Cognitive, social, and physiological determinants of emotional state. *Psychological Review, 69*, 379–399.

Schaible, T. D., & Jacobs, A. (1975). Feedback III: Sequence effects. Enhancement of feedback acceptance and group attractiveness by manipulation of the sequence and valence of feedback. *Small Group Behavior, 6*, 151–173.

Schein, E. H. (1961). *Coercive persuasion: A socio-psychological analysis of the "brainwashing" of American civilian prisoners by the Chinese communists.* New York: Norton.

Scherer, K., Wallbott, H., & Summerfield, A. (Eds.). (1986). *Experiencing emotion: A cross-cultural study.* Cambridge, England: Cambridge University Press.

Scher, S. J., & Cooper, J. (1989). Motivational basis of dissonance: The singular role of behavioral consequences. *Journal of Personality and Social Psychology, 56*, 899–906.

Schlenker, B. R. (1982). Translating actions into attitudes: An identity-analytic approach to the explanation of social conduct. In L. Berkowitz (Ed.), *Advances in experimental social psychology* (Vol. 15). New York: Academic Press.

Schmidt, G., & Weiner, B. (1988). An attribution-affect-action theory of behavior: Replications of judgments of help-giving. *Personality and Social Psychology Bulletin, 14*, 610–621.

Schneider, D. J. (1973). Implicit personality theory: A review. *Psychological Bulletin, 79*, 294–309.

Schofield, J. W., & Sagar, H. A. (1977). Peer interaction patterns in an integrated middle school. *Sociometry, 40*, 130–138.

Schofield, J. W. (1979). The impact of positively structured contact on intergroup behavior: Does it last under adverse conditions? *Social Psychology Quarterly, 42*, 280–284.

Schuman, H., Steeh, C., & Bobo, L. (1985). *Racial attitudes in America: Trends and interpretation.* Cambridge, MA: Harvard University Press.

Schwartz, G. E., Fair, P. L., Salt, P., Mandel, M. R., & Klerman, G. L. (1976). Facial muscle patterning to affective imagery in depressed and nondepressed subjects. *Science, 192*, 715–724.

Schwartz, S. H., & Howard, J. A. (1982). Helping and cooperation: A self-based motivational model. In V. J. Derlega & J. Grzelak (Eds.), *Cooperation and helping behavior: Theories and research.* New York: Academic Press.

Schwartz, S. H., & Howard, J. A. (1981). A normative decision-making model of altruism. In J. P. Rushton & R. M. Sorrentino (Eds.), *Altruism and helping behavior: Social, personality, and development perspectives.* Hillsdale, NJ: Erlbaum.

Schwartz, S. H., & Struch, N. (1989). Values, stereotypes, and intergroup antagonism. In D. Bar-Tal, C. Graumann, A. Kruglanski, & W. Stroebe (Eds.), *Stereotyping and prejudice: changing conceptions* (pp. 151–167). New York Springer-Verlag.

Schwarzwald, J., Amir, Y., & Crain, R. (1992). Long-term effects of school desegregation experiences on interpersonal relations in the Israeli defense forces. *Personality and Social Psychology Bulletin, 18*, 357–368.

Schwarzwald, J., & Cohen, S. (1982). Relationship between academic tracking and the degree of interethnic acceptance. *Journal of Educational Psychology, 74*, 588–597.

Sears, D. O. (1988). Symbolic racism. In P. Katz & D. Taylor (Eds.), *Eliminating racism: Profiles in controversy* (pp. 53–84). New York: Plenum Press.

Seashore, S. E. (1954). *Group cohesiveness in the industrial work group.* Ann Arbor, MI: Institute for Social Research.

Sharan, S. (1980). Cooperative learning in small groups: Recent methods and effects on achievement, attitudes, and ethnic relations. *Review of Educational Research, 50*, 241–271.

Shaver, P., Hazan, C., & Bradshaw, D. (1988). Love as attachment: The integration of three behavioral systems. In R. Sternberg & M. Barnes (Eds.), *The psychology of love* (pp. 68–99). New Haven, CT: Yale University Press.

Shaw, M. E., & Harkey, B. (1976). Some effects of congruency of member characteristics and group structure upon group behavior. *Journal of Personality and Social Psychology, 34*, 412–418.

Shaw, M. E. (1932). A comparison of individuals and small groups in the rational solution of complex problems. *American Journal of Psychology, 44*, 491–504.

Shaw, M. E. (1954). Some effects of unequal distribution of information upon group performance in various communication nets. *Journal of Abnormal and Social Psychology, 49*, 547–553.

Sheppard, B. M., Hartwick, J., & Warshaw, P. R. (1988). The theory of reasoned action: A meta-analysis of past research with recommendations for modification and future research. *Journal of Consumer Research, 15,* 325–343.

Sherif, C. W., Kelly, M., Rodgers, H., Sarup, G., & Tittler, B. I. (1973). Personal involvement, social judgment, and action. *Journal of Personality and Social Psychology, 27,* 311–327.

Sherif, C. W., Sherif, M., & Nebergall, R. E. (1965). *Attitude and attitude change.* Philadelphia, PA: Saunders.

Sherif, M., & Hovland, C. I. (1961). *Social judgment.* New Haven, CT: Yale University Press.

Sherif, M., & Sherif, C. W. (1953). *Groups in harmony and tension.* New York: Harper.

Sherif, M. (1935). A study of some social factors in perception. *Archives of Psychology, 27(187)* 1–60.

Sherif, M. (1966). *In common predicament: Social psychology of intergroup conflict and cooperation.* New York: Houghton Mifflin.

Sherif, M., Harvey, O. J., White, B. J., Hood, W. R., & Sherif, C. W. (1961). *Intergroup conflict and cooperation: The Robbers Cave experiment.* Norman: University of Oklahoma Book Exchange.

Sherif, M. (1936). *The psychology of social norms.* New York: Harper & Row.

Shoemaker, D., South, D., & Lowe, J. (1973). Facial stereotypes of deviants and judgments of guilt or innocence. *Social Forces, 51,* 427–433.

Shrauger, J. S. (1975). Responses to evaluation as a function of initial self-perceptions. *Psychological Bulletin, 82,* 581–596.

Shupe, L. M. (1954). Alcohol and crimes: A study of the urine alcohol concentration found in 882 persons arrested during or immediately after the commission of a felony. *Journal of Criminal Law and Criminology, 44,* 661–665.

Shweder, R. A. (1977). Likeness and likelihood in everyday thought. Magical thinking in judgments about personality. *Current Anthropology, 18,* 637–658.

Sidanius, J., Pratto, F., Martin, M., & Stallworth, L. (1991). Consensual racism and career track: Some implications of social dominance theory. *Political Psychology, 12,* 691–721.

Sidanius, J. (1993). The psychology of group conflict and the dynamics of oppression: A social dominance perspective. In S. Iyengar & W. McGuire (Eds.), *Explorations in political psychology* (pp. 183–219). Durham, NC: Duke University Press.

Sigall, H., & Landy, D. (1973). Radiating beauty: The effects of having a physically attractive partner on person perception. *Journal of Personality and Social Psychology, 28,* 218–224.

Sigall, H., & Ostrove, N. (1975). Beautiful but dangerous: Effects of offender attractiveness and nature of the crime on juridic judgment. *Journal of Personality and Social Psychology, 31,* 410–414.

Silverstein, B. (1989). Enemy images: The psychology of U.S. attitudes and cognitions regarding the Soviet Union. *American Psychologist, 44,* 903–913.

Simpson, J. A. (1987). The dissolution of romantic relationships: Factors involved in relationship stability and emotional distress. *Journal of Personality and Social Psychology, 53,* 683–692.

Singer, J. L., & Singer, D. G. (1981). *Television, imagination, and aggression: A study of preschoolers.* Hillsdale, NJ: Erlbaum.

Sivacek, J., & Crano, W. D. (1982). Vested interest as a moderator of attitude-behavior consistency. *Journal of Personality and Social Psychology, 43,* 210–221.

Skowronski, J. J., & Carlston, D. E. (1989). Negativity and extremity biases in impression formation: A review of explanations. *Psychological Bulletin, 105,* 131–142.

Skrypnek, B. J., & Snyder, M. (1982). On the self-perpetuating nature of stereotypes about women and men. *Journal of Experimental Social Psychology, 18,* 277–291.

Slavin R. E., Wodarski, J. S., Blackburn, B. L. (1981). A group contingency for electricity conservation in master-metered apartments. *Journal of Applied Behavioral Analysis, 14,* 357–363.

Slavin, R. E. (1985). Cooperative learning: Applying contact theory in desegregated schools. *Journal of Social Issues, 41*(3), 45–62.

Smelser, W. T. (1961). Dominance as a factor in achievement and perception in cooperative problem solving interactions. *Journal of Abnormal and Social Psychology, 62,* 535–542.

Smith, E. E. (1961). The power of dissonance techniques to change attitudes. *Public Opinion Quarterly, 25,* 626–639.

Smith, E. R., & Miller, F. D. (1983). Mediation among attributional inferences and comprehension processes: Initial findings and a general model. *Journal of Personality and Social Psychology, 44,* 492–505.

Smith, K. D., Keating, J. P., & Stotland, E. (1989). Altruism reconsidered: The effect of denying feedback on a victim's status to empathetic witnesses. *Journal of Personality and Social Psychology, 57,* 641–650.

Snyder, C. R., & Fromkin, H. L. (1980). *Uniqueness: The human pursuit of difference.* New York: Plenum.

Snyder, M., Tanke, E. D., & Berscheid, E. (1977). Social perception and interpersonal behavior. *Journal of Personality and Social Psychology, 35,* 656–666.

Snyder, M., & Frankel, A. (1976). Observer bias: A stringent test of behavior engulfing the field. *Journal of Personality and Social Psychology, 34,* 857–864.

Snyder, M., & Jones, E. E. (1974). Attitude attribution when behavior is constrained. *Journal of Experimental Social Psychology, 10,* 585–600.

Snyder, M., & Swann, W. B. Jr. (1978). Hypothesis- testing processes in social interaction. *Journal of Personality and Social Psychology, 36,* 1202–1212.

Snyder, M., & Swann, W. B., Jr. (1976). When actions reflect attitudes: The politics of impression management. *Journal of Personality and Social Psychology, 34,* 1034–1042.

Snyder, M., & Tanke, E. D. (1976). Behavior and attitude: Some people are more consistent than others. *Journal of Personality, 44,* 501–517.

Snyder, M., & Uranowitz, S. (1978). Reconstructing the past: Some cognitive consequences of person perception. *Journal of Personality and Social Psychology, 36,* 941–950.

Snyder, M. (1981). On the self-perpetuating nature of social stereotypes. (pp. 183–212) In D. L. Hamilton (Ed.), *Cognitive processes in stereotyping and intergroup behavior.* Hillsdale, NJ: Erlbaum.

Snyder, M. (1979). Self-monitoring processes. In L. Berkowitz (Ed.), *Advances in experimental social psychology* (Vol. 12). New York: Academic Press.

Snyder, M. (1974). The self-monitoring of expressive behavior. *Journal of Personality and Social Psychology, 30,* 526–537.

Snyder, M. (1984). When belief creates reality. In L. Berkowitz (Ed.), *Advances in experimental social psychology* (Vol. 18). Orlando, FL: Academic Press.

Sokolov, A. N. (1963). *Perception and the conditioned reflex.* Oxford, England: Pergamon Press.

Sorrentino, R. M., King, G., & Leo, G. (1980). The influence of the minority on perception: A note on a possible alternative explanation. *Journal of Experimental Social Psychology, 16,* 293–301.

South, S. J. (1991). Sociodemographic differentials in mate selection preferences. *Journal of Marriage and the Family, 53,* 928–940.

Spencer, S. J., & Steele, C. (1992). The effects of stereotype vulnerability on women's math performance. Paper presented at the annual meeting of the American Psychological Association, Washington, D.C.

Sprecher, S. (1989). The importance to males and females of physical attractiveness, earning potential, and expressiveness in initial attraction. *Sex Roles, 21,* 591–607.

Sprecher, S. (1986). The relation between inequity and emotions in close relationships. *Social Psychology Quarterly, 49,* 309–321.

Srull, T. K., & Wyer, R. S. (1980). Category accessibility and social perception: Some implications for the study of person memory and interpersonal judgments. *Journal of Personality and Social Psychology, 38,* 841–856.

Srull, T. K., & Wyer, R. S. (1979). The role of category accessibility in the interpretation of information about persons: Some determinants and implications. *Journal of Personality and Social Psychology, 37,* 1660–1672.

Srull, T. K. (1981). Person memory: Some tests of associative storage and retrieval models. *Journal of Experimental Psychology: Human Learning and Memory, 7,* 440–463.

Stall, R., Coates, T., & Hoff, C. (1988). Behavioral risk reduction for HIV infection among gay and bisexual men. *American Psychologist, 43,* 878–885.

Stangor, C., Sullivan, L., & Ford, T. (1991). Affective and cognitive determinants of prejudice. *Social Cognition, 9,* 359–380.

Stangor, C. (1990). Arousal, accessibility of trait constructs, and person perception. *Journal of Experimental Social Psychology, 26,* 305–321.

Stasser, G., Kerr, N. L., & Bray, R. M. (1982). The social psychology of jury deliberations: Structure, process, and productivity. In N. L. Kerr and R. M. Bray (Eds.), *Psychology of the courtroom* (pp. 221–256). New York: Academic Press.

Stasser, G., Kerr, N. L., & Davis, J. H. (1980). Influence processes in decision-making groups: A modeling approach. In P. B. Paulus (Ed.), *Psychology of the group influence* (pp. 431—447). Hillsdale, NJ: Erlbaum.

Stasser, G., & Titus, W. (1987). Effects of information load and percentage of shared information on the dissemination of unshared information during group discussion. *Journal of Personality and Social Psychology, 53,* 81–93.

Stasser, G., & Titus, W. (1985). Pooling of unshared information in group decision making: Biased information sampling during discussion. *Journal of Personality and Social Psychology, 48,* 1467–1478.

Stasson, M. F., Kameda, T., Parks, C. D., Zimmerman, S. K., & Davis, J. H. (1991). Effects of assigned group consensus requirement on group problem solving and group members' learning. *Social Psychology Quarterly, 54,* 25–35.

Staub, E. (1989). *The roots of evil: The origins of genocide and other group violence.* New York: Cambridge University Press.

Steele, C. M., Hopp, H., & Gonzales, J. (1986). Dissonance and the lab coat: Self-affirmation and the free choice paradigm. Unpublished ms., University of Washington.

Steele, C. M., & Liu, T. J. (1983). Dissonance processes as self-affirmation. *Journal of Personality and Social Psychology, 45,* 5–19.

Steele, C. M. (1988). The psychology of self-affirmation: Sustaining the integrity of the self. In L. Berkowitz (Ed.), *Advances in experimental social psychology* (Vol. 21, pp. 261–302). San Diego: Academic Press.

Steiner, I. D. (1972). *Group process and productivity.* New York: Academic Press.

Stephan, W. G., & Stephan, C. W. (1985). Intergroup anxiety. *Journal of Social Issues, 41*(3), 157–175.

Stephan, W. G. (1986). The effects of school desegregation: An evaluation 30 years after *Brown.* In M. Saks & L. Saxe (Eds.), *Advances in applied social psychology* (Vol. 3, pp. 181–206). Hillsdale, NJ: Erlbaum.

Sterling, B., & Gaertner, S. L. (1984). The attribution process of arousal and emergency helping: A bidirectional process. *Journal of Experimental Social Psychology, 20,* 586–596.

Sternberg, R. J. (1986). A triangular theory of love. *Psychological Review, 93,* 119–135.

Sternberg, R. J. (1988). Triangulating love. In R. J. Sternberg & M. L. Barnes (Eds.), *The psychology of love* (pp. 119–138). New Haven, CT: Yale University Press.

Stewart, J. E. (1980). Defendant's attractiveness as a factor in the outcome of criminal trials: An observational study. *Journal of Applied Social Psychology, 10,* 348–361.

Stogdill, R. M. (1972). Group productivity, drive, and cohesiveness. *Organizational Behavior and Human Performance, 8,* 26–53.

Stoner, J. A. F. (1968). Risky and cautious shifts in group decisions: The influence of widely held values. *Journal of Experimental Social Psychology, 4,* 442–459.

Stoner, J. A. F. (1961). *A comparison of individual and group decisions involving risk.* Unpublished master's thesis, Massachusetts Institute of Technology.

Stone, J., Aronson, E., Crain, A. L., Winslow, M. P., & Fried, C. B. (in press). Inducing hypocrisy as a means for encouraging young adults to use condoms. *Personality and Social Psychology Bulletin.*

Stone, W. F. (1967). Autokinetic norms: An experimental analysis. *Journal of Personality and Social Psychology, 5,* 76–81.

Storms, M. D. (1973). Videotape and the attribution process: Reversing actors' and observers' points of view. *Journal of Personality and Social Psychology, 27,* 165–175.

Stouffer, S. A., Suchman, E., DeVinney, L., Star, S., & Williams, R. (1949). *The American soldier: Adjustments during Army life* (Vol. 1). Princeton, NJ: Princeton University Press.

Strack, F., Martin, L., & Stepper, S. (1988). Inhibiting and facilitating conditions of the human smile: A nonobtrusive test of the facial feedback hypothesis. *Journal of Personality and Social Psychology, 54,* 768–777.

Suls, J., & Wills, T. (Eds.). (1991). *Social comparison: Contemporary theory and research.* Hillsdale, NJ: Erlbaum.

Sumner, W. G. (1906). *Folkways.* New York: Ginn.

Swann, W. B., Jr., Giulano, T., & Wegner, D. M. (1982). Where leading questions can lead: The power of conjecture in social interaction. *Journal of Personality and Social Psychology, 42,* 1025–1035.

Swann, W. B., Jr., Griffin, J. J., Jr., Predmore, S. C., & Gaines, B. (1987). The cognitive–affective crossfire: When self-consistency confronts self-enhancement. *Journal of Personality and Social Psychology, 52,* 881–889.

Swann, W. B., Jr., Pelham, B. W., & Krull, D. S. (1989). Agreeable fancy or disagreeable truth? Reconciling self-enhancement and self-verification. *Journal of Personality and Social Psychology, 57,* 782–791.

Swann, W. B., Jr., Stein-Seroussi, A., & Giesler, R. B. (1992). Why people self-verify. *Journal of Personality and Social Psychology, 62,* 392–401.

Swann, W. B., Jr., Stein-Seroussi, A., & McNulty, S. E. (1992). Outcasts in a white-lie society: The enigmatic worlds of people with negative self-conceptions. *Journal of Personality and Social Psychology, 62,* 618–624.

Swann, W. B., Jr., & Ely, R. J. (1984). A battle of wills: Self-verification versus behavioral confirmation. *Journal of Personality and Social Psychology, 46,* 1287–1302.

Swann, W. B., Jr. (1987). Identity negotiation: Where two roads meet. *Journal of Personality and Social Psychology, 53,* 1038–1051.

Swann, W. B., Jr. (1984). Quest for accuracy in person perception: A matter of pragmatics. *Psychological Review, 91,* 457–477.

Swann, W. B., Jr. (1983). Self-verification: Bringing social reality into harmony with the self. In J. Suls & A. G. Greenwald (Eds.), *Psychological perspectives on the self* (Vol. 2, pp. 33–66). Hillsdale, NJ: Erlbaum.

Swann, W. B., Jr. (1985). The self as architect of social reality. In B. Schlenker (Ed.), *The self and social life* (pp. 100–125). New York: McGraw-Hill.

Swann, W. B., Jr. (1990). To be known or to be adored: The interplay of self-enhancement and self-verification. In R. M. Sorrentino & E. T. Higgins (Eds.), *Handbook of motivation and cognition* (Vol. 2, pp. 408–448). New York: Guilford Press.

Sweeney, P., Anderson, K., & Bailey, S. (1986). Attributional style in depression: A meta-analytic review. *Journal of Personality and Social Psychology, 50,* 974–991.

Swingle, P. G., & Gillis, J. S. (1968). Effects of the emotional relationship between protagonists in the prisoner's dilemma. *Journal of Personality and Social Psychology, 8,* 160–165.

Szybillo, G. J., & Heslin, R. (1973). Resistance to persuasion: Inoculation theory in a marketing context. *Journal of Marketing Research, 10,* 369–403.

Tajfel, H., Billig, M., Bundy, R., & Flament, C. (1971). Social categorization and intergroup behaviour. *European Journal of Social Psychology, 1,* 149–178.

Tajfel, H. (Ed.). (1978). *Differentiation between social groups.* London: Academic Press.

Tajfel, H., Nemeth, C., Jahoda, G., Campbell, J., & Johnson, N. (1970). The development of children's preference for their own country: A cross-national study. *International Journal of Psychology, 5,* 245–253.

Tajfel, H., & Turner, J. C. (1986). The social identity theory of intergroup behavior. In S. Worchel & W. Austin (Eds.), *Psychology of intergroup relations* (pp. 7–24). Chicago: Nelson-Hall.

Tajfel, H., & Wilkes, A. L. (1963). Classification and quantitative judgment. *British Journal of Psychology, 54,* 101–113.

Tajfel, H. (1969). Cognitive aspects of prejudice. *Journal of Social Issues, 25,* 79–97.

Tajfel, H. (1970). Experiments in intergroup discrimination. *Scientific American, 223*(2), 96–102.

Tajfel, H. (1979). Individuals and groups in social psychology. *British Journal of Social and Clinical Psychology, 18,* 183–190.

Tajfel, H. (1978). The psychological structure of intergroup relations. In H. Tajfel (Ed.), *Differentiation between social groups: Studies in the social psychology of intergroup relations.* London: Academic Press.

Tajfel, H. (1981). *Human groups and social categories.* Cambridge, England: Cambridge University Press.

Tanford, S., & Penrod, S. (1984). Social influence model: A formal integration of research on majority and minority influence. *Psychological Bulletin, 95,* 189–225.

Tassinary, L. G., & Cacioppo, J. T. (1992). Unobservable facial actions and emotion. *Psychological Science, 3,* 28–33.

Taylor, D. M., Wright, S., Moghaddam, F., & Lalonde, R. (1990). The personal/group discrimination discrepancy: Perceiving my group but not myself to be a target for discrimination. *Personality and Social Psychology Bulletin, 16,* 254–262.

Taylor, D. M., & McKirnen, D. J. (1984). A five-stage model of intergroup relations. *British Journal of Social Psychology, 23,* 291–300.

Taylor, S. E., & Brown, J. D. (1988). Illusion and well-being: A theory of cognitive adaptation. *Psychological Bulletin, 103,* 193–210.

Taylor, S. E., & Crocker, J. (1981). Schematic bases of social information processing. In E. T. Higgins, C. P. Herman, & M. P. Zanna (Eds.), *Social cognition: The Ontario Symposium* (Vol. 1). Hillsdale, NJ: Erlbaum.

Taylor, S. E., & Fiske, S. T. (1975). Point of view and perceptions of causality. *Journal of Personality and Social Psychology 32,* 439–445.

Taylor, S. E. (1981a). A categorization approach to stereotyping. In D. L. Hamilton (Ed.), *Cognitive processes in stereotyping and intergroup behavior* (pp. 83–114). Hillsdale, NJ: Erlbaum.

Taylor, S. E. (1983). Adjustment to threatening events: A theory of cognitive adaptation. *American Psychologist, 38,* 1161–1173.

Taylor, S. E. (1975). On inferring one's attitudes from one's behavior: Some delimiting conditions. *Journal of Personality and Social Psychology, 31,* 126–131.

Taylor, S. P., & Gammon, C. B., & Capasso, D. R. (1976). Aggression as a function of alcohol and threat. *Journal of Personality and Social Psychology, 34,* 938–941.

Taylor, S. P., & Gammon, C. B. (1975). Effects of type and dose of alcohol on human physical aggression. *Journal of Personality and Social Psychology, 32,* 169–175.

Taylor, S. P., & Leonard, K. E. (1983). Alcohol and human physical aggression. In R. G. Geen & E. I. Donnerstein (Eds.), *Aggression: Theoretical and empirical reviews* (Vol. 2, pp. 77–101). New York: Academic Press.

Tedeschi, J. T. (Ed.). (1981). *Impression management theory and psychological research.* New York: Academic Press.

Tedeschi, J. T., Schlenker, B. R., & Bonoma, T. V. (1971). Cognitive dissonance: Private ratiocination or public spectacle? *American Psychologist, 26,* 685–695.

Tedeschi, J. T., & Rosenfeld, P. (1981). Impression management theory and the forced compliance situation. In J. T Tedeschi (Ed.), *Impression management theory and social psychological research.* New York: Academic Press.

Tennov, D. (1979). *Love and limerence.* New York: Stein & Day.

Tennyson, A. (1842). Come not, when I am dead.

Terborg, J. R., Castore, C., & DeNinno, J. A. (1976). A longitudinal field investigation of the impact of group composition on group performance and cohesion. *Journal of Personality and Social Psychology, 34,* 782–790.

Tesser, A., Martin, L., & Mendolia, M. (in press). The role of thought in changing attitude strength. In R. E. Petty & J. A. Krosnick (Eds.), *Attitude strength: Antecedents and consequences.* Hillsdale, NJ: Erlbaum.

Tesser, A., Millar, M., & Moore, J. (1988). Some affective consequences of social comparison and reflection processes: The pain and pleasure of being close. *Journal of Personality and Social Psychology, 54,* 49–61.

Tesser, A., & Brodie, M. (1971). A note on the evaluation of a "computer date." *Psychonomic Science, 23,* 300.

Tesser, A., & Cowan, C. L. (1975). Some effects of thought and number of cognitions on attitude change. *Social Behavior and Personality, 3,* 165–173.

Tesser, A. (1978). Self-generated attitude change. In L. Berkowitz (Ed.), *Advances in experimental social psychology* (Vol. 11). New York: Academic Press.

Tesser, A. (1988). Toward a self-evaluation maintenance model of social behavior. In L. Berkowitz (Ed.), *Advances in experimental social psychology* (Vol. 21, pp. 181–227). San Diego: Academic Press.

Tetlock, P. E. (1979). Identifying victims of groupthink from public statements of decision makers. *Journal of Personality and Social Psychology, 37,* 1314–1324.

Thibaut, J. W., & Kelley, H. H. (1959). *The social psychology of groups.* New York: Wiley.

Thomas, K. W., & Pondy, L. R. (1977). Toward an "intent" model of conflict management among principal parties. *Human Relations, 30,* 1089–1102.

Thurstone, L. L., & Chave, E. L. (1929). *The measurement of attitudes.* Chicago: University of Chicago Press.

Thurstone, L. L. (1928). Theory of attitude measurement. *Psychological Bulletin, 36,* 222–241.

Tice, D. M. (1992). Self-concept change and self-presentation: The looking glass self is also a magnifying glass. *Journal of Personality and Social Psychology, 63,* 435–451.

Tilker, H. A. (1970). Socially responsible behavior as a function of observer responsibility and victim feedback. *Journal of Personality and Social Psychology, 14,* 95–100.

Tomkins, S. S. (1962). *Affect, imagery, consciousness. (Vol. 1.) The positive affects.* New York: Springer-Verlag.

Tomkins, S. S. (1962). *Affect, imagery, consciousness.* New York: Springer.

Torrence, E. P. (1966). Some consequences of power differences on decision making in permanent and temporary three-man groups. In A. P. Hare, E. F. Borgatta, and R. F. Bales (Eds.), *Small groups: Studies in social interaction* (Rev. ed., pp. 600–609). New York: Knopf.

Touhey, J. C. (1979). Sex-role stereotyping and individual differences in liking for the physically attractive. *Social Psychology Quarterly, 42,* 285–288.

Travis, C. B., & Yaeger, C. P. (1991). Sexual selection, parental investment, and sexism. *Journal of Social Issues, 47,* 117–129.

Travis, L. E. (1925). The effect of a small audience upon hand-eye coordination. *Journal of Abnormal and Social Psychology, 20,* 142–146.

Travis, L. E. (1928). The influence of the group on stutterer's speed in free association. *Journal of Abnormal and Social Psychology, 23,* 45–51.

Triandis, H. C., Bontempo, R., & Villareal, M. (1988). Individualism and collectivism: Cross-cultural perspectives on self-ingroup relationships. *Journal of Personality and Social Psychology, 54,* 323–338.

Triandis, H. C. (1989). The self and social behavior in differing cultural contexts. *Psychological Review, 96,* 506–520.

Triplett, N. (1898). The dynamogenic factors in pacemaking and competition. *American Journal of Psychology, 9,* 507–533.

Trope, Y. (1986). Identification and inferential processes in dispositional attribution. *Psychological Review, 93,* 239–257.

Turner, J. C., Hogg, M. A., Oakes, P. J., Reicher, S. D., & Wetherell, M. (1987). *Rediscovering the social group: A self-categorization theory.* Oxford: Blackwell.

Turner, J. C., Hogg, M., Oakes, P., Reicher, S., & Wetherell, M. (1987). *Rediscovering the social group: A self-categorization theory.* Oxford: Basil Blackwell.

Turner, J. C., Hogg., M., Turner, P., & Smith, P. (1984). Failure and defeat as determinants of group cohesiveness. *British Journal of Social Psychology, 23,* 97–111.

Turner, J. C. (1985). Social categorization and the self-concept: A social cognitive theory of group behavior. In E. Lawler (Ed.), *Advances in group processes* (Vol. 2, pp. 77–122). Greenwich, CN: JAI Press.

Turner, J. C. (1991). *Social influence.* Milton Keynes, England: Open University Press.

Turner, M., Pratkanis, A., Probasco, P., & Leve, C. (1992). Threat, cohesion, and group effectiveness: Testing a social identity maintenance perspective on groupthink. *Journal of Personality and Social Psychology, 63,* 781–796.

Vallacher, R., Messé, L., & Fullerton, T. (1987). Is equity ever motivating? Reward and task structure effects on group performance. Paper presented at the meeting of the American Psychological Association, New York.

Vancouver, J. B., & Ilgen, D. R. (1989). Effects of interpersonal orientation and the sex-type of the task on choosing to work alone or in groups. *Journal of Applied Psychology, 74,* 927–934.

Vanneman, R. D., & Pettigrew, T. F. (1972). Race and relative deprivation in the urban United States. *Race, 13,* 461–486.

Varela, J. A. (1971). *Psychological solutions to social problems.* New York: Academic Press.

Vasta, R., & Copitch, P. (1981). Simulating conditions of child abuse in the laboratory. *Child Development, 52,* 164–170.

Vinokur, A., & Burnstein, E. (1974). The effects of partially shared persuasive arguments on group-induced shifts: A group-problem-solving approach. *Journal of Personality and Social Psychology, 29,* 305–315.

Voss, H. L., & Hepburn, J. R. (1968). Patterns in criminal homicide in Chicago. *Journal of Criminal Law, Criminology, and Police Science, 59,* 499–508.

von Baeyer, C. L., Sherk, D. L., & Zanna, M. P. (1981). Impression management in the job interview: When the female applicant meets the male (chauvinist) interviewer. *Personality and Social Psychology Bulletin, 7,* 45–52.

Walker, I., & Pettigrew, T. F. (1984). Relative deprivation theory: An overview and conceptual critique. *British Journal of Social Psychology, 23,* 301–310.

Wallach, M. A., Kogan, N., & Bem, D. J. (1962). Group influence on individual risk taking. *Journal of Abnormal and Social Psychology, 65,* 75–86.

Wallbott, H. G. (1991). Recognition of emotion from facial expression via imitation? Some indirect evidence for an old theory. *British Journal of Social Psychology, 30,* 207–219.

Walster, E., Aronson, V., Abrahams, D., & Rottmann, L. (1966). Importance of physical attractiveness in dating behavior. *Journal of Personality and Social Psychology, 4,* 508–516.

Walster, E., Walster, G. W., Traupmann, J. (1978). Equity and premarital sex. *Journal of Personality and Social Psychology, 36,* 82–92.

Walster, E., Walster, G. W., & Berscheid, E. (1978). *Equity: Theory and research.* Boston: Allyn & Bacon.

Walster, E., Walster, G. W., & Berscheid, E. (1978). *Equity: Theory and research.* Boston: Allyn & Bacon.

Walster (Hatfield), E., & Festinger, L. (1962). The effectiveness of "overheard" persuasive communications. *Journal of Abnormal and Social Psychology, 65,* 395–402.

Waters, H. F., & Malamud, P. (1975, March 10). "Drop that gun, Captain Video." *Newsweek,* pp. 81–82.

Watkins, M. J., & Peynircioglu, Z. F. (1984). Determining perceived meaning during impression formation: Another look at the meaning change hypothesis. *Journal of Personality and Social Psychology, 46,* 1005–1016.

Watts, B. L., Messé, L. A., & Vallacher, R. R. (1982). Toward understanding sex differences in pay allocation: Agency, communion, and reward distribution behavior. *Sex Roles, 8,* 1175–1187.

Webb, E. J., Campbell, D. T., Schwartz, R. D., Sechrest, L., & Grove, J. B. (1981). *Nonreactive measures in the social sciences* (2nd ed.). Boston: Houghton Mifflin.

Weber, R., & Crocker, J. C. (1983). Cognitive processes in the revision of stereotypic beliefs. *Journal of Personality and Social Psychology, 45,* 961–967.

Wegner, D. M., Wentzlaff, R., Kerker, R. M., & Beattie, A. E. (1981). Incrimination through innuendo: Can media questions become public answers? *Journal of Personality and Social Psychology, 40,* 822–832.

Wegner, D. M., & Crano, W. D. (1975). Racial factors in helping behavior in an unobtrusive field experiment. *Journal of Personality and Social Psychology, 32,* 901–905.

Weigel, R. H., Vernon, D. T., & Tognacci, L. S. (1974). Increasing attitude-behavior correspondence by broadening the scope of the behavioral measure. *Journal of Personality and Social Psychology, 30,* 724–728.

Weigel, R., Loomis, J., & Soja, M. (1980). Race relations on prime time television. *Journal of Personality and Social Psychology, 39,* 884–893.

Weiner, B., Amirkhan, J., Folkes, V., & Verette, J. (1987). An attributional analysis of excuse giving: Studies of a naive theory of emotion. *Journal of Personality and Social Psychology, 52,* 316–324.

Weiner, B., Frieze, I., Kukla, A., Reed, L., Rest, S., & Rosenbaum, R. (1971). *Perceiving the causes of success and failure.* Morristown, NJ: General Learning Press.

Weiner, B., Graham, S., & Chandler, C. (1982). Pity, anger, and guilt: An attributional analysis. *Personality and Social Psychology Bulletin, 8,* 226–232.

Weiner, B., Perry, R., & Magnusson, J. (1988). An attributional analysis of reactions to stigmas. *Journal of Personality and Social Psychology, 55,* 738–748.

Weiner, B., & Handel, S. (1985). Anticipated emotional consequences of causal communications and reported communication strategy. *Developmental Psychology, 21,* 102–107.

Weiner, B., & Kukla, A. (1970). An attributional analysis of achievement motivation. *Journal of Personality and Social Psychology, 15,* 1–20.

Weiner, B. (1985). An attributional theory of motivation and emotion. *Psychological Review, 92,* 548–573.

Weiner, B. (1979). A theory of motivation for some classroom experiences. *Journal of Educational Psychology, 71,* 3–25.

Weiner, B. (1986). *An attributional theory of motivation and emotion.* New York: Springer-Verlag.

Weld, H., & Roff, M. A. (1938). A study in the formation of opinion based upon legal evidence. *American Journal of Psychology, 51,* 609–628.

Wells, H. G. (1905). *A modern utopia.* London: Chapman & Hall.

West, S. G., Whitney, G., & Schnedler, R. (1975). Helping a motorist in distress: The effects of sex, race, and neighborhood. *Journal of Personality and Social Psychology, 31,* 691–698.

White, G. L., Fishbein, S., & Rutstein, J. (1981). Passionate love and misattribution of arousal. *Journal of Personality and Social Psychology, 41,* 56–62.

White, G. L., & Mullen, P. E. (1990). *Jealousy: Theory, research, and clinical strategies.* New York: Guilford Press.

White, G. L. (1980). Physical attractiveness and courtship progress. *Journal of Personality and Social Psychology, 39,* 660–668.

White, R. K. (1977). Misperception in the Arab-Israeli conflict. *Journal of Social Issues, 33*(1), 190–221.

White, R. K. (1970). *Nobody wanted war: Misperceptions in Vietnam and other wars.* Garden City, NY: Doubleday.

Whittaker, J. (1963). Opinion change as a function of communication-attitude discrepancy. *Psychological Reports, 13,* 763–772.

Wicker, A. (1969). Attitudes vs. actions: The relationship of verbal and overt behavioral responses to attitude objects. *Journal of Social Issues, 25,* 1–78.

Wicklund, R. A., Cooper, J., & Linder, D. E. (1967). Effects of expected effort on attitude change prior to exposure. *Journal of Experimental Social Psychology, 3,* 416–428.

Widmeyer, W. N., & Loy, J. W. (1988). When you're hot you're hot! Warm–cold effects in first impressions of persons and teaching effectiveness. *Journal of Educational Psychology, 80,* 118–121.

Wilder, D. A., & Shapiro, P. N. (1984). Role of outgroup cues in determining social identity. *Journal of Personality and Social Psychology, 47,* 342–348.

Wilder, D. A., & Shapiro, P. N. (1989). Role of competition-induced anxiety in limiting the beneficial impact of positive behavior by an out-group member. *Journal of Personality and Social Psychology, 56,* 60–69.

Wilder, D. A., & Thompson, J. E. (1980). Intergroup contact with independent manipulations of in-group and out-group interaction. *Journal of Personality and Social Psychology, 38,* 589–603.

Wilder, D. A. (1986). Cognitive factors affecting the success of intergroup contact. In S. Worchel & W. Austin (Eds.), *Psychology of intergroup relations* (pp. 49–66). Chicago: Nelson-Hall.

Wilder, D. A. (1984). Intergroup contact: The typical member and the exception to the rule. *Journal of Experimental Social Psychology, 20,* 177–194.

Wilder, D. A. (1981). Perceiving persons as a group: Categorization and intergroup relations. In D. L. Hamilton (Ed.), *Cognitive processes in stereotyping and intergroup behavior* (pp. 213–257). Hillsdale, NJ: Erlbaum.

Wilder, D. A. (1977). Perception of groups, size of opposition and social influence. *Journal of Experimental Social Psychology, 13,* 253–268.

Wilder, D. A. (1978). Reduction of intergroup discrimination through individuation of the outgroup. *Journal of Personality and Social Psychology, 36,* 1361–1374.

Wilder, D. A. (1986). Social categorization: Implications for creation and reduction of intergroup bias. In L. Berkowitz (Ed.), *Advances in experimental social psychology* (Vol. 19, pp. 291–355). New York: Academic Press.

Williamson, G. M., & Clark, M. S. (1989). Providing help and desired relationship type as determinants of changes in moods and self-evaluations. *Journal of Personality and Social Psychology, 56,* 722–734.

Williams, K. B., Harkins, S., & Latané, B. (1981). Identifiability as a deterrent to social loafing: Two cheering experiments. *Journal of Personality and Social Psychology, 40,* 303–311.

Williams, R. B., Barefoot, J. C., Califf, R. M., Haney, T. L., Saunders, W. B., Pryor, D. B., Hlatky, M. A., Siegler, I. C., Mark, D. B. (1992). Prognostic importance of social and economic resources among medically treated patients with angiographically documented coronary artery disease. *Journal of the American Medical Association, 267,* 520–524.

Willis, R. H., & Levine, J. M. (1976). Interpersonal influence and conformity. In B. Seidenberg & A. Snadowsky (Eds.), *Social psychology: An introduction* (pp. 309–341). New York: Free Press.

Willis, R. H. (1972). Diamond model of social response. In W. S. Sahakian (Ed.), *Social psychology: Experimentation, theory, and research.* Scranton, PA: International Textbook.

Wills, T. A. (1981). Downward comparison principles in social psychology. *Psychological Bulletin, 90,* 245–271.

Wilson, E. O. (1978). *On human nature*. Cambridge, MA: Harvard University Press.

Wilson, E. O. (1975). *Sociobiology: The new synthesis*. Cambridge, MA: Harvard University Press.

Wilson, J. P., Aronoff, J., & Messé, L. A. (1975). Social structure, member motivation, and productivity. *Journal of Personality and Social Psychology, 32,* 1094–1098.

Wilson, L., & Rogers, R. W. (1975). The fire this time: Effects of race of target, insult, and potential retaliation on black aggression. *Journal of Personality and Social Psychology, 32,* 857–864.

Wilson, T. D., & Linville, P. W. (1982). Improving the academic performance of college freshmen: Attribution therapy revisited. *Journal of Personality and Social Psychology, 42,* 367–376.

Winter, L., & Uleman, J. S. (1984). When are social judgments made? Evidence for the spontaneousness of trait inferences. *Journal of Personality and Social Psychology, 49,* 904–917.

Witte, K. (1992). Putting the fear back into fear appeals: The extended parallel process model. *Communication Monographs, 59,* 329–349.

Wolfgang, M. E., & Strohm, R. B. (1956). The relationship between alcohol and criminal homicide. *Quarterly Journal of Studies on Alcohol, 17,* 108–123.

Won-Doornink, M. J. (1979). On getting to know you: The association between the stage of relationship and reciprocity of self-disclosure. *Journal of Experimental Social Psychology, 15,* 229–241.

Woodall, W. G., & Burgoon, J. K. (1983). Talking fast and changing attitudes: A critique and clarification. *Journal of Nonverbal Behavior, 8,* 126–142.

Woodworth, R. D. (1938). *Experimental psychology*. New York: Holt.

Wood, J. T. (1984). Alternative methods of group decision making: A comparative examination of consensus, negotiation, and voting. In G. M. Phillips & J. T. Wood (Eds.), *Emergent issues in human decision making* (pp. 3–18). Carbondale: Southern Illinois University Press.

Wood, J. V. (1989). Theory and research concerning social comparisons of personal attributes. *Psychological Bulletin, 106,* 231–248.

Wood, W., Rhodes, N., & Biek, M. (in press). Working knowledge and attitude strength: An information-processing analysis. In R. Petty & J. Krosnick, *Attitude strength: Antecedents and consequences*. Ohio State series on attitude and persuasion (Vol. 4). Hillsdale, NJ: Erlbaum.

Wood, W. (1987). A meta-analytic review of sex differences in group performance. *Psychological Bulletin, 102,* 53–71.

Wood, W. (1982). The retrieval of attitude-relevant information from memory: Effects on susceptibility to persuasion and on intrinsic motivation. *Journal of Personality and Social Psychology, 42,* 798–810.

Worchel, S., Andreoli, V., & Folger, R. (1977). Intergroup cooperation and intergroup attraction: The effect of previous interaction and outcome of combined effort. *Journal of Experimental Social Psychology, 13,* 131–140.

Worchel, S. (1986). The role of cooperation in reducing intergroup conflict. In S. Worchel & W. Austin (Eds.), *Psychology of intergroup relations* (pp. 288–304. Chicago: Nelson-Hall.

Word, C. D., Zanna, M. P., & Cooper, J. (1974). The nonverbal mediation of self-fulfilling prophecy effects in interracial interaction. *Journal of Experimental Social Psychology, 10,* 109–120.

Word, C., Zanna, M., & Cooper, J. (1974). The nonverbal mediation of self-fulfilling prophesies in interracial interactions. *Journal of Experimental Social Psychology, 10,* 109–120.

Worth, L. T., Mackie, D. M., & Asuncion, A. G. (1989). Distinguishing cognitive and motivational mediators of the impact of positive mood on persuasion. Unpublished ms., cited in Mackie and Worth (1990).

Wright, S. C., Taylor, D. M., & Moghaddam, F. M. (1990). Responding to membership in a disadvantaged group: From acceptance to collective protest. *Journal of Personality and Social Psychology, 58,* 994–1003.

Wyer, R. S., & Srull, T. K. (1986). Human cognition in its social context. *Psychological Review, 93,* 322–359.

Yaryan, R., & Festinger, L. (1961). Preparatory action and belief in the probable occurrence of future events. *Journal of Abnormal and Social Psychology, 63,* 603–606.

Yerkes, R. M., & Dodson, J. D. (1908). The relation of strength of stimulus to rapidity of habit-formation. *Journal of Comparative Neurology and Psychology, 18,* 459–482.

Zaccaro, S. J. (1984). Social loafing: The role of task attractiveness. *Personality and Social Psychology Bulletin, 14,* 99–106.

Zajonc, R. B., Adelmann, P. K., Murphy, S. T., and Niedenthal, P. M. (1987). Convergence in physical appearance of spouses. *Motivation and Emotion, 11,* 335–346.

Zajonc, R. B., Heingartner, A., & Herman, E. M. (1969). Social enhancement and impairment of performance in the cockroach. *Journal of Personality and Social Psychology, 13,* 83–92.

Zajonc, R. B. (1980). Compresence. In P. B. Paulus (Ed.), *Psychology of group influence* (pp. 35–60). Hillsdale, NJ: Erlbaum.

Zajonc, R. B. (1965). Social facilitation. *Science, 149,* 269–274.

Zajonc, R. B. (1968). The attitudinal effects of mere exposure. *Journal of Personality and Social Psychology, 9,* 1–27 (Monograph and supplement 2).

Zajonc, R., Adelmann, P., Murphy, S., & Niedenthal, P. (1987). Convergence in the physical appearance of spouses. *Motivation and Emotion, 11,* 335–346.

Zajonc, R., Murphy, S., & Inglehart, M. (1989). Feeling and facial efference: Implications of the vascular theory of emotion. *Psychological Review, 96,* 395–416.

Zander, A. (1985). *The purposes of groups and organizations*. San Francisco: Jossey-Bass.

Zanna, M. P., & Cooper, J. (1974). Dissonance and the pill. An attribution approach to studying the arousal properties of dissonance. *Journal of Personality and Social Psychology, 29,* 703–709.

Zanna, M. P., & Pack, S. J. (1975). On the self-fulfilling nature of apparent sex differences in behavior. *Journal of Experimental Social Psychology, 11,* 584–591.

Zanna, M. P., & Rempel, J. K., (1986). Attitudes: A new look at an old concept. In D. Bar-Tal & A. Kruglanski (Eds.), *The social psychology of knowledge*. New York: Cambridge University Press.

Zanna, M. P., & Sande, G. N. (1987). The effects of collective actions on the attitudes of individual group members: A dissonance analysis. In M. P. Zanna, J. M. Olson, & C. P. Herman (Eds.), *Social Influence: Ontario Symposium* (Vol. 5). Hillsdale, NJ: Erlbaum.

Zanna, M., Crosby, F., & Loewenstein, G. (1987). Male reference groups and discontent among female professionals. In B. Gutek & L. Larwood (Eds.), *Women's career development* (pp. 28–41). Newbury Park, CA: Sage.

Zarate, M. A., & Smith, E. R. (1990). Person categorization and stereotyping. *Social Cognition, 8,* 161–185.

Zebrowitz, L. A. (1990). *Social perception.* Pacific Grove, CA: Brooks/Cole.

Zillman, D., Bryant, J., Cominsky, P. W., & Medoff, N. J. (1981). Excitation and hedonic valence in the effect of erotica on motivated intermale aggression. *European Journal of Social Psychology, 11,* 233–252.

Zillman, D., Katcher, A. H., & Milavsky, B. (1972). Excitation transfer from physical exercise to subsequent aggressive behavior. *Journal of Experimental Social Psychology, 8,* 247–259.

Zillman, D. (1983). Transfer of excitation in emotional behavior. In J. T. Cacioppo & R. E. Petty (Eds.), *Social psychophysiology: A source book* (pp. 215–240). New York: Guilford Press.

Zillman, D. (1984). *Connections between sex and aggression.* Hillsdale, NJ: Erlbaum.

Zillman, D. (1988). Cognition-excitation interdependencies in aggressive behavior. *Aggressive Behavior, 14,* 51–64.

Zillman, D. (1979). *Hostility and aggression.* Hillsdale, NJ: Erlbaum.

Zimbardo, P. G. (1965). The effect of effort and improvisation on self-persuasion produced by role-playing. *Journal of Experimental Social Psychology, 1,* 103–120.

Zimbardo, P. G. (1969). The human choice: Individuation, reasons, and order versus deindividuation, impulse, and chaos. In W. J. Arnold and D. Levine (Eds.), *Nebraska symposium on motivation* (Vol. 17, pp. 237–307). Lincoln: University of Nebraska Press.

Zuber, J., Crott, H., & Werner, J. (1992). Choice shift and group polarization: An analysis of the status of arguments and social decision schemes. *Journal of Personality and Social Psychology, 62,* 50–61.

Zuckerman, M., DePaulo, B., & Rosenthal, R. (1981). Verbal and nonverbal communication of deception. In L. Berkowitz (Ed.), *Advances in experimental social psychology* (Vol. 14). New York: Academic Press.

Zuckerman, M. (1979). Attribution of success and failure revisited, or: The motivational bias is alive and well in attribution theory. *Journal of Personality, 47,* 245–287.

A

Abelson, R. P., 82, 148
Abrahams, D., 256
Abrams, D., 379, 448, 450, 458
Abramson, L., 181
Adamopoulos, J., 430
Adams, K. C., 34
Adelman, P., 123
Adelmann, P. K., 261
Adorno, T. W., 351, 472
Ainsworth, M., 270
Ajzen, I., 31, 32, 79
Alessi, C., 46
Allbright, L., 262
Allen, A., 39
Allen, K. M., 410
Allen, M., 45
Allen, V. I., 374
Allen, V. L., 377
Alley, T. R., 108, 124
Allison, S. T., 240, 250
Alloy, L. R., 181
Allport, F. H., 408
Allport, G. W., 2, 19, 25, 126, 161,
    163, 447, 462, 465, 472, 474, 478,
    480, 489, 495, 508
Amir, Y., 488, 508
Amirkhan, J., 179
Ancok, D., 484
Andersen, S., 336
Andersen, S. L., 217
Anderson, A. B., 415
Anderson, C., 315, 316
Anderson, C. A., 175, 181, 183
Anderson, D., 315
Anderson, J. A., 123
Anderson, K., 181
Anderson, N. H., 130, 139, 140, 419
Andreoli, V., 511
Anthony, T., 471
Apple, W., 50
Archer, D., 119–120, 475
Argyle, M., 266
Aristotle, 25
Arkoff, A., 53
Arms, R. L., 318

Aronoff, J., 411, 412, 419
Aronson, E., 14, 19, 61, 82, 83, 90,
    92–94, 102, 104, 136, 252, 512
Aronson, J., 131
Aronson, V., 256
Asch, S. E., 127, 128, 141, 142, 144,
    364, 372–375, 377, 385, 388
Ashmore, R. D., 134, 257, 278
Askling, L. R., 427
Asunsion, A. G., 60, 470
Atkins, J., 191
Austin, W., 517
Axelrod, R., 250, 252
Axsom, D., 76, 91–92

B

Back, K., 263
Baer, J., 141
Baer, R., 384
Bagby, R. M., 83
Bailey, S., 181
Bakan, D., 249
Baker, S. M., 152
Bales, R. F., 425
Bandura, A., 181, 317, 318
Baral, R. L., 262
Barbee, P. L., 294
Bargh, J. A., 154, 155, 160
Barios, M., 475
Barnes, M., 259
Barnes, M. L., 278
Barnes, R., 178
Barnes-Nacoste, 514
Baron, R. A., 305, 310, 316
Baron, R. M., 116, 117, 118, 333
Baron, R. S., 428, 431, 433, 438
Barrett, L., 322
Barrios, A. A., 130
Bar-Tal, D., 259, 465, 480
Bashner, R., 478
Bassett, R., 382
Bassili, J. N., 115, 117
Batson, C. D., 292–293, 298, 301

Batson, K. C., 240
Bauman, D. J., 294
Baumeister, R. F., 409
Baumgardner, M. H., 45, 52
Baumrind, D., 17, 351, 357
Beattie, A. E., 341
Beatty, S. E., 90
Beauvois, J. L., 382
Beecher, H. K., 330
Belch, G. E., 59
Belch, M. A., 59
Bell, P. A., 316
Bem, D. J., 30, 39, 96–99, 102, 104,
    217, 381, 432, 476
Bem, S. L., 155, 166, 210, 336
Benassi, M. A., 136
Berglas, S., 218
Berkowitz, L., 83, 228, 310, 311, 318,
    322, 325
Bernstein, S., 210
Berry, D. S., 118, 118, 124
Berscheid, E., 134, 238, 257–260 268,
    269, 272, 335
Bersoff, D., 146, 166
Betancourt, H., 177, 179
Bettencourt, B. A., 515
Bettman, J. R., 168, 180
Bickman, L., 290
Biernat, M., 466, 480
Billig, M., 482
Birrell, P., 467
Bishop, D., 215
Bishop, G. D., 432
Bither, S. W., 55
Black, J. B., 148
Blackburn, B. L., 246
Blair, I., 177, 179
Blake, R. R., 511
Blanchard, F. A., 415, 474
Blaney, N., 512
Blascovich, J., 410
Blau, P. M., 233
Blehar, M., 270
Bless, H., 60
Bobo, L., 495, 496, 498
Bogardus, E. S., 487
Bohner, G., 60, 60
Bond, R., 154
Bonoma, T. V., 95
Bontempo, R., 226

Bootzin, R., 488
Borden, R., 451
Borgida, E., 146, 166, 175, 190
Bornstein, R. F., 278
Boster, F. J., 433
Bouchard, T. J. Jr., 411
Bourhis, R. Y., 484
Bower, G. H., 148, 156
Braddock, J. H., 510
Bradshaw, D., 270
Braly, K. W., 149, 463
Bray, R. M., 429
Breckler, S. J., 40
Breckler, S. T., 26
Brehm, J. W., 52, 88, 379
Brekke, N., 175
Bretl, D. J., 475
Brewer, M. B., 14, 19, 147, 152, 159,
    245, 247, 252, 259, 441, 449, 453,
    458, 469, 483, 502, 510, 514, 515,
    517
Brewer, W. F., 157
Brickman, P., 456
Brickner, M. A., 419
Brigham, J. C., 464, 465, 471
Bringle, R. G., 274
Brock, T. C., 56
Brodie, M., 257
Bromley, S., 290, 488, 490, 498
Bronfenbrenner, U., 506
Brophy, J. E., 178
Brotzman, E., 358
Brousseau, K. R., 426
Broverman, D., 151
Broverman, I., 151
Brown, J. D., 181, 183, 219, 222, 228
Brown, R., 433, 515, 517
Brown, V., 475
Brown, Y., 398
Bruner, J. S., 133, 147, 153, 157
Bruun, S. E., 246, 413, 417
Bryant, J., 315
Buchanan, D. R., 256
Bugelski, R., 472
Buller, D. B., 331
Bullock, M., 114
Bundy, R., 482
Burgoon, J. K., 51, 331
Burgoon, M., 50, 55, 381
Burnstein, E., 433
Burwitz, L., 408
Bury, A., 83
Bush, M., 381
Bushman, B. J., 321
Buss, A. H., 304
Buss, D. M., 259, 275
Buunk, B., 274
Byrne, D., 6, 13, 264, 264

C

Cacioppo, J. T., 29, 40, 45, 65, 68, 69
    72, 73, 76, 79, 378, 382, 401
Calder, B. J., 31
Callahan-Levy, C., 249
Campbell, D. T., 14, 29, 40, 370, 373,
    385, 469, 476
Campbell, J., 441
Canavan, P., 250
Cantor, J., 475
Cantor, N., 149, 152, 166
Cantril, H., 3–4, 12
Capasso, D. R., 323
Caporael, L. R., 259
Carli, L. L., 378
Carlsmith, J. M., 14, 19, 84, 86, 93, 96,
    98
Carlson, M., 293, 295
Carlson, R., 249
Carlston, D. E., 140, 144
Carment, D. W., 408
Cartwright, D., 425
Cartwright-Smith, J., 122
Case, N., 276
Case, R. B., 276
Castore, C., 415
Catalan, J., 381
Chaiken, S., 34, 46, 74, 76, 79
Chaikin, A. L., 255, 265
Chammah, A. M., 248, 252
Champion, D., 191
Chan, G., 427
Chandler, C., 178
Chanowitz, B., 478
Charlin, V., 293
Charng, H., 301
Chase, J., 505
Chave, E. L., 25
Chein, I., 509
Cheng, P. W., 190
Chertkoff, J. M., 428, 484
Childress, S. A., 325
Cialdini, R. B., 294, 380, 381, 382,
    398, 402, 451, 473
Cimbalo, R. S., 267
Clark, K. B., 453, 509
Clark, M. P., 453
Clark, M. S., 238, 239, 255, 301
Clark, N. T., 381
Clark, R. D. III., 286, 399
Clarkson, F., 151
Coates, T., 442
Coffman, T., 495
Cohen, A. R., 86

Cohen, C. E., 158
Cohen, E. G., 513
Cohen, J. L., 409
Cohen, S., 276, 510
Collins, B. E., 30
Collins, M. E., 509
Cominsky, P. W., 315
Comstock, G. D., 452
Condon, J. W., 265
Cook, D. A., 245, 382
Cook, K. S., 272
Cook, S., 509
Cook, S. W., 415, 508, 510, 511, 517
Cook, T. D., 46, 69, 467
Cooper, H. M., 333
Cooper, J., 83, 90, 91–93, 99–102, 104,
    337, 489, 505
Cooper, W. H., 134, 144
Copitch, P., 311
Copper, C., 471
Cottrell, N., 409
Courtright, J. A., 437
Cowan, C. L., 34
Craig, K. D., 109
Crain, A. L., 83
Crain, R., 488
Cram, F., 496
Crane, M., 210
Crano, W. D., 19, 30, 36, 86, 265,
    290, 291, 332, 333, 334, 378, 381,
    385, 400, 447, 490
Croak, M. R., 515
Crocker, J., 147, 448, 452, 453, 454,
    458, 486
Crocker, J. C., 163, 511
Crosby, F., 290, 456, 458, 488, 490,
    493, 498
Cross, T., 114, 124
Cross, W. E., 452
Crott, H., 433
Crow, K., 60
Crowley, M., 290
Croyle, R., 99
Crutchfield, R. S., 377
Cunningham, J. A., 83
Cunningham, M. R., 294
Curtin, T. R., 467
Cutting, J. E., 117

D

D'Agostino, P., 203
D'Agostino, P. R., 155

Dalrymple, S., 358
Darbey, B. L., 381
Darby, B. K., 294
Dardis, G., 504
Darley, J. M., 160, 221, 282–286,
    292–293, 342, 343, 446, 491
Darwin, C., 29, 109
Dashiell, J. F., 408
Davis, J. A., 220
Davis, J. H., 419, 427, 429, 430, 433,
    434
Davis, K. E., 194, 196
Davitz, J. R., 108
Dawes, R. M., 25
Dawson, M. E., 28
Deaux, K., 146, 162, 166, 181
DeBono, K. G., 47
Deci, E. L., 196
Deffenbacher, J. L., 55
DeJong, W., 176
DeNeve, K. M., 316
DeNinno, J. A., 415
DePaulo, B., 121, 124
Derlega, V. J., 255, 265
Dermer, M., 268
Dertke, M., 494
Desforges, D., 515
Deutsch, M., 224, 250, 509
Devine, P. G., 83, 152, 477, 478, 480
DeVinney, L., 455
Dillard, J. P., 381
DiMatteo, M. R., 119–120
Dion, K., 134, 260
Dion, K. K., 257
Dion, K. L., 431, 438
Dobbs, A. R., 316
Dodson, J. D., 408
Doise, W., 10, 19, 432
Dolich, I. J., 55
Doll, J., 31
Dollard, J., 305, 309, 310
Doms, M., 395–396
Donnerstein, E., 492
Donnerstein, E. I., 322, 325
Donnerstein, M., 492
Donoghue, J., 192
Doob, A. N., 88
Doob, L. W., 305, 309
Dougherty, D., 114, 124
Dovidio, J., 469, 476, 515
Dovidio, J. F., 282, 286, 288, 301, 489,
    491, 495, 498
Downing, J. W., 34
Downs, A. C., 136
Drenan, S., 505
Dubé-Simard, L., 456
Dull, V. T., 152, 159
Dunand, M. A., 321

Duncan, B. L., 161
Durso, F. T., 162
Dusek, J. B., 333
Dutton, D. G., 492

E

Eagly, A., 74, 134, 135
Eagly, A. H., 79, 151, 257, 258, 278,
    290, 308, 320, 378, 464, 476, 480
Earley, P. C., 433
Eberly, S., 276
Echabe, A. E., 162
Edwards, C., 191
Edwards, K., 515
Eisenberg, N., 120
Ekman, F., 124
Ekman, P., 108–110, 112–115
Ellemers, N., 452
Ellen, P. S., 32
Elliott, A. M., 478
Ely, R. J., 342
Emswiller, T., 162
Endler, N. S., 377, 412
Epstein, J. L., 510
Epstein, V., 250
Erb, H. P., 60
Erber, R., 156
Erdley, C. S., 155
Erikson, G., 452
Eron, L. D., 320, 325
Esses, V. M., 462
Evans, M., 158
Evans, N., 476
Evans, S., 258
Exline, R. V., 108
Eysenck, H. J., 308

F

Fair, P. L., 29
Faling, V., 267
Farino, A., 176
Fazio, R. H., 33–35, 83, 92, 101, 102,
    104, 505
Feather, N., 172
Fein, S., 316

Feingold, A., 135, 258
Feingold, P. C., 50
Feldman, S., 172
Fenton, M., 384
Ferris, C. B., 50
Feshbach, S., 52, 306
Festinger, L., 93, 57, 77, 82–84, 86, 89,
    96–99, 104, 219, 222, 228, 263, 286,
    376, 379, 444, 458
Fiedler, F., 215
Filion, D. L., 28
Fincham, F. D., 175
Fincher-Kiefer, R., 203
Fireman, B., 364
Fischer, G. W., 511
Fishbaugh, L., 378
Fishbein, M., 31, 32
Fishbein, S., 257
Fisher, J. D., 442
Fiske, A. P., 255, 278
Fiske, S. T., 140, 146, 147, 151, 166
    200, 478
Flacks, R., 443
Flament, C., 482
Flay, B. R., 46, 69
Fleischer, R. A., 428
Fleming, J. A., 342, 343
Flowers, M. L., 437
Fode, K. L., 330
Folger, R., 511
Folkes, V., 177, 179
Folkes, V. S., 260
Ford, T., 462, 464
Forgas, J. P., 156
Försterling, F., 181, 183, 190
Forsyth, D. R., 415, 421, 426, 428, 438
Frager, R., 383, 384
Frankel, A., 197
Frankel-Brunswik, E., 351
Fraser, S., 380
Freedman, J. H., 380
Freedman, J. L., 83, 320
Freeman, S., 451
Frenkel, O. J., 88
Frenkel-Brunswik, E., 472
Freud, S., 307
Frey, D., 319
Frey, D. L., 291
Frey, K. S., 219
Fried, C., 93
Fried, C. B., 83
Friedman, H., 151
Friedman, H. S., 120
Friesen, W. V., 108, 110, 112–115
Frieze, I., 169
Frijda, N. H., 60
Fromkin, H. L., 379
Fufall, A., 493

Fulero, S., 158, 467
Fulker, D. W., 308
Fullerton, T., 419
Funder, D. C., 142
Furnham, A., 172
Futoran, G. C., 426

G

Gaertner, S., 319
Gaertner, S. L., 286, 288, 290, 291,
    301, 489, 491, 495, 498, 515
Gaes, G. G., 292
Gaines, B., 224
Gammon, C. B., 323
Gamson, W. A., 364
Gardner, R. C., 474
Garza, E. G., 513
Geen, R. G., 315, 321, 325
Geiselman, R., 259
Geller, E. S., 50
Gerard, H. B., 90, 370, 510
Gergen, K., 220
Gibson, J. J., 116
Gies, F., 475
Giesler, R. B., 224
Gifford, R. K., 467
Gilbert, D. T., 202
Gillen, B., 191
Gillig, P. M., 45
Gillis, J. S., 250
Gilmore, R., 505
Ginosar, Z., 50
Ginsburg, R. B., 127
Giuliano, T., 341
Glick, P., 161, 494
Goethals, A. R., 265
Goethals, G., 130
Goethals, G. R., 93, 198, 220
Goldberg, L. R., 134
Gonzales, J., 95
Gonzalez, A., 512
Goodwin, R., 259
Gorenflo, D. W., 447
Gouldner, A., 240
Graetz, K., 504
Graham, J., 177
Graham, S., 178
Granberg, D., 79
Graumann, C., 465, 480
Graves, N., 358
Grayson, B., 117, 118
Graziano, W. G., 258, 336

Green, S. K., 256, 259
Greene, D., 191, 195, 196
Greenwald, A. G., 40, 45, 52
Grev, R., 294
Griffin, G. W., 437
Griffin, J. J. Jr., 224
Gross, P. H., 160
Groth, G., 259
Grove, J. B., 29, 40
Gruder, C. I., 46
Guetzkow, H., 418
Guillon, M., 395
Guimond, S., 456
Gumpert, P., 250
Gurtman, M., 469
Guzzo, R. A., 162

H

Hacker, H. M., 495
Hackman, J. R., 426, 434
Haddock, G., 462
Haight, N., 259
Halamaj, J., 46
Hale, J. L., 433
Hall, E. T., 108
Hall, J. A., 110, 119–120, 124
Hamill, R., 210
Hamilton, D. L., 141, 146, 151, 166,
    202, 205, 467, 468
Hamilton, V. L., 351, 365
Hancock, R. D., 379
Handel, S., 179
Hansen, C. H., 117
Hansen, R. D., 117, 192
Hardin, G., 243, 252
Hardy, C., 417
Hardy, D., 191
Harkey, B., 411
Harkins, S., 374, 405, 417
Harkins, S. G., 47, 69, 415, 417, 419,
    421
Harlow, T., 122
Harnish, R. J., 47
Harper, N. L., 427
Harris, B. A., 278
Harris, M. J., 331, 334, 346
Harris, R. J., 240
Harris, V. A., 196, 197
Harrison, A. A., 250
Hartley, E. I., 472
Hartwick, J., 32
Harvey, O. J., 501

Haslam, S. A., 153
Hass, R. G., 44, 172, 495
Hastie, R., 160
Hastorf, A., 176, 177
Hatfield, (Walster). E., 257, 259, 260
Hatfield, E., 278
Haugtvedt, C. P., 65
Haythorn, W., 411
Hazan, C., 270, 271
Hazareth, A., 175
Heider, F., 169, 183, 198, 199
Heilman, M., 146, 166
Heilman, M. E., 162
Henderson, M., 266
Hendricks, M., 488
Hendy, H. M., 478
Henley, N. M., 117, 124
Hennigan, K. M., 46
Hensley, T. R., 437
Hepburn, J. R., 323
Herbert, T. B., 276
Herek, G., 437
Herman, C. P., 61
Heslin, R., 55
Hewstone, M., 152, 163, 190, 464,
    470, 515, 517
Hicks, A., 76
Higgins, E. T., 153, 155, 163, 217, 228,
    476
Hill, C. T., 272
Hilton, J. L., 342, 343
Hinkle, S., 384
Hirokawa, R. Y., 426
Hirt, E., 452
Ho, H-K, 441
Hoff, C., 442
Hoffman, C., 141, 476
Hofling, C. K., 358, 359
Hogg, M. A., 379, 400, 415, 448, 449,
    450, 458
Holland, T. T., 351, 358
Holman, R. H., 59
Holtzworth-Munroe, A., 168
Homans, G. C., 233
Hood, W. R., 501
Hogg, M. A., 486
Hopkins, A., 146
Hopkins, N., 152
Hopp, H., 95
Hoppe, R. A., 429
Hornik, J. A., 429
Hornseth, J. P., 429
House, P., 191
Hovland, C. I., 42–45, 48, 50, 51, 58,
    64, 65, 400
Howard, J., 467
Howard, J. A., 289
Howard, J. W., 469

Howard, W., 291
Hoyle, R., 504
Hu, L., 471
Hubert, S., 140
Huesmann, L. R., 320, 325
Huesmann, R., 320
Hunter, J. E., 381
Hurst, N., 476
Huth, P., 437
Hymes, R., 484

I

Ickes, W., 178
Ilgen, D. R., 405
Inglehart, M., 122
Inkster, J. A., 89
Insko, C., 473
Insko, C. A., 53, 504, 505
Insko, V. M., 53
Iritani, B., 475
Irvine, A. A., 200
Isen, A. M., 59–60, 293
Isenberg, D. J., 431
Izard, C. E., 121

J

Jacklin, C. N., 308
Jackson, J., 409, 417
Jackson, J. M., 415
Jacobs, A., 415
Jacobson, C. K., 358, 359
Jacobson, L., 331, 332
Jacobson, N. S., 168
Jahoda, G., 441
James, W., 208, 209, 212, 216, 219, 222, 225, 227
Jamieson, D. W., 139
Janis, I. L., 44, 49, 52, 53, 58, 59, 434, 435, 437, 438
Jaspars, J., 190
Jaspars, J. M., 175
Jastro, J., 334
Jennings, (Walstedt) J., 475
Jensen, C., 467
Jervis, R., 505

John, O. P., 516
Johnson, C. E., 430
Johnson, D. F., 258
Johnson, D. W., 513
Johnson, G., 288
Johnson, N., 441
Johnson, P. B., 474
Johnson, R. T., 513
Johnston, L., 163
Johnston, R. E., 111–112
Jonas, K., 464
Jones, C. R., 153
Jones, E. E., 130, 131, 176, 179, 180, 194, 196, 197, 201, 202, 205
Jones, E. E., 218, 370
Jones, J. M., 492, 498
Jones, R. A., 52
Jones, S., 223
Jones, S. C., 335
Jorgenson, D. O., 250
Joseph, G., 333
Josephson, W. D., 321
Joule, R. V., 382
Judd, C. M., 34, 471
Julian, J., 215
Jussim, L., 142, 332

K

Kahle, L. R., 90
Kahneman, D., 190
Kaiser, C., 390
Kalgren, C. A., 35
Kameda, T., 434
Kanekar, S., 175
Kanki, B., 393
Kao, C. F., 73
Kaplan, M. F., 428, 433
Karabenick, S. A., 378
Karau, S. J., 414, 417
Kardes, F. R., 34
Karlins, M., 495
Karraker, K. H., 258
Kashima, E., 199
Kashima, Y., 199
Kassin, S., 190
Katcher, A. H., 313
Katz, D., 149
Katz, I., 172, 495
Katz, L. D., 141
Katz, P., 498

Katz, P. A., 463, 474, 511
Katz, R., 427
Kaye, D., 59
Keating, C., 109, 118
Keating, J. P., 297
Kelley, D. J., 294
Kelley, H. H., 44, 131, 187, 192, 193, 205, 233, 239, 249, 252, 376, 443, 507
Kelly, G. A., 155
Kelly, H. H., 241
Kelly, M., 36
Kelman, H. C., 45, 351, 365, 376
Kelsey, R. M., 410
Kennedy, C., 452
Kennedy, J. F., 434, 507
Kennedy, L., 134
Kenny, D. A., 262
Kenrick, D., 259
Kenrick, D. T., 294
Kerckhoff, A. C., 263
Kerker, R. M., 341
Kernis, M., 258
Kernis, M. H., 259
Kerr, N. L., 246, 413, 415, 417, 419, 428, 433, 438
Ketcham, K., 165, 166
Khrushchev, 507
Kidd, R., 178
Kiesler, S. B., 262
Kimata, L., 259
Kimes, D., 475
Kinder, D. R., 495
King, A. S., 338
King, G., 396, 476
King, G. A., 155
King, R., 368
Kipnis, D. M., 264
Kirchner, P., 59
Kitayama, S., 226, 228
Kite, M. E., 464, 480
Kleck, R., 122
Klerman, G. L., 29
Klineberg, O., 474
Knapp, M. L., 50
Know, R. E., 89
Knurek, D., 310
Koenig, K., 443
Koeske, G., 400
Kogan, N., 432
Koletsky, S., 177
Komorita, S. S., 248
Koulack, D., 66
Kozlowski, L. T., 117
Kramer, R. M., 245
Krantz, S. E., 156
Krauss, R. M., 50, 250
Kraut, R. E., 111–112

Kravitz, D. A., 248
Krismer, K., 83
Kriss, M., 199
Krueger, J., 467
Kruglanski, A., 465, 480
Kruglanski, A. W., 194, 400, 402
Krull, D. S., 202, 225
Kukla, A., 169, 175
Kulik, J. A., 190
Kumar, P., 160
Kwan, J., 397

L

Lage, E., 389, 392, 395
Lagerspetz, K., 308
Laird, J. P., 122
Lake, R. A., 492
Lalonde, R., 456
Lalonde, R. N., 453
Lambert, W. E., 474
Lamm, H., 431, 432, 438
Landers, D. M., 408
Landy, D., 136, 259
Lane, I. L., 249
Langer, E., 478
Langer, E. J., 173, 174
Lanzetta, J., 122
Lanzetta, J. T., 115–116, 427
LaPiere, R. T., 30–31
Larrick, R. P., 316
Larsen, R. J., 275
Lassiter, G. D., 200
Lasswell, H. D., 43
Latané, B., 282–286, 405, 417, 491
Lau, R. R., 168, 180
Laughlin, P. R., 419, 426, 427, 430, 433
Lawton, M. P., 264
Leavitt, H. J., 418
Lee, J-Y, 441
Lefkowitz, M. M., 320
Leippe, M. R., 45, 52
Leirer, V. O., 141
Lemyre, L., 486
Lennon, R., 120
Leo, G., 396
Leonard, K. E., 323
Leone, C., 34
Le Page, A., 318
Lepper, M., 162, 195, 516
Lerner, M. J., 473
Leve, C., 437

Leventhal, G. S., 242
Leventhal, H., 29, 53
Levin, P. F., 293
Levine, J. M., 383, 388, 402, 415
LeVine, R. A., 469, 476
Levinson, D. J., 351, 472
Levinson, R. M., 493
Levi-Strauss, C., 232
Levy-Loboyer, C., 311
Lewin, K., 442
Lewis, S. K., 381
Leyens, J. -P., 321
Liberman, A., 34, 74, 76, 79
Liebrand, N. G., 484
Liebrand, W. B. G., 246
Likert, R., 27
Lilli, W., 451
Lilly, T., 474
Linder, D., 50
Linder, D. E., 90
Linville, P. W., 174, 211, 212, 511
Linz, D., 322
Lippman, W., 149
Liu, T. J., 94
Loewenstein, G., 456
Loftus, E. F., 164, 165, 166
Lombardi, W., 154
Longo, L. C., 257, 278
Loomis, J., 474
Lord, C., 515
Lord, C. G., 83, 162
Lord, K., 219
Lorenz, K., 307
Lowe, J., 119
Loy, J. W., 132
Luce, R. D., 247
Luhtanen, R., 448, 486
Lui, L., 152, 159
Lumsdaine, A., 43
Lydon J. E., 139
Lykken, D. T., 114
Lyons, P. M., 136

M

Maass, A., 398, 399, 402, 471
Maccoby, E. E., 308
MacCoun, R., 484
MacCoun, R. J., 247, 413, 428
Mackie, D., 470
Mackie, D. M., 59–60, 400, 402, 432, 433

Madden, T. J., 32
Magargee, E. I., 428
Magnusson, D., 412
Magnusson, J., 176
Maheswaran, D., 76
Major, B., 452–454, 458
Makhijani, M., 134
Makhijani, M. G., 257, 278
Malamud, P., 320
Malamuth, N. M., 322
Malloy, T. E., 262
Malpass, R. S., 471
Mandel, M. R., 29
Mandell, W., 50
Manis, M., 466, 480
Mann, J., 515
Mann, L., 49
Markus, H., 155, 156, 176, 209, 210, 212, 213, 215, 225, 228, 408
Marsh, H. W., 219
Martens, R., 408
Martin, J. P., 456
Martin, L., 34
Martin, M., 495
Martin, R., 399
Marx, K., 232
Maslach, C., 379
Mason, J., 516
Mathewson, G. C., 90
Mavin, G. H., 155
Mayseless, O., 398
Mazur, A., 109
McArthur, L., 124
McArthur, L. A., 189, 190
McArthur, L. S., 116
McArthur, L. Z., 50, 117–119, 199
McCane, T. R., 123
McCauley, C., 437
McClintock, C. G., 250, 484
McConahay, J. B., 474, 495
McDermott, M., 276
McDougall, W., 8
McGee, M. G., 38
McGuire, C. V., 220
McGuire, W. J., 25, 40, 50, 54–55, 82, 220, 378
McKirnen, D. J., 457
McManus, J. A., 151
McNeil, S. P., 250
McQueen, L. R., 250
Medoff, N. J., 315
Meek, D., 433
Meeus, W. H. J., 359–363, 365
Mehrabian, A., 108
Meichenbaum, D. H., 55
Meindl, J. R., 473
Mellon, P. M., 332, 334
Mendolia, M., 34

Merton, R. K., 334
Messé, L. A., 30, 86, 240, 248, 249, 413, 419, 484
Messick, D. M., 240, 245, 247, 252, 272
Mikula, G., 249
Milavsky, B., 313
Milgram, S., 17, 190, 296, 306, 351–358, 365
Millar, M., 222
Millar, M. G., 30, 258
Miller, A., 191
Miller, A. G., 355, 365
Miller, C. E., 428, 428, 433
Miller, D., 176
Miller, D. T., 346
Miller, F. D., 202
Miller, G. R., 50
Miller, J. A., 382
Miller, J. G., 199
Miller, M. D., 55
Miller, N., 293, 295, 431, 438, 441, 510, 514, 515, 517
Miller, N. E., 305, 309, 472
Miller, R. L., 381
Mills, J., 89, 238, 238, 255
Minturn, A. L., 153
Mischel, W., 141, 149, 152, 166
Moe, J., 473
Moghaddam, F., 456
Moghaddam, F. M., 457
Moll, A., 334
Montanari, J. R., 437
Monteith, M. J., 478
Montepare, J. M., 117
Moore, J., 222
Moore, J. S., 258
Moorhead, G., 437
Moreland, R., 155
Moreland, R. L., 415
Moriarty, T., 291
Morris, C. G., 426, 434
Morse, S., 220
Moscovici, S., 389–392, 395, 402, 432
Moser, G., 311
Moss, A. J., 276
Mousaw, P., 267
Mouton, J. S., 511
Mowrer, O. H., 305, 309
Moyer, K. E., 306
Mudrack, P. E., 415
Mugny, G., 390, 392, 394–395, 398, 399, 402
Muir, S. K., 256
Mullen, B., 191, 471, 471
Mullen, P. E., 274
Mummendey, A., 305, 325, 399
Murphy, S., 122, 123

Murphy, S. T., 261
Murray, A., 456
Murrell, A., 515
Murstein, B. I., 255, 260, 262
Musser, L. M., 336
Myers, D. G., 431, 432, 438

N

Nacoste, R., 473
Naffrechoux, M., 389
Nahemow, L., 264
Nail, P. R., 383, 385
Napolitan, D. A., 198
Neale, M. C., 308
Nell, E. B., 55
Nelson, C., 137, 161, 494
Nelson, D., 6, 13
Nelson, T., 466, 480
Nemeth, C., 441
Nemeth, C. J., 393, 397, 398, 402
Neuberg, S. L., 147, 342, 345
Newcomb, T. M., 5–6, 7–8, 12, 82, 443, 458, 508
Newell, K. M., 408
Nezlek, H., 258
Nezlek, J., 258
Ng, S. H., 484, 496
Nias, D. H. B., 308
Nicholls, J. G., 180
Niedenthal, P., 123
Niedenthal, P. M., 261
Nisbett, R. E., 134, 190, 195, 196, 201
Northcraft, G., 177
Norvell, N., 513
Novick, L. R., 190
Novick, N., 219
Nurius, P., 212, 228

O

O'Connell, M., 493
O'Keefe, D. J., 61
O'Sullivan, C. S., 162
Oakes, P., 448, 458
Oakes, P. J., 153, 400, 486
Odbert, H. S., 126

Oleson, C. D., 240
Oleson, K. C., 298
Olson, J. M., 61, 228, 480
Omoto, A. M., 268
Orive, R., 447
Orne, M. T., 351, 358
Orr, S. P., 115–116
Osgood, C., 507
Osgood, C. E., 27, 30
Ostrom, T. M., 419
Ostrove, N., 136
Otten, C. A., 290
Otten, S., 305
Oyersman, D., 215

P

Pack, S. J., 339
Pallak, M. S., 245, 382
Palmer, J. C., 164
Panitch, D., 335
Papageorgis, D., 54–55
Papastamou, S., 390, 394–395
Papciak, A. S., 250
Park, B., 130, 144, 471
Parker, J. D. A., 83
Parker, J. W., 219
Parks, C. D., 434
Patrick, C. J., 109
Patten, S. C., 351
Patterson, M. L., 108
Paulus, P. B., 438
Pavelchak, M. A., 151
Peabody, D., 134, 137
Pelham, B. W., 202, 216, 225
Penner, L., 494
Penner, L. A., 290
Penrod, S., 322, 400
Peplau, L. A., 272, 275, 278
Perdue, C., 469
Perez, J. A., 390, 398, 399, 402
Perlman, D., 275
Perri, M., 258
Perry, R., 176
Personnaz, B., 395
Pessin, J., 408
Peterson, P. D., 66
Pettigrew, T. F., 456, 470, 474, 496
Petty, R., 374
Petty, R. E., 45, 47, 56, 57, 65, 68, 69, 72, 73, 76, 79, 378, 400–401

Peynircioglu, Z. F., 141
Phillips, D. P., 321
Picciotto, S., 177
Pierce, C. M., 358
Pietromonaco, P., 154
Piliavin, J. A., 286, 289, 292, 301
Pilisuk, M., 503
Pittenger, J. B., 258
Platow, M. J., 484
Polmar, N., 328
Pomare, M., 515
Pondy, L. R., 507
Post, D. L., 199
Postman, L. J., 161
Powell, M., 239
Powell, M. C., 35
Pratkanis, A., 437
Pratkanis, A. R., 40, 45, 61
Pratto, F., 160, 259, 495
Predmore, S. C., 224
Prentice-Dunn, S., 319, 491
Priest, R., 263
Probasco, P., 437
Pruitt, D. G., 432
Pryor, J. B., 151, 199
Pyszczynski, T. A., 268

Q

Quattrone, G. A., 471
Quigley, B., 292

R

Raaijmakers, Q. A. W., 359–363, 365
Radelet, M., 494
Radlove, S., 191
Raiffa, H., 247
Ramsey, S., 515
Rank, S. G., 358, 359
Rapoport, A., 248, 252
Raskin, D. C., 29, 114
Razran, G. H. S., 59
Reed, C. F., 330
Reed, L., 169
Reeder, G. P., 151
Regan, D. T., 33, 34

Rehm, J., 451
Reicher, S., 448, 458
Reicher, S. D., 400
Reifman, A. S., 316
Reis, H., 258
Reitan, H. T., 377
Rempel, J. K., 27, 35, 40
Rest, S., 169
Rhine, R. J., 66
Rhodes, N., 58, 379
Rhodewalt, F., 218
Rholes, W. S., 153, 163
Richards, J., 219
Richardson, K. D., 473
Riger, A. L., 181, 183
Riggio, R. E., 120
Rillet, D., 394–395
Rimé, B., 321
Rissman, A. K., 429, 433
Robinson, J., 50
Roby, T. B., 427
Rock, L., 130
Rodgers, H., 36
Rodriguez, R., 73
Roff, M. A., 341
Rogers, P., 119–120
Rogers, R. W., 319, 319, 491
Rohrkemper, M. M., 178
Rokeach, M., 473
Ronis, D. L., 52
Rosenbaum, R., 169
Rosenberg, M., 208, 209, 215–217, 452
Rosenberg, M. J., 82
Rosenberg, S., 137
Rosenfeld, P., 95
Rosenkrantz, P., 151
Rosenthal, A. M., 282
Rosenthal, R., 119–121, 124, 330–334, 346
Ross, D., 317
Ross, E. A., 8
Ross, L., 162, 191, 196, 198, 205, 217
Ross, M., 31
Ross, S. A., 317
Roth, J., 173
Rothbart, M., 158, 467, 469, 471, 516
Rotter, J. B., 170
Rottman, L., 256
Routh, D., 152
Rovira, D. P., 162
Ruberman, W., 276
Rubin, Z., 267, 272
Ruble, D. N., 219
Rule, B. G., 316
Runciman, W. C., 495
Runciman, W. G., 456
Runyan, D. L., 433
Runyan, D L., 432

Rusbult, C. E., 272, 273
Rushton, J. P., 307, 308
Russell, D., 168
Russell, G. W., 318
Russell, J. A., 114
Russell, P., 180
Russo, E. M., 388, 402
Rutstein, J., 257
Rutte, C. G., 245
Ruvolo, A., 213
Ruvolo, C. M., 151, 166
Ryan, C., 471
Rytina, S., 364

S

Sachdev, I., 484
Sadalla, E., 259
Sadler, O., 34
Saegart, S. C., 264
Safilios-Rothschild, C., 269
Sagar, H. A., 161, 510
Saks, M. J., 304
Salovey, P., 511
Salt, P., 29
Sampson, E. E., 226
Samuelson, C. D., 245
Sanbonmatsu, D. M., 34
Sande, G. N., 88
Sanders, G. S., 421, 433
Sandilands, M. L., 318
Sanford, R. N., 351, 472
Sanna, L. J., 408, 417
Sansone, C., 34
Santee, R. T., 379
Santos, S. J., 513
Sarup, G., 36, 79
Sattler, D. N., 413
Sawyer, J., 263
Saxe, L., 114, 124, 259, 488, 490, 498
Schachter, S., 4–5, 13, 219, 312, 445
Schachter, S. S., 263
Schaerfl, L. M., 250
Schaible, T. D., 415
Schein, E. H., 355
Schell, A. M., 28
Schenker, C., 191
Scher, S. J., 93
Scherer, K., 110, 113
Schlenker, B. R., 95, 104
Schmidt, G., 179
Schmitt, D. P., 259

Schnedler, R., 290
Schneider, D. J., 134, 144
Schofield, J. W., 161, 510
Schopler, J., 504
Schreiber, H. J., 399
Schuman, H., 495
Schwarswald, J., 488
Schwartz, G. E., 29
Schwartz, R. D., 29, 40
Schwartz, S. H., 289, 473
Schwarz, F., 60
Schwarz, N., 60
Schwarzwald, J., 510
Scott, R., 176
Sears, D. O., 474, 495
Sears, R. R., 305, 309
Seashore, S. E., 415, 415
Sechrest, L., 29, 40
Segall, M., 109
Seligman, C., 381
Seligman, M., 181
Semmelroth, J., 275
Sentis, K., 210
Sentis, K. P., 240
Severance, L. J., 66
Shaffer, D. R., 294
Shapiro, P. N., 450, 503
Sharan, S., 513
Shaver, K., 130
Shaver, P., 270, 271
Shaw, M. E., 377, 404, 411, 418
Sheffield, K., 43
Sheppard, B. M., 32
Sherif, C. W., 36, 487, 495, 501
Sherif, M., 8, 36, 65, 369–372, 374,
    375, 385, 487, 495, 501, 504, 516
Sherk, D. L., 339
Sherman, J., 398
Sherman, S. J., 151, 166
Shippy, T. A., 426
Shoemaker, D., 119
Shope, G. L., 315
Shotland, R. L., 408
Showers, C. J., 409
Shrauger, J. S., 223
Shupe, L. M., 323
Shweder, R. A., 126
Sidanius, J., 259, 488, 495
Siegal, M., 199
Sigall, H., 136, 259
Sikes, J., 512
Siladi, M., 210
Silverstein, B., 505, 517
Simpson, J., 421
Simpson, J. A., 273, 275, 278
Singer, D. G., 321
Singer, J., 312
Singer, J. L., 321

Sivacek, J., 36, 381
Skelton, J., 218
Skinner, B. F., 96, 232
Skowronski, J. J., 140, 144
Skrypnek, B. J., 338
Slavin, R. E., 246, 512, 513
Sloan, L., 451
Smelser, W. T., 412
Smith, E. E., 86
Smith, E. R., 155
Smith, J., 155
Smith, K., 384
Smith, K. D., 297
Smith, P. M., 486
Smith, T. L., 25
Snapp, M., 512
Snyder, C. R., 379
Snyder, L., 471
Snyder, M., 38, 164, 197, 258, 268,
    335, 338–340, 342
Snyder, R., 493
Soja, M., 474
Solomon, L., 224
Sorrentino, R. M., 379, 396
South, D., 119
South, S. J., 259
Spaulding, K., 471
Spencer, S. J., 181
Spiegel, N., 258
Sprecher, S., 256, 257, 272, 278
Sriram, N., 467
Srull, T. K., 146, 154, 155, 160, 166
Stahelski, A. J., 249, 507
Stall, R., 442
Stallworth, L., 259, 495
Stangor, C., 156, 462, 464
Stanley, J. C., 14
Star, S., 455
Stasser, G., 419, 434
Stasson, M. F., 434
Staub, E., 301, 325, 351, 365
Steeh, C., 495
Steele, C., 181
Steele, C. M., 94, 95, 102, 104
Steffen, V. J., 308, 320
Stein, M. I., 117, 118
Steinberg, J., 294
Steiner, I. D., 418–419, 421
Steinleitner, J., 451
Stein-Seroussi, A., 224, 342
Stephan, C., 512
Stephan, C. W., 488
Stephan, W. G., 488, 510
Stepper, S., 122
Sterling, B., 288
Stern, P. C., 252
Sternberg, R. J., 269, 278
Stewart, J. E., 136

Stiff, J., 45
Stogdill, R. M., 415
Stone, J., 83, 86, 93
Stone, W. F., 374
Stoner, J. A. E., 433
Stoner, J. A. F., 431, 432
Stonner, D., 315
Storms, M. D., 201
Story, J., 191
Stotland, E., 297
Stouffer, S. A., 455
Strack, F., 122
Streeter, L. A., 50
Strodtbeck, F. L., 425
Stroebe, W., 465, 480
Strohm, R. B., 323
Struch, N., 473
Suchman, E., 455
Sullivan, J. J., 245, 382
Sullivan, L., 462, 464
Suls, J., 219, 228
Summerfield, A., 110
Sumner, W. G., 441
Sunderland, J., 486
Sussman, M., 429
Swann, E. D., 38
Swann, W. B., 216
Swann, W. B. Jr., 224, 225, 339, 340,
    341, 342, 343, 346
Swap, W. C., 264
Swedlund, M., 393
Sweeney, J., 248
Sweeney, P., 181
Swingle, P. G., 250
Szybillo, G. J., 55
Szymanski, K., 417, 421

T

Tagiuri, R., 133
Tajfel, H., 441, 448, 449, 457, 458,
    465, 479, 482, 484, 496, 497, 504
Tanaka, K., 199
Tanford, S., 400
Tanke, E. D., 38, 258, 335
Tannenbaum, P., 27, 82
Tassinary, L. G., 29, 40
Taves, P. A., 101
Taylor, B. R., 316
Taylor, D., 498
Taylor, D. M., 456, 457
Taylor, L. W., 34

Taylor, S. E., 102, 146, 147, 153, 166, 181, 183, 200, 222, 228
Taylor, S. P., 323
Teasdale, J., 181
Tedeschi, J. T., 95, 96, 292, 433
Telesca, C., 47
Tennov, B., 269
Tennyson, Alfred Lord, 350
Terborg, J. R., 415
Terwilliger, R., 53
Tesser, A., 30, 34, 70, 221, 222, 257
Testa, M., 454
Tetlock, P. E., 437
Thein, R. D., 160
Thibaut, J., 505
Thibaut, J. W., 233, 239, 241, 376
Thomas, K. W., 507
Thompson, J. E., 511
Thorne, A., 451
Thurstone, L. L., 25, 78
Tice, D. M., 218
Tilker, H. A., 356
Tittler, B. I., 36
Titus, W., 434
Tognacci, L. S., 32
Tom, D. Y. H., 333
Tomaka, J., 410
Tomkins, S. S., 121, 261
Torrence, E. P., 428
Tota, M., 154
Touhy, J. C., 259
Traupmann, J., 272
Travis, C. B., 259
Travis, L. E., 408, 408
Treyens, J. C., 157
Triandis, H. C., 226
Triplett, N., 407
Trolier, T. K., 467
Trope, Y., 50, 197, 202
Trost, M., 159
Turnbull, W., 346
Turner, J. C., 153, 400, 448, 449, 452, 457, 458, 486, 504
Turner, M., 437
Turner, T. J., 148
Tushman, M., 427
Tversky, A., 190
Tyler, R., 469, 476

U

Uleman, J. S., 202
Ulrich, K., 494
Uranowitz, S., 164

V

Vallacher, R., 419
Vallacher, R. R., 240, 249
Van Avermaet, E., 395–396
Vancouver, J. B., 405
Vanderklok, M., 191
Van Doosje, B., 452
Van Knippenberg, A., 452
Van Leeuwen, M., 516
Van Leeuwen, M. D., 383, 385
Vanneman, R. D., 456, 496
van Run, G. J., 246
Varela, J. A., 426, 434
Vasta, R., 311
Vaughn, 474
Verette, J., 179
Vernon, D. T., 32
Villareal, A., 59
Villareal, M., 226
Vincent, J. E., 294, 381
Vinokur, A., 433
Vivekananthan, P. S., 137
Voelkl, K., 454
Vogel, S., 151
Vogel, D. A., 258
von Baeyer, C. L., 339
Voss, A. L., 323

W

Wade, C., 379
Walder, L. O., 320
Walker, I., 456
Walker, M., 451
Wall, S., 270
Wallach, M. A., 432
Wallbott, H., 110
Wallbott, H. G. S., 123
Walster, E., 134, 238, 240, 256, 269, 272
Walster, G. W., 238, 260, 269, 272
Walster, H. E., 57
Walters, G., 495
Ward, L., 130
Warshaw, P. R., 32
Warwick, D., 443
Waters, E., 270
Waters, H. F., 320
Watkins, M. J., 141
Watts, B. L., 29, 240, 249

Waugh, G., 290
Webb, E. J., 29, 40
Weber, R., 163, 511
Wegner, D. M., 290, 341, 342, 490
Weigel, B., 474
Weigel, R. H., 32, 415
Weiner, B., 168–171, 175–179, 183
Weiss, J. A., 426
Weiss, W., 44–45
Weitz, B. A., 168, 180
Weld, H., 341
Well, H. G., 3
Wells, G. L., 56
Wells, H. G., 449–450
Wentzlaff, R., 341
Werner, J., 433
West, S., 516
West, S. G., 290, 398, 402
Westen, D., 275
Wetherell, M., 400, 448, 458
Whalen, P., 493
Wheeler, D., 381
Wheeler, L., 258, 259
White, B. J., 501
White, G. L., 257, 260, 274
White, R. K., 505, 507
Whiteside, H. D., 242
Whitney, G., 290
Whittaker, J., 377
Wicker, A., 31
Wicklund, R. A., 50, 90
Widmeyer, W. N., 132
Wiggins, E. C., 26
Wilder, D. A., 374, 450, 466, 467, 503, 511, 515, 516
Wilke, H., 245, 452
Wilkes, A. L., 465
Williams, C. J., 35
Williams, K., 405, 409, 418
Williams, K. B., 417
Williams, K. D., 414, 417
Williams, K. K., 69
Williams, R., 455
Williams, R. B., 276
Williamson, G. M., 238
Willis, R. H., 383
Wills, T., 219, 228
Wills, T. A., 222
Wilson, D., 76
Wilson, E. O., 297, 307
Wilson, J. P., 411, 412, 419
Wilson, L., 319
Wilson, T. D., 134, 174
Winslow, M. P., 83
Winston, W., 220
Winter, L., 202
Witt, P. N., 330
Witte, K., 53
Wodarski, J. S., 246

Wolfgang, M. E., 323
Won-Doornink, M. J., 266
Wood, J. T., 428
Wood, J. V., 222, 228
Wood, W., 34, 35, 58, 379, 412, 413, 421
Wood, W. W., 378
Woodall, W. G., 51, 331
Woodworth, R. D., 114
Worchel, S., 50, 93, 421, 511, 513, 514, 517
Word, C., 489
Word, C. D., 337, 338
Worth, L., 470
Worth, L. T., 59, 60
Wright, S., 456
Wright, S. C., 457
Wyer, R. S., 146, 154, 155, 166

Y

Yaeger, C. P., 259
Yaryan, R., 89

Yates, S. M., 34, 76
Yerkes, R. M., 408

Z

Zaccaro, S. J., 419
Zajonc, R., 122, 123
Zajonc, R. B., 261, 264, 408
Zalk, S. R., 511
Zander, A., 404, 425
Zanna, M., 456, 489
Zanna, M. P., 27, 33, 35, 40, 61, 88, 93, 100
Zanna, M. P., 101, 102, 139, 141, 228, 337, 339, 462, 480
Zarate, M. A., 155
Zavalloni, M., 432
Zebrowitz, L. A., 142, 144, 151
Zebrowitz-McArthur, L., 119
Zillman, D., 257, 305, 312, 313, 315, 452
Zimbardo, P. G., 56, 296
Zimmerman, S. K., 434

Zion, C., 161, 494
Zuber, J., 433
Zuckerman, M., 121, 124, 181
Zukier, H., 142, 144
Zuwerink, J. R., 478

A

Accessibility, attitude-behavior
consistency and, 35–36
Accuracy, vs. expectancy, 332–333
Actor-observer bias, 201
Actual self-concept, 216
Additive tasks, 418
Administrative obedience, 359–362
Affect-effort theory of expectancy, 334
Affiliation and uncertainty study
(Schacter), 4–5, 11
Affordances,
defined, 116
nonverbal communication and,
116–117
overgeneralization and, 118–119
African Americans,
disidentification, 453
media and, 474
minority self-esteem and,
452–455
Agentic-communal motives, 249
Aggression, 304–324
alcohol and, 323
based on instinct or inheritance,
307–309
cognitive neoassociationism
of, 311
cues to, 318
defined, 304–305
displaced, 310, 472–473
erotic violence, 322
ethological approach to 307
excitation transfer theory,
312–315
frustration-aggression theory,
309–312
heat and aggressive crime,
315–317
hostile, 306
inheritance theories, 307–309
instrumental, 306
intention, 305
media violence and, 321–322
pornography and, 315
public events, 321–322

race and, 319
social learning theory of, 317–318
sociobiological approach to,
307–309
television and, 320–321
types of, 305–306
AIDS, cognitive dissonance and, 94
Alcohol, aggression and, 323
Alcoholic disinhibition, 323
Altruism, 282
as social norm, 240
American Psychological Association, 15
Anger, attribution theory and, 177–178
Anticonformity, 383–384
Appearance, effect of, on expectations,
335–337
Arousal,
in arousal-cost-reward model,
287–289
cognitive dissonance and, 99–100
frustration and, 311
group performance and, 408–409
misattribution of, 288–289
Arousal-cost-reward model, 286–293
arousal, 287–289
costs and rewards, 289–292
costs and rewards:nonnormative
factors, 292–293
gender and, 290
mood, 293
race or ethnicity, 290–291
relationship between helper and
victim, 291
responsibility assignment, 291–292
time constraints, 292–293
Asch's line study
normative social influence and,
375–376
public compliance and, 377
Aschematic, 209
Assimilation, in confirmatory bias, 161
Assimilation effect, 66
Attachment theory of love, 270–271
Attention, information-processing
and, 146
Attitudes, 24–39. *See also* Prejudice;
Stereotypes
Bennington study, 7–8, 11
cognitive component, 462
in cognitive dissonance theory, 83

emotional component, 462
evaluation approach, 27–28
facial electromyogram (EMG)
galvanic skin response, 28–29
psychophysiological approaches,
28–29
in self-perception theory, 97
similarity and interpersonal liking,
5–7
standard definitions of, 30
three-part distinction, 26–27
Thurstone's approach, 25
toward social groups, 462–465
unobtrusive methods, 29
Attitude-behavior consistency, 30–31
accessibility, 35–36
direct experience, 33–34
ego involvement, 36
extremity and mere thought,
34–35
generality/specificity of attitude
and behavior, 31–32
individual differences/self-
monitoring, 38–39
intention, 32–33
knowledge, 35–36
vested interest, 36–37
Attitude change,
elaboration-likelihood model
(ELM), 68–73
heuristic-systematic model, 74–78
models of, 64–78
See Counter-argumentation;
Persuasion
social judgement theory, 65–68
Attraction, law of, 6–7, 11
attitude similarity, 264–265
beauty and goodness, 257–258
excitation transfer theory, 257
factors that influence initial
attraction, 255–262
first impressions, 256
from attraction to liking, 262–266
market value of physical
attractiveness, 258–259
matching hypothesis, 260
physical attractiveness, 256–257
physical proximity and, 262–264
role of physical similarity,
260–262

Attractiveness, sales and, 47–48
Attribution/Attribution theory, 168–182
    achievement motivation and, 180–181
    actor-observer bias, 201
    anger and, 177–178
    attribution and social inference, 186–196
    attribution-emotion-behavior link, 179
    attributions, emotions and social behavior, 177–180
    attributions and success in college, 174
    attributions of motivation, 194–195
    augmentation principle, 193
    causal attributions and poverty, 172
    causal inference from single observations, 192–193
    controllability, 170
    controllability and social stigma, 175–177
    controllability in classroom, 175
    controllability in courtroom, 175
    controllability of cause, 174–177
    correspondent inference theory, 193–194
    covariation principle, 187–190
    depression and, 181
    discounting principle, 193
    external locus, 169
    fundamental attribution error, 196–201
    illusion of control, 181
    internal locus, 169
    judgements of success and failure, 170–171
    locus of cause: internal-external distinction, 170–171
    manipulation attributions; strategies and social interaction, 179–180
    one-stage vs. two-stage model of, 201–203
    overjustification effect, 195–196
    person attribution bias, 196–201
    pity and, 178–179
    self-attributions, 180–181
    self-efficacy, 181
    in self-perception theory, 97
    self-serving bias, 180–181
    stability, 169
    stability of cause: expectations for future, 172–174
    structure of perceived causes, 169–177

Audience, characteristics, in counter-argumentation
        individual differences in intelligence and self-esteem, 58–59
        mood, 59–60
Augmentation principle, 193
Authoritarian personality, 472
Autistic hostility, 508
Autokinetic effect, 8, 369–372
    conversion and, 377
    informational social influence and, 370, 372, 375–376
    normative social influence, 371, 372
Averaging, in social decision schemes, 427
Aversive consequences, 92–93
Aversive racism, 489–490

B

Baby-faced adults,
        nonverbal communication, 118–119
        stereotype of, 118–119
Base-rate fallacy, 190–191
Basking in reflected glory (BIRG), 451–452
Bay of Pigs, 434–435
Behavior,
        attitude and, 26–27
        self-perception theory and, 96–99
Behavioral style, 392
Behavior control, 242–243
Behavior matrix, 235–236
        behavior control, 242
        fate control, 241
        prisoners' dilemma, 247–248
        tragedy of the commons, 244
Belief congruence theory, 473
Bennington study, 7–8, 11
Biased information search, 339–342
        innuendo effect, 341–342
Blind trials, 329
Body image, self-schemas and, 210, 211
Bogardus Social Distance Scale, 487
Boomerang effect, 66
Brown v. Board of Education of Topeka, 509–510
Bystander intervention, 280–300. See also Helping

arousal-cost-reward model, 286–293
barriers crossed to help, 286
diffusion of responsibility, 282, 283–285
epileptic seizure study of, 283–285
murder of Kitty Genovese and, 280–282
pluralistic ignorance, 283, 285–286
research on, 282–286
smoke-filled room study, 285–286

C

Categorization,
        as basis of stereotypes and prejudice, 465–471
        in-group bias, 469–470
        out-group homogeneity, 470–471
Category accentuation, 465–467
Causal schemata, 192–193
Central (processing) route, 68–69
Change-of-meaning effect, 141–142
Children, self-fulfilling prophecy, 336–337
Classroom,
        academic performance and social class, 332–333
        attribution controllability and, 175
        cooperation in, 512–513
        expectancy effect and, 331–332
        expectation-versus-accuracy hypotheses, 332–333
        transmission of expectations in, 334
Cognition, attitude and, 26–27
Cognitive algebra, 139–140
        evaluative rating, 139
        extremity effect, 140
        negativity effect, 140
        weighted average, 140
Cognitive dissonance, 82–102
        AIDS experiment and, 94
        alternations to basic theory, 92–95
        arousal and, 99–100
        aversive consequences revision, 92
        commitment and, 86, 88
        effort justification, 89–91
        free choice, 87–89
        hypocrisy theory, 93

importance of theory, 82–83
impression management theory, 95–96
insufficient justification, 86
misattribution paradigm, 100–101
motivating properties of dissonance, 99–101
overjustification effects, 102
postdecision regret, 87
preconditions, 85–86
replacements to basic theory, 92, 95–102
reverse incentive effect, 84–85
self-affirmation theory, 94–95
self-perception theory, 96–99, 102
theory of, 83–85
weight loss and, 91–92
Cognitive neoassociationism of aggression, 311
Cohesion, group performance and, 415–416
Collective self-esteem, 448
Combinational procedure, 418
Commitment, 270
cognitive dissonance and, 86, 88
low-ball technique and, 382
Committed images, 217
Communal relationships, 238–239
attitude similarity, 264–265
commitment and, 273
defined, 255
equity theory, 272
vs. exchange relationships, 255
factors that influence initial attraction, 255–262
from attraction to liking, 262–266
investment and, 273
investment model, 272–274
jealousy and, 274–275
measurement of liking and love, 266–269
persistence and dissolution of, 271–276
physical attractiveness, 256–257
physical proximity, 262–264
reciprocity, 239
satisfaction and, 273
self-disclosure, 265–266
Communication, source of, 43–49
and counter-argumentation, 43–49
attractiveness and, 47–48
expertise, 44
multiple sources, 47
role playing and, 48–49
sleeper effect, 44–46
trustworthiness, 44
Communication and Attitude Change

Program, 43
Companionate love, 269
Competition, conflict and, 504–505
Competitive choice,
communication and, 249–250
in prisoners' dilemma, 247
Compliance, 384, 390, 392
compliance-gaining strategies, 380–383
Conclusion drawing, 49–50
Condom usage, cognitive dissonance and, 94
Confirmatory biases, 160–163
assimilation, 161
discounting, 162–163
Conflict,
intergroup competitiveness, 504–505
mirror image, 506–507
realistic group conflict theory, 501–503
reducing through contact experiments, 511–515
robbers cave experiment, 501–503
superordinate goals, 502
Conformity,
Asch's line study, 372–377
defined, 376
minority influence, 388–401
number of accomplices and, 373–374
public compliance and, 376
uncertainty and social comparison theory, 446–447
See also Social influence
Conjunctive tasks, 418, 420
Consensus,
base-rate fallacy, 190
in covariation principle, 187–188
failures of, 190–192
false consensus rate, 191–192
Consensus formation, in social decision schemes, 427
Conservation,
group incentives and, 246–247
as social dilemma, 245
Consistency,
illusion of, 190
in covariation principle, 188
minority influence and, 392
vs. rigidity, 393–394
Contact hypothesis, 508–509
amount of contact, 511
cooperation, 511–513
personalization, 515
salience, 514–515
status equality, 513–514
Contrast effect, 66

Controllability, in attribution theory, 174–177
in classroom, 175
in courtroom, 175
defined, 170
pity and, 178–179
social stigma and, 175–177
Control mechanisms, 241–243
behavior control, 242–243
fate control, 241–242
Control phase, in group decision making process, 426, 427, 434
Convergent thinking, minority influence, 397–398
Conversion, 376–377, 384
Cooperation,
improving, 511–515
status equality, 513–514
Cooperative choice,
communication and, 249–250
in prisoners' dilemma, 247
Cooperative interdependence, 508, 511
Correlations, 12
negative, 12
positive, 12
Correspondent inference theory, 193–194
Costs,
nonnormative factors, 292–293
normative factors, 289–292
in outcome values, 237
in social exchange theory, 233
Counter-argumentation, 43–60
characteristic of audience, 58–60
message and, 49–55
setting, 55–58
source of communication, 43–49
Courtroom,
attribution controllability and, 175
physical attractiveness and sentencing, 136
Covariation principle, 187–190
consensus, 187–188, 189
consistency, 188, 189
covariation defined, 187
deviations from, 190–192
distinctiveness, 188, 189
establishing covariation, 187–188
failures of consensus, 190–192
illusion of consistency, 190
Crime,
attribution controllability and, 175
confessions and perspective effect, 200
heat and aggressive crimes, 315–317
Criminal justice system, racism and, 494–495

Crossracial identification, 471
Cultural differences,
    fundamental attribution error
        and, 199
    salience and, 199–200
    self-image and, 225–226

D

Debriefed, 16
Deception, 15
    detection of, 120–121
    paralinguistic cues and, 113
    polygraph and, 113–114
    in research, 15–16
Decision making. *See* Group decision
    making
Decoding, nonverbal
    communication, 109
Deindividuation, 245
Delegating, in social decision
    schemes, 427
Delinquency,
    possible selves and, 215
    self-concept and, 215
Demand characteristics, 14
Dependent variable, 13
Depression, attribution theory and, 181
Desegregation, 509–511
Diagnosticity, defined, 186
Diffusion of responsibility, 282, 283–285
Direct experience, attitude-behavior
    consistency and, 33–34
Direct influence, minority influence
    and, 395–396
Discounting, in confirmatory bias,
    162–163
Discounting principle, 193
Discrimination, 482–497
    aversive racism, 489–490
    collective self-esteem, 486
    fraternal deprivation, 495–496
    institutionalized, 492–496
    interpersonal, 486–492
    minimal intergroup situation,
        483–486
    nonverbal behavior, anxiety and
        ambivalence, 488–492
    positive distinctiveness, 486
    racial, and helping, 290–291
    realistic group conflict, 495
    reverse, 492
    rules of fairness and, 484–485

social distance, 487–488
social identity theory and, 486
symbolic racism, 495–496
Disidentification, 453
Disjunctive tasks, 418, 419
Displaces aggression, 310, 472–473
Dissonance. *See* Cognitive dissonance
Dissonance theory, 508
Distinctiveness, in covariation
    principle, 188
Distraction, setting and persuasion,
    55–57
Distress, in empathy-altruism model,
    298
Divergent thinking, minority influence,
    397–398
Dominance, nonverbal communication
    and, 109
Door-in-the-face effect, 381
Double blind trials, 329
Double minorities, 399–400

E

Efficiency principle, 75–77
Effort justification, 89–91
    weight-loss and, 91–92
Ego involvement,
    attitude-behavior consistency, 36
    social judgement theory and, 65
Elaboration, information-processing
    and, 146
Elaboration-likelihood model (ELM),
    68–73
    ability, 70
    central vs. peripheral processing,
        68–69
    vs. Heuristic systematic model,
        77–78
    message factors, 70
    motivation, 69
    need for cognition, 72–73
    processes of resistance and change,
        70–72
    sleeper effect and, 72
EMG. *See* Facial electromyogram
    (EMG)
Emotion,
    facial feedback hypothesis,
        121–122
    James-Lange theory of, 121–122
    recognition of, and facial
        expressions, 114–116

Emotional expression. *See* Nonverbal
    communication
Empathic joy hypothesis, 297–298
Empathy, 297
    defined, 121
    in empathy-altruism model, 298
    nonverbal communication and,
        121–123
    as social norm, 240
Empathy-altruism model, 298–299
Empathy-joy hypothesis, 298–299
Encoding, 157–159
    consistencies, 157–159
    expectancy and, 157–159
    information-processing and, 146
Enemy, image of, 505–507
Energy conservation, low-ball technique
    and, 382–383
Equality, as social norm, 240
Equity,
    equality, 240, 249
    gender differences and, 240, 249
    as social norm, 240
Equity theory of relationships, 272
Erotic violence, aggression and, 322
Ethics, research and, 15–17
Ethnocentrism, 441, 469
Evaluation apprehension, 409–410
Evaluation approach to attitude, 26–28
    Likert scales, 27
    Osgood's semantic differential,
        27–28
Evaluation phase, in group decision
    making process, 425–427, 434
Evaluative rating, in cognitive
    algebra, 139
Exchange relationships, 238–239
    vs. communal relationships, 255
    defined, 255
Excitation transfer theory, 257, 312–315
Expectancies, 328–346
    accuracy vs. expectancy in
        classroom, 332–333
    affect-effort theory of
        expectancy, 334
    appearance and, 335–337
    biased information search,
        339–342
    encoding and, 157–159
    experimenter bias, 330–331
    gender and, 338–339
    on the job, 338
    placebo studies, 329–330
    poverty and academic
        performance and, 332–333
    race and, 337–338
    teacher's and lower social class
        children, 332–333

transmission of expectation in
classroom, 334
See also Self-fulfilling prophecy
Expectancy effects, 328–329
classroom, 331
Experimental realism, 14–15
Experimental research, 12–14
correlation and, 12
validity, 14–15
variables and, 13
Experimenter bias, 330–331
Expertise, perception of, social influence
and, 378–379
Expertise, source credibility and, 44
*Expression of the Emotions in Man and
Animals, The* (Darwin), 109
External locus, in attribution theory,
defined, 169
Extremity effect, 140
Extrinsic motivation, 194–196
undermining intrinsic, 195–196
Eyewitnesses,
crossracial identification, 471
testimony, memory
reconstruction, 164–165

F

Faceism, 475
Faces, baby, and nonverbal
communication, 118–119
Facial electromyogram (EMG), 29
Facial expression. *See* Nonverbal
communications
emotional experiences and,
121–122
emotion recognition and,
114–116
Facial feedback hypothesis, 121–122
Facial stereotypes, 119
False consensus rate, 191–192
Fate control, 241–242
Fear-arousing messages, 52–54
Feelings, attitudes and, 27
Field research, 11
First impressions, 256
Flexibility, minority influence and,
394–395
Foot-in-the-door effect, 355, 380–381
Fraternal deprivation, 456, 495–496
Free choice, 87–89
Free riding, 417

Friendship,
attitude similarity, 264–265
rules of, 266
self-disclosure, 265–266
study on formation, 5–6
Frustration,
arousal and, 311
defined, 311–312
prejudice and, 472–473
Frustration-aggression theory, 309–312
displace aggression and, 310
frustration in, 309–310
revised edition, 310–312
Fundamental attribution error, 196–201
actor-observer bias, 201
defined, 196
language and culture, 199
roles and, 198

G

Galvanic skin response (GSR), 28–29
Gender differences,
cultural differences, 110
in group performance, 412–413
in helping, 290
interpretation of nonverbal
behavior, 120
mate selection and, 259
nonverbal communication
and, 110
social influence and, 377–378
social norms and, 240, 249
Gender identity, 449
Gender schematic, 155
Gender stereotypes, 150–151, 161,
463–464
media and, 474–475
social-role theory, 475–476
Gestalt perspective, 128
Getting acquainted study (Newcomb),
5–6, 11
Global self-esteem, 216
Graduated and reciprocated initiatives in
tension-reduction (GRIT), 507
Group decision making, 424–437
averaging, 427
consensus formation, 427
context, 425
control phase, 426, 427
decision making and, 427, 434
decision making in juries, 429

delegating, 427
discussion and, 426–427, 434
evaluation phase, 425–427
experimental studies of, 425–428
group dynamics, 424–425
group polarization, 430–434
groupthink, 434–437
initial individual preferences,
428–429
majority, 427, 430
orientation phase, 425–426, 434
plurality, 427, 430
process of, 424–428
quality, 425
social decision schemes, 427–428
task solution certainty, 429–430
threats to quality decisions,
434–437
voting, 427
Group incentive, 246
conservation and, 246–247
Group performance, 404–420
commitment and cohesion,
415–416
evaluation apprehension, 409–410
evaluation effects, 417–418
free riding, 417
general arousal, 408–409
homogeneity of performance, 415
motivation loss, 419
participant behavior, 416–418
performance information effects,
416–417
personal beliefs, 413–415
personality characteristics and,
411–412
process loss, 419
sex composition of group and,
412–413
social facilitation, 407–408
social inhibition, 407–408
social loafing, 406
task demands, 418–420
why people work in group
settings, 404–406
Group polarization, 430–434
informational social influence,
433–434
normative social influence, 433
social decision schemes, 432–433
Group processes, defined, 9–10
Groups. *See also* In-groups
Group setting, 404
Groupthink, 434–437
bases of, 435–436
cohesiveness, 435–436
decision pressure, 435–436
defined, 435

illusion of invulnerability, 436
illusion of morality, 436
isolation, 435–436
leadership style, 435–436
mindguards, 436
pressure and, 436
research evidence for, 437
self-censorship, 436
symptoms of, 436–437

H

Halo effect, 134–136, 259
  physical appearance and, 134–136
Heat, aggressive crime and, 315–317
Helping. *See also* Bystander intervention
  barrier crossed before, 286
  empathic joy hypothesis, 297–298
  empathy-altruism model, 298–299
  gender differences, 290
  image repair hypothesis, 294
  mood and, 293, 294–295
  motives for, 294–299
  negative-state relief
    hypothesis, 294
  race or ethnicity and, 290–291
  relationship between helper and
    victim, 291
  responsibility assignment, 291–292
  time constraints, 292–293
  urban environment, 295–297
Heuristic processing, 74–75
Heuristic-systematic model,
  efficiency principle, 75–77
  vs. elaboration-likelihood model,
    77–78
  heuristic processing, 74–75
  sufficiency principle, 75–77
  systematic processing, 74
Hostile aggression, defined, 306
Hovland's message-learning approach,
  42–43
Hypocrisy theory, 93
Hypotheses, 10
Hypothesis-testing research, 10–11

I

Idealized images, 217
Ideal self, 217

Ideal self-image, 216
Illusion of control, 181
Illusion of invulnerability, 436
Illusion of morality, 436
Illusory correlations, 467–468
Image repair hypothesis, 294
Implicit personality theory, 133–139
  descriptive meaning, 137
  evaluative bias and, 134–136
  halo effect, 134–136
  intellectual competence, 139
  social desirability, 139
Impression formation, 126–144
  category accessibility and, 154
  classroom study of trait centrality,
    131–133
  cognitive algebra, 139–140
  gestalt perspective, 128
  halo effect, 134–136
  implicit personality theory,
    133–139
  intellectual competence, 139
  personality traits, 126
  physical attractiveness and,
    134–136
  primacy effect in, 128–131
  social cognition and, 146
  social desirability, 139
  trait centrality, 131
  wholistic impressions, 141–142
Impression management theory, 95–96
Independence, and social influence,
  383–384
Independent variable, 13
Indirect influence, minority influence
  and, 395–396
Individual processes, defined, 9
Informational social influence, 370, 372
  group polarization and, 433–434
  vs. normative social influence,
    375–376
Information-processing,
  attention and encoding, 146
  elaboration, 146
  organization, 147
  retrieval, 147
  social cognition and, 146–147
  storage, 147
Informed consent, 15
In-group bias, 469–470
  rules of fairness and, 484
In-group minorities, 399–400
In-groups,
  basking in reflected glory (BIRG),
    451–452
  changing sexual behavior and, 442
  defined, 441
  disidentification, 453

distinctiveness and, 449–451
  ethnocentrism, 441
  fraternal deprivation, 456
  importance of, 444–445
  membership groups, 442–444
  minority self-esteem, 452–455
  need for out-groups, 45–451
  positive distinctiveness, 452
  positive identity, 451–452
  relative deprivation, 455–456
  social comparison theory,
    444–447
  social identity theory, 447–449
Inheritance theories of aggression,
  307–309
Innuendo effect, 341–342
Inoculation hypothesis, 54–55
  stress and, 55
Instinctive drive to aggression, 307
Institutionalized discrimination, 492–496
  racism and, 492–494
  sexism, 492–494
  symbolic racism, 495–496
Institutional Review Boards (IRB), 16
Instrumental aggression, defined, 306
Insufficient justification, 86
Intelligence,
  academic performance and social
    class, 332–333
  expectancy effect and, 331–332
  persuasion and, 58–59
Intention,
  aggression and, 305
  attitude-behavior consistency and,
    32–33
Interdependence, 232
  behavior matrix, 235–236
  mutual fate control, 242
  nature of outcome values in,
    236–237
  outcome values and, 235
  social exchange and, 234–236
Intergroup attitudes, 462–479. *See also*
  Prejudice; Stereotypes
  categorization, 465–471
  ethnocentrism, 469
  in-group-out-group
    categorization, 468–471
  personality factors, 472–473
  social learning factors, 474–476
  unconscious prejudice, 476–478
Intergroup competitiveness, 504–505
Intergroup discrimination, 483–484
Intergroup relations, 500–516
  contact experiments, 511–515
  contact hypothesis, 508–509
  desegregation, 509–511
  discrimination, 482–497

ignorance and misperception in, 505–507
intergroup competitiveness, 504–505
intergroup contact, 508–516
mirror image, 506–507
realistic group conflict, 495
robbers cave experiment, 501–503
superordinate goals, 502
Internal locus, in attribution theory, 169
defined, 169
Internal validity, 14
Interpersonal discrimination, 486–492
nonverbal behavior, anxiety, and ambivalence, 488–492
reverse discrimination, 492
social distance and, 487–488
Interpersonal processes, defined, 9
Intimacy, 269
Intrinsic motivation, 194–196
undermining, 195–196
Invasion of privacy, 16
Investment model, of relational development, 272–274

J

James-Lange theory of emotion, 121–122
Japanese, self-image and, 226
Jealousy, 274–275
Juries, decision making in, 429

K

Kinesics, 108
Kitty Genovese, bystander intervention and, 280–282
Knowledge,
attitude-behavior consistency and, 35–36
attitudes and, 27

L

Laboratory research, 11

Language, fundamental attribution error, 199
Latitude of acceptance, 65–68
Latitude of rejection, 65–68
Law of attraction (Byrne & Nelson), 6–7, 11
Learned disinhibition, 323
Levels of explanation, 9–10
group processes, 9–10
individual processes, 9
interpersonal processes, 9
Lie detector text, nonverbal communications and, 113–114
Likert scales, 27
Liking,
attitude similarity, 264–265
from attraction to liking, 262–266
measurement of, 266–269
physical proximity, 262–264
relationship closeness inventory, 268–269
scales for, 267–268
self-disclosure, 265–266
similarity of attitude and values, 5–7
Loneliness, physical health and, 276
Love,
attachment theory of, 270–271
commitment and, 270
companionate, 269
forms of, 269–270
intimacy, 269
measurement of, 266–269
passionate, 269
relationship closeness inventory, 268–269
scales for, 267–268
triangular model of, 269–270
Low-ball technique, 381–383
commitment and, 382
energy conservation, 382–383

M

Majority, in social decision schemes, 427, 430
Matching hypothesis, 260–262
Mate selection, sociobiological theory of, 259
Media, stereotypes and, 474–475
Membership groups, 442–444
reference groups, 442–444
Memory, scripts and, 148

Mental representations, 146–147
Mere exposure hypothesis, 264
Message, in counter-argumentation, 49–55
delivery, 50–51
drawing a conclusion, 49–50
fear arousal, 52–54
inoculation hypothesis, 54–55
one-sided vs. two-sided, 51–52
quality of, and distraction, 57
Message-learning approach (Hovland), 42–43
Mindfulness, 478
Mindguards, 436
Minimal intergroup situation, 483–486
Minority influence, 388–401
behavior style and, 392
consistency and, 392
convergent and divergent thought, 397–398
conversion, 392
definition of minority, 399–400
diffusion of influence effects, 398–399
direct vs. indirect influence, 395–396
double minorities, 399–400
flexibility and, 394–395
in-group minorities, 399–400
modes of influence, 390–392
originality and, 392, 395
out-group minorities, 399–400
rigidity, 393–394
symmetry vs. asymmetry, 389–390
Minority self-esteem, 452–455
prejudice and, 454
Mirror image, 506–507
Misattribution,
cognitive dissonance and, 100–101
defined, 100
in excitation transfer theory, 312–313
heat and aggression, 316–317
Mixed-motive situation, 243–244
Modern Utopia, A (Wells), 449–450
Mood,
helping and, 293, 294–295
persuasion and, 59–60
schema accessibility and, 156–157
Moral images, 217
Motivation,
attributions of, 194–195
elaboration-likelihood model and, 69
overjustification effect, 195–196
possible selves and, 212–213

undermining intrinsic, 195–196
Motivation loss, 419
Mutual fate control, 242

N

National stereotypes, 463–464
Nature of Prejudice, The (Allport), 462
Need for cognition, 72–73
Negative correlation, 12
Negative-state relief, 294, 298–299
    urban environment study and, 295–297
Negativity effect, 140"New look", 147
Nonverbal communication, 108–123
    accuracy of interpreting expressions, 119–120
    baby-faces and, 118–119
    controllability of, 112–113
    cultural influences, 110
    decoding, 109, 114–123
    defined, 108
    detection of deception, 120–121
    ecological perspective and, 116–117
    emotional recognition, 114–115
    empathy and, 121–123
    evolutionary perspective, 109
    facial feedback hypothesis, 121–122
    gender differences in decoding, 120
    gender influences and, 110
    interpreting nonverbal messages, 114–123
    James-Lange theory of emotion, 121–122
    kinesics, 108
    nonverbal leakage, 112–113
    nonverbal messages as affordances, 116–117
    occupation and nonverbal sensitivity, 120
    overgeneralization of affordances, 118–119
    paralinguistic, 108
    polygraph and, 113–114
    Profile of Nonverbal Sensitivity (PONS), 119–120
    proxemics, 108
    sending nonverbal messages, 109–114
    as social interaction and, 110–112

transmission cues, 109
    universality of, 109–110
Normative social influence, 371, 372
    group polarization and, 433
    vs. informational, 375–376
Norm formation study (Sherif), 8, 11
Norms,
    autokinetic effect and, 369–372
    defined, 369
    formation of, 369–370
    informational social influence, 370, 372
    normative social influence, 371, 372
    social, 240–241

O

Obedience, 350–364
    administrative, 359–362
    defined, 351
    ethical objections and generalizability to Milgram's research, 365–358
    forces for compliance or resistance, 363–364
    Milgram's research on, 351–356
    obedient nurse study, 358–359
    personal responsibility, 356, 362
    physical proximity and, 355–356
    rebellion, 356
    social support and, 363–364
Occupation, nonverbal sensitivity and, 120
One-sided message, 51–52
Organization, information-processing and, 147
Orientation, in group decision making process, 425–426, 434
Originality, minority influence and, 392, 395
Osgood's semantic differential, 27–28
Ought self, 217
Outcome values,
    costs, 237
    rewards and, 236–237
Out-group minorities, 399–400
Out-groups,
    defined, 441
    homogeneity of, 470–471
    need for, 450–451
Overjustification effect, 102, 195–196

P

Pain, nonverbal communication and, 109
Panic, war of the world study, 3–4, 11
Paralinguistic, 108
Paralinguistics, deception and, 113
Passion, 269
Passionate love, 269
Perception, 157
    ecological perspective of, 116–117
Perception of expertise, social influence and, 378–379
Performance information effects, 416–417
Peripheral (processing) route, 68–69
Personal constructs, 155–156
Personal identity, 457
    defined, 448
    gender identity and, 449
Personality,
    authoritarian, 472
    group performance and, 411–412
    implicit personality theory, 133–139
    stereotype/prejudice formation, 472–473
Personality traits, 126, 149
    centrality of, 131
Personalization, 515
Persuasion,
    attractiveness and sales, 47–48
    characteristics of audience, 58–60
    message and, 49–55
    multiple sources and, 47
    role playing and, 48–49
    setting, 55–58
    source of communication, 43–49
Physical appearance,
    attractiveness and sentencing, 136
    expectations, 335–337
    halo effect and, 134–136
Physical attractiveness, 256–257
    beauty and goodness, 257–258
    excitation transfer theory, 257
    halo effect, 259
    market value of, 258–259
    matching hypothesis, 260
    role of physical similarity, 260–262
Placebo,
    defined, 329
    studies, 329–330
Planned behavior, theory of, 32–33
Pluralistic ignorance, 283, 285–286

social comparison theory, 286
Plurality, in social decision schemes, 427, 430
Political change, reactions to, 496
Polygraph, nonverbal communication and, 113–114
Pornography,
    aggression and, 315, 322
Positive correlations, 12
Positive distinctiveness, 452
    discrimination and, 486
Possible selves, 212–214
    delinquency and, 215
Postdecision regret, 87
Poverty,
    causal attributions, 172
    expectancy effect and school performance, 332–333
Prejudice,
    authoritarian personality, 472
    belief congruence theory, 473
    categorization and, 465–471
    displaced aggression, 472–473
    frustration and, 472–473
    in-group bias, 469–470
    mindfulness, 478
    minority self-esteem and, 454
    out-group homogeneity of, 470–471
    overcoming habit of, 478
    personality factors, 472–473
    relationship to stereotype, 464–465
    scapegoat theory of, 472–473
    self-esteem and, 473
    social learning factors, 474–476
    unconscious, 476–478
Primacy effect, in impression formation, 128
Priming effect, 153–155
subconscious priming, 154
Principles of Psychology (James), 208
Prisoners' dilemma, 247–250, 503–504
    communication, 249–250
    competitive choice, 247
    cooperative choice, 247
    gender, 248–249
    relationships, 250
    threat and, 250
Private acceptance, 376–377, 384
Process loss, 419
Profile of Nonverbal Sensitivity (PONS), 119–120
Prototypes, 151–152
Proxemics, 108
Psychology of Interpersonal Relations, The (Heider), 169
Psycholphysiological approaches,

attitude and, 28–29
    facial electromyogram, 29
Public acceptance, 384
    group cohesiveness and, 379
Public behavior, 390
Public compliance, 376

R

Race, self-fulfilling prophecy, 337–338
Racial identity, self-esteem and, 452–455
Racial stereotypes, 161
Racism,
    aggression and, 319
    aversive, 489–490
    helping and, 290–291
    symbolic, 495–496
Random assignment, 13
Realistic group conflict theory, 495, 501–503
Reasoned action, theory of, 32
Rebellion, obedience and, 356
Reciprocity, 265
    in exchange relationships, 239
    as social norm, 240
Reconstructive memory, 163–165
    eyewitness test and, 164–165
Relationship closeness inventory (RCI), 268–269
Relationships. *See also* Communal Relationships; Exchange relationships; Social exchange
    attitude similarity, 264–265
    breakup and loneliness, 275–276
    commitment and, 273
    communal, 238–239
    communal vs. exchange, 255
    equity theory of, 272
    exchange, 238–239
    factors that influence initial attraction, 255–262
    from attraction to liking, 262–266
    investment model, 272–274
    investments and, 273
    jealousy, 274–275
    measurement of liking and love, 266–269
    persistence and dissolution of, 271–276
    prisoners' dilemma and, 250
    satisfaction and, 273
    self-disclosure, 265–266

Relative deprivation, 455–456
Research,
    blind trials, 329
    classic studies, 3–8
    debriefing, 16
    deception and, 15–16
    double blind trials, 329
    ethics and, 15–17
    experimental, 12–14
    experimenter bias, 330–331
    field, 11
    hypothesis testing, 10–11
    invasion of privacy and, 16
    laboratory, 11
    sex differences and, 377–378
Research methodology, 12–15
    correlations, 12
    validity and, 14–15
    variables and, 12–13
Resegregation, 510
Responsibility, personal, and obedience, 356, 362
Retrieval, information-processing and, 147
Reverse discrimination, 492
Reverse incentive effect, 84–85
Rewards,
    nonnormative factors, 292–293
    normative factors, 289–292
    in outcome values, 236–237
    in social exchange theory, 233
Rigidity, vs. consistency, 393–394
Risk-taking decisions, 432–433
Role playing, 66
    persuasion and, 48–49
Role schemas, 148

S

Scapegoat theory of prejudice, 472–473
Schema accessibility, 152–157
    external factors, 152–153
    internal factors, 153–157
    mood, 156–157
    personal constructs, 155–156
    person categories, 153
    priming effects, 153–155
    self-schemas, 155
    situational cues, 152
Schemas,
    defined, 147, 148
    prototypes, 151–152
    scripts, 148

stereotypes, 149–151
traits and, 149
Schematic, 209
Schematic processing, 157–165
  assimilation, 161
  confirmatory biases, 160–163
  consistencies, 157–159
  discounting, 162–163
  encoding, 157–165
  expectancy and, 157–159
  inconsistencies, 159–160
  reconstructing memory, 163–165
  selective attention and recall,
    157–160
Schematic traits, 209
School desegregation, 509–511
Schools,
  academic performance and social
    class, 332–333
  expectancy effect and, 331–332
  expectation-versus-accuracy
    hypotheses, 332–333
  transmission of expectations
    in, 334
Scripts,
  memory and, 148
  role schemas, 148
Self-affirmation effect, vs. self-fulfilling
    prophecy, 342–343
Self-affirmation theory, 94–95
Self-attributions, 180–181
  achievement motivation and,
    180–181
Self-complexity, 210–212
  buffering effect of, 212
Self-concept, 208–227
  cross-cultural perspectives on,
    225–226
  defined, 209
  delinquency and, 215
  maintaining and protecting self-
    image, 222–226
  possible selves, 212–214
  self-complexity, 210–212
  self-esteem, 215–217
  self-evaluation maintenance,
    221–222
  self-perception theory, 217–218
  self-schema, 209–212
  theory of social comparison, 219
Self-consistency vs. self-enhancement,
    223–224
Self-disclosure, 265–266
Self-efficacy, 181
Self-enhancement
  vs. self-consistency, 223–224
  social comparison and, 222
Self-esteem,

collective, 448, 486
discrimination and, 486
global, 216
measuring, 215–217
minority, 452–455
persuasion and, 58–59
prejudice and, 473
self concept, 215–217
social comparison and, 219–220
social identity and, 452
Self-evaluation maintenance theory,
    221–222
Self-fulfilling prophecy, 334–339. See
    also Expectancies
  children and, 336–337
  defined, 334
  effects of appearance on
    expectations, 335–337
  effects of race on expectations,
    337–338
  high stakes and, 343–345
  on the job, 338
  vs. self-affirmation, 342–343
  sex-typed jobs and, 338–339
Self-image,
  cross-cultural perspectives on,
    225–226
  maintaining and protecting,
    222–226
  self-enhancement vs. self-
    consistency, 223–225
  self-verification, 224–225
Self-monitoring, attitude behavior
    consistency and, 38–39
Self-perception theory, 96–99, 102,
    217–218
  attitudes, 97
  attribution, 97
Self-schema, 155, 209–212
  aschematic, 209
  schematic, 209
  schematic traits, 209
  self-complexity, 210–212
Self-serving bias, 180–181
Setting, in counter-argumentation,
    55–58
  overheard communications, 57–58
  situational distractions, 55–57
Sex-typed jobs, self-fulfilling prophecy
    and, 338–339
Shift-to-risk phenomenon, 431
Sleeper effect, 44–46
  elaboration-likelihood model
    (ELM), 72
Social change, 456–457
  fraternal deprivation, 456
Social class, expectancy effect in
    classroom and, 332–333

Social cognition, 146–165
  defined, 146
  information-processing and,
    146–147
  mental representation, 146–147
  "new look", 147
  prototypes, 151–152
  roles and, 148
  schema accessibility, 152–157
  schemas and, 147
  schematic processing, 157–165
  scripts and, 148
  selective attention and recall,
    157–160
  stereotypes, 149–151
  traits, 149
Social comparison, 390
  theory of, 219–222
  defined, 219
  distinctiveness and, 220
  downward comparison, 222
  self-enhancement, 222
  self-esteem and, 219–220
  self-evaluation maintenance,
    221–222
  shock research, 4–5
  upward comparison, 222
Social comparison theory, 219–222,
    444–447
  conformity and, 446–447
  pluralistic ignorance and, 286
  uncertainty and, 445–446
Social decision schemes, 427–428
  group polarization and, 432–433
Social distance, interpersonal
    discrimination and, 487–488
Social exchange, 232–251
  agentic-communal motives, 249
  behavior control, 242–243
  communal relationships, 238–239
  control mechanisms, 241–243
  deindividuation, 245
  exchange relationships, 238–239
  fate control, 241–242
  gender differences and, 240, 249
  group incentives, 246–247
  interdependence and, 234–236
  mixed-motive situation, 243–244
  nature of outcome values in,
    236–237
  prisoners' dilemma, 247–250
  reciprocity, 239
  regulating, 237–241
  social dilemmas, 244–245
  social norms and, 240–241
  tragedy of the commons, 243–245
  transformations, 239–240
Social exchange theory, 232–234

behavior matrix, 235–236
costs and rewards in, 233
outcome values, 235
Social facilitation, 407–408
distraction and, 410–411
evaluation apprehension, 409–410
general arousal and, 408–409
Social identity, 439–458
defined, 448
gender identity and, 449
Social identity theory, 447–449
discrimination and, 486
gender identity, 449
positive distinctiveness, 452
Social inference, 186–204
actor-observer bias, 201
attributions of motivation, 194–195
augmentation principle, 193
causal inference from single observation, 192–193
correspondent inference theory, 193–194
covariation principle, 187–190
defined, 186
diagnosticity, 186
discounting principle, 193
fundamental attribution error, 196–201
one-stage vs. two-stage model of attribution, 201–203
overjustification effect, 195–196
person attribution bias, 196–201
Social influence, 368–385
anticonformity, 383–384
Asch's line study, 372–377
autokinetic effect, 369–372
compliance-gaining strategies, 380–383
compliance to majority, 390, 392
conformity, 376–377
conversion, 376–377
conversion to minority, 392
defined, 368
door-in-the-face effect, 381
foot-in-the-door effect, 380–381
gender and, 377–378
group decision making, 424–437
group performance, 404–420
independence and, 383–384
individual differences in susceptibility to, 379
informational 370, 372
informational vs. normative, 375–376
low-ball technique, 381–383
minority influence, 388–401
normative, 371, 372

obedience, 350–364
perception of expertise, 378–379
resistance to, 383–384
social comparison, 390
social identity, 439–458
stimulus ambiguity, 377
task difficulty, 377
two-process theory of, 390
Social inhibition, 407–408
Social judgement theory, 65–68
assimilation effect, 66
boomerang effect, 66
contrast effect, 66
ego involvement and, 65
latitude of acceptance, 65–68
latitude of rejection, 65–68
Social learning theory, of aggression, 317–318
Social loafing, 406
Social mobility, 457
Social norms, 240–241
altruism, 240
costs and rewards, in helping, 289–292
empathy, 240
equality, 240
equity, 240
reciprocity,, 240
Social Psychology (McDougall), 8
Social Psychology (Ross), 8
Social psychology,
applying, 17–18
classic research in, 3–8
defined, 2–3
history of, 8–9
hypothesis-testing research and, 10–11
levels of explanation, 9–10
Social stereotypes, 149–150
Social stigma, attribution controllability and, 175–177
Sociobiological approach, to aggression, 307–309
Source credibility, 44
Stability, in attribution theory, 169–170, 171
defined, 169
expectation for future and, 172–174
Status equality, 513–514
Stereotypes, 149–151, 462–463
belief congruence theory, 473
categorization and, 465–471
facial, 119
gender, 150–151, 161, 463–464
illusory correlation, 467–468
in-group bias, 469–470
learning, 467–468

national, 463–464
out-group homogeneity, 470–471
personality factors, 472–473
racial, 161
relationship to prejudice, 464–465
self-esteem and, 473
social, 149–150
social learning factors, 474–476
social roles and, 475–476
unconscious prejudice, 476–478
Stigma, defined, 175–176
Stimulus ambiguity, 377
Storage, information-processing and, 147
Stress, inoculation against, 55
Students,
academic performance and social class, 332–333
expectancy effect and, 331–332
Study of panic (Cantril), 3–4, 11
Subconscious priming, 154
Sufficiency principle, 75–77
Superordinate goals, 502
Symbolic racism, 495–496
Systematic processing, 74

T

Task demands, 418–420
additive tasks, 418
combinational procedure, 418
conjunctive tasks, 418, 420
disjunctive tasks, 418, 419
task divisibility, 418
task goal, 418
Task divisibility, 418
Task goal, 418
Task solution certainty, 429–430
Teachers,
academic performance and social class, 332–333
affect-effort theory of expectancy, 334
expectancy effect and, 331–332
expectation-versus-accuracy hypotheses, 332–333
transmission of expectations in, 334
Television, aggression and, 320–321
Threat, prisoners' dilemma and, 250
Thurstone scale, 25–26
Tow-process theory, 390
Tragedy of the commons, 243–245

Trait centrality, 131
    classroom study of, 131–133
Traits, 149
Transformations, social exchange and, 239–240
Transmission cues, nonverbal communication, 109
Triangular model of love, 269–270
Trustworthiness, source credibility and, 44
Two-sided message, 51–52

U

Uncertainty,
    conformity and, 446–447
    shock research, 4–5, 11
    in social comparison theory, 445–447

Unconscious prejudice, 476–478
Unobtrusive methods, 29
    attitude and, 29

V

Validity,
    external, 15
    internal, 14
    research and, 14–15
Variables, 13–14
    dependent, 13
    independent, 13
Vested interest, 49
    attitude-behavior consistency, 36–37
Visual perspective, fundamental attribution error and, 199–201
Voting, in social decision schemes, 427

W

War of the world study, 3–4
Weighted average, in cognitive algebra, 140
Weight loss,
    cognitive dissonance and, 91–92
    effort justification and, 91–92
Wholistic impressions, 141–142
    change-of-meaning effect, 141–142
    resolving inconsistencies, 142

Photo Credits